'Few things about the]   oldiers
who were shot at daw   irst to
make use of the court martial   i bring a
welcome sense of perspective to the subject'   Gary Sheffield, *Mail on Sunday*

'Corns and Hughes-Wilson have amassed an unprecedented collection of case
histor*ic* . . . These make compelling, often moving reading'
Max Hastings, *Evening Standard*

'A grimly fascinating read . . . exactingly researched and closely argued'
Daily Telegraph

'an ex ellent book . . . Corns and Hughes-Wilson have written a powerful book'
Joanna Bourke, *Independent*

'An important and moving book that will provoke much discussion'
Good Book Guide

' . . . shows in chilling detail how the military mind dealt with the misfits who
seemed to threaten the battle morale of their comrades'   *Sunday Times*

'The au' are scrupulous in trying to understand the period in its own terms'
Sunday Telegraph

Colonel John Hughes-Wilson is a military historian, author and broadcaster. He lectures on 'Military Law in Action'. Cathryn Corns is a clinical scientist with a passionate interest in military history.

Blindfold
and Alone

British Military Executions in the Great War

CATHRYN CORNS &
JOHN HUGHES-WILSON

CASSELL

To the m[...] War,
[...] means of their passing

Cassell,
an imprint of The Orion Publishing Group Ltd
Orion House, 5 Upper St Martin's Lane
London WC2H 9EA

An Hachette UK Company

3 5 7 9 10 8 6 4

Copyright © Cathryn Corns and John Hughes-Wilson 2001

First published in Great Britain
by Cassell 2001
This Cassell Military Paperbacks edition 2005

British Library Cataloguing-in-Publication Data
A catalogue record for this book is available
from the British Library

ISBN 978-0-3043-6696-5

Printed and bound in Great Britain by
Clays Ltd, St Ives plc

www.orionbooks.co.uk

CONTENTS

PART THREE

ILLUSTRATIONS

Maps

Documents

Photographs
Contemporary pictures from the Imperial War Museum, London (numbered) and modern pictures.

The Coward

I could not look on Death, which being known,
Men led me to him, blindfold and alone.
RUDYARD KIPLING

FOREWORD

This is an important and timely book about an aspect of war which has haunted me – there is no other word for it – almost all my adult life. Although, taken in the round, the Second World War was a far larger historical event, the First World War has somehow burned itself deeper into our national consciousness. In a sense the Western Front is a metaphor for the war as a whole: a strip of murdered nature separating the old world from the new.

The war's terrible impact on British society – as Cathryn Corns and John Hughes-Wilson point out, three out of five families were directly involved – did not help rational analysis. Charles Carrington, brave participant and shrewd observer, thought that its history was speedily hijacked. Instead of the war he remembered it was a case of: 'Every battle a defeat, every officer a nincompoop, every soldier a coward.' It was not until the twentieth century drew to its close that the debate became genuinely comprehensive, with Brian Bond, Tim Travers, Robin Prior, Trevor Wilson, Paddy Griffith and John Bourne among the scholars whose work has changed the way we think about the war.

Or has it? As any historian who has tried even mildly to be revisionist about Field Marshal Sir Douglas Haig on television will acknowledge, there is a corpus of opinion which is not overly interested in the facts because it has already made up its mind. Point out that it was more dangerous to be a British general in the First World War than the Second; that just over half the British soldiers who fought had volunteered to do so; or that in its war-winning offensive in the last hundred days of the war the British Army captured twice as many Germans as the French, Americans and Belgians put together, and your interlocutor will disagree on the grounds that, as Field Marshal Sir William Robertson used to put it, he has heard different.

Controversial though the war as a whole remains, it has no single aspect that generates as much heat as the execution of British soldiers, and we ought not to be surprised that this is so. The whole ghastly process inspires revulsion. The victim, so often a volunteer, and in many cases worn down by the miseries of trench life and the impact of battle, was strapped to post or chair and shot by a firing party often composed of men from his own unit: what was intended as demonstrative justice made reluctant accomplices of all involved. The machinery of military bureaucracy ground home the lesson: execution of the sentence was promulgated in routine orders and (initially) notified to next of kin, and campaign medals were forfeit.

Such mournful episodes have become the vital ground around which the ideologically committed or personally involved have staked their own hard wire of interpretation and, in the process, often unwittingly, have helped create one of the war's most formidable redoubts of myth and misunderstanding. Thus it is sometimes said that under-age soldiers were routinely shot; that courts martial were 'kangaroo courts' composed of officers separated by social class and military experience from the men they judged; and that senior officers used executions as a way of concealing their own mistakes. That such demonstrable errors have become part of the debate underlines the need for this book, the first to examine the court martial records in full and, no less importantly, place the trials in the context of their own time and of the army which conducted them.

The result is a painstaking and compassionate survey which charts cases from those where the evidence is clear and the offence one, like murder, for which the offender would have been executed had he been a civilian; through those where men accused of capital offences under military law were justly convicted by that law as it then stood; to some where the circumstances of trial or offence do indeed suggest a miscarriage of justice. The authors conclude that the unlucky, the shell-shocked and the rogues alike were, as Dr John Reid, then Minister for the Armed Forces, told Parliament in 1998, 'all victims of war'. Most of them who, in the words of one veteran, 'tried and failed' deserve our sympathy: and sometimes they found, blindfold and alone, that courage which had earlier deserted them in circumstances which we can scarcely guess at.

Richard Holmes

ACKNOWLEDGEMENTS

This book grew out of the seminar held at the Royal United Services Institution, Whitehall in November 1997 chaired by the doyen of British military historians, Professor Sir Michael Howard, MC. The audience, which included the authors of two seminal works on the subject, was both knowledgeable and articulate and generated a thought-provoking discussion which subsequently appeared in the *RUSI Journal*. It is only proper, therefore, to acknowledge the debt we owe to the Director, Admiral Richard Cobbold, and the staff of the RUSI, in particular its Librarian, John Montgomery, for their unfailing help and encouragement.

Books like this do not get written without the help, generosity and kindness of others. Amongst the many people who have helped us, Judith Beresford who spent quite literally hours in the Public Record Office devilling on our behalf and without whose encyclopaedic knowledge of the First World War records this book could not have been written, and Monica Tasker whose proof-reading and editing experience proved invaluable, deserve special thanks and praise.

Among the various other sources we consulted, the staff of the Imperial War Museum's Reading Room and Photographic Archive, the National Army Museum, the National Film Archive and Richard Davies, the Archivist of the Liddle Collection at the University of Leeds, have all contributed to a marked degree towards the new material in the book. The various members of the Public Record Office staff have as always – and with unfailing patience – helped us to find that 'last little bit of information'.

All professional disciplines, especially the law, seem arcane and inaccessible to the layman: military law perhaps even more than most. Professor Gerry Rubin, Professor of Law at the University of Kent at Canterbury, has helped us to unravel what at times really did look like, in George Bernard Shaw's memorable phrase, 'a conspiracy to confuse the layman'.

At the end of the day, as with nearly all human endeavours, someone has to turn high-flown thoughts and words into reality. In our case it was Gill Smith, as rapid and accurate a typist as any author could wish, who actually did the work of transforming scribbles and drafts into a readable manuscript. Our grateful thanks go to her, and to our eagle-eyed copy editor Gillian Kemp. Last but not least, we owe a sincere debt of gratitude to Nick Chapman and Keith Lowe of Cassell Military books for having the vision to back a potentially contentious project. To them, and to all those who have contributed to a better understanding of a complex and emotive subject, go our most sincere thanks. We could not have done this without their help.

Acknowledgement is also made to the Keeper of the Records for permission to reproduce Crown copyright material in the Public Record Office and to the Keeper of the Liddle Collection, University of Leeds who gave permission to reproduce quotes from material in the collection. The authors are also grateful to the Senior Archivist at the Imperial War Museum for permission to quote from material in the collection and to Mrs Verity Walker for permission to use material from the diary of Capt. Westmacott. The authors have made every attempt to obtain copyright for material quoted in this book. In the event that we have accidentally infringed anyone's copyright then we would request that person to contact the publishers.

PART ONE

CHAPTER 1

THE LOST WORLD

What a Society gets in its armed services is exactly what it asks for,
no more and no less. What it asks for tends to be a reflection of what it is.
When a country looks at its fighting forces it is looking in a mirror; the
mirror is a true one and the face that it sees will be its own.

GENERAL SIR JOHN HACKETT

'The past is a foreign country; they do things differently there.' Thus L. P. Hartley, as a traveller from a far-off shore, sadly viewed his vanished world before 1914.[1] Today, when visiting foreign countries, we marvel at the strange sights and comment on the many differences from our own homes. We may not always like what we see, yet we do not seek to alter the way the inhabitants live their daily lives, or demand that in faraway places they conduct their affairs only in ways acceptable to us.

Why is it therefore that when we visit the equally foreign terrain of the past, we with increasing frequency insist on imposing our modern scale of values, and observe events of long ago through the distorting lens of our modern ideas of what is right or wrong? Even looking back only eighty years, at the generation before 1914, it is almost impossible for us to understand their often alien world. The truth is that however much we may disapprove of them, we can no more change the past than we can stop the world spinning. All we can do is note our great-grandparents' actions, marvel or despair at the events of long ago, and resolve to learn from others' mistakes in the past. In the old Arab proverb, 'Spilled water cannot be replaced in a smashed jug.' Except in the nightmare world of *Nineteen Eighty-Four* the past is always the past and therefore unchangeable.

Of all past events, the First World War seems to keep a disproportionate hold on our modern imagination. If any event can be truly said to have altered history, then the events of 1914 catapulted themselves across the globe. It was the Great War that changed lives, ruined empires, and destroyed idealism for

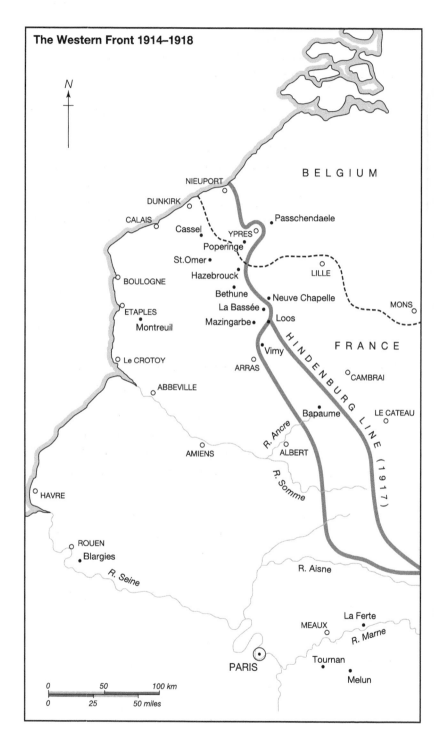

The Western Front 1914–1918

ever. There is a very clear difference in attitudes between those of 1914 and those of 1920. Philip Larkin's phrase in 'MCMXIV', 'Never such innocence again', succinctly sums up the loss of idealism and hope that remains as our enduring legacy from 1914–18. This sense of loss is further encouraged by the outpourings of ex-public school subalterns, who effectively hijacked the experience of the Western Front for their own memoirs, leaving us a literary memory rather than a cold historical analysis.

The Great War destroyed a stable European-centred world where institutions and values which had flourished for hundreds of years seemed not only permanent but also unquestionable. Four years of war – a war that moreover could have been avoided – ripped values, empires and men's lives brutally apart.[2] In Professor Eric Hobsbawm's phrase, the Great War of 1914–18 was the 'first of the twentieth century wars of secular religion'.

But savage religious wars of one kind or another had been ripping Europe apart for centuries before 1914. The real significance of the First World War was its revolutionary consequences for upheaval and change. Its struggles convulsed continents and its outcome ruined lives, toppled empires and changed the world for ever. By 1919, after the slaughter and upheaval of what was effectively a European civil war, the post-Versailles Treaty world looked a different place. According to Barbara Tuchman, a pair of iron gates had closed on a vanished world.

> The Great War of 1914–18 lies like a band of scorched earth dividing that time from ours. In wiping out so many lives … destroying beliefs, changing ideas and leaving incurable wounds of disillusion it created a physical as well as a psychological gulf between two epochs.[3]

While there would undoubtedly have been dangerous tensions between the great powers of Europe and their rulers, those tensions could hardly have had more dreadful consequence than those left in the wake of the four terrible years of the First World War. Even a short war, 'over by Christmas' in the words of the millions cheering off their soldiers from London, Paris, Berlin, Vienna and St Petersburg, would have been a blessing compared with the four long-drawn-out years of the greatest calamity the world had ever seen. Ten million soldiers would not have gone to their deaths and millions of others would have been spared the terrible physical – and mental – mutilations that would blight the rest of their lives.

The sheer scale of the killing, much of it voluntarily endured, that went on during the war is also incomprehensible to us today in a political climate that regards one single body bag as a public relations failure. Even after the terrible slaughter of the Great War's legacy, Hitler's war, the casualties of 1914–18 horrify. Britain and her imperial allies lost 996,230 men killed. But Britain has no monopoly of disaster: far from it. One million Frenchmen became casualties *by the end of 1914 alone* (300,000 of them killed before Christmas), and by the end of the war 5.6 million French soldiers had been killed or wounded. Germany lost 2,000,000 killed by the time she surrendered, starved out and broken politically, economically and militarily, in November 1918. The Great War's losses may have been 'made good' by 1930 as academic statisticians and demographers claim but the true loss could never be replaced. John Keegan puts his finger on the real tragedy for above all, 'it damaged civilisation, the rational and liberal civilisation of European enlightenment and through the damage done, world civilisation also'.[4] That sense of a civilization lost for ever still haunts us to this day.

This combination of a cataclysmic event, a loss of values and innocence, plus dreadful human cost (three out of five British families were directly affected by the war) helps explain our fascination with the lost world of 1914. This in its turn has spawned a rich crop of British myths. Many of these are, like so many myths, almost impossible to counter. To take but a few examples: 'the uniquely dreadful experience of the trenches' – in fact no worse than Italy in 1943–4, as many men who fought in both wars have pointed out. 'The unparalleled casualties' – any veteran of the dreadful 1944 slogging match in Normandy would disagree, as would veterans of fighting the Japanese in Burma on being told that 'the fighting in the First War was particularly horrific'; and, last but not least, 'Those poor young men sent off and forced to fight …' – a particularly cruel myth, as the British fought most of the Great War with an army of only too willing volunteers.[5] It is to no avail. As a unique horror story the First War has been popularized by too many for too long until it grips our imagination. As we tour the endless rows of headstones only one hour from Dover the full cost becomes apparent. But amongst those hundreds of thousands of headstones from that lost world are a few – a very few – of men who fell for their country, but were executed by their own side for failing to meet the challenge.

No single topic relating to the First World War seems to generate as much heat as the issue of those soldiers executed for military offences. In French country graveyards credulous schoolchildren listen wide-eyed to half-truths relayed by indignant young schoolteachers. Every modern author or screenplay about the Great War appears to feel the need to include an obligatory execution scene in the interests of dramatic licence. No subject has inspired so much public interest – or so much misinformation.

The first book to raise publicly the issue of the capital courts martial was *The Thin Yellow Line*, by William Moore, who in 1974, without access to the trial transcripts, identified many of the core issues.[6] Then, in 1983, Judge Anthony Babington, an experienced lawyer and ex-soldier, was given access to the then closed court martial records and allowed to summarize the information relevant to the cases.[7] Although Babington took great care to preserve the anonymity of the executed men, by referring to 'Private C of a Scottish Regiment', it subsequently became possible to relate the details of the cases to the names of the executed men. In fact, most of these names were already accessible in the public domain [8] but they were not widely known until Julian Putkowski and Julian Sykes published *Shot at Dawn* in 1989.[9] By comparing war diaries, newspapers and other records these two authors managed to identify the names of 361 men executed between 1914 and 1920 under authority of the British Army Act. Their book relied heavily on Babington's previous work for details about individual cases and occasionally errors crept in, such as in the cases of Philip Oyns and Alexander Reid, both described as deserters whereas both were in fact executed for murder.

In 1998 Gerald Oram produced a detailed listing of all the death sentences passed by courts martial between 1914 and 1924, extracting these from the registers of courts martial.[10] This is a painstaking work and a valuable reference tool, but is not immune from errors, such as cases where the dates suggest that an execution preceded the trial, or where the compilers of the original registers made transcription errors, such as in the case of Pte Earp, shot in 1916 for quitting his post, but who in the index is shown as a deserter.

Overseas, the cases of the executed Canadians and New Zealanders have been well described in books by A. B. Godefroy [11] and Christopher Pugsley.[12]

Nowadays most of the relevant details can be read in the primary sources, mainly as court martial records held in the Public Record Office.[13] However, even when reviewing this primary material, care is needed. The information in the files varies widely, and papers which were present at some time are no longer always in the file: an example is Herbert Burden's conduct sheet, which was put into evidence in 1915 but is no longer available. At some point, in the manner of all official papers, the files appear to have been weeded, and it is notable that for most of the trials in 1917 the recommendations by the commanders of the different formations are now no longer among the papers. This sometimes makes it difficult fully to appreciate the detail of a trial. In other cases, it is clear that medical certificates and other supporting documents have not been retained in the files. For example, occasionally the documents refer to a paper marked 'A' and put into evidence, which, eighty years later, turns out not to be in the file. On examining such cases, it is often only at the third or fourth reading of the transcript that the full significance of the missing piece of evidence or statement becomes apparent.

It is also very clear from the transcripts that the most damning evidence in a trial was nearly always given by NCOs and other soldiers. Although officers often gave evidence, this was usually corroborating events already described by junior ranks who had witnessed events at first hand, rather than directly convicting. Indeed, in one case (Pte Hawthorne; see Chapter 15), concern was actually expressed during the confirmation process that

> the convicting evidence having been given by officers, and only junior
> ones, a very deep feeling against the officers as a whole may be engendered
> and the battalion will consequently become valueless.[14]

What is absolutely clear is that these capital courts martial were not some form of oppressive class warfare, or some deadly social control of the working class by brutal officers. Of all the canards and myths this is perhaps the most ill-informed. In an organization that prided itself on pure paternalism and care for its soldiers based on the Victorian values of the public school and muscular Christianity the idea that regimental officers would 'oppress' *their* soldiers reveals only ignorance or prejudice. In the stern world of 'The Regiment' everyone lived by a tough set of rules and punishments and understood the uncompromising standards demanded.

The courts martial were nothing more or less than the result of the legitimate application of military law as voted into statute by Parliament like any other law. The *Manual of Military Law,* 1914, merely laid out the legal regulations under which *all* ranks in the trenches – officers, NCOs and soldiers alike – lived and died. Men were punished for a variety of offences, almost invariably related to a failure to carry out a duty. Most failures were hushed up or kept within the company and only a tiny minority of offences on duty ever went to a court martial. Reading the letters and memoirs of the Western Front makes it clear that the majority of officers felt a deep compassion for the hardships endured by their soldiers, and preferred to wake the sleeping sentry – or in some cases let the exhausted man sleep – rather than bring a charge, and certainly not a court martial. (There can be few who have served in the infantry at any time who can honestly say that they have not dozed off on sentry.) When soldiers were charged, the offence was always considered a grave one, and they were usually convicted on evidence from their own ranks, seeming to have engendered scant sympathy from their comrades at the time. With the passing of the years surviving veterans appear to have become more tolerant and sympathetic to the failings of their long-dead comrades as the distorting prism of time and compassion blurs emotions. The view at the time however tended to be less forgiving. To quote just one, a battalion doctor summed up the prevailing view:

> I think that it was absolutely essential. It was setting a bad example to the men. They had begun to feel that you only had to walk off during a battle and then come back afterwards and you escaped death or mutilation ... I think that it was a necessary punishment ...[15]

After a court martial the papers were reviewed at every level of command, up to the commander-in-chief, the legally empowered confirming authority. At the time this was felt to be a good legal safeguard, akin to the then new Court of Criminal Appeal. These provided at least four levels of review of sentence by senior officers and legal advisers. In nearly all of the cases, comments have been added after the trial – many in the same handwriting. It is not possible to tell who added these comments, but it seems likely that this happened when the lawyers working for the Deputy Judge Advocate General (DJAG), checking the legality of the proceedings and sentence, reviewed the cases. These comments did in no way affect the outcome of the trial, but may well have affected the outcome of the confirmation process.

Eyewitness accounts of events, particularly those dating from several years after the war ended, have to be treated with great caution. Many can be shown to be inaccurate in one or more details, and some turn out on examination to be downright fabrications. This is not to imply that men 'invented' a good story, although hearsay and rumour would have spread the word among the British Expeditionary Force as fast as any modern web site, once the shocked members of a firing squad had drowned their feelings gossiping with their mates in the wet canteen.

There is no doubt either that old soldiers' tales often grow more vivid and detailed with the passage of time, and memory plays tricks as the perception of events changes over the years. For example, the band leader Victor Silvester's much-quoted tales of taking part in firing squads as a young soldier appear to bear absolutely no relation to recorded facts.[16] Pte Kennedy's recollections of the cases of Ingham and Longshaw are inaccurate in some details, but that is not to say that his basic information is invalid. Likewise, Sir Gordon Macready's recollections of *five* men being executed together in 1915 cannot be substantiated, although *four* men were executed at Dickebusch at the time he mentions. What is clear is that all these individuals were trying to recall the intensity of great events at a time when life and death heightened every sense and emotion in a distant world.

It is a world hard for us to recreate or understand. Life as it was lived before 1914 stands very firmly on the far side of the 'band of scorched earth' described by Barbara Tuchman. Our last links with this lost world are a very few *very* old men and women, or the images captured for us now only in the photographs or on scratchy cine films. This cine-past of the years before 1914 looks like an alien, overdressed experience to our modern eyes. Despite our best efforts, the people of our great-grandparents' generation are populating a foreign landscape and a society whose views and values are frequently as alien to us as any far distant country.

Yet this alien world of 1914 was also, paradoxically, wrestling with some very familiar problems. The challenges of modernization, poverty, mass communications, consumerism, welfare taxation and wealth redistribution were uppermost in every politician's mind in the early years of last century. The question of Ireland dominated British newspaper headlines between 1910 and 1914 as surely as they do today. An explosion of economic growth, rising living standards and persistent demands for political reforms exercised the chattering classes of the 'Golden Age' at smart dinner tables throughout Europe.

In some ways it really *was* a golden age. Even for the poorest families whose sons 'went for a soldier', things had never been better. The standard of living, greater disposable incomes and general availability of goods meant that a genuine consumer society had emerged by 1900–1914, particularly for the new suburban middle class. People flocked to the city, despite its overcrowding and shortcomings, where they lived better, with better clothes, real schools, access to a doctor and plentiful entertainment. Despite its undoubted pockets of slum poverty, life in the city was better and people voted with their feet.

They were attracted principally by the wages available from the explosion in industry, manufacturing and service industries that revolutionized Europe from 1850 onwards. This urbanization was not just a consequence of industrialization. It also reflected the rapid growth of European populations. For example, in 1870 Britain's population stood at 26 million; by 1911 it had grown to 41 million, a growth of nearly 60 per cent in just forty years. Growth, progress and change were all on the march in 1914.[17]

Most of the people moving to the towns, or, in Britain's case, the second or third generation of urban dwellers, were incomparably more knowledge-able and better educated than their parents and grandparents. The knowl-edge revolution of the late nineteenth century was distilled into a spate of Education Acts, which were in turn met with dissent from the surprisingly small – by modern standards – pool of middle class taxpayers. They grumbled not just at the use to which their taxes were now being put but also, more significantly, at the very principle of 'unprecedented state interference in the rights and duties of parents'.[18]

They might have saved their breath. By 1907 state intrusion into people's lives was here to stay. State education of the masses until 14 years of age was a fact, and society was infinitely better off because of it. By 1914 virtually every child left school at 14 able to read as well as write in a neat round hand, as any glance at the soldiers' letters of the Great War can prove. (Even that last bastion of feudalism, the Imperial Russian Army, reflected this change. In 1880 only 22 per cent of Russian recruits could read and write; by 1913 the figure had increased to 68 per cent.[19]) At the start of the twenty-first cen-tury, when Britain conceals the worst literacy record in Europe except for Poland, with over 7 million adults admitting 'serious difficulties in reading and writing', it is important to remember that the generation that met war in 1914 treasured literacy as a universal goal and had effectively achieved it.[20]

Ever alert, the marketplace recognized this opportunity to make money. Just as the state, and the growing army of liberal reformers busily involved in 'improving the lot of the poor/the working man/the East End/orphans /prostitutes/the homeless' (to name but a few of the reformist committees and institutions of 1900–1914), realized that 'the few could impose their own higher standards on the many … and were able to explore their grip on, and access to, the methods of mass communication to achieve it', so did the ever vigilant market forces of commercialism.[21] For a population who could all read, advertisers offered a remarkable array of inducements to buy the won-drous products now on offer. Any contemporary photograph of urban life in 1900–1914 invariably has its ubiquitous advertisements in the background, exhorting the literate masses to buy happiness and joy by the exclusive use of their product. Television invented neither mass advertising nor the consumer society.

The products themselves reveal much about people's expectations and social attitudes, and reflected the massive social changes taking place. The new urban masses had not only consumer needs: they also had, more importantly (from the sellers' point of view), lots more money to spend. 'Disposable income' was for the first time widespread in society. 'Trickle-down economics' may be fashionable or derided today but in the period between 1880 and the outbreak of the First World War the theory was validated many times over and its practical application obvious in every back street corner shop.

These new urban consumers' needs were catered for by a bewildering proliferation of new goods and services, offers, recreation, travel and entertainment. The whole process was encouraged by a mass media promoting 'consumerism' for the first time to the bourgeois middle classes and their faithful imitators, the growing and increasingly prosperous working class. Hardly surprisingly (given the combination of available money plus a literate population with leisure and a massive range of new goods and services), an identifiable 'popular mass culture' began to emerge for the first time between 1880 and 1914.

By far the most popular leisure activity was still drinking. The average working man was more likely to be socializing, drinking in the pub, café or *Gasthaus* than ever before. But appearances are deceptive. Unlike the Hogarthian excesses of *Gin Lane*, the well-paid working man of Edwardian times was no longer attempting to anaesthetize himself from an otherwise unendurable existence. The pub and the music hall often represented not the desperation of the poor but the aspirations of an increasingly prosperous society.

This increasingly sophisticated society tended to seek its pleasures in a myriad of other ways. The Edwardian scene was rich, in terms of not just money, but also diversity. For the upper classes and the really wealthy, diversion was to be found in the traditional social round of horse racing, field sports, the 'Season' and a restless programme of travel, to Cowes, the Riviera or Vienna. For the growing middle classes, 'progress' now brought them too the inestimable blessing of safer, affordable and reliable travel, previously the monopoly of the rich. In their millions they flocked to their own seaside and other resorts, free from worry. In fact, by 1914, any Briton with money could

> proceed abroad to foreign quarters, without knowledge of their religion, language or customs, bearing coined wealth upon his person, and would consider himself greatly aggrieved and much surprised at the least interference. But, most important of all, he regarded this state of affairs as normal, certain and permanent, and any deviation from it as aberrant, scandalous and avoidable.[22]

In Keynes's analysis of both the laissez-faire state of mind of the pre 1914 traveller, and also the loose borders of pre 1914 Europe, whether from Sheffield to Scarborough or Lille to Le Touquet, lies another important clue to the very different way of thinking for all classes before the Great War: a sense of permanence and unfettered liberty. The society that went off to war in 1914 was securely founded on hundreds of years' solid bedrock of established custom, practice, precedent and beliefs. Whether it was 'God, King and Country', '*La République*' or '*Unser Kaiser und Vaterland*', older, unshaken values underpinned the increasingly complex, progressive society revealed to us in pictures, books and people's lives. Centuries of years of social stability and economic structures remained basically unchanged, if not completely unchallenged. The Edwardian world was an ordered place with the certainty that stemmed from an unshaken belief in the institutions that made up a long-established society. All classes (and most people) knew their place. Even the most fiery radicals and revolutionaries acknowledged the fact of an ordered and structured society, if only the better to attack it.

This rigid acceptance of caste was not only widely held, but formally taught. For example, a well-known French school textbook of 1907 stated as a guide for French state teachers:

My good 13-year-old boy, your tasks are to learn your trade, to obey your parents and your bosses ... to cast your vote without personal interest, to carry out your military national service with modesty and sincerity, to work hard, and to raise your children ... [23]

Before the Great War few people questioned this view of the young male's social role and prospects.

This acceptance of a broadly unchanged and only slowly evolving social and political order had important spin-off effects. First it encouraged the universal acceptance of authority, secondly it promoted the growth of institutions the better to climb the permanent trellis of the existing social order.

Authority in 1914 was everywhere. The modern cult of sturdy, anti-authority individualism based on individuals' 'rights' would have been little understood before the First War. A Briton's 'rights' were seen as primarily freedom and property. The Englishman in particular may have felt his personal liberty more keenly then from behind the bastion of his own front door but, by and large, he elected to merge his personal sovereignty into that of the group. By our present-day standards, people in the lost world of pre 1914 were much more sociable and lived in a society with much more obviously defined communities, groups, extended families and even neighbours. Clubs and institutions of every kind flourished to an astonishing degree, for all classes and conditions of men and women, before the First World War.

The first and foremost of these institutions was the trade union. Just as the most pervasive – if involuntary – organization for most people's lives was the office, mill or factory of their workplace, then the most important voluntary organization tended to be that associated with it. Acceptance of the rigid authority of the master, boss or overseer bred counterbalancing and parallel organizations, frequently equally hierarchical and authoritarian. But this desire to 'join' was not just confined to protecting the 'rights' of skilled labourers' jobs or the workplace; it went hand in hand with an equally powerful drive to better oneself, or even others, in order to make the world a better place. This almost evangelical zeal permeated society at nearly every level and sometimes found surprising expression. For example, the converts to the new secular faith of the Independent Labour Party preached its message with an almost religious fervour:

> A cycle corps ... was formed ... and audiences were gathered on village greens by the singing of the choirs; then short and simple addresses on Socialism were given. On these country jaunts the cyclists distributed leaflets and pasted slips on gates, even sticking them on cows, bearing such slogans as 'Socialism: the Hope of the World'.[24]

Thus did the new mobility of the mass-marketed people's transport ally itself with the almost Wesleyan desire to improve others in Edwardian England.

This powerful desire to socialize and join groups that so marked the decades before the Great War found expression in a dense thicket of groups and organizations. In those far-off days before the solitary vices of television and the computer claimed our undivided attention, people joined organizations. Baden-Powell's Boy Scout movement, church or chapel, the Mothers' Union, sports clubs, self improvement institutes, the Territorial Army, choral societies, the YMCA, the Temperance League, the Boys' Brigade, brass bands and working men's clubs all flourished. This desire to combine with others permeated all levels of society. Just as royalty could be worshipful masters of the Grand Lodge of England's Masonic Craft, so too could their loyal, if socially distant, subjects emulate them as members of the Royal and Ancient Order of Buffaloes, or their local Mechanics' Institute. In 1914 people 'belonged'. The men who went off to war in 1914 were from a generation of 'joiners'.[25]

One fictional, but quite clearly autobiographical, source of support for this structured view of society before 1914 is *A Chronicle of Ancient Sunlight* by Henry

Williamson. In this panorama of life in the years from 1900 to 1930, Williamson's fictional (and slightly 'wet') hero, Phillip Maddison, belongs to the Boy Scouts, goes to the local grammar school, joins the Territorial Army and finds himself going off to war in 1914. His middle-aged, middle class father feels duty bound to be a special constable. As a record of suburban English social structure, lives and attitudes before the First World War Williamson's broad sweep has never been bettered, and gives a far more accurate view of society, as it was, than any retrospective scholastic social history. More importantly, Williamson's later treatment of the horrors of war is more accurate in its portrayal of men's reactions than the more self-conscious and shocked reactions of the generally more upper class 'war poets', who had never experienced 'real life' or the rough brutalities of the workplace before they volunteered for the Front.[26] (It is a sad comment on pre 1914 standards of health and safety at work that casualties from industrial accidents in mill and mine often matched 'quiet days' on the Western Front.)

Williamson's account reinforces the 'vigorously literary' climate of his day, when for a brief period classical education and popular education coincided.[27]

If increased knowledge, greater economic choice, and a general desire to form associations to better their lives were the mainsprings of Edwardian social life, then there were two darker forces lurking in the wings of pre 1914 society: the spectre of poverty and the problems of political change.

Nowadays, when we look back at pre 1914 Europe, and Edwardian Britain in particular, we tend to concentrate on social problems like prostitution or the plight of the poor. But as a way of understanding pre 1914 society, this narrow focus does not stand up to too deep a scrutiny, any more than drugs or the 'underclass' define life for most people today. The fact is that the great majority of our great-grandparents did *not* live in urban squalor by the standards of their time. The Rowntree of York study of 1899 and Charles Booth's findings in his *Life and Labour in London* of 1889 calculated that 8 per cent of the population were so poor that 'they could not guarantee food, shelter or clothing' (the classic historic definitions of human needs) and another 22 per cent were in fact living in 'secondary poverty', which Booth identified as 'living by hand to mouth week to week'. The army of 1914 was drawn from a society in which about one in twelve of Britons had to struggle every week just to get by.[28]

Yet all this was at a time when real wages were rising and real prices were falling. The conundrum of how to address this disparity was the great Edwardian domestic political issue. Poverty and the redistribution of wealth in a highly unequal society obsessed the prosperous political classes in the years following the Boer War. By 1906 a new Liberal government, bent on social reform, introduced major social legislation designed to change society for ever, culminating in 1909, when the radical Liberal Chancellor Lloyd George introduced the 'People's Budget', specifically targeted 'against poverty and squalor'. At a time when Britain was rearming at a prodigious rate to meet the escalating German naval challenge, this increased scale of government spending was breathtaking. If nothing else, it demonstrates just what a rich country Britain was in the years before the First War and just how effective were the social reformers' efforts. In 1909 for the first time in peacetime, government spending on social programmes exceeded that on defence.[29]

As with so many revolutions, the poor wanted more. Led by the new trade unions, now protected from the legal consequences of their actions by law, organized labour began a militant campaign of strikes and stoppages of savage intensity to wrest power, money and influence from the governing and propertied classes. British industry, already feeling the terminal effects of German and American competition, became both polarized and paralysed in the period 1906–14. Social order broke down, in some cases very seriously indeed:

> In 1911 there was a general strike in Liverpool ... as near revolution as anything I have seen in Britain ... For three months nothing moved in Liverpool. The dockers did not handle any cargoes. The railway porters came out. The tramway men went idle. Even road sweepers declined to work. Some troops were sent into the city to maintain order, but increased disorder because they were stoned by the strikers and ordered not to shoot, even in self defence ...[30]

Nowadays we tend to forget just how violent was the political turmoil and social upheaval so prevalent before the First World War, not only in Britain, but all over Europe. The long-established tectonic plates of the old political order were shifting uneasily as a score of grievances, political issues and economic reforms forced change onto reluctant governments. In Britain it was the suffragettes, social reform and Ulster; in France the extreme left; in Germany the demands of the Reichstag; and in Austria-Hungary, most disastrous for all, the pressures of nationalism. Despite the golden economic climate, change and violence were everywhere abroad. In the words of R. J. Unstead, 'Beneath the gaiety and comfortable assurance, there was strife.'[31]

One of the ironies of the period is precisely this contrast between the stability of 'God, King and Empire' on the one hand and the violent, almost revolutionary changes being forced through society at the same time. The certainties of Empire, Free Trade, the 'rich man in his castle, the poor man at his gate' seem to us to fit uneasily with the ever-present newspaper reports of strikes, impending civil war in Ireland, the attacks of the suffragettes and the social disorder of the 1900s. As Jose Harris noted, writing of Edwardian Britain:

> ... nothing in the sociological theories of the period quite prepares one for the extraordinary co-existence of extreme social inequality with respect for and observance of the law, of growing public disorder with fierce defence of civil liberties, and of endemic structural and economic change with social and institutional cohesion, that characterised British society for most of the period 1870 to 1914.[32]

From the above it is clear that British society immediately before the Great War was a very different world to our own. Great wealth coexisted alongside deep poverty, and the apparent calm of a century of order was sometimes keeping the lid on a potential eruption of social strife. It was a complex network of classes, organizations and powerful pressure groups held together by an apparently well-ordered and stable society. Our distant view of such societies – such as France in 1789 – inevitably veers towards the general and the quickly grasped caricature, ideally simplified on screen to make complexities easier to comprehend and represent. It is difficult to understand the nuances of another time.

To take one example, 'class'. Class differences seem so clear-cut, so divisive, so easy to see in the old films and books that we assume that class must have been a major source of social discontent in the pre 1914 world. That is often a mistake. The most cursory glance at the real lives of most people and the writings of the time proves that 'class' was by no means a *disabling* problem for our Edwardian grandparents. Using our modern values, we just assume that it was. On the contrary: not only did our Edwardian forebears accept 'class' as part of their society, they accepted it as part of the immutable order of things and a constructive framework of social order. In many cases, and at some surprising levels, they even approved of it. For example, in 1910 the relatively new Labour Party made a clear distinction between the 'real' working class and the 'unemployables', talking of 'those who are allowed ... to wander about parading their sores and propagating their kind'. Even the TUC itself called the 'unemployable' 'a menace to the State'.[33]

Not only did acceptance of class provide a social fabric, this same class structure helped to pull the country together at times of crisis. 'Class differences' were certainly no bar to the enthusiastic reception to the news of the outbreak of war in 1914. The shared bonds of nationalism far transcended ideas of social class or economic self-interest. This realization shocked socialist radicals throughout Europe on the outbreak of war, who had believed – or hoped – that the 'international brotherhood of the working man' would somehow triumph over national tensions. They were sadly mistaken. The murder of Jaurès in Paris on 31 July 1914 effectively killed any dreams of international class solidarity as well as a Socialist icon. The radicals of the Left, like a later vociferous minority of protestors against the Falklands War of 1982, were swept away on a tidal wave of national fervour, fuelled by genuine nationalist enthusiasms for a war, and egged on by a rabidly jingoistic press. National ties counted for more than class war.

Many of the 1914 attitudes and excesses of nationalism and patriotism can be explained away by ignorance. In an age when, despite a burgeoning press and some very limited tourism for the rich, 'abroad' was unknown territory for the majority of citizens, ignorance and fear of foreigners was the norm. The age of CNN and global communications has made us very different to the generation that confronted the world crisis in 1914. Despite the influence of the mass media of the day (which had a yellow press to rival our own), few people in 1914 were interested in 'abroad'. Insulated by a hot summer, trouble in Ireland, domestic diversions and a general ignorance of the world about them, even the shooting of the Archduke Franz Ferdinand at Sarajevo on 28 June 1914 scarcely stirred a ripple in the popular press. To find a parallel today we have to go to the hedonistic young students on a provincial American campus to discover anything remotely comparable to the blissful ignorance with which the 1914 generation went to war, secure in their own delusions of supremacy and oblivious to great events in the wider world.

There were other key attitudes that differentiated the men – and women – of 1914 from us. Nationalism sprang not just from Darwinian ideas of racial superiority and Nietzschean influences on educated thought, but also from the unifying symbol of 'the British Empire'. British national consciousness was inextricably entwined with imperial glory, rights and responsibilities. For even the poorest British family, save for a tiny minority of political cranks or activists, the Empire was a source of stability, self-belief in their superiority, pride, or stern duty. Half the globe coloured pink really meant something in a way that we today find incomprehensible, if not downright embarrassing. We are different people. In a post-colonial era, with the humiliations of Singapore, Cyprus and Suez to look back on, it is almost impossible for us to realize just how strong a unifying feature 'the Empire' was. But imperial ties were a genuine force in 1914 and were sufficiently powerful to pull hundreds of thousands of new Canadians, Australians, New Zealanders and South Africans from the white colonial dominions back across the oceans to volunteer to fight – and to die – for 'the mother country'.

Britons were not alone in these imperial attitudes. Although arriving late amid the comity of nations, the Kaiser's post-1871 New German Empire made special efforts to drum up pan-Germanic and imperial solidarity too. In a phrase from a German history schoolbook of 1908,

> The Empire is unified, powerful and respected in the world. The differences between classes no longer exist. All paths are open to personal industry and talent. All people can take part in their government ... The condition of the lower classes has improved.[34]

It could have been written about Britain.

Nationalism and the Empire were but one of the widely held attitudes that make the generation that rushed to the colours in 1914 so foreign to us today. Britons then held a different set of shared values based on their own perceptions of property, society and the law, down to a common cultural identity centred on church, school, clubs and work. These attitudes were not only broadly held; they were also often sharply at variance with our present-day values. To take just one example, 'property' and 'property rights' still stood at the heart of English law far more than our present legal view of individual or 'human' rights.

This view of British society as a group of increasingly prosperous, literate, free individuals with legal rights to property, labour and free association and ruled by a stratified hierarchical oligarchy went very deep in 1914. It was a society held together by shared values such as imperialism and national pride, reinforced by a powerful mass media, and driven by a strong impulse by all classes for economic self-interest in a climate of growing economic prosperity. Only those on the fringes of society, such as the very poor, were excluded from this general drive towards progress. This view of a coherent if different Edwardian society should not obscure the very real tensions and antagonisms that existed like fault lines within Britain and which very nearly brought the country to the brink of *civil* war in 1914. Pre 1914 Great Britain had its own problems. They were however handled very differently from the way in which we deal with our political problems today.

For example, there was much less government. The law, medicine and the universities genuinely regarded themselves as free organizations effectively independent of the state and were deeply traditional in every way. Even on the major institutions of the state, the impact of government in Edwardian Britain reflected a very different emphasis from today. Organizations like the civil service (a much smaller organization in 1914), the judiciary and to a marked degree the armed forces were surprisingly free from direct governmental, and certainly political, interference both within their own cloisters and in the day to day performance of their duties. Nowhere, paradoxically, was the impact of government less welcome than in the two core organs of the state totally funded by the taxpayer, the Royal Navy and the Army. Both the armed services were fiercely traditional and proud of their independence from political meddling. Although a highly technical and radical service in 1914, even the Royal Navy still remained deeply conservative in the attitudes of its officers and men, especially in the area of internal discipline.

The army was even more so. As John Keegan has pointed out, war is primarily a social activity and all armies are 'genuinely social organisations governed by their own social laws'. Every army reflects the society from which it is drawn, from the introverted (and sometimes downright strange) rites of the Prussian-German General Staff to the Victorian ethos of prefectorial 'service', public school values and organizational behaviour which characterized the pre 1914 army.[35]

The four years of war that followed in 1914 were to transform the pre-war army, like every other institution of Edwardian Britain, from the tiny, self-governing and insulated organization that went to war into something much bigger and more impersonal. In 1914 the British Army was a small (less than 250,000 strong), socially exclusive organization, split half between the UK and half overseas. Its officer corps was tiny, and, after the hard lessons of South Africa, professionally well qualified for modern warfare. Its commanders were men who had fought and succeeded on active service (French, Haig, Smith-Dorrien, Plumer, Allenby, Byng) and all of them knew each other well. It was an army that 'was recruited from the bottom of society but led from the top', in J. F. C. Fuller's well-worn phrase, and the social values of the officer corps were essentially those of the king and court. The effect was of a self-governing stolid élite, obsessed by horses and field sports, far removed from the pressures and clamour of everyday life. Most officers stayed out of politics, despised politicians and the middle classes and were interested mainly in 'the Regiment', promotion and active service for God, King and Country with a bit of adventure and fun thrown in.

'The Regiment' was the be-all and end-all of the army in 1914. Officers and men alike joined a regiment, trained with a regiment, served overseas with their regiment and focused their complete lives around 'the Regiment'. In fact, in one very real sense, 'the Army' as an organization did not really exist as a permanent entity. It was the regiments that made up the army that were legally the permanent organizations, for every year Parliament had to vote an Army Act to allow the government to maintain its standing army. On the back of this annual parliamentary bill rested the whole legal system of military law and King's Regulations.

This concentration on the regiment meant that all ranks were effectively psychologically bonded onto a small (an infantry battalion was only about 1,000 strong) world that fed them, clothed them, worked them hard, trained them, looked after their welfare, and, if they transgressed its own special rules, punished them. Ruled over wherever it was in the world by a commanding officer with the summary powers of a magistrate and the confidence to exercise his power if required, the regiment was the officer's and soldier's universe. The regiment's standards were a reflection of the society of the day, when capital punishment was an accepted penalty in both peace and war for soldier and civilian alike. In the same way that flogging was acceptable to Wellington's army a hundred years before, the indignities of Field Punishment No. 1 and the final sanction of capital punishment were accepted by the British Army of 1914–18 and regarded as normal.

The soldiers who joined this mini-society were all seven-year volunteers, mostly recruited from the intelligent and ambitious youth of the working class.[36] Most regular soldiers volunteered to escape the tedious, back-break ing or futureless manual work that was on offer in the first decade of the twentieth century. According to the official statistics, in 1913 manual labourers comprised 68 per cent of the recruits and only 3 per cent were 'clerical'.[37]

These impressionable young men, anxious to please, were only too easily moulded by a training tradition whose corporate memory extended back over two centuries and was designed to recreate civilians swiftly into the army's image. Like fledglings 'imprinting' on their parents, the working class recruit came to rely on the regiment, his NCOs and his officers – but above all his mates, or 'chums' in the jargon of the time – for a life offering welfare, security and, in the final analysis, survival in battle. In the army, those who survived the rigours of training found a new home in their regimental pride, a sense of belonging to an institution that was greater than any individual, a job they could master (the fire of British riflemen shocked the Germans so badly at Mons they claimed they had run into an army of machine guns) and a life they could enjoy among men of their own kind. The regiment gave these men a well-ordered, secure and clearly directed world ruled by a hierarchy that reflected fairly accurately the distribution of power and influence in Edwardian society and epitomized its values.

The old regular army was an insulated world regulated by its own rules and customs within a deeply hierarchical structure. It was a world where officers and men knew and trusted each other, and with the self-assurance that comes from being members of a competent, confident group apart. At the apex of the pyramid was the commanding officer (CO), a colonel who effectively represented 'the Squire'. From him flowed promotion, patronage, praise and blame, but, above all, direction to the little world that was the regiment. Under him came the officers: the senior major, four or five company commanders (majors or captains) and up to twenty younger officers – platoon commanders, controlled by a captain adjutant plus the supporting officers: a padre, a quartermaster and a doctor. In a society where not only economic but also educational inequalities were much more marked, the officers tended to be relatively well educated – compared with the soldiers – and selected from the scions of 'good families', 'county set', 'new money' or sons of the regiment. To be an officer in a smart regiment was a prestigious thing in 1914, and to fit in with the rowdy, haughty and critical set of the officers' mess, a private income was essential, particularly for the cavalry or Guards.

Under the officers were the non-commissioned officers – corporals who had done more than seven years commanding sections of ten or more men: and sergeants, hardbitten, long-service regulars 'going for their pension' at twenty-two years, who were the iron rods that ruled the platoons. The sergeants, and above them the four or five sergeant majors under the regimental sergeant major (RSM), ran the regiment on a day to day basis. Officers may have made the decisions and given the orders, but it was the NCOs who ensured that they were carried out. It was the NCOs, and particularly the senior NCOs, who watched the men like hawks and in the final analysis dealt with any problems 'on the shop floor' of regimental life. Officers managed by exception. They may have been the fount of authority but they freely delegated it to their NCO subordinates. The key was that everyone knew each other and had been tried and tested over several years. The RSM was usually of the same age and service as the CO and both would have known each other in the regiment for twenty-odd years. Young platoon commanders were exhorted to 'listen and learn from your sergeant ...'. In a status-conscious world that relied on mutual respect and everyone knowing their role in the system, the regiment – and the army – was a microcosm of Edwardian Britain.

Such a closed, insular system had many drawbacks. But it was designed to do one thing, and one thing only: go anywhere in the world and fight until recalled. The regiment was a self-contained flexible machine for fighting, as competent and as self-governing a little world as a Roman legion.

It was also a world of rigid standards and high expectations. Soldiers were expected to carry out their orders to the letter and do as they were told: failure to do so in the pre-war army would result in an instant disciplinary charge and appearance before the company commander or (much worse) the commanding officer. Most soldiers had spent some time in the guardroom at some point of their careers. NCOs were expected to ensure that the soldiery did their duty without mercy or favouritism; and the officers were expected to lead their soldiers from the front and, above all, look after their men. Woe betide the young lieutenant who failed to inspect his men's feet in an infantry battalion that relied for its mobility on marching 20 miles a day, every day if necessary, or who failed to ensure that his men were properly fed and bedded down before he took himself off to the mess! Weeks of extra duties – without any right of appeal – would swiftly follow, summarily dispensed by a curt adjutant. If an officer failed to live up to the expectations of his brother officers or consistently failed in his duties he would be invited to leave, or, if he failed to take the hint, exiled to some dreary staff post far from the regimental home. These standards – which were universally understood and accepted – extended to every area of the officer's and the soldier's life.

Fashionable though it may have become to deride our grandfathers' values and behaviour, it was a world of formidable courage. In an age that has come to believe in wars without casualties and no body bags – except for the enemy – it is chilling to record that the 100,000 strong BEF that went to France in August 1914 had suffered 96,000 casualties by the end of the year; and not in the mud of the trenches either.[38]

Most of these casualties were a result of the often ignored mobile warfare which characterized the autumn fighting of 1914, or in the bitter defence around Ypres as winter set in. These BEF losses were made good first by the Territorial forces, then the Kitchener volunteers until, by 1917, conscription provided the bulk of the army. By 1918 the old army had expanded by fourteen times its original strength and there were very few survivors from the lost world of 1914. But in spirit and in discipline it was the same army, reflecting the same values by which the old regulars had marched off four years earlier to fight and die.

The truth was that the hundreds of thousands of volunteers who enthusiastically flocked into the recruiting offices in 1914 and 1915 were very different men from the recruits who had 'gone for a soldier' in the pre-war days of peace. As the new armies mushroomed overnight, the surviving professionals were swamped by the flood of enthusiastic amateurs. These last survivors of the ordered world and historic practices of the old regular army could only meet the challenge of Kitchener's new mass citizen army by inculcating their own tried and tested military values as quickly as possible in the middle of a war that had completely overwhelmed them. It was a transfer of values, dedication, working practices, pride and discipline that would have far-reaching consequences for many of the 'new armies'. For the rest of the war, the British Army was effectively forced to ignore the magnificent potential of its well-educated new citizen army, and train them, treat them, fight with them and expect them to behave as if they were exact replacements for the long-vanished regulars of 1914.

In a far-off age that seems vaguely familiar to us, but is in reality only a familiar landscape inhabited by vanished ghosts with alien attitudes, values and beliefs, nothing symbolizes that lost world of pre 1914 Britain so much as the men of the old regular army. Whatever we may think from the pictures we have seen, the men who went off to war in 1914 came from a world that is a long-dead foreign country to us now. It was a closed world, mustachioed, confident, built around the horse, and populated by tough, solid working class men led by a semi-aristocratic snobbish élite, the whole bound together by comradeship, mutual trust, pride in the regiment, a clear hierarchy and, above all, old-fashioned standards of behaviour backed up and enforced by a ferocious code of discipline.[39, 40]

CHAPTER 2

THE HISTORY AND DEVELOPMENT OF MILITARY LAW

It is not the general that punishes severely ... he only adminsters the laws of the military. Do this and he will be loved, he will be feared; but, above all, he will be obeyed.

MARÉCHAL COMTE DE SAXE, 1732

All armies need discipline. It is the core value that distinguishes the uniformed, regulated fighting force from an armed mob. In order to control an army and order its activities, there has to be an accepted set of rules by which that army can regulate the conduct of its members. Although these rules have varied from age to age and have inevitably reflected the prejudices of different societies over the years, at heart they all share one common purpose: control.

This concept of control is what really distinguishes military law from civilian law. Theoretically the civilian law is concerned with an abstract concept called 'justice' and increasingly today with the rights of the individual. As early as AD 430 Vegetius, the Roman military writer, spelled out with brutal clarity the difference between civil and military codes of justice – the primary purpose of military law is to ensure that the will of the commander is obeyed at all times.

Such ideas go back to the very earliest times. There is evidence that Egyptian pharaohs had a uniform set of laws to discipline and control their armies, and by the time of Christ, according to Tacitus, the Romans had already codified their basic military law. Significantly, the fount of this military law was the elected political magistracy. Their republican legitimacy as 'imperators' was translated in time of war into legal authority over the soldier-citizens conscripted to make up the republic's legions. As the empire later developed, the system became even more formalized, until by the fifth century the Emperor

Justinian had a 'Digest and Codex of Military Laws' published for the regulation of his widely spread army. In addition to the historic need to control the armies a new principle was recognized and codified – even in states where civilian control was theoretically paramount, the military have a special need for self-regulation. The need for instant obedience, strict discipline, and the unchallengeable authority of the commander in time of war meant that even for the most liberal democracy there has been a widespread acknowledgement that the military forces needed powers of self-regulation within a separate code of justice. Even the advent of that most humanitarian organization, the European Court of Human Rights, has explicitly recognized the existence and importance of a separate judicial code for the military. In 1976 a group of Dutch soldiers tried to sue the Dutch Army for the suppression of an underground newspaper criticizing the military authorities, which they claimed denied them their rights under the European Convention on Human Rights, 1950. The court found against them. In a landmark decision it ruled that 'the freedom of expression guaranteed by Article 10 applies just as much to servicemen as it does to other persons within the contracting States [of the Treaty]. However, the proper functioning of an Army is hardly imaginable without legal rules to prevent servicemen from undermining lawful authority [and discipline].'[1]

Part of this is caused by the nature of warfare. Just as civilian society has rules, or laws, to control the day to day conduct of its members and to regulate their activities, so too does that other expression of a society, its army and armed forces. Nothing has changed fundamentally since Vegetius spelled it out in Roman times. The reason is clear: the unique requirements of soldiering and campaigning. For a tribune commanding an ill-paid, restless and often mutinous bunch of well-armed men on the distant frontiers of the empire, the ability – and the right – to dispense justice had to be delegated, swift and exemplary if he were not to lose control over his legion. For armed, aggressive men, whose core values were blood, iron, drink, discipline and gambling, clear and firm authority was a cornerstone of everyday life. This need for delegated power, and the legitimacy of such authority far from home, runs through all concepts of military law. Military justice often has to be summary justice if an army or a ship of war is to survive as a disciplined entity in times of trouble, far from home.

This distinction between military and civilian law was also clearly recognized in the concept of 'martial law' (a much misunderstood and misused phrase) which historically has placed civilians under the control of the military commander for some period, usually following a military occupation, to control disorder or to enforce order in a crisis. (Where civil law cannot operate, then military law is used. Nature – even the law – abhors a vacuum.) The military's laws have invariably been recognized as quicker, more brutal and more effective in restoring a situation than civil law. 'Martial law' can therefore be seen as a crude reflection of the virtues – and vices – of military law: swift, uncompromising and little concerned with the rights of the peacetime citizen or individuals' rights. When the Goths and Vandals are pouring over the city walls intent on killing and raping, civilians do what the legionary commanders tell them if everyone is to survive – or else. It is a crude but clear-cut proposition. It also reflects the very core purpose of military law: 'Do as you're told, if the army is to survive as an army.'

As medieval society developed in Europe the maintenance of discipline within its squabbling armies was enforced by 'articles of war', promulgated as special ordinances by the sovereign using the royal prerogative as a legal basis. In 1189, for example, the English king Richard I published a charter to regulate the conduct of his army going to crusade in the Holy Land. And by the time of the Tudors, military justice in England had, significantly, been delegated to the Court of the Constable and Marshal, with clear orders to enforce a code of discipline on the army when it was raised 'as ordered by the King's most sovereign majesty'.[2]

As the wars of religion spread across Europe in the sixteenth and seventeenth centuries national commanders and, more importantly, mercenary commanders began to set down their own rules for their particular army or armed band. From the Condottieri of Renaissance Italy to Frundsberg's Landsknechte of the 1500s, separate codes of military laws sprang up to try to control the marauding soldiers of a continent permanently at war.

The most influential of these was the code set down by Sweden's warrior king Gustavus Adolphus from 1630 onwards. As champion of the Protestant cause Gustavus brought the values of the new religion to bear on his soldiers. Military law was a high priority in his reforming zeal, alongside discipline, regular pay and a well-ordered administrative machine that brooked no corruption or defiance of authority.[3]

Where Gustavus led, others followed. Wallenstein, his Catholic adversary, emulated many of the Swede's reforms, as did Oliver Cromwell, who ordered the English New Model Army firmly on Gustavus's theories and practice. Although many of the disciplinary offences of the New Model Army were merely the offences of any soldier on active service from time immemorial, the great difference lay in their codification into English and their consistent application through a uniformly regulated disciplinary system. The New Model Army can truly be said to be the historic foundation of Britain's – and America's – code of military law.

There remained but one crucial reform to turn the English Parliament's statutes for regulating Cromwell's highly efficient, well-armed, powerful and politically dangerous army in time of war into a permanent code of military law. Until the 'Glorious Revolution' of 1688, all 'Articles of War' had been strictly temporary, issued under the sovereign's prerogative for the period of an emergency. Thus, even as late as Monmouth's rebellion of 1685, King James II authorized temporary Articles of War, just as his predecessor Richard II had done in 1385 and Charles I had done in 1642 at the start of the English Civil War.

The growth of a standing army in time of peace and the danger of new political rebellion worried English libertarians. In March 1689 Parliament debated and passed the first Mutiny Act, which embodied four important principles. First, civilians were exempt from military – or 'martial' – jurisdiction; secondly, it recognized the concept of, and specified, some purely military crimes, such as desertion and mutiny; thirdly, it authorized specialist courts martial to ensure that the military could discipline and regulate itself quickly; and, perhaps most important, it was (with annual parliamentary review) eventually to become a permanent code of law.[4]

At the end of Marlborough's wars in 1712, the Mutiny Act was allowed to expire and replaced by an Act 'for better regulating the forces to be maintained in Her Majesty's [Queen Anne's] service'. This Mutiny Act of 1712 was a more wide-ranging and explicit code of military law. In it a number of specific military offences were identified as *military crimes* and the power to try them, and to punish, delegated to the military authorities by the Crown acting in Parliament.[5] Over the next century these powers were further codified, until by the Napoleonic Wars the Crown exercised complete statutory control over all British armed forces worldwide by means of the Mutiny Act and statutory Articles of War issued under royal prerogative.

By 1879 the inconvenience of having two separate codes for the army led to a single consolidating measure, the Army Discipline and Regulation Act of that year. Two years later, as part of the wide-ranging army reforms of the late Victorian period, the first Army Act of 1881 became law. Thus, in the words of Mr Justice Blackstone a century earlier, Parliament had finally agreed with his earnest wish 'that it might be thought worthy of the wisdom of

Parliament to ascertain the limits of military subjection and to enact (proper) Articles for the Government of the Army'.[6]

With the 1881 Army Act 'military law' as we know it in Britain became a fully integral part of the legal system of justice. It also, with reviews in 1887, 1894, 1899 and 1907, led to the sixth edition of the authoritative *Manual of Military Law* published by HMSO for the War Office in February 1914. This was the 'bible' of military law that the British Expeditionary Force took to France in 1914.

CHAPTER 3

MILITARY LAW IN 1914:
THE *MANUAL OF MILITARY LAW*

The function of the Court Martial is to preserve security by preserving the armed forces in a state of discipline. Just that. If it can be done with justice, so much the better; but it must be done.

JOHN TERRAINE

The 1914 edition of the *Manual of Military Law* (MML) is a formidable red tome. Its 908 pages cover everything from 'Abandonment of Post' to the status of 'Yorkshire, Ridings'. Three inches thick and weighing nearly 3 pounds, the *MML* was most certainly not to be found in every soldier's – or indeed every officer's – knapsack. Weight and bulk apart, the *MML* is an impressive document. It is divided into three main sections:

Part 1 is the history and background to military law

Part 2 is the law, or the Army Act itself and its supporting statutory rules and regulations

Part 3 is a miscellany of statutory regulations, ranging from the Railway Regulation Act of 1842 to the first Official Secrets Act of 1911.

Only the details of Parts 1 and 2 need concern us.

Part 1 is particularly interesting, as it is an explanatory commentary on the law as it then stood (1914) in the statutory Army Act. Although it carries no legal weight as an authority, Part 1 goes to considerable lengths to explain the thinking and philosophy behind the law, and would have been an invaluable guide to officers seeking to interpret and unravel the legalistic wording of parliamentary law. For example, in Part 1, Chapter III, paragraph 13, it discusses 'Desertion', the principal capital offence of WW1:

The criterion between desertion and absence without leave is intention.

The offence of desertion ... implies an intention on the part of the offender either not to return to his Majesty's service at all, or to escape some particularly important service...[1]

To further help to clarify desertion, the *Manual* adds an important amplification to guide interpretation of the statute, and one that has a particular significance in many of the cases. Paragraph 14 says:

It is obvious that the evidence of intention to quit the service may be so strong as to be irresistible, as, for instance, if a soldier is found in plain clothes on board a steamer ... in the case ... there could be no doubt of the intention ...[2]

This lengthy explanation explains and illuminates the law, and, more importantly, the commonsense thinking behind it. For a harassed captain straight out of the trenches, tired, muddy and bottling up his shock and grief at the horrific sights and sensations of war, Part 1 would have been a godsend. If he had been ordered – as many were – to report next day back to brigade headquarters in some farmhouse behind the lines to be a member of a court martial, he would have found much to help him in his search for understanding. For example, paragraph 15 of Chapter III on 'Desertion' goes on:

Nor can desertion invariably be judged by distance, for a soldier may absent himself ... to a very considerable distance, and yet the evidence of an intention to return may be clear; whereas he may scarcely quit the camp ... and the evidence of intention not to return ... may be complete.[3]

To further amplify the law and to dispel any doubts as to the intention of the Act, Part 1 goes on in explanatory detail to spell out the common man's interpretation of 'Desertion' before moving on (in paragraph 21) to 'Fraudulent Enlistment' and then to the niceties of 'Embezzling' (paragraph 24) and 'Theft from a Comrade' (paragraph 23).

These paragraphs explaining 'Desertion' are particularly interesting. Paragraph 16 makes the clear point that deliberate absence from an important service, even though the soldier comes back after it is over, suggests 'desertion' in law. Even *attempting to desert* is desertion ('such as "climbing over a barrack wall in plain clothes" '). And in Part I paragraph 20 Chapter III the commentary advises the reader that 'A soldier charged with desertion may be found guilty of attempting to desert or being absent without leave' as a lesser charge. For the harassed regimental officer, fresh from the line, battalion headquarters' much thumbed copy of the *MML* 1914 must have seemed like the ultimate crib on military law. Even the list of subjects of Part 1 is a useful guide to officers forced to confront unfamiliar – and arcane – aspects of their profession. The chapter headings are:

1. Introductory
2. History of Military Law
3. Offences and Scale of Punishments
4. Arrest and the Summary Powers of a Commanding Officer ...
5. Courts Martial
6. Evidence
7. Offences Punishable by Ordinary Law
8. Powers of Courts of Law in relation to Courts Martial and Officers
9. History of the Military Forces of the Crown
10. Enlistment
11. Constitution of the Military Forces of the Crown
12. Relation of Officers and Soldiers to Civil Life
13. Summary of the Law of Riot
14. The Laws and Usages of War

One of the more revealing aspects of the *MML*'s priorities is the hierarchy and scale of punishments contained in Part II of the 1881 Army Act itself, as annually approved by Parliament. There is a clear order of precedence and a related severity of punishment, which reveals very clearly the military's disciplinary priorities and the thinking behind the law. 'Discipline' (Part 1 of the Army Act 1881) not unnaturally heads the list, with 'Application of the Act' (Part VI) bringing up the rear.

Part 1 of the 1881 Act itself is graded very clearly, with 'Mutiny and Sedition' as the most serious offences. Interestingly, this whole grouping of the Act is carefully structured into 'offences punishable by death', 'offences (in relation to the enemy) not punishable by death' and, significantly, 'offences punishable more severely on active service than at other times'. The army has always made the point – in common with most other armies' codes of military law – that the same offence can carry different penalties depending on circumstances. Thus desertion in peacetime is an administrative nuisance dealt with by a scale of minor punishments ranging up to imprisonment. However, desertion – or even unauthorized absence from the firing line – in the face of the enemy is a capital charge. The key words are 'when on active service'. So, for example, sleeping on sentry on an exercise may earn a rebuke, a fine, imprisonment or, even today, a good kick in the ribs in most armies. But to repeat the offence *on active service* in a front line trench in close proximity to the enemy was a potentially capital charge in 1914. The sleeping sentinel is guilty of hazarding his sleeping comrades' lives: sleeping on sentry is not the same as a nightwatchman dozing off on some suburban building site.

This also emphasizes the specifically military nature of many military law offences. Not bothering to turn up for work, refusing to obey the bosses' instructions and arguing with the office manager or foreman are all robust civilian symbols of the sturdy independence of labour in a free market. Today many of these 'rights' are even enshrined in statute. But to try them in a shell-torn trench on a dark night in war – any war – would be to invite swift and condign retribution. If the unforgiving enemy did not take advantage of such disputatious ill discipline, then an equally unforgiving senior NCO or officer would ensure that it did not happen twice. This usually meant a capital charge, as for example Section 6 of the Army Act itself clearly spells out:

> Every person who ... being a soldier acting as sentinel ... sleeps, or is
> drunk, at his post ... shall on conviction by court-martial ... if on active
> service ... suffer death or such less punishment as in this Act mentioned.[4]

The gravest military charge of all in the *MML* was, unsurprisingly, 'assisting the enemy', by for example abandoning a position, shamefully casting away arms, or showing cowardice before the enemy. The *Manual* spells out in some detail the legal thinking behind these charges. For example, the adjective 'shamefully' in the charge 'shamefully casting away arms' is carefully defined in a legal footnote:

> [This charge] must show the circumstances which make the act
> [of throwing away personal weapons] in a military sense shameful. The
> word 'shamefully' is held to mean by a positive and disgraceful dereliction
> of duty, and not merely through negligence or misapprehension or an
> error of judgment.[5]

This wording (which was doubtless consulted and pored over in the well-known case of Lance Sgt Willie Stones, executed for his part in the chaotic breakdown of discipline in the 19th Durham Light Infantry in November 1916, near Arras) also reveals another significant difference between civilian and military law. Most of the civil law is concerned with facts and objective reality; but military law has a number of clearly defined subjective, or behavioural, offences for which (apart from 'recklessness') there are few civilian counterparts, and which reflect specifically military values.

Chief of these is cowardice. Section 4 of the Army Act spells it out briefly and succinctly:

> Every person subject to Military Law who … (7) Misbehaves or induces others to misbehave before the enemy in such manner as to show cowardice, shall on conviction by court martial be liable to suffer death, or such less penalty as is in this Act mentioned.[6]

Now 'cowardice', like so many aspects of human behaviour, is often in the eye of the beholder. It is an essentially subjective judgement. Is the soldier, swallowing, white-faced, hands shaking and wetting his trousers before dashing over the top of a trench into the angry bullets of a machine gun scared? Is he exhibiting fear? Is this cowardice?

Or is the same soldier, weeping with fear and screaming in panic as he runs blindly forward into mortal danger, bullets kicking up dust round his feet, in reality a hero? He looks scared. Fear is infectious. Others may be induced to follow his example, and be 'induced to misbehave'. But our terrified soldier has conquered his fear. Fear, panic, terror – all go into the equation of 'cowardice'. It is perhaps the *outcome* that is the true arbiter of cowardice, such as refusing to obey the order to attack, or running away in fear. Cowardice is in fact the individual's reaction to his (very natural) fear, not the fear itself, despite its only too obvious manifestation. Fear is not cowardice.

The truth is, cowardice can be hard to prove; but other charges such as deserting a post, or disobeying a lawful order, are not. These are clear-cut, black and white matters of fact. For example: 'Did the accused go forward in the attack?' 'No Sir, he lay crying in the bottom of the trench and refused a direct order to advance along with the rest of the platoon …' The offence – suitably substantiated – is proven, and the prosecution rests. The soldier has disobeyed an order in the face of the enemy.

This may be one of the reasons why there were so few (18) charges of cowardice compared with so many charges of the more easily proved desertion (266). This search for an objective charge such as desertion is clearly mirrored in the pattern of court martial charges between 1914 and 1918. The emphasis changes from cowardice in 1915 to, for example, quitting post by 1918.

Other factors may also be at play, reflecting both the nature of military society in 1914–18 and the more subtle, deeper complexities of the masculine psyche. To be a coward has always been a matter of shame in most warrior societies. It strikes at the core value behind the group's very existence and purpose. In military law 'cowardice' is as fundamental an offence as is 'heresy' or 'apostasy' in the Church's canon law. The result is that a charge of 'cowardice' will probably only be proffered as a last resort, either because there is no alternative or because the needs of unit cohesion, or unit shame, demand that an example be made. This aspect, as well as the extra difficulties of proving the charge, may lie as much behind the charges of cowardice as any other reason. To be a 'coward' in a military unit was – and is – unacceptable, and a matter of shame to the coward's comrades. It's a hard thing to prove, but, like sin in the priesthood, a soldier knows it when he sees it. Even the Army Act itself gamely ends up attempting to define the indefinable by a footnote to the statutory clause (note 9 to Section 4):

> *Misbehaves*. This means that the accused, from an unsoldierlike regard
> for his personal safety in the presence of the enemy, failed in respect of
> some distinct and feasible duty imposed on him by a specified order or
> regulation, or by the well understood custom of the service, or by the
> requirements of the case, as was applicable to the position in which he
> found himself.[7]

The modern jurist or liberal twenty-first-century human rights lawyer would probably pounce on the ambiguities, and the legal possibilities contained within that word 'unsoldierlike'. But between 1914 and 1918 all those involved knew just what it meant both behind, and in front of, the court martial table. In a world where any 'disgraceful conduct' ('of a military or social nature')[8] (Section 16 of the Army Act) meant instant cashiering for officers (dismissal with disgrace and prohibition from holding any post under the Crown for life), all concerned knew the rules.

In the next section, Section 5, of the Army Act, Parliament described a list of offences not to be punishable by death, even though committed in the face of the enemy. Surprisingly, these include leaving the line without order for a specific purpose (such as taking wounded to the rear) (subsection 1) and corresponding with the enemy. If nothing else, section 5 clearly demonstrates the parliamentary draftsmen's intention not to allow the military authorities a free rein in all aspects of military law.

Section 6 however is uncompromising and brutally clear. Entitled 'Offences Punishable More Severely on Active Service than at Other Times', section 6 warns that plundering, leaving a guard or post without orders, striking a sentinel, impeding the military provost or even breaking into a civilian house in search of plunder can all be punishable by death if committed 'on active service'. Significantly, the very first explanatory footnote to the Act reinforces this point: 'The punishments ... vary widely according to the offences committed on active service or not on active service.'[9]

It is this explicit recognition that an army's *raison d'être* is to fight – and that the standards required in war, and not in peacetime barracks, are the paramount rules – that colours the next two sections of the Act: Section 7 ('Mutiny') and Section 8 ('Striking a Superior'). These are two essentially military offences (even punching the foreman in civil life is only common assault) and both could be punishable – on active service – by execution.

'Mutiny' is brief and to the point. 'Every person subject to military law who ... causes or conspires with other persons to cause any mutiny or sedition ... in His Majesty's forces', or who 'joins in, or, being present, does not use his utmost endeavours to suppress any mutiny ... shall on conviction by Court Martial be liable to suffer death or such less punishment as in the Act ...'[10] Astonishingly, mutiny is not defined in the Army Act 1881 at all. Any soldier, officer – or lawyer – would have had to look back to Part 1 of the *MML* where a helpful definition of mutiny is given to guide officers applying the law, as part of those offences 'which from their importance or relative frequency require a more detailed notice than others ...'[11] Here mutiny is spelled out as 'collective insubordination, or a combination of two or more persons to resist or induce others to resist lawful military authority'.[12] Not only therefore is Section 7 clear, but in footnote 5 it spells out the precise meaning of 'utmost endeavours' in the wording of the Act: '*Utmost Endeavours*. This does not necessarily mean the utmost of which a person is capable (to prevent a mutiny), but such endeavours as a man might reasonably and fairly be expected to make.'[13] Yet again, the essential fairness of the Parliamentary legal drafter shines through, and any fear of military collective charges is nipped in the bud.

'Striking a Superior Officer' (Section 8) is, quite logically, closely paralleled by Section 9, 'Disobedience to a Senior Officer'. Section 9's paragraphs list disobeying 'in such a manner as to show wilful defiance of authority ...' and, even more to the point, just 'disobeying any lawful command' as potentially capital offences on active service.

The explanatory footnotes go into some detail as to what is and is not a lawful command. Religious scruples are specifically excluded as an excuse for disobedience, and one wonders quite how the modern trend towards the 'civilianization' of military law and modern human rights legislation can possibly square with the unregulated and brutal exigencies of the battlefield either in

1914 or today. War is about killing people and destroying things – not a moral debate.

Interestingly, the footnotes spell out an important point: the man who *says* 'I will not do it' – or words to that effect – does not necessarily disobey a lawful command. That is insubordinate *language*. Actual non-compliance with the order must be separately proved.

So far the 1914 Army Act has run through the pantheon of serious military offences: assisting the enemy; shamefully casting away arms; cowardice; quitting post; leaving the battle line; mutiny; striking or disobeying a superior officer and insubordination. But Section 12 was the offence that prescribed and led to the majority (266, or 80 per cent) of 1914–18 executions.

The consequences of desertion are clearly set out by Parliament:

> Every person subjected to military law who ... Deserts or attempts to desert His Majesty's service ... shall on conviction by court-martial, if he committed such offence when on active service or under orders for active service, be liable to suffer death, or such lesser punishment ...[14]

Again, the precise *definition* of desertion is discussed in Part 1 Chapter III of the *Manual*. For desertion to be proved, intention or clear evidence of an intention not to return, or to avoid a particular service, is all that is required of the prosecuting military authorities. To avoid any possible doubt, footnote 11 to Section 12 of the Act states clearly:

> To establish desertion it is necessary to prove some circumstance justifying the inference that the accused intended not to return to military duty ... or intended to avoid some important particular service, such as active service, [or] embarkation for service abroad ...[15]

The majority of the capital courts martial in the Great War (and 266 out of 306 executions) were to be for precisely this offence.

The 1881 Army Act of Parliament, which was re-approved by Parliament in 1913, as reflected by the *Manual of Military Law*, was clear, totally legal and uncompromising. Moreover, the law made no allowance for individual weakness, human frailties or the shock of the new industrial battlefield. Only a plea of 'mental abnormality' could be a defence – and the mentally abnormal were not recruited for the army in 1914.

CHAPTER 4

MENTAL HEALTH IN
BRITAIN IN 1914

Medicine is the art of keeping the patient amused while nature effects a cure.

MOLIÈRE, 1673

Psychiatry as we know it had not been invented in 1914. Before the Great War 'mental illness' was an unknown concept and the attitude towards mental breakdown of soldiers has to be set against the attitudes prevailing at the time. In 1914 a person was considered either mad or sane – there was no grey area – but even the Edwardian definition of madness needs closer examination.

In early times insanity was regarded as demoniac possession, and in general, unless dangerous, the madman remained at liberty, surviving as best he could. From the mid seventeenth century there was a growing tendency for society to remove from sight any deviant individuals – including the physically or mentally handicapped, those with mental aberrations, the destitute, the homeless, the blind, deaf or dumb, abandoned children and the tubercular. The violent were shackled and manacled, and visiting the lunatic asylums, such as Bedlam, was a form of entertainment. However, by the end of the eighteenth century thinking about the mentally afflicted was changing – Philippe Pinel in France, Dorothea Dix in America and William Tuke in Britain were all leading the way towards the establishment of more humanitarian treatment for these unfortunate individuals. In the mid nineteenth century lunatic asylums sprang up throughout the UK, designed to house the insane poor in the belief that, given proper moral treatment and appropriate occupation, these individuals could be cured. However, there was no distinction made between mental disease and mental deficiency, so there was no distinction between the acutely insane (potentially curable) and the chronic insane (unlikely to be cured), and by the turn of the century the institutions were overcrowded with the chronically insane and mentally deficient. Many of these cases had already spent years in workhouses and had deteriorated both mentally and physically to the point that by the time that they entered the asylum there was no hope of cure.

By the end of the century the failure to achieve a humane cure had led to the mentally ill becoming isolated both socially and geographically in massive mental institutions, usually in semi-rural areas, with high walls, long corridors, prison-like rules, and locked 'wards'. The concept of restraint had replaced moral treatment and the medical superintendent had become a form of prison guard. This, then, was the situation in England just before the war started in 1914.

Whether you were admitted to an asylum or looked after privately depended on social class and the degree of insanity. Many extended families of the day, even the Royal Family, included a dotty aunt or an eccentric uncle who probably harboured a mild degree of mental instability. If a member of a well-off family became too difficult or violent, a 'nurse' or handler might be employed to keep them under control, and if this was not adequate they could be sent to special, secure, private institutions. On the other hand, the poor had no choice and either got by as best they could, or were committed to an asylum or were arrested for vagrancy and sent to prison.

The occupants of such a pre-war lunatic asylum covered every possible type of patient, from the so-called feeble-minded to the unfortunate individuals with epilepsy (for which there was no treatment at the time) and to the frankly insane and the 'morally degenerate' – masturbation was seen as a sign of mental weakness and homosexuality was considered clearly deviant and grounds for incarceration. The social code of the day was, by our standards, brutal. The Mental Deficiency Act of 1913 allowed a local authority to certify as insane and incarcerate a pregnant woman who had been deemed 'immoral', that is to say, unmarried. This Act was not finally repealed until the 1950s and many of the stories of these unfortunate women came to light in the 1980s when the asylums were emptied of their occupants.

Reading a textbook of psychiatry written in 1911 is a revealing and salutary lesson in how attitudes have changed and how far we have moved in terms of understanding disorders of the mind. The main emphasis at the time was on the 'feeble-minded' – the term used by the Royal Commission which looked into mental health in the early years of the century. There are many pictures of patients demonstrating various defects, photographed in a way that today we would regard as frankly degrading – serving to emphasize the 'sub-human' nature of these patients. This view was reinforced by the fact that the psychiatrists responsible for them were called 'alienists', i.e. dealing with alien beings, non-humans. The patients referred to suffer from a variety of disorders – mentally handicapped people, people with epilepsy, but also those suffering from syphilis or described as suffering from moral degeneracy. Chillingly, amongst the descriptions of degeneracy and idiocy is a mention of mirror-writing done by a left-handed 'idiot': 'mirror-writing occurs in idiots who are capable of a limited degree of calligraphic achievement but are incapable of learning to write properly'.[1] Dyslexia, too, was an indication of feeble-mindedness and many dyslexics were incarcerated alongside the insane.

Another factor to consider is that in pre-war Britain a significant number of the inhabitants of an asylum would have been suffering from 'general paralysis of the insane' (GPI), the name then given to tertiary syphilis. Estimates suggest that in 1914 about 10 per cent of the inhabitants of an asylum had this condition, which is associated with abnormal mental states and delusions. After the advent of penicillin this disease largely disappeared but it was extremely common in 1914 – Paul Ehrlich's 'magic bullet', salvarsan, had only been discovered in 1909 and come into widespread use a year later, too late to treat those infected at the turn of the century who were now suffering from GPI during the final stages of the disease. (Incidentally, salvarsan was derived from a dyestuff, an offshoot of the great German organic chemistry industry, and during the Great War the drug became virtually unavailable and a substitute had to be used to treat the explosion of venereal cases between 1914 and 1918.) Among the 'degenerates' housed in the asylums would also be alcoholics, some brain-damaged from the effects of drinking methanol, or wood alcohol, some with delirium tremens.

A manual of psychiatry published in 1916 showed little change in thinking from the end of the nineteenth century and defined a class of people it called 'constitutional neuropaths'.[2] These 'neuropaths' included people with 'sexual anomalies' – a term which covered a wide range of sexual behaviour from eroticism, frigidity, bestiality, necrophilia, masturbation, sadism, masochism and sexual inversion (which would include homosexuality and transvestism). Individuals with tattoos also fell into this group; as tattoos were often observed on criminals and the insane, they were considered a sign of acquired degeneracy.

There is great emphasis on sexual behaviour in the psychology books of the time, in consequence of Freud's contention that sexual factors were at the root of all neuroses. Baden-Powell's advice in *Scouting for Boys* sums up the thinking of the time. 'Should it [masturbation] become a habit it quickly destroys both health and spirits; he becomes feeble in body and mind, and often ends up in a lunatic asylum.'[3]

De Fursac's book also describes the concept of 'moral insanity', which includes 'weakness of judgement', 'absence of perseverance' and 'impulsiveness', and suggests that people with these defects benefit from working in (or detention in) agricultural colonies, which had the added advantage of being self-funding.[4] Indeed, Sherlock's 1911 book on the feeble-minded provides a plan for an 'Industrial Colony' for 2,000 persons, partly based on the Rev. H. W. Burden's Colony Scheme which appeared in the report of the Royal Commission on the feeble-minded, with space to accommodate male and female patients (strictly segregated) and children.[5] Such colonies were built and some survive today, converted into hospitals.

Not all of those whom we would now class as mentally ill finished up in the lunatic asylum. Many occupied the prisons, from the psychopaths to the socially inadequate who engaged in petty crime – these people filled the Victorian and Edwardian jails. There was no plea of diminished responsibility or insanity and if found guilty of a crime these unfortunate individuals served their sentence in prison, there being nowhere to house the criminally insane at that time. The social misfits and the inadequates found guilty of petty crime were labelled as 'criminally degenerate', a phrase encountered in some of the First World War capital courts martial, which needs to be set against the prevailing opinions of the day. Today in our climate of 'political correctness' such a phrase is unthinkable, but in 1914 it was considered an apt description for the mentally ill or subnormal petty criminal.

There is no doubt that class had a part to play in the attitudes towards the insane. The upper classes could suffer from madness – King George III had established that – and the well-off – even Winston Churchill's father – were by no means immune from the scourge of syphilis, but to a large extent were protected from the labels applied to the lower classes. An upper class Englishman could pay to indulge in a range of sexual vices, but a working class man indulging in the same fashion would be labelled depraved and degenerate – although the Oscar Wilde case had shown that even class did not always protect you from the law. Also, an educationally backward child of the poorest working classes, given minimal schooling and no education at home, was programmed to fail and stood a good chance of having to turn to theft to survive, and then being classed as criminally degenerate. Thomas Salmon, the American expert on war neurosis, writing after the war pointed out that in the UK insanity and pauperism had always been closely associated.[6] There was also a view that the undernourished, pale, rachitic town dweller was less mentally robust than his country counterpart, that mental deficiency was a concomitant of physical inferiority. Indeed, Charles Moran Wilson (later famous as Lord Moran, Churchill's doctor) expounds this view in describing the breakdown of a sergeant in his regiment: this man had just escaped being obliterated by a shell and not surprisingly was in a state of shock. Moran wrote:

> His lip trembled and he was trying to keep his limbs still … He asked me to send him to the transport for a day or two … But it was plain to me the game was up and he was done. When this sort of thing happens to a good fellow it is final … And now he must be hurried away to the base to a shell-shock hospital with a rabble of mis-shapen creatures from the towns.[7]

In mainland Europe and in the United States there had been some changes in the way in which mental illness was perceived and treated. In France the work of Jean-Martin Charcot and Josef Babinski had recognized that some nervous disorders, such as hysteria and neurasthenia, could be cured and they established outpatient clinics for their treatment – indeed, these were so successful that hysteria reached almost epidemic proportions in certain classes of society and, once divorced from the taint of 'lunacy', attained social respectability. Clifford Beers, an American who had spent some time in mental institutions, created a stir in 1908 when his book *A Mind That Found Itself* was published, castigating those in charge of such institutions.[8] Largely in consequence of Beers's efforts, the National Committee on Mental Hygiene had been formed and started to change the way in which the mentally sick were perceived and treated.

Writing in 1909, William White pointed out: 'When the student of medicine passes to the study of insanity, he crosses a scientific frontier, and enters an entirely new province of knowledge.'[9] White also attempted to provide a robust definition of insanity, settling on: 'Insanity is a disease of the mind due to disease of the brain manifesting itself by a more or less prolonged departure from the individual's usual manner of thinking, feeling or acting and resulting in a lessened capacity for adaption to the environment.'[10] This was, by the standards of the day, a very far-seeing view.

White also described the classical groupings of patients with mental disease and gave an extremely detailed protocol for the examination of a patient with 'insanity'. This included a detailed personal and family history, a full medical history, a detailed physical examination and psychological testing – a protocol which could have been usefully applied by many of the doctors in the Great War, had they been aware of these theories. White also recognized that each of the different groups of disorders had a different prognosis, and that in some cases patients with short-term disorders had a good chance of full recovery. He simplified the classification of the causes of psychiatric illness into two main groups, each having two subdivisions. First, there were the predisposing causes, which could be subdivided into individual causes, such as family history or general causes. Secondly, there were the 'exciting' causes, which included both physical and mental stress. This was a very simple and practical division.

He also included a chapter on the psychoneuroses (the group of disorders into which war neurosis fits). Neurasthenia was discussed, White describing this as constitutional, or acquired by exhausting or debilitating conditions. He advised a rest cure for these patients and wrote: 'this group of cases is especially favourable for a rational psychotherapy'.[11] The hysterical disorders were also described, with a subdivision into motor (paralysis, contractures) and sensory (parasthesia), and again, hypnotherapy was advocated as part of the cure.

There is no doubt that in the years preceding the war Britain lagged far behind in the field of psychotherapeutics. In 1913 Charles Dana saw the future, writing that neurology had passed from the microscope and the autopsy suite to the study of psychoneuroses and that the neurologist now had to contend with 'subjective states and the importance to all neuroses of environment, education ... the character, temperament and social conditions of his patients', because, in his view, 'nervous diseases are so largely social'.[12] Most doctors in Britain were slow to adopt these changes in thinking and in 1914 the general view in England on mental illness had changed little since the preceding century.

Titles, too, have changed with time – terminology before 1914 was different to that today. Psychiatry, as we understand it, had not yet branched from the main tree of medicine. In 1914 a psychiatrist was the medical superintendent in charge of a lunatic asylum – hardly a proper doctor by the standards of many of his colleagues. The doctors practising what we would now call psychiatry – such as Charles Myers and William Rivers – were medical practitioners with an interest in the whole nervous system who did not distinguish between neurology, neurophysiology and psychiatry as we now do. They were usually described as neurologists, mainly concerned with the physiology of the nervous system and experimental psychology, and referred to their work on the mind as 'neuropsychiatry'. The foundations of psychoanalysis had been laid by Sigmund Freud and Carl Jung between 1907 and

1911, and valuable though this technique later became in the treatment of shell shock, it was still in its infancy in 1914. Such ideas were not widely accepted as a legitimate technique and few doctors in Britain were trained in its use before the war.

The state of pre-war psychiatry can be summed up by the case of Virginia Woolf, who became mentally ill in 1913; her husband Leonard sought the opinions of the foremost men of the day – Henry Head, the neurologist at Cambridge, mentor to both William Rivers and Charles Myers, was called in, among others. None of these eminent men could offer either a cure or useful advice, and later Leonard Woolf commented in his biography that the inability of these doctors to identify, understand or treat her illness 'throws light upon the chaotic condition of medical knowledge about insanity in 1913'.[13] This is an important background against which to view the medical understanding, treatment and advice about shell-shocked soldiers during the Great War.

Even in 1917 Elliot Smith and Pear were bemoaning the lack of proper psychiatric facilities in Britain. In Germany, they pointed out, there were clinics for mental and nervous disease, to which patients could present themselves for treatment, in the same way as to a clinic for a physical condition, without any social stigma attaching to them. However, in Britain there was nothing comparable, and it was only when a patient became 'insane' that they received treatment. They wrote:

> If, however, we consider the attitude of the general public in this country towards the malady of insanity we find a mixture of ignorant superstition and exaggerated fear. From these springs a tendency to ignore the painful subject until a case occurring too near home makes this ostrich-like policy untenable. The sufferer is removed to a 'lunatic' asylum …

They concluded: 'the community treats the sufferer well, when, but not before, he has become a lunatic'.[14] This fact was one of those which made 'shell shock' such a difficult concept for the average member of the public to comprehend in 1914–18. In a society that equated mental illness with lunacy, shell shock victims were regarded with scant sympathy, as weaklings at best and degenerates at worst. It was many years until this attitude changed in Britain, and we still see it today. Whilst in the US there is popular acceptance of 'having therapy', such behaviour is still regarded as slightly peculiar by many Britons. In Britain we still tend to regard American servicemen having post-traumatic stress disorder counselling and therapy as being a bit 'soft', and some of the social stigma of mental breakdown still remains in our society, even into the twenty-first century.

Given that this was the state of the infant science of psychiatry and psychoanalysis in 1914, great strides were made in the recognition and treatment of mental illness during the war. With the benefit of the retrospectoscope (a useful medical instrument which allows us to apply hindsight) we may feel that these changes were too slow and inadequate, but in fact they represented huge advances in this fledgling branch of medicine. Some of the treatments used in shell-shocked men were, by our modern standards, barbaric, but many of the early neuropsychiatrists were still wedded to their strongly held medical background of experimental neurophysiology. They firmly believed that the symptoms of shell shock were caused by abnormal physiology and therefore to achieve a cure this abnormal physiology had to be corrected. It was only a few pioneering souls who readily made the jump from experimental neurology to therapeutic psychoanalysis, recognizing that it was the sights, sounds and smells that the soldiers had encountered which had caused psychological changes, and that the physical manifestations were secondary to these. That the physical changes which were the external manifestation of the underlying psychological damage could only be reversed by treating the patient's mental state was not apparent to many pre-war doctors.

War is a great catalyst for change. Many of the advances of the twentieth century stemmed in one way or another from war, and those made in medicine were no exception. During the Great War huge strides were made in the management of wounds, the infant science of blood transfusion was developed; new techniques were developed in surgery – neurosurgery became a new speciality and Howard Gilles rebuilt the shattered faces of men using his new plastic surgery techniques. At the same time other men were coming to understand that the mind could suffer invisible wounds which made a man a casualty of war, just as much as those whose bodies had been broken by high explosive, and set about evolving new treatments for the psychiatric casualties produced by the conflict. But as the BEF set off for war in 1914, neither its officers nor its doctors knew that. What we call post-traumatic stress disorder (PTSD) was unknown. The British soldier – the embodiment of Imperial Man – was expected to be brave and tough, whatever the strain of battle.

CHAPTER 5

THE SHOCK OF BATTLE

No man, however he may talk, has the remotest idea of what an ordinary infantry soldier really endures.

SGT H. GREEN

No one who has not been shot at or subjected to hostile shellfire for long periods of time can begin to have the slightest conception of what battle is really like. No amount of academic theorizing can begin to equate to the experience of some unseen gunner trying to blow you to bloody fragments. Nothing can quite describe the stomach-tightening tension, or the thudding jar that goes from the soles of your feet to your head as a shell lands nearby, or the brutal concussion of sound that sings in the ears for days. Worst of all is the fear of not knowing if the next one will land on you or when it will end. From the squares at Waterloo to the boggy hills of the Falklands, soldiers have known what it is like to be 'pounded'. And when that pounding goes on day after day without respite, when the sight of your friends as Edmund Blunden memorably recalled: 'as gobbets of blackening flesh, the earth wall spattered with blood, the eye under the duckboard, the pulpy bone ...' becomes almost commonplace, a reaction sets in.[1] Man's biology was not designed for protracted fighting and drawn-out horrors. The bravest spirit quails from the desolation of interminable violence and waiting for death by surprise.

War was not always so. For centuries man has understood the reality of death in battle. Homer, in the *Iliad*, gives a vivid description of a soldier's death:

> Meriones pursued Pheraklios and stabbed him low in the back, the spearhead driving through bone to burst his bladder. Pheraklios dropped screaming to his knees and death was a mist about him.[2]

Although the bloody truth about the horrors of the battlefield had been well understood since Homeric times, warfare was seen as an essentially episodic event. It was perceived as a series of battles punctuating – even defining – great events. In Osbert Sitwell's words, before 1914

> we were still in a trough of peace which had lasted a hundred years between great armed conflicts. In it ... wars [were] only a brief armed version of the Olympic Games ... There was no more talk of extermination or of fights to a finish than would occur in a boxing match ... [3]

But the Great War of 1914–18 brought a new dimension to man's comprehension of war. The impact of the Great War, with its industrial and production line scale of violence, was to change all that. Even the most thoughtful and professional soldiers were surprised by the intensity of the fighting that erupted in 1914. The impact of the machine gun, massed artillery and, above all, the sheer scale of the casualties between August 1914 and the comparative lull brought on by the first winter trench lines shook the planners. The BEF which went to war 100,000 strong in August 1914 had suffered 96,000 casualties by 31 December 1914, 50,000 of them in the bitter fighting around Ypres in October and November 1914 alone.[4]

As Anthony Farrar-Hockley points out: 'Foul weather multiplied these burdens on human endurance ... In later years old soldiers recalled that winter on the Somme or in Flanders sapped their vitality even more than the run of battle.'[5] This was not the war the BEF had expected.

Every army – like any other institution or individual – is a prisoner of its own experience. For the French and German armies, whose most senior generals still had youthful memories of the Franco-Prussian War in 1870, both sides were determined to get it right for the next round of fighting. For these major continental armies that meant three things: mass, manoeuvre and firepower, and all their training and equipment were geared to some mighty new clash on the borders of France. Both France and Germany prepared for that.

The long European peace from 1871 to 1914 hid a major arms race. These supposedly idyllic decades of peace and prosperity were, in fact, periods of preparation for the next continental clash of arms. Both France – determined to regain her lost provinces of Alsace and Lorraine on 'the blue line of the Vosges' – and Germany, equally conscious of French intentions, geared their armies for a war many felt was inevitable. Thanks to Napoleon and his nineteenth-century legacy, such a campaign was equally inevitably bound to be a clash between mass armies culminating in a gigantic decisive battle. Guglielmo Ferrero, musing after the Great War, saw the problem with the icy clarity of hindsight, that unfailingly accurate analytical tool:

Restricted warfare was one of the three loftiest achievements of the 18th century. It belongs to that class of hot house plants which can only thrive in an aristocratic and qualitative civilisation. We are no longer capable of it. It was one of the fine things that we lost in the French Revolution.[6]

The key to these mass continental armies was compulsory conscription. The revolutionary *levées en masse* had been converted and formalized by the end of the nineteenth century into social and military policy by both France and Germany. The young man was taken into the army by law, drilled, disciplined, trained in his duties to the state, then discharged back into society after two or three years as a (supposedly) model citizen. Even the United States of America, whose whole *raison d'être* was individual liberty, democracy and freedom, was forced to yield to the impulse to conscription during its bloody struggle to coerce the secessionist southern states between 1861 and 1865. Between them, the Union and the Confederacy conscripted no fewer than 2.25 million of their supposedly free citizens to fight for their respective causes. Before 1914, of the European powers only Britain, protected by her high-tech navy, could choose not to conscript her citizens, and even that policy was bitterly opposed by some hard-headed visionaries before the war. British resistance to forcing citizens to fight would eventually yield to the harsh imperatives of mass industrial warfare: Conscription was enforced in 1916.

The lessons of the American Civil War were plain to see. Unfortunately, and for a variety of reasons, the European military professionals chose to ignore them. As early as the battle of Second Manassas (or Bull Run) in 1862, Stonewall Jackson's Virginians, lining a ditch, cut down three times their number of charging Union infantry by a 'blizzard of fire'. Napoleonic tactics just did not work against modern rifled weapons. By 1864 the Union's Col. Theodore Lyman observed:

Put a man in a hole with a good battery on a hill behind him and he will beat off three times his number, even if he is not a very good soldier.[7]

The truth is that the American Civil War pointed the way to the future of warfare. Nearly all the horrors of the Great War were visited upon the warring states: conscription, rapid-firing weapons, mass casualties, trench warfare, economic blockade, industrial production and deliberate attacks on civilian populations. With them all went a previously known but now much more prevalent phenomenon: battle stress and the breakdown of discipline.

It was after the debacle at Bull Run that Union generals complained that the civilian authorities in Washington were diluting military law and that this had led to a lack of discipline among the soldiers.[8] As a condemned soldier had right of appeal to Washington, this delayed the legal process and the impact of a swift execution as an example was reduced. This did not stop the Union army using capital punishment, and they executed 267 men for a variety of military offences, mostly desertion. Indeed, on 4 September 1863 five men from the 27th Kentucky Regiment were shot for this offence, presumably together – a strong example to other men of the regiment. (The strangest execution for desertion also took place during the Civil War. On 5 September 1864 Pte William Dowdy decided to move his bedroll whilst on board the steamer *Effie Deans*. As a result, he was charged with absenting himself from his company until apprehended by his commanding officer on 6 September, and was shot – even though he never left the vessel.[9])

Most European observers failed to understand the lessons of the War between the States: 'It was dismissed as a transient phenomenon due to uniquely North American circumstances.'[10]

If Europeans wanted more clues to the true nature of future warfare, then the Russo-Japanese War of 1904–5, on the borders of Mongolia, Korea and Manchuria, gave even more specific signposts. Dug into stinking trenches, protected by barbed wire, living and fighting in contact with the enemy for the duration, and attacking without cover across open ground on the heels of massed artillery bombardments, the Russo-Japanese fighting around Port Arthur could have been a rehearsal for the horrors of 1914–18. It was widely misinterpreted or, worse, ignored. Instead of realizing that firepower now dominated the battlefield, killing unprotected attackers in great numbers, many western analysts of the fighting concluded that modern war would be brief but cataclysmic. From the facts of Tsarist Russia's near collapse into political and economic chaos as a result of the war, most commentators also concluded that a war could now be won only by throwing everything into the attack as hard as possible and then keeping going to the last man – which was, after all, how the Japanese had won.[11]

The problem was that much of the Russo-Japanese War was seen as a series of sieges. No one in 1914 imagined a whole war without flanks, a complete battlefield characterized only by opposing lines of trenches from horizon to horizon. The effort in labour alone was unimaginable. The problem was that no one had made the single most fundamental calculation: that if you put all the millions of conscripted European infantrymen into the battle line, shoulder to shoulder, it would stretch the whole length of the Franco-German border. They would quite simply fill all the space available. There could be no flanks.

The consequences of such a combination had been predicted with startling clarity by a French civilian, I. S. Bloch, as early as 1897. His 'War of the Future in its Technical, Economic and Political Relations', written before the Russo-Japanese War, is remarkable for its prescience:

> At first there will be increased slaughter on so terrible a scale as to render it impossible to get troops to push the battle to its decisive issue. They will try to, thinking that they are fighting under the old conditions, and they will learn such a lesson that they will abandon the attempt forever. Then ... we shall have ... a long period of continually increasing strain upon the resources of the combatants ... Everyone will be entrenched in the next war.[12]

Bloch's oft-quoted remark that the 'entrenching tool will be as important as a rifle in the next war' is often taken out of context, or used to imply some mass stupidity amongst all the generals of all pre 1914 armies. The truth is that no one even began to conceive that there might be absolutely no possibility of a war without flanks or movement. It is hard not to sympathize with the intelligent and ultimately, by 1918, victorious General Foch as he ruefully surveyed the wreckage of his first big command in northern France in late autumn 1914: 'They have sent me here to manoeuvre, but things are not going very brightly. This eternal stretching out in a line is beginning to get on my nerves!'[13]

The inevitable consequence of continuous lines was continuous contact with the enemy. Continuous contact meant continuous danger, continuous enemy fire and a continuous strain on the combatants. It also meant that any attack must be perforce a frontal attack across an obstacle belt into massed machine gun firepower or worse. That would mean massed casualties.

If there was one army among the pre First World War combatants that had experienced a war of manoeuvre, adapted and trained its soldiers to fight and win a war of manoeuvre, and prided itself on its battle readiness to do so again, it was the British Army. Tiny by continental standards but superbly equipped and trained as a result of early humiliations at the hands of the Boers in South Africa between 1899 and 1902, the British Army was ready for war. What it was not ready for by the time of First Ypres (October–November 1914) was the type of continental war in which it had found itself embroiled. It lacked reserve manpower, heavy artillery, and an industrial base geared for the mass production of ammunition. The new war was not what politicians, planners or general staffs had anticipated.

This new war came as a shock to all ranks. By the end of 1914 Lt J. A. Liddell, the Regular machine gun officer of an infantry battalion, was writing home:

> It's a war with no glamour or glory. Modern weapons are too deadly …
> the whole art of war has altered … now it's all digging trenches … Then
> a bombardment with enormous shells for a couple of days until trenches
> and men's nerves are smashed to ribbons, and a surprise rush in the
> middle of the night.

Later he wrote to a friend: '… This is a dreadful war …' And 'You don't know how boring and nerve-wracking this trench business is.'[14]

This was a view shared by many senior officers on all sides. This new war, a huge siege, was not what they were trained for. Most shattering of all was the sheer scale of the casualties and the haemorrhaging of the BEF. While the French had lost nearly 1 million men by the end of 1914, the BEF had suffered, percentage wise, even more grievous losses. By the end of 1914 the BEF had suffered 96,000 casualties. A new army was needed, and quickly. On 3 December 1914 Captain E. W. S. Balfour, Adjutant of the 5th Dragoon Guards, wrote in an eerie prophecy of the Somme and beyond:

> There's not much left of the old (regular) army, and the new campaign
> is going to have to be fought and won by a great half-trained National
> Army …[15]

The truth is that the British Army which went to war in 1914 was a very different animal to the British Army which emerged bloodied but victorious in 1918. For a start it had become eight times larger: 2,075,000 in 1918 against 247,000 in 1914; and over fourteen times its original strength would have passed through its ranks by the end of the war. Peter Simkins, the former senior historian of the Imperial War Museum, in fact identifies no fewer than four British armies during the First World War: the Regular Army, the Territorial Forces, Kitchener's volunteers and the conscripts. These can be quite clearly identified as the war progressed; and by 1918 the remnants of all four groups had melded themselves into a coherent but very different fighting force from the one that marched so light-heartedly into Belgium in 1914. All four elements had experienced and been bloodied by the shock of battle and shared in a common experience that we can only guess at. By 1918 everyone involved knew that it was no 'boxing match'. Modern industrial warfare, and particularly modern firepower, was a truly horrific experience.

Modern commentators on war often speak of the 'RMA', the revolution in military affairs, as being spawned by the age of information technology and the computer. The truth is that the first 'RMA' really took place during the Great War: the application of massive indirect firepower on an industrial scale for the first time. Computers and communications are only designed after all to place ordnance – even nuclear missiles – more effectively on the target. It is the firepower that kills and terrifies. As early as 1914 the realization by all sides that the problems of breaching obstacles and neutralizing enemy machine guns and artillery could only be solved by the application of massive firepower forced commanders to invest heavily in artillery as a battle-winning tool. The consequences of the vast attritional experiments of Verdun and the Somme in 1916 (once industry had delivered the weapons) were truly horrifying for those on the receiving end. Guns were massed wheel to wheel behind the lines and fired for days on end.[16]

It was the sheer obliterative concussion of shells landing nearby and the random selection of their victims that eventually wore down and destroyed even the most hardened of nerves. Sgt Collins of the 1/22nd Londons (the Queen's) later wrote of a 1917 bombardment:

> Not far in front of our trench I came across a couple of our lads who had gone completely goofy, from the concussion. It was pitiful. One of them welcomed me like a long-lost friend and asked me to give him his baby. I picked up a tin hat and gave it to him. He cradled it as if it were a child, smiling and laughing ... while the shells were exploding all around him ...[17]

Any French or German soldiers at Verdun or Messines could have testified to the same shattering experience of being shelled as if a chain flail was beating the ground blasting all before it and inexorably coming towards *you*. Although Pte S. Bagnall's account comes from the Second World War rather than the First, as a personal description of what it is like to be on the receiving end of an artillery bombardment it cannot be bettered:

> I could feel the exact spot in the small of my defenceless back where the pointed nose of the shell would pierce skin and gristle and bone and explode the charge that would make me feel as if I had a splitting headache all over for about a fiftieth of a second before I was spread minutely all over the earth and hung up in the trees. I held my breath and

tried to press deeper into the earth and tensed every muscle as though by sheer will power I could abate the force of that disintegrating shock, cheat death, defy God, pleading 'Oh God, have mercy on me please, don't let me die. Please, please, don't let me die ...[18]

From the first trenches in October 1914 to the end in 1918, all those involved on the Western Front were aware that they were involved in something unspeakably shocking and brutal, well outside the experience of any living person. To quote Capt. Dillon of the 2nd Battalion Ox. & Bucks., who wrote as early as 24 October 1914:

I don't care one farthing as far as I am concerned, but the whole thing is an outrage on civilisation. The whole of this beautiful country devastated. Broken houses, broken bodies, blood, filth and ruin everywhere. Can any unending everlasting Hellfire for the Kaiser, his son and the party who caused this war repair the broken bodies and, worse, broken hearts which are being made? Being made this very minute within a few hundred yards of where I am sitting. Well, them's my sentiments.[19]

It was the sheer scale and brutality of this new industrialized warfare, added to its unremitting tempo of twenty-four-hour operations and battle, seven days a week, that overwhelmed individuals. Add to it all the lice, the rats, the rotting bodies, the stench, fear, cold and hunger, day in and day out, the exhaustion of humping 60-pound loads for miles through narrow trenches, and even the toughest spirit would quail in despair before turning to religion, fate, the bottle or just running away from the horror of it all.

But in 1914 no one knew that: the war was going to be over by Christmas. Men with strong nerves would just have to endure the shock of battle – however long it lasted.

CHAPTER 6

SHELL SHOCK: A BRIEF HISTORY

Stoddart says that English psychiatry is far behind that on the continent.

CLARENCE FARRAR, 1904

The condition which became known as 'shell shock' during the Great War has existed for as long as man has gone to war, but the changing nature of war has led to a change in both the frequency of the condition and the way in which cases present. In 1997 Hans Binneveld wrote: 'One can no longer imagine a battlefield without psychiatrists and psychologists. Their presence is due to the fact that participation in a war, for many of those involved, is an extremely traumatic experience.'[1]

Although there were descriptions of psychological trauma in early warfare, such as that described by Herodotus at the battle of Marathon,[2] and Shakespeare wrote of it describing Hotspur's night terrors,[3] the condition did not become widely recognized in Europe until the seventeenth century. During the Thirty Years War (1618–48) Spanish doctors described Spanish soldiers who had been conscripted to fight in the Netherlands as suffering from *estar roto*, meaning to be broken, in a state of despair.[4] In 1678 a Swiss doctor, Johannes Hofer, wrote about this condition, calling it *nostalgia*.[5] The Germans also recognized a similar condition which they called *Heimweh*, or 'longing for home'. In the succeeding years many European armies recognized the existence of this condition amongst their soldiers and it was a common concept in the era of pre-industrial warfare.

During the Napoleonic campaigns French soldiers were frequently described as suffering from nostalgia and the condition was particularly prevalent during the retreat from Moscow. The enlightened Dominic Larrey, surgeon to Napoleons armies, regarded it as a form of insanity, but other doctors of the day considered that it was an extreme form of melancholy.[6] Malingering was also a problem in the French Army at this time, as soldiers diagnosed with nostalgia were exempted from further military service.

Men in Wellington's army also suffered from similar symptoms, but the

British Army of the day was more concerned with the rooting out of malingerers, and Hector Gavin wrote in 1836 on how to identify men who faked blindness, stammering, dumbness and paralysis; but he also recognized that fear could make a man genuinely ill.[7]

Any one soldier's involvement in these early wars was generally short. Although an army might be in the field for many months or even years, actual episodes of fighting were relatively brief. Even Wellington's Peninsular campaign lasting from 1808 to 1814 involved relatively few, short, pitched battles.

Russian military doctors encountered psychiatric casualties in the Crimean War of 1853–6 and remained interested in the phenomenon after this war ended, but western countries paid the subject little attention until the American Civil War of 1861–5.

This conflict represented the change from the old pattern of warfare to the new. Although the individual battles were short (Gettysburg lasted less than three days), modern weapons – rifles, shrapnel shells – and the use of trenches provided pointers to the future development of war. The American Civil War also demonstrated the psychological impact of this new technological warfare. In the first year of the Civil War the Union Army diagnosed 5,213 cases of nostalgia – an incidence of 2.34 cases per 1,000 soldiers – and by the end of the war nearly 10,000 men of the Union Army had been diagnosed as suffering from the condition.[8]

William Hammond, a Union surgeon who became one of the pioneers studying mental illness, investigated the cause of nostalgia in the soldiers. He observed that many of those affected were young, and wrote: 'Youths of this age are not developed and are not fit to endure the fatigues and deprivations of Military life. They soon break down, become sick and are thrown upon the hospitals.'[9] Taking a remarkably modern and enlightened view, he suggested that the minimum recruiting age should be raised to 20 and that men should undergo psychological screening before entering service. On the other hand, at the same time, some army officers were proposing the formation of a 'malingerers' brigade' composed of the men who had displayed cowardice – an idea only abandoned when it became apparent that officers as well as men were affected.

The men with nostalgia were discharged from the army but with no provision for their treatment or cure. Between 1861 and 1862 six men out of every thousand troops were discharged from service with 'insanity', inundating the civil asylums. This led, in 1863, to the War Department ordering that no more men were to be discharged on grounds of insanity and instead these men were to be detained in a military asylum. This measure effectively stopped any faking of psychiatric symptoms, as service at the front appeared preferable to such an asylum.[10] The scale of the problem is demonstrated by the fact that of every 100 men discharged from the Union Army, as a result of 'nervous disease', 20.8 suffered from paralysis.[11]

Dr Silas Mitchell was a neurologist working with men who had gunshot wounds, but who also displayed symptoms of nervous shock. Medical knowledge of the day could offer no explanation so he evolved a physiological explanation – that the bullet, in damaging a nerve, transmitted a shock to the spine, which was then redirected to other nerves, leading to collapse, paralysis and other symptoms.[12] Another theory developed to explain some of the symptoms was that of 'windage', that the wind of a shell passing close to a soldier's spine could cause paralysis. In cases where no external physical injury could be seen, these theories were adopted as the explanation for the symptoms.[13] Although the observations made during the Civil War led to advances in neurology in the United States, the psychologically traumatized soldier was, effectively, labelled 'insane' and forgotten.

The British Army encountered psychological breakdown amongst men serving in South Africa in the Boer War (1899–1902) but took little interest in them, calling them insane and sending them home with the other casualties of war. A London surgeon, Charles Morris, wrote of the mental casualties under his care:

> A most remarkable evidence of the privation, exhaustion and mental strain that many had to pass through was seen in the cases of neurasthenia that occurred. It was terrible to see the condition of fine strapping men, produced in this way, which led them to shrink from the slightest touch and to shed tears like children.[14]

The British medical establishment and army had been warned of the consequences of modern war, but took little heed.

It was the Russo-Japanese War of 1904–5 which established some of the modern principles of military psychiatry. Russian doctors had come into contact with psychiatric casualties during both the Crimean War and the Russo-Turkish War of 1877–8 and were also aware of the problems of psychological breakdown amongst soldiers during the American Civil War and the Franco-Prussian War of 1870–71. By 1904 they were more advanced in the field than any other nation. During the war of 1904–5, 2,000 battle shock casualties were identified, but many thousands of other psychologically traumatized men overwhelmed the medical services. The problem was exacerbated by the fact that when troops realized that the insane were being evacuated many others feigned psychiatric symptoms in an attempt to escape front line service. One of the key features of the Russian approach was treatment of the casualty close to the battle zone – the concept of proximity that today is one of the cornerstones of the management of battle stress – and a forward specialist hospital was established just behind the lines at Harbin in Manchuria. However, the treatment regimes were not greatly effective, with only 54 out of 275 officers treated being returned to the front, and 51 out of 1,072 enlisted men.[15]

By 1905 the doctors of the Russian Army had recognized that mental collapse amongst its soldiers was related to the stresses of war and Dr Paul Jacoby proposed the theory that the advances in weapons technology were adding to the stresses of combatants. He advocated that in future campaigns every army should have special psychiatric units for neurological casualties, as prompt treatment led to a better chance of recovery.[16]

These innovations in medical care of the psychologically traumatized were reported in the French and German medical journals, but were largely ignored in Britain. The Russian medical services in general enjoyed a poor reputation, and their advances in this field were largely neglected by the medical profession in Britain. However, doctors in the United States took note, and after reviewing the treatment of soldiers with mental disorders during the Russo-Japanese War, R. L. Richards wrote, with great foresight:

A future war will call at least equally large numbers of men into action. The tremendous endurance, bodily and mental, required for the days of fighting over increasingly large areas, and the mysterious and widely destructive effects of modern artillery fire will test men as they have never been tested before. We can surely count then on a much larger percentage of mental diseases requiring our attention in a future war.[17]

CHAPTER 7

SHELL SHOCK AND THE GREAT WAR

It is for us, not for our children, to act in the light of this great lesson.

G. ELLIOT SMITH AND T. H. PEAR, 1917

When war broke out in 1914 none of the belligerents was prepared for large numbers of psychiatric casualties. Most of the countries involved expected the war to be over by Christmas, but the reality was a war that turned out to be unlike anything ever experienced before. The new technological warfare with weapons of mass destruction and the introduction of chemical weapons resulted in casualties on a scale never before conceived. In addition, the very nature of trench warfare increased the psychological strain on the men involved. Whilst trenches offered some element of safety to the men within them, they were also a form of confinement, imprisoning men who were being shelled and fired upon by an enemy they could not see, nor retaliate against. Other factors added to the strain – the cold, the wet, poor food, the lice and the decaying corpses all contributed to the psychological pressures on the soldier.

The first psychiatric casualties began to arrive at the base hospitals after only a few weeks. They were admitted with the physically wounded, and often left unattended, as no one knew what to do with them. Even today mental breakdown carries a certain stigma, and the general public tends to regard mental illness as only marginally removed from insanity. In 1914 the divisions were clear: you were mad or you were sane. These traumatized men were therefore insane, in the same way that during the Russo-Japanese War mental breakdown had been regarded as 'insanity', albeit potentially curable. As the trench lines stabilized and the psychologically affected became a steady stream the War Office started to try to find a way of dealing with these men.

An editorial in the *Lancet* in December 1914 first highlighted the medical problem.

It is no doubt somewhat early in the day to attempt to draw conclusions of wide applicability as to any connection between the stress and strain of the war and the development of hysteria, neurasthenia, traumatic psycho-neurosis and so on. Nevertheless, those who are coming into contact with the nervous side of the cases retired from the war are beginning to notice the frequency with which hysteria, traumatic and otherwise, is showing itself.[1]

Before the Great War medicine did not have the plethora of subspecialities with which we are familiar today, where every disease sometimes seems to have its own 'ologist'. Medicine and surgery were separate entities, with their separate Royal Colleges, but other specialities operated within these broad divisions. The neurologists, whose interest extended to psychology as well as to the anatomy and functionality of the nervous system, regarded themselves as physicians, not psychiatrists. It is also important to realize that although pre-war medical students received some training in neurology, they were given no training in psychology or psychiatry apart from, at best, a brief visit to a lunatic asylum.

Charles Myers was an eminent neurologist who, on the outbreak of war, offered his services to the army. Rejected as being too old (he was 42), he went to France as a civilian, working at the Duchess of Westminster's Hospital at Le Touquet. Here, in November 1914, he encountered the first of many cases of battle shock, which were to lead to his descriptions of 'shell shock'.

The first cases which Myers encountered all had one feature in common: their acute mental breakdown had been precipitated by being in close proximity to an exploding shell, hence the name he gave to their condition. Initially Myers and others believed that the condition arose from close proximity to shell blast and that this was an essential component for the development of the condition. These doctors, like those in the American Civil War, sought a physical explanation for the psychological symptoms. Other doctors across Europe were applying their own labels to the condition: '*Kriegsneurosen*' in Germany and '*la confusion mentale de la guerre*' in France. Myers's original theory was that the vibrations of an exploding shell could produce some kind of 'molecular commotion' in the brain, leading to the symptoms seen. Other doctors proposed that the explosion of a shell drove microscopic particles into the brain, or released carbon monoxide, causing the condition.

In 1915 Myers published the first of a series of three articles in the *Lancet* on the subject of 'shell shock'.[2] Later he pointed out that even at this stage of the war

... I was careful to point out the 'close relations of these cases to hysteria'; and I did not suppose, as Lt Col. (the late Sir) Frederick Mott was then attempting to show, that they arose from the effects of minute cerebral haemorrhages or other microscopically visible lesions. I attributed them, as they are now generally attributed, to mental 'repression' and 'dissociation'.[3]

In March 1915 Myers joined a team of doctors investigating war-induced lesions of the nervous system, whose principal duty was to select which cases of nerve shock should be evacuated to the UK. His duties also came to include 'examining and giving court martial evidence on soldiers charged with desertion, suicide, drunkenness or other crimes', showing that even within seven months of the outbreak of war, the army was beginning to understand the importance of psychological factors in some specific military offences.[4]

The army puzzled over how to classify these invisible wounds, and at the end of 1915 introduced two categories. The first was 'shell shock – wounded', to be applied if a man's condition was due to an enemy shell. In this case he was regarded as wounded in action and entitled to wear a wound stripe. The second category was 'shell shock – sick', applied to a man who had broken down without a shell being the direct cause. These men were treated as other 'sick' and not entitled to a wound stripe. The introduction of these categories was unhelpful and led to delays whilst attempts were made to establish into which group a man came, when prompt treatment would have been more beneficial.

As more and more men who had not been in contact with shell blast presented themselves, Myers and others became convinced that war neurosis could not solely be ascribed to a near miss from a shell and proposed to the Director General Army Medical Services that the term 'shell shock' should be dropped. Unfortunately, by then the term was in widespread use and had been adopted to cover all the neuropsychiatric symptoms resulting from battle stress. The continued use of this expression throughout the war obscured, rather than clarified, the real issue and led to confusion in the minds of many doctors, as it still does amongst many people nowadays.

The soldiers suffering from war neurosis tended, by doctors and public alike, to be labelled 'neurasthenic' or 'insane' – the label sometimes varied depending on a man's social class. Terms such as 'hysteria' were also used, but this label was perceived as having undesirable connotations: in Edwardian Britain, women – the weaker sex – suffered from hysteria. Men who became 'hysterical' were therefore not 'real' men – Imperial Man was strong, patriotic, heroic and psychologically robust, and did not suffer from 'hysteria'. Even well into the war there was still a firm view that men, particularly officers, with shell shock just needed to 'pull themselves together'. The neurologist-cum-psychologist had a dilemma. People were either sane or mad – and the mad were deemed incurable. Even at the end of the war few non-specialist doctors could distinguish between the concept of short-term mental breakdown and chronic incurable insanity. Myers described the problem: '... In the case of prisoners: from the military standpoint a deserter was either insane and destined for the madhouse or responsible and should be shot.'[5] This view comes across in many of the court martial transcripts where a doctor reports that he has examined a man but could find no signs of insanity.

Myers describes another case which illustrates the problems suffered in trying to deal with the concept of mental deficiency – an element in several of the cases of capital courts martial. It concerned

> ... a very young soldier charged with desertion, who had been sent down to Boulogne for a report on his responsibility. He was so deficient in intelligence that he did not in the least realise the seriousness of his position. My only course, I thought, was to have him sent home, labelled 'insane'; and the sequel was that he was returned to France with a report saying that no signs of insanity were discoverable in him.[6]

By mid 1916 Myers had seen over 2,000 patients with shell shock and numerous men with other mental disorders. He noted that many of these men had a 'nervous' disposition, but went on to say that even those with the strongest nerves were not immune to breakdown. Many doctors were of the opinion that some men were predisposed to shell shock by virtue of heredity – that those with a family history of mental disorders were more likely to suffer from the condition. The history of a man would therefore be gone into to establish whether family predisposition was at the root of his nervous collapse. This led to such comments as 'mother died in an asylum' in some of the court martial records, when attempts were being made to judge whether a soldier was responsible for his actions.

Another important observation made by Myers was the discovery that shell shock was more of a problem in military units with poor discipline. He was not implying that the application of discipline per se prevented mental breakdown, but indicating that a well-trained man in a good unit, with confidence in his officers and NCOs and the support of equally well-trained comrades, was far less likely to break down.

In an attempt to put war neuroses into perspective two of the doctors working with shell shock cases published a book in 1917, drawing attention to the fact that the problems of shell shock were the everyday problems of nervous breakdown, which existed before the war and would continue to exist after its end.[7] They also tried to end the myth that a man with shell shock had 'lost his senses', making the point that the real problem was in fact that their senses were functioning with painful efficiency but had been overwhelmed by the sights, sounds, smells and horrors of the battlefields.

Shell shock patients fell into two main classes: those affected by shell concussion, who might also have physiological changes to their nervous system, and those men suffering from purely mental shock. This latter group could be divided into patients with objective symptoms, such as blindness, mutism, paralysis or contractures, and those with subjective symptoms, i.e. the purely mental symptoms, such as neurasthenia. Elliot Smith and Pear wrote that the subjective disorders,

> which are apt to go unrecognised in a cursory examination of the patient, are frequently more serious than the objective, and are experienced by thousands of patients who to the more casual observer may present with no more signs of abnormality than a slight tremor or stammer, or a depressed or excited expression.[8]

It is these subjective disorders which gave the army such a problem. To many senior officers a deserter suffering from these symptoms was not, in the classical way, shell-shocked; after all, by the latter stages of the war, such a man would be in no worse state than many of his colleagues in the trenches – indeed, many front line officers were suffering from the same symptoms. If other soldiers could do their duty, then so could this man, leading to a fundamental, if hidden, conflict between the army and the medical profession. However, in other areas the changing nature of war casualties was being taken seriously. *The Times History of the War* reported in 1916:

> From this time onwards interest in the nervous affection of battle became profound. Neurologists were attached to the military hospitals, and nerve cases were studied as closely and as carefully as were surgical and medical cases. It was realized that the coming of the high explosive shell ... had wrought a revolution in the types of war injuries and so in war medicine.[9]

The objective disorders – paralysis, mutism and so on – had a clear physical component. The cause of the problem might be psychological, but the manifestations were physical and this led to physiologically based attempts at a cure. In Germany in 1915 large numbers of psychologically traumatized men had flooded into the civilian psychiatric hospitals, labelled 'insane'. Fritz Kaufman, a German doctor, less concerned about the welfare of the men than about the cost to the state of supporting them, introduced a form of electrotherapy combined with verbal suggestion. His treatment programme ran on military lines: these men were soldiers and discipline was central to the cure. Kaufman told his patients that the cure would be painful, but that they would be cured. There was no debate, no opportunity to resist (unlike with hypnotherapy) – they would be cured whether they liked it or not. He was less concerned with the welfare of the individual patient than with the need to save the state money and it is unlikely that he expected his 'cures' to be returned to military service.[10]

French doctors used similar techniques, where rewards and punishments were used to achieve the same effect. The rationale of these treatments was that if he did not get better, a soldier was resisting the authority of the doctor and that such resistance was insubordination, which would not be tolerated.

In Britain a civilian doctor working at the National Hospital for the Paralysed and Epileptic developed a similar technique. Although Lewis Yealland's techniques were given a bad press in Pat Barker's *Regeneration* trilogy,[11] and his methods seem to modern eyes inhumane, he achieved cures. Most, but not all, of his patients were NCOs or private soldiers suffering from objective disorders – paralysis, mutism, etc. – and he was well aware that his patients' physical symptoms had a psychological cause, but believed that only when the physical manifestations had been cured could the psyche then be healed. His main concern was, as a doctor, to return these damaged men to a normal life; he was not an army doctor and it is unlikely that he expected his patients to be returned to the front line.

Yealland's methods were described by a colleague in the preface to his book:

> His principle has been a straightforward one, and is based on the belief
> that a disorder originating in suggestion should yield to counter-suggestion,
> that the precise method of counter-suggestion is really immaterial so long
> as it is strong enough, and that line of treatment must be varied according
> to the mental attitude of the patient …

He also realized that it was essential to recognize when to start the cure, with exhausted men being given a chance to rest and recuperate first.[12]

Many of his patients had already undergone treatment in France or Britain and were considered hopeless cases, with symptoms lasting for months or years. The core of his treatment was the use of verbal suggestion in a tightly controlled environment, and to that extent his treatment was psychological, not physiological. Patients were not allowed to ask questions, or to deny that they wanted to get better. They were told that the treatment was invariably successful, and that the length of time needed to achieve a cure was in the hands of the afflicted man himself. By exerting his authority, reinforced with electrode treatment, Yealland achieved cures. Patients were told that the application of the electrodes would be painful (although in several cases he used only the mildest current) and that it was up to them how quickly the cure was effected.

Watching jerky, silent black and white films of Yealland's patients, one focuses only on the pain inflicted by the electrical treatment, and the psychological basis of the treatment is overlooked. It is difficult to remember that the purpose of this doctor's treatment was to make dysfunctional men, doomed to life in institutions or living as invalids, into human beings again. This he achieved, and if to our eyes his treatments seem inhumane, many of his patients were grateful to him.

Yealland's technique had another bonus – it sorted out the malingerers from those suffering from genuine hysterical paralysis. He always carried out a detailed physical examination of the patient before carrying out his treatments, so as to establish with reasonable certainty that a condition was hysterical and not organic, and this also identified some potential malingerers. Malingering was a serious problem for doctors and was extremely common – Alan Sichel at No. 58 Ophthalmic Centre Military Hospital proved that up to 11 per cent of his patients were falsifying their symptoms and military doctors were warned to look out for men trying to evade their duties in this way.[13] In 1913 Sir John Collie had published a book on malingering and how to recognize it, which when reprinted in 1917 was nearly twice as thick and contained sections on self-inflicted wounds and shell shock.[14] J. C. Dunn, relating his experiences in dealing with a malingerer, wrote: 'He had taught me that the first duty of a battalion medical officer in War is to discourage the evasion of duty. That has to be done not seldom against one's better feeling, sometimes to the temporary hurt of an individual, but justice to all the other men, as well as discipline demands it.'[15] Under these circumstances it is hardly surprising that on occasion a man genuinely traumatized by his experiences was given 'medicine and duty' by a harassed battalion medical officer. At the start of the war the standard excuse given for a military offence was: 'I was drunk and didn't rightly know what I was doing', but by 1916 men often claimed shell shock as a defence at courts martial, these claims frequently having no foundation. This led, inevitably, to some men who were genuinely suffering from a mental breakdown being convicted of offences for which they were not truly responsible, and in some cases being shot.

Whilst Yealland was practising his techniques in London, further north the army was trying a different technique. Maghull Hospital in Liverpool had been built as a modern colony for epileptics in 1912 but during the war had been taken over for shell shock cases and in total nearly 4,000 men received treatment there. In charge was Richard Rows, a doctor with a keen interest in the new Freudian methods of psychoanalysis. Under him were assembled a team of some of the greatest neurologists and psychologists of the day, including William Rivers, Grafton Elliot Smith, Tom Pear and William Brown. Maghull was an ideal location. The hospital was new and comprised several mock-Georgian villas giving patients a degree of quiet and space. The patients were kept busy, either on the hospital farm or in the kitchens, or taking part in 'constructive relaxation', such as playing cards, billiards and so on.

It was at Maghull that the 'talking cure' was born. The patients – all 'other ranks' – were stiff-upper-lipped working class men who would not have dreamed of discussing their fears and anxieties with strangers, and yet were persuaded to talk and to recognize their own individual psychological blocks and to face and overcome them. It is a measure of the army's anxiety regarding the shell shock problem that it was prepared to fund and support what was, effectively, an experiment. In fact the experiment was so successful that by 1917 other doctors were sent to Maghull to study the techniques used so that they could be applied on a wider basis.[16]

Through Pat Barker's books [17] and the film *Regeneration*, William Halse Rivers has recently received the fame he richly deserves as one of the pioneers of psychotherapy in the treatment of shell shock. Others deserve similar recognition, but through his contact with Siegfried Sassoon at Craiglockhart, Rivers is the name synonymous with this method of treatment.

Born in 1864, Rivers was the only son of a clergyman who coincidentally offered treatment for stammering – among his clients was Charles Dodgson, better known as Lewis Carroll; ironically, William Rivers himself had a stammer which even his father's methods failed to cure. The young Rivers decided on medicine for a profession and studied at St Bartholomew's Hospital in London, qualifying at the age of 22. He subsequently developed an interest in physiology and neurology which led to his studying under various experts both in England and abroad. One of the men he met was Charles Myers. By 1908 Rivers and Myers had become interested in the subject of psychology and it was largely through them that this subject became a separate academic discipline at Cambridge.

As a result of their interest in anthropological neurology, Rivers and Myers went on an expedition to the Torres Straits, and Rivers later went to south-western India to study the Todas. Had it not been for the war Rivers probably would have remained primarily interested in this line of research, but events were to overtake him.

In 1914 he went to a conference in Australia and then continued on to the New Hebrides, where he stayed until 1915. The outbreak of war seems to have made little impression on him, although at the age of 50 and with the war supposedly to be over by Christmas there was little reason for him to return to England. On returning to England in spring 1915, when it appeared that the war was not going to be over quickly, he spent some months decid-ing what type of war service to undertake, before joining the Maghull Military Hospital in Liverpool as a civilian physician.

When Rivers joined the staff of Maghull, identifying, understanding and treating the severe emotional disturbances due to war trauma was a high priority. Hundreds of men passed through the hospital with the condition that would become known as 'war neurosis', described with such perception by Wilfred Owen as the 'men whose minds the Dead have ravished'.[18] The doctors at Maghull found themselves not only fighting on the scientific and medical front, attempting to understand and relieve the symptoms of the sufferers, but also fighting public and official opinion which viewed such psychological breakdown with scant sympathy.

In 1916, when 52 years old, Rivers was commissioned as a captain into the Royal Army Medical Corps and in October was sent to Craiglockhart Hospital for Officers, in Edinburgh. There had recently been a change in 'top brass' at the hospital and Rivers formed part of the new team assembled to deal with the shell-shocked patients. His technique was to try to understand each of his patients, and to help them to help themselves – by talking to them of their dreams and helping explain them, by persuading them to write and to live as normal a life as possible, free of some of the constraints of military discipline. He described the processes as 'Autognosis' in which the subject learned to understand himself and 'Re-education' – 'to understand how knowl-edge of himself may be utilised and … to turn energy into more healthy chan-nels'.[19] He described the underlying principles of his approach:

Of greater interest and more importance is the process by which the patient is led to understand how the disorder has developed ... If the patient learns that his disease is only the expression of an exaggeration of a wide-spread trend of feeling, thought or action, his condition will no longer appear mysterious, terrifying or horrible, but will assume proportions which can be faced rationally and dispassionately.[20]

In all, Rivers was only at Craiglockhart for just over a year, but in that time he met and treated Siegfried Sassoon, who ensured Rivers's subsequent fame. Sassoon also had a stammer, and a rapport was clearly established between the two men – the degree of which is indicated by the fact that the first chapter of *Sherston's Progress*, describing Sassoon's introduction to Craiglockhart, is simply entitled 'Rivers'. When Sassoon left Craiglockhart after passing his medical board, he wrote:

I had said goodbye to Rivers. Shutting the door of his room for the last time, I left behind me someone who had helped and understood me more than anyone I have ever known. Much as he disliked speeding me back to the trenches, he realised that it was my only way out and the longer I live the more right I know him to have been.[21]

The two men continued to meet after the war and Rivers made such a deep impression on Sassoon that the latter wrote in his diary in 1952: 'I should like to meet Rivers in the next world.'[22]

At the end of 1917 Rivers left Craiglockhart and moved to London, as psychologist to the Royal Flying Corps based in Hampstead, where he spent a lot of time getting to understand the mental qualities required for military aviation and the problem of 'wind up'. During this time he wrote several papers on his methods of treatment which, together with works by other contemporary psychiatrists, laid the foundation for modern treatment of post-traumatic stress disorders.

During the battle of the Somme, war neuroses became a major issue.[23] Early in the battle, at Daours, Philip Gibbs, the war correspondent, noted 'shell-shocked boys weeping or moaning, and shaking with an ague'.[24] Then on 9 July ninety men of the 11th Battalion, Border Regiment were ordered to go on a trench raid. This battalion had attacked on 1 July and lost all their officers and 500 other ranks, and the remaining 250 men had been put under the temporary command of an officer from another unit and been used for carrying parties and general fatigue duties. Of the ninety, thirty men reported sick, saying that they had shell shock. The officer commanding, Capt. Palmer, arranged for a sick parade at 11 p.m., and the men were examined by Lt Kirkwood, the MO. He wrote out a certificate: 'In view of the bombing raid to be carried out by the 11th Border Regiment, I must hereby testify to their unfitness for such an operation as few, if any, are not suffering from some degree of shell shock.'[25]

Despite this, Brigade ordered the raid to go ahead, but the men moved so slowly and reluctantly to the jumping-off point that Second Lt Ross, in charge of the party, realized that there was 'a great lack of offensive spirit in the party', and as it was by then impossible to stick to the original timetable, he cancelled the raid. When this was reported back, the four sergeants in the party were arrested and a court of inquiry convened. At this, Lt Kirkwood explained that he believed the men to be totally demoralized after 1 July and that they had not had time to recover their equilibrium. This view was not accepted by either brigade or divisional commanders, the latter saying that the MO was to blame for the debacle and that he had been relieved of his duties.

Gen. Hubert Gough, commanding the Reserve (later Fifth) Army, wrote:

> It is inconceivable how men, who have pledged themselves to fight and uphold the honour of their country, could degrade themselves in such a manner, and show an utter want of manly spirit and courage which, at least, is expected of every soldier and Britisher. The conduct on the part of Lieutenant Kirkwood RAMC shows him to be totally unfitted to hold a commission in the army, or to exercise any military responsibility. Immediate steps must be taken to remove Lieutenant Kirkwood from the service.[26]

Although the ADMS asked Gough to reconsider, he was adamant. In the file is a note by Surgeon General Sir Arthur Sloggett, Director General Army Medical Services. It concludes: 'The whole case is deplorable. The MO appears to have been made a scapegoat.' Even when the medical profession was beginning to realize the problems of battle stress, it was plain that some army commanders still considered that a British soldier should be immune to such weakness.

In mid 1916 Charles Myers, continuing his pioneering work in France, was promoted to lieutenant colonel and moved to St Omer, through which all 'mental' and '?mental' cases from First Army passed. He noted in his subsequent book that of the men seen, a third were returned to duty, with only one case of relapse.[27]

By now he had established three fundamental principles for the management of shell shock: promptness of action, suitable environment, and psychotherapeutic measures.[28] He believed that all regimental medical officers (RMOs) should be trained in basic psychological techniques and that they could deal with many patients near the front line. The remainder should be evacuated to special receiving centres within the appropriate army area, these centres being as remote from the scenes of warfare as possible, out of range of shellfire but preserving the mental 'atmosphere' of the front. Treatment should first of all be rest and sleep (but men should not be allowed to brood in solitude about their condition), followed by psychotherapy. An important part of this involved reassuring the soldier that he was not about to be sent to a lunatic asylum, nor returned to the front until he was cured. Myers advocated that as soon as possible after men had been treated, whilst convalescing, they should be restored to a military atmosphere, with gradually increasing discipline. In his view the prognosis was worse for men who had been physically buried or lifted by a shell, and he believed that in some of these cases there had been unidentified neurological trauma. He also noted that the very young were affected more than older men, and he made the observation: 'It is the common experience of Regimental Medical Officers that a man who has twice broken down under shell fire is useless at the front thereafter.'[29]

Myers felt strongly that men with shell shock should not be evacuated to the base areas. He quotes various RMOs:

We have found in certain units that the condition became fashionable, if not catching.

... We have seen too many dirty sneaks go down under the term 'shell-shock' to feel any great sympathy for the condition.

At all times while in the trenches men are arriving at the Aid Post, and on enquiries as to their condition the invariable answer is 'shell shock'.[30]

An Assistant Director of Medical Services wrote to Myers:

'Shell shock' should be abolished. The men have got to know the term and will tell you quite glibly that they are suffering from 'shell shock' when really a very different description might be applied to their condition.[31]

Myers was involved in continual struggles with the army. When he suggested to the Director General Army Medical Services that the term 'shell shock' be dropped no action was taken, except the recirculation of the 1915 instructions on the labelling of men 'shell shock – wounded' or 'shell shock – sick'. This led to men being detained in receiving centres being labelled as 'NYD?N' (not yet diagnosed, ?nervous) or 'NYD? shell shock' whilst information was obtained from their units as to whether they should be labelled 'W' or 'S', which delayed their treatment and reduced the likelihood of a complete cure.

In August 1916 Myers's title was changed to Consulting Psychologist, with responsibility for the Fourth and Fifth Armies, with Lt Col. Gordon Holmes (who had little experience of 'mental' cases) taking over responsibility for all the other areas. This led to conflict and Myers's ultimate departure from France, and he returned to England in 1917 to continue his work there. Disillusioned, he refused to contribute to the *Official History of the Great War*, or, sadly, to give evidence to the post-war 'Shell Shock Committee', and only published his Great War experiences in 1940.

By 1918 the army was struggling to deal with the numbers of men apparently suffering from shell shock or neurasthenia and was beginning to realize the impact of paying pensions to men suffering from no physical wounds. In January 1918 instructions were issued attempting to staunch the flow of men being inappropriately discharged from the service on grounds of 'nerves'.[32] Entitled 'Special Medical Board to determine discharge from the Army on account of shell shock, neurasthenia &c', these ordered that 'No soldier suffering from one of the above-mentioned disabilities will be discharged as medically unfit by a medical board unless one member of the Board is a neurologist and concurs in the finding.' In March instructions were issued relating to medical boards on 'Neurasthenic Officers' (reinforcing the idea that ordinary soldiers suffered from shell shock, whilst officers had neurasthenia): 'No officer suffering from shell shock, neurasthenia, functional nervous disorders or epilepsy will be marked permanently unfit for military service unless one member of the Board has special knowledge of disease of the nervous system and concurs in the finding.'[33]

The British Army – and other armies engaged in the conflict – had discovered that men's nerves could take only so much, and that shell shock (and its successor, post-traumatic stress disorder) was to be a feature of all future conflicts. Psychological casualties would be a major factor in all wars. Elliot Smith and Pear ended their book with the words: 'It is for us, not for our children, to act in the in the light of this great lesson.'[34] Sadly, the next generation was left to relearn the lessons of the Great War, and both medicine and the law had to acknowledge, painfully, that doctors in battle are often called upon to interpret military law whether they like it or not.

CHAPTER 8

MILITARY LAW IN ACTION 1914–18

Come here my Son. Better I execute the punishment upon thee personally,
than God should visit the consequences of thy crimes upon our whole Army.

KING GUSTAVUS ADOLPHUS OF SWEDEN, 1630

For most of the army, contact with military law took place at the lowest level, the platoon, then the company, the regiment or battalion. Platoon discipline in 1914 tended to reflect the hierarchy and custom of the Edwardian factory or shipyard: it was brutal, informal and fierce. Such informal discipline has existed since time immemorial. To take but one First World War example from an Irish regiment:

> I got a new draft the other day ... undesirables and old soldiers. Tried
> some tricks on the young fellow (i.e. a fledgling platoon commander).
> I said, nice and quiet to the Sgt Major ... 'just beat them into shape'.
> I don't like writing things on men's conduct sheets. When we get them
> into the trenches we'll see if they come up to our standards or not ...[1]

Such behaviour was not driven by brutal sadism, but was a short cut to much-needed discipline within an essentially paternalistic system. Being belted by an NCO for stepping out of line was infinitely better than being formally charged and, in an age when the foreman ruled by his fists, was accepted and understood. (To this day deputies and overmen down the pit carry a heavy stick, as a badge of office, just as did Roman centurions. It is not entirely decorative.)

The next step up was the company commander's 'Table', 'Memoranda' or 'Orders'. Company commanders could dispense summary punishments ranging from fines, 'confined to barracks', 'restrictions of privileges', extra drills and parades, limited imprisonment in the unit guardroom or (in the field) field punishment (FP).

Field punishment was intended as a physical punishment to replace flogging.

In an age when corporal punishment was as normal as any other – birching young offenders was a magistrate's choice, and anything from a smack round the head to a formal beating was the norm to discipline recalcitrant schoolboys – physical punishment was regarded as part of life's rich pattern. Tying a soldier to a post in full public view was considered merely as making a public example of a man guilty of a serious offence.

Although field punishment seems positively barbaric to our more enlightened eyes, only fifty years earlier in 1864 hangings and floggings in the armed services were still public affairs. By 1914 the alternative, field punishment, and particularly the most severe, FP No. 1, or 'crucifixion', was considered by the harsh discipline of the pre-war regular army as a more humane and enlightened alternative for a regimental malefactor who often felt that he had got off lightly. In most cases field funishment worked and men were only too anxious to avoid the humiliation of being publicly tied to a wagon wheel or post for two hours while their mates went about their business.[2]

Part of the problem was that not everyone shared the pre-war regulars' standards. For a boyish clerk who had volunteered and then run foul of the sergeant major, and particularly for the easy-going and vociferous Australians, the sight and experience of field punishment seemed both brutal and shocking.

Above the disciplinary level of the company commander came the battalion or regimental commander, or commanding officer (CO), who had effectively a magistrate's powers of summary justice. He could lock a man up for twenty-eight days, award FP No. 1 and strip NCOs of their rank (and pay). A commanding officer's award on a regimental conduct sheet could never be expunged. For a soldier to go before his CO was a serious business, because the next step, following the time-honoured question to the accused on being found guilty, was 'Do you accept my award/punishment, or do you wish to elect to go forward to be tried by court martial?'

Knowing the formidable powers of a court martial most soldiers – if they knew themselves to be justly convicted – chose to accept their CO's award, however unpleasant. What was true in 1914 is still true today.

Colouring all military justice in 1914 was a completely different attitude to both authority and punishment. This did not just apply to soldiers. Officers, NCOs and men all understood the rules by which their closed military community, the regiment, prospered and survived. Across the years it is difficult to understand these 'social dynamics'. But unless we comprehend how other people worked together in a different world long ago, we will fail to grasp just why many things happened the way they did. Above all, we must be careful not to make the adolescent historian's mistake and judge other cultures by our modern-day values and standards. Compassion or distaste for distant events should not blind us to the realities and customs of the past.

In the far-off foreign world that was 1914–18, the officer, non-commissioned officer or soldier charged with the offences set out in the *Manual of Military Law* would have been aware of several things. First, there was an inherent reluctance to charge senior non-commissioned officers unless they had committed a very serious or blatant offence. There was even more resistance to formally disciplining officers within fighting units (although unofficial punishments of officers were widespread and severe ('twenty-eight days extra duties' could be – and were – awarded to young officers at the slightest whim and without any right of appeal whatsoever). To do so publicly advertised the failures of the unit, regiment and, implicitly, the army itself. For an officer or senior NCO to be formally charged meant that the offence was regarded as serious enough by the individual's commanding officer to be dealt with as a public example. Publicly charging an officer or senior NCO was tantamount to admitting that they should not be officers or NCOs. Thus, whereas a soldier who fell asleep on sentry might be kicked awake, charged and punished, the sergeant in charge of sentries in the line who fell asleep would be cautioned and watched like a hawk by his officers and fellow NCOs. The platoon commander who slept through the rounds of his sentries in the line would be given extra duties, shamed by his colleagues, laughed at by his men and the incident overlooked – once. But should he repeat it, the young officer was almost invariably dismissed as 'a worthless officer' and sent back to some depot as yet another failed front line officer, with all the social stigma and odium which that represented at the time. An officer or senior NCO who was formally charged and court-martialled could expect a searching examination and little mercy. He was as guilty of 'letting the side down' as of any formal charge, and would normally receive a harsh punishment intended primarily to disgrace him. The key psychology lay in the 1914 attitudes towards leaders and led: soldiers could afford to fail, and were indeed expected to do so; senior NCOs and officers were not permitted to fail in their duties. Leaders who failed were ruthlessly dismissed by the standards of the old pre 1914 regular army.

The second aspect colouring military discipline when soldiers were charged was simply the issue of guilt. 'If the offender was not guilty of an offence, then why had he been put on a charge?' ran the thinking. More delicate, legalistic souls more used to the niceties of modern law may wince at such an approach, but it has coloured regimental discipline within most armies for centuries, and to a degree still colours it to this day. On the shop floor of army life the presumption of innocence is different from that usually seen in civilian courts. For example, a guardsman who drops his rifle very publicly, or faints on the Queen's Birthday parade ('Trooping the Colour'), will, even today, find himself standing to attention in front of his company commander's table, with the sergeant major breathing warmly down his neck – it is just not acceptable and there had better be a good excuse. If a soldier can prove that (a) 'the rifle sling broke, Sir, and was defective', or (b) 'the regimental medical officer has examined me and discovered that I've got anaemia left over from our time in Belize/The Balkans/Sierra Leone', then the soldier *might* get away with it. But despite any legal presumption of innocence, the onus is on him to explain his 'unsoldierlike' and unacceptable behaviour, not for his superiors to prove his guilt. He dropped his rifle on a public parade and *he should not have done so.*

Like it or not, there is little or no presumption of innocence at the summary justice level of the army. The truth from time immemorial is that soldiers inhabit a different world; they have to do dreadful things on behalf of the rest of society, and their standards of behaviour are different. As a result of these uncompromising standards, and despite the law which states that an accused person is innocent until proven guilty, soldiers usually are not formally charged unless they are considered to have committed some offence. As a principle, little has changed over the years. In a dark, wet, mud-filled trench, full of frightened men, screaming wounded and sudden violent explosions, men have to do as they are ordered immediately and without question. Any failure to obey orders or do your duty is unacceptable if the group is to live, but failure by the officers and NCOs was especially disastrous. In 1914 these rules were no different, and the standards of behaviour equally well understood.

This thinking coloured most regimental discipline, formal and informal. The majority of disciplinary cases went unreported outside the regiment and were dealt with within the unit. So a bolshy soldier would get extra fatigues or field punishment; a drunken corporal might lose a stripe and the extra pay it brought; the sergeant who got lost with the company stores all night would get a formal reprimand and extra duties; and the young officer who took his platoon down the wrong trench and got muddled up with the Royal Loamshires in the brigade attack would get an informal reprimand from a harassed company commander or commanding officer, and be warned not to do it again once he had finished his round of extra duties. The point is, relatively few offences ever got outside the regiment, battalion or unit. Lieutenant colonels, as commanding officers, had wide legal powers under the Army Act and they used them to ensure that *their* standards were met. So, by the standards of the day and by regimental thinking, for any individual to be charged with a 'court martial offence' represented a very serious matter indeed.

The Army Act of 1914 lists the powers of courts martial under the 'Arrest and Trial' sections, s45 to s68. In 1914 there were four types of court martial: the Regimental Court Martial (RCM), District Court Martial (DCM) the General Court Martial (GCM) and the Field General Court Martial (FGCM). The arbiter of these was, in the first instance, an individual's commanding officer. Under Section 46 of the Army Act, the powers of the commanding officer ('CO') are listed in great detail, covering nearly three whole pages.

The CO of a unit, usually a lieutenant colonel, had the power to deal with any disciplinary charge. First, he had the authority to instigate a court of inquiry to establish the facts of a case; he could then dismiss it, or deal with it summarily by selecting an appropriate charge within his powers (e.g. using Section 40, 'Conduct to the Prejudice of Good Order and Military Discipline'), instead of allowing a capital charge of disobedience to go forward to a court martial. The CO's powers of discretion were enormous. Most COs, with one eye on their own officers and another on the morale of their NCOs and men, were extremely reluctant to wash regimental dirty linen in public. However, as the war developed and external factors intervened (such as military police arresting a deserter in Boulogne and sending him back to his unit with a report to divisional HQ) then a unit commander would be forced to acknowledge publicly his soldiers' crimes or to make an example. Divisional and brigade commanders would be expected to demand fairly tersely what had happened to an individual who had figured in an official police deserters report.

Equally, a soldier found malingering in the picket lines of another unit could not be hushed up; it was too public within the brigade. A CO faced with this sort of problem had the dilemma of choosing between his own neck (as a tough CO), the overall good of his regiment and the needs of the wretched individual under arrest. The greater requirements of the group usually prevailed in such cases.

One of the key powers of a CO was therefore contained in the words:

> An offender shall not be liable to be tried by Court Martial for any offence
> which has been dealt with summarily by his Commanding Officer ...[3]

There can be little doubt that the majority of commanding officers, in the majority of cases, kept the disciplinary procedures tightly contained within their own units. However, if their summary powers were not sufficient then the next step up was the court martial. In 1914 a Regimental Court Martial was the lowliest form of court martial.

Regimental Courts Martial are today non-existent, but in those days could be convened by any regular officer designated as a 'commanding officer' with the rank of captain or above. The board had to consist of three officers each of whom must have held a commission for at least one year. The powers of an RCM were carefully proscribed. It could not impose sentences of more than forty-two days' detention, and punishments of death, penal servitude or more than six weeks' imprisonment were forbidden. The RCM was essentially, as its name implies, the regimental court of last resort if the summary powers of the commanding officer were not sufficient.[4]

The RCM was a low-level legal instrument and is best thought of as a kind of 'board of inquiry'. It was not used for disciplining soldiers for offences on active service on the Western Front, although many RCMs took place in units training or based in the UK.

A District, or General, Court Martial was a different matter and the subject of the utmost gravity. A General Court Martial could be convened only by an authorized general officer on behalf of the Crown, and had to consist of not fewer than five officers – nine in the UK – all of whom had held the rank of captain or above. Its younger brother, the District Court Martial, consisted of three officers, and its powers were carefully circumscribed. No sentences of death were allowed, and it could not try officers. GCMs and DCMs were the army's peacetime courts and formal instruments of justice.

The real instrument of swift justice on active service was the Field General Court Martial, a curious hybrid of the General, the District and the Regimental Court Martial. Section 49 spells out the duties and responsibilities of the FGCM.

The panel at a Field General Court Martial was to comprise not fewer than three officers, unless the convening officer (normally the brigade commander in a capital case) was satisfied that this number was not available for operational reasons. The president was normally an officer of field rank (a major or above) and the other members were usually a captain and a lieutenant. The accused man's CO was not permitted to sit on the panel, although other officers from his battalion could, and frequently did.[5] An explanatory note to the relevant section of the Army Act spells out the legal intention behind the law on FGCMs:

(1) The object of this section is to provide for the speedy trial of offences committed abroad or to try such offences by an ordinary court martial on active service where it is not practicable with due regard to the interests of discipline and of the service. A field general court martial can try any offence committed on active service ... [6]

Under Section 51 of the Act the accused had an absolute right to object to the composition and members of any court martial panel, so an FGCM including officers of his own regiment could be either a source of scrupulous fairness or a grievance. A court martial, even an FGCM, was also totally bound by the same civilian rules of evidence and standards as any civil court, and by equally strict legal procedures.[7]

However, any court martial was empowered to find an accused guilty of a lesser charge. Thus, for example, to the occasional bafflement of civilian barristers, a court martial could acquit a soldier of the specific charge of desertion but find him guilty of the lesser charge of attempting to desert, or absence without leave (offences with which he had not been charged) and punish him accordingly.[8]

The aims and purpose of the FGCM are fairly clear from the Act. It was intended as an emergency court when the army was detached or engaged on active service overseas. Moreover, although a relatively junior officer (e.g. an isolated detachment commander) could, in theory, convene an FGCM, only the commander-in-chief of the detached forces could confirm any sentence of penal servitude or death. There is both an explicit and an implicit acknowledgement in Sections 49–54 that the FGCM is intended as an exceptional operational measure. For example, the wording of Section 49:

if in the opinion of the [detachment commander] ... it is not practicable that such offence be tried by an ordinary Court Martial ...[9]

The FGCM was in fact intended for the speedy trial of offences committed on active service, in faraway places. Although only occasionally mentioned in the Act, the realities of operations in the far-flung corners of the Empire, far from London and the Royal Courts in the Strand, pervades this part of the *Manual of Military Law*. There is a certain irony that a piece of legislation primarily intended for use on the veldt or the Hindu Kush should find its main source of employment less than a day's travel from Charing Cross Station.

What is quite clear, however, is that the FGCM was a formally and legally constituted judicial instrument. It was not a 'paramilitary kangaroo court' or a 'hasty and illegal tribunal', to highlight two of the criticisms levelled against it by some modern press accounts of the trials. It was a carefully thought out measure, designed to do precisely what military law was intended to do: delegate the power to control troops' behaviour, especially over specifically military offences, down to the detached commander fighting the enemy. Any especially grave sentencing (such as death) had to be unanimous (with the junior officer giving his opinion first to avoid senior officers 'directing' the proceedings), and was strictly controlled and subject to confirmation by the most senior officer in the theatre of operations, invariably a senior general, or the commander-in-chief, who held a formal royal warrant legally empowering him to dispense justice. Only the commander-in-chief in a theatre of war could authorize a sentence of death and, in a further restriction of an FGCM 's powers, subsection (d) states: 'Where a FGCM consists of less than three officers, the sentence shall not exceed ... Field Punishment ... or imprisonment.'[10]

The FGCM was by the standards of its day a practical and important tool of military law. To prevent abuse its powers were carefully constrained and its findings were subject to confirmation by a superior legal authority. Although there was no court of appeal for men sentenced by court martial, there was no automatic right of appeal in civilian life in 1914 either. The civilian Court of Criminal Appeal itself had only been instituted in 1907. In 1914 appeals were only permitted if there were clearly defined reasons, such as new evidence, or procedural errors in the legal process at the trial. With its many tiers of scrutiny, the military system was felt in many ways to be theoretically fairer than civil law as it then stood.

Three other criticisms have been raised against the FGCM as a procedure during the war: its speed of operation; lack of legal expertise amongst its members; and the claim that the trials were unfair, class based and biased.

To deal first with this last criticism, most eloquently voiced in *The Thin Yellow Line*,[11] *For the Sake of Example*[12] and, most critically of all, *Shot at Dawn*:[13] the truth is that such criticisms tend to be based on modern emotional reaction to the trials rather than historical fact. Biased and unfair many trials may seem by our contemporary standards, but the great majority appear to have been conducted in accordance with the legal rules of the time. There are very few, if any, arguments over guilt or innocence in the records of the time and, most revealingly, there is not one example of an officer or soldier wrongly convicted of the offence with which he was charged. To quibble over the exigencies of procedure or the harshness of sentences handed down over eighty years ago makes no more sense than it does to query the justice of Great-uncle Jack, being transported to Australia for stealing a sheep in 1840. The law at the time was the law at the time. And as for the complaint that courts martial were 'class based', it is clear that all justice in the early years of the twentieth century from magistrates' courts to courts martial was 'class based'. The whole of society in Edwardian Britain was class based, the law especially. In 1910 the mine owners of South Wales, sitting as magistrates, thought nothing of fining their own miners for going on strike without notice, and even ordered the fines deducted from their workers' wages! The courts martial merely reflected the paternalistic standards and *mores* of their age, and the hierarchy of society of the day. Crucially, no one at the time felt that there was a vendetta against working class soldiers. Such ideas are a later invention of modern social commentators looking back in indignation at some of the stranger ideas of the early social and racial theorists.

The real argument is in fact not over any alleged injustice of the verdicts themselves but over the severity of the sentences handed down and sometimes their seemingly arbitrary nature. It is here that the first criticism, about the speedy and sometimes superficial nature of the trials, becomes the most worrying aspect of many of the cases. The idea of a frightened young man on trial for his life being dealt with in some French farmhouse during a single morning worries fair-minded people. But in the 1914–18 war the FGCM was intended as a swift instrument, not as a lengthy and painstaking judicial procedure. Implicit behind this modern criticism is a demand for some more considered and deliberate legal alternative based on today's civilian procedures. Only by removing the accused, all the witnesses and character referees (many of whom were already dead or lying wounded in hospitals all over France and the British Isles) to some legal chambers and courtroom far behind the lines could this demand for 'slower and more measured justice' be met. Such a demand would, at the time, have been met by derision. For a hard-pressed infantry battalion CO with only half a dozen surviving officers, and still burying some of the witnesses, to be asked to detach chunks of valuable manpower from the battle line to deal with lawyers worrying about the human rights of one of his soldiers who had failed in his duty or run away would have been the final straw in 1914–18. To those involved at the time, such a concept would have been seen as naive, incomprehensible and insulting to the dead who had just fallen in the last battle. As early as December 1914 the staff of 4 Division sent a formal note of protest against the DJAG's lofty rulings on courts martial in the field, saying 'that it is doubtful if the DJAG realises the difficult conditions under which courts martial have to be conducted in the front lines'.

The prime purpose of the army was to kill Germans and push the invaders back out of France and Belgium. The most basic reading of the contemporary record supports this view.[14] Most fighting units found it both difficult and burdensome to support FGCMs held only 10 miles away and taking just one single working day of officers' time, let alone anything longer. This view of the court martial as an irritating distraction from the real business of the war is powerfully reinforced by the contemporary writings, with innumerable reports of the difficulties of detaching officers, NCOs and soldiers to attend an unpleasant duty.

By far the most potent criticism of the field courts martial is the lack of legal expertise by court martial members. Even at the time it was felt that as much expertise as possible was needed. The ponderous attempts to follow the rules in the arrangements for FGCMs seem to have reflected this desire to do things as formally as possible despite the difficult circumstances.

The idea, however, that somehow FGCMs were held by an impromptu group of officers dispensing arbitrary justice in a muddy trench and were over in a few minutes is pure fiction. The courtroom would always be far enough back to be out of enemy fire, and while the surroundings may have been temporary (in at least one case the trial was held in a converted French café and as the court was cleared thirsty soldiers flooded back in), every effort appears to have been made to obey the letter of the law even to the point of solemn pedantry.

A room near brigade headquarters would be cleaned out and three or five officers of various regiments would sit behind a table. Often an officer-lawyer from the Judge Advocate's Branch was there to advise them on law and procedures. As the war progressed, more and more professional lawyers appeared in the army's ranks, and many were transferred to act as court martial officers (CMOs), as legally qualified advisers to courts martial.

The prosecutor was almost invariably the adjutant (or administrative captain) of the accused's unit. For a harassed adjutant of a battalion just out of the line this must have been a thoroughly time-consuming and unpleasant job. The prisoner was entitled to ask for a defending officer, quaintly termed 'the prisoner's friend'. There were no hard and fast rules about the appointment of a defending officer. A bewildered soldier often chose a popular or respected officer from his own company to represent him, despite the latter's total ignorance of the law. Some men chose qualified barristers and solicitors, now in uniform, to act in their defence, and in many courts martial the accused man defended himself. This may be because he was not offered a prisoner's friend, although most men would have been aware of their rights in this respect, and at trials where a CMO was present it must be assumed that the man had elected to defend himself. In 1914 this was considered normal. Most civilians hauled up before the magistrate would have defended themselves and the same principles were true for courts martial. In many cases the accused soldier may not even have wanted a defending officer to speak for him or may have thought it pointless.

The delay in bringing an accused man to trial also varied dramatically, and was the subject of much testy enquiry by higher authority. In the middle of a war, however, administrative and especially legal matters always took second place to operational priorities. Delays often appear to have been caused by the demands of the battlefield or a time-consuming hunt for solid – and surviving – witnesses or evidence.

For the accused, waiting for the court martial was always an ordeal. Whilst some cases, such as the first man to desert, Highgate, or Short the Etaples mutineer, were tried with almost indecent haste, others, like Sub Lt Dyett, waited weeks for the ponderous bureaucratic machinery of the BEF to determine their fate.

In every case the procedure was broadly the same once the court martial had been convened, the correct number of suitably qualified officers assembled, and a suitable location prepared. The accused was marched in beltless and hatless under escort, the charge was read out and the accused man asked to plead.

After Byers' suicidal guilty plea early in 1915 (see Chapter 24) no soldier was permitted to plead guilty to a capital charge – an automatic plea of 'not guilty' was read into the record to give the accused a defence whether he liked it or not. The prosecution's witnesses were heard on oath and cross-examined, frequently by the accused prisoner himself, and then the defence put its case. In many cases this was just a statement on oath, or sometimes not on oath, by the defendant. In many cases the only defence was 'I didn't realize it was so serious, sir,' or (the old soldier's defence), 'I didn't know what I was doing, sir,' often (although not always) tied to the suggestion that the accused had been drunk at the time and was therefore not responsible for his actions.

From the surviving court martial papers, it is clear that the accused was cross-examined carefully, and the courts' desire to get to the root of the matter shines through. For a young subaltern sitting with a major or a captain to try a nervous, tongue-tied young soldier on trial for his life must have been an ordeal for all parties. One of the problems was that as officer casualties mounted in 1914 and 1915, the supply of experienced regular officers with any knowledge of military law and the competence to sit on courts martial began to dry up. The trials became even more stilted and it is painfully apparent that in most cases the courts were pedestrian, if not positively pedantic in their adherence to the *Manual of Military Law* and the Rules of Procedure. In a process unfamiliar to all, everyone 'stuck by the book' and followed it with painstaking thoroughness, frequently stopping to consult the *Manual*. Sometimes the notes in the transcripts and the questions to the prisoner reflect these inexperienced and amateur attempts to dispense justice fairly.

In order to assist the court in its deliberations and provide a much-needed level of legal expertise, experienced lawyers were drafted in as specialist CMOs as the war progressed. For example, Haig's staff spelled out the duties of the CMO in March 1916:

> The duty of the Court Martial Officer is to keep the Court straight on matters of law and procedure, and in order to do this his rank ought not to be too junior, otherwise he will not carry sufficient weight with the President, who is usually of Field Rank.
>
> For instance, it is particularly necessary for him to check the tendency of many Presidents to ask irregular questions which lead to inadmissible replies, and therefore cause proceedings to be quashed. It is almost impossible for a subaltern, who is probably the junior member, to fulfil his duty in such respects effectively, or even with propriety.[15]

Despite this professional legal assistance, the proceedings were further slowed by the need to record all the evidence in a laborious longhand, which must have reduced any razor-like cross-examination to a snail-like pace. On the other hand the painful slowness of the proceedings clearly gave even the dullest soldier time to think. Once all the evidence had been heard and all witnesses cross-examined, the accused or his defending officer were invited to make a closing address, and the court cleared to consider its verdict behind closed doors. (If there was a formally qualified judge advocate present he summed up the proceedings before the court retired.)

Court martial members are sworn to secrecy by oath, and it is difficult to reconstruct what happened in what was effectively 'the jury room'. In his personal account written long after the war Charles Carrington alludes to some of the pressures of the time:

> When under instruction young officers were taught that in the conduct
> of proceedings the first duty of the court was to ensure that the prisoner
> had every advantage to which he was legally entitled, that every member
> of the court was to consider himself the prisoner's friend; but that the
> prerogative of mercy was no concern of theirs [i.e. the court's]. The
> court should not hesitate to pronounce a heavy sentence if the case was
> proved; and there were many military crimes for which the normal
> penalty was death.[16]

Carrington was clearly troubled by this even while writing in 1965, when he was well into his seventies. He goes on to give us some hint of the pressures in the closed court considering its verdict.

> A memory that disturbs me is the hint or warning that came down from
> above, … that morale needed a sharp jolt, or that a few severe sentences
> might have a good effect. It was expedient that some man who had
> deserted his post under fire was shot to encourage the others. Sometimes
> discipline would be screwed up a couple of turns: death sentences would
> be confirmed and executed.[17]

Clearly such considerations weighed heavily with the court when considering their verdict, particularly if they felt the offence had been proved. When the panel discussed its verdict behind closed doors it was mandatory for the most junior officer present to give his opinion first so that it could not be said that he merely endorsed the views of more senior officers. The level of inexperience was sometimes shocking. In his memoire of his experiences as a young volunteer officer, Guy Chapman relates of his first court martial:

> … the accused was an elderly pioneer sergeant of the 60th, the charge,
> 'drunk in the trenches'. He was duly found guilty. As he was marched out
> I hurriedly turned to the pages of the *Manual of Military Law* and found
> that the punishment was death … So when [the President] turned to me
> as the junior member of the court and demanded my sentence, I replied,
> 'Oh death, I suppose.' Major Keppel blenched and turned to my opposite
> number, Gwinnell. Gwinnell who was as young and unlearned in

expediency as myself answered as I had, 'Death I suppose!' Our president ... groaned; 'But my boys, you can't do it.'

'But Sir', we protested ... 'It says so here.' It was only after an appeal from the President that we allowed ourselves ... to punish the ruffian by reduction to the rank of Corporal ...[18]

This account by Chapman is revealing for another reason: it reveals the sheer ignorance among the new amateur officer corps in France. The dramatic expansion of the army had produced a serious dearth of experienced officers, particularly among the junior line or regimental officers. While a new subaltern fresh from training could learn about his men and how to live and survive in battle fairly quickly, much of the deeper professional background competence of the regular officers had died with them. Whether it was the procedures for ordering new socks for his soldiers, indenting for ammunition or rum, or the complicated rules of King's Regulations, detailed knowledge of how the army worked as an organization was lacking. Nowhere was this more true than in the more esoteric professional disciplines, of which military law was one example. While a pre-war officer 'gentleman cadet' may have prided himself on not taking his military law classes very seriously at Sandhurst, at least he had been forced to pass an exam; and a couple of years of regimental soldiering meant that he had a journeyman's feel for the way the system worked and what was right and proper. Officers who wished to progress in the army had to pass professional examinations, of which the 'Military Law' paper was a notoriously difficult hurdle for the busy regimental officer. The merest glance at the exam papers or the pre 1914 professional textbooks reveals just how detailed and technical was the level expected.[19]

The problem was that by 1915 no one had found the time to train the thousands of new officers in a skill that was at best highly peripheral to their brief career as fighting officers and at worst a waste of valuable time. Most new officers learned their military law at the FGCM.

Once the verdict was agreed the accused was marched back in and the finding read out. If it was 'guilty' then the accused (or his defending officer) was invited to make a 'statement in mitigation of punishment'. These were usually fairly emotional, 'I'm sorry ...', 'I didn't realize it was so serious ...', 'Give me another chance ...', 'I'd had pains in my legs ...', 'I never meant to do it ...', 'I didn't know what I was about ...', to quote just some of the examples in the case papers, but by and large they seem to have fallen on stony ground, especially if the court's examination of the accused's regimental conduct sheet revealed a bad disciplinary record. In a world in which the death rate for British soldiers in action was never less than 2,000 men a week, and averaged 400 dead per day for over four years, the fate of one soldier who had failed in his duty – or worse, was a persistent source of trouble – seems to have been met with hard-nosed impartiality at best and a ruthless lack of compassion at worst. Anyway, went the thinking, it was up to the confirmation process to temper justice with mercy.

Once the war had settled down to static trench fighting from late 1914, a system of confirmation of sentencing emerged. The court martial papers were sent 'upward' starting with the accused's commanding officer, who had to give his views on the accused's record, his discipline and his value as a fighting man. Most COs seem to have recommended merciful treatment, and where they do not it is revealing ('A worthless soldier …' 'No value as a fighting man …' 'Surly, disrespectful and a constant source of trouble …'). Usually, however, a commanding officer pleaded for his soldier and as nine out of ten death sentences were not confirmed and reduced to lesser sentences, these pleas for mercy appear to have been heard much more often than not. No self-respecting officer wanted to wreck the spirit of the units in the trenches.

The next recommendation on the papers was usually the brigade commander's. As he was the authority who had convened the court martial, his comments usually included a remark about the discipline in the unit from which the convicted man came. Again, this could be revealing ('An example needs to be made …' 'Discipline is not good in this unit …'). Divisional, corps and army commanders subsequently appended their various recommendations ('I recommend mercy …'; 'this is a good unit and no example is necessary', or 'I recommend that the sentence be carried out …') and the papers found their way to the Adjutant General's Branch at GHQ of the BEF. There the papers would be scrutinized by the DJAG's team and then placed, with a recommendation by the Assistant Adjutant General for discipline, before the commander-in-chief, French or Haig, who were the only men in France with the ultimate legal power of a royal warrant to confirm a death sentence. For theatres of war other than France and Flanders the confirming officer would be the local commander-in-chief, e.g. C.-in-C. Mediterranean Expeditionary Force. It is to the credit of all these commanders that they refused to confirm 89 per cent of the 3,000 death sentences placed before them.

Once the sentence was confirmed or otherwise, it was promulgated. This was usually done in front of the man's unit on parade, and as Charles Carrington drily recorded usually took the form of: 'The sentence of the

Court was – death! ... (Dramatic pause.) Commuted by the Commander-in-Chief to three months field punishment.'[20]

But for one in ten convicted soldiers the sentence was not commuted. The wretched man was led away under escort and executed by a firing squad, sometimes (although this was unusual) from his own unit, at dawn next day.

The shootings of the First World War seem to exercise a curious fascination for some, which, when the figures are compared with the endless numbers of men killed in action, seems somehow inappropriate. Paradoxically, there is nothing like the same clamour about the civil executions by hanging in the UK at the time. The fact is, the military – and civil – legal system of the time had the death penalty for specified crimes, and they used it: in the military's case extremely sparingly.

The grisly business of the final sanction of military justice in 1914–18, shooting at dawn, has been pored over by many both in fact and in fiction. Again, like all things military it followed a clear set of instructions and a clear ritual. The unfortunate man was given the services of a chaplain and was usually offered alcohol or even opiates by a merciful RMO to deaden the waiting during the night before. He usually wrote letters home or talked to the priest or his guards. (One of the ironies is that most of the condemned men exhibited a remarkable sangfroid and even stoic bravery in the face of certain death.) At dawn he was led out with an MO and chaplain, tied to a post or a chair, blindfolded; a scrap of paper was pinned over his left breast and then a firing party of twelve men, almost as distressed and sick as the convicted man, fired a single volley at about 15 to 20 yards' range. If the unfortunate man was still breathing or kicking spasmodically, the officer responsible for carrying out the sentence, usually the Assistant Provost Marshal of the division in question or the officer in charge of the firing party, stepped forward and fired a *coup de grâce* at short range into the victim's brain to finish him off. The firing party was marched off, usually in a state of shock, and stretcher bearers took the body to bury it nearby, usually in a properly marked grave. Murderer, deserter, coward or mutineer are all today buried alongside their comrades in the Commonwealth War Graves Commission cemeteries in France and Belgium.

The best descriptions of such executions can be found in fiction in Len Deighton's *Declarations of War* and in Stanley Kubrick's film *Paths of Glory*. Accurate factual accounts are harder to come by. Rumour and gossip abounded. For example, Victor Sylvester's claims to have participated in five firing squads at Etaples as a young soldier are demonstrably false, as are many of the wilder stories. The best description comes from an APM himself.

In December 1915 Captain T. H. Westmacott was appointed Assistant Provost Marshal of the 1st Indian Cavalry Division. His duties included attendance at military executions, of which he witnessed three which affected him deeply. His diary includes a full description of two of these executions, withholding the name of the soldier concerned. His diary reads:

14 April, 1916. I ... received orders to attend the execution of a deserter in the Cheshire Regiment. The man had deserted when his battalion was in the trenches and had been caught in Paris. He was sentenced to death, but the sentence was remitted, and he was sent back to his battalion. He did so well in the trenches that he was allowed leave to England. He deserted again, and after being arrested was sent back to his battalion, where he was again sentenced to death. This time he was shot ... I found Coates, the firing party and a company of the Cheshires drawn up opposite a chair under a railway embankment. The condemned man spent the night in a house about half a mile away. He walked from there blindfolded with the doctor, the parson and the escort. He walked quite steadily on to parade, sat down in the chair, and told them not to tie him too tight. A white disc was pinned over his heart. He was the calmest man on the ground. The firing party was 15 paces distant. The officer commanding the firing party did everything by signal, only speaking the word 'Fire!' The firing party was twelve strong, six kneeling and six standing. Before the condemned man arrived, the firing party about turned after grounding arms, and the OC firing party and the APM mixed up the rifles and unloaded some of them.

On the word 'Fire!' the man's head fell back, and the firing party about turned at once. The doctor said that the man was not quite dead, but before the OC firing party could finish him with his revolver he was dead, having felt nothing. The company was then marched off. The body was wrapped in a blanket, and the APM saw it buried in a grave which had been dug close by, unmarked and unconsecrated.[21]

This soldier was Pte J. E. Bolton of 1st Cheshires. The place of his execution was minutely described in the trial papers and it would seem that despite Westmacott's recollection the grave was marked in some way, as Bolton now lies buried in the CWGC cemetery at Roclincourt.

Westmacott's diary recorded a complete case in bare detail some three months later. It is worth quoting in full.

26 June, 1916. A Sowar in the 29th Lancers shot the Wordi Major (native Adjutant) of the Regiment dead. He then threw away his rifle, tore off most of his clothes, and rushed off to the HQ of the Lucknow Brigade, where he happened to catch General Morton Gage, the Brigadier, in the street. He told the General a long story, but as the General was British service he could not understand a word. The man was a Delhi policeman, and a Jat, who enlisted for the period of the war. He is a sulky kind of fellow but there is no doubt that the Wordi Major, who was an absolute rotter, goaded the wretched fellow to desperation.

After this date we moved down to the neighbourhood of Doullens for the battle of the Somme. Until the 13th of July the man was in my charge and I had to drag him about with DHQ until that date, very hard luck on the man. He behaved very well the whole time and one day he said to me, 'Sahib, I am quite certain now that I shall not be shot, as you have kept me so long.'

19 July. Had a long ride of about 28 miles to Villers Chatel, north of Aubigny, Yadram, the murderer, riding with me under escort the whole way. On arrival, orders came in for his execution.

20 July. Rode over to the Lucknow Brigade HQ and to the 29th Lancers and arranged everything including the place of execution.

Sent Yadram to the Regiment under escort to have the sentence promulgated. Gibbon, the Divisional Chaplain, was a great nuisance, as he obtained leave from the Divisional Commander to visit Yadram during the night. As Yadram was a Jat and not a Christian we all considered it a great piece of impertinence on Gibbon's part.

21 July. Got up at 2.45am and went over to the 29th Lancers with Gordon, the General's ADC, and Winckworth, my assistant. The Regiment was drawn up dismounted in hollow square with the firing party and the chair in front. The firing party consisted of twenty men, five from each squadron. They grounded arms and faced about and moved three paces to the rear, while I mixed up the rifles and unloaded some of them. Then they marched back and picked up their arms. The prisoner was then brought up under escort blindfolded with a white disc pinned over his heart, and he sat down in the chair. As Sergeant Walsh, my provost sergeant, was tying him to the chair, he shouted in Hindustani, 'Salaam, O Sahibs! And Salaam, all Hindus and Mahometans of this regiment!

There is no justice in the British Sirkar. I did this deed because I was abused. Those of you who have been abused as I was go and do the same, but eat your own bullet and do not be shot as I shall be.'

Then the OC firing party gave the signal, and the party came to the present, and on the word 'Fire!' they fired a volley. The regiment and the firing party then faced about and marched off. Five bullets had gone through the disc, but the man still breathed, and I had to shoot him through the heart with my revolver, a horrid job. The grave had already been dug at the firing point, and Yadram was put straight into it and the grave was filled in and levelled by a fatigue party from the regiment.[22]

Once an execution had been carried out the whole event was publicized in General Routine Orders (GROs) which were circulated to all units and formations. The deaths were far from hushed up; they were widely advertised as a deliberate example to encourage others not to commit the same offence.

These executions then were military justice's final sanction. Other armies of the Great War did exactly the same, although with varying frequency. The Germans record only forty-eight legal executions between 1914 and 1918 (although in a curious reversal, the German Army shot nearly 15,000 of its own men in the Second World War). The French Army executed several hundred men during the war and condemned 629 men to death purely as a result of the 1917 mass mutiny. Indeed, in the autumn panic before the Marne in 1914 the French high command actually lost count of the number of soldiers executed and has never revealed the true total. The Italians admit to shooting 750 of their soldiers, many of them after the Caporetto debacle of 1917. Even the tiny Belgian Army executed 12 soldiers before instituting its notoriously harsh 'companies disiplinaire' from 1915 onwards.

The British Army's use of capital punishment on active service between 1914 and 1918 then turns out to be the norm for armies of the day. Indeed, it can be argued strongly that the death penalty was used only in a minute percentage of cases. During the period 4 August 1914 to October 1918 there were approximately 238,000 courts martial resulting in 3,080 death sentences. Of these only 346 were carried out, which break down into the following categories of offences on active service:

Mutiny	3
Desertion	266
Cowardice	18
Disobedience of a lawful order	5

Sleeping at post	2
Striking a superior officer	6
Casting away arms	2
Quitting post	7
Murder	37

Of the two main military offences, there were 551 courts martial for cowardice, with 3.3 per cent resulting in execution; and there were 7,371 for desertion of which about (records differ) 3,000 resulted in sentence of death, of which 266 were executed (3.6 per cent of the total tried). No fewer than 5,250,000 men served in the British Army in the First World War of whom 750,000 were killed and 1,500,000 wounded.[23]

These statistics show with lucid clarity just how sparingly the final sanction of military law was employed by a massive army fighting for its life. The questions then remain: how and why was it used; and was it successful as a disciplinary policy?[24]

PART TWO

CHAPTER 9

THE BRITISH EXPEDITIONARY FORCE AND THE FIRST EXECUTION

However skilful the manoeuvres, a retreat will always weaken the morale of an Army.

NAPOLEON, MILITARY MAXIMS

The army that sailed for France in August 1914 had more in common with Wellington's army a century before than with Montgomery's only thirty years later. The flickering black and white films of the day reveal images of another era, more nineteenth than twentieth century. Groups of cheerful, heavily moustached young men grin at the camera. The officers cluster in little groups at the dockside and startled horses are swung into space to be lowered gently into the holds. The gun carriages with their spindly wheels look positively Napoleonic. The scene is redolent of a past age.

The customs, practices and attitudes of the men who made up the British Expeditionary Force reflected this. The general officers commanding the corps had been born in the 1860s (Douglas Haig, commanding the BEF's I Corps, was born in 1861). Even the 35-year-old professional infantry company commanders or their company sergeant majors would have been born in about 1880, joined the army in 1900 and formed their views during Edward VII's reign. The BEF may have been a modern army by the standards of 1914, but it was peopled and ruled by men with very old-fashioned ideas of what was right and proper.

They were also very hardy men. The sunburned soldiers who swung down the long, dusty French roads in 1914 were not only those of a different generation but a much tougher generation than the young men of today. To march 20 miles a day with a 40-pound pack, greatcoat, rifle and ammunition was the norm. With the exception of the unlucky reservists mobilized and sent to France at short notice, whose feet rapidly blistered red raw, the

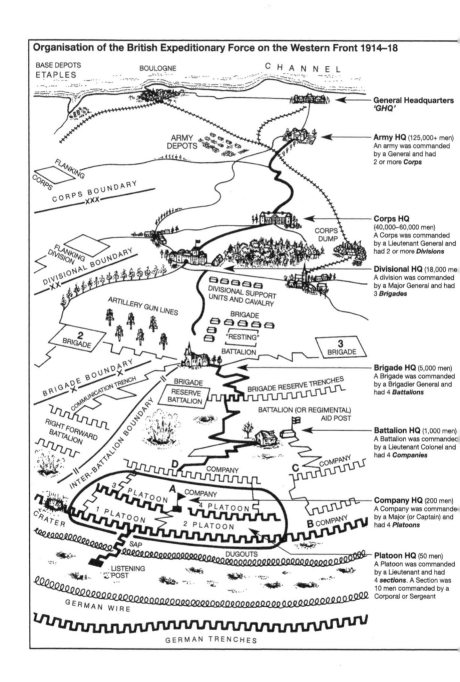

Organisation of the British Expeditionary Force on the Western Front 1914–18

BASE DEPOTS
ETAPLES

BOULOGNE

C H A N N E L

General Headquarters
'GHQ'

ARMY DEPOTS

Army HQ (125,000+ men)
An army was commanded
by a General and had
2 or more *Corps*

FLANKING CORPS

CORPS BOUNDARY
XXX

FLANKING DIVISION

CORPS DUMP

Corps HQ
(40,000–60,000 men)
A Corps was commanded
by a Lieutenant General and
had 2 or more *Divisions*

DIVISIONAL BOUNDARY
XX

DIVISIONAL SUPPORT
UNITS AND CAVALRY

Divisional HQ (18,000 me)
A division was commanded
by a Major General and had
3 *Brigades*

ARTILLERY GUN LINES

BRIGADE

2 BRIGADE

"RESTING"

BATTALION

3 BRIGADE

BRIGADE BOUNDARY
X

COMMUNICATION TRENCH

BRIGADE RESERVE BATTALION

BRIGADE RESERVE TRENCHES

Brigade HQ (5,000 men)
A Brigade was commanded
by a Brigadier General and
had 4 *Battalions*

RIGHT FORWARD BATTALION

INTER-BATTALION BOUNDARY

BATTALION (OR REGIMENTAL)
AID POST

Battalion HQ (1,000 men)
A Battalion was commandec
by a Lieutenant Colonel and
had 4 *Companies*

D COMPANY

COMPANY

C COMPANY

3 PLATOON

A COMPANY

COMPANY

1 PLATOON

4 PLATOON

2 PLATOON

B COMPANY

Company HQ (200 men)
A Company was commande
by a Major (or Captain) and
had 4 *Platoons*

CRATER

SAP

DUGOUTS

Platoon HQ (50 men)
A Platoon was commanded
by a Lieutenant and had
4 *sections*. A Section was
10 men commanded by a
Corporal or Sergeant

LISTENING POST

GERMAN WIRE

GERMAN TRENCHES

average soldier in the BEF was not only used to hardships but expected them.[1] The endless tramp in the blazing sun, bawling out a variety of songs, both profane and sacred (the Welsh regiments were addicted to hymns), the smiles and cheers of the local civilians and the ordered routine of sleeping rough in the fields, well fed by the quartermaster, were almost precisely the experiences of Wellington's army a century before.

The soldiers who made up the BEF were generally a pretty tough lot by today's standards, schooled in a more independent and brutal world. Leaving school at 14, working on the farm or in a factory and then enlisting for a soldier at 17 or 18 was the normal pattern. The induction into life in the depot and then the Edwardian barrack room, with its uncompromising discipline, endless drill, drink and tribal loyalties, would have come as little surprise to a recruit used to the petty brutalities of the foreman, the shipyard or the mill. Service in a garrison town or even in India would have completed the recruit's education into the realities of life. The average age of the BEF's soldiers may have been only 21, but these hard-drinking, hard-working and tough young men were no innocents abroad.[2]

Such a man was Private Thomas Highgate of 1st Battalion, the Queen's Own Royal West Kents. With the rest of 13 Brigade, they had dug themselves 'excellent trenches by the railway bridge' near Mons on 23 August and waited with a mixture of 'curiosity and trepidation' for what might happen next.[3] At 11 a.m. the Fusilier battalion of the Brandenburg Grenadiers debouched in mass formation onto the open fields in front of the Royal West Kents. What happened next was a savage education for both sides in the realities of modern warfare. The West Kents' rifles opened a disciplined storm of fire that ripped the German regiment to shreds, effectively destroying it as a fighting unit and leaving 'moaning bodies piled high'.

Retaliation was swift. The Germans' divisional and corps artillery opened up on the British infantry positions and subjected the stunned soldiers to a barrage for which their training and experience had not prepared them. As the 5.9 inch (150mm) German shells thundered down to burst in mind-jarring crashes among their ranks, the Kents pulled back, taking with them as many of their wounded as they could and leaving the mangled bodies of their comrades behind, reduced to huddled lumps of blood and offal. It was, for both sides, a shocking experience. Thus began for Thomas Highgate the retreat from Mons.

Over the next two weeks the BEF pulled back no less than 200 miles. Although in the words of one battalion diarist: 'the marches were not excessive ... only about 16 or 20 miles a day',[4] it was 'the lack of sleep' and 'constant urgency to keep retreating' that wore the battalions down. Despite officers' best efforts, in the confusion, alarms and minor skirmishes of the retreat, soldiers fell out with blistered feet, heatstroke and exhaustion; they disappeared into woods to relieve themselves on a night march and got back to discover their company gone; platoons took the left fork instead of the right at a crossroads in the dark, and found to their consternation that by dawn they were miles away and in another division's line of retreat. In the words of Capt. Brownlow, R.A.:

> I have no clear recollection, it remains in my mind as a blurred nightmare, in which shadowy figures slept as they rode or walked, in which phantom gun teams halted in sleep, checking for miles a ghostly stream of men in which the will to move wrestled with the desire to sleep.[5]

Slowly the retreating BEF fell into the normal condition of any army retreating under pressure: organized chaos, as a horde of formed units, individual companies, wagons, horses and 'a positive football crowd of stragglers' all flooded south towards the Marne.

The commander-in-chief of the BEF was Field Marshal Sir John French, a temperamental Irish cavalry officer. Already he had suffered the humiliation of seeing his French allies apparently abandon him and force his army into ill-considered retreat. His friend, and chosen ally as commander of II Corps, Gen. Grierson, had died of a heart attack on the way to France and been replaced by another officer, Gen. Smith-Dorrien, whom he heartily detested and suspected of being a War Office plant to spy on him. Finally, to add insult to injury, it looked as if his proud army was disintegrating into chaos, as the tired and dispirited soldiers began to loosen the bonds of formal pre-war discipline. In the words of the assistant provost marshal of 5th Division on 25 August: 'March discipline bad – and charged many men with entering cafes and drinking while on march.'[6]

Ever mercurial, Sir John overreacted. In particular he was worried about stragglers. As early as 25 August, the day before Smith-Dorrien's II Corps turned on its German pursuers at Le Câteau, the Provost Marshal of the BEF was ordered by the Adjutant General to check on stragglers. Col. Bunbury's report, coming as it did from a cynical military policeman, was in fact deeply reassuring. He told the Commander-in-Chief that 'there was no such thing as wilful shirking'. Some men 'had been throwing away their packs, saying that they cannot march and fight in them, but all retain their belts, pouches, entrenching tools and bayonets'.[7] Spirits were high.

The Provost Marshal also reported a discussion he had had with a straggling private soldier of the South Lancashire Regiment, 'who asked me if I could direct him to his unit ... He knew of a few groups of men seeking other troops ...', but all 'were moving in the right direction and eager to rejoin their regiments'.[8]

Bunbury advised the C.-in-C. that 'there was not the slightest thought among the men to shirk the marching and the fighting, and all were in good heart and keen to fight'. He concluded his report by admitting that 'all arms units [were] all together' but 'no fuss, no confusion' ... and 'All eagerly seeking to return to their units.'[9]

In some ways French was right to be alarmed. On paper, by 5 September 1914 the BEF had lost nearly 20,000 men: killed, wounded, missing in action or just plain disappeared. Despite the reassuring report by the Provost Marshal, by 30 August the BEF had no fewer than 2,923 reported stragglers alone out of a total strength of over 100,000. Of these over 291 came from a single battalion, the 1st Royal Warwicks, and 246 from the 2nd Argyll and Sutherland Highlanders. Highgate's battalion, the 1st Royal West Kents, reported only 10.

With two of his Regular commanding officers about to be court-martialled for giving up and offering to surrender their battalions, the War Cabinet breathing down his neck, and his French allies' apparently unrealistic plans, Sir John French was, by the standards of the day, in 'a blue funk'. The C.-in-C. had further been angered by the forceful visit paid him at Paris on 31 August by Lord Kitchener, Secretary of State for War, to put some backbone into him. Now to see his beautiful army falling apart was the last straw.

On 4 September he burst into print in BEF orders, which would eventually filter down to every soldier in the army.

> The C in C views with grave displeasure the straggling which still
> continues ... and has reason to think that in certain cases sufficient effort
> is not being made to rejoin units ... All ranks will in the event of being
> detached from their units use every effort to [rejoin] ... and [will face]
> severe punishment if there is reason to suppose that every effort has not
> been made to rejoin.[10]

It was in this fevered atmosphere of retreat, confusion, tension and uncertainty at all levels that the BEF's long nightmare came to an end near the banks of the River Marne, south-east of Paris on 5 September. In the phrase of one officer, 'I would never have believed that men could be so tired and hungry yet still live.'[11] Weary beyond measure, on 5 September 1914 the Royal West Kents stopped in a stubble field a mile south of Tournan. Next day Pte Thomas Highgate deserted.

The first that the BEF, busy with the preparations to advance on the Marne, knew about it was a telegram received by the General Staff at 8.55 a.m. from the French authorities, 'Civilian reports an English deserter in plain clothes at the farm of M. Poirier, Rue de la Martry, Tournan and can you deal?' Across the telegram, an unknown senior staff officer had written 'Instruct the Colonel Commanding 2nd Army Corps Troops to [arrange] F.G.C.M.'[12]

To an army in retreat, obsessed by stragglers, looting, desertion and beginning its epic counter-attack across the Marne that same day, Highgate had become just another administrative problem to be dealt with before the army moved on: but it was a problem that the pre-war regular army knew well and for which well-rehearsed legal and administrative procedures existed. These procedures had changed little in principle from Wellington's day, when summary justice on the line of march for desertion and plundering received a drumhead court martial, followed by an equally rapid hanging by the roadside by the provosts as an example to the rest of the army marching past. Justice was swift, brutal, but well understood by the pre-war army.

With astonishing rapidity Lt Gen. Sir Horace Smith-Dorrien, the commander of II Corps, ordered a court martial convened, and on the very afternoon of his arrest, Highgate was medically examined by Capt. Moss of the Royal Army Medical Corps, judged to be in 'sound mental and bodily health, fit to undergo punishment', and found himself on trial for his life, charged with 'When on active service, deserting His Majesty's Service'. Crucially, Smith-Dorrien filled out the Army Form 49, the Declaration of Military Exigencies under Rule of Procedure 104, stating that 'The proximity of the enemy rendered it inexpedient to observe the provisions of rules 4 c, d, e, 5, 8, 13, 14.' These rules, especially 13 and 14, guaranteed the defendant 'proper opportunity of preparing his defence, and a copy of the summary of evidence against him'. It was tough, but it was legal. Smith-Dorrien's attitude (which was almost certainly shared by his staff) was that II Corps had a battle to fight.

The court assembled at Château Combreux, just south of Tournan, and under the presidency of the colonel commanding II Corps's attached troops, plus a captain and a lieutenant from the Cameron Highlanders, heard the evidence. Highgate, undefended, pleaded not guilty.

The principal witness at the trial was a Thomas Fermor, an Englishman, gamekeeper to Baron Edward Rothschild whose estate bordered Tournan. Fermor told the court that he had gone searching for his bicycle in Tournan on the morning of 6 September 1914, and 'on information received I went towards the Madeleine' (mis-spelled 'Medlin' by the president in his hand-written transcript of the court martial) 'and found the accused there dressed in civilian clothes'. Fermor testified on oath that Highgate said: 'I have lost my army and I mean to get out of it,' or words to that effect. At the court martial Highgate challenged Fermor in cross-examination, implying that Highgate's remark really meant he wanted to get back to his unit. Fermor had then searched Highgate, found his army pay book and taken him to a nearby woodshed (probably in the Rue Martry) where his discarded uniform was discovered, but no rifle or ammunition. Fermor then handed his prisoner over to the Gendarmerie at the *mairie* in Tournan, where Highgate was later collected by a staff officer, Capt. Milward of the 53rd Sikhs. According to Milward, Highgate said on being taken into custody: 'I left my bivouac this morning and remember nothing more', the fairly universal response of the hard-drinking, pre-war regular soldier to a disciplinary charge.

Highgate, still clad in the stolen, ill-fitting French civilian clothes in which he had been arrested, declined to cross-examine, but elected to make a state-ment on oath to the court in his own defence.

His story was simple. He claimed to have left his regiment on the line of march as they set off north that morning to 'ease' himself. By the time he came back, the regiment had moved on. In his own words:

> I got strolling about, went down into a farm, lay down in an empty house and have a slight remembrance of putting some civilian clothes on, but I do not remember exactly what happened until the man came down to arrest me. I was coming back to see if I could find my clothes and my Regiment, but I was taken to the police station ...

The prosecutor, the assistant provost marshal of II Corps, asked Highgate only two questions, the first about his statement to the gamekeeper. To the second question he got a damning reply: 'I cannot say why I was in civilian clothes.'

The court martial swiftly found Highgate guilty of deserting His Majesty's forces on active service, and sentenced him to death. Within four hours, the corps commander as convening officer had endorsed the verdict and the very next day the commander-in-chief confirmed the sentence.

What happened next seems to our modern eyes particularly grisly, but should be seen in its historical context. At dawn on 8 September the Assistant Adjutant and Quartermaster General (AA and QMG) of 5th Division drafted an urgent note in his field notebook:

> To Brig. Gen. 15th Inf Bde:
> (Order A-471 September 8th)
> The Proceedings of FGCM on Pte T. J. Highgate RW Kent are forwarded herewith. The Lt. General [i.e. Smith-Dorrien, the II Corps Commander] would like you to arrange for the death sentence to be promulgated and carried out at once, as publicly as convenient ...
> 5 a.m., 8.9.14.[13]

At 5.10 a.m. he drafted a separate order to the divisional Provost Marshal (Order A-472):

> (1) ... Explain to (Comd) 15 Bde that he is asked to arrange [the execution] as his Brigade Group is marching past.
> (2) Prisoner to be given 3/4 of an hour – after being informed of his sentence – alone with a clergyman.
> (3) Burying party to remain behind. [Note: the BEF was advancing across the Marne]
> (4) Carrying out of sentence to be <u>as public</u> as possible ...[14]

In a final sad twist the assistant provost marshal of 5th Division replied to divisional HQ at 07.15, after the execution:

> ... I interviewed [the accused] and in the presence of a C of E clergyman read out the sentence of death to Pte. Highgate of R W Kent's at 6.22 a.m. on 8th September 1914 ... In the presence of one company of the Dorset and Cheshire Regiments I promulgated and carried the sentence into effect at 7.7 a.m. Death was instantaneous ...[15]

Highgate left a sad legacy. In the trial documents at the Public Record Office there still exists his AB64 or paybook with his scrawled 'Soldier's Short Will' inside:

> If I get killed all I have to come from the government for my services I leave to Miss Mary MacNulty, No. 3 Leinster St., Phibsborough, Dublin.

Even as the burying party shovelled the earth onto Thomas Highgate's now anonymous grave on the outskirts of Tournan, the headquarters of the BEF was already leaving. On the morning of his execution his regiment was

SCHEDULE.

Date 6th September 1914   No.

Name of Alleged Offender (a)	Offence charged	Plea	Finding, and if Convicted, Sentence (b)	How dealt with by Confirming Officer
o 10061 Pte Thomas James Highgate P. West Kent Regt.	When on Active Service Deserting His Majesty's Service	Not Guilty	Guilty. To suffer death by being shot.	Confirmed H S Smith-Dorrien General Comg 2. Corps 6. Sep/14. Confirmed J D P French F. M C-C.

H S Smith-Dorrien General Comg 2nd Corps —

Sentence executed at 7.7 a.m. on 8th Sept. 1914

f.d Monteith Capt
R. P. M. 5 Th Div.
7.15 a.m. 8.9.14

(a) If the name of the person charged is unknown, he may be described as unknown, with such addition as will identify him.

(b) Recommendation to mercy to be inserted in this column.

H S Smith-Dorrien
General
Convening Officer,
II Army Corps.

A B Dunsterville Colonel
Comdg II Army Corps Troops
President.

Sir John French's confirmation of the execution of Thomas Highgate, the first death sentence to be confirmed during the war.

advancing 20 miles away to the north, pushing across the Petit Morin near La Ferté sous Jouarre, where today stands the magnificent memorial to the missing of the battle of the Marne.

Highgate's case has roused some controversy since his unremarked death in the first month of the war. In the winter of 1999–2000 a fierce debate broke out among the villagers of his native village of Shoreham in Kent as to the desirability of adding his name to the town's war memorial. Passions ran high, with the Royal British Legion opposed to an 'executed deserter's name being included among the ranks of the fallen heroes of two World Wars'. Despite the local vicar's referendum, and a debate in the national press, the decision was eventually taken not to carve his name on the memorial.

Ironically, the decision flew in the face of Highgate's contemporaries. In the 1919 House of Commons debate on the commemoration of the executed men Col. Lambert Ward said: 'I ask the House not to dismiss this petition with the remark that these men were cowards and deserved their fate. They were not cowards in the accepted meaning of the word ...'[16] The irony of it all was that Highgate's name was already on the Roll of Honour near his home in Catford, south London.

Even by the rough and ready standards of the early BEF, Highgate's hasty summary trial and execution does not appear to have met the basic theoretical requirements of military justice. While there can be little doubt that he intended to desert – being found inexplicably in civilian clothes away from his regiment which had been ordered to advance seems to constitute clear proof of an 'intention to permanently avoid a military duty' – the corps commander's haste in convening the court martial and the peremptory removal of a fully considered defence under the Rules of Procedure because of 'the exigencies of the service' must inevitably leave a lingering sense of unease. However, there seems little doubt of his guilt by the standards of the day. Thomas Highgate got rough justice, but justice nonetheless.

But Highgate's execution served another purpose in a hard-pressed army teetering between defeat and victory. There can be little doubt that the chastened spectators of the Cheshires and Warwicks who witnessed the execution would have gone back to their regiments and passed on the word, which would then have spread through the extended family that was the BEF like wildfire. Even for a war that was going to be 'over by Christmas', desertion was not an option.

CHAPTER 10

THE EARLY CASES

When we speak of strict discipline, it means that everyone in the
army, regardless of rank, must observe discipline and no infringements
are allowed.

GENERAL VO NGUYEN GIAP, 1961

As the BEF and its shaken and sullen commander-in-chief advanced cautiously north to the Marne, the Aisne and eventually (by November) to the Channel coast, the ponderous but inevitable bureaucratic instincts of an army reasserted themselves. After the chaos of the great retreat came order.

As early as 10 September the BEF's 'Army Routine Orders' published a terse six-line entry under BEF order 'No. 75, Courts Martial', announcing Highgate's 'death by being shot', sandwiched between orders on 'Supply Columns – Ammunition Packs' and 'Storage of Base kits and Reserve Baggage'.[1] Such an order was more than just the publication of a factual event: it was also intended as a warning to other potential Highgates.

By 19 September both Sir John and the BEF had settled down having pushed the Germans north to the Aisne. The commander-in-chief had obviously mused on the subject of discipline and discussed it with his adjutant general. On that day the Royal Engineers Printing Unit produced an addendum to the BEF's orders which gives a fascinating insight into both the BEF's and Sir John French's thinking on discipline.

GENERAL INSTRUCTIONS

The Commander-in-Chief has had under consideration certain sentences recently awarded by Courts-Martial. It would be improper for him to interfere in any way with the discretion of a Court-Martial as to the sentence to be awarded, but, at the same time, he is of the opinion that the unequal sentences awarded by Courts-Martial for similar crimes show that many officers do not sufficiently appreciate the precise quality of the offences with which they have to deal.

He wishes to point out that certain offences which in peace time are adequately met by a small sentence, assume, on active service, a gravity which wholly alters their character.

This principle is fully recognized in Military Law; for instance, in the case of desertion, the Army Act in time of peace, permits a maximum sentence of two years' duration only, whereas on active service, a Court is allowed to award a sentence of death for the same offence. Similar considerations apply to cases of looting and to other offences specified in Sections 4 and 6, Army Act.

The Commander-in-Chief wishes to impress upon all officers serving upon Courts-Martial that it is their duty to give weight to consideration of good character, inexperience and all other extenuating circumstances, but that, at the same time, they are seriously to consider the effect which the offence in question may have upon the discipline of the Army, upon which its safety and success depend, and if they come to the conclusion that a sentence, however severe, is necessary in the interests of discipline, no feeling of commiseration for the individual must deter them from carrying out their duty.[2]

Sir John was right to be concerned about discipline. As the casualty list mounted, and the old regular army shredded away, some of its soldiers and even the occasional regular non-commissioned officer began to calculate the odds and decide that the horrors of modern war were not for them, despite the possible consequences. The commander-in-chief's views would have been known, as regimental officers passed down the message, but for some it was not enough.

One man who apparently did not get the message was Pte George Ward of the 1st Battalion, Royal Berkshires. On 24 September, only three weeks after Highgate's execution, he was tried for cowardice. In yet another hasty FGCM he was tried within a day of his offence and shot two days later. The trial documents are some of the shortest in the courts martial records, the evidence being recorded on a single page.[3]

What is interesting is that we can make a very rare comparison with one of the cases where the death penalty was remitted. Ward was tried by the same panel as another man from the same regiment, Cpl Victor Prior, also charged with cowardice, and the details (such as they are) of his trial are in the same file as Ward's. Generally the court martial records of the men who were found guilty but not executed (the majority of the cases), have not survived. The Prior and Ward cases therefore are one of the few chances we have today to get some insight into the minds of the senior officers who confirmed the sentence and see what influenced their judgement.

According to the evidence presented at his trial, on 16 September Pte Ward of the Berkshires withdrew, without orders, from the firing line on the line of the River Aisne as the Germans pulled back north from the Marne. He was seen walking back by his company sergeant major, who asked him where he was going, to which Ward replied that he had been wounded, but then disappeared. The sergeant major then testified: 'I next saw accused at 10 a.m. September 23rd at Oeuilly. The accused was not wounded.' Sgt Maj. Vesey confirmed that Ward had reported back to him at Oeuilly at noon on the 23rd and that he was fully armed and equipped. That was the total evidence against Ward. He appears to have made no defence to the charge; the word 'Defence' has been scribbled out on the 'Precis of Evidence' in the case. It would appear that he was arrested on his return on the 23rd and tried the following day, and it seems unlikely that he was offered the services of a prisoner's friend, or an opportunity to prepare a defence. Even a regular, such as Ward, probably did not realize the seriousness of what he had done – by returning, fully armed, he may have expected summary justice from his CO, not the full panoply of an FGCM.

Four days after Ward had left the line, on 20 September 1914 Cpl Victor Prior and a small section of 1st Berkshires were detailed to hold a forward post on the Aisne. The outpost was shelled and one soldier wounded, whereupon the section retired. An officer, Lt Hanbury, saw the whole incident and testified at the trial. Like Ward, Cpl Prior was charged with cowardice. Three other members of the 1st Royal Berkshires were indicted on the original charge sheet but their names were later deleted. The factors that influenced these charges of cowardice would have been clear to the military mind of 1914: Cpl Prior was the responsible NCO in charge who had allowed his section to retire from the battle without orders and Ward had run away from his duty and had been missing for seven days.

Both Prior and Ward pleaded not guilty, but both were found guilty and sentenced to death. What followed thereafter was revealing. Cowardice, as a subjective charge, is often hard to prove. Later in the war, as the application of military law evolved to meet the needs of both discipline and justice, both men would almost certainly have been arraigned on different charges. Cpl Prior, for example, was clearly guilty of the objective offence of 'quitting post' without due authority, and Ward of desertion, having abandoned the battle line for nearly a week. However, for the 1914 regulars, 'cowardice' was a very tangible thing and was viewed and dealt with differently, and cowardice was the charge against both men.

Both Sir Douglas Haig, then a lieutenant general and commanding I Corps and his commander-in-chief, Sir John French, felt that an example was necessary. On 25 September 1914 Haig minuted the Adjutant General of the BEF: 'I am of [the] opinion that it is necessary to make an example in order to prevent cowardice in the face of the enemy as far as possible. I therefore recommend that … Pte Ward 1 Royal Berks be shot, and that … Cpl Prior of the same regt. to two years Impt [sic] H.L. [Hard Labour].'[4] The commander-in-chief agreed. He wrote (of Cpl Prior) on the court martial papers: 'I commute the sentence to 2 years. It is not a real case of cowardice but it was more deserting post.' As Cpl Prior had stayed with his company and fought on after pulling back without orders, this seems reasonable. Ward, who had stayed away from the battle, had his fate sealed by the single word 'Confirmed', and he was executed by the banks of the River Aisne at Oeuilly on the evening of 26 September as the Berkshires marched off. His grave has been lost but, like Thomas Highgate, his name is commemorated on the memorial to the missing of the BEF at La Ferté sous Jouarre.

That Ward was shot as an example is without question. Whether the example was clear enough is a matter of conjecture. From the moment the BEF had arrived in France some men had been calculating their chances. Such a man was Cpl George Latham of the 2nd Battalion, Lancashire Fusiliers. Arriving in France on 22 August, and immediately plunged into the confusion of the retreat from Mons, Cpl Latham decided to quit after only three days. The day after II Corps's bloody and old-fashioned battle at Le Câteau on 26 August 1914, more than ten days before Highgate's, crime and a month before Ward's, Cpl Latham deserted.

Unlike the unfortunate Highgate, Latham went to considerable lengths to stay absent and to cover his tracks. His CSM testified later at the court martial that Cpl Latham had been absent from a roll call as the 2nd Battalion fell back on 27 August 1914.[5] Latham's story is of particular interest as it shows both the confusion of the early days of the BEF and the way in which the net closed on deserters as the trench lines crystallized and military order was reimposed.

After leaving his unit on 27 August the NCO somehow managed to stay on the run behind the lines until the night of 6–7 November 1914. He was then arrested and handed over to the Military Mounted Police for escort to his brigade, now at Chapelle d'Armentiéres. That night Latham promptly slipped his guards and escaped.

By 23 November Latham had somehow found a warm and cushy billet in the house of a Madame Cambier in the Rue d'Armentiéres, Nieppe, just behind the front line. Doubtless banking on the theory that the best way to hide was to blend in with the background, Cpl Latham seems to have 'billeted' himself with Mme Cambier and walked freely around the town in his uniform. Luck ran out for him however when a month later, on 21 December 1914, a Pte Robb of his own battalion recognized him in the street at Nieppe.

Alerted by this chance encounter, the net closed in. At the court martial held at Le Bizet, just over the Belgian border, on 11 January 1915 the full story emerged. Latham had, with remarkable insouciance, asked for his mail from England to be forwarded to a Madame Chilbrae at an address in Nieppe. If we read between the lines at the court martial, the most likely interpretation seems to be that Latham had originally 'visited' (his own word) Mme Chilbrae and then, sometime in late November, had transferred his affections to Mme Cambier, who lived in the same road. This time Latham's luck ran out for good when, on 21 December, Mme Chilbrae walked up to the military policeman on duty at 4th Division's headquarters in Nieppe, gave him a bundle of newspapers and letters addressed to 'M. Latham' and 'shopped' the British corporal. It looks as if Pte Robb was used to identify the NCO, and a military police squad promptly descended on the house of Mme Cambier and arrested Latham.

Latham's defence was novel. In a brief statement to the court he claimed to have been sent back 'on a cart' from the fighting at Ligny in August 1914 to a base at Compiègne, east of Paris, where he claimed he was subsequently evacuated to a depot at Le Mans. After a month at Le Mans he then said that he had been sent forward to rejoin his regiment, where 'I was met by someone, I don't know who, to conduct some ambulances … I lost my way and was taken prisoner by the Germans.'

Latham testified that he then escaped and was handed over to his divisional and brigade headquarters once he had regained the British lines. 'Being ashamed of myself, I escaped … and went to Nieppe. I remained there until I was apprehended.'

The court martial, consisting of a gunner major from a mountain battery, an infantry captain from the King's Own and a lieutenant from the Royal

Artillery, did not believe a word of it and found Latham guilty of desertion. He had been absent for three months, was living with a Frenchwoman and showed no intention of rejoining his regiment.

On 22 January 1915 Cpl Latham became the first NCO in the BEF to be executed for a military crime. He lies buried at Trois Arbres cemetery in Belgium. Cpl Latham was quite clearly guilty of desertion. His sentence was equally clearly intended to set an example.

Cpl Latham was not the only long-term deserter in the BEF by the beginning of 1915. At least two others would join him eventually from the old, regular, army. Thomas Harris of the Royal West Kents and Drummer Frederick Rose of 2nd Battalion, Yorkshire Regiment (who remarkably managed to stay absent from 18 December 1914 until he was arrested two years later in a police raid on a house in Hazebrouck on 1 December 1916) were two deserters who managed to avoid the army for a remarkably long period. The army's attitude to such men is summed up by the brigadier general commanding 12th Infantry Brigade, who forwarded Latham's court martial conviction and sentence to higher headquarters with the terse statement: 'In my opinion, the severest measures possible are necessary to stop the frequent cases in which men avoid fighting by going absent.'[6]

As the war dragged on from 1914 into the New Year everyone realized that this was going to be a long haul. With the old army of autumn 1914 now a lifetime away, the commanders of the BEF realized that the hastily trained volunteers arriving in France were going to need strong leadership and ruthless discipline if they were to be of any use on the battlefield.

Obedience to orders was the only way the army knew to ensure that the new drafts and the new armies would fight.

CHAPTER 11

DISOBEDIENCE

You men have bitched about this chickenshit drilling. But it's all for one reason: instant obedience to orders and alertness ... if a man wants to stay alive on the battlefield, then he must be alert!

GEORGE S. PATTON, 1943

D isobedience strikes at the heart of the army's core existence. A soldier must obey a command without question: in battle there is not time to debate an order – right or wrong, it must be carried out. Without obedience of that nature an army cannot function. To the non-military eye disobedience is an irritation; to the army commanders of 1914 it was a capital offence, only one step removed from mutiny – collective disobedience – the most serious of all military offences. The wording of the charge was precise: 'Disobeying in such a manner as to show a wilful defiance of authority, a lawful command given personally by a superior officer, in the execution of his office'.[1]

During the Great War five men were executed for disobedience. Some of these executions were for apparently minor offences but they struck at the nerve centre of the army's structure. Amongst the old regular army and soldiers generally there would always be an element of 'grousing'; muttering into their moustaches, the old regulars might complain amongst themselves but they knew the boundaries past which they could not step. There would be 'minor' disobediences – delay in carrying out an order when out of the line, *sotto voce* comments which if overheard by an officer might lead to a few days in the guardroom, but man and officer knew the boundaries.

The man with the doubtful privilege of being the first soldier to be executed for disobedience during the war was Pte Patrick Downey of the 6th Battalion, Leinster Regiment. This battalion had been formed at Dublin in August 1914 and had first seen action in Gallipoli, but after only a few weeks (during which time eighty-one men were killed in action)[2] it was re-routed to Salonika, arriving there in October 1915. It would appear that within two months the battalion had a serious discipline problem, as on 1 December 1915 six soldiers were tried by FGCM for discipline-related offences.[3]

Pte Patrick Downey was charged with 'disobeying a lawful command in such a manner as to show wilful defiance'; Pte Thomas McMahon was charged with using insubordinate language to a superior officer; Ptes James Creegan, Patrick Lee and Fred Thompson were charged with disobeying a lawful command given by a superior officer, and Pte Michael Bergin was accused of both using insubordinate language and disobeying a lawful command. None of the individual offences in itself was serious, but the overall effect was to weaken the battalion as a fighting unit. Disobedience on this scale quickly labels a battalion as 'unsatisfactory' and action was needed to prevent such behaviour from spreading and potentially turning into mutiny.

There was no field officer available to sit as president at the court martial and the panel consisted of a captain and two second lieutenants. The evidence in all six cases was extremely brief.[4] It transpired that on 23 November McMahon and Bergin had been ordered on baggage fatigue but had refused to work until after they had eaten their breakfast. Both were found guilty. On the following day Bergin and Creegan, when out on patrol, refused to fall in when ordered but did so eventually. Again both were found guilty. On 27 November Lee and Thompson, who were in Hasanli, did not return to the company HQ when ordered to by their CSM, and were found in a house in the village the next morning. Again both were found guilty. These five men were sentenced to a variety of punishments, the most severe being imprisonment with hard labour for one year, given to Bergin.

The real scapegoat for the battalion's collective indiscipline was to be Pte Patrick Downey. He had a bad military record. His character was described on his AF B122 as 'very bad'. On 25 November he had been tried by FGCM for insubordination and had been given eighty-four days' FP No. 1. He also had a previous conviction for disobedience, another for disregarding orders, and had commited six other offences.

On 26 November, the day after his previous court martial, his sergeant ordered him to fall in for fatigues. Downey replied: 'No, I won't fall in.' CSM Bagnall again ordered him to fall in and still Downey refused. Bagnall tried again, and once more Downey refused. His captain then ordered him to put on his cap, and Downey replied: 'No, I won't.' It seems clear that at this point Downey was fed up with soldiering. This was a pointless display of childish disobedience and the army was not going to tolerate it. On top of the other minor discipline problems of the last few days, drastic and immediate action was required to prevent the risk (real or imaginary) of having the whole battalion refusing to work.

The summary of evidence was taken four days later and Downey was court-martialled on 1 December 1915. He pleaded guilty to the charge, and was sentenced to death. His only plea in mitigation was that he had never been in prison in civil life, and that he had previously served for two months with the 5th Battalion of the Royal Munster Fusiliers. His age at the trial was given as 19 years 9 months, and he had served for fifteen months, suggesting that he had joined up in September 1914.

It can only be presumed that Patrick Downey did not realize that he had pushed the army too far, and thought that by pleading guilty he might get off with a prison sentence which would get him away from the front. The inexperienced officers who made up the court martial panel incorrectly accepted Downey's guilty plea and sentenced him to death, as in the Byers case ten months earlier. They had probably gone to Salonika with the 1914 *Manual of Military Law* and not realized that procedures had changed in consequence of the Byers case. Downey should have been made to plead 'not guilty' and the evidence heard. When the conviction went for confirmation the finding should have been quashed and a retrial ordered.

However, Lt Gen. Brian Mahon, commanding the British Forces in Salonika, wrote about the case to GHQ, Mediterranean Expeditionary Force:

> Under ordinary circumstances I would have hesitated to recommend that the Capital Sentence awarded be put into effect as a plea of guilty has been erroneously accepted by the Court, but the condition of discipline in the battalion is such as to render an exemplary punishment highly desirable and I therefore hope that the Commander in Chief will see fit to approve the sentence of death in this instance.

Gen. Monro did confirm the sentence, despite concerns as to its legality, and the disobedient Pte Patrick Downey was executed at dawn on 27 December at Eurenjik.

Patrick Downey appears from his army record to have had a bad character – it is rare for a soldier's character to be described as 'very bad' without some good reason. His actual offence seems relatively trivial and, although he was not shot simply for refusing to put on his cap, he had overstepped the boundaries established by the army. From the evidence presented in the other cases at the court martial and the comments made by Lt Gen. Mahon, the 6th Leinsters had a discipline problem which needed addressing by prompt action.

Pte Downey had committed a capital offence (whether we like it or not, disobedience of this sort was punishable by death, according to the statute of the day) and an example was needed to stem potential mutiny. Downey had a bad record and, in the military mind, was expendable. He therefore provided the necessary example to the rest of his battalion and the division. By our standards he was treated harshly and by the legal standards of the day his conviction should not have stood, but even if a retrial had been ordered the final outcome might still have been the same. Downey and others in his battalion had gone too far and, rightly or wrongly, he paid the price.

Sgt John Robins was a regular. His battalion, the 5th Wiltshires, had landed in Gallipoli on 17 July 1915 and established their bivouac camp at Gully Beach. In August, with the 6th Leinsters, they had attacked at Chunuk Bair and had suffered considerable casualties.[5] Although the battalion continued its normal front line duties it was not again used in an attack. At the beginning of December 1915 Robins and his battalion were in trenches at Suvla Bay and on the 3rd of that month, Sgt Robins refused to go out on patrol with Second Lt MacMillan.

In consequence he was charged the following morning with 'disobeying in such a manner as to show wilful defiance of authority, a lawful command given personally by his superior officer in the execution of his office'. Two days later, on the 7th, he stood trial by what appears to have been a hastily convened FGCM.[6]

The evidence presented was brief. Two witnesses gave evidence for the prosecution and Robins conducted his own defence. Second Lt MacMillan told the court that he warned Sgt Robins to accompany him on patrol, but Robins replied that he was not well enough to go. As Robins had not previously reported sick, MacMillan sent him to see the doctor, who reported that he was fit for patrol. MacMillan then again ordered Robins to go with him, but Robins said: 'I am not well enough. I will not go.'

The second witness was Pte Allsworth, who was asleep in the bay in which Robins was. He told the court that he was woken up by hearing Robins say: 'I am not well enough to go on patrol.' Robins cross-examined this witness, and elucidated that Allsworth had not heard any order given to Robins.

In the summary of evidence the medical officer had been listed as a witness, and had said: 'At 6.00 p.m. on 3/12/15 I took Sgt. Robins' temperature and felt his pulse. They were both normal. He complained of nothing definite whatever, except a general feeling that he was unwell. I gave him some medicine and told him to carry on.' When this summary of evidence was taken, Robins had declined to cross-examine the doctor. The medical officer did not therefore give this evidence in person at the trial, but instead submitted a written statement, which should not have been allowed. It is doubtful whether it affected the outcome of the case, but it is another example where a capital court martial in the MEF lacked the legal input seen in France.

Sgt Robins called no witnesses, declined to give evidence, and called no character witnesses. He made a statement saying he had served eight and a half years in India and had since suffered from bouts of fever, and that on 3 December he had been unwell for several days, made worse by the wet weather. He said: 'I have been out here nearly five months and this is the first trouble I have ever been in. I have always done my duty. This would not have happened if I had been quite well. At the time I did not realize the seriousness of what I did.'

Some idea of the conditions can be gained by the fact that Robins's conduct sheet could not be produced, as it had been lost in the recent flood. However, the adjutant said that to the best of his knowledge, apart from an entry on home service, Robins had a clean sheet.

On the basis of the evidence produced in court, the death sentence appears somewhat harsh and it might be expected that it would have been commuted by the Commander-in-Chief, especially in view of the fact that the battalion had suffered badly from sickness in December.

In his letter recommending that sentence be carried out, the acting CO of the 5th Wiltshires wrote that he had previously spoken to Robins about neglecting his duty and that the soldier had been impertinent to Second Lt MacMillan on another occasion. He ended: 'His appearance is slovenly, and his manner with the men bad. Generally speaking, I do not consider him a good NCO.' The brigade commander also recommended that sentence be carried out.

Maj. Gen. Maude, commanding 13th Division, hit the nub of the issue: 'The offence of which the accused has been convicted is on active service such a grave one and especially when committed by an individual holding the rank of sergeant that I have no alternative but to recommend that the law be allowed to take its course.' As this offence took place on the Mediterranean front, sentence was confirmed by Gen. Monro, commanding the MEF.

In the court martial papers there is a detailed note as to how and where the execution should be carried out, instructing that the firing party be made up of men of a different battalion (the 8th Cheshires). The staff captain of 40th Brigade wrote: 'The sentence is to be carried out at 8 a.m. tomorrow;

the execution to take place at a point on the beach 400 yards north of the mouth of Gully Ravine.'

Sgt Robins was an NCO, and was therefore expected to set an example to the other men. In a situation such as this it was almost inevitable that he would be tried by FGCM for his offence. It was not, to the observer eighty-five years or more distant, a particularly serious offence, but it was one which hit at the fundamental core of the army's structure. Perhaps Robins did feel unwell, but as an old soldier he knew the consequences of refusing an order. Continuing to refuse to go on patrol after being seen by the doctor was inviting trouble.

Perhaps old soldier Robins was unimpressed by the new Second Lt MacMillan, seconded from another battalion, but in the front line this was a fatal mistake. Even young, inexperienced officers must be obeyed or the next step is that a group of men refuse an order and that is but one step from mutiny – the prospect of which often concerns commanders far more than the prospect of any attack by the enemy.

In September 1915 a new Deputy Judge Advocate General was appointed to the MEF and at the end of December he wrote in his War Diary: [7]

During the month of December two death sentences were ordered by the C-in-C to be carried out: 1st re 16743 Pte. H. Salter, 6th East Lancashire Regt. tried on November 22nd for desertion; 2nd No. 227 Pte. J. Downey, 6th Leinster Regiment sentenced on 1st December for Wilful Defiance. The latter was a case from Salonika and it was particularly requested by the GOC that this sentence be carried out in view of the marked tendency towards insubordination which has recently been evident from the proceedings of Courts Martial in that command. These are the only two death sentences that have been carried out in the M.E.F. since I joined the force in September and only one had been carried out before that. Between 25th April and 31st December 101 men had been sentenced to death but in every case except those mentioned above the C-in-C had refused to confirm the death sentence.

Although it appears that Monro's decision to confirm the sentences on Robins and Downey was unduly harsh, the other ninety-nine men whose sentence was commuted were probably grateful for his benevolence.

The next two cases of disobedience, on the Western Front, also occurred close together. On 22 April 1916 three privates from the 9th Battalion, Cheshire Regiment stood trial for 'disobeying in such as manner as to show a wilful defiance of authority, a lawful command given personally by his superior officer in the execution of his office'.[8] The case bore many similarities to that of Pte Hawthorne (see Chapter 15), executed for cowardice a few months later.

On the night of 14–15 April 1916 a wiring party consisting of a sergeant, a corporal and eight men was due to go out into no-man's-land. There was some grumbling among the men that it was too light, and when they arrived at company HQ the sergeant reported this to Second Lt Kenyon, who said that they must go out. He led the party forward but was followed only by the NCOs. The company commander, Lt Walton, then ordered the men to follow him over the parapet, making it clear that if they did not do so they would be charged with disobedience and might be sentenced to death. This officer then led the party into no-man's-land, followed by the NCOs and five of the men. Ptes Cuthbert, Dineen and Bate remained behind and were placed under arrest.

The full picture emerged during the trial. It transpired that there had been a general agreement amongst the men, almost certainly including the NCOs, that it was dangerously light, and that they should all refuse to go out. However, when ordered out by the officer, the NCOs had obeyed, with the other men following when threatened with a court martial. The company quartermaster sergeant, giving evidence for the prosecution, said that he heard Pte Cuthbert say that he would rather be shot than go out wiring that night. Although this was not substantiated by any other witness it became a damning statement.

Pte Cuthbert made a statement (not on oath) on behalf of all three men saying that on the way up to the company HQ, word had been passed back from Sgt Carruthers for all the men to refuse to go out as it was too light. Two of the privates from the working party gave evidence for the defence, supporting this statement. As Second Lt Kenyon was shot and wounded, the men may well have been right that it was not a good night for working in the open.

All three men were found guilty and sentenced to death; all three had previous minor offences on their conduct sheets. Dineen and Bate had enlisted in November 1914 and Cuthbert in March 1915. Bate was the only defendant to have a serious previous offence, when he had gone absent in the UK after discharge from hospital in July 1915 and had remained at large for two months. Lt Walton told the court that the men were all new to the battalion, having been drafted from the King's (Liverpool) Regiment, and that none of them had previously given any trouble.

The key letter post-trial was that sent from Maj. Gen. Bridges, commanding 19th Division. He wrote: '… Pte Cuthbert is considered by his commanding officer to be an undesirable man and likely to be a source of corruption in the regiment. The other two men … were in the Commanding Officer's opinion, led astray.' He continued: 'I consider that an example is necessary and I strongly recommend that the Death Sentence be carried out in the case of Pte Cuthbert.' This was supported by Maj. Gen. Landon, commanding XI Corps.

Gen. Monro, who had confirmed the sentence in the two earlier cases of men executed for disobedience, was now in command of First Army. He wrote: 'I regard this as a case where an example is necessary. These men deliberately refused to obey an order owing to the element of danger attached to it. I recommend that sentence be carried out in all three cases.' Fortunately for Pte Dineen and Pte Bate, Haig did not agree with this waste of manpower and commuted their sentences. He may have been influenced by a note which accompanied the papers, from Lt Col. Gilbert Mellor, DJAG First Army, who commented that the disobedience was encouraged, if not directly caused, by the gross misconduct of the NCOs of the party.

Pte James Cuthbert was executed '500 yards south of Enguinatte church'. He was clearly shot as an example to others who might try to avoid potentially dangerous duty in the front line. Cuthbert had overstepped that fine line between soldiers' 'grousing' and outright disobedience and his fate no doubt had a salutary effect on the other men of his division. Perhaps the final word on Cuthbert's execution should be left with the writer of the 9th Cheshires War Diary who on 15 April, the night after Cuthbert's offence, wrote: 'Weather fine with a moonlight night, much work to be done, but too light to wire in front.'[9] It was a soldier's duty to obey orders.

Shortly after Cuthbert's execution, another soldier decided that he had seen enough of the army and its discipline. Like Patrick Downey in Salonika, Driver John William Hasemore pushed the army beyond its breaking point and paid the ultimate price. Hasemore had joined the army in June 1915 and was serving in the relative safety of the Field Artillery. He had kept a clean record until 1 April 1916, when he was court-martialled for disobeying a lawful command and was given twenty-eight days' FP No. 1. Whilst serving this punishment he challenged authority once more and found himself in front of another court martial.[10]

On 30 April 1916 Hasemore (spelled Hasemere on all the court martial documents) was charged on four counts. The first charge was one of 'using insubordinate language to a superior officer' and the evidence given was that on 4 April, just after he had started his punishment, Hasemore was carrying some horse rugs to the company office. Bombardier Furhman told the court that Hasemore who kept dropping the rugs, had said: 'Go tell the sergeant major I refuse to do any more work,' and that he had then walked into the guardroom and lain down. Furhman reported this to the sergeant major. No other evidence was presented on this charge.

The second charge was one of 'disobeying a lawful command in such a way as to show wilful defiance', and the events giving rise to this followed on from the earlier episode. Sgt Eager told the court that he had gone into the guardroom and ordered Hasemore to get on with his work but he had refused. When again ordered to work, Hasemore replied: 'They could not make a slave out of me in the British Navy and they can't make a slave of me in the British Army.' Eager repeated his order and when it was not obeyed for the third time, placed Hasemore under arrest.

These two incidents led to Hasemore being put up for trial by FGCM, but if he had kept his head down and got on with his work he might well have got off with a fairly minor punishment. However, Hasemore was fed up with the army and a few days later fatally overstepped the mark. On 11 April, when his battery was moving from the front line into reserve, Hasemore was under arrest and was at the rear of the column, under guard. He would not keep up with the rest of the men and Second Lt Steven ordered him to march properly. Hasemore replied: 'I will not fucking well march.' The officer halted the column, waited for him to catch up and then ordered that Hasemore be tied to the limber by means of a rope around his waist. Whilst this was being done, Hasemore sat in the road and said: 'You are having a fine old game with me. I will not fucking well soldier in France. I have finished with soldiering.' As the section moved off he cut the rope. He then asked the officer if he could march without being tied, and was allowed to do so, but again he dropped behind.

The section had to be halted again and this time the exasperated officer ordered that Hasemore be tied to a limber with his hands tied behind his back. Well roused by now, Hasemore resisted and told the sergeant tying him that if it were not for his stripes he would smash him and that he 'would kick his fucking bollocks in'. To the officer he said: 'You dog, you pig, you rotten fucking bastard, it is men like you who spoil the British army. Call yourself a British officer.' Hasemore emphasized his point by kicking the sergeant. After the limber had moved a few yards, he threw himself to the ground and Second Lt Steven then had him placed on a limber. When the column next halted, Hasemore complained that his hands were tied too tightly, but the officer refused to loosen them. Hasemore's response was to shout: 'When I am free I'll get my revenge, you sod.' These words led to the fourth charge of using threatening language to his superior officer.

This version of events was supported by all the witnesses, and Hasemore, who defended himself, did not challenge it. In his defence he made a statement, not on oath. He told the court that Bombardier Furhman had kept nagging him, and he had then said that he would do no more work until he had seen the sergeant major. On the third and fourth charges he said: 'On the line of march I lost my head and really cannot say what happened.' Sgt Eager gave a character reference for Hasemore, saying that he had been in his section for six weeks and his work had been satisfactory. In mitigation, Hasemore told the court that he had been at sea all his life and that he could speak German, Spanish and Italian.

Maj. Gen. Hickie, commanding the 16th (Irish) Division, recommended that the sentence be carried out on the basis that the crimes were deliberate, repeated and took place in public on the line of march. He also noted that Hasemore's actions were in direct defiance of authority rather than against any particular officer or NCO. The corps commander agreed, and Gen. Monro, who had been instrumental in the confirmation of all three executions for disobedience which had taken place to date, concurred, writing: 'I recommend that the sentence be carried into execution – this driver appears to possess no sense of discipline.'

Driver John Hasemore may have decided to soldier no more, but termination of contract is not an option for a soldier in the midst of war. He paid the ultimate price for his continued, ill-considered disobedience and was shot in the abattoir at Mazingarbe at 4.25 a.m. on 12 May 1916. The question left unanswered is why this 1915 volunteer, who had nothing on his 'crime sheet' until 1 April, suddenly rebelled against authority.

It was to be another nineteen months before the final execution for disobedience took place.[11] Rifleman William Slade had joined the army in February 1916 and had been posted to the 2/6th Londons. His record showed a history of disobedience. In November 1916 he had been confined to barracks for not complying with an order but, more seriously, in August 1917 had been tried by FGCM for disobeying an order and had been sentenced to three months' FP No. 1. Whilst serving this sentence Slade had another brush with authority. Like Hasemore, he pushed his luck too far on two separate occasions.

Rifleman Slade was court-martialled on two charges. The first was:

disobeying in such a manner as to show a wilful defiance of authority a lawful command given him personally by a superior officer in the execution of his office, in that he in the Field on October 6th 1917, when ordered by Lance Corporal Collins to go on parade did not do so and said 'I refuse' or words to that effect, although warned of the consequences of such disobedience.

At the trial two corporals gave evidence on this charge, which was not disputed by Slade.

The second charge was more serious as it occurred near the front line:

Disobeying in such a manner as to show a wilful defiance of authority a lawful command given him personally by a superior officer in the execution of his office, in that he at Canal Bank West, near Ypres, on 26th October 1917 when ordered to parade to march to a forward area did not do so although warned of the consequences of such disobedience.

Lt Wylie described the incident to the court.

Slade's company had been ordered to fall in, ready to go up the line, and Slade had refused to do so. Lt Wylie was told of this, went to Slade's dugout and ordered him to put on his equipment and parade. When he did not move or reply, the officer told him that if he disobeyed this order he would be tried by court martial. Slade made no response so the lieutenant waited about five minutes, then told him that he would give him two minutes to get on parade. Slade still made no reply and was put under arrest.

Rifleman Slade called no witnesses in his defence and only made a brief statement on oath: 'I am not responsible for my actions. Since Bullecourt, the scenes I saw there have worked on my mind.' When cross-examined by the court he said that he had not reported sick. After Slade had made his statement the prosecution appears to have called another witness, Capt. Paline of the RAMC, who said: 'I saw the accused on the Canal Bank about five days ago. I talked to him for about ten minutes. I examined him for mental deficiency in this way. I saw no signs of mental derangement.'

Character evidence was given by the adjutant, who told the court that Slade had arrived in France in January 1917 and had been a stretcher bearer at Bullecourt in May 1917, where he did his work well. Until his court martial on 10 August 1917 he had borne a good character.

The formation commanders' recommendations are no longer in the file. The only comments which appear are those made by Field Marshal Haig, who wrote: 'I do not confirm the finding on the first charge. I confirm the finding on the second charge. I confirm the sentence.' This gives an insight into Haig's character and sense of justice – as Slade had been sentenced to death on both counts, the busy commander-in-chief might well have simply scrawled 'Confirmed' and left it at that. However, Haig, meticulous in detail, quashed the finding on the first charge – of disobeying the order to go on parade on 16 October – but does confirm sentence for the much more serious offence in the front line.

This is a case where the margins between disobedience and cowardice are blurred and there are similarities between Slade's case and that of Rifleman Bellamy, who was executed for cowardice in 1915. The different charges in the two cases may have arisen because by 1917 the army was much more rigorous about framing charges. It was easier to prove objectively the charge of disobeying an order than to prove cowardice.

The case of Rifleman Slade raises some questions. He seems to have been a good soldier until his first exposure to battle at Bullecourt in spring 1917. The sounds, sights and smells of that bloody battlefield had left him shaken, perhaps even to the extent that death at the hands of a firing squad was preferable to living through another similar experience. It may also be said that the medical profession failed him. By late 1917 shell shock was known and recognized, and yet the doctor who examined him said only that he had been examined for 'mental deficiency' – harking back to the pre-war concept of mental illness and not recognizing the symptoms of a man suffering from battle shock.

What do we, over eighty years later, make of these executions? Three of these five men refused to carry out duties in the front line, coming close to a charge of cowardice: refusal to go on patrol or a wiring party was clearly unacceptable to an army at war. The other two cases, Pte Downey and Driver Hasemore, were different, being a simple refusal to carry out orders. The truculent behaviour of several men of the 6th Leinsters demonstrated that there had been a complete breakdown of discipline in that unit – a problem which had to be dealt with if the battalion was to be any use as a fighting force. Pte Downey's bad record and his pointless display of disobedience meant that he became the necessary example to bring the rest of his unit into line. Although the letter of the law was not followed, and he was allowed to plead guilty, it is unlikely that this materially altered the outcome of the case. Driver Hasemore presented the army with a problem. No army at war could overlook his protracted surly and uncooperative behaviour. We do not know why this man suddenly rebelled, but rebel he did and paid the price so that others were not encouraged to follow his example of unilaterally deciding to terminate his contract with the army.

CHAPTER 12

SLEEPING AT AND QUITTING POST

No human being knows how sweet sleep is but a soldier.

COL. JOHN S. MOSBY, 1887

At some time almost every soldier in the army has dozed off in the small hours of a boring sentry duty. Many will not have been caught, others will have received a sharp kick and a reprimand from the sergeant. A few will have been dealt with more severely. But when on active service – those critical four words – the offence is one of the most serious military crimes: leaving a post without orders, or sleeping at post, are offences which can endanger an entire military unit, however exhausted the sentry. In war, everyone is tired beyond belief but the sleeping sentry is risking his comrades' lives. Pre-war, at home in the UK, such an offence was not generally punished very severely but at the front these offences were regarded as extremely serious and were punishable by death.

In the official statistics of the war the offences of quitting post and sleeping at post are not separated, but in total there were 6,567 courts martial 'in the field' for these two crimes.[1]

The numbers of death sentences and executions for these two offences are:

Offence	No. of death sentences	No. of executions	Percentage carried out
Quitting post	82	7	8.5 per cent
Sleeping at post	449	2	0.4 per cent

The first death sentence during the Great War awarded by a court martial in the field was given to Pte A. Whittle of the 2nd Dragoon Guards for sleeping at post on 23 August 1914, the first day of engagement with the enemy. Whittle, however, was reprieved and the sentence commuted to two years' imprisonment with hard labour. More cases were to follow and by the end of 1914 thirty-nine men had been sentenced to death for this offence, although none were actually executed.

The problem diminished slightly through the winter, but the number of convictions and death sentences rose again in the summer and autumn, many of them in Gallipoli.

	France & Flanders	*Gallipoli*
June	11	0
July	26	2
August	31	1
September	31	10
October	50	27

The number of death sentences awarded for sleeping at post in Gallipoli is but a tiny percentage of the cases which occurred. The DJAG (Dardanelles) wrote in his war diary on 31 July 1915 that cases of men sleeping at post continued to be frequent, although in nearly every case it was shown to be directly due to the exhaustion of the men, who were living in tents under the hot sun.[2] On 30 September 1915 a new DJAG took over and wrote: 'Charges of sleeping at post represent a very large proportion of the cases on the peninsula and it seems that the excessive periods of duty for which sentries are posted is to a considerable extent the cause of the prevalence of this offence.'

The situation in France was also sufficiently bad for General Routine Orders to carry a statement about discipline:

DISCIPLINE: The Commander-in-Chief regrets to notice a prevalence of the most serious and dangerous offence of 'sleeping on the post'. It has not been necessary up to the present time to carry out the extreme penalty in relation to this offence, but the number of cases which have recently occurred have caused the Commander-in-Chief to decide that he will have no alternative but to carry out the extreme penalty in the future. This order is to be read out three times.[3]

After this the number of courts martial for sleeping at post declined and the number of death sentences fell but still remained at around ten per month in 1916, although no executions were carried out. There were various reasons for this. If a man fell asleep, standing up at his post, it was reasonable to assume that he was not wilfully shirking his duty as a sentry, but had accidentally fallen asleep, perhaps after a long march or spell without adequate rest. These factors could be, and were, used in mitigation.

In dangerous or exposed positions it was customary to post two men together as sentries, often on a staggered duty, to ensure that the men at the post were alert. It was two men on such a sentry duty who finally faced a firing squad for having fallen asleep. Pte Thomas Downing and Pte Robert Burton were serving with the 6th Battalion, South Lancashire Regiment in Mesopotamia when the incident occurred, on 6 February 1917. They were charged on the day of their offence and court-martialled the next day.[4]

The evidence was not contested by the men, who were tried separately, although the evidence given was similar in both cases. Sgt Miller told the court that he had posted Pte Downing as a sentry in a forward post for a two-hour duty at 1 a.m. on 6 February. At 2 a.m. Pte Burton was posted with him for a two-hour duty. At 2.45 a.m. the sergeant and Second Lt Jackson visited the post and found both men asleep. The court was told that both men were found sitting down, leaning against the parados, with their rifles nearby. Sgt Miller woke them by kicking them on the legs. Evidence was given that neither man had previously reported sick and that neither had been on fatigues since midday on 5 February.

In his defence Downing said: 'I was very tired on the morning in question. I was awake till about 2.30 a.m. when a patrol of the East Lancs went through the line returning to their lines at the rear.' Burton said: 'I have been out with the battalion since the beginning but recently have been much troubled with indigestion and pains in my head. I wanted to stick the thing out and so have not reported sick. I have been feeling very tired and run down recently.'

Both men had joined up in the first rush of patriotic fervour in August 1914. Downing had been wounded in Gallipoli and had then been invalided to India and had only recently returned to the battalion. The adjutant, Capt. Ward, said that Downing had generally done good service with the battalion and said of Burton: 'the accused has done good service with the battalion throughout the war'. Neither man had any entries on his conduct sheet.

After sentencing, during the confirmation process, the CO of the 6th Somersets wrote that Downing had been wounded in Gallipoli in August 1915 and had rejoined the battalion at Amara in November 1916. He added: 'While serving in the Battalion he has always done his work in a soldierly manner and has never given the slightest trouble.' Of Burton, he wrote: 'He has always done his work in a most satisfactory manner and has never given any trouble.'

Brig. Gen. O'Dowda, commanding 38th Brigade, commented of both men: 'There appear to be no extenuating circumstances beyond his character and

I consider that sentence should be carried out.' Maj. Gen. Cayley, GOC 13th Division, took a more lenient view: 'There are no extenuating circumstances but in view of Pte Downing's excellent record and as an appreciation of the good work done by his Battalion during the present operations I recommend that the sentence be commuted to one of 5 years penal servitude and suspended.' He wrote the same of Pte Burton.

However, Lt Gen. Marshall, commanding III Indian Corps, wrote of Downing: 'In view of the fact that the accused (together with his fellow sentry) was found sitting down in the trench, I am unable to see any extenuating circumstances and do not recommend any suspension of sentence in this case.' In respect of Pte Burton he wrote: 'The actual fact of Pte Burton being found sitting down shews such a want of appreciation of his duties as a sentry, responsible for the lives of his comrades that although the accused bears a good character I am unable to recommend suspension of sentence.'

Lt Gen. Maude, C.-in-C. of the British forces in Mesopotamia, confirmed sentence on these two August 1914 volunteers. Ex-Sgt Crutchlow has said that three men were executed, and the day before the incident the battalion had marched over 30 miles and that these men had been unlucky enough to be selected for sentry duty.[5] In his recollections he also says that the battalion CO had pleaded with Lt Gen. Maude to commute the sentences, but that Maude had refused. In fact, the battalion war diary makes it clear that no great distance had been marched the day before Burton and Downing's offence, and again, old soldiers' recollections are unreliable.[6]

These two men, both with excellent records, were shot at Bassuoia on 19 February 1917. It is ironic that had they been deserters on the Western Front, their sentences would have almost certainly, at this stage of the war, been commuted. Instead, Downing and Burton were shot as a reminder to all men serving in the army that sleeping at post was a capital offence and was regarded as a most serious crime. The two men were undoubtedly guilty of the crime for which they were executed, and neither made any attempt to deny what had happened, but by signing their death warrants Gen. Maude almost certainly deprived the British Army of two good soldiers who, like many others, had suffered a temporary lapse. With hindsight we can only say that both were unlucky.

Leaving a post without orders, like sleeping on post, is a very specific and serious military offence. This offence forms part of the continuum of offences ranging from disobedience through to cowardice, and cases which appear to be superficially similar were tried for either cowardice (as in the case of L Cpl

Holland; see Chapter 14), or quitting post, depending on local views as to the most appropriate charge. Quitting a post is an objective assessment – a man is either at his post or he is not, and there are no shades of grey. If he was not at his post the army was generally unconcerned as to the reason why he was absent: absence was absence. Despite this, relatively few death sentences were carried out for this particular military crime, a total of seven men being executed for this offence.

Although several men had been sentenced to death at the end of 1914 for quitting their posts , none was executed.[7] In January 1915 a Pte Cunningham of the Essex was sentenced to death for leaving his post on two occasions, but his sentence was commuted to ten years' penal servitude. The first execution occurred at the beginning of 1915, when Cpl George Povey and several other men from the 1st Battalion, the Cheshire Regiment were court-martialled.[8] The men were all tried separately, but the evidence was the same in all the cases. In Povey's case three witnesses gave evidence, their total testimony comprising fewer than 100 words. At about 2.30 a.m. on 28 January 1915 the battalion was holding the line near Wulverghem. There was a sudden panic in the front line when someone shouted that the Germans were in the trench. Hearing this, several men, some of whom had been asleep, ran towards the rear before being stopped at a support point, when they were ordered to return to their post.

Cpl Povey's defence was that he had been asleep when the panic started, and woke hearing the words: 'Clear out lads, they're on us.' He saw several men running away and followed them, but when he reached the support point and was ordered back to the front line, he went. He also told the court that when stopped, he had all his arms and equipment with him.

The panic had apparently arisen when a German – seemingly alone – had crept right up to the front line trench and had pulled a rifle out through a loophole in the trench. It has to be suspected that the men were asleep in the small hours of a freezing cold January night and were startled into wakefulness by this event, and panic ensued.

All the men were found guilty. Povey, the NCO, was sentenced to death and the other men were given ten years' penal servitude, with recommendations to mercy. The brigade commander took note of the recommendations and reduced the sentences of imprisonment. Maj. Gen. Morland, commanding 2nd Division, and Lt Gen. Fergusson, II Corps, recommended that the sentence on Povey be carried out. The army commander, Sir Horace Smith-Dorrien, wrote: 'This is a very serious case indeed and I agree with the Corps Commander's opinion that the death sentence should be carried out in the case of No. 10459, Cpl G Povey of the 1st Battalion, Cheshire Regiment.'

Although not specifically mentioned, the clear implication is that Povey was executed because he was an NCO and should have stemmed the panic instead of joining in. In this, the case parallels that of McDonald and Goggins (see Chapter 13) late in 1916. The *Manual of Military Law* lays out very clearly that an NCO, as a rule, should be punished more severely than a private soldier concerned with him in the commission of the same offence.[9] The army had set the standard by which its NCOs would be judged. Cpl Povey was executed at St Jans Cappel on 11 February 1915,[10] but his grave was lost during the war and he is commemorated on the Menin Gate.

The next execution for quitting post took place in Gallipoli. Thomas Davis was serving with the 1st Battalion of the Munster Fusiliers, which had taken part in the original landings at Cape Helles in April 1915 and had taken heavy casualties – so much so, that for a short while they and another depleted unit, the 1st Battalion Dublin Fusiliers, were amalgamated into a combined unit, the 1st Battalion 'Dubsters'.[11]

On 20 June 1915 Pte Davis had been posted as a headquarters guard at 1 a.m. for a two-hour tour of duty. At 2.30 a.m. L Sgt Bradshaw had checked the post and found Davis missing. After searching for him unsuccessfully, he posted another guard. Neither Bradshaw nor Pte Borleigh, who was on duty from 3 to 5 a.m., saw Davis again until sometime between 5 and 5.15 a.m. At his trial Davis was not defended and did not contest the evidence. In his defence he made a statement to the court (which consisted of two captains and a lieutenant, no field officer being available to act as president). Davis said that he had been posted as a flying picket around headquarters and at 2.15 a.m. he had sudden stomach cramps and had to use the latrine. He said that he was there about two hours and as he was leaving he had a further attack.[12]

After the court had considered its finding, the adjutant gave information about Davis's previous record. He said that Davis had been sentenced to death at the beginning of May but this had been commuted to ten years' penal servitude; the crime for which this was awarded was not stated. A few days after this, he had been given twenty-eight days' FP No. 1 for being absent from his picket. It has been stated elsewhere that promulgation of Davis's first death sentence occurred after his execution, but this is clearly not so.[13] The confusion seems to have arisen from the Registers of Courts Martial [14] extracted by Oram.[15] This shows that five men of the Munsters were sentenced to death for cowardice, three on the 3rd or 4th of May and Pte P. Davis and Pte O'Leary on 4 July 1915. In all five cases, sentence was commuted to ten years' imprisonment. In four cases the place of trial is given as Mesopotamia, although the battalion was in Gallipoli. It therefore appears that there were transcription errors in the original ledger and Pte P. Davis was actually tried on 4 May, and that 'P' is a transcription error for 'T'.

The court decided not to believe Davis's version of events and sentenced him to death. Under other circumstances, given the prevalence of dysentery on the peninsula, his story might have been given more credence, but his previous offences counted against him. Pte Davis was shot on Gully Beach on 2 July 1915.

It was to be a year before another man was executed for the same crime. In July 1916 Pte Arthur Grove Earp of 1/5th Warwicks was shot by a firing squad despite a recommendation for mercy by the court.[16] He had been tried on 8 July 1916 charged with 'When on active service leaving his post without orders from his superior officer in that he on June 26th when belonging to the left post garrisoning Carench [*sic*] trench under No. 443 Sgt Williams, left his post without orders from his superior officer.'

Two witnesses gave evidence for the prosecution. Sgt Williams explained to the court that he took his platoon into Carency trench at 4 a.m. and that Cpl Golby was put in charge of the left post garrison to which Earp belonged. The sergeant and the corporal both told the court that they had personally warned the men that they were not to leave the post until they were relieved. Pte Earp was at his position at 12.30 p.m. but Cpl Golby noticed that he was missing at about 1 p.m., and he was still absent when the sergeant returned at 1.30 p.m. Sgt Williams searched for him unsuccessfully and Earp was not seen again until 2.30 a.m. on 27 June, when Cpl Golby said that the missing man reported to him in Botha dugout, behind the front line.

Under cross-examination by Earp, Sgt Williams said that the platoon had been doing twenty-four-hour periods of duty in the front and reserve lines for four days and 'they had a particularly trying time of it as the great bombardment was in progress and there was a lot of retaliation'. Cpl Golby told the court: 'The accused was in a highly nervous state when we went onto the post. The trenches were shelled heavily from about 4 a.m. for about two hours. When the accused reported to me at 2.30 a.m. on June 27th he told me that he couldn't stand the shelling so went to Botha dug-out.'

In his defence, Earp said that when the trenches were being heavily shelled he got into the dugout: 'I was feeling giddy and did not know what I was doing. After the shelling ceased, I walked out and went a little way down the communication trench, the shelling then started again and I could not get back.' He added: 'The next time our platoon went up into the front line I was sent out of the trenches by Capt Gell as I was unable to stand the shelling.' Sgt Williams, giving evidence for the defence, told the court: 'The accused was always of a nervous disposition and was very nervous on that morning in particular. He had been sent down to the base for three or four months and on June 26th had been back with the regiment about three or four months.' No one asked of the sergeant why Earp had been sent to the base. The implication was that he was suffering from shell shock or 'nerves', but if so, this important point was never brought out at the trial, even by the defendant himself.

His records showed that Pte Earp had joined up as a Kitchener volunteer in September 1914. There were no entries on his conduct sheet and his

Forwarded.

I strongly recommend that the sentence be carried out & I concur with the Brigadier; & the evidence of previous conviction for the same offence in the Battalion does not support the contention of the G.O.C. Div & of the Corps Commander that an example is not necessary. On the contrary, it appears that an example is very necessary. This is a very serious military offence & if it is passed over the standard & courage of the British soldier is likely to be lowered.

17. 7. 16.

Headquarters Res.Army.

General,
Commanding Reserve Army.

General Gough's comments on the Earp case, recommending that an example was necessary

SCHEDULE.

Date *July 8* 19*16*. No.

*t more
an six
mes to
entered
one form.*

Name of Alleged Offender (a)	Offence charged	Plea	Finding, and if Convicted, Sentence (b)	How dealt with by Confirming Officer
N° 2676 Pte A. G EARP 1/5 R. War Reg.	When on active service leaving his post without orders from his superior officer on June 26. 1916 *alternative charge* When on active service conduct to the prejudice of good order and military discipline on June 26. 1916	Not Guilty. Not Guilty.	Guilty. Sentence Death. Recommendation for mercy. The court recommend the accused for mercy owing to the intense bombardment which the accused had been subjected to on account of his good character.	Reserved. B. CWent Brg Gen 11th July 1916 Confirmed. D. Haig. Gen¹.

† How can we give this plea is allowed D.H.

(a) If the name of the person charged is unknown, he may be described as unknown, with such addition as will identify him.

(b) Recommendation to mercy to be inserted in this column.

B. CWent. Brg Gen   F. S. Hanson Maj
Convening Officer.   President.
Cmd⁵ 143 Inf. Bde   1/7 R. W

Sir Douglas Haig's ('D. H.')despairing comment, and his confirmation of the death sentence on Pte Arthur Earp

character was 'good'. In view of this and the intensity of the bombardment going on at the time, the court recommended him to mercy.

Brig. Gen. Dent, commanding 143th Brigade, recommended that sentence be carried out as three other men from the same battalion had been convicted of the same offence only three weeks earlier and in those cases sentence had been commuted. In addition, another man was awaiting trial on the same charge. (The cases he referred to were those of Ptes Giles, Hatton and Scrivener, whose sentences were commuted to two years' imprisonment.)[17] The implication was clear: unless drastic action was taken, this type of behaviour would spread and Earp's death was necessary as an example to others.

The commander of 48th (South Midland) Division, Maj. Gen. Fanshawe, disagreed. He wrote: 'The battalions of the Brigade have done well and I do not think that an example is necessary.' The GOC of VIII Corps, Lt Gen. Aylmer Hunter Weston, a man not known for leniency, concurred with the recommendation to mercy but Gen. Hubert Gough, commanding the Reserve (shortly to become Fifth) Army, disagreed: 'The evidence of previous convictions for the same offence in this battalion does not support the contention of GOC Division that an example is not necessary. On the contrary, an example is very necessary. This is a very serious military offence and if it is passed over the state of courage of the British soldier is likely to be lowered.'

The court martial documents arrived on Douglas Haig's desk in the aftermath and recriminations of the first day of the battle of the Somme and the commander-in-chief was in no mood for tolerance. He confirmed the sentence and wrote, almost despairingly it seems: 'How can we ever win if a plea like this is allowed?' He also wrote a firmly penned note to the Adjutant General, adding under Gough's comments: 'This opinion, in which I fully concur, is to be communicated to the Corps and Divisional commanders.' Like naughty schoolboys, Lt Gen. Hunter Weston and Maj. Gen. Fanshawe were called to task and reminded of their military responsibilities. Each signed 'noted' beneath Haig's comments. For a general officer this was a humiliation designed to drive home a message from the Commander-in-Chief to his subordinates, of whatever rank, not to be 'soft'.

Pte Arthur Grove Earp went to his death before a firing squad as an example to others that, no matter how bad the conditions, orders must be obeyed, and that for a soldier duty outweighs all personal considerations. There are similarities between this case and that of Harry Farr. Although it is not made clear at the trial, Earp seems to have been evacuated from the front line with shell shock or nerves, and, like Farr, Earp complained that he could not stand the noise of the guns – which on the eve of the battle of the Somme, when the bombardment could be heard in England, must have been tremendous. Perhaps in these more enlightened times Pte Earp might have been recognized as having a psychological breakdown, but not by the rough and ready standards of 1916.

Pte Earp was as much a victim of the failure of the Somme offensive as the thousands who died on the opening week of the battle, just as surely as were Lawton and McCubbin (shot for cowardice a week after Earp), executed by commanders fearful of a complete breakdown in discipline among the new, unproven, citizen army. The only solution was to reinforce the standards of the old, regular army: a firm reminder to the men of the Kitchener battalions that the army was not an extension of civilian life. This, to the commanders of the time, was the only way that control of the new army could be maintained and the war won.

The case of the last man to be shot for leaving his post without orders was rather different to the other cases in this category. Pte Thomas Hopkins was executed on 13 February 1918, over two months after his trial and five months after his fatal offence.[18] On 1 September 1917, Pte Hopkins was in the trenches for the first time. He had joined the Lancashire Fusiliers in September 1916 and had been posted to the 1/8th Battalion in August 1917. At 2 a.m., when the gas alarm was given, Hopkins was standing next to Sgt Caldwell and Cpl Cowell. When the 'Gas clear' call was given he was missing, although all his equipment was left where he had been standing. He was not seen again by the battalion until 9 or 10 September, although details of his arrest and whereabouts were not given at his trial.

Hopkins compounded his misdemeanours by escaping from the bivouac in which he was being held prisoner during the night of 18–19 September. Again, details of his whereabouts and subsequent re-arrest were not given but he was back in confinement at Coxyde, near the coast, on 10 October. The evidence given was that Hopkins was being held in a cubicle within a hut and, whilst briefly left unguarded, had escaped through a window. The NCO of the guard saw him escaping, but confessed at the trial: 'I did not take any action as it was customary to use the window as an exit as the door was at the other end of the hut and it meant passing through several cubicles to get to it.' Despite being pursued, Hopkins made off into the dunes around Coxyde. He was rearrested and, although the summary of evidence was taken on 2 November, he did not stand trial until 3 December 1917.

The army took great care in framing the charges. On 6 October (before the prisoner's last escape attempt) the GOC 42nd Division had written to Fourth Army for advice on preparing the charge sheet. He wrote:

> Re offence on 1st September. There appears to be no 'intention' to support a charge of desertion in as much as the man made his way to the second line of his Battalion. Would a charge of Cowardice with an alternative charge under Army Act section 4 (2) stand?

The reply from the DAAG was that the charge should be: 'Without orders from his superior officer leaving his post in that he on or about 1 September 1917 without orders from his superior officer left his post in the trenches.' Hopkins was tried on this charge and two of escaping.

His defence to the first charge was: 'I had been lying about and the weather was cold so I went down a road into a town. I had no pay and had been hand-cuffed for six or seven months, no friends in the regiment.' In his plea of mitigation he said that he was 27 years old and was a boiler cleaner in civilian life. He had joined up on 4 September 1916 and been sent to No. 23 Infantry Base Depot on 20 July 1917, joining the 1/8th Lancashire Fusiliers on 8 August.

Hopkins's 'crime sheet' showed a string of minor offences in the UK: refusing to work, refusing to obey an order, being drunk and improperly dressed. More seriously, on 29 April he had been charged with attempting to desert and given 112 days' detention, and it was whilst serving this sentence that he was sent to France. Since arriving abroad he had had one brief absence and 'was out of bounds' on 3 August.

The court found him guilty and Hopkins was sentenced to death, but the court was clearly concerned about his mental condition. The president wrote:

> The Court desire me to state for the information of higher authorities that while they have no reason to think that the accused was not responsible for his actions, he appears to be of a very low mentality and they would suggest the desirability of some further medical report beyond the certificate furnished that he was fit for trial and to undergo hard labour.

This was followed up and on 16 December it was arranged for the prisoner to be taken to Wimereux, near Boulogne, to be seen by a specialist in mental diseases. In this case there was no question of shell shock – this had been Hopkins's first exposure to action; the question was quite simply whether he was mentally competent and responsible for his actions. He was examined by Capt. Montgomery, who wrote on 22 December that Hopkins had never been in an asylum and that there was no history of insanity in the family, and that he worked as a boiler cleaner earning 24/- a week. The MO noted in his report that Hopkins had many convictions in civilian life and that he was dull and morose and seldom spoke. Dr Montgomery wrote: 'Patient is below average intelligence and is a criminal degenerate.' He went on: 'In my opinion patient is responsible for his actions. He knew that what he was doing was wrong when he went away from the trenches, his object being to avoid military service.' He ended: 'In my opinion patient is fit for service. Patient is sane.'

The doctor had followed up the question of civil convictions and on 14 January 1918 the Chief Constable of Birkenhead wrote: 'So far as can be ascertained there is no insanity in the family, but in May 1910 the medical officer of HM Prison, Knutsford reported that he was mentally deficient and it is believed that he improved mentally prior to his enlistment in the army.' Hopkins had a bad character in civilian life, with a series of convictions from 1909 to 1915, mainly for theft. In addition it was noted that he had a further thirty-two summary convictions for vagrancy, drunkenness and assaults on police.

The divisional, corps and army commanders all recommended that sentence be carried out. General Horne, GOC First Army, wrote:

> I have given this case very careful consideration. The acts were deliberate without a doubt, and the offence of leaving the trenches after or during a gas alarm is a very serious one. The man has a very bad character both in civil life and in the army. He is probably useless as a soldier. For the above reasons I feel it my duty to recommend that the sentence be carried out. I am quite aware that the general worthlessness of the man is inclined to influence above decision, but I have given due weight to this point and see no reason to allow it to alter my opinion. I do not think it affects my judgement.

On 31 January the papers were sent to the DJAG for his view on the legal aspects. He wrote that the case would have been more satisfactory if some evidence had been given as to the accused's movements after leaving the trenches and the date and time of his arrest. However, he felt that there was sufficient evidence to support the conviction. When the Commander-in-Chief confirmed the sentence on 4 February 1918, Hopkins was still in hospital at Wimereux and an escort was sent to bring him back to Gorre, where he was shot by firing squad on 6.20 a.m. on Wednesday 13 February 1918.

The case illustrates several points. By 1917–18 the army was generally very careful about framing charges, making it less likely that an incorrect charge would lead to acquittal or quashing of a conviction. The prisoner was medically examined, albeit perfunctorily, before his trial. After conviction considerable attempts were also made to check if Hopkins was legally and mentally responsible for his actions, and therefore that the conviction was safe on medical grounds. His civilian record was enquired into, establishing the truth of his statements to the doctors. On the other hand, the actual court martial proceedings were not as complete as they might have been, with little evidence about his initial arrest or rearrests.

The case itself is problematical. It is apparent that Hopkins was of below average intelligence but this, in itself, does not make him unfit for active service (after all, by definition, half the population are of below average intelligence). The legal and moral question was fundamental to both military and English criminal law: was the man responsible for his actions? If so, then he was culpable. If not, then he should be considered 'guilty but insane' and not executed. This was the law of the time and cannot be changed retrospectively by attempting to apply our current values. From our modern perspective the word 'degenerate' has a certain specific meaning, but the term has undergone a clear change in emphasis in the last eighty years. 'Criminal degenerate' was a perfectly acceptable description of a petty criminal of low IQ in 1918, whereas now the word has moved along the scale from being a commonly used phrase to encompassing only extremes of behaviour. 'Physically degenerate' was also a frequently used expression to describe anyone whose physical standards were below the norm. It is like the words 'cripple' and 'idiot' – no longer 'politically correct', fallen into disrepute and disuse – but in 1914 Nietzschean notions of 'Imperial Man' and similar ideas were intellectually respectable. Weaklings and degenerates were of questionable value – even as cannon fodder.

CHAPTER 13

THE BANTAMS AND THE 19TH DLI

Leave soldiers in a defensive position long enough and they begin to scare themselves to death.

HARRY H. SUMMERS, 1989

O n the outbreak of war the minimum height requirement for army recruits was 5 feet 3 inches. Many smaller men, especially those in the industrial and mining areas, wanted to join up too but were not allowed to serve their country. Eventually Alfred Bigland, MP for Birkenhead, obtained permission from the Minister for War, Lord Kitchener, for the raising of a 'Bantam' battalion. Men between 5 feet and 5 feet 3 inches would be accepted for service in this unit provided they had a minimum chest measurement of 34 inches (an inch more than the normal minimum, thereby ensuring that these were fit, sturdy men). The response was overwhelming and the first Bantam battalion, the 15th (Service) Battalion of the Cheshire Regiment, was filled immediately. Other battalions soon followed, including the 18th Highland Light Infantry, the 15th Sherwood Foresters, the 19th Durham Light Infantry, and others. These were formed into three brigades, the 104th, 105th and 106th, which together made up the 35th (Bantam) Division under the command of Maj. Gen. Reginald Pinney.

Initially the ranks of the Bantams were filled by the small, tough men from the pits and the factories of Britain's industrial heartlands, Glasgow and the Welsh valleys. Small though these men were, they soon gained the respect of the larger men as fighting troops. However, there is no doubt that they were viewed with scepticism by some commanders. At the beginning of the war the archetypal hero, the man literally to look up to, was 'Imperial Man'– tall, strong, sturdy – and these small men did not meet that exacting standard. The battalions of the 35th Division arrived in France in late January and early February 1916 and were introduced to trench life in the area of the old 1915 battlefields before moving south to the Somme, where they were blooded in battle for the first time. Initially the reinforcements were adequate to maintain the physical standards necessary for a soldier, but after the losses on the Somme the standards of recruits fell dramatically and many of the new drafts were weak, undersized boys and men. The days of the experimental Bantam division were numbered.

The first Bantam soldier to be executed was Pte James Archibald of 17th Battalion Royal Scots, who deserted after three and a half months in the trenches before his unit had been in serious action. He had joined up in June 1915 and arrived in France with 106th Brigade on 31 January 1916. In May of that year his unit was in the trenches near Richebourg.

On 14 May 1916 Archibald had been warned that when his battalion went into the line that night he was to be posted as a sentry.[1] At about 6.30 p.m. Archibald was given a grenade rifle to carry in addition to his normal equipment, and his battalion started to move forward. During the march Archibald went missing and was still absent when the sentries, of which he should have been one, were posted.

The following afternoon an elderly French lady stopped two soldiers of the Lancashire Fusiliers and asked them to look in her barn some distance behind the lines. When they did so, they found Pte Archibald asleep. They questioned him, discovered he was an absentee and had no equipment, and arrested him.

Archibald was court-martialled on 24 May and the panel included two officers from his battalion. The accused soldier made little attempt to defend himself. He made a statement, not on oath: 'When I was marching along in single file I felt queer and do not remember anything until I found myself near the barn. This was at night and I thought I had better go into the barn and lay down till morning. And I remember nothing till I was woken up next day.'

The court found Pte Archibald guilty and, although he had been absent for less than twenty-four hours, sentenced him to death, it appearing that he had deserted with the clear intention of avoiding front line duty. He had only one entry on his conduct sheet, for the relatively unusual 'Neglect of duty in the trenches', for which he had received twenty-eight days' FP No. 1 on 25 April, a sentence he would have still been serving at the time of his desertion.

After the trial, Lt Col. Cheales wrote, as part of the confirmation process,

This man was not a man who gave much trouble neither was he in any way a man whom one would pick out as a good man. He is considered by his Platoon Commander to be of poor intellect, and I consider that he is a typical slum product of a low level of intelligence. From a fighting point of view, Pte Archibald was of not much consideration. He was noted in his Company roll book as an unreliable man.

The CO added: '… I am doubtful that he realised the gravity of the offence he was committing', but then went on to say that the men of his battalion had been made aware of cases where the death penalty had been inflicted.

Brig. Gen. O'Donnell, commanding 106th Brigade, wrote:

The 17th Battalion Royal Scots is very well conducted. It contains a proportion of rough characters and lately there has been a certain amount of insubordination especially when orders are issued for heavy work in the trenches. I am reluctantly compelled to state that I think an example is necessary in the interests of discipline of the Brigade.

Division and Corps commanders also recommended execution, although Lt Gen. Haking said: 'I see no reason against carrying out the death sentence except the youth of the man.' At some point after the trial the question of Archibald's age must have been raised, as a telegram dated 26 May informed the brigade that he had given his age on attestation as 19.

At this stage of the war, 35th Division was part of First Army, commanded by Gen. Monro, who wrote: 'This appears to me to be a bad case. The man in question not only evaded duty but threw away his arms and equipment. I recommend that the sentence be carried out.' Pte James Archibald became the first Bantam soldier to be executed. Sentence was promulgated at 4 p.m. on 3 June in front of men from his battalion and Archibald was shot at Loisne as dawn broke on 4 June 1916, just a month before the first day of the Somme battle. The Bantams now had their disciplinary example.

The Bantam Division's first exposure to a full-scale offensive was in July 1916 when 35th Division moved to the Somme. Although not involved in the fighting on 1 July, they were used in the next phase of the attack in mid July. Cpl Jesse Wilton was one of the men who found the confusion of the battlefield far removed from the simplicities of recruiting posters and the training grounds at home. Wilton was older than most of the soldiers at the front. He was a 40-year-old who had joined the 15th (Service) Battalion of the Sherwood Foresters on its formation in February 1915 (although the certified copy of his conduct sheet produced at the trial gives his date of enlistment as February 1916, this appears to be a transcription error). The battalion arrived in France in February 1916 and during the succeeding months Wilton had performed well enough to earn his stripes. By July the battalion was serving on the Somme. The facts presented at the trial were straightforward.[2] At 3 a.m. on 19 July Lt McIntosh had ordered Wilton and ten men to garrison an isolated forward post at Arrow Head Copse, in no-man's-land, for a forty-eight-hour period. These men were told that this post was to be held 'at all costs'. At 10 p.m. on the following night, forty-three hours after having been posted, Cpl Wilton and his men arrived back in the front line trench.

Pte Daniels, who had been one of the outpost, described what had happened. He said that there had been heavy machine gun fire and shelling all day, and that on the evening of the 20th Cpl Wilton had said to him: 'What had we better do?' Daniels had replied: 'I leave it to you.' A little later Wilton had said: 'I think we had better go now. I think the Germans are coming on.' The party then returned back to the British front line along a communication trench, the privates following instructions from their NCO. Pte Hughes, who was in the front line when the men arrived back there between 9.30 and 10 p.m., told the court that Cpl Wilton had said to him: 'Look out, the Germans are coming.'

Wilton defended himself. He did not contest any of the evidence but in a statement to the court told them that whilst he and his men were at their post there was heavy shelling and machine gun fire and that when he took his men to the front line trench he reported to the company commander. He stated: 'My nerves and the nerves of my men were very much shaken.' Alongside this, in the trial proceedings, a later note has been added: '?casualties', apparently questioning whether any of the men had been wounded. Under cross-examination, Wilton confirmed that he had been told to hold the post until relieved. His conduct sheet showed that he had a clean record.

Arrow Head Copse was an unpleasant place to be on 19–20 July 1916. On the 19th, the 15th Foresters had been told that on the following day they were to attack on a 1,000-yard front, from Maltz Horn Farm to Arrow Head Copse. Early on the 20th, Lt Col. Gordon, commanding the battalion, sent a message to brigade HQ to say that his men were badly shaken from shelling and gas. They had been in gas masks for the last four hours and only two companies were fit to attack. These two companies, supported by men from 23th Manchesters, attacked at 5 a.m. but the rising sun exposed the attackers and they made little progress. A second attack took place at 10.45 a.m. but there was an extremely hostile bombardment. The 15th Foresters lost 49 officers and men killed and 155 wounded as a result of this attack.[3]

Cpl Wilton was found guilty of quitting his post and was sentenced to death, but with a recommendation to mercy. After the trial the papers went to his commanding officer for his views. Lt Col. Gordon wrote:

> BEHAVIOUR: Indifferent, as an NCO he is a failure, being too familiar with his subordinates, and surly and morose to his superiors, resenting any assistance offered him. IN ACTION: Has hitherto been good having volunteered on several occasions to go on reconnaissance patrols and on wiring parties. Chief cause of complaint is that NCOs will not assert themselves as they come from the same class of men as those in the ranks and think too much of their position after the war when they will all be in the workshops again. I consider the case of this man to be serious. He apparently discussed the matter with his men before deserting his post. There was nothing to prevent him from sending a message to his company commander asking for orders, a comparatively easy matter for him to do. I can see no favouring cause as regards his actions, which in my opinion were deliberate.

From the individual's CO this was a particularly damning recommendation. The Brigade, Division and Corps commanders were all in favour of execution, as was Gen. Rawlinson, commanding Fourth Army.

What does not emerge at any point, either during the trial or subsequently, was that Wilton was not the only man in the battalion to be tried for this crime. The records show that on the same day that Wilton was tried, Pte Moffit was also sentenced to death for quitting his post, but this was reduced to five years' penal servitude.[4] It therefore appears that, like Cpl Povey, L Cpl Hawthorne and L Cpl Holland (all executed for cowardice), Cpl Wilton was shot as an example to other NCOs of the 'new army', to remind them that it was their duty to reinforce discipline, and that they would be especially culpable in situations such as this. The *Manual of Military Law* makes it clear that if an NCO and a private soldier commit the same offence, 'a non-commissioned officer should as a rule be punished more severely than a private soldier concerned with him in the commission of the same offence'.[5] L Cpls McDonald and Goggins of the 19th DLI were to discover this later in the year after a similar episode. The old, regular army expected high standards of its NCOs and viewed the easy informality of the 'Chums' and 'Pals' of Kitchener's amateur, 'civilian' new army with suspicion.

By the end of August 1916 commanders were already beginning to express concern as to the poor quality of reinforcements being sent to the Bantam battalions. In mid August, when the 16th Cheshires were in the line preparing for an attack under difficult conditions, with artillery falling short, their commanding officer (Lt Col. Clayton) was forced to write to the brigade commander asking for his men to be relieved. It is an astonishing document:

> Dear General,
>
> I am ashamed to say that the Battalion is quite demoralised. I do not think that they would stand up against anything, and I honestly think it would be safer to get them relieved if possible. Company commanders tell me that very few men would follow their officers over. They are quite hopeless.[6]

This is one of the greatest admissions of failure that a commander can make – that his men cannot be relied on to hold the line. An event such as this could not be overlooked.

In a report after the failed attack, the commander of 105th Brigade described one of the reasons for the failure of the attack as:

> (iii) The class of man we are now getting, who are no longer the 'Bantam' proper, but are either half-grown lads, or are degenerates. Col. Clayton's and the Brigade Major's reports show the state of affairs among the men. The officers did well and did everything in their power to rouse the men. [7]

Lt Col. Davson wrote of this problem:

> But when losses occurred, the men who were sent to take their places, were in most cases, not 'Bantams' at all, as the term was originally understood, but under-developed men, who had previously been rejected by the commanders, and who were unfitted, both morally and physically, to take their places in the fighting ranks of the British Army.[8]

The 18th Battalion of the Highland Light Infantry were in the front line at Montauban on 17 July 1916 and were in action at Delville Wood on 19 July. After a short spell in reserve, they moved into the trenches north of Maricourt on the 26th.[9] At about 5 p.m. on that evening, Pte Hugh Flynn was with the rest of his battalion, but when the rations were issued an hour later, he was found to be missing.[10] He was next seen at St Pol on 5 August and was returned to his unit, when he was charged with desertion and tried at Arras on 27 October 1916. The story which emerged was somewhat unusual.

The court heard from two witnesses that Flynn had gone missing on 26 July, and then Pte Robson, of the Royal Army Service Corps, told them of a meeting with Flynn on 5 August. Robson had been walking along the road at Auxi-le-Château when Flynn went up and spoke to him. Flynn asked

Robson where he could join the army, and told him that he had stowed away on a boat from Folkestone and had then walked to Auxi from Frévent. Clearly confused by this, Robson asked Flynn why he was wearing army uniform. Flynn replied that he had got it at St Omer and added that if he couldn't join the army at Auxi he intended to go to Boulogne to get on a boat to England. The rather puzzled Robson took Flynn to the nearby Third Army School of Instruction and handed him over to the adjutant.

Flynn remained in the guardroom at the Army School for some time, carrying out various chores, presumably whilst his story was investigated. They must have been unaware that they had a deserter on their hands, as Flynn's name appears on a printed list of absentees 'up to and including 10 September'.[11] In this he is described as aged 21, 5 feet 1 inch tall, with black hair, grey eyes, dark complexion and stout build. Eventually the truth was discovered and he was taken back to his unit on 19 September.

Flynn, who was defended at his trial, made a statement on oath in his defence. In it he said he remembered being in Dublin Trench and that heavy shelling was going on and he asked to see the MO, but had been refused permission. He could remember nothing else until he found himself in Corbie, when he decided that the best thing to do would be to join another regiment to make a fresh start. After being cross-examined, he added to his earlier statement, saying that he had said nothing to Robson about going to Boulogne or getting back to England.

When his conduct sheet was presented to the court, Flynn was found to have several minor offences against him, all but one in the UK. He had volunteered for army service on 19 April 1915. He was found guilty of desertion and sentenced to death.

The papers then went up through the formation commanders for confirmation. His commanding officer did not have a good opinion of the soldier: 'From a fighting point of view, I consider him a useless soldier. His nerves cannot stand shelling. I have seen him myself … hiding in an old gun pit trembling with fear.' However, he was also fair to the soldier, saying: 'I consider that Pte Flynn did not deliberately run away so as to avoid duty. The shelling was severe at the time and his nerves could not stand it.'

Brig. Gen. O'Donnell, commanding 106th Brigade, agreed that the crime was not deliberate, 'but was the outcome of a cowardly disposition' and that sentence should not be carried out. However, Maj. Gen. Landon, commanding the Bantam Division, disagreed and recommended execution. Lt Gen. Haldane, the corps commander, criticized the CO of 18th HLI:

The statement of the officer commanding 18th Battalion Highland Light Infantry was considered most unsatisfactory. From his own statement it would appear that this officer had been aware, for some time, of the man's constitutional weakness as regards shell fire, and should have taken steps, when he first noticed it, either for him to be withdrawn from the line or such disciplinary action as was necessary. If this had been done, the man would not have now been placed in the grave position he now is at the present moment.

Haldane then recommended the sentence be carried out, but added a hand-written note to the typed letter, reiterating some of his earlier points and pointing out that Flynn's known weakness under fire might be construed as extenuating circumstances.

Gen. Allenby was less sympathetic and suggested that sentence should be carried out, and Sir Douglas Haig confirmed this on 11 November 1916. Pte Hugh Flynn was executed at 6.35 a.m. on 15 November 1916.

Another soldier from the same battalion deserted a few days after Flynn. On 29 July Pte John McQuade was attached to 106th Trench Mortar Battery as a shell carrier at Carnoy. At 2 p.m. on that day the men had been paraded and warned that they would be going to the trenches shortly. At 5 p.m. the battery fell in and McQuade was found to be missing. Although two witnesses at his subsequent trial say that this soldier was missing from 29 July until 5 August, no evidence of his arrest was given at the trial, only that he was brought back to his battalion from Corbie on 'about' 15 August.[12]

On 31 August the battalion was marching from Authieux to Sus St Léger when McQuade fell out, saying that he could go no further. At Sus St Léger at 9 p.m. the roll was called and McQuade was absent. His name appears on the same list of absentees as Flynn's, and he is described as aged 30, 5 feet 2 inches, with a dark complexion, slender face and knock knees.[13] On 10 September he and another soldier reported to L Cpl James of the military police at Fontinettes, saying that he wanted to get to his machine gun unit at Camiers. As McQuade had no movement order he was taken to nearby Fort Risbon, at Calais, and handed over. The following day an escort was sent to Calais to fetch the man back to his unit.

McQuade was taken back to Arras and tried on two separate counts of desertion. He was undefended at his trial, and made little effort to defend himself. On the first charge he made no statement in his defence and called no witnesses, and did not challenge any of the evidence. His only statement in defence of the second charge was to say that he had fallen out on the march with sore feet.

He did not have a good record. He had enlisted on 10 May 1915 and had collected a few minor entries on his conduct sheet in the UK. More seriously, he had gone missing from his draft when it moved from Boulogne to Etaples and then on 5 July 1916 had been tried by FGCM for disobeying an order. For this crime he had been sentenced to one year's hard labour, but sentence had been suspended and he had returned to duty.

The court found McQuade guilty and sentenced him to death. As part of the confirmation process his CO was asked to give his opinion of the soldier. He wrote a damning reference:

> This man has been while in this battalion absolutely useless as a soldier, his fighting qualities are nil. So little is he to be depended on, the O.C. Company has always requested me to leave him behind when going into action. I therefore sent him to the Trench Mortar battery for carrying purposes ... He has been a perpetual nuisance to his O.C. Company ... he is always deficient of his kit etc. I left the man behind when we came to France and he was sent up to join the battalion on 6th June 1916. I am of the opinion that both crimes of desertion were deliberate to avoid service.

The other commanders all agreed, but when the papers reached Third Army HQ the DAAG intervened, to say that in view of the lack of evidence about arrest on the first charge, the finding should be reconsidered, as a conviction only of absence was justified. The court was therefore reconvened to reconsider its finding and sentence. It revoked its earlier finding, deciding that McQuade was guilty of the lesser crime of absence, but decided that the original sentence of death should stand. There is a strange tailpiece to the case. On the court martial schedule Haig has written 'Confirmed, 1 November 1916' and signed in the usual way. However, he has then crossed this out and initialled the change. No doubt this was because the original finding had been changed, but there is now no document in the file indicating that sentence on McQuade was confirmed.

The Bantam Division was, however, to suffer a far more serious breakdown of discipline before the end of the year, and one that would result in three executions in one unit. At the end of August, 35th Division was moved out of the front line Somme area into the line around the city of Arras, on the Third Army front. The line taken over by the division consisted of a three-brigade front, with 'I', 'J' and 'K' sectors taken over by 104th, 105th and 106th

Brigades respectively. The sectors were divided into a total of seven subsectors, corresponding to battalion fronts. When in the line, the 19th DLI held 'K2' subsector at the extreme left of the division and in front of the village of Roclincourt.[14]

The system of front line trenches generally consisted of a 'fire trench', a 'support line' and a 'reserve line'. The fire trench was the main line of defence with saps running forwards towards the enemy line for sentry or listening posts. In 'K' Sector, where portions of the line around the old mine craters had been badly damaged by the enemy's bombardment, the support or 'close support' line was strongly held and only outposts were maintained in the front line. The quality of the front line wire varied considerably.

In front of 'K' Sector there were mine craters (from right to left) Katie, Kent, Kick, Kite and King. These craters were all consolidated and held by the British. In 'K' Sector, from New Street to Wednesday Avenue there was a close support trench (Spook Avenue). This line however had been so continually bombarded and badly knocked in that it had been abandoned. The support line in 'K' Sector was known as the 'Works Line' and contained the following small works: E, F, G, H, I, K, L. The wire along this line was good on the whole. The reserve line in 'K' Sector was known as the 'Redoubt Line' and contained Observatory Redoubt, Thelus Redoubt and the Defences of Roclincourt Village. This line was in a fair state of repair, as were also the works. (see map page 160.)

There were numerous communication trenches in all three sectors. Under corps orders, the main communication trenches in 'K' Sector were Sunday, Wednesday and Cecil Avenues. The heads of Sunday and Wednesday Avenues required constant attention as they were continually bombarded and damaged by enemy trench mortar fire. Cecil Avenue had been made good only from the front line back to the 'Works Line'. From that point, communication to the rear was maintained by Father's Footpath and Bogey Avenue leading back into Roclincourt, behind the British line.

When 35th Division took over these sectors in September 1916, the Commander Royal Engineers of the division issued a list of the principal works to be carried out, in order of urgency, and the first item on his list was 'The construction of heightened fire-step suitable for the Infantry of this Division'.[15]

Although there were no great offensives in this area, there was a lot of activity with trench raids and counter-raids and use of gas. By November bad weather and enemy action meant that many of the trenches were in poor condition and waterlogged.

On 21 November the enemy activity increased and artillery action exposed the 'Pope's Nose' (a German position opposite 'K' sector), showing it to be a concrete emplacement. 'Aerial torpedoes' were used, as well as trench mortars, and there were several German attempts to cut the British wire. The last episode in which the division took part as a Bantam unit occurred on 26 November, and it was something of a fiasco. On the same night that a large trench raid had been planned by 19th DLI, the Germans carried out their own trench raids on all three brigade fronts. The outcome of these events was that no fewer than twenty-six men were sentenced to death on various charges and that three NCOs were executed.

The events of that night are barely mentioned in the battalion war diary [16] and get only brief mention in the war diary of 106th Brigade.[17] This is revealing, as there was a full-scale divisional inquiry into what happened and a detailed report in the war diary of 35th Division.[18] An understanding of the sequence of events is important in the light of the subsequent courts martial, and the following is extracted from this divisional war diary.

The diarist noted that the two lines were very close together in the K2 sub-sector, the outer lip of King Crater being only 50 yards from the enemy line, and that the wire around the crater was very thin. Normally there would be two sentry groups of six men at the southern and northern entrances to the crater, but because of the planned British raid, the line was actually held by the following men of the 19th DLI:

Post 'A': Cpl Stevenson + one man
Post 'B': L Cpl Hopkinson, Pte Harding and Pte Hunt
Post 'C': L Cpl McDonald, Pte Ritchie and Pte Spence, who were all on duty, and L Cpl Goggins, Pte Forrest, Pte Davies and Pte Dowsey, who were in a nearby dugout.

At 2.15 a.m. Lt Mundy and L Sgt Stones of 19th DLI visited post 'A' and then entered the crater on their way to post 'B'. Just inside the crater they ran into some German raiders who seemed to have got in from the north (see map overleaf). Lt Mundy was shot and Sgt Stones ran back to post 'A'. He then went on down the communication trench to the junction of two communication trenches, Bogey and Wednesday Avenues. Cpl Stevenson from post 'A' went into the crater and brought in the dying Lt Mundy. After shooting Lt Mundy the Germans had moved on to post 'B', where Pte Hunt stood his ground and was taken prisoner. But L Cpl Hopkinson and Pte Harding ran down the front line to 'C' post, shouting: 'Run for your lives, the

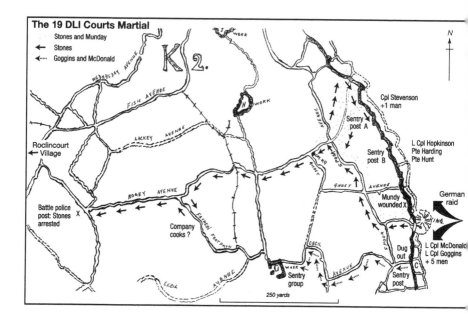

The 19 DLI at Roclincourt: showing the movements of Lance Sergeant Willie Stones and Lance Corporals Goggins and McDonald on the night of 25–26 November 1916, based on the map put into evidence at the court martial of L Sgt Stones (PRO WO 71/535). Sgt Stones and Lt Mundy visited post 'A', then went back to post 'B' via King Crater, where Mundy was shot. Stones went back to post 'A' to raise the alarm before going back to company HQ and then back to the battle police post

Germans are on you.' Pte Harding shortly afterwards returned to his post, but L Cpl Hopkinson was finally stopped by the 19th DLI battle police well to the rear, at the junction of Bogey and Wednesday Avenues (at the same place as Sgt Stones), where, like Stones, he was found to be without his rifle. On hearing the shouted warning, the whole of the party at post 'C' had left their post and been stopped by a sentry at 'G' work, in the support line.

At some point after the men left 'B' and 'C' posts, Second Lt Harding and Sgt Napier (officer and NCO of the watch, according to the diarist) were doing their rounds in the dark, apparently unaware of what had happened, when they ran into the German raiders north of Cecil Avenue (another communication trench). Both were shot, although the NCO managed to get to

LEFT Sir John French, the mercurial first Commander-in-Chief of the BEF from August 1914 to December 1915 (IWM Q 69149)

BELOW Field Marshal Sir Douglas Haig, Commander-in-Chief of the BEF from December 1915 until the end of the war. Haig refused to confirm nine out of ten of the death sentences awarded at Field General Courts Martial (IWM Q23642)

OPPOSITE TOP Sir Charles Monro with Lord Kitchener. General Monro, as Commander-in-Chief of the Mediterranean Expeditionary Force from September 1915, confirmed several of the death sentences in that theatre of war (IWM Q13585)

LEFT Battle conditions – 1. Infantry dug in forward of the front line after an attack (IWM Q11678)

ABOVE Battle conditions – 2. The MO of the 14th East Yorks at work. The Regimental Aid Post was usually about 500–1000 yards behind the front line (IWM Q11545)

OPPOSITE TOP Battle conditions – 3. 'In Brigade Reserve': a working party 'resting' out of the front line (IWM Q1616)

LEFT Battle conditions – 4. 'Going up the line' from forward Brigade Headquarters (about half a mile behind the front line trenches): the Ancre Valley, winter 1916, the road from Beaucort to Hamel (IWM Q1568)

ABOVE Battle conditions – 5. A Royal Artillery support gun line, usually about 2 miles behind the front line (IWM Q104)

ABOVE Battle conditions – 6. A typical Brigade or Divisional HQ:
the headquarters of 63 (Royal Naval Division) during the battle of the
Ancre, at Englebelmer, November 1916. Sub Lt Dyett returned to his
billet in this area (IWM Q66820)

RIGHT Battle conditions - 7. Rear transport lines and Divisional HQ
were based in the ruins of Ypres. 'The Salient' in Flanders was the
heart of the BEF's operations in that area for four long years
(IWM Q11759)

OPPOSITE LEFT Battle conditions – 8. 'Out of the line': Dickebusch Huts. It was in this area that nine men were executed, including the 'Worcester Four' and Herbert Burden (IWM Q10482)

LEFT Mass training at the notorious 'bull ring' Base Depot at Etaples. Raw recruits and experienced veterans alike were subjected to a harsh induction to life with the BEF in France (IWM Q33328)

ABOVE Loisne Chateau: Ptes Arthur Wild and Herbert Crimmins were tried here in 1916 after going absent just before the Battle of the Somme (Copyright held by Cathryn Corns)

OPPOSITE ABOVE Château Combreux at Tournan, where Pte Thomas Highgate was tried for desertion in September 1914 (Cathryn Corns)

ABOVE La Ferme de Champneuf, near Le Crotoy, where Sub Lt Edwin Dyett was court-martialled, and where he waited to hear his fate (Cathryn Corns)

LEFT One of the cells in the Town Hall at Poperinge, used to house men awaiting execution or trial (Cathryn Corns)

ABOVE The abattoir at Mazingarbe. Eleven men were executed on this site during the Great War (Cathryn Corns)

BELOW The grim asylum at Armentières, scene of several war-time executions (Cathryn Corns)

ABOVE RIGHT Locre Church in 1915. Ptes Byers, Evans and Collins were executed near here in February 1915, and were buried in the churchyard (IWM Q49379)

BELOW The estaminet at Duisans Halt, where Pte Edward Bolton of the 1st Cheshires spent the night before his execution
(Cathryn Corns)

ABOVE The railway embankment at Duisans where Pte Bolton was executed. The arrangements for this execution were described in detail by the APM, Captain Westmacott (Cathryn Corns)

RIGHT The execution post now on display at the Town Hall in Poperinge. This post is said to have been used for the execution of Coolie Wang in 1919 (Cathryn Corns)

LEFT 2nd Lt John Paterson. A deserter, Paterson was executed for the murder of Sgt Harold Collison, the military policeman who tried to arrest him (Public Record Office WO 339/111890)

BELOW A French officer administers the *coup de grâce* to an executed German prisoner, who was tried by drum-head court martial after attacking his French escort (IWM Q49340)

ABOVE The public mass-execution of twenty-one mutineers of the 5th Native Light Infantry in Singapore, February 1915
(IWM Q82506)

LEFT The grave of Pte Albert Ingham in Bailleulmont Communal Cemetery Extension, with its unique inscription chosen by his father. Ingham is buried next to Pte Alfred Longshaw; the two friends joined up, served and finally deserted together
(Cathryn Corns)

the stretcher bearers' dugout. The German raiders then went a short way up Cecil Avenue, bombing dugouts, before returning to their lines.

In the meantime Lt Howes, who was in charge of the counter-attack platoon in the company HQ dugout (at the junction of Ghost and Bogey Avenues), had been alerted by Sgt Stones and had ordered his platoon to follow him down Ghost Avenue and over the top across the open ground to the front line trenches. However, only four men followed him and he had to return for the rest.

Despite the German attack the raid by the DLI, about 700 yards to the north of King Crater, went ahead, with over fifty men taking part.[19] Two officers and seven other ranks managed to get into the German trenches but the remainder were held up by British artillery shells falling short in no-man's-land and on the German line. Casualties for this foray were one officer wounded, two other ranks killed and seven wounded. The brigade war diary describes the situation:

> … the remainder of the raiding party did not follow. Some confusion had apparently occurred at the gap [in the German wire] and the wrongful use of the order 'GET BACK' had caused the remainder to run back to our lines. Our artillery barrage which had opened by this time, was very short and the retiring raiders suffered several casualties from it, resulting in their becoming so demoralized that it was impossible to collect the men and make them return.[20]

The brigade war diary summarizes the total casualties up to midnight on 26 November as '3 officers wounded (Lt Mundy since died), 2 other ranks killed, 11 wounded and one missing'.[21] Sgt Napier died of his wounds on the 28th.

The events of that night had been a military shambles and 19th DLI came out of it particularly poorly. The death knell had already been sounded for the 35th (Bantam) Division and the events of 25–26 November were an unfortunate end to the Bantam experiment. Lt Col. Davson, in the *History of the 35th Division*, wrote:

> So ended a busy night, and also the last in which the Bantams took part as a 'Bantam' division. Although the general result of the enemy raids was much to be deplored it may be said to have had one good effect. It brought forcibly to notice that which commanding officers had been reporting for some time, namely that the major part of the recently received reinforcements could not be trusted to hold the line.[22]

In the eyes of GHQ and the staff, 35th Division had been found wanting.

However, the aftermath of these events was not yet over for several men of 19th DLI. On 24 December L Sgt Joseph William (Willie) Stones was sentenced to death for casting away his arms and running away from the front line and L Cpl Hopkinson for quitting his post. Then, on 28 December, L Cpls Goggins and McDonald and four private soldiers were sentenced to death for quitting their post and, finally, on 30 December a further eighteen men from the battalion were sentenced to death for cowardice. The total tally of death sentences was twenty-six – of which three were carried out. Had the other sentences been carried out, the application of military law would have resulted in more casualties than the German raid.

The trial of Sgt Willie Stones took place at Foufflin Ricametz on Christmas Eve 1916.[23] The composition of the court martial panel was slightly unusual. Panels were normally composed of a major, a captain and a lieutenant, but this case was presided over by Lt Col. G. B. J Riccard (17th Royal Scots), who sat with three captains, including Captain W. Briggs (the CMO for Third Army). Stones was charged with 'when on active service shamefully casting away his arms in the presence of the enemy in that he in the front-line trenches K2 sub-sector in 26th November 1916 when an NCO of the watch and attacked by the enemy shamefully cast away his rifle and left the front line and ran away'. The NCO was defended at his trial – not by some callow subaltern, but by Capt. Warmington, a 40-year-old London solicitor serving in 'Y' company of 19th DLI. The evidence presented at the trial is interesting and relevant to the wider question of capital courts martial and the Bantam battalions.

The first witness was Lt Howes, who on the night of 25–26 November was in the company HQ dugout at the junction of Ghost and Bogey Avenues at 2.15 a.m. (see map). He heard a voice calling down one of the entrances and in consequence of what the CSM reported to him, he collected men and bombs and started to move towards the front line. However, he found that only four men had followed him so he returned to get the others. At this point he saw Sgt Stones standing in Bogey Avenue. He told the court: 'He was standing there and seemed very much upset. I can't say whether he had a rifle. The place where I saw accused was about 150 yards, by the trench, from the front line. The accused was NCO of the watch on that night. As such it was his duty to be in the front line with the officer of the watch.' This was a crucial point; the NCO of the watch should not have left the front line without permission. Under cross-examination Howes said: 'The officer of the watch was

Lt Mundy' and 'It was at company HQ that I saw the accused. I couldn't say whether it was the accused that I heard.' He put a plan of the trenches into evidence. (see page 160)

CSM Holroyd, Stones's immediate superior as a senior NCO, told the court that he had been in the company HQ when the alarm was raised. He had then gone to the front line, where he did not see Stones, who was the NCO of the watch from 1 to 3 a.m. Acting Sergeant Staff gave evidence that Stones had relieved him in the normal way as NCO of the watch at 1 a.m. Further important evidence came from Pte Pinkney, who had just come off guard duty at 2 a.m. and was in the company office when Stones arrived to give warning that 'the Huns were in King crater'. He said that Lt Howes ordered the men to get bombs and to follow him into Ghost Avenue. Pinkney told the court: 'Accused wanted to warn the HQ cook. He asked me if I would show him the way to Father's Footpath [a communication trench] 'where the cooks were. When we got to HQ we looked in two dug-outs but could not find the cook.' He went on: 'When we were coming out, accused took ill. He seemed to have lost the use of his legs. He sat down for a good while and tried several times to get up.' Stones then asked Pinkney to go with him to find the doctor and they went along the trench until they were stopped at the junction of Bogey and Wednesday Avenues, at the rear of the trench system, by the battle police, who ordered them back up the line. Pinkney said: 'After staying there a good while accused came back with me. He tried two or three times to get back to the company office but could not manage it. After we got a little way past Father's Footpath he seemed to go off all again, but could not find the use of his legs.' Pinkney then took Stones into a dugout in Father's Footpath, covered him up and reported to the company office where he was. Pinkney did not remember whether or not Stones had his rifle with him. Cross-examined by the court, Pinkney stated: 'When I first saw accused he came running. He seemed properly put about. He seemed excited. There didn't seem to be anything the matter with his legs then.'

The next witness was Sgt Foster, who had mounted a regimental police battle post at the junction of Bogey and Wednesday Avenues to 'stop unauthorised people coming down the line'. These Battle Police were not Military Police 'redcaps', but men from the front line battalion posted to control movement of troops into and out of the front line. At 2.30 a.m. he had halted Pinkney and Stones (who was behind Pinkney) and asked Stones what they were doing. Foster said of Stones:

He was in a very exhausted condition and trembling. He said that he had been out on patrol with Lt Mundy and they had met four or five Germans. The enemy shot Lt Mundy who ordered accused to run and save his life. I noticed accused had no rifle or bayonet. I questioned him as to where they were. He said that the Germans were chasing him down the trench and he dropped his rifle and bayonet crossways across the trench. I ordered him to go up the line at once. He asked for permission to smoke and have a rest. I ordered him up the line, he hesitated but then he went.

In the war diary of the 35th Division it says that Stones was stopped by the battle police, and the diarist wrote: 'The Police report him in a pitiable ["terrible" has been deleted] state of terror.'[24]

Under cross-examination, Sgt Foster stated: 'I am certain that accused said he was "out on patrol" with Mr Mundy. Accused seemed as if he had been running. He was afraid. He could hardly walk, he seemed thoroughly done up.'

The defence then handed in a statement from the battalion medical officer, which said that Stones had reported with rheumatic pains in his legs on two occasions. Stones's defending officer then made a statement to the court that there was no evidence that the accused had shamefully cast away his arms in the presence of the enemy, and that only one witness, whose evidence was not corroborated, had said that he saw Stones without his rifle. (The *Manual of Military Law*, however, is clear on this point: 'Generally speaking, it is legally open to a court to convict an accused person upon the evidence of one credible witness …'[25]) He said that no evidence had been presented that Stones had run away from the line; he had gone to HQ to raise the alarm and this was within his duties and did not constitute running away. The court closed to consider this defence submission but declined to accept it and the case continued, with Stones giving his evidence.

L Sgt Stones described what had happened on patrol:

There was a shot, Mr Mundy fell, 'My God, I'm shot. For God's sake sergeant go for help and tell Mr Howes.' I did so. I came to a dug-out before I got to company HQ and I gave the alarm there also.

He described Mr Howes leading out his bombers and went on: 'I did not see the officers' cook.' Stones told the court that Pte Pinkney had been the last man out after Lt Howes and that he asked the former where the cooks were. He said they had searched for the cooks, but when they got to the end of

Father's Footpath his legs had given way, so he said to Pinkney: 'I wonder if the doctor has anything to nourish us up and take the pain away from my leg.' They then went further back from the front line in the direction of Roclincourt and ran into Sgt Foster's battle post. Stones then described how, after being ordered back by the sergeant, he could not walk properly and had to hold onto the sides of the trench. He described how his legs gave way as they reached Father's Footpath and Pinkney had to help him up. He told the court that he had then stayed in his dugout until about 3 p.m. when he tried to go on duty, but that his legs gave way again at stand-to at about 4.15 p.m. After that he was excused further duties and when relieved had trouble walking back to his billet, and had reported sick the next day.

Stones then underwent a lengthy cross-examination. He described in more detail what had happened in King Crater: 'We were patrolling the trench. The shot that hit Lt Mundy was from the enemy. When I saw them I had rifle and bayonet. I had the bayonet but not the rifle when I got to the junction of Bogey and Wednesday Avenues.' He said that he had tried to run back to company HQ to raise the alarm but couldn't, as his leg was stiff. He said: 'I wanted to warn the cook because the enemy could get round to the right of the crater – I thought they might get the company HQ. There was a sentry group posted on the right of the crater. So far as I knew it was still there.' This is a very important piece of evidence as it indicates that Stones did not know of the stampede from the sentry posts and therefore expected the other sentries still to be in place, protecting the front line.

Re-examined by his own defending officer, he said: 'As I turned to go, the Huns were stepping over Mr Mundy. I put my rifle across the trench so as to stop them from getting across at me so that I could get a lead of them to warn the men.' He added that on the 26th when in his dugout, he was in severe pain and couldn't lift up his head, but when an NCO was needed for the 3 to 5 p.m. duty he volunteered. He further explained his actions in the crater: 'I saw four or five Germans … my rifle was loaded. I didn't fire because the safety catch was on and the cover over the breech. My bayonet was not fixed. … I had the breech cover on when on patrol because I never had any orders to take it off. I cannot say how long it would have taken me to take it off.' Asked why he wanted to find the cook, Stones replied: '… the company was weak and I wanted to get all the men I could. It didn't occur to me to send Pinkney by himself because I was properly upset.'

CSM Holroyd gave evidence in Stones's defence: 'From the time of the raid until we came out Sgt Stones had to be excused duty because he was too ill to do it. He was the last man in the company I ever expected to shirk his duty.' The medical officer gave evidence for the defence, saying that he had attended Stones on 29 November, three days after the incident, when he complained of muscular rheumatism. In his opinion the condition was not serious and he had given him embrocation. He said: 'The accused had no temperature', and this statement is underlined in the original court martial transcript and appears to have been considered important, perhaps on the basis that if he were really ill he would have had some physical signs, such as a temperature – which demonstrates how different 1916 medicine was to that practised today.

Capt. Warmington then addressed the court for the defence, pointing out the salient features of the case. Lt Mundy had ordered Stones to get help; he had put his rifle across the trench and at no point had Stones tried to hide, in fact he had reported to company HQ and to his CSM, and his whereabouts had been known at all times. Capt. Warmington ended by saying that the evidence was not strong enough for a conviction and that Stones had been acting under orders from a superior officer.

After the court had considered its finding, but before deciding on sentence, character evidence was produced. His conduct sheet had no entries and showed that Stones had enlisted on 10 March 1915. Lt Howes told the court:

I have known accused for over a year. I have found his character as a soldier at all times excellent. His work in the trenches has always been good not only in getting the men to do the work, but in setting them an example. On the Somme he behaved well. He got his first stripe before leaving England. Accused has been nearly 11 months in France.

The court found L Sgt Willie Stones guilty of shamefully casting away his arms in the presence of the enemy and of leaving the front line and running away, and sentenced him to death. Despite his good character, there was no recommendation to mercy.

Finding and sentence, as always, were passed up the chain of command for the views of the unit commanders. Maj. Greenwall, currently commanding the 19th DLI, was unable to give an opinion on Stones's character but attached a reply from his company commander, 'on whose statements I can thoroughly rely'. His company commander wrote of Stones:

He came out with the Battalion in February as a Lance Corporal showing ability to handle men he was promoted over the heads of senior NCOs in the company. He has done good work in patrols and when in charge of wiring parties. I have personally been out with him in No Man's Land and I always found him keen and bold. In the trenches he never showed the least sign of funk. He has always been in my company and I have therefore had countless opportunities of seeing him under all circumstances I can safely say that he was the last man I would have thought capable of any cowardly action. He has been in a very poor state of health recently.

This last sentence is marked heavily in the papers.

Lt Col. Dent, the CO of the 19th DLI but now temporarily in command of 106th Brigade, recommended commuting the sentence because of the NCO's previous good record. Both Stones's company and battalion commanders had therefore done everything possible to save him from the firing squad. However, Maj. Gen. Landon, now commanding 35th Division, wrote: 'In my opinion there is no reason on which to base a recommendation that the sentence should be commuted.' Lt Gen. Haldane of VI Corps and Gen. Edmund Allenby, commanding Third Army, endorsed this view.

The Stones case raises many questions and chief among them has to be whether this man was accorded the basic right of English – criminal and military – law: of being innocent until proven guilty. It is impossible to tell whether Willie Stones dropped his rifle and ran in terror from the Germans, or whether he jammed his rifle across a narrow part of the trench to slow down pursuit. Given his previous good record, and the comments of his senior NCO and officers, he might have expected to be given the benefit of the doubt. The burden of proof was on the prosecution, to demonstrate that the rifle had been 'shamefully cast away in the face of the enemy', and this they arguably did not do. 'Shamefully' in this context has a specific meaning under the Army Act, explained in the *Manual of Military Law*:

> The particulars of the charge must show the circumstances which make the act in a military sense shameful. The word 'shamefully' is held to mean a positive and disgraceful dereliction of duty and not merely through negligence or misapprehension or error of judgement.[26]

However, what is often overlooked is that there was more to the charge than just this since it also included the much more serious allegation 'and left the front line and ran away'. This is almost identical to the specimen charge in the *Manual of Military Law*: '… in that he … when on outlying picquet, and attacked by the enemy, shamefully cast away his rifle, left his picquet and ran away'.[27] Stones's orders from the dying Mundy appear to have been 'Go for help and tell Mr Howes', which he did. Had he remained at company HQ or returned to the front line he would almost certainly not have been charged. However, it was demonstrated in court that Stones had not only left the front line but had then gone back some considerable distance before being stopped by the battle police and at a time when he was NCO of the watch and should have been in the front line. It is this fact which probably led to his death.

The charge appears to have been framed exceedingly carefully and it is probable that legal advice was sought from the DJAG. If he had been charged with cowardice the charge might not have stood up to investigation and he could not be charged with quitting post, as he had not been in a post to quit. It is almost possible to hear the questions being asked: 'Can we do this fellow for cowardice?' 'I think not, difficult to prove.' 'Well, did he have his rifle when he was stopped?' 'No.' 'Well what did he do with it? Let's ask the DJAG if we can charge him with casting away his arms then.' Stones was the only soldier on the Western Front to be charged with this offence, the only other case in the First World War being that of a West African soldier, under very different circumstances.

Stones seems to have been tried less for the offence in the charge but more as an NCO who appeared to be frightened and who ran away. Several people said that he was shaken and looked upset and that seems to have been equated to fear and thence to cowardice. But this was not the charge against him. Stones was not to know that after Lt Mundy had been shot there was wholesale panic in the front line, and that all the other sentries had bolted. The feeling is left that Stones was shot for several reasons – that he left his dying officer and did not return with help, that he did not go back to the front line having raised the alarm, and thirdly that he was stopped by the battle police a long way behind the front line (the junction of Wednesday and Bogey Avenues is over three-quarters of a kilometre from the front line). So far as the army was concerned, Sgt Stones, the senior NCO responsible for the sentries and pickets in the front line, had run away from his place of duty whilst under attack by the enemy.

The question may be asked as to why a relatively experienced NCO patrolling in a 'hot' area, knowing that a raid was imminent, had the breech cover on his rifle. Stones said under cross-examination that he had not been ordered to remove the cover, which at first sight appears a curious omission when moving around front line trenches in the dark. However, Stones and Mundy were on a routine patrol in a muddy trench on a November night with no reason to suspect any German activity. The main concern would have been to keep the rifle dry and the bolt free from mud. Equally, it would seem that Mundy did not have his revolver drawn, reinforcing the view that this was a simple routine patrol.

In August 2000 the Service Record for Sgt Willie Stones became available.[28] These show that this 5 feet 2 inch, 23-year-old miner had enlisted at West Hartlepool in March 1915. Only a few weeks later Mrs Stones wrote to the Infantry Records Office at York, concerned that her allotment of 21/- shillings a week had been cut to only 17/6 for herself and two children, after the death of the couple's 2-year-old daughter. Already, it seems, the family was suffering hardship through Stones's decision to serve his country. After his death the Ministry of Pensions wrote to the York records office to inform them that Mrs Stones was not entitled to a pension, and that she should be informed of this. Isabel Stones was now left with two children and no means of providing for them or herself. A few months later, in October 1917, she married a civilian, Arthur Jones. After the war, in September 1919, the pension arrangements were reviewed, and Mrs Stones (now Mrs Jones) was awarded a remarriage gratuity of £5 and a pension of 6/8 for one of her children (the latter to increase to 10/-). Sgt Stones's other dependent child was awarded a pension of 5/- a week, rising to 10/- from 3 September 1919.

On the same day as Stones, L Cpl Hopkinson was also tried, found guilty of quitting his post and sentenced to death. He had been one of the men at sentry post 'B' who, on seeing the German attackers after Mundy had been shot, had fled. It was possibly L Cpl Hopkinson and Pte Harding whom the men at post 'C' heard, leading to the panic at that post. It is known from the divisional war diary that Hopkinson was stopped by the battle police at about the same spot where Stones was stopped, and that he was also without his rifle.[29] This NCO was reprieved and his sentence commuted to fifteen years' penal servitude. The details of his trial have not survived, leaving the question as to why this NCO, on that night of panic, escaped with his life, whilst all the other NCOs who were convicted suffered the death penalty.

Other trials were to follow that of L Sgt Stones. Six of the men who had been at post 'C', to the south of King Crater, faced a court martial on 28 December 1916 on a charge of quitting their post. On sentry had been Pte Ritchie and Pte Spence, while L Cpl Goggins, L Cpl McDonald, Pte Davies, Pte Forrest and Pte Dowsey had taken cover in a dugout about 20 yards from the sentry group. When the alarm was raised by Hopkinson and Harding, fleeing from 'B' post, all of these men except Pte Spence, who gave evidence for the prosecution, left the front line. At their trial Capt. Warmington again appeared as counsel.[30]

The evidence that emerged was consistent with events described by the divisional war diary account of events that night, except that this said that McDonald had been one of the sentry group, whereas he stated that he was in the dugout.[31] CSM Austin told the court that on 23 November 1916 Cpl Wilson, who was one of the NCOs detailed for duty, had fallen sick and been replaced by L Cpl McDonald. He told the court that Pte Todd had also been one of the sentry group and had since been wounded, but this name does not appear in the war diary. The CSM said that two men should have been on the fire step and the others in the dugout taking shelter from the bombardment. He said that he would have expected there to be a sergeant and a corporal on the fire step, although no sergeant is mentioned as being at the post. He added that the post was about 25 yards to the right of the crater and the dugout was about 20 yards from the post.

The next witness was Second Lt Bryce of 17th Battalion, Royal Scots. This officer had been in command of the 'G' work, which was about 200 yards behind the front line, and had posted a sentry in Cecil Avenue in front of the 'G' work. At about 2.15 a.m. this sentry shouted that two NCOs and four men of the Durhams were at his post and the officer went outside where he saw that the NCOs had no rifles. When questioned it appeared that some of the men thought that their NCOs were leading them out of the line. The officer took their names but could only remember the two NCOs and Ptes Dowsey, Forrest and Davies. He was certain that the soldiers in the court were the same men. He said: 'All the men were in a state of excitement' but under cross-examination admitted that 'I should expect men to be in a state of excitement after being bombarded for three days by trench mortars.' He gave these men no instructions and no bombs and they all waited on the fire step, but he mentioned that he had twice found Goggins in a little bomb shelter. Pte Kidd, who was the Royal Scots sentry, said: 'The men came down the trench at a fair pace, they were not running.'

The final prosecution witness was Pte Spence, who was a member of the 'C' sentry post. His name had not appeared on the summary of evidence, but the trial transcript notes that the accuseds' counsel did not object to his evidence. Spence said that he had been on sentry duty with Pte Ritchie from midnight to 2 a.m. Someone had come along the trench and after that he saw no more of his sentry group until they all came back together half an hour later. At one point he had been knocked over by a trench mortar and when he got up he saw the Germans in the trench, so went into the next bay to tell the West Yorkshires, who were on the right.

All of the accused men gave evidence in their defence. L Cpl McDonald, who had not been on sentry at the time (and was unfortunate to have been a member of the sentry group at all, standing in for the sick Cpl Wilson), was standing-to in the sentries' dugout when he heard someone running down the trench, shouting: 'Run for your lives, the Hun are on top of you.' He then went towards the front line but saw no one, so went down Cecil Avenue to the 'G' work to get bombs. He said that he was last out of the dugout and followed the other men 'to see where they were going'. Cross-examined, he admitted that he knew that his company HQ was not at 'G' work and was not sure why he went there.

L Cpl Goggins was at the top of the dugout steps when he heard men rushing about, and hearing this told the others in the dugout to stand-to. He heard a shout of 'Run for your lives, the Hun are on top of you!' and had the impression that the front line had been taken and the Germans were between them and the front line. His evidence is then a little confused. He said that he was in charge of the group but was knocked down by the people rushing out (but does not say from where) and then went to warn the men in the dugout. He said: 'I did not go to the front line to see if my sentries were there because so many people had gone past' (this section is heavily marked in the trial transcript). He said he had given no orders for the men to leave the dugout, that his sole object in going to the 'G' work was to get bombs and that when he was found in the bomb shelter he was trying to get bombs for a counter-attack.

Pte Forrest added little. He had also heard the shout telling them to run, had followed the others to 'G' work, and said that he had his rifle when he arrived there. Pte Ritchie explained that he had been on sentry with Spence when someone shouted 'The Huns are in the front line – run for your lives.' When he looked, Spence had disappeared so he followed the others. He said that he had rifle and bayonet with him when he got to 'G' work. Pte Dowsey told the court that he had been in the dugout and when he came out he could see nothing because it was so dark. He tried to block the trench with the trapdoor of the dugout but then heard L Cpl McDonald coming. He got the impression that the front line was occupied by Germans, so the best idea seemed to be for them all to go into the reserve trench. He also had all his equipment with him when stopped by the sentry. Under cross-examination he said: 'I was in a queer state owing to being overworked.'

Pte Davies was on the stairs when he heard men rushing past and heard them shout. He said: 'I fell down the stairs with the shock.' He had gone towards the 'G' work where he met Goggins and Ritchie; he had all his equipment with him. He told the court:

I did not see the other men leave the dug-out, there was a candle in the dug-out. There were three men and a sergeant and an officer in the dug-out. The sergeant and the officer were both wounded. I did not know which way I was going. For all I knew I might have been going towards the front line. I lost my head altogether.

Capt. Warmington addressed the court on behalf of the six men. He said that as there was a raid planned for that night the front line was very thinly held, and these men knew this and were therefore right to go to the reserve line for help. He said: 'All their statements agree, all have given evidence on oath. Confinement they have already had and this charge is sufficient penalty for any unintentional mistakes they may have made.'

After the court had considered its verdict, the character evidence was given. This showed that all of the men were original Bantams, five having joined in the first week of March 1915, and Dowsey in July 1915. Four of the men were miners, McDonald a labourer and Forrest a chimney sweep. They all had a clean record except for Goggins, who had been a sergeant in the UK and lost his stripes for being absent from camp when under orders for active service.

All the men were found guilty and sentenced to death, although Pte Ritchie was recommended to mercy, 'it appearing to the Court that he is a person of low mental development and that he has been rejected by the ADMS on account of his nerves'.

Writing after sentence, Lt Oliver, their company commander, said their general conduct was good and they had never given any trouble. Although none had done anything special, all were quite up to the average and had done everything asked of them. He wrote that Goggins and Ritchie appeared to suffer from nerves but not enough to give concern in the trenches, although Ritchie had recently been rejected by the ADMS on account of his nerves. This latter sentence was a reference to the fact that between 8 and 21 December 1916 the men of the Bantam battalions had been inspected as to their fitness for infantry service, a total of no fewer than 2,784 men being weeded out by this process as being unfit. This weeding out had been proposed in August while the division was still on the Somme, but had been delayed.[32] The men under trial had all been inspected. Pte Ritchie had been rejected on medical grounds. Goggins, McDonald, Davies, Forrest and Dowsey had all been rejected as unfit, owing to their physique, being unable to carry out all the normal duties of an infantry soldier. Forrest and McDonald had been recommended for a labour battalion and the others for tunnelling companies (they were all miners). These were all original Bantams who had met the necessary standards of fitness for recruitment and yet were now rejected – the Bantam experiment was about to end.

Although the court martial had been convened by Lt Col. Dent, temporarily in charge of the brigade but normally the CO of the 19th DLI, by 1 January Brig. Gen. O'Donnell was back in command of 106th Brigade and he wrote: 'In each case the men have been found guilty of the charge and have been sentenced to "death". I am doubtful, however, if the evidence is sufficient for a conviction.' This opinion cannot have been shared by the DJAG, who would have inspected the papers before sentence was confirmed by the Commander-in-Chief. He continued: 'The battalion however has not done well in the fighting line. They suffered somewhat severely from heavy shelling while in the Somme fighting in July and were very shaky in the advanced trenches before Guillemont in August.' He finished: 'I am reluctantly compelled to recommend that should the finding be confirmed the sentence should be carried out for the purpose of example and to show that cowardice in the presence of the enemy will not be tolerated in the British Army.'

At this stage of the war the Bantam Division was commanded by Maj. Gen. Landon, who had taken over from Maj. Gen. Pinney, the original commander, in September. He wrote:

> The two NCOs and four privates have been found guilty of a most serious crime. They appear to all be equally culpable as soldiers but the NCOs must be held as having especially failed in their soldierly duties, and responsibilities. There are, however, some 4000 men in the Division of whom 334 are in the Durham L.I. who are recommended for transfer as being unsuitable mentally and physically for Infantry Soldiers and it is probable that any of them would have behaved similarly under the circumstances described in the proceedings of the Court Martial. In view of the mental and physical degeneracy of these men I consider that although the sentence passed on all six is a proper one, the extreme penalty might be carried out in the case of the two NCOs only and the sentence of the four privates be commuted to a long term of penal servitude, and this I recommend.

These men had all been on duty at sentry post 'C' and all told the same story of three or four men rushing past shouting 'Run for your lives, the Hun are upon us', or something similar. The running men were probably L Cpl Hopkinson and Pte Harding from 'B' post, who could be said to have initiated the panic. The two NCOs who were executed had gone about 200 yards from their front line post to 'G' work, and yet were shot, whilst the NCO from 'B' post, stopped by the battle police well behind the lines, had his sentence commuted. This inevitably leads to speculation. Could it perhaps be that Goggins and McDonald had been rejected by the corps commander as unfit, whilst the other NCO whose sentence was reduced had not been rejected?

The sentences on the four privates were commuted to fifteen years' penal servitude, but sentence on L Cpls Goggins and McDonald was confirmed by the Commander-in-Chief on 11 January 1917 and these two men, with L Sgt Stones, were shot at 7.35 a.m., in the snow at Roellecourt, near St Pol, on 18 January 1917.

A further eighteen men of the same battalion were tried on 30 December 1916 for cowardice, almost certainly relating to incidents on the same night, and were sentenced to death. The records of these trials have not survived and we can only speculate as to whether these were men involved in the unsuccessful raid on the German trenches or in another incident. Later these men's sentences, including that of L Cpl Dempsey, were reduced to ten years' penal servitude, this NCO escaping the fate of Goggins and McDonald. One of these men was Pte J. S. Dunn, whose records provide some details [33] – he was charged with cowardice relating to the raid, 'in that he did not enter the enemy's trenches as ordered'. This soldier continued to serve in the infantry, but deserted on 18 November 1918, rejoining his unit on 26 August 1919. He was tried for desertion and sentenced to detention, whereupon his suspended sentence of ten years' penal servitude was put into execution after being reduced to two years' imprisonment with hard labour. He was finally discharged from the service in April 1920.

There were also higher-level casualties of this incident. Lt Col. Bertie Dent, commanding the 19th DLI on the night of 26 November, had been a major in the regular army in 1914, and could have expected rapid promotion as the army expanded during the war. He had taken over command of the 1/7th West Riding regiment in December 1915 and in May 1916 had been given temporary promotion to brigadier general and put in command of 143rd Brigade. However, he seems to have failed at this level and returned to command the 19th DLI at his substantive rank of lieutenant colonel. After the events of November 1916 he was transferred to take command of 35th Division Depot Battalion, later becoming CO of the 16th Cheshires (also originally a Bantam battalion). He did not reach substantive rank of colonel until 1919 and eventually retired from the army in 1927, only then being given the rank of 'Hon. Brigadier General'. The failures of the 19th DLI may have reflected poor command as well as failings amongst the men themselves.

The events of the night of 26–27 November 1916 were a classic example of the chaos and confusion of war. Without experienced officers or NCOs, and lacking confidence in their own ability, there seems little doubt that the men of at least one company in 19th DLI's front line trenches panicked and fled in the dark. For the army this was unacceptable; scapegoats had to be found and an example made. Willie Stones, the sergeant of the guard, and the two corporals in charge of the advanced post and dugout, paid the price. It was intended to be a harsh example to the rest of the army. Whether Sgt Stones indeed 'shamefully cast away his rifle and ran away' that night at Roclincourt we shall never know. Doubts remain. Professor Gerry Rubin, expert on military law at the University of Kent, believes that the prosecution did not prove their case and that Stones's conviction is unreliable.[34] The feeling on reading the trial documents is that whatever the truth about Stones's rifle, the court regarded his guilt as proven by the fact that he, the NCO of the watch, was stopped in a communication trench some 700 metres behind the front line.

Willie Stones's great-nephew, the late Tom Stones, was angry about how his great-uncle was treated by the army, and demanded his uncle's medals, which were not awarded because of his execution. Stones was not unique in this, as none of the executed men's families received their medals after the war, and medals were withheld from other men for a variety of reasons. It may seem that there was an intrinsic flaw in a system which allowed Pte Hopkinson, and others equally culpable, who were sentenced to death but reprieved, to receive their medals whilst those who served their sentence and were shot were not entitled to any recognition of their previous good service to their country.

We will probably now never know the full truth about the real events of that dark night in the trenches. In their own way Sgt Stones, Cpl Goggins and Cpl McDonald were every bit as much casualties of the Great War as any of their comrades shot or blown up by enemy action, and it may be kindest to view them too as victims of war and certainly not as cowards who ran away in the dark.

CHAPTER 14

COWARDICE – THE EARLY YEARS

A coward, when he is taught to believe that if he ... abandons his colours
he will be punished by death, will take his chance against any enemy.

GEORGE WASHINGTON, 1776

If Great War executions are mentioned in a general group, the immediate response is: 'Oh, the men shot for cowardice', implying that the perception is that the majority of executions took place for this offence. In fact, only eighteen men, sixteen on the Western Front, were shot for this particular military crime, compared with 266 for desertion. Whilst trials for desertion showed a degree of consistency during the war, the trials for cowardice were much more sporadic. Cowardice is a much less clear-cut crime than desertion: evidence of a long absence, or being at a distance behind the lines or being found in civilian clothes are all reasonable proof of a soldier's intention deliberately to absent himself from the fighting; cowardice is harder to substantiate. It could be said that the difference is that desertion is an objective assessment, whilst cowardice is a subjective accusation and harder to prove. To further complicate the issue, most experienced soldiers' views of cowardice are ambivalent. For example, Rowland Fielding wrote in 1919:

> Though I have never actually come across it, I seem to have been reading all through the war of soldiers being shot for so-called cowardice, and I would like to say to you that I disapprove in almost every case of this method of dealing with a trouble which is generally the result of nervous collapse, and may be uncontrollable. The best of men have their ups and downs in war, as in peace. I will go further and say there are men who are capable of the bravest actions, and yet whose nerve may break down under certain conditions of strain, especially when they have been kept too long in the battle line. It may be argued that it is as reasonable to shoot one man for a temporary lapse as it is to give another a V.C. for a momentary heroic impulse. Perhaps it is. Both alternatives are open to

criticism. The true test of a soldier is his average behaviour under the tearing stress of war during a long period. It is the same in all walks of life. Of course, as you know, the justification for these shootings is believed to be that they deter other soldiers from running away. Surely that is a poor reason to give in our army! [1]

In reviewing the cases of the men shot for cowardice some features become apparent. In many cases the charge of cowardice actually arose out of a refusal to obey a direct order, such as refusing to leave a dugout to go on patrol; indeed, 'refusal to obey a lawful command' is often framed as the alternative charge. Although few of the soldiers claimed shell shock as a defence in the cases of desertion, some of the men executed for cowardice appear to have been suffering from battle fatigue. The earlier executions for cowardice (1914 to 1916) differ from the later ones in that the men executed for cowardice early in the war could equally well have been charged with desertion, with intent to avoid a specific duty. Later in the war this type of offence was dealt with as desertion, and the framing of cowardice charges appears to shift towards men who specifically refused to take part in some dangerous activity.

Amongst the executions for cowardice there are several cases that cause concern. Even by the legal and moral standards of the day some of these men appear to have been treated harshly.

The time-line and pattern of executions for cowardice during the war are also interesting. The number of death sentences awarded for this offence is fairly steady from the start of 1915 through to late 1916, when the numbers rise suddenly as a result of the conviction and sentencing to death of eighteen members of the 19th Battalion, Durham Light Infantry after the debacle at Roclincourt (see Chapter 13). However, the proportion of death sentences carried out varied during the war, notably in the last half of 1916 when nine British soldiers were executed, out of a total of fifteen throughout the war. The implications are that not only were the men in the trenches under huge strain from the battle of the Somme, but there was a growing unease, amounting to phobia, amongst the commanders ever fearful of unit breakdowns or even mass disobedience.

The first man executed for cowardice was George Ward, whose case was discussed earlier, with the other early executions in the BEF. After his execution no further death sentences were carried out for cowardice until mid 1915, when Pte Oliver Hodgetts of the 1st Worcesters was the first of three cases, being shot in June. [2] Hodgetts was a pre-war regular, whose battalion had been in Cairo when war broke out.[3] They arrived in France on 6 November and went into action almost immediately, and by the end of the year had lost forty-two men killed, a small number compared with the original BEF regular battalions, who had suffered 600 to 700 casualties.[4] In mid January 19-year-old Hodgetts went absent when his battalion was preparing to march to the trenches, and was given three days' FP No. 1. This did not deter him from trying to go absent a second time, and on 17 February 1915 he deserted again. Brought back to his unit, he was tried by FGCM. The records of that trial have not survived, but Hodgetts was given a sentence of ninety days' FP No. 1, an exemplary sentence by the standards of the old regular army.

Less than a month into his sentence, the 1st Worcesters were involved in the battle of Neuve Chapelle. Two days into the fighting Hodgetts decided that he had seen enough of war and made his way to the rear. He was fortunate not to be charged with desertion, but the key witnesses had been killed in the battle and his CO charged him with the lesser offence of leaving the firing line without permission and gave him a further twenty-eight days' FP No. 1.

The 1st Worcesters did not have much of a rest, as on 9 May they took part in the battle of Aubers Ridge. At 4 a.m. the battalion moved into the assembly trenches and all the men were present. When the roll was called again at 9 a.m. Hodgetts was missing. The unit were heavily engaged in the battle and suffered 235 casualties before they left the assembly trenches.[5] Fleeting glimpses were seen of Hodgetts over the next few days. On 10 May he was seen a little way behind the firing line, claiming that he was going to get attention for a bad ankle. The following day he was seen 'loitering about' in the rear when he said that he had lost his company. On 13 May he reported himself to his CSM in billets at Laventie, saying that he had sprained his ankle. Knowing Hodgetts's previous record, Sgt Major Morgan put him under arrest and arranged for him to be seen by the battalion medical officer.

On 22 May Hodgetts was tried by FGCM for 'misbehaving before the enemy in such a way as to show cowardice'. Unusually, two members of the court martial panel, Maj. Arden and Lt Conybeare, were officers from his own battalion. Despite his previous experience of a court martial, Hodgetts chose not to be represented at his trial. Three witnesses give evidence that he had not been in the firing line when he should have been, and told of the various sightings of him. The battalion MO also reported that he examined Hodgetts on the 13th and found no sign of an ankle injury. The defendant chose not give evidence on his own behalf or call any witnesses, although he did make a statement that whilst moving to the breastwork at the double he tripped and hurt his ankle, remaining where he fell all day. He claimed that he had then gone to the rear to look for the doctor but had not been able to find him. Hodgetts added: 'There was a lot of shell fire going on and I was quite dazed and not aware of what I was doing.'

Hodgetts was found guilty and sentenced to death; there was no recommendation to mercy. After the trial, as part of the post-trial confirmation process his CO, Lt Col. Grogan, wrote:

> The character of Pte Hodgetts from a general point of view is not good.
> From a fighting point of view he is quite worthless. This is the 3rd
> attempt he has made to get away from his unit. During the action at
> Neuve Chapelle he absented himself in the heat of the fight. When
> apprehended I spoke to him pointing out the serious nature of his offence
> and how he ought to be very grateful that owing to the death of various
> witnesses he was not to be tried by a FGCM and I strongly ordered him to
> pull himself together. In my opinion on this last occasion at Rue Petillon
> he deliberately absented himself with the sole motive of saving his own
> skin and this in spite of the fact in view of his previous records an attempt
> was made to keep a watch on him. Thus his previous conduct has been
> bad, he has once already been convicted of desertion on active service by
> FGCM. He has been with the Expeditionary Force for 5 months.
> Furthermore this is not an isolated case, and for the sake of an example
> and of acting as a deterrent in the future, I would respectfully submit that
> it would be a pity if a lenient view of this military crime in this case
> prevailed.

The other commanders in the chain of confirmation all recommended execution. Although the divisional commander made the point that the sentence should be carried out as a deterrent and a warning to others, Hodgetts appears to have been shot primarily as an incorrigible deserter rather than as an example and, as the CO's remarks make clear, was effectively beyond the patience of even the most tolerant regimental family.

Oliver Hodgetts was a pre-war soldier who once exposed to war seems to have discovered that soldiering was not for him. He was tried by the standards of the pre-war British Army and in the absence of a tenable defence was sentenced to death. A telling point at the court martial was that his battalion was in action continuously throughout 9, 10 and 11 May and took heavy casualties. Hodgetts was not with his unit, where he should have been, and was unequivocally, by the standards of the time, a coward evading his duty while his comrades risked their lives. He had been given two previous chances and this was one offence too many. This is a case where the army is seen to demonstrate its pre-war standards of discipline, yet at the same time these are tempered by well-meaning but ineffectual attempts to turn a man into a fighting soldier.

It is probable that later in the war Hodgetts would have been tried for desertion rather than cowardice, as he was absent for some days and clearly intended to avoid a specific, dangerous duty. However, early in the war the charge of desertion seems to have been used in cases where men either were absent for some time, or were found in the rear, or in civilian clothes when intention to desert permanently could be shown. The case of the incorrigible deserter Oliver Hodgetts is, therefore, different to the 1916 cowardice cases. There are many similarities between this case and that of Pte Herbert Chase, who was to be executed a few days later.

Chase was also a regular soldier, serving with the 2nd Battalion of the Lancashire Fusiliers, who formed part of the original BEF, landing on 22 August 1914. The newly formed 4th Division arrived too late to take part in the battle of Mons, but did take part in the rearguard action at Le Câteau on 26 August, where they formed the left flank of the defence. At this point Pte Chase seems to have decided that he too had seen enough of war and deserted. He managed to avoid detection for some time and was not recaptured until October 1914, but managed to escape and remained at liberty until December, when he was arrested and faced an FGCM.[6] Despite his three months on the run he was charged with absence without leave and escaping, rather than desertion. The papers of this first court martial have not survived and we can only speculate at the reasons for the lesser charge.

Chase was found guilty and sentenced to three years' imprisonment, later commuted to two years. He served the first few months of his sentence in the military prison at Rouen, but on 6 May 1915 was released under the new Suspension of Sentences Act. This Act had been introduced in 1915 as a means of ensuring that being sent to prison was not an alternative to fighting in the trenches, and one can imagine that many of the men released from prison – however harsh this may have been – were less than enthusiastic about returning to the perils and insecurities of the front line.

Less than two weeks after his release Chase went into action with his battalion at Shell Trap Farm in the Ypres Salient. On the morning of 24 May 1915 he was asleep in his trench when he heard the cry: 'Gas!' This new

German terror weapon had first been used not far from the Lancashires' current position on 22 April and British front line troops were understandably very nervous of this new weapon, so the alarm 'GAS!' tended to be shouted on the faintest suspicion.

About an hour after this alarm, the battalion was ordered to reinforce the front line and Chase was found to be missing. As a result he found himself facing his second court martial in less than six months. His trial was not one that inspires confidence in the military legal process, even given the exigencies of the battlefield in spring 1915. No field officer was available to serve as president so two captains and a lieutenant formed the court martial panel. Three witnesses gave evidence for the prosecution: the private who had woken Chase at 3 a.m., the lance corporal who found him missing at 4 a.m. and an RAMC private who reported that he had found Chase in a dazed and exhausted condition by the side of the road to Vlamertinghe at 4.30 a.m.

Chase gave in a written statement in his defence, saying that he and others had been compelled to leave the trench on account of gas used by the enemy. On oath, he told the court that he remembered being woken at about 3 a.m. but did not remember anything else until he found himself in hospital and said that he had not felt well the previous evening and had told Pte Davis this – a fact confirmed by this soldier's testimony to the court. Despite these elements of doubt the court found Pte Chase guilty of cowardice and sentenced him to death.

After the trial, as the sentence went up the chain of command for confirmation, irregularities crept in. Maj. Gen. H. Wilson, GOC 4th Division, wrote:

(1) It will be observed in the Proceedings of No 2779 Pte Chase 2nd Lancashire Fusiliers that no evidence was called by the Prosecution to prove the condition of Pte Chase when found at Vlamertinghe 'in a dazed and exhausted condition'

(2) Enquiries have been made and the following facts elucidated: –
a. Pte Chase went to the 12th Field Ambulance Dressing Station where he was recognised by Sgt Smith RAMC and No 6895 Pte AT White (v. statement marked A and B attached)
b. A number of men were examined by Capt Stewart RAMC, and found free from gas poisoning and sent from the Dressing Station of No 12 Field Ambulance to 'the farm occupied by Capt Shelley', the collecting post for stragglers (v. statement marked C attached)

(3) As the Court had completed the Proceedings and had recorded their finding and sentence when the Proceedings reached this office, no action has been taken in the direction of reassembling the Court.

These three statements from RAMC personnel are attached to the proceedings. This evidence was not produced at the trial, and its subsequent introduction was quite irregular. Statement 'A' by Sgt Smith of the RAMC says that he saw Chase at No. 12 Field Ambulance dressing station on 24 May, and that 'he did not appear to be very sick and I thought that there was very little wrong with him'. Pte Whittle of the RAMC made a similar statement, marked 'B' in the papers; Smith and Whittle had both worked with Chase previously, so recognized him. Statement 'C' was made by the MO commanding No. 12 FA dressing station, and says: 'On Monday 24th May a large number of men came to the dressing station at No. 12 F.A. saying that they had been gassed. I examined these cases and a proportion were found either by myself or another M.O. to be free from any signs of gas poisoning.' This doctor does not specifically mention that Chase was one of these men. Chase appears to be just one of many soldiers who had fled the front lines in fear of gas.

During the confirmation process the commander of 12th Infantry Brigade wrote: '… I am very strongly of the opinion that the sentence should be carried out without delay … I feel that if immediate examples are not made of men who quit their trenches the fighting quality of the Brigade will deteriorate.' Maj. Gen. Edmund Allenby, GOC V. Corps, commented: 'I doubt whether the evidence substantiates the charge. If it does, however, I recommend that the sentence be carried out.'

Gen. Sir Herbert Plumer, commanding Second Army, thought that the evidence did substantiate the charge and that the case deserved the extreme penalty, but he also wrote:

But it is well-known that there were others equally guilty who have not been arrested. After the warning by the Commander-in-Chief it is well-known that being affected by guns will not be sufficient as any excuse and that the extreme penalty will in future probably be carried out. In this case I recommend that the sentence be commuted.

However, it is clear that Plumer was not in full possession of all the facts when this was written, as later he wrote:

Since writing the aforegoing minute of 2nd June it has been brought to my notice that Pte Chase has been tried before for absence from the trenches … if I had known it I should have recommended that the sentence be carried out.

Chase's earlier record effectively condemned him to death.

Herbert Chase was shot at the abbey of St Sixtus in Proven on 12 June.

It has been said that visitors on guided tours to the monastery are shown the place of execution and the bullet marks in the wall,[7] but on a visit in 1997 the authors were told that this was within the enclosed part of the monastery, and not open to view. There is doubt about whether this was really the site of Chase's execution, as the war diary for the A&QMG of 4th Division describes the execution:

12 June 1915 Pte Chase Lancashire Fusiliers executed at San Sixte for cowardice. The confirmation of the sentence was received on June 9th but it took some time to get the firing party and representatives of units back to San Sixte and to prepare a suitable place, a clearing had to be made in a wood, and it was impossible to carry out the execution till today at 4.30 a.m. The sentence was promulgated at 4 p.m. yesterday to give the man a few hours of daylight to write his letters and to make arrangements. A chaplain visited him at 4.15 p.m. yesterday and again at 3.45 a.m. this morning. The execution was carried out without a hitch. Death was instantaneous.[8]

The third and final execution for cowardice on the Western Front in 1915 occurred in July. Hodgetts and Chase had both absented themselves from their place of duty, this being construed as cowardice, whereas Bellamy's case was effectively one of disobedience, which in the face of the enemy constituted cowardice.

Bellamy was a 34-year-old reservist who had joined the army in 1898, and in 1915 was back serving with the 1st Battalion of the King's Royal Rifle Corps (KRRC) in the trenches in front of Cambrin. The charge against him was extremely specific:

The accused No. 3319 Pte W. Bellamy, 1st Bn K.R.R. Corps, a soldier of the Regular forces is charged with: When on active service, misbehaving before the enemy in such a manner as to show cowardice, in that he, at Cambrin, France, on 24th June 1915, after having been ordered by Lance Corporal Kay, of the same battalion, to get up on the parapet in the fire trench and open fire, refused to do so, saying 'I can't get up I am too shaky.'[9]

The area around Cambrin was an unpleasant place to be in 1915. The British and German trenches ran close together, and 'normal wastage' was always high. In addition, both sides were engaged in mining activities, and the front line area resembled a lunar landscape of shell holes, mine craters and the detritus of war. On 24 June 1915 two further mines were exploded and Bellamy's company was ordered to stand-to, but Bellamy refused to leave his dugout.

For this specific act of disobedience, construed as cowardice, Bellamy was tried by FGCM on 2 July 1915; the case was brief, with just two witnesses for the prosecution. The platoon sergeant, Sgt Robertson, had ordered Bellamy to come out of his dugout and to open fire on the Germans after the first mine had exploded. This order was given three times but Bellamy refused to come out. The second witness was L Cpl. Kay, who had ordered his section to open rapid fire on the enemy, but Bellamy did not do so and remained in his dugout.

In his defence Bellamy made a statement alleging that he had suffered from nervous debility in the past and that the least shock upset his nerves. He also said that he had been examined twice in 1913 by doctors, and after the explosion of the first mine his nerves were so shaky that he did not know what he was doing. This is an interesting case as it is the first case of cowardice which raised the possibility of shell shock as a defence.

As in the case of Herbert Chase, there were some irregularities in the court martial, prompting Brig. Gen. Daly, commanding 6th Brigade, to write to the DJAG. He made the points that the evidence was not taken down correctly at the trial, and might appear to have been given by a third person; and that as a medical defence was made the man should be examined by a medical board; and proposed a retrial. His letter ends: 'As the extreme penalty has been awarded I am anxious that the proceedings should, in every particular, be valid.' This sentence demonstrates the degree to which the senior officers were concerned about ensuring that even the hastily convened FGCMs were conducted to the necessary standards.

The DJAG advised that a retrial was unnecessary but that a medical board could be arranged during the confirmation process, if required. This exchange of correspondence provoked a flurry of activity at Corps HQ. Maj. Gen. Landon wrote: 'I am doubtful whether the evidence as recorded is sufficient to legally sustain conviction on a charge of cowardice, but if the conviction can be upheld I recommend that the sentence of the Court be carried out.' Landon also entered into the debate as to how evidence at courts martial should be taken down. In the court martial record there is a copy of a circular issued by Corps HQ in November 1914 giving instructions on how to take down evidence, using the third person.

Unfortunately, in the opinion of his CO, Rifleman Bellamy had a bad character, both in general and as a fighting man. The brigade commander, in his report to Division, said that in his opinion the man should be given a medical board to assess whether there were any medical grounds which could constitute extenuating circumstances, but added: 'The case is in my opinion a very bad one and merits the extreme penalty.' Bellamy was subsequently examined by a medical board of three doctors but they found no mental abnormality and emphasized that in their view he was not suffering from nervous debility. Rifleman Bellamy was shot at 3.39 a.m. at Le Quesnoy on 16 July 1915.

There seems to be little doubt that Bellamy refused to obey an order, and had he been tried for that crime he would have undoubtedly been found guilty. However, the charge of cowardice is less tenable and there is no clear evidence, apart from the fact that he was shaking and refused to place himself in harm's way, that Bellamy actually displayed cowardice. Brig. Gen. Daly wrote to the divisional commander: '... I have ascertained that Rfm. Bellamy bears a bad character as a fighting man, and on a former occasion, left his post without permission', and it may be this statement which led to the soldier being executed. As Bellamy's regimental conduct sheet was not produced at the trial it is not possible to show whether he had been convicted of a previous offence, but such a damning 'back channels' statement emphasizes the army's system of parallel reporting.

These last two courts martial leave an air of unease; in both cases the confirming officers question the adequacy of the evidence, and yet the conviction was allowed to stand. It is easy to say that both men were probably guilty anyway – they probably were, but in neither case was the guilt clearly demonstrated in court. In both cases alternative charges could have been used – Chase quit his post without orders, and Bellamy clearly disobeyed a lawful order – and yet it was the charge of cowardice on which both men were convicted. The evidence available to us strongly suggests that both of these men were shot as much for their previous record as for their current crime.

L Cpl James Holland was the first man to be shot for cowardice in 1916. He was one of the thousands of volunteers who had flocked to the colours in August 1914 and in May 1916 he was serving with the 10th Cheshires on the Arras front, near Mont St Eloi. Holland, along with four privates, had been detailed to hold a position in the outpost line, forward of the front line in no-man's-land. They took up their position on 8 May at 2.30 a.m. and were ordered to remain there for twenty-four hours, having been warned that the position was to be held at all costs. Holland had been told that 'if anything unusual happened a man was to be sent back to report'.[10]

Late in the afternoon Holland went to see the sergeant at the next post, complaining of a severe headache and asking to be relieved, but was told to talk to the officer when he next came round. Shortly after this, confusion reigned at the outpost. Pte Santley was on duty in the post whilst the other three privates dozed nearby. He suddenly saw two men, whom he believed to be French, a few yards away and challenged them but could not understand their reply. In his evidence Santley said: 'I did not fire at him as I was not sure that he was a German.' Perhaps a hardened regular, out since Mons, would have shot first and asked questions later, but the 10th Cheshires was a service battalion of inexperienced Kitchener volunteers. Santley looked round for Holland, but could not see him.

A mass stampede then seems to have occurred. Holland and all four of the privates left their position and made a dash back to the main front line. On the way back, Holland paused to fire off a shot in the direction of the interlopers. The evidence is confused. Santley alleged that he remained at his post and all the others ran, whereas the other men said that all five of them ran back to the main trench system. When they arrived back at company HQ, Capt. Ellerton relieved the post and put all the men under arrest.

In consequence of these events L Cpl Holland was charged with 'misbehaving before the enemy in such a manner as to show cowardice', with the alternative charge of 'leaving his post without orders from his superior officer', and was tried by FGCM on 17 May. The four privates were not charged and gave evidence for the prosecution. The case was a lengthy one, with ten prosecution witnesses. The main evidence was not in dispute: the men should have been in the outpost line but had left their position.

In his defence Holland said that he thought that the whole post had been rushed, and that he heard a shout: 'We're all prisoners.' He said he found himself alone and went back to raise the alarm, stopping to fire off a shot as he went. The other point of note in his defence was that he said he was being treated for piles and suffered violent headaches in consequence, and being medically unfit meant that he had no control over himself when this affair took place.

After the finding two witnesses gave evidence of Holland's good character.

His conduct sheet was produced and described as a 'clean sheet'. Capt. Ellerton, the company commander, described Holland as an efficient NCO and as having a good character.

The court found James Holland guilty of cowardice and sentenced him to death. He was 'strongly recommended to mercy on grounds of ill-health at time of offence and long hours of duty'. Brig. Gen. Heathcote, commanding 7th Brigade, did not support this recommendation and wrote: 'The state of discipline in his battalion is not good and I do not make any recommendation in mitigation of punishment which I recommend should be carried out.' However, GOC 25th Division did not agree, and suggested that sentence be commuted 'on account of Holland's state of health and good character'.

L Cpl James Holland was shot on 30 May 1916; in the few days between trial and execution he must have reflected bitterly that his promotion to lance corporal was to cost him his life.

Holland's is one of the cases which mark the change from the old regular army to the new citizen army. Here was a volunteer, who had joined up in the first flush of patriotism in August 1914. He had done well and earned his promotion, and yet paid the ultimate price for one brief lapse. A volunteer had been measured against the standards of the old regular army and found wanting. This was a standard by which others were to be judged in 1916.

CHAPTER 15

COWARDICE AND THE BATTLE OF THE SOMME

All men are timid on entering any fight. Cowards are those who let their timidity get the better of their manhood.

GEORGE S. PATTON, 1943

On 1 July 1916 the eager volunteers of Kitchener's army were thrown into the fray in one of the bloodiest battles ever fought by the British Army. The Kitchener men's units had been trained in the UK for the great offensive of 1916 and for many, this was their first real action of the war. They were to discover that the schoolroom stories of the gallant deeds of Tommy Atkins in Victoria's army were to have little relevance to twentieth-century warfare. They were told that the great bombardment which preceded the battle would have killed all the Germans, and that all they had to do was to walk across no-man's-land and into the German trenches – it would, literally, be a walkover. The reality was different. As the men of the new army rose from their trenches, they were cut down in a savage hail of German machine-gun fire and 1 July 1916 went into history as the day that the British Army suffered 60,000 casualties. The battle lasted through the summer, finally drawing to a close in the mud in November. No fewer than nine of the eighteen executions for cowardice took place in the latter half of 1916 and the battle of the Somme played a major role in many of these.

The first two executions for cowardice in the second half of 1916 involved a Kitchener unit, the 17th (Service) Battalion, Sherwood Foresters. Known as the Welbeck Rangers, this north Nottinghamshire battalion had been formed in mid 1915, and arrived in France in March 1916 as part of the build-up for the Somme offensive. They quickly found themselves in the front line, at Richebourg L'Avoue, near Festubert. On the night of 3–4 July the 17th Foresters and the 16th Rifle Brigade had carried out a successful trench raid.[1] However, the raiding party left some equipment behind in no-man's-land, and on the following night a party from the Foresters was ordered to go out to retrieve it.

This was a difficult piece of line to man and to hold. The two front lines were fairly close at this point, being 200 to 250 yards apart. The area had been heavily fought over in 1915 and the trench line was not continuous, with parts having been fortified and known as 'islands'. The events of the night of 4 July took place near a spot known as No. 10A island.

On that night Lt Posener planned to take a group of men out into no-man's-land to retrieve the trench ladders left there on the previous night. One of the party selected was Pte George Lawton (or Lowton), whose behaviour led to his being charged with cowardice, with a secondary charge of disobedience 'in such a manner as to show a wilful defiance of authority'.[2]

At his trial on 19 July the prosecution produced two witnesses. The first was Lt Posener, who gave evidence that at about 10 p.m. on 4 July he ordered Lawton and others to go out with him into no-man's-land, but Lawton refused, saying that he had a wife and five children. The officer again ordered Lawton to go with the party but getting no response put him under arrest, and sent him to No. 10A Island. A little later Posener gave Lawton another chance, but Lawton still did not join the party when it went out. Under cross-examination by the court, the officer said that it was a dark night and that there was no shelling and that the trench bridges that were to be brought in were only 75 yards from the German line. He also admitted that all the members of the party appeared to be nervous.

The second witness, Sgt Smith, gave evidence similar to that of Lt Posener, but added that Lawton had said: 'I dare not go, as it is a sudden death to go out there tonight and I have a wife and five children at home.'

Lawton's defence was brief. He told the court that he had been with the 10th Foresters at St Eloi in February 1916 and had been buried by a shell explosion and had suffered injuries to his leg and back and spent a month in hospital at Etaples. In his evidence he stated: 'Until this happened to me, I feared nothing, but this accident has fairly upset me. If I am out on listening post I am fair fit to drop. On the night of 4th July I was still suffering from the effects of the February affair.' He told the court that he had enlisted in September 1914 and had come to France in December 1915.

Lawton also handed in a written statement in mitigation – this document makes sad reading over eighty years later as he pleaded for his life, saying that the incident in February had upset his nerves. He ends his pathetic plea with:

'Indeed, Sir, when our Officer warned me to go out on a Fatigue Party, I felt shocking nervous.'

Lawton's conduct sheet has no entries, and the court, despite awarding the death sentence, did so with a strong recommendation to mercy on account of his previous good character and his being buried by a shell explosion in February. The members of the court also recommended that Lawton be examined by a medical board to ascertain the condition of his nerves. In this the court martial panel appear to be behaving scrupulously fairly. On the evidence produced, Lawton appeared to be guilty of the charge, but in view of his defence they clearly wanted to establish whether he was responsible for his actions.

The medical board sat on 22 July and found Lawton 'in good health in every way'. By the standards of 1916, this is what might have been expected. 'Shell shock' was recognized by the medical establishment by this time, but only in its more extreme form. Men shaking and twitching uncontrollably were understood to be suffering from this condition, but those without physical symptoms were unlikely to be diagnosed. The doctors of the day examining George Lawton (who no doubt appeared normal when out of the line) were not in a position to recognize what we now know as post-traumatic stress disorder. In 1916 fighting soldiers were expected to overcome their fear.

As Lawton's papers went up the chain of command it seems that the various formation commanders felt compassion for the man. The officer commanding 117th Brigade recommended commutation of sentence, as did Maj. Gen. Cuthbert, GOC 39th Division. Lt Gen. Haking, the XI Corps commander, recommended that sentence be commuted to five years' penal servitude, as the man had previously served well and, significantly, 'because no example was necessary'. In the papers which went to Gen. Monro, commanding First Army, there is even a Suspension of Sentences Act form, completed, ready for Monro to sign.

Monro, as in other cases, disagreed with his subordinates, minuting the papers with brutal clarity:

> There are no extenuating circumstances of any significance. The Private
> Soldier deliberately declined to face a duty on the grounds of his being a
> married man with children. Before the Court Martial he urged Shell
> Shock as being the cause of his conduct – the medical authorities regard
> him as being in good health – there is nothing to show that if clemency
> were extended to this Private Soldier that he would do his duty in future.
> I recommend that the sentence of the Court be inflicted.

In the light of this, the Commander-in-Chief confirmed sentence and Lawton was executed on 29 July with another member of his battalion, Bertie McCubbin.

George Lawton appears to have been unfortunate in several respects. Although he had joined the 10th Battalion of the Sherwood Foresters on 6 September 1914, after his injuries in February 1916 he was posted, not back to his comrades, but to the 17th Battalion. There is no doubt that such a posting would have been as difficult for the 'transferee' as it was unwelcome. Effectively the volunteer had been dislocated from his friends with whom he had joined and trained. If he had gone back to his mates in the 10th, perhaps they would have helped him overcome his nerves. Instead he was posted to a new battalion, where he probably struggled amongst strangers to hide his fear and had no old friends to help him. This is a pattern repeated in other cases, where a man finished up in front of a firing squad soon after being posted to a strange battalion, and speaks, obliquely, of the very real strength of the British regimental system – and its potential fragility.

On the same day that Lawton was tried, the same court martial panel heard another charge concerning a soldier of 17th Foresters. Three days after Lawton had refused to go out into no-man's-land, Pte Bertie McCubbin refused a similar duty. The facts emerged at his trial; two witnesses gave evidence for the prosecution.[3]

Sgt Scotney told the court that he was the sergeant in charge of No. 11 Island in the trenches at Festubert. In response to a report from a lance corporal, Scotney went to McCubbin and said: 'Pte McCubbin, you go out on listening patrol; it is your turn to go.' McCubbin replied: 'I can't go over, I've got very bad pains in my inside.' Scotney reported these events to Lt Tomkies, who placed McCubbin under arrest. Under cross-examination by the court, the sergeant explained what the duty entailed: 'He would have to go about 40 yards over the parapet in order to reach the position. He would have had to remain there for one hour. It was rather a light night. The enemy trenches were, in my opinion, 200 to 300 yards away.' Scotney also told the court that McCubbin had been receiving treatment for 'a bad face', but that he had not previously complained of stomach pains.

The second witness was Second Lt Tomkies, who explained that he was in charge of No. 11 and 11A Islands. At about midnight, after hearing from Sgt Scotney, Lt Tomkies went to McCubbin and told him: 'You must go over the parapet to your listening post; if you do not do so I shall have you placed under arrest: do you quite understand the consequences of not obeying this order?' McCubbin replied: 'I do.' Tomkies again ordered McCubbin to go to his post, but he did not do so and replied: 'I cannot do so, my nerves won't let me; if I go over I shall be a danger to the other man who is out there as well as to myself.'

When he had been put under arrest, McCubbin then told Tomkies that he had pains in his insides, which had started during the evening.

McCubbin, like Lawton, handed in a written statement in his defence and one wonders whether this course of action was suggested by someone in the battalion. In his letter, which clearly demonstrates the high standard of literacy among the Kitchener volunteers, McCubbin writes:

> During my stay in the Annequin Trenches I had my nerves shattered by a shell which burst on the railway which runs above our trenches bursting three yards away. I have never been right since my nerves being completely ruined. This being the case I put the plea forward that my case not being a blank refusal to an officer but as nervousness on my part being made worse by the incessant bombardment which has been going on here lately. I have never been had up before my company officer or Colonel before until now this being the first time and I have always tried to play my part while I have been in the army. I have also a father somewhere in France leaving my mother at home with six brothers and sisters and always thinking if anything had to happen to us two what would become of them which does not help me to get on a deal. So I also put forward a plea that if you deal leniently with me in this case I will try and do my bit and keep up a good reputation.
> Your Humble Servant
> Pte B. McCubbin.

In court Bertie McCubbin made no real defence, except to say that he had pains in his inside that night.

Capt. Brookfield gave testimony as to McCubbin's character: this was a mixed blessing, considering the charge – cowardice – as he said that the accused man had always done his duty quite well but in the last six months 'he has become unsteady generally, and also unstrung'. The adjutant produced McCubbin's conduct sheet, which showed no entries, and told the court that McCubbin had been suffering from boils on his face, and that he had been on duty in the trenches for *twenty-six* days prior to 7 July.

Like Lawton, McCubbin was found guilty and sentenced to death, with a strong recommendation to mercy on account of his previous good character and his condition of health. Again, the brigade, divisional and corps commanders all recommended commutation of the death sentence, but that unswerving disciplinarian, Gen. Monro at First Army, disagreed, writing:

> I have given careful consideration to this case and as a result I cannot support the recommendation of the GOC XI Corps – if toleration be shown to Private Soldiers who deliberately decline to face danger, all the qualities which we desire will become debased and degraded. I recommend that the sentence of the court be inflicted.

Yet again, the half-completed Suspension of Sentences form bears poignant testimony to how close Bertie McCubbin came to a reprieve from the firing squad.

The two volunteers were shot together at Lone Farm, an advanced dressing station, on 30 July 1916 at 5 a.m. McCubbin's death certificate contains the chilling statement: 'death was not instantaneous'.

These two cases give rise to several questions. In both cases, there were only two witnesses for the prosecution, and neither man had a 'prisoner's friend' to help him with his defence. The evidence in neither case was disputed – both men clearly refused to carry out a duty in the front line, and in both cases there was an alternative charge of disobeying an order. Both men claimed that previous shell explosions had affected their nerves, and Lawton could show that he had spent time in hospital after being buried by a shell. We now cannot tell whether these men were truly traumatized by their experiences or whether this seemed a plausible excuse for their behaviour, but reading their sad letters in mitigation, our twenty-first-century knowledge suggests that these volunteers were treated harshly even by the standards of the time. This conclusion is supported by the strong recommendations for mercy by the formation commanders.

Monro's recommendation seems to have been the crucial factor responsible for these sentences being confirmed by the Commander-in-Chief. The other unit commanders had all recommended commutation of the sentence. The commanders closest to the action, who knew the battalion, pointed out that there was no need for an example and that the men's previous good records should allow them another chance, and yet Monro's view that sentence be carried out prevailed. The fatal ingredient in their offences may have been the timing of their defiant actions: after the debacle of the first day of the Somme and the perceived inadequacies of the new volunteer army, high command was not likely to take a lenient view of cowardice before the enemy.

A personality like Haig's, troubled by the failure of his great Somme offensive, would support one of his army commanders.

Other men shot for cowardice in 1916 were equally victims of the failures of the battle of the Somme. On the day after Lawton and McCubbin were executed, Pte Frederick Hawthorne was tried by FGCM for the same offence.[4] Hawthorne was serving with a Territorial unit, the 1/5th South Staffordshires, but seems to have been a volunteer as he enlisted on 12 September 1914, and by July 1916 had been promoted to lance corporal.

On 1 July the 1/5th South Staffordshires took part in the frontal asault on Gommecourt, intended as a diversion to the main strike by Rawlinson's Fourth Army further south.

The attack, by 46th (North Midland) Division, met strong opposition. Gommecourt was a well-defended strongpoint, and John Masefield in *The Old Front Line* wrote: 'It is doubtful if any point in the line in France was stronger than this point of Gommecourt.'[5] The defences were built around a position called the Quadrilateral, with 50 yards depth of barbed wire in front of it and a well-armed central fortress, the Kern redoubt. The 1/5th South Staffordshires were in the second wave, supporting the assault battalions of 1/6th South Staffs and 1/6th North Staffordshires. However, when the attack started, they were caught by the German counter-barrage and had difficulty moving beyond the communication trenches.[6] Total casualties for the battalion were recorded as 177 officers and men. A second attack was organized, but was cancelled.

Later the 1/5th South Staffordshires were detailed to carry out a trench raid, and a party of men was specially trained for this between 11 and 14 July. Cpl Hawthorne was one of the men selected for the raid, and was NCO in charge of No. 1 Sap party. On the night of 14 July at about 8.45 p.m. the raiding party marched from their billets to the trenches and were assembled ready for action by 11.20 p.m. Just after midnight, Second Lt Speed went to Hawthorne's dugout and told them to be ready to move at 1.40 a.m.[7]

When zero hour arrived, the lieutenant moved the wiring party out of its dugout and then moved on to Hawthorne's Sap party but when told to move out Hawthorne protested, saying: 'It's too light.' Second Lt Speed then called over Second Lt Hatlin as a witness, and again ordered Hawthorne and his party out. At the court martial, Speed alleged that Hawthorne had said: 'It's too light, it's bloody murder', but that he did move his party into position behind the wiring party. By the time that all the men were in position, there was general grumbling and Second Lt Speed had to keep repeating his orders to advance as the raiding party filed forward in the narrow communication trench.

When Speed ordered the wiring party to advance out of the trench into no-man's-land, Hawthorne's Sap party should have followed on immediately, but the Sap party did not move and Second Lt Hatlin was sent back to the adjutant to report on the situation. In consequence of the refusal of the Sap party to go out, the raid had to be cancelled and it was probably this fact which sealed Hawthorne's fate.

Frederick Hawthorne was tried by FGCM on 31 July 1916 charged with 'when on active service misbehaving before the enemy in such a manner as to show cowardice', with the unusual alternative charge of 'when on active service, previously to going into action using words calculated to cause alarm and despondency'. At the trial, evidence was given by the two young officers, the sergeant responsible for 'A' party, which should have moved out behind the Sap party, another NCO of this party and two men in Hawthorne's group. The evidence was consistent, that there was general grumbling about the lightness of the night, which seemed to have spread from the Sap party.

In his defence Hawthorne said that when they were moving into position his party was delayed by some of the wiring party returning for tapes which they had forgotten. When they had closed up again and the order was given to move out of the trench only eight of the wiring party went forward, the other three coming straight back. Hawthorne said that at this point there was general complaining amongst all the men that it was too light, and when Second Lt Speed ordered them out of the trench no one moved. Hawthorne admitted that when ordered out of the dugout he had said; 'It's too light.'

Evidence of the accused's good character was given by Second Lt Snape, in whose platoon Hawthorne served, and his regimental 'crime sheet' had no entries. Capt. Lamond, adjutant of the battalion, gave evidence that Hawthorne had served with the BEF since March 1915, and stated: 'I have never found any fault with him as an NCO during that period.'

In the court martial papers there is a three-page letter from Brig. Gen. H. Williams, commanding 137th Brigade. He gave a detailed description of the conditions on the night in question, saying that although the moon was nearly full, it was low in the sky and that the working party would not have been between the moon and the enemy, and that at 1.45 a.m. the moon was covered by cloud. He did make the point that on coming out of a dark dugout it may well have appeared light to Hawthorne. Brig. Gen. Williams went on to say that discipline in the 1/5th South Staffordshires was not as good as in the other battalions in his brigade and that morale had been shaken by the losses at Gommecourt. Damningly, he added that the standard of NCOs in the brigade was very inferior and wrote: 'the chain of responsibility – even for a Territorial Unit – can hardly be said to exist, and it is quite clear from the evidence in this case that discipline was entirely lacking as far as Lance Corporal Hawthorne was concerned'.

Brig. Gen. Williams's comments may well have been an attempt to demonstrate his authority following the abortive attack on Gommecourt. After this debacle the brigade commanders of 137th and 139th Brigades had both given evidence to a court of inquiry and the effectiveness of Williams's brigade had been questioned.[8]

Maj. Gen. Thwaites, commanding 46th Division, took a different view. He said that although there was nothing to say in mitigation of Hawthorne's sentence, carrying it out could have an undesirable effect:

(i) the temperament of these Staffordshire men is such that an extreme example may tend to produce a sullen and dispirited attitude.

(ii) the convicting evidence having been given by officers, and only junior ones, a very deep feeling against the officers as a whole may be engendered and the battalion will consequently become valueless.

(iii) I am not convinced that the raid was organised in the best possible way and this may have tended to produce a want of confidence by the men in their leaders. I am doubtful whether the officers, as a whole, inspire confidence ... I recommend that the death sentence be commuted without suspension of sentence.[9]

However, Lt Gen. Snow, commanding VII Corps, disagreed, saying: 'An example is needed and I therefore recommend that the sentence be carried out.' Edmund Allenby, commanding Third Army, concurred and L Cpl Hawthorne was executed at Warlincourt.

A remarkable and poignant note written by Maj. Gen. Thwaites is appended to the court martial proceedings. Unusually for a divisional commander, he appears to have attended the execution and felt sufficiently strongly to write: 'I should like to place it on record that Lance Corporal Hawthorne met his death like a man and a soldier.' One can only wonder at the sense of duty or other psychological process that motivated a major general to attend an execution personally and to write such a comment. To judge from his earlier note, the most likely explanation is a strong sense of identity with one of his Staffordshire men, whom he was powerless to spare.

L Cpl Frederick Hawthorne should have acted differently on that July night. As an NCO he did have a responsibility to carry out the attack as ordered, instead of joining in the grousing about the light. It is impossible not to feel that Hawthorne, like L Cpl Holland, was being measured against the standard of the pre-war regular army NCOs and found wanting. Had he been a less good soldier and not earned his stripe, it is likely that Hawthorne would have escaped the firing squad. The failure of the attack at Gommecourt also had a direct bearing on this man's fate – the battle of the Somme had claimed another victim.

A few days before Hawthorne's execution another soldier risked a similar fate. The case of Pte John Bennett, a regular serving with the 1st Battalion, Hampshire Regiment, has parallels with the case of Herbert Chase in 1915. Bennett had joined 3rd Hampshires in June 1914 but because of his youth he was not sent to France until November 1915.[10] On 1 July 1916 the 1st Hampshires suffered heavy casualties in the attack on Redan Ridge, with 320 killed, including the commanding officer.

On 8 August 1916 the battalion was serving in the Ypres Salient. At about 10 p.m. that night the gas alarm sounded and Bennett was seen putting on his smoke helmet. Half an hour later when his platoon was ordered to move forward he was found to be missing. In the early hours of the following morning he was seen about three-quarters of a mile in the rear, when he told another soldier from his battalion that he had lost his nerve and had climbed out of the trench, and when he had returned his company had gone.[11]

In due course Bennett was placed under arrest and was tried for cowardice on 16 August. The evidence was brief – just three witnesses saying that Bennett had gone missing between 10 and 10.30 p.m. on the 8th and had not been seen again until 2.15 a.m. on the 9th. In his defence he said that he did not hear the gas alarm, but saw others putting on their helmets, so put on his own. When ordered to stand-to he stood in the doorway of his dugout to stay under cover from shelling, and he said that he then climbed out of the trench into a shell hole without knowing what he was doing and that he did not remember what happened after that. He also said: 'I am given to understand that I am awaiting a medical inspection since a previous occurrence of this sort.'

Unfortunately Pte Bennett had a long crime sheet. In the UK he had several entries for not complying with an order and had been tried by FGCM in July 1916 for desertion. On that occasion he was found guilty of the lesser charge of absence without leave and given two years' imprisonment with hard labour. The date of his offence is not clear in the records, but as he was awaiting trial from 8 July until the 20th it would appear that this offence occurred during the Somme fighting and it is probable that the 19-year-old Bennett took part in the 1 July attack. Despite his record the court recommended Bennett to mercy, but gave no reasons for their recommendation.

His commanding officer, Major Armitage, wrote that there were no officers available to give any information about Bennett's character as they were all new, but he had taken the views of the CSM ('a most reliable man') and wrote: 'the man is absolutely useless ... As soon as any shelling starts or there are any signs of an attack he goes all to pieces and as far as I can gather seems to go practically off his head through sheer terror.' Major Armitage also wrote that although Bennett had been with the BEF for nine months, the greater part of this had been spent in hospital or with the transport. He continued: 'In my opinion the crime was not deliberately committed ... but rather through the fact that the man was in such a nervous state and so frightened that he did not know what he was doing.' He concluded: 'I would further point out that a man of this sort is a positive danger to have anywhere near the firing line; behaviour of this sort easily spreads and on critical occasions his conduct is such that he might easily start a panic among his comrades.'

Brig. Gen. Rees, commanding 11th Brigade, recommended commuting the sentence as the state of discipline in the battalion was good, and because 'the man was apparently too terrified to know what he was doing and therefore can hardly be described as deliberately avoiding the duty in question'. This is a good example of the importance of intention in military (and criminal) law at the time. If a man could be shown to be not responsible for his actions, under the McNaghten rules he would be found insane in a criminal court. Military law followed the same principles: if a man was so deranged (i.e. insane) as to be not responsible for his actions, he could not be responsible for forming an intention to avoid a duty.

However, Maj. Gen. Lowther, commanding 4th Division, disagreed, as did Lt Gen. Hunter-Weston. On 19 July 1916 Hunter-Weston had been rapped on the knuckles by Douglas Haig for being too 'soft' in the case of Pte Earp. He was not going to make the same mistake when asked a month later to give an opinion in the case of Pte Bennett. He wrote: 'Cowards of this sort are a serious danger to the Army. The death penalty is instituted to make men fear running away more than they fear the enemy. In the interests of the Service I recommend that the Death Sentence be carried into execution.' Herbert Plumer, commanding Second Army, concurred. Meticulously the DAAG made enquiries as to the truth of Bennett's statement that he was awaiting a medical report and he attached a note to the proceedings: 'Enquiries have been made as to the accused's statement that he was awaiting medical inspection and the Division inform me that it is untrue.'

John Bennett was executed at Poperinge on 28 August 1916. From the account given by his commanding officer it appears that this young soldier was completely terrified under fire – not shell-shocked by the definitions of the day, but simply too frightened to behave rationally. Maybe his experiences on the Somme on 1 July had unhinged his mind to the extent that he really was incapable of rational behaviour – but it is easy to take this view eighty-five years distant from the events.

A few days before Bennett's peremptory flight from his trench, another man was acting in a way that was to lead to another trial for cowardice.[12] Pte James Anderson was serving with the 8th Loyal North Lancashires near Beaumont Hamel on the Somme on 4 August 1916 and had been detailed as one of a working party carrying rations to the front. According to the evidence, which was uncontested, Anderson set off with a carrying party at around 10.30 p.m. to go to Gordon Trench. When the party reached Peche Street, Anderson started to go back towards Hamel, passing Lt Copeman, who was at the rear of the party. When asked where he was going Anderson was alleged to have replied: 'I am going out. I can stick it no longer. My nerves are gone.' Under cross-examination by the court, Copeman admitted that he did not give Anderson any orders to rejoin the working party. When the party returned to billets at Mesnil, Anderson was found asleep in his dugout.

In view of his statement, Anderson was examined by the battalion medical officer, who gave evidence to say that he could find nothing wrong with him and found no evidence of nervous breakdown. He added: 'If the accused had suffered from shell shock there would have been some evidence of it at the time I examined him.'

Anderson elected to make a statement to the court, not on oath. He said that in January 1916 he had been buried in a dugout and had a nervous breakdown. He had then spent some weeks at No. 10 hospital before rejoining his battalion, the 12th King's Liverpool. In March he had been sent to hospital with chronic bronchitis and after two months was sent to the 8th Loyal North Lancashires, on 24 July 1916. He said that on the night of the incident his nerves were 'all shook up' owing to the shelling.

Almost no character evidence was forthcoming. Anderson had joined the battalion on 24 July and they had moved to the trenches on the 29th with the incident taking place on 4 August. Only a temporary conduct sheet was available, with no entries. Anderson had asked for two officers from his previous regiment to give a character reference, but unfortunately one had been killed and the other wounded, so they were not available. In mitigation, Anderson said that two of his brothers had been killed in France and another wounded at Gallipoli. He also mentioned that he took part in the battle of Loos in 1915. He was an early volunteer, having enlisted in September 1914.

In view of his short service with his new battalion, little could be said in mitigation. Brig. Gen. Onslow, commanding 7th Brigade, wrote that this was the first time that Anderson had been under fire with the battalion and that nothing was known of his previous character. He wrote:

> The Commanding Officer has no personal knowledge of this man, but he is of the opinion that the man was so frightened of shell fire that he deliberately preferred to take his chance of the consequences rather than remain under it. I am of the opinion that the man is not worth keeping, his character and action is well-known throughout the battalion and, therefore, for the sake of example the extreme penalty should be inflicted.

The other commanders all confirmed that sentence should be carried out and Anderson was shot on 12 September. This seems to be another case where a psychologically traumatized man had been removed from his original battalion and his friends and sent to a new unit where he was unable to cope with the mental strain.

Less than two weeks later another soldier decided to opt out of a working party in the front line and was to suffer the same fate as James Anderson. Albert Botfield had enlisted in the early days of the war, on 1 September 1914, and in September 1916 was with a pioneer battalion, 9th South Staffordshires.

On the evening of 21 September 1916 Botfield's platoon paraded prior to going to work, digging new trenches south-east of Pozières. When they were about 500 yards short of their objective, Cable Trench, a shell burst near the company at about 7.15 p.m. and Botfield ran away. According to evidence given by Sgt Warmington, he searched unsuccessfully for Botfield while the rest of the platoon went on. When they returned to billets at 4 a.m. Botfield was not in his bivouac but was seen returning at 7.30 a.m. The broad facts were uncontested at the trial. A corporal and private also gave evidence that they had seen Botfield running away. Evidence was also given about Botfield's movements between 6.30 and 7.30 a.m.[13]

Botfield, who had no prisoner's friend, made a statement to the court on oath. His version of events was that when the shell burst he jumped into the trench and after things quietened down he went to look for his party, but met a man who told him he was going in the wrong direction. He then sat down and went to sleep until about 4 a.m. Botfield said that he had worked in Cable Trench before.

Under cross-examination his story changed slightly. He said that after he met the man (who 'had some red stuff on his shoulders') he went straight back to his bivouac, arriving at 4.30 a.m. Botfield was then questioned by the court, and said: 'I was nervous that's why I took so long to come home and also the reason why I did not try and go on to Cable Trench after the shelling.'

When Botfield's previous record was presented to the court, after the finding, it transpired that he was no stranger to court martial proceedings. The adjutant of the battalion said that he did not know how long Botfield had been in France, but on 6 January 1916 he had absented himself from his reinforcement draft and had remained at large until captured in Boulogne a week later; for this offence he had been tried by FGCM, which found him guilty of absence and gave him ninety days' Field Punishment No. 1. In June he had two episodes of absence and had been given twenty-eight days' FP No. 1. Two months later Botfield again went absent and was tried by FGCM for desertion, but was found guilty of the lesser offence of absence without leave, the sentence of ninety days' FP No. 1 being confirmed on 8 September. It is therefore probable that he was serving his field punishment sentence at the time of his final offence.

In view of the evidence and his previous record, Botfield was sentenced to death, and this was endorsed by all the unit commanders. By the time that the trial took place his unit had moved to the Ypres Salient and Botfield was executed at Poperinge on 18 October 1916.

Although the case appears to have been straightforward, the battalion war diary suggests that Botfield's, statement that he had worked in the area before could not be entirely true as Cable Trench (which was not a trench in the true sense, but a cable-carrying conduit) was only started on that day.[14] However, the 9th South Staffs had worked in the Pozières area in July and August; and on the way up to work on the new trench Botfield probably followed a similar route to that taken in the summer, hence his statement. However, this probably does not materially alter the facts of the case: after the shell exploded, the other members of the party had no trouble in carrying out the work for which they were detailed and it appears that Botfield took the opportunity to slip away.

Field Marshal Douglas Haig had confirmed two death sentences for cowardice on the same day, and ten minutes after Pte Botfield faced a firing squad at Poperinge, Harry Farr was to meet his death in similar fashion at Carnoy, on the Somme.

Harry Farr was a pre-war regular soldier who, according to his conduct sheet,[15] had enlisted on 8 May 1908, but when war broke out was a reservist [16] and had arrived in France with the 2nd West Yorkshire Regiment on 5 November 1914. This battalion had been in Malta when the war broke out and did not arrive back in England until 25 September, and was sent to France from Southampton on 4 November.[17] The battalion took part in the battle of Neuve Chapelle on 10 March 1915 and it seems probable that Harry Farr was involved in the fighting there.

The battalion war diary reported that on 7 May 1915 they received details of a proposed attack and that all men were issued with respirators or masks as protection from gas.[18] The following day they took up positions in the assembly trenches, and the bombardment started preparatory to the assault at 5.40 a.m. on 9 May. The 2nd West Yorkshires left their forming-up trenches but became pinned down by continual shellfire in E trenches and were eventually ordered back, with the planned night attack being cancelled. On the 10th they moved forwards to the E trenches again, but once more the attack on Aubers Ridge was cancelled.

On 11 May 1915 Harry Farr was evacuated to Boulogne with shell shock where it appears that his nerves were so badly affected that he could not hold a pen.[19] He was sent to the 1st West Yorkshires on 20 October 1915 and his company commander said that Farr served continuously with the 1st Battalion between October 1915 and October 1916. This unit was not involved in the initial phases of the Somme battle but they were moved to that front in August and on 16 September took over the front line just in front of the Quadrilateral. On the 18th they attacked this position, taking 151 casualties, but just before this attack took place, Harry Farr's nerves gave way.[20]

The evidence at his trial was largely uncontested by Farr, who had no prisoner's friend.

The first witness was RSM Haking, who said that at about 9 a.m. on 17 September 1916 Farr went to him in the transport lines, telling him he had fallen out from his company sick on the previous night. Haking told Farr to report sick at the dressing station but when Farr went there they refused to see him as he was not wounded. He reported back to Haking, who ordered him to go up to the front line with a ration party that evening, but at 11 p.m.

Haking saw Farr still at the transport lines. When asked why he was still there, Farr replied: 'I cannot stand it.' When Haking told Farr that he would have to go to the trenches that night, he replied: 'I cannot go.' Haking then told QMS Booth to take Farr up to the trenches under escort. After a short distance Farr started to struggle with the escort and screamed. When Haking again told Farr that he would have to go up, or be tried for cowardice, he replied: 'I am not fit to go to the trenches.' Haking said he would take Farr to see the medical officer, but he refused to go, saying: 'I will not go any further that way.' After a further struggle with his escort Haking told them to let go. When they did so, Farr ran back to the transport line and Haking placed him under guard. Company QMS Booth, Pte Farrar and L Cpl Form all confirmed these events.

In his defence Harry Farr made a statement on oath. He said that on his way up to the trenches on 16 September he fell out sick, but the sergeant from whom he had asked permission had now been wounded so could not give evidence. He reported himself to the RSM at 9 a.m. and went to the dressing station as ordered but as he was not wounded they would not see him. When ordered up with the ration party he set off with them but then fell out sick; as he was in the rear of the party he could not get permission to fall out. Farr then described his conversation with CSM Haking in rather more colourful (and more believable) language than described by the NCO, but the substance of the conversation was the same. According to Farr, Haking said: 'You are a fucking coward and you will go to the trenches – I give fuck all for my life and I give fuck all for yours and I'll get you fucking well shot.' Although the language used and its apparent aggression is shocking eighty-five years later, it was normal for the trenches in 1916, and even the army of today is little different. Haking appears to have been acting with compassion, doing his best to cajole, order or bully Farr into doing his duty and avoiding the inevitable consequences of failing to obey an order. Farr told the court that he only struggled with his escort when they started to shove him about, and that if this had not happened he would have gone forward.

The court then asked Farr if he had an opportunity of reporting sick between 16 September and 2 October (the date of the trial). He replied that he did have that opportunity, but had not reported sick, because 'being away from the shell fire I felt better'.

Acting Sgt Andrews gave evidence for the defence and said that Farr had reported sick with nerves about April 1916 and that the MO kept him at the dressing station for a fortnight. He had reported sick for the same reason again on 22 July, but had been discharged the following day. The doctor who had treated Farr was unable to give evidence as he had been wounded.

After finding him guilty the court heard the character evidence. Farr's 'crime sheet' had only one entry, in the UK, when Farr had overstayed his pass for a few hours. Second Lt Marshall gave evidence as to Farr's character, and said: 'I have known the accused for the last six weeks. On working parties he has three times asked for leave to fall out and return to camp as he could not stand the noise of the artillery. He was trembling and did not appear in a fit state.'

After the trial, his company commander wrote: 'I cannot say what has destroyed this man's nerves but he has proved himself on many occasions incapable of keeping his head in action and likely to cause a panic. Apart from his behaviour under fire his conduct and character are very good.'

Brigade, division and corps commanders all recommended that the sentence be carried out. Lt Gen. Lord Cavan, commanding XIV Corps, added: 'The GOC 6 Division informs me that the men know the man is no good.'

Farr was seen on 2 October (the date of the trial) by the battalion MO, who certified that Pte Harry Farr was fit to undergo the strain of trial by FGCM. There must then have been some post-trial correspondence, as on 7 October the doctor, Capt. Williams (RAMC), wrote to the adjutant of the battalion: 'I hereby certify that I examined no. 8871 Pte. H. Farr 1st West Yorks on October 2nd 1916 and that in my opinion both his general physical and mental conditions were satisfactory.'

Farr was executed at Carnoy at 6 a.m. on 18 October. His typed death certificate is signed by Dr A. Anderson, Captain, RAMC – the signature is shaky and gives the impression that the doctor was shocked by the execution.

What should one make of the Farr trial? It is a case that has sparked much publicity, with Harry Farr's widow, Gertrude, telling the heart-rending story of her struggle to cope after his death, with a young daughter and no pension. His daughter has taken up the campaign to obtain a pardon for Harry Farr. From the army's point of view, he had a fair trial: the evidence of his refusal to go up to the front line was not contested and this constituted cowardice. In the light of his claim of shell shock he should have been examined by an expert in the condition but instead the army sought the advice of the hard-pressed MO who had examined him to see if he was fit for trial. Few people reading the trial transcript over eighty years later would dispute that Harry Farr was shell-shocked. Harry Farr was failed not by the army, but by the standards of medical knowledge of the day. When he was examined by the doctor he was away from the line, at Ville-sur-Ancre, and he appeared to be normal, because away from the noise of the guns he was all right. By the standards of medical knowledge at the time, anyone who was shell-shocked had suffered a complete mental breakdown, and did not miraculously recover just because they were away from the guns.

If only Harry Farr had gone forward with RSM Haking to see the MO in the front line, the story might have been different. Perhaps if he had been examined under shellfire it would have been obvious that the man was traumatized. By refusing to go to see the MO at that point, Farr may have signed his own death warrant. He was also unfortunate that he displayed the failure of his nerves just as the battalion was about to go into serious action against the Quadrilateral. On 17–18 September the battalion and brigade had far more to worry about than one soldier whose nerve had failed him, and this was probably subconsciously reflected in the court martial. Harry Farr was undoubtedly a victim of the battle of the Somme, just as much as the other men of his battalion who died on that battlefield.

A short distance along the line from Farr's battalion at that time, also engaged in the Flers-Courcelette attack, the 47th Division were attempting to take High Wood. On 15 September the 1/6th Londons (the 'Cast Iron Sixth') had taken heavy casualties in capturing the German trenches known as the Cough Drop and the position was held by just 100 men and two officers over the next few days. By 18 September Robert Loveless Barker had seen enough, and his behaviour on that day resulted in his standing trial on a charge of cowardice.[21]

The court martial was convened when the battalion was back at rest on 26 September 1916. Cpl Haacke described how when ordered to stand-to on the morning of the 18th Barker refused to come out of his funk hole and covered himself up with sandbags, saying: 'I won't come out for you or anyone else.' He then told the court that when the Germans counter-attacked on the 19th Barker got out of the trench and ran to the rear. Three other corporals give similar evidence. Barker not seen by his battalion again until 22 September, after they had been relieved, when he reported to the orderly room and handed in a medical certificate. This was from 4th London Field Ambulance, dated 22 September 1916 and saying 'for discharge today', the implication being that Barker had been detained in the Field Ambulance.

In his defence Barker (who was supported by a prisoner's friend – the first of the men shot for cowardice who availed himself of his right in this respect) made a long statement. He made no real defence to the incident on the 18th, saying that he left the funk hole after the third order to do so. He said that when the Germans attacked on the 19th he decided to warn the Lewis gunners in the trench behind him that the Germans were attacking. Having done so, he stopped there to clean his rifle. When he tried to go forward again the trench was blocked. Later he went over the top and got into a shell hole and waited for it to quieten down, when he went back to his trench where he found that his battalion had been relieved. Barker then went to No. 4 Field Ambulance to have his eyes bathed (he probably spent the night of 21st–22nd at the Field Ambulance). Barker emphasized under examination by his prisoner's friend that his sole motive in leaving the trench was to warn the Lewis gunners. Three soldiers from the Lewis gun team gave evidence on Barker's behalf, saying that he had arrived and warned them of the German attack.

After the finding, Rifleman Barker's conduct sheet was presented to the court. The soldier had shown a previous desire to avoid action, and had been tried for desertion on 8 June 1916 when he had been sentenced to death. This was later commuted to five years' penal servitude and suspended.

Brig. Gen. Hampden, commanding 140th Brigade, endorsing the sentence, wrote:

> I am of the opinion that this case is a plain one and that cowardice in the face of the enemy was shewn. The man is a degenerate and from reports I have received does not seem to realise the gravity of his offence. For this reason his presence in the ranks is a danger. I do not feel justified in recommending any remission of sentence under the circumstances but I regret having to make this decision as I have a very high opinion of the fighting qualities of all ranks in the 6th London Regt. They are cheery and trustworthy however unpleasant and difficult the conditions may be in which they are situated and the spirit of the Bn is excellent. Rfn Barker enlisted prior to mobilisation.

Lt Gen. Pulteney, commanding III Corps, wrote '… In view of the report of GOC 104th Inf. Bde. Regarding this man's mental condition and the high fighting qualities displayed by the 6th Battalion London Regiment I consider that no example is necessary.' Gen. Rawlinson, commanding Fourth Army, did not agree and recommended that the sentence be carried out and this was confirmed by the Commander-in-Chief. Rifleman Barker was executed by firing squad at Busseboom at 6.45 a.m. on 4 November.

There was to be one more execution for cowardice in 1916. On 9 October Reginald Tite, serving with the 13th Royal Sussex on the Somme, left his battalion trenches under fire. The battalion's front ran from Watling Street to Beaumont Hamel Road and it was in this area that Tite's nerves failed him.

Although his charge sheet had been prepared on 12 October Reginald Tite was tried on 2 November 1916. He was charged with 'When on active service misbehaving before the enemy in such a manner as to show cowardice in that he in the field on the ninth day of October 1916, during a bombardment of the enemy trenches and when under the enemy's fire, left the trenches without permission from his superior officer.' The court martial records note that Tite objected to the president of the court, Major Heagerty, as he belonged to his own battalion, but the court overruled this objection.[22]

Pte Dacey, who was in charge of the Lewis gun team which included Tite, told the court that on the morning of 9 October Pte Tite had asked his permission to leave the trench. Second Lt Evans refused permission but showed him a safe place and told him to stay there during the planned trench mortar demonstration. A short while later Tite could not be found, but he reported back at about 12.30 p.m. He was then put on periscope duty while Dacey and an officer went to look at a new position for the gun. Tite left his trench and went to see Sgt Benford and told him that he could not stay in the line. Benford told him to go back, as it was a serious matter to leave the line, but Tite replied that he could not stick it. Lt Evans then told Sgt Benford to put Tite under arrest.

In his defence Tite made a statement, not on oath. He said: 'I wish to state that I am very queer when I am in the line. I can't sleep and I can scarcely eat anything. When there is a bombardment on I seem to take leave of my senses. I run about from one bay to another and I have to clear out of the line altogether.'

When the character evidence was presented, it transpired that Tite had already faced an FGCM for disobeying a lawful command on 1 August and been sentenced to four years' penal servitude, which had been suspended.

Pte Tite was sentenced to death. Despite his claim to mental problems he was not examined by a doctor, apart from the usual pre-trial examination. The RAMC captain who saw him made no reference to his mental state, and wrote: 'I have this day examined no 4242 Pte Tite and find that he is physically fit.' This is another case where a man appears to have been broken psychologically by the battle of the Somme, but whose condition went unrecognized.

CHAPTER 16

COWARDICE – THE LAST CASE

I've been scared in every goddam war I've fought in.

GEN. NORMAN SCHWARZKOPF, 1993

Reginald Tite was the last man to be shot for cowardice in 1916 and ended the spate of executions for this crime, although in December twenty members of the 19th DLI were sentenced to death for cowardice after a series of military disasters on the Arras front (see Chapter 13). It was nearly a year until the next and final execution took place for this crime.

Pte James Adamson was tried on 31 October 1917 at the Rue du Four de St Adrian, Arras. Like Rifleman Barker he had the assistance of a prisoner's friend at his trial. Adamson was a volunteer who joined the 3rd Battalion of the Cameron Highlanders in March 1915, but at the time of his offence was serving with the 7th Battalion. His charge sheet makes the offence clear:

When on active service misbehaving before the enemy in such a manner as to show cowardice in that he in the trenches on 28th July 1917 having previously been warned, refused to and did not take part in a raid on the enemy's trenches at 7 p.m. on the date aforesaid, for fear of his personal safety.

A second charge was also made:

When on active service disobeying in such a manner as to show a wilful defiance of authority a lawful command given personally by his superior officer, in the execution of his office in that he at Bivouac Camp on July 30th 1917 when personally ordered by Company Sergeant Major Anderson his company sergeant major to get ready to proceed to the trenches, did not do so, although the order was repeated.[1]

For reasons which are unexplained there was a delay in bringing Adamson to trial. The summary of evidence was taken on 9 August 1917 but his trial did not take place until 31 October 1917 when the circumstances of Adamson's offences emerged. On 28 July 1917, in the line east of Ypres, A Coy was to take part in a bombing raid at 7 p.m., this raid being led by Capt. Jenkins. This officer was subsequently wounded and did not give evidence at the trial but four witnesses described the events. When his company had been warned for the raid, Adamson complained to Capt. Jenkins that he had a sore knee and could not take part. Jenkins had then warned him of the penalty for not going over. The raid went ahead but when Sgt Morgan returned to the British front line he found that Adamson had never left the trench. Under cross-examination, Morgan said: 'The accused told me that he was too frightened to go over and that he was frightened to go down to the supports, and that he would go there with no other body than myself.'

L Cpl Baird told the court that he heard Capt. Jenkins warn Adamson of the seriousness of his crime and the penalty he would suffer, and said that the accused said he would be willing to take his punishment if he got justice.

The battalion MO gave evidence to say that Adamson had reported sick on 30 July but had not gone sick on the 28th or 29th. When he examined Adamson on the 30th the doctor found nothing wrong with his knees which would have prevented him doing his duty on the 28th. Under cross-examination the MO said that on the 30th Adamson had complained of bleeding piles and back pains, but, again, this would not have prevented him from doing his duty on the 28th.

In his defence Adamson explained to the court that on the night of 23–24 July he had fallen into some barbed wire and torn his knees (this was a kilted regiment, so the story rings true). He went into the line and reported sick to the orderly sergeant the next day and was called before Capt. Jenkins, who told him to carry on as the company was soon to be relieved. Adamson said that on the 26th the CSM (since killed) had relieved him from being one of a carrying party because of his knees. When warned for the raid he had told the platoon sergeant and Capt. Jenkins that his knees were too bad, but was told he would have to go on the raid. Adamson admitted that he had not taken part, and had stayed in the British front line, but denied that he had told Sgt Morgan that he was frightened.

The court decided to proceed with the second charge, and in evidence heard that on 30 July 1917 A Coy was told to get ready to go to the trenches, by the CSM, since killed. Adamson did not get dressed, despite being ordered to do so, saying that he was not fit to stand. He was then arrested and, having dressed, marched back to the details camp. Sgt Mead said that Adamson made no complaint about being unable to walk to the details camp, and that he could stand and walk quite well. L Cpl Ogston also gave evidence that Adamson had no difficulty in marching back to the details camp. The battalion doctor gave evidence similar to that given previously, adding that Adamson had some scratches on his knees but nothing to hinder him from doing his work. He had examined him again on 16 August and found him fit for duty.

Adamson's defence was brief. He said that he had been given some ointment for his piles, and was not fit when told to get dressed. He told the court that he first arrived in France in March 1916, was wounded on the Somme on 22 August with the 7th Cameron Highlanders, and had been invalided home to England, rejoining the battalion in March 1917.

His conduct sheet had several entries, mainly relating to offences committed in the UK. Between 31 May 1915 and 29 February 1916 he had been charged with reporting sick without a cause, insolence, and using insubordinate language (for which he was tried by DCM and sentenced to one year's imprisonment with hard labour and discharge with ignominy, commuted to detention for six months without discharge). He broke out of barracks when warned for his draft on 29 December 1915 and whilst still at Invergordon had refused to go on parade and been charged with not complying with an order. He then went to France with the 7th Battalion and served on the Somme in August but was soon in trouble again, as on 3 August 1916 he was charged with disobedience and using improper language to an NCO. After being sent back to the UK wounded he was charged with overstaying his pass on two occasions and creating a disturbance in the barrack room. On New Year's Eve 1916 he went missing for four days until arrested in Kirkcaldy.

Adamson was found guilty of the first charge of cowardice, but not guilty of the second. As is the case with several of the 1917 court martial files, the letters regarding sentence are no longer with the trial transcript and there is no explanation for the delay in bringing him to trial. Adamson was shot near Arras on 23 November 1917, four months after his offence, and there is an eyewitness account of the execution by G. S. Chaplin.[2]

James Adamson was, from his record, a difficult character and gives the impression of being a rather truculent individual, resisting authority; and he made no real defence to the charge of cowardice. Unlike the 1916 cases he does not allege shell shock, or even sheer terror, just damaged knees, which whilst probably sore and uncomfortable were not considered an adequate reason for not doing his duty. Like many other men in the trenches, he also suffered from piles – but painful and unpleasant though this condition is, many others with the same complaint put up with it and carried on. The evidence produced in court showed that he had failed in his duty, and with his previous record this was enough to ensure sentence of death.

There were no further executions for cowardice in the war (Louis Harris, the last man to be shot before the Armistice, was charged with cowardice and was found not guilty of that charge but found guilty of and executed for desertion). Pte James Adamson has the dubious distinction of being the last man officially shot by the British Army for cowardice in the face of the enemy.

What, in summary, do we make of the cases of the fifteen *British* soldiers executed for cowardice?

The first man to be shot in 1915, Oliver Hodgetts, could equally well have been charged with leaving his post. He had made two earlier attempts to desert, which undoubtedly counted against him. He offered no real excuse for his behaviour and by the regular army standards of the day was clearly guilty, and even with hindsight it is hard to find any extenuating circumstances.

Herbert Chase also had a bad record, with a long previous absence, and again could well have been charged with leaving his post. The court martial proceedings were short and some damning evidence was added, improperly, to the file after the trial. Gen. Allenby, the corps commander, commented that he was doubtful that the evidence substantiated the charge, but the proceedings were reviewed by the army's legal arm and they must have felt that the evidence was sufficient for conviction. However, by the standards of the day Chase, like Hodgetts, appears guilty of the crime alleged and made little attempt at a defence.

William Bellamy also had a bad character, which undoubtedly contributed to his death. His trial was brief and again during the confirmation process one of the commanders, Maj. Gen. Landon, wrote that he was doubtful whether the evidence was sufficient legally to sustain a conviction. At his trial Bellamy made some claim to 'nerves' but was examined by a medical board who found nothing wrong. If examined by a twenty-first-century panel of doctors he might have been found to be suffering from PTSD, but by the medical standards of the day he was fit for duty. These three cases were all tried before the army tightened up on its legal process and before courts martial officers were available to help the panel through the correct procedures, but although the evidence was scanty, the cases appear – just about – to be proven.

In 1916, however, the cases take on a different aspect and raise some concerns. In two cases, those of L Cpl Holland and L Cpl Hawthorne, the men were effectively executed because they were NCOs. In both cases these junior

NCOs were held to be guilty of cowardice whilst private soldiers who committed the same offence at the same time escaped punishment. However, this is in accordance with the principle established in the *Manual of Military Law*, which states: 'For example, a non-commissioned officer should as a rule be punished more severely than a private soldier concerned with him in the commission of the same offence.'[3] The comments added by the commanders at all levels show that the NCOs of the new volunteer army were being judged – and found wanting – against the standards of the old regular army. Both of these men could claim to have been badly treated by an army which had not yet learned how to deal with the transition from a professional to a citizen army.

The great Somme offensive gave rise to cases which, with hindsight, can be recognized as shell shock, or battle stress. Two otherwise good soldiers, Lawton and McCubbin, both claimed bad nerves in their defences and in both cases all the formation commanders recommended commutation of sentence, until the chain of confirmation reached that stern disciplinarian Gen. Monro. Both of these cases seemingly deserved a second chance and leave a feeling that the scales of justice were unfairly weighted against these men.

In the cases of Anderson and Farr, both men could show a history of shell shock and Anderson was particularly unfortunate in being transferred to a new unit just as he was most in need of the comradeship of the trenches. Both men seem to have been treated harshly, even by the standards of the time, and no one today would question that they were not fully responsible for their actions under fire. The real criticism in both cases is that the two men were not properly medically examined after their trials, when their history of shell shock had emerged. Given the standards of medical knowledge of most front line doctors of the day, it is unlikely that either man would have been recognized as suffering from shell shock in the conventional, 1916, sense but their symptoms should have been recognized by one of the experts in mental disease increasingly called on to give evidence in such cases.

The other four men shot for cowardice in 1916 all had previous convictions. Pte Bennett may have had some claim to shell shock, but it is doubtful whether he was any more affected by the conditions on the Somme than the others in his battalion. If it had not been for his previous conviction for desertion he might have been dealt with more leniently, but in the midst of the battle of the Somme the army was in no mood for leniency.

Botfield, Barker and Tite all had previous convictions for serious military offences and had all been tried by FGCM before, and again suffered the extreme penalty in consequence of a crime committed on the Somme front. The latter two both demonstrated signs of nerves, but it is difficult to tell from reading the transcript of a trial whether these men were shell-shocked or simply – like many others – frightened.

There is no doubt that the battle of the Somme exerted a dual influence on the executions for cowardice in the second half of 1916. This battle was, literally, the blooding of the 1914 volunteer soldier where these men met the new technological warfare and found it to be a far cry from the nineteenth-century warfare they had read about at school. Some of these men were unable to cope with the reality of war and gave way. At the same time, the surviving pre-war regulars were beginning to show the strain of nearly two years at the front. Their endurance was being put to the test and some had drained their bank account of courage.

The high command in 1916 was also learning how to handle its new citizen army and was still trying to treat these men in the same way as it had dealt with the regulars in 1914 and 1915. Unsure of the quality of the new army and doubtful of its fighting skills, the senior commanders were nervous after the failure of the initial Somme offensive and an instinctive – but inappropriate – response was to reinforce discipline along pre-war lines, in an attempt to make the volunteers into 'proper' soldiers.

With the benefit of hindsight, we may now, at the start of the twenty-first-century, feel that several of the men shot for cowardice in 1916 were harshly treated, the best-known case being that of Harry Farr. Certainly in reviewing the transcripts of the cowardice trials one has more sympathy with the executed men than in the majority of the cases of desertion.

Cowardice in 1916, and now, is a subjective issue, and it was the only capital offence in the Great War where this was the case. All the other offences are objective and capable of definitive proof.

In the context of cowardice, it is easy to think that the 'chateau generals' living in comfort miles behind the lines had no appreciation of the front line horrors endured by the average soldier. Whilst there were undoubtedly good generals and bad generals in the British Army, the majority were more in touch with the realities of war than is generally understood. Seventy-eight men holding general officer rank died in the war, the majority of them by shell or small arms fire, indicating their proximity to the enemy.[4] For example, during the battle of Loos three divisional commanders were killed in the front line, and during the Somme battle Maj. Gen. Ingouville-Williams, commanding 34th Division, was killed whilst reconnoitring the ground. Many of the men who had reached this rank were personally brave – several of them held decorations for gallantry and knew what it was like to be under fire – but their own bravery sometimes meant that they had little sympathy for those who were less psychologically robust than themselves.

If some of these men did not receive justice, the cause was multifactorial. Some of the courts martial were hastily convened and lacked legal input, in some cases the view of one formation commander (such as Gen. Monro) outweighed comments by other commanders, and in other cases medical boards were not convened when they might have been. The outstanding sadness of the cases involving men whose nerves had been shattered by battle is that the medical services simply did not know how to deal with mental breakdown unless it was so obvious as to be unmistakable. To the average doctor Harry Farr, when out of the line, would probably have seemed like any other soldier – tired, showing signs of strain, perhaps nervous if there was a sudden noise. If men such as he had been diagnosed as suffering from shell shock the army would have been seriously depleted of manpower. It would be another thirty or forty years before the scale of mental trauma suffered by these men would be understood.

CHAPTER 17

LONG TIME AWAY:
DESERTION – THE REAL PROBLEM

A perfect shield adorns some Thracian now.

I had no choice, and threw it in a wood.

Oh well, I saved my skin, so let it go!

A new one's just as good!

ARCHILOCHUS, 648 BC

The widely-held belief that most soldiers were executed for cowardice is mistaken. By far the most serious disciplinary problem confronting the BEF was desertion.

An unknown member of the War Office summed up desertion after the war in an official report on the subject:

'Desertion' is dealt with in Section 12 of the Army Act, and is defined as absence without leave with the intention either of never returning to the Service at all or avoiding some particular onerous or dangerous duty. It differs from cowardice in that it involves a definite and specific intention. It need not occur in the presence of any danger and is more likely to be the result of a calculating regard by a man for his own safety than cowardice which is inspired by fear in the presence of actual danger.[1]

David French says that in 1928 the military members of the Army Council 'accepted that cowardice may be a momentary impulse, but insisted that desertion was a "cold blooded and deliberate crime of the meanest description"'.[2]

The crucial difference between absence without leave and desertion was always the intent. The *Manual of Military Law* was quite clear that in some instances intention to desert permanently is clear, such as if a man is found in plain clothes heading away from his unit.[3] However, it goes on to point out

215

that length of absence itself is not conclusive of intention, nor can intent be judged solely by a man's distance from his unit. A man may be only briefly absent or found only a short distance from his unit, but other circumstances, such as being in plain clothes like the first deserter, Highgate, or without his equipment, make his intention clear. It is for these reasons that at most capital trials the prosecution goes to considerable lengths to prove that by being absent a man misses front line trench duty, and therefore is 'avoiding some particular onerous or dangerous duty'.

Absence and desertion were very serious problems during the war. Postwar statistics show that the overall desertion rate between 1914 and 1918 was 10.26 per 1,000 men – so that in an army of 1 million men, there were over 10,000 absentees – the equivalent of a whole division of troops.[4] The size of the problem was already becoming apparent by mid 1915, when instructions were issued by the War Office, drawing attention to the fact that there had been 1,251 desertions from the Expeditionary Force and over 20,000 desertions from the new army, reserve and other regular units. It continued:

> Desertion during active service is one of the most serious crimes a soldier can commit, a fact which does not appear to be everywhere sufficiently appreciated by the officers who as presidents and members of courts martial have to deal with this offence, as sentences in not a few cases have been exceedingly lenient.[5]

This was followed in August 1915 by another instruction drawing attention to the matter and showing that 46 per cent of cases dealt with in July had resulted in sentences of less than three months.[6] Such instructions, encouraging officers to deal more harshly with deserters, were quite improper, as the court martial panel was specifically empowered to deal with each case on its merits as it saw fit, not to 'follow orders' as regards sentencing.

As the war progressed, lists and descriptions of absentees were printed and circulated to assist in the identification of deserters. These lists were long documents, including many hundreds of men. Some have been preserved in various war diaries and provide interesting descriptions of the absentee soldiers as well as demonstrating the scale of the problem.[7]

In total during the war there were a total of 126,818 courts martial for desertion and absence. In the field there were 7,361 courts martial for desertion and 37,034 for absence, and in the UK there were 31,269 courts martial for desertion and 51,154 for absence. Of these absentees, only 266 were actually executed – a tiny fraction of the total deserters.

Some deserters, even from the earliest days of the war, managed to evade the searching arm of military justice for a very long time indeed. The case of Drummer Rose of the Yorkshire Regiment is remarkable among those deserters who were apprehended, as his two-year absence stands as some kind of record. If 'intention' to desert (as required by the Army Act) needed to be proved, Rose's period of absence from December 1914 to December 1916 would seem to be a reasonable proof of a clear intention to dodge the dangers of the front line.[8]

Rose was a drummer with the 2nd Yorkshires who had joined the army as a regular soldier in 1909. He had fallen out in the dark as the battalion was marching up to the line at Fleurbaix on the night of 19 December 1914; the 2nd Yorkshires had been out since October 1914. At the court martial Company Quartermaster Sergeant E. J. Keane testified that he saw Rose at the battalion rear echelon ammunition checkpoint and asked him why he was not with his company. Rose claimed that he had hurt his leg and was trying to catch up. The CQMS next saw the accused on 16 December 1916, two years later.

Rose's story was unusual. At his court martial before three infantry officers and a court martial officer on 18 February 1917 he pleaded not guilty and made a statement that he was 'very sorry to have disgraced the regiment' and that he 'had never meant to stay away for so long'. He told the court that he had received news from home that his brother had died and his father 'had taken to drink' – a not uncommon occurrence in 1914 – and as a result he had been very troubled about his mother's financial state. To add to his woes, he said, he had got a girl pregnant 'just before the regiment left for the front'. He added: 'I am very ashamed ... but I could not help it, as it is through having so much trouble on my mind that I did it.' Rose also asked the court to note that he was 'very impulsive and forgetful'.

Clearly unimpressed, the court cross-examined the soldier closely on his story. Rose claimed that 'he didn't remember leaving the Regiment', which after two years may well have contained some truth. Much more damaging was his admission that despite his emotional plea about family troubles he had not made any financial allotment to his mother. He claimed not to know how long he had been away from his regiment, or how he had fed and clothed himself over the past two years. Despite a succession of members of his old drum platoon to testify that they knew him as a 'good and steady soldier before the war' the court rapidly found Rose guilty of desertion and sentenced him to death.

In this they must have been influenced by the circumstances of Rose's arrest. He had been living in the deserters' favourite rat holes among the damaged houses and cellars of Hazebrouck just behind the lines and had been given away to the gendarmerie. 'Acting on information received', Gendarme Maréchal Antoine Dorge and his team of gendarmes raided a house at Pont Rommel. Whilst Dorge 'rattled the front door', Rose bolted out of the back, to fall into the arms of the waiting gendarme whom Dorge had prudently posted to watch the back door. Rose claimed to the Frenchman that he worked in the British military hospital, but a brief visit under escort exposed the lie and Rose was handed over to the military police to await judgement.

Any plea of mitigation was bound to be a counsel of desperation in a case like this. Brig. R.W. Morgan of 21st Infantry Brigade minuted divisional HQ: 'There is no officer left serving with the Battalion who was present when Rose deserted ... He immediately deserted [in 1914] undoubtedly with the deliberate intention of avoiding service ... I cannot discover any redeeming feature in this case.' Commanders of 30 Division, VII Corps and Third Army all agreed. After two years' absence there was no attempt to suspend the sentence or give Rose another chance. Drummer Rose was executed by firing squad on 4 March 1917. Perhaps the most charitable judgement on Rose is that he deserted hoping that the war would be over by Christmas, when he could then return to his unit without fear of serious reprisals. When it was not, the unfortunate drummer was trapped by his own actions and he had to carry on waiting, living on his wits.

While time is obviously a factor in Rose's case, the question that must have been on the court's mind was: how on earth had he survived so long? Another early desertion case shows just how resourceful determined deserters could be.

Cpl Frederick Ives of 3th Worcesters left his regiment only six weeks after Britain's declaration of war. On 10 September 1914 CSM Hodgkinson of 3rd Worcesters had marched Cpl Ives before the CO, where he was remanded on an unspecified court martial charge. On 13 September, whilst he was waiting for a summary of evidence to be prepared on this charge, Ives made a run for it from his trench whilst under shellfire. He was next seen nearly ten months later when he was arrested, dressed in plain clothes, by a Sgt Dyce of the Gordon Highlanders at Gournay en Bray on 24 June 1915.[9] Ives, who pleaded not guilty, gave his defence on oath. He claimed that he had been 'picked on' by the other NCOs and CSM of his new battalion as he had been transferred from the 4th Battalion of the Worcesters to the 3rd Battalion.

The 4th Worcesters were in Burma on the outbreak of war and it is reasonable to suppose that Ives was at home at that time and was drafted to join the 3rd Battalion when it sailed for France on 16 August 1914. Life for the junior NCO in his new battalion may not have been easy. The Worcesters had a reputation as a very close-knit, introverted regiment and rivalry between the individual battalions would have been keen.

Cpl Ives may very well have had a rough ride on arrival as a corporal in 3rd Worcesters, especially if he had fallen foul of his new CSM. He also claimed that he had 'lost his memory when he went away'. In an astonishing admission at the court martial, he then claimed to have 'worked in a manu-factory of munitions' during his absence. He also said that he 'had no inten-tion of leaving the country and intended to give himself up'. Although there have been some suggestions that he may have been shell-shocked, no evi-dence was produced at the court martial and, despite Ives's unusual contri-bution to the French war effort, he was rapidly found guilty and sentenced to death. Surprisingly, the court then recommended mercy, 'on the grounds that in his sworn evidence the accused states that he was suffering from loss of memory when he absented himself … and the possibility that such loss of memory may have resulted from heavy shell fire'.

Higher authority was unimpressed. Getting a civilian job and being away for nine months since the start of the war constituted desertion in early summer 1915, and even memories of shellfire were expected to wear off. Cpl Ives was shot at Ypres on 26 July 1915. The mystery remains: just how did Frederick Ives fend for himself behind the battle lines in provincial France for so long during the war? The obvious answer seems to be that, like so many other deserters, he found some lonely Frenchwoman to take him in, whose husband may have been away at the front, or dead. How else could he have got a job making munitions and found clothing and shelter? Whatever the truth, Ives took his secret to his grave. Today he lies buried with his comrades in the Perth (China Wall) cemetery in the Ypres Salient.

Some idea of how men like Rose and Ives survived can be found in Brig. Gen. Frank Crozier's memoirs:

> Hazebrouck was one of the towns where deserters were sheltered. When Hazebrouck eventually became a front-line zone … and the civil population and foodstuffs were evacuated, the deserters in hiding found themselves stranded in the cellars of houses which had been destroyed by gunfire. In their efforts to exist and escape capture those unfortunate men

turned bandit and looted and robbed the dumps at night for food. It was unsafe to venture through Hazebrouck alone at night, and unarmed, in 1918, even though the cellars were periodically combed.[10]

Another early deserter who managed to evade capture for nine months was Pte T. Harris of the Royal West Kents, who actually deserted before even Thomas Highgate. Unable to face the unpleasant reality of war, Harris disappeared in the confusion after Le Câteau, probably on 27 August 1914. But Harris was more ambitious than many of his fellow deserters. Not for him the rat-like existence in the ruined cellars at Hazebrouck, or even warming his feet at some recently bereaved Frenchwoman's fire: Harris moved in with an English family in Paris and even – the evidence can be seen quite clearly in the court martial papers, although it was struck out as inadmissible at the court martial – posed as a sergeant of the military police '*searching for deserters*'. As a plan this bold stroke was, sooner or later, bound to attract the attention of the real British military police in Paris doing just that, and Harris was arrested, posing as a detective, in plain clothes, at Bures on 28 May 1915.

At Harris's court martial at Dickebusch on 12 June 1915 the hard-pressed commander of 13th Brigade was unable – presumably because of officer casualties – to appoint the necessary three officers with more than one year's service, and the FGCM consisted of a senior major, a captain from Harris's own regiment and a second lieutenant.

Harris's defence is worth quoting in its entirety; on oath he testified:

> I was at the Battle of Mons and Le Cateau and my nerves were shattered by the sights I saw. I lost my memory and wandered away after Le Cateau. I don't remember anything until I found myself in Paris. In Paris I met some English people who persuaded me to stay with them and after a time I did not like to come back. I am very sorry I stayed away.

The deserter's wisdom in 'staying away' in the interests of personal survival was graphically endorsed. Not a single officer or senior NCO from his unit appears to have survived to testify at Harris's court martial nine months on, as his battalion had lost 516 soldiers dead in the nine months between the start of the war and June 1915. For a unit that went to war 1,000 strong, these are heart-stopping casualties, especially if we remember that for every man killed there are two others wounded. The RWKs had actually suffered a *150* per cent casualty rate in nine months. The new acting CO, Maj. Robinson, when asked for his recommendation, scribbled on a page of a field notebook:

I am not aware of [Harris's] personal characteristics and can find no-one who is now with the battalion who is. In my opinion the fact that he was in France during the whole period of his absence and is unable to show that he made any attempt to rejoin his battalion is sufficient evidence that his sole object was to avoid service.[11]

Harris was shot as a long-term deserter on 21 June 1915 and his grave, like that of Cpl Ives, is in Perth (China Wall) cemetery. No other members of the Royal West Kents were executed for the rest of the war.

Perhaps the best example of deserters surviving in France was the case of another long-term deserter much later in the war. To say that Pte Ernest Lawrence of the 2nd Battalion of the Devonshire Regiment was a resourceful rogue is not uncharitable. Lawrence, who was absent on no fewer than three occasions in 1917, had some remarkable adventures in his attempts to hide *inside* the BEF.

Finally caught and brought to justice on 4 November 1917, Pte Lawrence told an unusual story at his court martial.[12] On 5 March 1917 he had first absented himself from a forward ration party and made his way back to the safety and relative comfort of the No. 2 Infantry Base Depot at Rouen, well behind the lines. Here, on 11 March, Lawrence coolly reported himself to the orderly room and said that he had been posted from No. 8 Stationary Hospital at Rouen. Unfortunately, simple checks soon exposed this fiction and by 15 March his story had been unmasked. Sent back to his battalion as a prisoner on 15 April, he absconded on the night of 8 May 1917 from a front line working party of prisoners under escort at Gonnelieu. A week later, on 15 May, Lawrence turned up at No. 49 Infantry Base Depot at Le Havre on the Channel coast and reported to the orderly room asking to draw his pay. Asked for proof of identity, he went to get his pay book and returned with a forged and doctored AB64 pay book made out to a 'Pte Richards'. The suspicious orderly room clerk, Cpl Champion, reported the matter and searched the newly arrived soldier's kit to find the incriminating torn-out pages of an AB64 stolen from a Pte Richards. Lawrence was arrested.

At his trial later in the year, after he had finally been arrested for *yet another* offence of desertion, he offered a novel defence. Under oath Lawrence admitted that he had 'left his battalion' while awaiting court martial for his first attempt to desert. The next passage of testimony is highly unusual: 'I went to Rouen by train (in March 1917). I intended finishing plans of a trench mortar of my own design which had been favourably considered by the War Office, subject to alterations. My CO, Lt Col. Sunderland, was reluctant to assist me; hence my absence.' Lawrence openly admitted to having altered his pay book at Le Havre during his second attempt to desert, adding: 'It was a bold game to play, but I could not get any satisfaction as regards my plans ...'

A presumably bemused court then cross-examined Lawrence about his movement order to Rouen signed by Lt Col. Sunderland, produced in evidence. Lawrence admitted that he had forged it. The court then considered Lawrence's *third* charge of desertion. Following his arrest at Le Havre for forging an AB64 and absence in May 1917, an escort from his battalion had been sent to collect their errant soldier. On 23 May, while being loaded onto the motor lorry, Lawrence slipped his guard and fled, leaving the embarrassed regimental police escort to return empty-handed to 2nd Devons and admit that, yet again, their bird had flown.

Five days later, on 28 May 1917, the Royal Flying Corps Machine Shop at Pont de Larche gained a new employee. Lawrence, claiming to be 'Pte Shakespeare', reported to Sgt Goatcher RFC with a letter of authority posting him to the RFC and signed yet again by the ubiquitous Lt Col. Sunderland. Knowing only too well the turbulence and documentary confusion possible in a 2 million strong army, Lawrence was given a job in the RFC drawing office 'until the paperwork caught up'. Here he soon acquired an RFC uniform and, in his own words at the court martial, 'I interviewed the Adjutant and he told me that I would be tested ... and subsequently transferred to the RFC. I passed my trade test and all went well to Aug 9th when I was placed under arrest as an absentee ...' On this third desertion, Lawrence had effectively engineered his own transfer to the RFC!

Faced with this lengthy catalogue of absence and deception, the court sentenced Lawrence to death as a deserter. The usual confirmatory opinions were called for; Lt Col. Sunderland's successor as CO of 2nd Devons, Lt Col. Milton, was scathing: 'This man has been a constant source of annoyance and is absolutely untrustworthy ... he is sullen and inclined to be insolent.' The commander of 23rd Brigade drew attention to Lawrence's extensive previous crime sheet. It turned out that he had been convicted twice before: in December 1916, when a previous FGCM had awarded him forty days' FP No. 1 for absence without leave on active service, and on 2 March 1917 for falling out from a front line working party without permission, for which he had received twenty-eight days' FP No. 1. (Interestingly, Lawrence first deserted to Rouen in March 1917 just three days after this award by the CO, Lt Col.

Sunderland. It may have been that he could not face another month of FP.) Brig. Gen. Grogan's recommendation was uncompromising:

> Deliberate and carefully considered desertion is disclosed on three separate occasions. Such an example must have a dangerous influence on the fighting qualities of those with whom he comes into contact, and an exemplary punishment is required for the sake of deterrent.

This unequivocal opinion was endorsed by both the corps and the army commanders, and confirmed by the commander-in-chief. Pte Lawrence of 2nd Devons was shot – probably to his own surprise – at Ypres at 6.50 a.m. on 22 November 1917.

Lawrence's surprise – if indeed that was the case – may have been because he appears to have been relying on the fact that he was still serving in uniform in the RFC, therefore may have felt secure against any capital charge of desertion. If so, he was sadly mistaken. Serving in safety back with the RFC clearly constituted desertion from 'a specific (and hazardous) front line duty' with 2nd Devons risking their necks in the firing line.

CHAPTER 18

THE 'WORCESTER FOUR'

I'm more afraid of the effects of King Alcohol than all the bullets of the enemy.

STONEWALL JACKSON, 1862

At 4 a.m. on 26 July 1915 an event unique in the British Army of the First World War took place when four men were executed by firing squad simultaneously. The event was noted in the war diary of the A & QMG, 3rd Division; 'July 26th 4 men of 3rd Battalion Worcestershire Regiment sentenced to death. Execution carried out at 4 a.m. Some rain, heavy rain during night of 25/26.'[1] The four men had all been found guilty of desertion, and were Ptes Alfred Thompson, John Robinson, Bert Hartells and Ernest Fellows. It has been suggested that five men were executed together, the fifth man being Cpl Frederick Ives of the same battalion, and that the executions took place on the Ypres ramparts.[2] The evidence for this came from a statement by Sir Gordon Macready in his memoirs, in which he says that five men had been sentenced to death for desertion and it fell to him to arrange the executions, the APM being ill. He wrote: 'On a wet and windy morning just before daybreak, I had to see that the usual ritual was observed. Blindfolded, with a little paper target fixed to their chests, and bound to a wooden chair, these men were shot by firing squads from Regiments other than their own.'[3] He does not specifically mention where these executions took place but says that one man was an American and another a champion boxer, but his recollections appear faulty in this respect.

John Peaty states that the four men were shot separately,[4] but the war diary extract and the fact that the same APM (Maj. Rich) certified on the courts martial papers that all four executions were carried out at 4 a.m. strongly suggest that the four men were shot together. Cpl Frederick Ives had been executed four days earlier, at 4 a.m. on 22 July, this being noted on the court martial proceedings,[5] agreeing with his date of death on the Commonwealth

War Graves Commission database and his death certificate.[6] His execution was also noted in the war diary of the 4th South Lancs: 'Battalion furnished Promulgation Party and Firing Party for execution of 12295 Cpl F Ives 3/Worcester Regt. Charge desertion.'[7] At the time this battalion was near Busseboom, a mile south-east of Poperinge; the divisional HQ (where Ives would have been held in custody of the APM) was in the same area and the records of the CWGC show that although Cpl Ives is now buried in Perth (China Wall) Cemetery, his body was originally interred near Busseboom.[8] The scene of his execution at Busseboom is now marked by a plaque. The 4th South Lancs was a Territorial unit, attached at that time to 7th Brigade, and providing a firing party must have been an unpleasant task for these 'Saturday night soldiers'. The evidence therefore contradicts the suggestion that Ives was shot on the Ypres ramparts.

The other four men deserted from their unit as two separate pairs, and it was only chance that led to their simultaneous execution. On 15 June 1915 Bert Hartells and Ernest Fellows, along with the other men of their platoon, were issued with extra ammunition ready for an attack the following morning but by 5 p.m. both were missing. On 8 July the military police found the pair in Hondeghem, halfway to Dunkirk, wearing uniforms but without their equipment. When questioned, they said that they had left their unit, near Ypres, two days previously.[9] In fact, by 8 July, the men had been absent for three weeks.

They both used drunkenness as a defence. Hartells said that at about 2.30 p.m. on 15 June he had gone out for a drink, met a friend and drunk two or three bottles of wine, 'and not being used to drink I became the worse for it and instead of returning to my bivouac I wandered away. I then got ill and took another drink to put me right again, this made me worse.' He said that he then met another friend and had some more drinks, then tried to find his battalion. He told the court that he did not intend to desert as he had a wife and children.

Ernest Fellows's defence was similar; he too said that he went for a drink on 15 June, and: 'I had my drink and met several friends and had more than was good for me.' He said that when he left the estaminet he lost his way, and had been trying to find his battalion when found in a barn by the military police – he carefully did not remind the court that he had been absent for three weeks before his capture, giving the impression that his absence had lasted only a few days. Like Hartells, he said that he had not intended to desert, being a married man with children.

Pte Hartells was a pre-war regular who had enlisted in 1904 and arrived in France in August 1914. However, his service record showed that he had a previous conviction for absence, from 25 November 1914 to 4 February 1915, and his character was described only as 'fair'. Fellows had enlisted in September 1914, and had gone to France in December. His 'crime sheet' showed only two minor offences and his character was described as 'very good'. Although from this it appears that he was a 1914 volunteer, his regimental number suggests that he may have been a reservist.

Both men were found guilty of desertion and sentenced to death. After the trial the battalion CO wrote of Hartells: 'This man has always done his work well in the trenches,' and said that his previous absence had been from the transport lines and that he had not avoided any dangerous duty. Of Fellows he said: 'This man has done his work well whilst in the trenches. He appears to be rather simple and stupid and easily led wrong.' Brigade, division, corps and army commanders all endorsed the death sentence, which was confirmed by Sir John French on 23 July 1915.

Pte Thompson and Pte Robinson were tried on the same day, by the same court martial panel. Like Hartells and Fellows these two men were tried separately, although the prosecution evidence was the same for both men.[10]

On 27 June Thompson and Robinson had both been present when their company commander had told them that they would be moving to the trenches that evening. When the battalion paraded at 8 p.m. they were missing. Eight days later, on 5 July, they were found at Abancourt, on a train going to Rouen. When discovered they had no travel passes, and told the NCO who found them that they had been put on the train by a French officer. He did not believe their story, and as they could not produce a pass, arrested them.

Robinson, in his defence, said that he had gone to Vlamertinghe, where Thompson had met some friends: 'We both got the worse for drink. I cannot remember what happened during the night. The next day we got brandy from a farmhouse and wandered along the road, we lay down that night in a damp field.' The next day, they went to a town that they discovered was St Roche, and reported to a French barracks, but had been unable to make themselves understood and had then gone to the station, where a French officer had put them on the Rouen train. As in the previous case, Robinson implied that he had only been absent for a couple of days, whereas he and Thompson were, in fact, missing for over a week. Robinson ended his statement: 'I did not intend to desert. I have been out in the country since August 1914 and finish my 13 years service in December this year.'

Thompson's defence was similar. He said that he had gone to buy bread when he met friends and had too much to drink. 'My two friends left me and I then wandered all night and the next day not knowing where I was going. I suffer from loss of memory owing to an accident that happened to me when I was 16 years old when I was knocked down by a horse and cart and had my skull fractured near my eyes. This always affects me when I have too much to drink.' He then gave the same story as Robinson about going to the French barracks and being put on the train.

The court was not persuaded by their defence and both were found guilty and sentenced to death, both being recommended to mercy by the court, Thompson 'on account of injury to his head which may have affected him' and Robinson 'on account of his good service during present campaign, he has been out since the commencement of the war.'

The surviving officer commanding 3rd Worcesters wrote about Robinson, after the trial: 'This man's character, both in the trenches and out, has not been satisfactory. His nerves have been bad for some time past,' and mentioned that he had joined the battalion in February 1915 (although he had gone to France in August 1914 with another battalion).[11] Brig. Gen. Ballard, commanding 7th Infantry Brigade, endorsed the recommendation to mercy. Of Thompson, his CO wrote: 'The conduct of this man both in and out of the trenches has until recently been good. Latterly it has been somewhat indifferent due no doubt to the fact that his nerves have been in a bad state for some time past.' Brig. Gen. Ballard again supported the recommendation to mercy. However, division, corps and army commanders all agreed that the death penalty should be carried out.

On 16 July the DAA & QMG of 3rd Division ordered a medical board to be assembled to investigate Pte Thompson's claim of loss of memory. However, the board found: 'There is absolutely no evidence to show that the injury referred to has any permanent effect upon this man's nervous system and are of opinion that he does not suffer from loss of memory as a result of this injury.'

Sentence on the two men was confirmed by the commander-in-chief on 23 July. A note on the court martial proceedings reads: ' Sentence on the above duly carried out at 4 a.m. 26th July', signed by the acting adjutant of the 1st Wiltshires, and endorsed by Maj. Rich, the APM of 3rd Division. A similar note is written on the proceedings of the Hartells and Fellows case.

Again the evidence is that these men were not executed in Ypres. At the time of the execution the 3rd Worcesters were in the front line at St Eloi and it is most unlikely that the number of men needed to furnish four firing parties would have been taken out of the line. The promulgation and confirmation of sentence were noted by a Second Lt Peel, adjutant of 1st Wilts, suggesting that this regiment provided the firing parties for the execution. On 26 July this unit was at Dickebusch Huts and the four men of the Worcesters were executed in that vicinity.[12] The records of the Commonwealth War Graves Commission show that these four men were buried about 1,000 yards north-west of Dickebusch, although their bodies were subsequently moved.[13] Their graves were originally near the farm of Marcel Coene, where other executed men were already buried.[14] Ptes Thompson, Robinson and Hartells were reburied in Aeroplane Cemetery, but Pte Fellows is buried with Cpl Ives in Perth (China Wall) Cemetery.

The evidence is, therefore, that these four men from 3rd Worcesters were executed together and that the apparent eyewitness account of five men being shot on 26 July 1915 is incorrect. The deaths were all confirmed by Maj. Rich, the APM, who had also witnessed Cpl. Ives's execution, which raises the question as to the reliability of Sir Gordon Macready's recollections – an example of how cautiously eyewitness accounts must be interpreted, especially when published long after the events to which they refer took place.

CHAPTER 19

BACK TO 'BLIGHTY' – THE HOME RUNS

How sweet to cast care to the winds ... and after wandering long to
come again to my own dear home.

CATULLUS, *c*.50 BC

Just as the Holy Grail of the escaping WW2 POW was a 'home run' from some Stalag in Germany or Poland, so the most desired outcome of the WW1 deserter from the Western Front was to get back across the Channel to the safety and security of the British Isles.

Back home, provided he kept his head down, the successful deserter was far more able to blend into the background. By careful manipulation of his identity, location and occupation, a deserter could virtually start a new life. Most deserters in the UK tried to keep a low profile, and for good reason. The authorities were always on the lookout for service deserters, of whom there were many, and every policemen in the land was on a permanent lookout for absentees and deserters from the forces. Regular lists were circulated to all police stations, and parents or relatives of known deserters could expect extra visits from the local constable and the occasional raid and search of attics and cellars by the military police. The life of the deserter staying in his home town or village was at best chancy.

Rifleman Peter Sands was a regular soldier who found that the easiest route back to the UK was with a legitimate leave pass in his pocket but was unusual in that he managed to make his way back to Belfast. After his arrest he was returned to his unit in France for trial, as was normal practice for a man who had deserted from active service abroad. The story emerged at his court martial on 30 August 1915, when he was tried for desertion, having been absent from his battalion, 1st Royal Irish Rifles, from 2 March 1915 to 7 July 1915.[1]

On 26 February, when his unit was at Laventie, Sands had been granted leave to the UK until 1 March. However, he failed to return and on 1 April was struck off the ration strength as an absentee. His trial was extremely brief, covering only a page and a half of foolscap paper. One witness gave evidence of Sands's going on leave, and the other put into evidence the official police report of his arrest in Belfast on 7 July 1915. In his defence, Sands said that he had reported at the Belfast depot on 2 March as he had lost his warrant. He alleged that he spoke to a Cpl Wright, No. 7663, who was unable to help. Sands went away and made no further attempt to rejoin his unit. He told the court: 'If I had intended to desert I would have worn plain clothes but up to the time I was arrested I always wore uniform.'

Rifleman Sands was found guilty of desertion and sentenced to death. The formation commanders all recommended that sentence should be carried out, despite the fact that he was described as having a good character and as a good soldier. Sands had been absent from the BEF for over four months, and this, combined with the distance from his unit, was taken as clear proof of his intention to desert. Gen. (as he then was) Douglas Haig, then commanding First Army, wrote: 'This is a bad case and I recommend that the extreme penalty be carried out.' Sir John French confirmed the sentence and Rifleman Sands was shot at Fleurbaix at first light on 15 September 1915.

Pte Joseph Edward Bolton was a pre-war regular who had enlisted into the Border Regiment in 1913, but had then been transferred into the 1st Cheshires, with whom he went to France in August 1914. After serving with the BEF for one month he deserted, on 22 September 1914. He was subsequently recaptured and tried for desertion by FGCM on 11 August 1915, implying that his absence had been a lengthy one. Bolton was sentenced to death, but Sir John French commuted the sentence to ten years' penal servitude, which was then suspended.

Amazingly, only three months later Bolton was allowed to go to England on leave, being due to return to his unit on 2 December 1915. Instead he took the opportunity to go absent again, and on 24 December a court of inquiry declared him to be a deserter. Eventually, on 22 February 1916 he was arrested at Balls Corn Mills, at Ince in Lancashire, where he was working under the name of Cunningham.

As was normal practice, Bolton was returned to his unit in France for trial by FGCM. He did not dispute any of the evidence presented at his trial and indeed made some unwise admissions, saying: 'I remained absent and did not report myself until I was arrested', 'I was in plain clothes when I was arrested', 'I realised I was missing duty in the trenches' and 'I did not mean to come back to this regiment. I meant to join another regiment.'[2]

In his sworn statement, Bolton said that he had gone to Victoria Station, Manchester, but missed his train back to France. Although he said that he then went to London and reported himself, he did not follow his orders to go to Southampton and instead returned to Lancashire. He explained that he was using the name Cunningham because this was his real name – he had only joined up under the name of Bolton because he had been in trouble at the time. One of his statements had the ring of truth about it: 'I got into further trouble with the regiment and was always being jeered at. That is one of the reasons I stayed away.' This throws an interesting light on the contemporary views of his fellow soldiers after his first desertion attempt – he was perceived, it seems, as having let down his 'regimental family'.

Pte Bolton was found guilty. In mitigation of punishment he said: 'I am sorry for what I have done and I ask for another chance to do better.' The court decided that he had already been given a second chance, and sentenced him to death. When the papers were passed up the chain of command for confirmation, all the formation commanders recommended that the sentence be carried into execution. His CO wrote: 'The discipline of the battalion is satisfactory except that absence from leave is prevalent. Sooner or later there is no doubt that a soldier of the battalion will be shot for absence amounting to desertion.' The men of the regiment were about to be given a stark reminder that unilateral termination of contract was not an option in the army.

The court martial documents carry detailed instructions as to the arrangements for the execution. Capt. Courtenay of 15th Brigade wrote to the CO of the 1st Cheshires:

> The sentence should be promulgated tomorrow afternoon ... The execution will take place at 5 a.m. on 14th inst., place will be notified later. You will arrange to have a grave dug at the site of execution, on evening of 13th inst, also to have two men with spades to fill in the grave after burial. The following will have to be provided by you a chair, blanket and two ropes.
>
> Your medical officer will be present and bring with him a bandage, a piece of white cloth to mark the heart and the death certificate ready made out, so that he will merely have to fill in whether death is instantaneous or not. The firing party will be found as under
>
> 1 officer & 6 men 1st Norfolk Regt
> 1 sergeant & 6 men 1st Bedfordshire Regt

The Divisional commander wishes 1 platoon from each company of your battalion to be present at the execution.[3]

The following day, Capt. Courtenay wrote again, regarding the place of execution:

...the place of execution of Pte Bolton will be on the road just W of the railway arch in L15A5/7 against the railway embankment. A room has been obtained at the Halte L9C5/1 to be used by the prisoner after promulgation. Please detail a guard of 1 Sgt and 3 men who will take over the prisoner from the Sergeant of the Divisional Guard for promulgation and who will then take the prisoner to the estaminet at the Halte and will remain as guard over him until the sentence has been carried out.[4]

Pte Joseph Bolton was shot at 5 a.m. in the prescribed place at Duisans, and was buried there. The medical officer completed his previously prepared death certificate: 'Death was practically instantaneous.' Bolton's execution was witnessed by Capt. Westmacott, the APM of the First Indian Cavalry Division, who noted the events in his diary, commenting that Bolton, tied to a chair with a white disc pinned over his heart, was the calmest man present.[5] Although Capt. Westmacott commented that the grave was unmarked, its location must have been noted as Bolton's body is now buried in Roclincourt Valley Cemetery (see page 101).

Pte William Watts of the 1st Battalion, Loyal North Lancs, also took the opportunity to go absent whilst he was on leave. On 8 November 1915 he collected the pay owing to him and set off home to Liverpool. His battalion expected him to return on 20 November, but it was the end of March before he returned under escort, having been arrested in the UK. It was clear to his commanding officer that Watts had deserted and that he should be charged with desertion, but when he investigated the case he found a woeful lack of a firm chain of evidence. Lt Col. Sanderson summarized the information available and wrote to higher authority for advice.[6] In outline the events appeared straightforward:

1. On 10 November Watts left on ten days leave.
2. On 22 November he saw a doctor who gave him a medical certificate for ten days.
3. On 29 November his equipment was found by police.
4. On 8 December his wife told police that she had not seen him since 27 November.

5. The civil police arrested Watts on 24 December in Liverpool.

6. He was sent to the rest camp in Southampton but deserted from there; there was no evidence available to confirm this.

7. On 6 March 1916 he was arrested in Liverpool and sent to Southampton on the 8th.

8. He spent from 13 to 24 March in hospital with a head wound.

9. He rejoined his battalion on 28 March 1916.

On 2 April Lt Col. Gilbert Mellor, DJAG at GHQ, advised that the two police documents detailing the arrests were admissible as evidence, but there needed to be a witness from the camp in Southampton. The camp was contacted, and replied that he had arrived there on 1 January but had escaped the following day. Unfortunately no one there could positively identify Watts and the DAA & QMG wrote to 2nd Brigade: 'The case will have to proceed as best it can without this evidence.'

The case now became even more complicated. On 25 January 1916 a court of inquiry into Watts's absence had been held, and had declared him a deserter. Gilbert Mellor deemed it advisable that one of the two main witnesses at the inquiry should give evidence at the trial. However, as so often happens in war, the principal witness had been killed and the other could not give direct evidence of desertion. Yet again the papers were sent to the DJAG. Once the official wheels of the army had been set in motion it would take more than a few technicalities to halt the legal process.

Lt Col. Gilbert Mellor replied that the second charge of desertion could not be proceeded with and prepared two carefully worded charges: first, desertion relating to the absence from 20 November to 24 December, and secondly, conduct to the prejudice of good order and discipline 'in that he on 6 March 1916 was apprehended at Liverpool dressed in plain clothes when his duty required him to be with the 1st Battalion Loyal North Lancashire Regiment on Foreign Service'. In the end the words 'dressed in plain clothes' were omitted as this could not be substantiated.

This resolved the legal niceties of the case. However, in the background Watts was claiming a history of insanity, as on 30 March a communication had been sent to the Chief Constable of Lancashire asking him to confirm (1) that Watts's father had died in an asylum and (2) that Watts's married sister was mentally defective. The answer was not helpful to Watts's case. His mother confirmed that her husband had indeed died in Rainhill asylum, where he had been detained suffering from religious mania, but she denied that her daughter suffered from any mental derangement. The police also visited the daughter and found her 'an intelligent woman for the class she belongs to'.

After all the preamble the court martial itself was brief. Only two witnesses gave evidence for the prosecution: the sergeant who had paid Watts before he went on leave and a subaltern who put into evidence the proof of Watts's arrest and the declaration of the court of inquiry.

Pte Watts's defence was brief. He told the court that when he arrived home on leave he had been told that his wife was 'carrying on with a black man'. His wife had, he said, told him that 'she did not want me and that it was only my money she wanted'. Being upset and not knowing what he was doing he had gone to London and been engaged on a ship. When he eventually got back to Liverpool he had been arrested.

After considering its finding the court heard that Watts was a regular, having served in the regiment since 1908. His conduct sheet showed a previous absence, in December 1914, of eight days. Sgt Manning testified that he had known Watts since 1908. 'He was a good soldier at the depot and in the company. He has been out since September 1914. He was in my company at the time of the Battle of Loos, where he suffered from the effects of gas and had to be admitted to hospital.'

Watts was found guilty on both charges and was sentenced to death. When asked for his opinion of the man during the confirmation process, Lt Col Sanderson said that he did not think that this soldier should be executed. He spoke well of Watts and alluded to the fact that his father had been in an asylum. The CO of this regular battalion did not think that an example was required, as discipline was good. He also pointed out that as Watts's desertion had occurred before the execution of Pte Hunter (see Chapter 24) from this unit 'he had not the benefit of the example given by that execution'. This view was supported by the brigade commander, but division and corps commanders disagreed. Gen. Monro was in command of First Army at that time and wrote: 'I recommend the execution of this case. The intention to desert is clearly substantiated', a view with which it is hard to disagree. Sentence was confirmed by General Haig, and Watts was executed at dawn on 5 May 1916. A harsh sentence on a man with a good record, but again it was the length of his absence as well as his distance from his battalion that proved a clear intention of deserting permanently.

In 1918 a young soldier from the Sherwood Foresters went on the run whilst home on leave. The story that emerged was a sad one. Pte Arthur Briggs had enlisted into the Foresters in January 1915 and had been sent to

Gallipoli, where he was promoted to lance corporal. In December 1915 he was evacuated sick, first to Mudros and then back to England, arriving home at the end of January 1916. In May 1916 he was in hospital in Newcastle, but went missing from there for fifteen days, then when discharged from hospital in August failed to report himself and was absent for another eight days. It would seem that Pte Briggs had discovered women, as an illegitimate child was born to his girlfriend in January 1917. Then in November he overstayed his leave pass and was arrested after a four-day absence by the civil police. On 7 February 1917 he returned to his unit.[7]

A year later, on 23 January 1918, he was given leave to return to the UK until 7 February. He went on leave with two other men from his battalion, the 9th Battalion, Sherwood Foresters, but failed to return on the appointed date. The only other evidence presented at his subsequent trial in July 1918 was that of his arrest in Edinburgh on 11 June 1918. This document described him as 26 years old, and said that he was in plain clothes at the time of his arrest.

Capt. Munday MC, a qualified solicitor serving in the battalion, defended Briggs. In defence, a lengthy written statement was handed in, describing the events which led to Briggs's desertion. Briggs explained that he went on leave intending to marry his girlfriend, but when he arrived home his parents objected strongly. However, he went ahead and was married on 2 February. His wife, who was in service, he said, was then sacked from her job. Briggs alleged that he had written to his regiment asking for an extension to his leave, but received no reply. After the trial this statement was followed up and a note in the file says that no letter was received.

As she had no family of her own and his family refused to help, Briggs walked from Sunderland to Edinburgh and found a job on a farm. His wife joined him there in May and found a job. Things were then made worse as he heard of the death of his father and brother. He said that he had decided to give himself up on 10 June, but was arrested before he could do so. At the end of his statement he added a note to say that his girlfriend had a child by him on 24 January 1917, when he was serving on the Somme. He ended his statement: 'This is a correct statement and I hope it will not be published broadcast [sic].'

Whether the court had any sympathy for the young soldier's alleged predicament we shall never know, but they found him guilty and sentenced him to death: again the length of his absence and the fact of his being in plain clothes proved his intention to remain absent.

When his CO was asked of his opinion of the man, during the confirmation process, he said that Briggs's character as a fighting man was 'poor' and 'his NCOs describe him as a coward'. The brigade commander commented that discipline in the battalion was poor and said: 'I recommend that sentence of death be carried out as the man is not a good soldier and an example in these cases is required.' The other commanders at division and corps level agreed, and Gen. Horne, commanding First Army, wrote that the offence of deserting while on leave was a common one and that there appeared to be no extenuating circumstances in the case.

Pte Arthur Briggs was executed at Bracquemout on 19 July 1918 at 4 a.m. His headstone carries the inscription 'Gone but not forgotten', selected by his family: whether his wife or mother we cannot tell, but interestingly the CWGC register for Hersin Cemetery describes him as 'son of Harriet Briggs'.[8]

Some of the more ingenious managed to get back to the UK without a leave pass. Two men of the 5th Dorsets, who appear to have deserted together, achieved this feat, although they found different means of reaching England.

On 26 September 1916 a party of twenty-five men from the 5th Battalion, Dorset Regiment were detailed to work at Mouquet Farm, supporting the Royal Engineers. Amongst them were Pte William Anderson and Pte John Lewis. On the evening of 28 September the roll was called and both men were present, but by next morning they were missing. At the men's subsequent trials there were difficulties in providing witnesses to the men's absence as, apart from Second Lt Trotter, all the other members of the party had become casualties.

It is not known where the two men went next. Although they both stood trial on the same day, 9 March 1917, their stories were entirely different.[9]

Anderson was tried on two charges, one of absence without leave and one of desertion. There was little evidence on the first charge. His absence at roll call on 29 September 1916 was described and a written statement put into evidence describing his arrest at Aveluy on 13 October. In it, L Cpl Jones of the military police stated that he saw Anderson enquiring where 11th Division was. Jones asked him how long it was since he had been with the division, and when Anderson replied 'a fortnight' he took him in charge. Anderson made no defence to the first charge of absence without leave.

The second charge, of desertion, related to 1 January 1917 when Anderson's unit was near Lancashire Dump, and two witnesses testified that he had not been seen by them after that date. Another witness gave evidence that Anderson had not been given any leave to go to the UK. He managed to leave France and find his way back to the UK, but his freedom did not last long. On 30 January 1917 Anderson was spotted in Fanshawe Avenue, Barking and arrested as an absentee. He told the police that he had lost his ticket and had written to ask for another, but this story did not hold up to investigation.

Pte Anderson chose to make no defence to what was patently a serious charge. After finding him guilty the court heard character evidence. His conduct sheet listed several fairly minor offences and CSM Gittens described him as a good soldier. As the sentence was passed up through the chain of command, all the formation commanders recommended that the sentence be carried out. Pte Anderson, his home run short-lived, was shot by firing squad at Beauquesne on 31 March 1917.

Pte John Lewis, who had gone missing on the same day as Anderson's first offence and who, by coincidence, was tried on the same day, presented a different story.[10] The evidence presented at his trial was extremely flimsy, and although he was found guilty and sentenced to death, a retrial was ordered.

This retrial took place on 6 April, and this time the army was taking no chances, appointing Capt. Griffith-Jones, an experienced CMO, to advise the panel. At the original trial four witnesses gave evidence and the trial covered two sheets of foolscap paper. At the retrial there were eleven witnesses and the transcript is nineteen pages long, making it one of the most detailed of the surviving records of courts martial for desertion.[11]

Evidence was given by several witnesses to show that Lewis had served with his battalion in Egypt and subsequently in France, and that in September 1916 he had been a member of a working party attached to the Royal Engineers. The reason for this amount of detail became apparent later. On 26 September Lewis had been with the working party near Mouquet Farm, on the Somme, working under continuous and heavy shellfire, but had not been seen by his unit since 28 September. The evidence presented left no doubt that the accused man was John Lewis and that he had gone missing from a very 'hot' part of the front line on 28 or 29 September.

The Town Major of Puchevillers then gave evidence. Lt Greaves had been the Town Major there since August 1916 and recognized the accused as the man he had ordered to be arrested at Puchevillers Station on 11 October 1916. He had seen Lewis at a billet used by some Railway Operating Department (ROD) men and had asked if there was anyone there other than ROD men. He said that Lewis had replied: 'I am Tom Jones and I come from Barking,' adding: 'I am a civilian and I crossed to France before the war.' When Lt Greaves pointed out that Lewis was in uniform, he claimed that he had found parts of it and had had to wear it. The officer had 'Tom Jones' arrested and he was detained in the Fifth Army Guard Detention Room pending enquiries.

'Tom Jones' remained there for some time, witnesses testifying that they had seen him there throughout October and November, and that the man was known as 'Tom Jones of Barking'. During his stay there, he was given work to do, and on one occasion objected, saying: 'I am a civilian and not a soldier and do not want to be one.' He said that he had been a stoker on board a ship and had landed in France three months before the war and had been going around with the troops since the war started. When he finally left the guardroom in December he still insisted that he was a civilian. What was omitted at this trial is what happened to Lewis when he left Puchevillers.

Pte Lewis made a statement, on oath, in his defence. He alleged he had no recollection of leaving the trenches at Mouquet Farm and said: 'I deny that I have ever stood in front of an officer in khaki and told him that I was a civilian, as far as I can say. That is all I have to say.' Under cross-examination he denied ever being at Puchevillers or Toutencourt (where his battalion had been prior to his going to Mouquet Farm). He added: 'I have learnt that I am not a civilian through my people telling me so. I have been told that I was in Egypt with this battalion but I have no recollection of being so.' Nowhere in the prosecution evidence does it refer to Lewis having been to England, but he alludes to it, mentioning that when he was taken to the police court in Folkestone his brothers and sisters recognized him and told him he belonged to the 5th Dorsets.

The court did not believe the story of loss of memory – the man had given a false name and particulars. A man with genuine loss of memory might forget his name and background, but on finding himself in uniform he was likely to realize that he must be a soldier and would not 'remember' a false name. Lewis was found guilty and sentenced to death. His military superiors could find no extenuating circumstances and he was executed on 19 April 1917.

The case contains elements of the bizarre. Reading the two trial transcripts is like looking at two entirely different cases. In the first trial, the key evidence relating to the desertion was that Lewis had left his battalion on the Somme and had been arrested in the UK, implying that he had deserted to England. However, in his defence at the first trial, he stated that he had been roaming around Puchevillers and had been taken to the guardroom by the Town Major. 'There I went before a Colonel and I wouldn't tell him where I belonged to,' Lewis said. He alleged that after two and a half months there, he had been sent to Boulogne and then to England, with two gunners, who on arrival at Folkestone handed him over to the military police. At that trial Lewis had said: 'I joined the battalion in Egypt in January 1916, I enlisted in April 1915. I am 20 next May, or 21, I can't remember which.' At this trial his memory of events after leaving his unit seems quite clear.

There is little doubt that Lewis and Anderson conspired together to desert in September 1916, and probably set off together. It seems beyond coincidence that Anderson was arrested in his home town of Barking following his second attempt at desertion in January 1917, while Lewis alleged that he came from Barking when masquerading as Tom Jones. At some point after leaving Mouquet Farm in September 1916 the two men split up, with Anderson being arrested at Aveluy in October and Lewis making his way to Puchevillers. One question remains: why did the APM put Lewis on the ship to England? He seems to have been sent back under some sort of escort, and the escort handed him over to the police immediately on arrival, so the suspicion is that he was sent back to the UK simply to be identified, and that this is why evidence of his arrest in the UK was not presented at the second trial. The army could hardly use the fact that Lewis had been arrested in the UK as showing intent to desert if they had put him on the boat themselves. In the end they did not need to. Despite his claims 'not to remember', the evidence of Lewis's sojourn at Puchevillers was quite enough to establish intent to desert his regiment and to send him before a firing squad.

CHAPTER 20

ALMOST MADE IT

How frightening the cost to succeed – but to fail is too awful to think about.

KRONENBURGER, 1964

For the soldiers trying to make a it back to Blighty the first problem was getting across the Channel. Travel control security at the BEF's main ports was tight, with special Field Security Teams from the newly formed Intelligence Corps supplementing the ever-suspicious eye of the Military Police. In addition, the army's 'Q (Movements)' staff and Travel Control Officers could be relied on to examine both officers' and soldiers' leave warrants and other papers carefully before permitting them to board the regular cross-Channel ferries.

Despite this, the rear echelons of the BEF and especially the port areas acted like a magnet for deserters heading for home. Although many by 1917–18 had opted for a life on the run, living a parasitic life scavenging around the huge base area camps such as Etaples and Boulogne, a few braver souls moved into the port towns, waiting their chance near the docks.

One such was a Pte James Briggs of 2nd Battalion, the Border Regiment. A re-enlisted special reservist, he arrived in France with a draft during the winter lull of 1914–15 and joined his battalion on 10 January 1915. Ten days later, when his battalion was at Sailly, the early morning roll was called and Briggs was found to be missing. He was next seen by a Cpl Mathews of the Worcesters at Le Havre. On the evening of 22 January 1915, alerted by a docker that 'there were soldiers in the Southampton boat', and knowing that boarding was not permitted before 9 p.m., Mathews searched the ship and found Briggs and a Pte Gardner hiding in the hold. Briggs told Cpl Mathews that 'we have been sent from No. 1 Hospital, Rouen, to go to the hospital ship'. As Mathews pointed out: 'They could not very well mistake the hospital ship as it is a very large boat and the mail boat a very small one.' When he discovered that Briggs had no movement order or travel warrant Cpl Mathews hauled the pair off to the local military hospital to check their story, which unsurprisingly turned out to be a pack of lies. Mathews arrested both men, and they were confined in Le Havre in a temporary guardroom.[1]

During the night of 30 January Briggs escaped from confinement by the simple expedient of removing two of the old boxes used to make the makeshift wall of the guardroom. Unbelievably he was next found drunk at 11 a.m. next morning in a bar in the Rue du Champs de Foire in Le Havre. This time he was confined to a more secure prison in the town jail.

Briggs put up no defence. Although on trial for his life he gave a monosyllabic 'No' to the court requests for an explanation. Verbatim, the transcript reads:

Do you apply to give evidence as a witness yourself?
No.
Do you intend to call any witness in your defence?
No.

In what must have been desperation the court then asked Briggs:

Have you anything to say in your defence?
No.

The court then closed to consider its verdict. Briggs's five previous convictions for absence were then revealed and Briggs invited to say something in mitigation of sentence. His statement was brief and far from the point:

I was taken from my house when I was 15 years old, and have never seen my parents since.

That was it. Pte James Briggs was found guilty and sentenced to death.

The trial papers went up through the chain of command for confirmation of sentence. Maj. Gen. Capper wrote: 'Pte Briggs only recently joined the battalion with a draft from England on 10 January 1915, there has been no opportunity of judging his fighting qualities. His general behaviour, from his records, is Bad.' Capper also commented that discipline in the battalion was bad. He ended: 'I cannot find any extenuating circumstances. The desertion was evidently planned and deliberate … This case is genuine desertion and an attempt to leave the country.' It may be thought that these comments were penned by some 'chateau general' far behind the lines. In fact, Maj. Gen. Capper was one of the seventy-eight British general officers who died on active service during the war. At the battle of Loos, on 26 September 1915, after a failed attack on the Quarries at Hulluch, Capper went forward to reorganize the attack personally and was mortally wounded by small arms fire. Capt. Bennett wrote of the incident: 'The rifle fire was hot and we were coming over, necessarily in small numbers at a time. As I ran across I overtook General Capper running with our men. He was actually joining in the assault. He must have been shot almost immediately as I did not see him again.'[2] No chateau general, this.

The sentence was confirmed by Sir John French, and Pte Briggs was executed at Rostraete at 7.30 a.m. on 6 March 1915.

Pte Briggs almost made it back to England. The anonymity of the base ports, teeming with soldiers, and the hope of an escape back home lured other deserters like a magnet. Some were probably waiting their chance to slip on board a ship, others just attempted to blend into the background, safe from the dangers of the front line.

Amongst the capital courts martial there are a few cases where justice seems to have been harsh, and there are other cases where a soldier with a good record deserted after a long period at the front. However, there are other cases where there seems little excuse and a man appears to deserve the full retribution of the law by any standards. One such man was Pte George Mills of the Duke of Cornwall's Light Infantry, who deserted without ever having seen action.[3]

It appears that Pte Mills enlisted in February 1915 and was posted to France only three weeks later. On 31 July his battalion, 2nd DCLI, was in the support line near Erquinghem and Mills, as an officer's servant, had been left behind in the billets. It had been arranged between him and the other servants that he would wait up until the officers returned from the front line at about 4 a.m., and one of the other men lent Mills his watch so that he would know the time. When the men arrived back at the billets, Mills gave the officers some tea.

Next morning he was missing, apparently taking with him various personal items and some cheques, belonging to two of the officers, and his comrade's watch.

On 2 August 1915 Mills presented himself at the APM's office in Boulogne, dressed as a Second Lieutenant. He told them he was Lt Mulock and had lost his leave pass to England, and wanted fresh papers. He was asked how he had come to lose them, and said that he had lost his pocket book whilst cycling. The suspicious APM enquired how, if he was only passing through, he came to have a bicycle. Mills did not make an adequate reply, and the APM asked him to return later, and in the meantime telegraphed the battalion.

On the same day Mills went to the Boulogne branch of Cox's Bank and asked the cashier to cash a cheque for £8. The cashier refused to pay such a large sum and Mills changed it to £5, signing the cheque as Lt Martin. The next day he went to the same bank and attempted to draw another cheque for £5 in the name of Albert George Battersby, but the cashier recognized him and asked whether or not he was Lt Martin. Mills replied that he was Lt Martin and that the cheque had been given him by a brother officer two months ago. The cashier pointed out that the cheque was dated 3 August and called for an escort to take 'Lt Martin' to the APM.

Mills was taken to the APM's office by the Port Security section of the recently formed Intelligence Corps, and was left in the outer office whilst the officer spoke with the APM. He tried to run away, but was caught by Sgt Lott, who had been in the outer office. He was then taken to the field punishment barracks and searched, when various items were found which had been reported as stolen.

In September 1915 Pte Mills was tried on eight charges: desertion, two charges of stealing goods from an officer, two charges of stealing money from an officer, two charges of forgery and one of stealing goods from a comrade.

Mills made an attempt to defend himself by saying that the other officers' servants were always drunk and fighting, and he suddenly took it into his head to run away. He said:

> The other servants were down on me because I did not drink or smoke. I
> dressed as an officer so as not to be stopped by the sentry of my regiment.
> I thought that Lt Martin would forgive me about the cheques and stop
> the money out of my pay. I intended to go home for a few days and come
> back again as all the other servants had had leave and I had had none.

He told the court that he had been 21 the previous November and that he had enlisted as a regular in London on 24 February 1915 and had arrived in France on 8 March, becoming Lt Martin's servant in May.

Mills was found guilty on all the charges and sentenced to death. After the trial, during the process of confirmation, his CO wrote that Mills had joined the battalion on 16 March, and had been made company orderly for three weeks and then an officers' servant. He wrote: 'This man has never been in action ... he has done very little work in the front trench line so his character from a fighting point of view can hardly be judged ... His behaviour as a soldier has been good.' The CO also mentioned that the company officers felt that the crime had been deliberate and that Mills had no intention of returning.

The brigade commander wrote: 'from the facts of the case it appears that the man knew very well what he was about'. Division, corps and army commanders all agreed and sentence was confirmed by Sir John French. Pte George Mills was shot in Boulogne on 29 September 1915 and is buried in Boulogne Eastern Cemetery.

A soldier with a bad record was executed in March 1917 after a singularly damning – and most unusual – condemnation by his brigadier general. Pte William Bowerman, was no young soldier who signed on in the first flush of patriotic enthusiasm but a 38-year-old married man who enlisted into the 1st Battalion, East Surrey Regiment in June 1915. He does not appear to have been an enthusiastic soldier. His conduct sheet runs to four pages, with a string of offences between February and December 1916: misconduct, insubordinate language, drunk, overstaying pass and absence all appear. In September 1916 he was absent from his unit at Rouen for six days and then, whilst a prisoner, broke out of camp. On 11 November, when his company was moving to the trenches, he went absent for two days – surprisingly, he was only sentenced to twenty-eight days FP No. 2. Then in December 1916 he was tried by FGCM for desertion, and sentenced to five years' penal servitude. This was commuted to two years' imprisonment with hard labour, and suspended on 1 February 1917.[4]

The next day Bowerman was being held under close arrest at his battalion HQ on the left bank of the La Bassée canal. He was escorted from the battalion HQ to the company HQ in the support line, and handed over to the acting CSM for duty in the trenches. At about 2 p.m. the CSM sent Bowerman to his platoon for duty but an hour later the platoon sergeant was unable to find him.

Just over twenty-four hours later, at 6 p.m. on 3 February, two NCOs of the military police were on duty in the Boulevard Daunau in Boulogne, and saw Bowerman. Although he was in uniform, they were suspicious and stopped and questioned him. Not satisfied with his answers, they arrested him.

At his court martial six witnesses gave evidence for the prosecution, providing a complete chain of evidence. It appears that this case had been put together very carefully. A CMO, Lt Carter (who, although a qualified barrister, was serving with the RAMC), sat on the court martial panel to ensure that the correct legal procedures were followed.

Bowerman, who was not defended, made a statement, not on oath, in his defence. ' I left the trenches because I was sent up without any dinner.' He also added – with a degree of plausibility – that his clothing was inadequate for the trenches: 'I had only a thin undervest on which I had not changed for about five weeks. I was verminous. I had a thin jacket which was torn in the sleeves and torn under the armpits and would keep out no cold weather. I had no leather coat or overcoat.'

While in the trenches he had gone down to the village to get a drink of water and 'a fit came into my head and I went right off'. He said that by 3.30 p.m. he was in Béthune and met some Canadian friends and went with them on the train to Boulogne. He concluded: 'I had no intention of trying to get away whatever.'

The court closed to consider its finding and then heard evidence of Bowerman's previous record. Not surprisingly, the accused man called no character witnesses. He was found guilty and sentenced to death.

As part of the normal confirmation process, the condemned soldier's CO was asked his view of the man. His statement endorsed the verdict of the court: 'This man's character is very bad. Whilst in the battalion he has caused endless trouble, being often insubordinate and on several occasions leaving the battalion when in or going into the trenches.' In his opinion, the crime had been deliberately committed.

Brig. Gen. Harold Fargus, commanding 95th Infantry Brigade, was not a man to mince words. He wrote: 'Very bad character and no good as a fighting man' and then went on to make what is, to our eyes, a most incredible statement:

I consider the extreme penalty should be inflicted because:

(a) the man has already deserted once on active service

(b) he has no intention of fighting for his country

(c) is quite worthless, as a soldier or in any other capacity and is better removed from this world.

Division and corps commanders both pointed out that this was Bowerman's second offence and said he should be executed. Lt Gen. Byng, commanding First Army, agreed.

Pte Bowerman was executed at 5.40 a.m. at Raimbert, on 24 March 1917. The death certificate is chilling, the medical officer noting that 'death was not instantaneous'. (The 'not' is underlined in the original.) The APM noted: 'Death was not instantaneous the coup de grace being given by the O/C firing party.' No doubt Brig. Gen. Fargus would have felt that this undesirable specimen of humanity could not even die properly. His grave was lost in the subsequent fighting, and he is commemorated on the Loos Memorial.

5th Division.

In accordance with Pamphlet S.S. ~~SS~~ 412. Part III
4 (5) I have to report as follows in the case
of the undermentioned man:

No 12341. Pte. BOWERMAN. 1st. E. Surrey

(i)   Very bad character and no good as a
       fighting man, has been with the Expeditionary
       Force since 8/4/16.

(ii)   State of discipline of the battalion is very
       good.

(iii) Attached.

(iv)   I consider the extreme penalty should be
       inflicted because:
       (a) The man has already deserted once on Active Service
       (b) He has no intention of fighting for his country.
       (c) Is quite worthless as a soldier or in any
           other capacity and is better removed from this
           world.

10/3/17   Harold Fargus. Lieut-Col.
                           commdg. 95th Infty Brigade

*Lt Col. Harold Fargus's comments in the case of Pte Bowerman, recommending that
sentence be carried out*

M.O. 1st E. Surreys.

I CERTIFY that No. 12841.

Private BOWERMAN W. of 1st EAST SURREY REGT

was executed by shooting at 5.40. a.m. on 24th inst.

March 1917 at RAIMBERT.

Death was not instantaneous

J.J. Jouerville Capt RAMC [TC]
M.D. (c 1st E. Surrey Regt

The medical officer's certificate, certifying the death of Pte William Bowerman, noting that death was not instantaneous

There can be no doubt that Pte Bowerman had, for whatever reason, deserted his unit whilst they were in the front line, and he was guilty as charged. Given his previous record it was almost inevitable that he would be executed. However, the case gives an uncomfortable insight into the minds of some army commanders of the day. Bowerman was, by the army's standards, an habitual criminal who had been legally sentenced to death, but Brig. Gen. Harold Fargus's statement smacks of eugenics. Just before the war the 'science' of eugenics was becoming an issue of public interest – and continued to do so after the war. In 1911 Col. Melville of the RAMC, and Professor of Hygiene at the Royal Army Medical College, had published an article in *Eugenics Review* in which he wrote: 'It may be that an occasional war is of service by reason of the fact that in time of danger the nation attends to the virility of its citizens.'[5] It would seem that if the war itself did not cull the less manly, then some others were prepared to do the culling.

Conscription was introduced in Britain for the first time in spring 1916, and brought under arms some men who might have preferred not to serve their country. Pte Ernest Horler appears to have been one such reluctant soldier. He enlisted on 23 May 1916 and it has been suggested that he was a conscript.[6] In December 1917 he was serving in the front line with 12th Battalion, West Yorkshire Regiment. On 3 December 'B' Company was paraded and told that they were to parade at 7 p.m. that evening ready for wiring work to be done in the support line. Horler was with 'B' Company when these orders were given, but failed to appear for the 7 p.m. parade.[7] The soldier made his way to Boulogne, where he surrendered himself the next day.

He was taken to Etaples to be returned to his unit, and on 14 December he was one of a draft of men being returned to the front. However, when the draft reached the railway siding, Horler was missing and could not be found. He stayed absent for nearly a month until 12 January 1918, when he was stopped by a member of the military police. Horler had no pass, nor pay book nor identity disc and was arrested.

At his subsequent court martial Horler was tried on two charges, of desertion and escaping. He did not contest the evidence, but did make a statement in his defence. After the evidence had been heard on the first charge and the prisoner asked if he wished to say anything, the court martial transcript notes: 'After warning, the accused gives evidence.'

Pte Horler admitted that he was present at the 3 p.m. parade and had been told to parade again at 7 p.m. and then told the court: 'I left the battalion because I was a sick man when I was sent to it. My heart is in a very bad state; the arteries are poisoned by an injection. My stomach is poisoned also. I have reported sick on different occasions for these ailments. I have been ill for a good many months and done my duty the whole of the time in the line and out. When I left the Battalion I did not know that the wiring party was going to the support line that night. I left because my condition has been getting gradually worse.'

The court then heard the evidence of the charge of escaping. This time Pte Horler made a statement, not on oath. He admitted going absent from the draft but explained that he had no intention of deserting and that he had lost his pay book and ID disc in the camp at Etaples.

After the court had considered its finding he made a plea in mitigation of sentence.

I have been ill. I have been deprived of pay and I am sure there is a lot due to me. I should like to apply for a medical board, on my physical and mental condition. Before joining the army I had a fine character. I have an aged mother and have to make her an allotment. My illness has told against me all the time. I appeal to the Court to see that my health is enquired into.

When his conduct sheet was produced it became apparent that Horler had previous experience of the court martial process. On 25 July 1917 he had been absent from his unit briefly, and on 28 July had been tried by FGCM for disobeying a lawful command and given fifty-six days' FP No. 1. Then in November 1917 he had been tried by FGCM a second time, this time for escaping and absence without leave, and been sentenced to two years' hard labour, which had been commuted to ninety days' FP No. 1. It was whilst serving this sentence that Horler made his bid for freedom.

On 30 January before his trial, Horler had been examined by a doctor and found fit to undergo trial by court martial – the standard medical examination at that stage of the war. After his trial, on 1 February he was again examined by the deputy ADMS of 3rd Division, the doctor commenting '... and find him suffering from no appreciable disease'. On the same day the battalion medical officer was asked to report on the condemned man's medical history. The doctor reported that Horler had seen him on five occasions:

Firstly with Bad feet
Secondly 'Rheumatic' – which did not exist
Thirdly Chill – easily remedied
Fourthly during Field Punishment stomach requiring purge
Fifthly Prior to disappearance reported that his heart was bad.
I examined him and found his heart normal.
On the morning of the trial he made no complaint of illness and on examination I found him to be suffering from no appreciable disease.

Asked for his view on the man, his CO replied that the soldier had only been in action once and 'Most of his time has been spent under arrest or as an absentee.' He had joined the battalion from another unit on 2 October 1917 and had been struck off the strength as a deserter on 14 December. In the CO's opinion desertion was deliberate.

Maj. Gen. Deverell, commanding 3rd Division, thought that the crime was deliberate and commented on the previous convictions. He concluded: 'The prisoner appears to be a worthless man who has continuously endeavoured to evade service.' The Corps Commander and Gen. Byng, of Third Army, agreed.

When the trial papers reached GHQ, Capt. Dowson, on behalf of the DJAG, noted that the surrender document put into evidence relating to Horler's arrest in Boulogne was not strictly admissible in evidence as it contained the phrase: 'as a deserter (or absentee without leave)'. However, he pointed out that this was merely a formal expression and cannot have affected the finding. He also thought that the evidence on the charge of escaping was 'scant, but I think sufficient'.

Pte Horler was, by coincidence, executed on the day his regiment was disbanded, 17 February 1918. It appears that the Infantry Records Office at York mistakenly followed the old procedure in these cases and Horler's mother had her allowance cut, which led to questions in Parliament.[8] It was also revealed that the soldier's whereabouts had been traced through letters sent to his mother which she had passed on to the military authorities.

In August 1918 a man who claimed to be a 46-year-old American citizen was shot. After his trial the brigade commander described him as 'one of the worst characters in the Army'. Henry Hendricks had joined 2nd Battalion, Leinster Regiment in February 1917 and gone to France on 31 May; according to his own statement, he had been wounded on 31 July 1917.

A year later, on 30 July 1918, he was tried on three charges: desertion, escaping and absence. The evidence presented was that he had gone missing from his unit on 16 September 1917, after only three and a half months at the front. He was found at Boulogne on 3 November, at a base details camp, where he was arrested, but before he could be returned to his unit for trial Hendricks managed to get himself admitted to hospital. Amongst the trial papers is a letter dated 21 May 1918, from the RAMC doctor commanding No. 7 Stationary Hospital, who said that Hendricks had been more or less constantly in hospital for the past six months, during which time he had twice escaped from custody. This doctor clearly believed that Hendricks was malingering, and described him as fit to stand trial.[9]

However, on 1 July 1918, when back with his unit, Hendricks escaped from custody in the regimental transport lines. Four days later he was picked up with another man, named Murphy, in Le Mesnil Boutry, by two French gendarmes. He told them that his name was Harry White and that he was an Australian serving with the Australian Imperial Force. Believing him to be an absentee, the Frenchmen handed him over to a British Intelligence officer.

Hendricks, who was defended, made only a token effort to explain his actions. He told the court that for the five days prior to his desertion in

September 1917 he had reported sick, but had been given 'medicine and duty', so had gone to Boulogne to get treatment. He added that he had been in hospital from 9 November 1917 to 28 March 1918, and had then gone to St Omer and been admitted to hospital there. He complained: 'I was put in leg irons and kept in irons two months. While in handcuffs I escaped.'

The court found Hendricks guilty on all three charges and sentenced him to death. Maj. French, CO 2nd Leinsters, wrote that he believed that the crime was deliberate and that the man was a bad character. Brig. Gen. Freyberg, commanding 88th Brigade, wrote: 'This man is one of the worst characters in the Army, he openly defies all authority and deliberately commits crime. He is the worst influence in his regiment and is valueless as a soldier. He has to be handcuffed while under arrest to prevent him escaping.' Someone later in the confirmation process has marked this with the comment: 'But look at conduct sheet.' In fact his conduct sheet shows only that on 30 August 1917 he was fined for gambling in his billet. The two other offences were committed when he was a prisoner, one of refusing to obey an order and the second, on 27 June 1918, 'Losing by neglect 1 pr. Government Handcuffs' – no doubt 'lost' in his bid to escape, for which he was deprived a month's pay.

The other commanders all recommended confirmation, although Field Marshal Haig noted on the papers that he did not confirm the finding on the charge of absence (relating to 1–5 June 1918), but that he did confirm finding on sentence on the first two charges.

Pte Hendricks was shot on 23 August 1918 at La Kreule; if his statement about being 46 years old was true, then he was the oldest man to be executed during the war. He was the third American to be shot, Frederick Arnold and Arthur Dagesse, both serving with Canadian units, having been executed in July 1918 and March 1918, respectively.

CHAPTER 21

THE PALS – JOIN UP TOGETHER, SERVE TOGETHER, DIE TOGETHER

One of the lasting truths about being a soldier is that friendships with comrades in arms are the deepest and most enduring of all.

GEN. FRED FRANK JR, 1998

The Pals battalions were – like the Bantams – a transient phenomenon of the Great War, until the aftermath of the battle of the Somme exposed the weakness of such a recruiting philosophy. When Lord Kitchener appealed to the country for 100,000 volunteers his call was answered within days and the first 'K1' units were formed, followed by the second and third hundred thousand volunteers K2 and K3 units. However, before the K4 units were formed there was a change in recruiting policy, when local organizations decided to help in the formation of the new army. Although the Pals battalions are generally thought of as a northern phenomenon, the first Pals unit was the 10th Royal Fusiliers, the 'Stockbrokers'. Lord Derby championed the scheme whereby local authorities took on the responsibility of housing, feeding and clothing the recruits until they were ready to be taken over by the army. Local recruiting committees were formed and men with similar backgrounds joined up together. Thus were formed such units as the Accrington Pals, the Hull Commercials and the Grimsby Chums. Later, when absorbed into the army's regimental structure, these took on a regimental identity: for example, the Accrington Pals became the 11th East Lancs.

These battalions, formed on the principle that friends could join up, train and serve together, made use of existing friendships and loyalties to bind the unit together. In the early days this worked well as the battalions were shaped into functional military units in the UK. For many of the Pals their first real exposure to action was the battle of the Somme, when they were thrown into action on 1 July 1916. For the 31st Division, composed entirely of Pals battalions, this was to be a literal blooding in battle as they attacked on the left wing of Rawlinson's Fourth Army.

On Saturday 24 June 1916 the preliminary bombardment for the battle of the Somme began. For seven days and seven nights the ground shook as the shells fell. The noise – which could be heard in England – was unremitting. All along the front line men wrote – for many their last – letters home. On 1 July at 7.20 a.m. the barrage stopped, the planned mines were blown. A few minutes later whistles blew and the khaki-clad men of Kitchener's new army went over the top. Along the 18 miles of British front, from Gomme-court in the north to Maricourt in the south, hell broke out on earth as 20,000 men went to their death.

The 'Pals' of the 31st Division went into action for the first time with 93rd Brigade attacking just south of the village of Serre. The *Official History* describes what happened: '

> ... the 15th West Yorks, leading, was almost annihilated by frontal fire
> and deadly enfilade fire from the sides of the re-entrant it was attacking.
> All the officers became casualties within the first few minutes, and the
> survivors of the lines of companies lay down in No Man's Land ...
> The 18th West Yorks in support was unable to make any headway.[1]

The brigade lost 598 dead, and took a total of 1,824 casualties. The 18th West Yorks (the 2nd Bradford Pals) had over 400 casualties, including their commanding officer.

However, two men of this battalion missed the attack. On 10 June 1916 Pte Herbert Crimmins and Pte Arthur Wild had been detailed as ration carriers. From that date until 30 June they were two of many detailed to carry stores, water and ammunition from the main store at Euston Dump to the ration dump in the assembly trenches. Every man had been instructed as to his duties on the day of the attacks – 1 July.[2]

At 11.45 a.m. on 30 June the ration party was ordered to parade at 5.45 p.m. and was issued with extra ammunition. Second Lt Thornton warned the men not to leave the camp. At 4 p.m. orders were received for the men to parade at 6 p.m. and Second Lt Thornton sent Sgt Breen to warn the ration party of this. Breen reported back to the officer, presumably to say that Crimmins and Wild were absent, but as the sergeant had been wounded on 1 July he was not available to give evidence. At 6 p.m. the roll was called, when it was confirmed that these two men were missing.

They were not seen again until 1 p.m. on 4 July when they surrendered themselves to Sgt Reader of the military police at Vignacourt. Neither man had his rifle or any equipment. They were arrested and on 21 August, after the battalion had left the Somme area, faced an FGCM at Loisne Château. Each of the two men was charged with 'When on active service deserting His Majesty's Service in that he, at Bus-les-Artois on 30th day of June 1916, after being warned for duty as a ration carrier, absented himself from his Battalion until 1 p.m. on the 4th day of July 1916, when he gave himself up to the Military Police at Vignacourt'. Crimmins and Wild were tried separately, by the same court martial panel, but the evidence in both cases was identical, and neither contested the facts presented.[3] Their defences, however, differed.

Pte Crimmins told the court that at 11 a.m. on 30 June he and Wild had gone into an estaminet for a drink, before returning to their unit at noon for dinner. They had then returned to the estaminet and remained there until closing time. Crimmins said: 'We then wandered along a road three or four miles and went into a cornfield and there fell asleep. When we woke up it was dark and we were afraid to go back and so went on to a village called Beauquesne.' They had then gone to Vignacourt to look for Wild's brother to ask for his advice. Finding that he was no longer there, they gave themselves up. Crimmins apologized to the court: 'I am very sorry for what I did. I had not the slightest intention of deserting. My father has been in the Army for twenty-seven years and I have five brothers now serving abroad. I have been in the trenches both before and after this occurrence and tried to do my best.'

Cpl Wise and Second Lt Thornton, who had given evidence for the prosecution, testified to Crimmins's good character. Wise said: 'He has been a good soldier and very good in his work.' Second Lt Thornton told the court: 'He has always worked well and on a recent tour in the trenches went out on wiring parties and did his work satisfactorily.'

In his defence, Pte Wild claimed that he had suffered from shell shock. He explained that when he had been working in a sap near Colincamps, a 'coalbox' had exploded alongside him. He had been severely shaken and taken out of the line to rest. He had been to see the MO, who had told him that he would be better in a few days. Under cross-examination he was asked why he had not returned to Bus when he woke in the field. He replied: 'Because I was frightened of the consequences of my absence and also thought I should not be able to stand the noise of guns.'

Other witnesses substantiated his story. Sgt Hustwick testified that at Colincamps three *Minenwerfers* had landed nearby, and said: 'I had to send the accused, Pte Wild, out of the sap as he was so shaken with shell shock and I did not see him again that night.' Second Lt Thornton said: 'Early in June 1916 the accused, Pte Wild, was in the front trenches at Colincamps when some "coalboxes" landed near him. He was taken out with shell shock and I assisted to get him out.' Subsequently, during shelling whilst working at Euston dump, Wild had been so badly affected that Thornton had sent him back to camp.

The court decided that Crimmins and Wild had deliberately deserted, and sentenced them both to death. In Crimmins's case they added: 'With a strong recommendation to mercy on account of his exceptionally good character', and in Wild's case: 'With a strong recommendation to mercy on account of the nervous condition of the accused due to the explosion of a trench mortar projectile in the near vicinity of the sap in which he was working in the Colincamps sector in the early days of June 1916.'

Both men had good records. Crimmins's conduct sheet showed that he had enlisted on 24 February 1915 and had no entries. Wild had enlisted on 1 March 1915 and his sheet had one minor misdemeanour shown. However, Lt Col. Carter, CO of the battalion, wrote of Crimmins: 'The character of this man … from a fighting point of view is indifferent.' He concluded: '… this soldier is a weak man, and … has in my opinion, been led away (possibly under the influence of drink) by Pte Wild. I think that the crime was committed deliberately, nevertheless, as he has shown himself to be of a nervous disposition when in the trenches.' Neither did Lt Col. Carter have a high opinion of Pte Wild: 'this man has always been of a rather lazy disposition, and one who needed driving the whole time to get the full amount of work out of him'. As to the claim of shell shock, the CO wrote: 'The case of shell shock which is mentioned in the evidence was nothing serious as I happened to be in the front line trench myself at the time.' In conclusion he said: 'In my opinion, of the two men Crimmins and Wild, Wild was the stronger character, and I think undoubtedly deserted deliberately, with the sole object of avoiding further active service.' This last statement appears unduly harsh, as the two men surrendered themselves voluntarily – albeit after the attack.

Brigade, division, corps and army commanders all concurred in the death sentences, and Sir Douglas Haig confirmed these on 1 September 1916. The two 'Pals' were shot together at Lestrem at 5.51 a.m. on 5 September 1916.

The sentence clearly shocked other men of this close-knit Pals battalion. In *Tommy Goes to War*, Pte George Morgan is quoted as saying that the two men had got drunk and wandered off, and expected to get a nominal sentence, but were shot. Morgan also recounted that the men were reported as being killed in action at the time, and remembered a letter in the local paper in which a lady was trying to find out what had happened to her brother. 'That is what happened to her brother', said Morgan.[4]

Undoubtedly these two men were victims of the Somme offensive, which they had sought to avoid. They knew that an attack was imminent, they had been issued with extra ammunition and warned to parade for the trenches that evening. On leaving the estaminet both men admitted to walking 3 or 4 miles before falling asleep in a field; there is therefore no reason why they could not have walked the shorter distance back to camp. It appears quite likely that Wild, who undoubtedly suffered from a degree of shell shock, probably made worse by the incessant bombardment which was going on, decided to 'opt out' of the attack on 1 July. Crimmins went along with his friend's plans, and once the attack was over they gave themselves up, expecting, perhaps, a dose of field punishment.

It is important to remember that the men of the new armies had been told that the attack on the Somme was going to be a 'walkover', that the Germans would all be dead in their bunkers. Crimmins and Wild probably thought that under these circumstances they would hardly even be missed. The reality was different. Their battalion took heavy casualties; the attack on that part of the line was a total failure. By going absent on the eve of this battle, these two men met the criteria for desertion defined in the *Manual of Military Law*: 'A man who absents himself … with a view to shirking some important service though he may intend to return when the evasion of the service is accomplished, is liable to be convicted of desertion.'[5]

The two 'Pals' of Kitchener's new army had been tried and found guilty by the standards of the regular army. Their treatment seems harsh, but the army commanders were still smarting from the setbacks of 1 July and were still coming to grips with the concept that the new citizen army had to be managed differently to the old regular forces. The weaknesses of the Pals concept became apparent in the aftermath of the battle of the Somme. After the failures of 1 July and the huge losses sustained by the new army, yellow casualty telegrams flowed in a steady stream to the Pals' home towns. As the pages of the local newspapers filled with casualty lists and whole streets went into mourning the scale of the losses could not be concealed. The heavy casualties affected not only the families at home but also the men themselves, who saw many of their friends dead or maimed; there was a backlash to the spirit of comradeship in these battalions.

A few months after Crimmins and Wild had been executed another two friends faced a firing squad in the aftermath of their experiences on the

Somme. These two friends from Manchester had come tantalizingly close to getting back to Blighty. Albert Ingham and Alfred Longshaw had worked together in the Salford Goods Yard of the Yorkshire and Lancashire Railways and, in the spirit of the 'Pals' battalions, had joined up together on 5 September 1914 into the 18th Battalion, the Manchester Regiment (the 3rd Manchester City Battalion). The two men had served together through the Somme campaign when they had attacked at Montauban on 1 July, when their division suffered over 3,000 casualties. On the 7th they attacked at Trônes Wood and then, at the end of the month, they had been involved in the fighting around Mansell Copse, Trones Wood and Guille-mont. The two friends were then transferred to the brigade machine gun company together.

The two men disappeared from their unit at Buire on the night of 5–6 October 1916, when they were under orders to go to the front line at short notice. At their trials evidence was given to show that both men were present when this warning was given. On 1 November at 9.30 a.m. Sgt Emment of the Intelligence Corps was on duty at Dieppe, where his duties involved examining shipping in the port. He visited a Swedish vessel, the *Belleville*, and recognized Ingham and Longshaw as not being part of the original crew. Both men told him that they were American citizens and refused to answer further questions. Not satisfied, Emment took them both to his office and interrogated them further, separately. Ingham insisted that his name was Sam Bostock, and that he was an American. Longshaw also insisted that he was an American who had reached France via Spain.[6]

However, by 3 p.m. Longshaw had had enough, and admitted that his name was Longshaw and that he had deserted from the machine gun com-pany of his regiment. Emment then went to the other man, and said: 'I want to question you again, Ingham', whereupon Ingham admitted that he belonged to the Manchester Pals. Both men then made statements, Ingham saying: 'Having lost most of my pals I decided to clear out with Longshaw.' He said that they had bought the civilian clothes which they were wearing when arrested, in a village on the way to Dieppe.

The two men were tried on 20 November 1916. They did not dispute the prosecution evidence. In his defence Ingham said:

> I was worrying at the time about the loss of my chums also about my
> mother, being upset, through hearing bad news of two of my comrades.
> I plead for leniency on account of my service in France of 12 months and

my previous good conduct. I beg for a chance to make atonement. I left with my chum firstly to see those at home and then to try and get into the Navy along with his other brother, who is serving there.

Longshaw told the court that he had gone absent with the intention of joining the Navy.

I was prompted to act like this by the state of mind caused by the wish to visit my people at home about whom I was greatly worried. Also my service on the Somme had reacted on my state of mind, which had become morbid and irrational, also the fact that practically all my comrades were gone induced me further to this act. Also all immediate prospect of leave was denied. My motive was first to visit home and then to join in the same unit of the Naval forces as my brother.

Longshaw asked the court for the 'chance to make full reparation in service to condone for his offence'.

Both men were found guilty and sentenced to death. The commanders of the various formations all supported the sentence. Brig. Gen. Lloyd wrote that 'A well thought-out plan of escape from service is disclosed and a man who commits such a crime deserves the extreme penalty.' In truth there was little that could be said. The very fact of their being found on board ship, attempting to leave France, testified to their intention to desert permanently from their regiment and their own evidence supported this.

Instructions given for their execution were that it was 'to be held at Bailleul-val and sentence to be promulgated at 3.30 p.m. before as many men as you have at Bailleulval'.

It seems that feelings ran high in the battalion as another man, Pte Hunt, had been shot for desertion only a month earlier. Pte Paddy Kennedy had witnessed Hunt's execution, and later commented on the cases of Ingham and Longshaw. However, he gets some of the facts clearly wrong and, as with all personal recollections, his memory may have been clouded by time. He believed that both men had taken part on both the Somme and Arras offensives, and had gone missing on 23 April 1917, then being found on an American ship in Rouen. Kennedy reported that just before the pair of 'Pals' were shot, Longshaw turned to Ingham and said: 'Well, good-bye Albert.'[7] The epitaph for these Pals had become 'enlist together, serve together and die together'.

The two friends were together as the fatal volleys rang out at 7.12 a.m. on

1 December 1917 and they are buried next to each other in Bailleulmont Communal Cemetery Extension. During the war it was reported that the men had died of wounds [8] but at some time later Pte Ingham's father discovered the truth, and when asked for his choice of inscription to be carved on his son's unusual red sandstone headstone defiantly chose the words: 'SHOT AT DAWN ONE OF THE FIRST TO ENLIST A WORTHY SON OF HIS FATHER'.

This is the only Commonwealth War Graves Commission headstone to carry any indication that the soldier resting there was executed. It is a fundamental principle of the Commission that all men should be treated equally in death, with no distinction made for civil or military rank, or the manner of a man's passing. The graves of the executed men who lie in the cemeteries of the Western Front, and further afield, are tended with the same care as those of other men who fell in service to their country. Sometimes VC holders lie a few graves away from an executed man, and at Hazebrouck a murdered Canadian lies two graves away from his murderer.

In 1922 the Imperial War Graves Commission (as it then was) wrote to the JAG at the War Office about the executed men:

> The Commission would be greatly obliged if they could be furnished with a list of soldiers who were executed by Field General Court Martial during the late War, with the dates of execution and if possible the places.
>
> It should be explained that the names of these soldiers are not given in the publication 'Soldiers Died in the Great War'. The Commission has however decided on consideration to erect headstones, of the usual pattern, over their graves without any reference to the manner of their death, or, if their graves are not known, to commemorate them in the same way as other officers and men whose graves are unrecorded, and it is therefore necessary to apply to you in this matter in order to be sure that the Commission's records are complete.[9]

The War Office indicated their agreement to this request and the Director of Records at the IWGC wrote back: 'The receipt of Major Barnes's 8/39 dated 18.4.22 is acknowledged with thanks. The forwarding of the list will be awaited and when it is received the greatest care will be taken to prevent any leakage of information.'[10] Another PRO file gives further insight:

> Burial procedure to be adopted after cases of judicial execution carried out under military arrangements
>
> ... Overseas cemeteries ... [are] not normally consecrated ... there

should be nothing to prevent the burial of a victim of judicial execution in a military cemetery

Soldiers who are judicially executed at a time when the death of serving soldiers qualifies them for war graves treatment are treated like other soldiers. But since executions for, say, desertions, are not made public, the question of public opinion being outraged at the burial side by side of a soldier executed for desertion and of another who died gallantly in action, does not arise.[11]

The evidence is that this was not part of a great cover-up campaign to pretend that men had not been executed, but a genuine concern to protect the dead men and their families. These men had paid their debt and were now entitled to be honoured with their comrades.

CHAPTER 22

EVADING HIS DUTY:
THE CASE OF SUB LT DYETT, RN

The training and selection of young officers is the most important duty I ... have been entrusted with in my career. Your duty as future officers is to ensure that you never betray the trust your soldiers will one day put in you.

ACADEMY SGT MAJOR J. C. LORD, ROYAL MILITARY ACADEMY SANDHURST, 1962

As the battle of the Somme petered out in the winter rains and mud of 1916, a second officer was executed for neglecting his duties in battle. It was a case that was to have considerable public ramifications and was to become a focus of indignant press stories under such headlines as 'The Tragedy of a Boy Officer'.[1] Careful scrutiny of the evidence, however, reveals a much more complicated story and one with some darker aspects than those reflected in the press and contemporary books. The case is really about the quality of officer selection in a mass army fighting a continental war.

As the well-educated son of a merchant navy captain, Edwin Dyett was automatically singled out for a commission. In 1914 the 'qualities' approach to leadership was the norm in all armies, and a mixture of good education and 'good breeding' was thought to be an automatic guarantee of leadership qualities. This approach to officer recruitment was not confined to the British armed services. The German and American armies followed a similar social philosophy. Such educational class distinction for officer selection was normal at the time. It was to take the disgraceful scenes at Dunkirk before the British adopted the 'socially scientific' approach of WW2 with War Office Selection Boards (WOSBs) to evaluate officer candidates on more functional and meritocratic grounds in the UK. So when Dyett volunteered for the Royal Navy in 1915, as befitted his family background he was promptly commissioned into the Royal Navy. But not as a sailor. Dyett was commissioned into the Royal Naval

(63rd) Infantry Division, apparently against his will. From his letters we know that he would have much preferred to have gone to sea as a 'proper' RN officer. But the pressure for infantry in France meant that the soldiers of the RN Division would be needed on the Western Front as the British war effort began to expand in 1916 to meet its continental obligations and RN officers found themselves fighting alongside the army in the trenches.

The RN Division was a unique organization with a unique spirit and ethos. First formed on Winston Churchill's initiative in 1914 to protect Antwerp and the Channel ports, in 1915 it had been transported to fight in the ill-fated Gallipoli Expedition (where Rupert Brooke the poet, one of the RN Division's many élite and well-connected officers, had died of an infected mosquito bite) before being evacuated at the end of 1915. By May 1916 the division had been recalled from the Mediterranean to France for duty on the Western Front and began the slow (and painful) process of integration into the army. As the summer and autumn of 1916 wore on, the RN Division was refitted and retrained for full offensive operations in France. Edwin Dyett was one of the new young infantry officers.

By October 1916 the Somme offensive had become a grinding battle of attrition designed to kill Germans, and to keep the enemy's reserves locked into the BEF's sector of the Western Front. As the weather broke in October and the autumn rains turned the shell-churned ground into a quagmire, Haig and the local army commander, Gough, decided on one last push to keep German attentions away from the Eastern Front and Verdun and to straighten the line before winter. The attack was planned along the narrow and marshy valley of the Ancre against strongly fortified German positions that had resisted all attacks since the ill-fated bloodbath of 1 July.

The RN Division was selected to assault north of the Ancre on a front of only 1,200 yards. For many of the RN veterans of 1914–15, this was the chance to show 'The Army' just how good the 'Navy's Infantry' was. The atmosphere was further heightened by clumsy Army attempts to alter proud naval traditions and what the officers of the regular army perceived to be the Navy's 'non-professional' approach. This potential rivalry was made much worse by the loss of the RN Division's trusted and well-liked commander, Gen. Paris, who was severely wounded in front line trenches in mid October. Paris was one of 224 British generals killed or wounded in WW1, thus dispelling the widely held – and erroneous – belief that all Great War generals fought only from comfortable chateaux safely behind the lines. (In contrast, only twenty-one British generals were killed in WW2.)[2]

The army promptly drafted a hard-nosed disciplinarian, Maj. Gen. Shute, as a replacement to 'get a grip on the RN Division'. Shute was initially very unpopular, and doggerel poems about 'that shit Shute' began to circulate as informal samizdats within RN Division officers' messes. In this taut atmosphere, with the troops exhausted by three weeks' back-breaking labour digging trenches along the Ancre and humping stores forward at night under the enemy's nose, the RN Division attacked on the north bank of the river just before dawn on 13 November 1916.

The attack had been planned to use the then new technique of the 'creeping barrage', with lines of infantry following the artillery's shells as the bombardment slowly advanced over the enemy trenches, smashing wire, bunkers and, it was hoped, Germans in its path.

Dyett's regiment, Nelson Battalion, was the left rear battalion of the 189th Brigade, packed with 3,000 assault troops into a tiny ravine, which is now, ironically, the site of the Ancre war graves cemetery. At 5.45 a.m. they advanced into the valley mist, following the left forward assault unit, Drake Battalion, into the full fury of a German counter-bombardment.

Almost immediately the attack broke down. Although the two leading battalions had surprised and overrun the Germans, taking hundreds of prisoners, the bypassed pockets of defenders fought on from their bunkers and trenches, sending machine gun bullets whipping sideways into the knots of naval infantrymen milling around in the fog. The German defensive artillery barrage blew mud, bits of wood and assaulting infantry men alike into the air. It was a scene of chaos and confusion, with the leading waves of attackers disappearing into the mist and the follow-on waves pinned down and being shot to pieces by an anonymous and unseen enemy. (For an excellent description see *The Royal Naval Division*, by Douglas Jerrold.[3])

Dyett had not been involved in the initial attack. In keeping with official BEF attack policy, he had been 'left out of battle' as part of the reserve of officers and men whose function was to provide instant replacements for battle casualties, or even a nucleus to re-form the unit should Nelson Battalion be reduced to a mere cadre by excessive casualties – an all too depressingly familiar experience for British infantry battalions fighting on the Somme in 1916.

Deciding just which officers to leave out and which to take into action posed an agonizing life or death choice for many COs. Balanced against a desire to take only 'the first team' into action must have been the need to conserve some of the very best young officers, whilst at the same time enabling their weaker brethren to gain experience in the hope they would survive and eventually mature into effective fighting officers. It is significant that Dyett was left out of Nelson's assaulting order of battle for Z day on 13 November 1916. The later evidence proves unequivocally that his CO suspected the young lieutenant might prove to be a weak link in the forthcoming battle. Events were to show that his judgement was only too correct.

As the attack spluttered on up the valley sides into the late morning of 13 November runners drifted back from the invisible battle front with news of heavy RN Division casualties: officers dead or missing, hundreds of wounded cowering in shell holes, a shortage of ammunition and bombs, and news of good progress, with German front line and reserve trenches now firmly in British hands. The brigade commander ordered the Nelson's two 'spare' officers to get up to the front line to find out what was happening. What happened then is a matter for dispute, but it cost Sub Lt Dyett his life.

On 19 December 1916 at Champneuf, near the Channel coast at Le Crotoy, Sub Lt Edwin Dyett RN was charged with

> … when on active service deserting his Majesty's service in that he in the field on 13th November 1916 when it was his duty to join his battalion, which was engaged in operations against the enemy, did not do so and remained absent from his battalion until his arrest at Englebelmer on 15th November 1916.

The alternative charge stated Dyett's crime in bald, unequivocal terms:

> Conduct to the prejudice of good order and Military Discipline in that he in the field on 13th November did not go up to the front line when ordered to do so.

Dyett pleaded not guilty to both charges.[4]

The trial was set for 10 a.m. on 26 December 1916 at a farmhouse in the village of Champneuf. The members of the court martial panel were:

> Brig. Gen. S. F. Metcalf, DSO of the Royal Artillery, officer commanding 18th Division, RA (president).
> Temporary Lt Col. C. T. Martin of 2nd Battalion, HLI
> Maj. F. R. Day of 8th Battalion, Norfolk Regiment
> Maj. H. P. M. Berney-Fickling of 8th Battalion, Norfolk Regiment
> Acting Lt Col. J. S. Collings-Wells of 4th Battalion, Bedford Regiment

The judge advocate (advising on legal procedure) was Capt. J. S. Griffith-Jones of 10th Battalion, South Wales Borderers, who had been a pre-war barrister. The prosecutor was Sub Lt Herbert Slade Strickland of Nelson Battalion and Dyett was defended by Sub Lt Cecil Cameron Travanion of Hawke Battalion, who pre-war had been a solicitor.

Dyett's court martial was therefore properly established and the accused was defended by someone with a full legal background. A judge advocate was present to ensure that correct procedure was followed and the court martial panel consisted of experienced officers. This was no kangaroo court.

Dyett's CO, Lt Cmdr E. W. Nelson of the Nelson Battalion, testified that Lt Truscott and Sub Lt Dyett were 'spare officers' in the attack and that he had ordered them to report to divisonal HQ for orders. Asked his opinion of Dyett, he said that 'he was a very poor officer who had asked for a transfer to sea service as he thought that he was not fitted for the firing line'. He stated that Dyett and Truscott were the only officers available to go up to the firing line and admitted that he was worried about sending Dyett forward as he felt that '[Dyett's] authority in command over men was not good'.[5]

The other officer from the battalion sent forward with Dyett on that day was Lt Cyril Truscott of the same battalion. He testified that he and Dyett had gone forward, by car, to brigade HQ, which was situated in Charles Street trench between Mesnil and Hamel, and that Dyett had remained outside the dugout whilst Truscott went in to receive their orders from the brigade commander. These were that the two officers 'were to join the battalion, which had last been heard of in the Green Line which was a trench on the Beaucourt side of Station Road' (i.e. well inside the German front lines).

The two officers made their way forward on foot the half mile or so to the ruins of Beaucourt Station, where they found Sub Lt Herring and a party of men. What happened then seems to be at the heart of the matter. Herring and Dyett were seen arguing and Truscott took charge of about twenty-five leaderless men of his battalion, and at about 5.45 p.m. led his party towards the Green Line, leaving Dyett arguing with Herring. Truscott and Dyett belonged to different companies and they were effectively independent agents and expected to find their own men when they found the battalion. Truscott next saw Dyett two days later, on 15 November, at the billets near Engelbelmer, 5 miles to the rear. He stated: 'The accused appeared to be normal when he was with me on 13 November. I noticed nothing strange in his demeanour' and 'I saw no signs of what is termed "cold feet" or any tendency on the part of the accused to desert.' (see map page 275)

Brig. Gen. Lewis Phillips, commanding 189th Infantry Brigade, was then sworn in and confirmed that at about 1.30 p.m. on 13 November Lt Truscott and another officer appeared at his brigade HQ dugout and were given 'cast-iron orders which applied to both officers'. Brig. Gen. Phillips was unable to identify Dyett as the second officer. On 15 November, when the brigade came out of the line and moved to Engelbelmer, Brig. Gen. Phillips sent for Dyett 'on the basis of information received' and, 'after his unsatisfactory explanation', placed him under arrest. Neither Dyett nor any other officer of Nelson Battalion had reported back to Brig. Gen. Phillips at any time on 13 or 14 November after the brigade commander had dispatched Truscott and Dyett forward with his orders. This was serious stuff: for a brigade commander to testify against a mere subaltern in his unit in 1914–18 was a truly devastating indictment.

Capt. A. R. Bare, Staff Captain 189th Infantry Brigade, 63rd (RN) Division, claimed he saw Truscott and Dyett at brigade HQ at about 1.30 p.m. He swore that he next saw Dyett at Engelbelmer at about 10 or 11 a.m. on 15 November whilst Nelson Battalion was still in the line. He ordered Dyett to report to brigade HQ. In cross-examination Capt. Bare testified that 'he knew that the Brigadier had received a note from Lt Herring concerning Dyett's conduct'.

It was the evidence of Sub Lt John Herring, Drake Battalion, the man with whom Dyett had argued in the dusk of 13 November 1916, that did for Dyett. On 13 November Herring had been in charge of a brigade ammunition dump well forward at Hamel, only 400 yards back from the fighting. He claimed that he ordered a group of about 200 men drifting rearwards from the fighting back into the firing line when he saw Truscott and Dyett at Beaucourt Station at about 5 p.m. Herring said that he ordered Truscott to take these men back up to the line (a pencilled note in the court martial record says: 'In the Navy does a Sub-Lt give orders to a Lt?'). Herring said that he also told Dyett to follow Truscott. Dyett allegedly replied: 'I am not the senior officer and I find such chaos here that I think that I had better go back and report to the Brigade.' The area around the ruined station was under sporadic shell-fire and numerous 'spents' and 'overs' from the fighting were landing in the deepening dusk. Herring said that Dyett acted as if he expected to find a battalion HQ to report to and that he 'did not appear to grasp the situation', adding, however, 'that Dyett did not appear to be agitated or frightened'.

When Herring walked back down the valley to Hamel dump he claimed that Dyett followed him back towards the rear. Once he got back to the brigade forward dump Herring wrote a note about Dyett to the Staff Captain at brigade HQ.

From the court martial papers Herring appears to have been cross-examined fairly rigorously. Herring said that he reported to the Staff Captain in writing 'that I had given orders to the accused to take some stragglers forward and he had refused'. He added: 'Accused was *not* in my opinion deserting in the face of the enemy. In my opinion accused was going back to headquarters to report that he found the place in a state of chaos.' Asked why there had been an argument between him and Dyett back at the station, he said: '[Dyett] appeared to resent me giving him an order.'

Sub Lt Ernest Gardner, a company commander in Nelson Battalion, testified that on 13 November he went forward with the battalion. Having advanced deep into the German lines they subsequently dug in 300 yards east of the Green Line. At about 6 p.m. on the 13th Lt Truscott appeared and the battalion stayed in this line until 15 November when they were relieved and marched back to Engelbelmer, arriving between 1 and 2 p.m. At no time did Gardner see Dyett during the operations.

Sub Lt Herring's assistant at Beaucourt Station on 13 November, Petty Officer Ames, saw Herring hand over 'about 200 men' to Truscott and later saw Dyett and Herring arguing at Beaucourt Station. He said that Herring told Dyett to help Truscott with the men, and Dyett said: 'I cannot take charge among all this chaos and disorder. I will return to Brigade for orders.' He last saw Dyett back at Hamel dump. Cross-examined, Petty Officer Ames said: 'Accused did not look as though he was afraid or in a funk. He looked as though he wanted to get out of it.' (This comment is underlined heavily in red in the court martial papers and may be the remark which killed Dyett.)

Lt Bernard Dangerfield, Nelson Battalion, testified that on 15 November at about 1 p.m. he met the battalion coming down from the line. When he arrived at Engelbelmer, Dyett was virtually the first person he saw, standing waiting at the gate of No. 79 billet. About an hour later Dangerfield saw Lt Truscott march into Engelbelmer with the rest of the battalion.

The defence called no witness and astonishingly Dyett did *not* give evidence on his own behalf.

In Dyett's defence Cecil Trevanion pointed out that the accused officer was of a highly neurotic temperament and had felt himself unfit to be an officer in the field, having made four separate applications for transfer into the Navy or Royal Naval Reserve. He also quoted the evidence of Dyett's company commander that Dyett had said 'his nerves prevented him from taking an active part in an advance' and had 'begged him to be kept at the base as he had no confidence in his powers of leadership'. The defence claimed that after losing his way in the dark and spending the night in a dugout, Dyett reported to Lt Cmdr Egerton, Royal Naval Volunteer Reserve, at Engelbelmer. Finally Trevanion said that Dyett's conduct throughout 'showed a great lack of initiative in not at once grasping the altered instruction and his return to Brigade HQ was for further enlightenment.' An unknown hand has minuted the court martial papers, 'But he did <u>NOT</u> go there.'

The judge advocate, Capt. J. S. Griffith-Jones, summed up, particularly making the point that Dyett had not been seen at all on the 14th and laid stress on the question of 'intent': did Dyett *intend* to desert or to avoid a particular duty? Griffith-Jones pointed out that a mistake or error of judgement does not amount to intent. Against the Judge Advocate's remark that 'The Accused did not report back to Brigade HQ' the '<u>NOT</u>' is heavily underlined.

The court found Dyett guilty of the first charge but not of the second, and sentenced him to death, but with a recommendation to mercy on two counts:

1. He was very young and has no experience of active operations of this nature

2. The circumstances – growing darkness, heavy shelling and the fact that men were retiring in considerable numbers – were likely to affect seriously a youth, unless he had a very strong character.

The papers went up the line for confirmation of sentence. The divisional commander, the unpopular Major General Shute, recommended mercy for his young officer, pointing out his youth and inexperience. However, the corps commander wrote: 'I see no reason why the sentence should not be carried out' and Hubert Gough, commanding Fifth Army, noted: 'I recommend that the sentence be carried out,' adding, 'If a Private had behaved as he did in such circumstances, it is *highly probable* that he would have been shot.' On 2 January 1917 FM Sir Douglas Haig confirmed the sentence.

Two days later, on the evening of 4 January 1917, Dyett was playing cards with two other officers when confirmation of the sentence arrived and he was told of the sentence and that he would be shot at dawn on the following day.[6] He spent an hour with the padre and wrote a letter home to his mother. Sub Lt Edwin Dyett was shot at dawn by members of his own battalion at 7.30 a.m. on 5 January 1917 at St Firmin, near the dunes of Le Crotoy.

Dyett's own story was clear, poignant and contained some significant gaps. Whilst under arrest on 13 December and awaiting trial, he wrote to a friend:

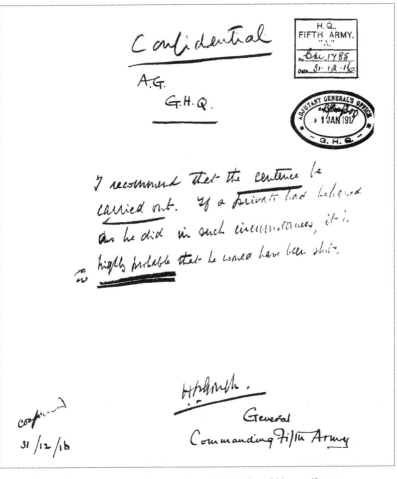

Confidential

A.G.

G.H.Q.

H.Q.,
FIFTH ARMY.
"A."
No. *1785*
Date. *31·12·16*

ADJUTANT GENERAL'S OFFICE
1 JAN 1917
G. H. Q.

I recommend that the sentence be carried out. If a *private* had behaved as he did in such circumstances, it is highly probable that he would have been shot.

[signature].
General
Commanding Fifth Army

copy
31/12/16

General Gough's comments in the case of Sub Lt Edwin Dyett RN – an officer was to be treated no differently to a private soldier

We went up the line and took over the right sector for four days; there we were relieved and returned to our billets, and my Company, with others, during the night took up our position, and things went fairly well until late in the morning, when I was detailed to go and replace casualties – you were in that scrap, so there is no need to explain how many. I crossed no-man's-land later in the afternoon, but could not find a man belonging to my unit. My companion went off with a crowd we met, but as I still held hope of finding the Company, I rambled about and lost touch with everybody, and my nerves, not being strong, were completely strung up.

DEATH WARRANT.

Temporary Sub-Lieutenant E.L.A. DYETT R.N.V.R. Nelson Bn

having been tried by General Court Martial, and sentenced
to death by shooting, the sentence will be carried out
between 7.30 and 8.30 a.m. at ...*ST. FIRMIN*......
on...*Friday 5th January 1917*.

C. D. Shute

Commanding 63rd R.N.Division.
....

3/1/17.

*Sentence duly carried out at ST. FIRMIN
at 7.30.A.M. on ~~FIRST~~ FRIDAY. JANY, 5th 1917*

C.S.W

*C. S. Walmesley Cap:
a.p.m.*

5/1/17.   63rd (R N) Div

The death warrant authorizing the execution of Edwin Dyett, with confirmation by the APM that sentence had been carried out

I met another officer, who says he ordered me to join up with the party,
but this I did not do, but wandered about still looking for my own unit.
In the meantime this gentleman went back and sent a startling message of
sorts to BHQ, with result that they are trying to kick me out of it, but up
to now [13 December] the evidence given is not strong enough to cause a
'sitting' and that is what happened to me in the biggest advance – luck,
isn't it? It makes me sick to think of it, and they have now kept me a

month hanging on. I am hoping for news any day now, and if there is nothing in it do not see why I should worry my people by telling them. Now I have all the Company letters to censor, so please excuse more. [7]

By Christmas Eve Dyett was still waiting for news but, like many others kept waiting for the law to take its course, he believed a court martial unlikely (in fact, it took place two days later, on the 26th). He wrote:

I hear that you are worrying about me more than is necessary. I will explain my present situation so as to relieve your mind. I was surplus, and was sent off at five minutes' notice. I went up with another officer of my Battalion who was senior by one ring. We reported ourselves at Brigade Headquarters as instructed by our Lieutenant-in-Command. At that time they had lost touch with the battalion, so we waited for an hour or so in their dug-out awaiting orders, which we got – at least, the other man got them, and then after a lot of trouble I got them to tell me what they were and we proceeded towards Boche overland. There was considerable hostile artillery, gas shells and tear shells falling all around us, and snipers were all over the place; we had very narrow shaves more than once. We could not find our units and rambled about.

When it was dark, we met a body of men with an officer in charge; they were wanted by Colonel Freyberg VC [Hood Battalion]; there was much confusion and disorder going on, and my nerves became strung up to the highest extreme. I found that my companion had gone off somewhere with some men. The officer who was leading the party we met was my 'one and only enemy', so we were not polite to each other, and as he is junior to me I practically ignored him except for telling him I was going back to BHQ, which I had left an hour or two before in daylight, but finding those places was not as easy a matter as I thought, with the result that I got lost for the second time. I found an NCO of the old A Company – we rambled about until he fell down for want of sleep, but I managed to get him along. Later my voice was recognised by some more men of the A Company who were lost; they attached themselves to me, saying they also were looking for BH Quarters. BHQ, however, were not to be found that night. My nerves were completely gone and my head was singing. About then we came across a funk hole, and there we stayed. However, my 'enemy' had gone back behind his supports and sent a startling message to BHQ concerning me. I have been under close arrest ever since *14th* (sic) November.

On 8th November I put in an application to the Commanding Officer telling him my reasons for wanting to return to sea on account of my nerves not being able to stand the strain. He told me he was just the same as I, so I let it slide at that, as I did not want everyone to say that I was trying to 'swing the lead' as others have done. I have obeyed orders, and that is all I care about it. Things are very one-sided just now, but as soon as I have my little say in the matter it will alter their colour altogether. Now that is as much as you can know of what happened as if you had found out yourself.[8]

This was Dyett's version of events. As far as he was concerned, he had only been absent for one night and was arrested on the *14th*, not the 15th. The reason for the argument with Herring was, according to an account published in 1983, that Dyett had caught Herring trying to smuggle a woman into the Royal Naval Division's camp at Blandford earlier that year – hence the reference to his 'enemy'.[9] The puzzle is: why did Dyett not call witnesses to prove his version of events? There was ample time between Dyett's arrest and his court martial. Could it have been that there was insufficient time to find these witnesses (and Egerton) between Dyett's learning on 24 December that he was to be tried and his court martial two days later?

However, another document exists which puts a different complexion on things – there was another witness to Dyett's conduct, who was not called to give evidence. An officer with Hood Battalion, Sub Lt J. H. Bentham, had been badly wounded in the attack and had little sympathy for Dyett. He subsequently wrote:

Suddenly a shell burst among us and when the smoke had cleared I found my two runners killed, wounded myself through the thigh and maiming [*sic*] nearly all the remainder. I gave my map and instructions to an NCO and told him to carry on. He was killed just as he left me. This was at exactly 6.15 a.m. We had certainly had a hectic half hour and now it was all over. One of my lads was wounded in the lung and was coughing up bright red blood and it wasn't long before he died. The remainder took what shelter we could in a crater as the enemy were plastering us with shells. Wave after wave of reinforcements passed us shouting, 'Got a blighty, lucky devil', etc. Then we got our first-aid packages and bandaged our wounds as best we could; my leg was pumping blood. At about 10 a.m. our Battalion Medical Officer McCracken came along and dressed our wounds. He poured iodine into my wound and told me that that would stop me laughing in church! He had to go with the Battalion but said some stretcher bearers would be along later.

Lying with our backs to the front, we could see reinforcements coming over the brow of a hill at the rear, not far away hidden in an isolated pocket was a German machine gun, who took a terrible toll of those men as they showed against the sky line. I tried to crawl and ascertain where this devil could be, but it was too far away so I shouted until someone came along and I told him and sure enough shortly afterwards the gun stopped. I had given my morphine tablets to the more seriously wounded to deaden the pain, but soon the effects wore off and they started moaning with the pain. It was now afternoon and no one had come along. We opened our iron rations and had something to eat, those of us who could do so, but one poor lad with a shattered arm and smashed shoulder blade was praying to die and begged us to put him out of his misery. The afternoon dragged on and I realised that stretcher bearers would not find us in the dusk which came down. German shells were still dropping all round we wondered if one would find us and finish us off.

My wound by now had set hard and numbed with cold I did all I could to cheer up the others. The night passed and it seemed a lifetime and we began to despair of being found at all as there was no signs of life whatsoever. Dawn came and turned into day and then an officer I knew to be one of the reserves came along. He looked white and scared and asked me where the front line was. I told him it must be a long way now but he would jolly well soon recognise it when he got there. Off he went and I never saw him again, but that same officer was later shot for cowardice. He had deserted his support troops who, without an officer, never arrived in the front line. *John Bull*, however, without knowing the true facts made a great fuss about it and placards were headed 'Shot at Dawn' and 'Tragedy of Young Boy Officer'.

Another badly wounded boy died that morning and others were of the opinion that we should perish there, it was now over 24 hours since we were knocked out. Thank God it wasn't raining. Our iron rations were finished and at 2 p.m., exactly 36 hours after being hit, a party of German prisoners under a guard came along with stretchers.[10]

If this is true, and there appears to be no reason for doubting it, then Dyett's case is seriously weakened. Why did he not get help sent to these men? Or are these the men referred to in his letter – and calling them as witnesses would have damaged, not improved, his case? The weight of all the evidence is that Dyett did not go up to the front line as his duty demanded, he did hide himself for nearly a day and a half whilst his brother officers and soldiers were getting killed in the fighting, and he even failed to get help for wounded men lying bleeding in the freezing November mud of no-man's-land. Officers are not expected to behave like that.

Dyett's case raises some interesting questions, both in terms of the facts and in terms of his trial. Although there can be little doubt that Dyett disappeared for a day and a half neither prosecution nor defence made any great point of it. That he was absent from the place of duty seems incontestable. The issue of his 'feud' with Herring – and the latter's 'sneaking' on him – seems also to have been ignored; just why did Herring's angry little note carry so much weight? After Dyett's execution rumours swept the Royal Naval Division that Dyett had been 'betrayed' by a brother officer, and A. P. Herbert's fictional pastiche cameo, *The Secret Battle*, hints darkly at bullying and breakdown.[11] It has also been said that Sub Lt Herring was 'universally disliked' in the battalion.[12]

In terms of his trial it beggars belief that Dyett was not called upon to testify, if only to explain his actions. However, if he had testified then his absence on the 14th could have been probed more deeply – with possibly embarrassing results for his defence, because he certainly was absent on that day, as a glance at the map opposite clearly shows.

It is the paucity of Dyett's defence that is so puzzling, and across the years we can only search for clues in the papers. Trevanion, although qualified as a solicitor, seems to have had little experience in advocacy or in appearing in a court such as this. He does not seem to have grasped his role as being for the *defence*. We can only speculate that he was a junior officer, appearing in front of much more senior men, and may have been more preoccupied with fear of displeasing them than with establishing the truth in a case that all knew was a bad one. Why did someone from his own battalion not defend Dyett? Were his officers unwilling, or was the court trying to be fair, so found a legally qualified prisoner's friend for him?

It all remains a mystery, except for the one crushingly obvious explanation, which an embarrassed group of officers and the man himself were trying to shield from public gaze at the time: Dyett *had* deserted his battalion and his men and skulked off for two days leaving them in the lurch. In 1916 this would have been unacceptable. By the code of the day this was not officer-like behaviour, and as Gen. Gough pointed out, the Army was

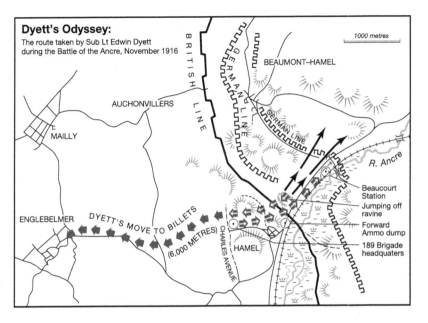

Dyett's Odyssey:
The route taken by Sub Lt Edwin Dyett
during the Battle of the Ancre, November 1916

1000 metres

BRITISH LINE

GERMAN LINE

BEAUMONT–HAMEL

AUCHONVILLERS

MAILLY

R. Ancre

ENGLEBELMER

DYETT'S MOVE TO BILLETS
(6,000 METRES)

CHARLES AVENUE

HAMEL

Beaucourt
Station
Jumping off
ravine
Forward
Ammo dump
189 Brigade
headquaters

shooting private soldiers for behaving in such a cowardly fashion.

Finally, it is absolutely clear that Dyett was not shell-shocked or suffering from battle fatigue – this cannot be used as an excuse in his case. This was his first real action, unlike others in his battalion who had been in Gallipoli. Although he was almost certainly frightened, his only excuse seems to be his claim that he had 'delicate nerves' – an excuse that no mere private soldier would dare to advance before battle. Officers are meant to set an example, however scared they may feel. Edwin Dyett's tragedy appears to be that he was not suited to his responsibilities. In the isolation and fear of the battle-field and, critically, away from the ever-watchful eyes of his soldiers, a lonely Dyett took the safe and easy option, drifting away from the fighting and back to the comfort and security of his billet.

On the night before he was to be executed, Dyett wrote one last letter home to his mother:

France January 4, 1917
Dearest Mother Mine, I hope by now you will have had the news. Dearest, I am leaving you now because He has willed it. My sorrow tonight is for the trouble I have caused you and Dad.

Please excuse any mistakes, but if it were not for the kind support of the Rev. W.C. – who is with me tonight, I should not be able to write myself. I should like you to write to him, as he has been my friend.

I am leaving all my effects to you, dearest; will you give my little – – half the sum you have of mine?

Give dear Dad my love and wish him luck. I feel for you so much and I am sorry for bringing dishonour upon you all. Give – – my love. She will, I expect, understand – and give her back the presents, photos, cards, etc. she has sent me, poor girl.

So now dearest Mother, I must close. May God bless and protect you all now and for evermore. Amen.[13]

There was an ugly after-note to the Dyett case. The 189th Brigade clerk, Petty Officer MacMillan, recorded, many years later: 'But the officer who had acted as prisoner's friend … carried on soldiering; and if he had not had his wits about him he might have paid dearly for the part he played in [Dyett's] trial.'[14] It turned out that the Brigade Major saw Trevanion's name had been 'left out of Battle' for the later attack on Gavrelle. According to MacMillan:

… He saw that the officer who had acted as 'Prisoner's Friend' … was on the Reserve list. At this his monkey rose [that is, he became angry], and in his most unbearing manner he told me to instruct the Battalion Commander concerned to 'send the hard-nosed bastard forward.'[15]

Fortunately Trevanion heard of this and managed to get himself evacuated as a casualty, but the story highlights a little-recorded and nasty fact of some military courts martial in WW1: for an officer to defend an accused man was seen in at least one case as an activity worthy of condemnation – subversive at best and a perversion of military regulations and discipline at worst. It is unlikely to have been an isolated incident. Being a 'prisoner's friend' may not have been such a risk-free duty after all. After the war, in 1919, the Darling Report on the whole court martial system observed tartly: 'evidence has been given before us … that in some instances, superior authorities have actively discouraged officers from appearing on the behalf of accused persons.[16]

Edwin Dyett lies buried in a lonely plot in the corner of the French communal cemetery at Le Crotoy in the Bay of the Somme. If any fair judgement can be made, it is that he was unequal to the strain of his responsibilities in battle and should never have been made an officer in the first place. Like so many of his braver, or more obedient, brother officers he too paid with his life (260 officers and 3,000 men of the RN Division became casualties in the battle of the Ancre).[17] Sub Lt Dyett failed in his duty as an offficer and paid the harshest penalty of all.

CHAPTER 23

A LONG WAY FROM HOME

Though it rain silver and gold in some foreign land and daggers
at home, yet it is better to be back in one's homeland.

MALAY PROVERB

Although the vast majority of desertions occurred on the Western Front, six men serving with British regiments were executed for desertion in other theatres of war, from where they had little hope of making the coveted 'home run'.

During the winter of 1914–15 war on the Western Front had settled into stagnation in the trenches which ran from the North Sea to the Swiss border. Winston Churchill and others had raised the idea of an indirect attack on the Central Powers to end the deadlock, by means of an attack on Constantinople. Originally rejected, this idea was reconsidered in January 1915 under pressure from Russia, which wanted to divert Turkish attentions from the Caucasus. When the original naval operation failed, the plans were modified to include amphibious landings along the Gallipoli peninsula on 25 April 1915. Bogged down in atrocious conditions, shelled by the Turks and with infection rife, the landings were eventually called off and the Peninsula evacuated at the end of the year.

The first man to be shot for desertion in operations away from the Western Front was Pte Harry Salter of the 6th Battalion, East Lancs Regiment, who deserted from his regiment in Gallipoli. This unit had not been involved in the initial landings on the Gallipoli peninsula in April but landed near Cape Helles, on 'V' Beach, as reinforcements on 7 July 1915. On the 17th of that month Gen. Sir Ian Hamilton saw the battalion 'either bathing or basking mother-naked on the hot sand' and noted how impressed he had been by the men's 'physique and class'.[1] In August they moved northwards into the Anzac area and were involved in some heavy fighting, losing 144 men killed in the month.[2] By 1 September the battalion strength was a mere seven officers and 311 other ranks.[3]

In November the battalion was doing alternate tours of duty between the front line at Green Hill and the reserve line at Chocolate Hill, but by 1 November Harry Salter had seen enough fighting on the Peninsula and deserted. The evidence at his eventual court martial was brief, only two pages long.[4]

CSM Fergusson told the court that 'On 1 November 1915 at Chocolate Hill the accused, Pte. Salter, absented himself from the battalion. I did not see him again until 21 November.' The next witness, Sgt Maj. Beard of the Essex Regiment, gave evidence that he was in charge of the police at Anzac and that Salter had been brought to him on 11 November, in uniform. On the 16th he handed his prisoner over to an escort from the 6th East Lancs, but on the way back to their battalion they became lost and whilst the escort was asleep, Salter escaped.

On the 18th he was again arrested at Anzac and taken to Sgt Maj. Beard, who again wired for an escort, but by the time that it arrived the resourceful Salter had escaped once more. However, he was arrested again on the following day, this time in an Australian uniform, and on 20 November Beard handed him over, no doubt with relief, to Cpl Foster, who took him back to his unit.

Salter, who was not supported by a prisoner's friend, made no defence to the charges of desertion and escaping. His conduct sheet showed that he had been sentenced to one year's imprisonment for 'when on Active Service leaving the ranks', this being suspended on 24 September 1915.

The officer commanding his battalion had little good to say about Pte Salter's qualities as a soldier: 'General character bad. His work unsatisfactory and he is a bad influence on his company. He has been absent twice on Active Service and has been transferred from one company to another at the request of his Company Commander.'

Brigade, division and corps commanders all recommended that sentence be carried out, and Gen. Monro, commanding the Mediterranean Expeditionary Force, confirmed the sentence. Pte Harry Salter was shot on 11 December 1915, a week before his battalion was evacuated from Gallipoli, and is buried in Green Hill Cemetery. As Salter made no attempt to defend himself no reasons ever emerged for his attempt to desert. He can have had no hope of getting home to the UK, or even of getting away from the fighting.

On 5 October 1915 two transport ships dropped anchor off the Greek port of Salonika – British troops were about to experience the frustrations of war in the Balkans. The situation was complex. The Anglo-French force was to support Serbia against Bulgarian attack, but as Serbia had no seaport all

Allied aid had to be landed at the – theoretically neutral – port of Salonika in Greek Macedonia. The Salonika campaign was one of the forgotten episodes of the Great War, tying up huge numbers of men for two years. The Germans called Salonika the 'Greatest Allied Internment Camp', Asquith called it a 'Wild Goose Affair' and Clemenceau labelled this forgotten army 'the gardeners of Salonika'. Sickness was rife: 481,000 men fell sick during the campaign and nearly 5,000 men lost their lives.

In May 1917 the 10th Battalion of The Black Watch was due to take part in an attack. On 6 May Pte Archibald Brown's company were warned that they were to proceed to the trenches that night, and although this order was subsequently cancelled the company did carry out some practice assaults in preparation for the real attack. At 8 a.m. on 7 May, Brown reported for duty to the orderly sergeant, but shortly afterwards went missing.[5]

The following morning L Cpl Parker of the Military Foot Police was on point duty in October Street, Salonika, where he saw the accused. As he was unable to produce a pass, Parker arrested him.

Brown was not defended at his trial. The core of his defence was that when the company was told that the move to the trenches had been cancelled this was spread around informally and that there had been no order to stand-by. The court did not find this an adequate excuse and Brown was found guilty and sentenced to death.

Brown had enlisted early in the war, on 12 September 1914, but seems not to have taken to soldiering. His conduct sheet showed a string of entries, the most serious being in February 1917 when he had been found guilty of striking a superior officer, for which he was under suspended sentence of one year's imprisonment.

The GOC of 77th Brigade wrote that Brown was 'good at his duties, but a shirker and a criminal character'. He continued: 'owing to his having been carrying out a term of IHL [imprisonment with hard labour] this is the first occasion on which he has been present with his battalion during an action'. He recommended that sentence be carried out, as 'the crime appears to be one of sheer cowardice deserting from his battalion on the eve of operations'.

The commanders of XIII Corps and 60th Division both agreed, and Gen. Milne, commander-in-chief of the Salonika army, confirmed sentence. Pte Brown was shot at 4.30 a.m. on 1 June 1917. This soldier cannot have expected to get very far from his unit, and it is probable that he simply intended to be absent for long enough to miss the engagement on 8–9 May, perhaps in the expectation of a further prison sentence – perhaps to be served in safety at home. In the event his unit took heavy casualties attacking the Bulgar positions and his absence was regarded as a deliberate attempt to avoid danger.

Another soldier also missed the attack that night. Sgt Harry Ashton was serving with the 11th Battalion, Scottish Rifles (The Cameronians) and his unit was due to attack the Bulgar positions near Doiran Lake. His company had been given detailed training for the attack and it was shown in evidence that Ashton had been present when the company commander went through the operational orders with his NCOs.[6] On the night of 7–8 May Ashton's company moved, under cover of darkness, into position at Wooded Point (see map). The men scattered in the wood and lay low all day. At 6 p.m. Capt. Scougal, the company commander, spoke to each platoon commander, ordering them to be ready to move out of the wood at 7.30 p.m.

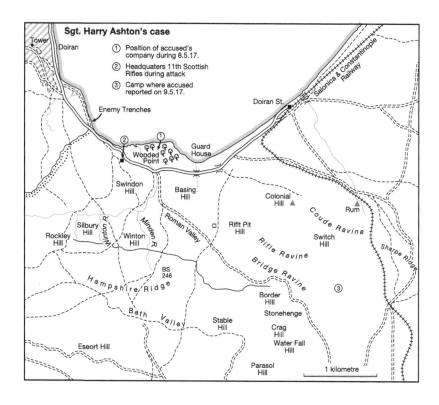

At Ashton's subsequent trial it emerged that his order was passed from man to man. As the company prepared to attack at 8.30 p.m. Sgt Ashton was found to be missing. The attack went ahead, lasting most of the night, until the company withdrew at about 5 a.m. on 9 May and went to Swindon Camp to collect their kit and then back to camp in the Gjol Ajak Ravine.

The key witness at Ashton's trial was L Cpl McCulloch, who had been in the wood with Ashton. He told the court that they had both fallen asleep and did not wake until the bombardment started between 9 and 10 p.m. The two men's accounts of what happened next were different. McCulloch said that when they woke they debated about whether to join their comrades and he alleged that Ashton had said: 'It would be a silly idea for us to try and find the company', but that he himself 'went off to try and find the boys'. He told the court that he left Ashton and went along the road to look for his unit and went as far as Doiran Camp, but could find no one, so returned to the wood. Ashton's version of events was that they both stayed in the wood all day, before going to Swindon Camp in the evening and then going back to Gjol Ajak Ravine, where they arrived at 11 p.m.

Sgt Ashton gave evidence on oath. He said that when he woke and found the other men gone he did not know what to do: 'The thought entered my mind of what the boys would think for I knew that the thought would be uppermost in their minds was that we deliberately intended to miss them.' He was subjected to an extremely lengthy cross-examination: during this it transpired that he was new to the company, having been with it only four days. When asked why he did not try to get in touch with his unit, he replied: 'Because I knew that they would think that I had missed them intentionally and I couldn't face them.' He also told the court that McCulloch had not gone to look for his unit, but had stayed in the wood. This allegation seemed to go down badly with the court martial panel, although there was no evidence or witnesses that McCulloch had, in fact, gone to Doiran Camp.

In mitigation Ashton said that he had enlisted on 9 September 1914 and after a spell as orderly room clerk had asked to go out to France, where he was wounded at Loos. He had been an NCO for thirty-three months and had no previous crimes to his name. He handed to the court a character reference from Capt. Low (then in hospital) which said: 'This man is clean and honest – works well if supervised but has no great command over men.'

The court chose to believe McCulloch's version of events in the wood and sentenced Sgt Ashton to death for desertion, but recommended him to mercy 'on the grounds of good character and previous service, subject to verification'.

This was actually Ashton's second trial on this charge. He had originally been tried for this offence on 21 May 1917, but the sentence had not been confirmed and a retrial was ordered. There were then delays as no suitable prosecutor could be obtained, and the retrial did not finally take place until 30 June 1917.

After the verdict the papers went to the unit commanders for their comments. The brigade commander made two crucial comments: '(a) This NCO is reported by his Commanding Officer to have performed his duties in a slack and unsatisfactory manner' and '(b) the state of discipline in the 11th Scottish Rifles is indifferent', a damning cue for tough action. His recommendation that sentence be carried out was endorsed by the divisional commander: 'I recommend that the sentence be put into execution on account of the grave nature of the offence and the fact that men of this battalion have committed crimes to avoid taking part in operations.' As in the case of Pte Brown, Gen. Milne confirmed sentence and Sgt Harry Ashton faced a firing squad on 8 July 1917.

In 1918 another soldier decided to avoid front line service on the battlefields of the Balkans. Pte Robert Young had been a reluctant conscript into the Army in March 1916. He had attempted to avoid conscription and had served a six-month prison term before being mobilized in May 1917. Less than a month later he had gone missing from camp and had been found guilty of stealing from a comrade, then in September 1917 he was tried by DCM for desertion in the UK. He was sent to Salonika where in January 1918 he joined the 11th Battalion Worcestershire Regiment. Two months later he was tried by FGCM for absence and stealing money from a comrade, and was sentenced to two years' imprisonment with hard labour. He served four months of this sentence in the military prison in Salonika before the balance was suspended and the reluctant soldier returned to his unit on 10 July.[7]

On 3 September 1918 the 11th Worcesters were in the front line. Their position was under heavy shellfire and Pte Young's dugout was blown in and his rifle and equipment lost, one man being killed. At 6.45 p.m. the platoon sergeants warned Young for duty after stand-to at 7.30 p.m. At 7.45 p.m. Cpl Cowley called the roll of men at his post and found Young missing.

At his trial, evidence was given that at about 7.00 p.m Young had bought some biscuits, then went back to his unit, before finally making off. At 8.15 p.m he was seen at the YMCA tent at Thom Hill, where he told Pte Pender: 'My platoon has got wiped out by shells and the remainder – twelve – are to come down to Mr Twentyman for a rest.' He remained there overnight and then went to the camp at Smol Hill. On the morning of 5 September he was seen in the recreation marquee at Smol Hill and was asked what he was doing there. Young replied: 'I have walked out of the line.' He was arrested and handed over to his battalion.

Pte Young was defended by Second Lt Sabin, who made a creditable effort at a defence. In a statement to the court Young admitted that he had been absent from 7.15 p.m. on 3 September to 11.30 a.m. on the 5th. He told the court that the shelling had been intense and that he had just left his dugout when it was blown in and Cpl Wallace killed. He had then helped carry Cpl Wallace's body to Gun Hollow. Because of the shelling he had missed dinner and bought the biscuits and shared them round. He said: 'While I was eating the biscuits I began to think over what had happened during the day. I became upset and went out of the camp. I went down to Smol, hardly knowing where I was going. I remained at Smol until apprehended two days later.' Under questioning by the prisoner's friend he said the sight of Cpl Wallace had upset him and the shelling had made him nervous. He insisted: 'When I left camp I did not realise what I was doing at that time and I had no intention of deserting. After a night's rest I realised what I had done, but I hadn't the courage to come straight back.'

The prisoner's friend then made a statement, saying that the prosecution had not proved an intention to desert and that the duty which Young had missed was not a particularly dangerous one.

After the finding, character evidence was presented to the court, with Young's regimental conduct sheet. The panel was informed that the accused man had been arrested in 1916 for not reporting under the Military Service Act; when offered the choice of going straight into the army or a prison sentence, Young had opted for the latter and had served a six-month sentence. The court was told: 'From that time he has had terms of imprisonment in the army because it was against his wish to serve.' Pte Young was found guilty and sentenced to death, but the court added a recommendation to mercy 'on the grounds that the accused was at the time suffering from mental strain and has expressed an intention of doing his duty in the future'.

None of the formation commanders could find a reason not to carry out sentence. His CO wrote that Young was known as a shirker and had a bad character, and that in his opinion the soldier had left the front line to get away from danger. Brig. Gen. Wingate noted: 'As we are on the eve of active operations and the example of one waverer may contaminate others at some critical moment, I recommend that the sentence be carried out.' Sentence was confirmed by General Milne, Commander-in-Chief of the Salonika force, and the unwilling conscript, Pte Robert Young, was shot by firing squad at Smol at 5.30 a.m. on 18 September 1918; only a few days later the Bulgarians sued for an armistice and fighting ceased on this front on 30 September 1918.

In January 1917 a man even further from home, in Mesopotamia, had tried to desert, and his trial on 2 February proved to be somewhat irregular, even though the court martial panel comprised a lieutenant colonel, a major and a captain. The evidence was presented out of sequence and is difficult to follow, but the order of events becomes clear.[8]

Pte Richard Jones was serving in Mesopotamia with 6th Battalion South Lancashire Regiment. On 21 January 1917 at 12.30 p.m. he was found to be missing, although his rifle and equipment were found. On the same day Jones reported to No. 39 Field Ambulance complaining of sore feet, but he did not have a sick report from his unit and the doctor found nothing wrong with him, and told him that he would be returned to his battalion later in the morning. Later Jones complained of dysentery, but the doctor examined his stools and found no sign of this condition. At the trial the MO of 6th South Lancs gave evidence that Pte Jones had not reported to him sick either on 21 January or at any date prior to that.

The next morning an NCO of the RAMC escorted Jones back to the transport lines of his battalion. Later, when put on parade, he was found to have no rifle or equipment and a transport officer detained him whilst further investigations were made. However, during the night of 22–23 January Jones escaped and on the 23rd was picked up at Imam, trying to obtain a railway warrant. No witness to this event was called at the trial. Instead the court accepted a written statement from Capt. Guthrie at Imam. This was headed: 'Certified that No. 10764 Pte R M Jones 6th Battalion South Lancashire Regt. was apprehended by the Military Authorities at Imam on the 23 January 1917.' Under this, Capt. Guthrie wrote that on the afternoon of 23 January 1917 Pte Jones had asked for a rail warrant to Sheikh Saad. The officer was suspicious, as Jones had no rifle or equipment, and arrested him pending further investigations. This evidence was, in fact, inadmissible and should have been given in person by the officer.

Pte Jones, who was not defended, did not challenge or deny this evidence – in fact, Jones did not challenge any of the evidence, and in his defence only said that when he reported sick his feet were sore and he had been feeling very poorly for several days. His case was not helped by his field conduct sheet, which showed six episodes of absence during the previous year. Despite the confused nature of the evidence, the court decided that Pte Jones had intended desertion and sentenced him to death.

After the trial his CO, Lt Col. Charlton, wrote: 'I have personally known No. 10764 Pte R.M. Jones since the day of his enlistment. During the whole of this period he has given continual trouble. Both kindness and disciplinary action have been without avail. He is the most useless soldier I have ever come across.' Brigade, division and corps commanders all failed to find any extenuating circumstances that would justify commuting sentence, and Lt Gen. Maude, commanding the British forces in Mesopotamia, confirmed sentence on 18 February 1917.

There was some consternation when the trial papers reached the DJAG, Indian Army Corps, and he wrote to the DAG at GHQ:

> The Court have accepted a written statement as to the accused having attempted to procure a Railway Ticket from Imam to Sheikh Saad instead of hearing the evidence of the Post-Commandant of Imam-al-Mansur himself. The document was of course, entirely inadmissible; the statement it contains was unsworn, and the accused could not cross-examine ... It is most unfortunate that in any case a Court should attempt to admit evidence in this manner, contrary to all principles of military and ordinary law, but it is particularly regrettable in case involving the extreme penalty ... It is however, too late now to rectify.

The letter then goes on to discuss the other, legitimate, evidence and ends: ' ... I am of the opinion that there was sufficient legal evidence ... to support their finding.'

The DAG immediately wrote to ensure that the members of the court martial panel were aware of their error. It is slightly surprising that a retrial was not ordered, and Capt. Guthrie called in person to give evidence. Instead, after confirmation by Gen. Maude, instructions were sent to say that Jones was to be shot by a firing party from his own battalion and that he was not to be told of his sentence until 7 p.m. the night before. Forty-year-old Pte Jones, who had enlisted in August 1914, was shot by firing squad on 21 February 1917, only two days after Ptes Burton and Downing of the same battalion had been executed for sleeping on sentry; all three executions took place at Nahr Bassouia. The death certificate noted that 'Pte R M Jones ... met his death by gun shot wounds at 7 a.m. on the 21st day of February 1917'.

After the war, when all the capital cases were reviewed in 1920, a note was added to the file: 'I am not satisfied that without the inadmissible evidence the accused would have been found guilty of desertion although there was evidence upon which he could be so convicted. This is, in my opinion, an unfortunate case.' That Jones was trying to desert seems clear from the story, but at the very least he should have been given a retrial to clear up any doubts as to the validity of the legal process.

Between Pte Jones's unsuccessful attempt at desertion and his execution, another soldier went missing in Mesopotamia. Pte George Cutmore was serving with the 2nd Battalion, The Black Watch and managed to remain at large for four months.[9]

After his capture and the taking of the summary of evidence the DJAG, Maj. Palmer, was asked for advice on framing the charge. He suggested that whilst desertion was appropriate, there should be an alternative charge of 'absent without leave'. In his letter he pointed out that 'The memorandum from the APM attached to the Summary of Evidence would not be admissible as evidence unless the accused surrendered himself voluntarily ...' Later, he wrote: 'In order to prove the charge as laid, it would be necessary to call at least one of the military police who apprehended the accused in Sheikh Saad.' The letter went on to say that if this were not possible, the charge should be amended to say: 'Until received over from an escort on 17 June 1917 and this fact should be proved.' The charge was amended to take this into account.

The trial was brief. Evidence was given that on 3 February 1917 Cutmore had been on a working party and on returning had been given permission to fall out but then went missing and was not seen again by his battalion until he returned under escort several weeks later. Another witness told the court that although Cutmore had originally been described as an absentee since 3 February, it had later been discovered that he had been admitted to hospital on 4 February and discharged on the 5th so that his absence originated on that date.

Despite the DJAG's comment, no evidence was produced about Cutmore's arrest, and if the accused man had said nothing it would have been difficult to prove the desertion charge. However, the private, who was not defended, made a statement and underwent a long cross-examination. He did not dispute any of the evidence, and his defence was brief: 'I had no intention of leaving the Regt. As I did, the reason why I did is because I had 200 Rs [currency], so I went away from hospital to Sheikh Saad where I admitted to the APM that I was an absentee from the Regt. I did not realise at the time what I was doing.' During cross-examination he said that he had won the money playing cards, and that during the four months of his absence he had been at the rest-camp at Sheikh Saad, but had never reported to anyone – amazingly, no one seems to have noticed him there. He was asked why he did not return to his unit when active operations began, but he denied realizing that active operations were taking place.

The soldier had a bad record and his crime sheet covered three pages, showing that Cutmore had enlisted in April 1915 and had been in trouble ever since. Most of the entries were for minor offences – dirty on parade, dirty rifle, 'committing a nuisance in the barrack room', but in March 1916 he had gone absent in the UK for nine days after breaking out of camp. He also had three charges of 'Losing by neglect his kit value 23/9'.

The length of Cutmore's absence was taken as proof of intention to desert and to miss active operations, and he was sentenced to death. The views of the army commanders are interesting. Lt Gen. Hobbs, GOC 1st Indian Army Corps, suggested that Pte Cutmore's bad record implied that his absence arose from a disinclination to work rather than cowardice, and therefore sentence should be commuted and suspended. On the other hand, a letter from the DJAG to Corps HQ says: 'The Army Commander has confirmed the Finding and Sentence ... as he considers that this is a clear case of constructive desertion.' He went on: 'The fact that the Black Watch has gained for itself such a brilliant record during this campaign would appear to the Army Commander to render it particularly desirable that such an unworthy member of the Regiment be removed from its ranks.' The message is clear: not only is Pte Cutmore guilty, he is an undesirable that the army would like to dispose of. As in other cases, an expendable man has been selected for the firing squad, not in this case as an example to his battalion, but so as to not weaken it as a fighting unit by having worthless men in the ranks.

Pte George Cutmore, who may have spent his last hours regretting his impulse to enjoy his winnings, was shot at 5 a.m. on 25 July 1917, on the left bank of the Tigris at Samarrah.

CHAPTER 24

YOUNG OFFENDERS

Youth is truly the season of credulity.

WILLIAM PITT, EARL OF CHATHAM, 1776

R eading the visitors' book at Locre Cemetery, the burial place of Joseph Byers, shows how strongly passions have been raised on the issue of the execution of under-age soldiers during the First World War.

To put this into context, young men have always joined the army under-age. A Punch cartoon published during the war sums it up: (see page 291)

> OFFICER (to a boy of thirteen who in his efforts to get taken on as a bugler has given his age as sixteen): 'Do you know where boys go who tell lies?'.
> APPLICANT: 'To the Front, sir'.[1]

Testimony to the number of these young men who lost their lives at the age of 15, 16 or 17 is to be found in the scores of cemeteries which mark the line of the Western Front.

In 1914 the school-leaving age was, for all but the privileged few, 14. A youth of this age would leave school with a working knowledge of the three Rs and, depending on his social status, would either find a job, such as manual or clerical work, or become an apprentice. By the age of 18 he would regard himself as a man of the world, and many girls of that age would be married and raising their first child. A man would not attain his age of majority until he was 21, but that had little impact on his everyday life; if he had brushed with the law he would have discovered that he had been legally responsible for his actions since the age of 14. Universal male suffrage was a recent phenomenon and he was unlikely to be concerned by his lack of franchise and, although he needed parental consent to marry, this was unlikely to be a significant problem. A young man who joined the army at the age of 17 or 18 would undoubtedly have considered himself a man, doing his bit for his country. At the start of the twenty-first century, when greater life expectancy and social change have permitted the young the luxury of extending juvenility so that many stay in full-time education to the age of 18 or 21, it is easy to forget the realities of 1914.

Another easily overlooked point is that we are used to having to prove our age and most people have their birth certificate. This was not the case before the Great War. A woman would probably keep her 'marriage lines' safe, but few had any record of their birth – in cases where a child was born a little too soon after marriage, the actual birth date might well be 'remembered' wrongly. Civil registration was introduced in England and Wales in 1837 but even as late as the 1880s and 1890s some births still went unrecorded. Most people depended on memory to work out their age and some were quite unaware of their true age.

The executions of young soldiers have to be set against this background. There is also the question of how the army dealt with the young men it recruited. In 1914, although it was possible to join the army under the age of 19, a soldier was not normally sent overseas until he reached this age. Hence, on the outbreak of war, when many youths tried to enlist, they were told to go away for a walk and come back the next day when they were 19. The army did not check ages on enlistment, but simply entered onto the attestation papers the age given by the man joining up. This was then signed by the applicant as being a true record of his details, and the age he had given became his 'official' army age.

The army recognized that there were many under-age soldiers in the ranks and did make attempts to deal with them. In September 1915 instructions were issued:

In future any application for the discharge of a soldier in the regular or territorial forces made by parent or legal guardian on the ground that the man is under 19 years of age and is therefore too young to serve ... will be dealt with ... in accordance with the attached instructions.

The order went on:

The age given by a soldier on enlistment is his official age, and battalion and company commanders should not make promises to parents that their sons will not be included in drafts for service until they are 19 (real age).[2]

The instructions given were that men under 17 would be discharged by their CO. If over 17, the soldier was to be held to serve, and draft letters to send to relatives were provided.

In June 1916 a revised instruction was issued and incorporated into First Army Routine Orders of 15 September 1916,[3] which were updated a month later by more explicit instructions:

502 – Soldiers Under Age

Disposal of Soldiers whose release from the Service is applied for on account of being under-age

The following revised instructions are notified for the guidance of all concerned in dealing with the case of a soldier whose release from the Service, or transfer to a Home Service Unit is applied for on the grounds that he is too young to serve:–

When the soldier was serving with an Expeditionary Force he was to be dealt with as follows:

(a) If under 17 years of age – he will be sent home ...
(b) If over 17 but under $18\frac{1}{2}$ years of age – he will be sent home, if he be willing ... If not willing to be sent home, his services will be utilized either behind the firing line, or he will be sent home at the discretion of the G.O.C.-in-C...If he is over $18\frac{1}{2}$ but under 19 years of age – he will not be sent home but will be posted to a Training or other Unit behind the firing line ...[4]

The orders went on to say that soldiers under 17 years were to be given no option of staying abroad, whilst those between 17 and $18\frac{1}{2}$ would be given the choice of transferring to a Home Service Establishment or remaining in foreign service (where they would be utilized behind the firing line). The orders also covered cases where the battalion officers knew a man to be under-age, but no application had been made by his family for his release.

Such applications were not always successful. George Coppard enlisted in the Queen's (Royal West Surreys) on 27 August 1914 when he was 16 years and 7 months old, and sailed to France in June 1915. In February 1916 his family applied to the War Office for his release, providing a birth certificate as evidence, but the reply, based on the model provided in the instructions of September 1915,[5] said that as Coppard had given an age of 19 years 7 months at attestation, this was his official army age and he could not be discharged.[6] On the other hand, James Tait joined the 10th East Yorks in April 1915, when he was $15\frac{1}{2}$, but his mother obtained his release in 1916 after demonstrating his true age to the War Office. Undeterred, he re-enlisted in the DLI as

OFFICER (to boy of thirteen who, in his effort to get taken on as a bugler, has given his age as sixteen): "Do you know where boys go who tell lies?"
APPLICANT: "To the Front, sir."

The eternal problem of the under-age soldier – a Punch *cartoon*

soon as he was 18.[7] Another young soldier, G. Adams, joined 1st Middlesex in March 1915, aged 16, and was discharged as under-age in January 1916. In a letter to his mother (who had asked for his discharge) he describes how he was asked by the CO if he wanted to stay in France or to go home – after the battle of Loos this young man decided to go home, but rejoined in December 1916.[8]

A notable under-age recruit was Victor Silvester. After his death in 1978 articles appeared saying that he had joined the army under-age and whilst at Etaples had read some confidential papers relating to men being shot and, as a punishment, had been made to serve on the firing squads for the next five executions.[9] In a *Guardian* article, apparently quoting Silvester, there is a gory description of an execution, where the condemned man, bleeding from a chest wound and tied to a chair, tried to make a run for it after a botched execution. Silvester is also quoted as having been reduced to screaming in his sleep and being physically sick until he was admitted to a military hospital and tied to the bed to prevent his escape.

The truth, revealed when Victor Silvester's army records were released in 2000, is rather different. He enlisted into the Argyll and Sutherland Highlanders on 4 September 1916, saying that he was 20 years and 7 months old, and that he had previously served for sixteen months (the regiment is illegible, but may say London Scottish).[10] However, he was discharged a week later on 12 September as being under-age. As he was only 16 at the time, it would seem that Silvester's father, the vicar of Wembley, had applied for his son's discharge. The young Silvester seems to have been determined to get to France as he then joined the First Aid Services and served with them in France from October 1916 to June 1917, entitling him to the British War Medal and Victory Medal.[11] It is surprising that such a young man would have been sent abroad with the Red Cross and it is possible that, yet again, he had lied about his age. Victor Silvester was re-enlisted into the Argyll and Sutherland Highlanders in January 1918, when he reached the age of 18, but as he did not reach the age of 19 before the end of the war, he did not serve abroad with the regiment.[12]

His story of having taken part in executions is, therefore, unsubstantiated. His description of a wounded man is somewhat fanciful, but may have been partly based on fact – perhaps a story told him by one of the wounded men who came under his care.

After the war the War Office reviewed all the cases of men under the age of 21 and listed them in the Summary of First World War Capital Courts Martial cases.[13] The ages given in this document are, of course, calculated from those given by the man on enlistment and may not be his true age. According to this list the youngest soldier shot was James Mitchell, an 18-year-old serving with the British West Indies Regiment, who was executed for murder in Palestine in 1917; under the criminal code of the day, he would have been liable to death by hanging if the offence had been committed in the UK. The record shows that eight men aged 19 were executed for military offences, the youngest being Herbert Burden (19 years 3 months) and Thomas Highgate (19 years 4 months), both, according to army records, being old enough for military service overseas. However, it is noted on one of the cases that William Hunter (official age 20 years 56 days) was only 17 years and 9 months old when he committed his fatal offence.

There is no doubt that the army had a difficult problem. Many men had joined up under-age, but the authorities had no way of establishing who these were unless either the soldier himself or his parents subsequently demonstrated his true age. Any under-age soldier accused of a capital crime could, in his plea of mitigation, tell the court his true age, but none of those executed appear to have taken this step. However, what we do not know is whether any of those sentenced to death but reprieved, or given a lesser sentence, were under-age and did demonstrate this to the court and in consequence had their punishment reduced.

If none of the executed men raised the issue of their age in their defence it is difficult to see what the army could have done. It is apparent from the trial documents that in many cases the man's records were consulted, but these would only have shown his 'army' age. If these showed him to be 19 or 20 and he had committed a capital offence for which he was sentenced to death there would be no reason to investigate further. It is only with the benefit of hindsight that we can identify that in some cases an under-age soldier may have been executed.

Publicity has centred on four cases of young men executed for desertion and each of these raises a different point of interest.

For many years, after the publication of the book *Shot at Dawn* highlighted the case, it appeared that Pte Joseph Byers, no. 15576 of the 1st Royal Scots Fusiliers, shot on 6 February 1915 at Locre, had been born in 1898 and was only 17 at the time of his execution, this being based on a birth certificate traced by the authors of that book.[14] However, this assumption has now been shown to be incorrect and there appear to have been two men called Joseph Byers. The Byers born in Scotland in 1898 was still at school in 1915, and went on to become a doctor, dying in 1965, and was clearly not the man executed at Locre in 1915.[15] There is therefore no reason to doubt that the Pte Joseph Byers shot at Locre was anything other than the 19-year-old the army believed him to be. Although the Commonwealth War Graves Register for Locre gives Byers's age at death as 17, this information was not in the original records and was added in recent years.[16]

The army records for Joseph Byers have not survived, but the Royal Scots Fusiliers Medal Roll for the 1914–15 Star show that he arrived in France on 3 December 1914 as one of a large draft of reinforcements.[17] His regimental number suggests that he had enlisted in late November, which implies that he was sent to the front after only three weeks' training. This would have been very unusual, as an untrained man would be a danger to himself and others and at this time there were still adequate supplies of reservists available to most battalions. This raises the possibility that Byers may have had some previous military training, perhaps as a Territorial or a Special Reservist, hence his prompt dispatch to France whilst some of the other men who enlisted at the same time as Byers did not go to France until the following March.

Byers served only five weeks in the trenches before committing the offence which led to his execution.[18] The facts of the case appear straightforward. He had been detailed to carry coke from Kemmel to the trenches on 8 January 1915, had fallen out to use the latrines, but did not return. He was next seen on 18 January between Ypres and Poperinge, when he was arrested by a French gendarme. On 30 January 1915 Pte Byers was tried by FGCM for attempted desertion. He was undefended at his trial and pleaded guilty to the charge, possibly not realizing the seriousness of his crime. Although the court then heard the outline of the evidence against Byers, this was unchallenged and, obviously, undefended. Also, the prisoner made no plea in mitigation of sentence. Byers and another soldier, Andrew Evans (tried on the same day for an unrelated offence), were both sentenced to death.

The unit commanders all recommended that the sentence should be carried out, but Gen. Sir Horace Smith-Dorrien, commanding Second Army, was concerned about the case and wrote to the DJAG:

> I should unhesitatingly have recommended that both Death sentences be carried out, but I think it right to point out that no. 15576 Pte J. Byers pleaded guilty and therefore no sworn evidence was taken and although this is legally correct it is just a question of whether when a death sentence is involved the Court should not make the man plead not guilty and take sworn evidence.

This point was noted and amendments made to the instructions for holding courts martial. In only one other case during the war was a man executed after a guilty plea (Patrick Downey in Salonika in December 1915).

It is usually said that the youngest soldier executed was Pte Herbert Burden of the 1st Northumberland Fusiliers.[19] Burden had gone to France in March 1915 and on 2 July was tried for desertion.[20] According to the evidence at the trial, on the afternoon of 26 June 1915 Burden had been warned for a working party digging trenches close to the front line but had then gone missing. He was subsequently seen in the transport lines of the 1st Battalion, Royal West Kents on 27 June and then again at Dickebusch Huts on the 28th, when he was arrested. In his defence Burden told the court that he had been to see a friend in the West Kents, with whom he had served in 1913.

Unfortunately Pte Burden had a bad record. References made to his regimental conduct sheet, produced at the trial but no longer with the court martial records, show that he had seven cases of absence in the UK as well as three miscellaneous other offences and one case of absence in France. After the sentence his commanding officer wrote: 'Has not been in action other than the usual trench sniping, went out on patrol twice ... of inferior physique, reported as untrustworthy. Joined BEF 28.3.15. Sick 12.6.15 to 23.6.15.' He went on to add: 'This man was punished for absence on 11th inst. and reported sick the next day.' The CO also wrote that there were no officers of his company left who knew him, but that his platoon sergeant said that he was a man who could not be trusted. There is no reference to Burden's age at any point in the court martial proceedings. Although the battalion had been in action at Hooge, when casualties had been high, the implication was that Burden did not take part in this operation.

In view of his record of absence, all the officers in the chain of confirmation recommended execution. Discipline was still being applied to the standards of the pre-war regular army and Pte Herbert Francis Burden was shot for desertion on 21 July 1915.

The case has been one of the cornerstones of the Pardons Campaign: a boy-soldier executed by the unfeeling high command. The facts as presented in *Shot at Dawn* are that Burden was an under-age volunteer serving with the Northumberland Fusiliers, shot at the age of 17, this age being based on the evidence of the birth certificate of a Herbert Francis Burden born in Lewisham, south London, on 22 March 1898.[21] However, there has previously been no other evidence to link these two men together.

What is actually known of Herbert Burden, no. 3832, 1st Battalion Northumberland Fusiliers, executed for desertion? On further examination the case becomes almost bizarre. The ascertainable facts are:

1. On his death certificate he is described as no. 3832 Herbert Francis Burden, aged 19 and born in England, suggesting a year of birth of 1896.

2. His age, quoted in the Summary of First World War Capital Courts Martial cases and presumably obtained from army records, was given as 19 years 3 months at the time of his trial.[22]

3. On the Medal Roll of the Northumberland Fusiliers for the 1914–15 Star it is noted that he was shot by order of FGCM and his medal was forfeited for desertion.[23]

4. At his court martial he claimed that when he was absent he had gone to see a friend in the Royal West Kents with whom he served in 1913 (in the trial transcript '1914' is changed to '1913').

5. After his trial, his CO described him as 'of inferior physique', which could either mean that he was young or, equally, could describe an under-nourished town-dweller.

6. His CO said that he joined the BEF on 28 March 1915; the Northumberland Fusiliers Medal Roll for the 1914–15 Star gives his date of disembarkation as 24 March.

7. His regimental number was 3832. By searching the Medal Rolls and *Soldiers Died in the Great War* is possible to identify men with numbers in close proximity to Burden's, and by then checking against service records for other ranks (where available), the Medal Rolls for the 1914–15 Star and the Silver War Badge Rolls it is possible to establish the date of enlistment of some of these men and the date they arrived in France.

The birth certificate of Herbert Burden

Herbert Burden's death certificate

Eight men can be identified with numbers close to Burden's, and these all enlisted into the regiment between February and June 1914. The implication from this is that Burden actually joined the army before the war, possibly around May 1914, and was then transferred to the BEF in March 1915 when, according to army records, he would have reached the age of 19.

The service records for executed Herbert Francis Burden of the Northumberland Fusiliers have not survived, his papers in common with many others being lost in the Blitz. However, a set of papers do exist for a man called Herbert Francis Burden and these are very interesting.[24] The question is whether this Herbert Francis Burden is the same man as the one who joined the Northumberland Fusiliers and was executed. This Herbert Francis Burden enlisted at Deptford on 23 November 1914 and joined the East Surrey Regiment as no. 11012. He gave his birthplace as Lewisham and his father's name as Arthur John Burden. The birth certificate of the Burden born on 22 March 1898 shows his place of birth as Silvermere Road, Lewisham and his father's name as Arthur Burden. It therefore looks extremely likely that this birth certificate belonged to the young man who enlisted in the East Surreys.

In the attestation papers this Burden is described as 19 years 240 days old (on 23 November 1914, this no doubt being calculated by the recruiting officer from a date of birth). He weighed 115 pounds (8 stone 3 pounds) and had an expanded chest measurement of 36 inches. His complexion was given as 'fresh' with dark brown hair and hazel eyes. The doctor described his physical development as 'good'. He also appears to have had two tattoos, one on his right upper arm and another on his left forearm, of clasped hands and 'Love Lilly' respectively. His employment was 'Carman' and his father's address was given as 8 Doggett Road, Catford.

This young man was posted to the 3rd Battalion of the East Surreys but when in barracks in Dover three weeks later, on 14 December, he deserted. On 11 January 1915 a court of inquiry sat and declared no. 11012, H. F. Burden, a deserter. This Herbert Burden then disappears from sight and there are no further entries for him. The problem is to prove a link between him and the executed Burden.

On 4 August 1915 the *Catford Journal* carried a report of a memorial service for 'Nine Catford men who have fallen' – among them, Herbert Burden.[25] A search of *Soldiers Died in the Great War,*[26] the Commonwealth War Graves Commission database [27] and General Register Office indices of army and navy deaths overseas and deaths in England and Wales shows that at this stage of the war only one other man of this name had died – he had served with the Dorsetshire Regiment, enlisting and residing in that county, and was killed on 24 August 1914; he is clearly nothing to do with the Lewisham Burden. The newspaper report thus appears irrefutably to link up the Lewisham-born Herbert Burden to the young man executed in 1915.

It would therefore appear that Herbert Francis Burden joined the Northumberland Fusiliers in or about May 1914, aged 16 years 2 months, but lied about his age, saying he was 18 years and 2 months old. He deserted from this regiment and returned to London, where in November 1914 he enlisted into the 3rd East Surreys at Deptford, saying that he was 19 years and 240 days old. Three weeks later he deserted from his new regiment and returned to the Northumberland Fusiliers. He then went to France with this regiment as soon as he reached the 'army' age of 19 (according to the records of the battalion). He was then shot in July 1915 for desertion. After his trial, the comment was made by his CO that the defaulter's sheet (no longer with the other records) 'shows he is much addicted to absence' and at the trial it was stated that he had seven cases of absence in the UK – one of these would appear to be his brief defection to the East Surreys.

There is no simple explanation as to why this young man joined the Northumberland Fusiliers, deserted, joined another battalion and deserted again. It is surprising that as a deserter he then enlisted in another regiment under his proper name and correct home address, unless he had originally given false details to the Northumberland Fusiliers. Several hypotheses can be proposed, but the truth will never be known. The Burden case is not quite as simple as the court martial proceedings and the Pardons Campaign make it appear.

It is interesting to note that at his trial, Burden was stated to have been found in the lines of the Royal West Kents, a regiment in which many men from the Lewisham–Catford area served, and it is probable that he did have friends in the regiment. The final twist to the story is that after the war, names of men were compiled for the war memorial in St Laurence's Church, Catford.[28] A roll of honour was compiled, including the names of Herbert Burden, and Thomas and Robert Highgate. This Thomas Highgate was the first man executed in the war, and his family lived in Brookdale Road, Catford[29] – the road next to Silvermere Road, where Burden had been born, and close to Doggett Road where his family lived, so these two men may have known each other. The war memorial screen which was eventually erected in St Laurence's Church (which was demolished in the 1960s) carried the name of the executed Thomas Highgate (along with the names of two of his brothers, Robert and Joseph), but Herbert Burden's name was not included.

The name of Herbert Morris does not appear on the list of soldiers executed under the age of 21 in the Summary of First World War Capital Courts Martial cases.[30] The only clue to his age is in the Commonwealth War Graves Commission register for Poperinge New Military Cemetery, where he is described as the son of William and Ophelia Morris of Riversdale, St Catherine, Jamaica, aged 17 (as this age was given in the original registers it may have been provided by his family and would therefore appear be accurate).[31] Pte Morris was from Jamaica and was serving with the 6th Battalion of the British West Indies Regiment. He had enlisted in December 1916 during a recruitment drive in the West Indies and arrived in France in April 1917. After a brief period of acclimatization the battalion moved to line of communication duties in the Ypres area.[32]

After only a few months at the front Morris seems to have decided that he could stand it no more. The evidence presented at his trial on 7 September 1917 told that on 20 August 1917 Morris was one of a group of sixty men warned that they were to go by lorry from their camp at Poperinge to Essex Farm, from where they would go to work with the artillery at Burnt Farm.[33] Although Morris was seen to get onto the last lorry of the convoy, he was missing when the group arrived at Essex Farm. The next morning he turned up at St Martin's rest camp in Boulogne saying that he had been sent there by mistake and was on his way to Le Havre. As he had no rifle, equipment or leave warrant, he was arrested.

Pte Morris, who had no prisoner's friend, made a statement in his defence, not on oath, saying: 'I am troubled with my head I cannot stand the sound of the guns. I reported to the Doctor and he gave me no medicine or anything. It was on Sunday 19.8.17 that I saw the doctor. He gave me no satisfaction.' Despite this defence, Morris does not appear to have been medically examined and the doctor did not give evidence at the trial.

Two of his officers gave evidence for the defence. Lt Andrews told the court: 'The accused has never given me any trouble. He is well behaved. I have known the accused for 6 months. His intelligence is higher than that of the ordinary men in my platoon.' Capt. Russell said: 'The accused has never given me any trouble and is a willing worker.'

Unfortunately Morris had left his unit on a previous occasion, his conduct sheet showing that on 16 July 1917 he had left his detachment and been found in Boulogne the following day. For this absence he was given fourteen days' FP No. 1. The court decided that the case had been proved, and sentenced him to death. In common with many of the court martial records from 1917 the commanders' recommendations are no longer with the trial transcript, and it would appear that sentence on this occasion was not suspended because of the previous attempt to desert. Young Pte Morris was shot on 20 September 1917 at Poperinge.

There is no mention of Morris's age during the trial, and he certainly did not raise it as a plea in mitigation. Even if the army had suspected that he was a young soldier and his records had been checked, these would only have shown his 'official' army age given on enlistment. With the benefit of hindsight it is easy to say that soldiers' ages should have been checked more thoroughly, but at that time, when birth certificates were not readily available, the army had to accept the information given it. As Morris's name does not appear on the 'young soldiers' list in the Summary of First World War Capital Courts Martial cases, it implies that he gave an age on enlistment which suggested he was over 21 at the time of his death.[34]

The youngest man *knowingly* executed by the British Army was Pte William Hunter of the 1st Loyal North Lancashire Regiment. His 'army age' at the time of his trial was 20 years 56 days, but during his trial he told the court that he was really 18. This appears to be the only case in which an under-age man's true age emerged at his trial.[35]

Pte Hunter was one of the many young men who flocked to the colours on the outbreak of war and was drafted into one of the regular battalions of the original BEF. The 1st Battalion of the Loyal North Lancs had been heavily engaged in the initial phase of the war, fighting at Mons, the Marne, the Aisne and several of the actions around Ypres. Hunter was sent to France on 4 January 1915, just after what the army believed to be his 19th birthday. By that time he had already had one brush with authority: on 12 December 1914 he was found missing from his billet in Felixstowe and was not picked up until 27 December. For this absence he was given fourteen days' FP No. 2.

On arriving at the front, Hunter seems to have served creditably until 6 August 1915, when he went missing en route to the trenches and was absent for three days, for which he received ten days' FP No. 1. Almost immediately, on 15 August, he left his unit again, surrendering himself three days later. This time he was tried by FGCM for desertion, but was found guilty of the lesser charge of absence without leave and sentenced to two years' imprisonment with hard labour; this was later commuted to one year, and the sentence suspended.

He served another month before his fatal offence. On 4 February 1916 he stood trial at Lillers on three counts, one of desertion and two of escaping. The court martial panel consisted of three captains and a lieutenant, there being no field officer available to act as president. However, one of the panel was Capt. D. Lane Ingpen of the 10th West Yorkshire Regiment, a barrister in civil life, who was CMO at several of the capital trials and who provided legal advice during the proceedings.

The evidence presented at the trial showed that on 22 September 1915, on the eve of the battle of Loos, the 1st Loyals had been ordered to get ready to proceed to the trenches. Hunter, who was in the guardroom at the time, was not actually present at the parade when this order was given, so could make the point that he was not aware of the imminent battle. He was not present the following evening, when the battalion paraded prior to moving into the line, and was not seen again until he was found by Maj. Samuel of the Royal Fusiliers at a farm at Bois Fontaine, Burbure, on 30 November 1915.

On the following day he was handed over to Sgt Lawton of the Military Foot Police and was locked in the guardroom at Lillers, but a few hours later he was found to be missing again. He remained at large until 4 December, when he was again found at Bois Fontaine. Again he was handed over to Sgt Lawton, who sent him under escort to Mazingarbe. Here he was put into the guardroom in the charge of Pte Duckworth of the 1st Loyal North Lancs, but his guard left Hunter for a couple of minutes whilst he checked on another room, and in that brief time Hunter escaped again. He was found, inevitably, in the woods near Burbure on 8 January by Sgt Lawton. This evidence was all uncontested.

Pte Hunter, who defended himself, called no witnesses in his defence, but made a statement on oath. He told the court that he came from Newcastle and had left school at 14 and gone to sea for two years but he had got into trouble and had jumped ship in Montreal. On arriving back in the UK he had joined the army, saying that he was 18, when in fact he was only 16. He had enlisted in a Lancashire regiment as he thought he would not be likely to come across people who knew him, but he did not get on with the other soldiers and had lost heart with soldiering.

In August, whilst at rest in Béthune, he had come across some friends and spent three days with them, this leading to his earlier trial for desertion. He then said:

My sentence was suspended and, being then free from detention, I had a good time with friends before the regiment was back in the trenches. During this time I got in league with a young woman, and I did not like to leave her. I did not realise the seriousness of what I was doing in remaining absent from my regiment. While I was in the guard room I heard a lot of tales about men being shot for offences like mine and I got into such a state of mind that I did not know what to do.

He went on:

Now I realise that I have played the fool all along and I am sorry. I ask the court to be lenient with me. I am young and have always been easily led. I am not afraid of the trenches, and if leniently treated I hope to make a good soldier.

Under cross-examination he told the court that he did not go absent to avoid duty in the trenches, but unfortunately he made some damning admissions: 'During the two months when I was absent it did sometimes occur to me that my regiment would probably be in the trenches and that I was missing the trenches. I did not give myself up, because I was having a good time and thought that I would stay away a bit longer. If I had not been arrested, I should still have stayed absent.' This last sentence is heavily underlined in the trial proceedings and may have been the final deciding factor in the case. He also told the court that he was 18 on 27 December 1915. The court found him guilty of all the charges and sentenced him to death, with a strong recommendation to mercy 'on grounds of extreme youth, service in the field and likelihood of being a good fighting man'.

Here is a case which crystallizes the army's dilemma with under-age soldiers. On first seeing the trial papers, knowing that this was a young soldier, the initial reaction is one of pity – a poor young man, thrown in at the deep end, serving through 1915 with a regular battalion, unable to cope with the horrors of war, and who had run away and been tried by FGCM. At his first opportunity he had run away again, desperate to get away from the slaughter. But then, reading Hunter's own evidence, a different picture emerges, that he had effectively run away from his comrades and his soldierly duties to have a good time with a woman and had no intention of going back, coincidentally missing the battle of Loos at which 130 men of his battalion lost their lives. This 18-year-old was no innocent abroad: he had spent two years at sea and had made his way back to the UK after jumping ship. This was not a fresh-faced youth straight out of school thrown in at the deep end of life, this was a man young in years but with considerable experience.

How did the army deal with him? It is not clear from the records whether they checked his claim as to his age, but they seem to have accepted it at face value. His CO, Lt Col. Sanderson, who had been wounded at Loos, wrote:

> Pte Hunter's company commander states that for the past 4 months (his period in command of the company) he has hardly seen the man, who has been in the guard room or a state of absence most of the 4 months.
> I do not know the man myself but I am of the opinion that
> (a) his character as a fighting man is 'NIL' as he intends to do no fighting
> (b) he would carry on as he has done heretofore, and avoid all trench work or fighting.

Brig. Gen. H. F. Williams, commanding 2nd Infantry Brigade, was also in favour of execution, as the state of discipline in the battalion was unsatisfactory. He also mentioned that he had established that Hunter's NCOs considered that he was not a good character. Williams also believed that it was not coincidence which led Hunter to desert on the eve of the battle of Loos and that this was a case of deliberate desertion. The divisional commander, Maj. Gen. Holland, also recommended that the sentence be carried out. However, Lt Gen. Sir Henry Wilson, commanding IV Corps, wrote: 'I think that this man ought to be shot except that he is very young, only 17¾ last

September and therefore I recommend that the sentence be commuted to 5 years penal servitude, not to be suspended.' That stern disciplinarian Gen. Monro did not agree: 'I recommend that the death sentence be put into execution. The man is very young, but his commanding officer says he is no good as a fighting soldier.'

In the court martial file there is a detailed note from the DAA & QMG of 1st Division, describing how the sentence was to be carried out. It is also apparent from this that Hunter seems to have made another bid for freedom after his trial, but this was short-lived and young William Hunter was shot by a firing party from his own regiment at 6.58 a.m. on 21 February 1916.

This trial raises several points. Unlike any of the other under-age soldiers, Hunter drew attention to his youth at his trial and this seems to have been accepted. The army therefore knew that he was only 18 when executed, and yet this was not sufficient to reduce his sentence. As George Coppard noted, his official age was his army age, and he was tried and punished on the basis of that age.[36] It also appears that he either was a pre-war regular or had enlisted very early in the war and, serving in a regular battalion in a regular formation, was tried and judged by pre-war regular army standards. A year later he might well have been given a second chance. He was undefended at his trial. Would he have made such a damning statement if he had the support of a prisoner's friend? Another important point, which recurs time and again in the capital courts martial, is that an example appeared to be necessary and the army selected for this purpose a man who was expendable. The brigade commander's comments on the discipline in the battalion indicate that an example was needed and it was the statement by his commanding officer that Hunter's value as a fighting soldier was nil which decided, as much as anything, his fate. An example needed to be made and here was a man who was expendable since he had no value as a soldier. In that context his age became immaterial.

James Crozier was a young Irishman who rushed to join the colours in September 1914. According to Brig. Gen. Frank Crozier, then a major in the 9th Royal Irish Rifles, this young shipyard apprentice arrived at the West Belfast recruiting office with his mother, who pleaded with him not to join up, saying that she would tell the officer that he was only 17.[37] Interestingly, Crozier does not appear on the 'young soldiers' list in the Summary of First World War Capital Courts Martial cases [38] and the only evidence of his age is from Frank Crozier's recollections, which were written some twenty years after the events.

As these are wrong in some other details of the case, it may be unwise to place too much confidence in Brig. Gen. Crozier's statements. In *The Men I Killed* he wrote that whilst the boy was signing his attestation, he spoke to the mother and told her not to worry and that he would look after her son.

In due course the 9th RIR went to France, arriving at Boulogne in October 1915, when James Crozier's 'army age' was 19. Frank Crozier describes the first six months in the line:

> six months passed – six months of front-line life in winter. Rain, rain, rain! Rain and rain and mud and slush and shells. Four days 'in' and four days 'out'... Hell. Sentry go, patrol duty in No-Man's-Land, wet uniform, eternal digging, eternal pumping out, ration parties, carrying parties, working parties. Mining-sniping-bombing. Up to the middle in mud and slush for four days on end; then another four days cleaning, drilling, sleeping and getting dry again. But considering all things, the food was good. One of the marvels of the war, was not that the men got good food in beastly, filthy surroundings in the trenches, but that they got food at all ...[39]

At the end of January the weather worsened: '... General Winter took a turn for the worse and for a week – the most trying week of that trying winter of 1915–16 – conditions became such as to be unfit for man or beast in the open. And in the open were we.'[40] On 31 January young James Crozier had put up with enough and went missing. Four days later he was picked up.

Frank Crozier is wrong in his recollections when he says James Crozier was caught at the coast in civilian clothes and with no equipment, a fortnight after leaving his unit. However, his observation that 'Crockett [his pseudonym for Crozier], fed-up, cold, wet to the skin and despondent had sneaked off from the line' probably accurately describes how the young man felt.[41] The details of the events were uncontested at the trial.[42] The 9th RIR went into the line at 7 p.m. on 31 January 1916. Crozier was warned at 8.30 p.m. not to leave his dugout as he was due to go on sentry. At 8.45 p.m. he had disappeared. On the morning of 4 February he was seen in the mechanical transport lines at the 7th Ammunition sub-park, which was about 25 miles to the rear. He had no cap badge or equipment and no pay book. On questioning he admitted he was a deserter and was arrested. He was not, as stated by Babington, admitted to a field ambulance behind the lines, but was examined after his trial.[43]

In his defence, Rifleman Crozier said that he had felt very ill on the day, that he went into the line and did not remember being warned for duty or leaving the trenches. He made no mention of his age. However, when cross-examined by the adjutant, and asked if there was any bombardment going on at the time, Crozier fell into the trap, saying that there were rifle grenades bursting nearby; he also said that he felt ill before going into the line but had not reported sick. There is an interesting – and relevant – difference between the summary of evidence and the evidence given at the trial. In the summary of evidence, Cpl Brightmore of the MMP stated: '... I examined the accused. He had no rifle or paybook. During the whole time I was in charge of him, his behaviour was peculiar. I asked him where he had been since leaving the trenches, he was unable to tell me.' The last two sentences do not appear in the evidence given at the trial; perhaps if Crozier had had the support of a prisoner's friend this omission would have been noticed.

After the evidence had been presented and the court had considered its verdict, a copy of his regimental conduct sheet was produced showing Crozier's character as 'Bad', which was damning. He had two charges of absence against him whilst in France, one from a working party and one from his billet. There are no details of dates or punishment, but the most recent entry was noted as being on 21 January 1916.

After sentence his CO, Lt Col. Frank Crozier, the same man who said he had promised the young man's mother that he would look after him, was called upon for his recommendations. He wrote:

> (1) From a fighting point of view, this soldier is of no value. His behaviour has been that of a 'shirker' for the past three months. He has been with the Expeditionary Force since 3/10/15. (2) I am firmly of the opinion that the crime was deliberately committed with the intention of avoiding duty in the Redan, more particularly as he absented himself shortly after the case of another soldier had been promulgated for a similar crime. The officer commanding the man's company is of the same opinion. Sentence was remitted in the case mentioned to 2 years I.H.L.

Frank Crozier was a tough disciplinarian who made no bones about the fact that military duty was paramount above all else. In his book he said:

> I invariably warned everybody connected with my command, whatever size it happened to be, that from me they might expect no mercy in matters relating to the safety of the line ... or leniency from the British Command, were I to fail or they to fail me.[44]

Frank Crozier came from a military family; duty was expected and duty was done, even if the duty might conflict with one's nature as a man. His comments on James Crozier are no more nor less than expected from such a man – the young deserter had a bad character, the action had been deliberate, and execution could be the only outcome. The only real contemporary criticism that could be made was that he did not reveal what he believed to be the man's real age. However, the possibility remains that Frank Crozier's recollections regarding the young soldier were incorrect.

Brig. Gen. Withycombe, commanding 107th Brigade, in recommending that sentence be carried out also wrote: 'The discipline of the 9th R.I. Rifles is good for a service battalion' – summing up the regular army view of the new volunteer army. When Withycombe's letter reached Division, a vigilant staff officer noted that although Crozier had introduced a medical element into his defence, he had not been seen by a doctor. A medical examination was arranged, and Lt Col. Fawcett, commanding No. 108 Field Ambulance, wrote on 18 February 1916 that he had examined Rifleman Crozier, had found him in sound health in mind and body, and that there was no evidence to show that he had recently been other than sound in mind and in body.

Rifleman James Crozier was shot by men of his own battalion. Frank Crozier found the duty unpleasant but unavoidable. He wrote of his namesake: 'He was brave. He showed no malice. He was cheerful almost to the end. I made him drunk, some hours before the execution to ease his living misery.'[45] He attended the execution: 'I saw the execution; and the whole battalion heard it on parade, a wall screening the victim from the men's view. Death, despite all the precautions, was not instantaneous owing to nervousness, the firing party fired wide.'[46]

Frank Crozier also reports that before the execution the military police were afraid that the battalion might mutiny and refuse to shoot, and had reported this to the APM. Crozier dealt with this by confining the MPs to their billet and by making sure that the APM remained in his office until the execution was over. Brig. Gen. Crozier also provides an epitaph for his namesake, Rifleman James Crozier: 'He was no rotter deserving to die like that. He was merely fragile. He had volunteered to fight for his country … at the dictates of his own young heart. He failed. And for that failure he was condemned to die – and he did at the hands of his friends, his brothers, with the approval of his church'[47] and 'To us, what was he? He was poor Crockett [Crozier]. And we never made up our minds for whom we were sorrier – him, or ourselves. Such is war.'[48]

CHAPTER 25

SHELL SHOCK AND DISCIPLINE

... a psychoneurosis may be produced in almost anyone if only his
environment be made 'difficult' enough for him ...

G. ELLIOT SMITH AND T. H. PEAR, 1917

It is easy for us to criticize the front line doctors of the war, saying that they should have recognized the shell-shocked and traumatized men. We have to remember, though, that the battalion medical officer had to be surgeon, physician, GP and psychiatrist to the men and had to meet the army's expectations of him. Many of these doctors were young men, scarcely qualified, being expected to take on roles beyond their skills and experience. They also had to have a sharp eye for the malingerers, who had a fine set of tricks to dupe the inexperienced doctor. It is not surprising that sometimes they made mistakes. Lord Moran describes the dilemma:

> ... a man reported sick and I sent him back to duty. The following day he
> came back again and again I sent him back. But the day after he was still
> among the morning sick. 'It's no good sir,' he said, 'I can't stand it no
> longer'. Once more I thoroughly examined him; there was nothing wrong
> with him physically and he was sane enough. He was simply tired – but so
> were others. Once more I sent him back, the next day he was killed.[1]

This was the pressure on the MO. If he sent such a man away sick, the next day there would be a trickle of such cases, and then a flood. However much sympathy he might have for an individual, a doctor also had his duty to the army: to maximize its fighting potential. Moran's use of the words 'he was sane enough' is interesting. If a man appeared sane, he was fit for duty. Only when the psychological breakdown was so great as to render him obviously insane was he likely to be evacuated with shell shock, given the state of medical knowledge of the average battalion doctor. The MO also had to be a detective. Malingering, in and out of the trenches, was an ever-present problem. Self-inflicted wounds were the most obvious form of self-injury, but there were other, less obvious tricks: adding egg white to urine to mimic kidney disease (one still used by patients today), eating cordite to cause an irregular heartbeat, eating picric acid to imitate jaundice, injecting turpentine under the skin to cause abscesses, rubbing horse manure onto the gums to mimic scurvy are but a few.[2] Some men went to extraordinary lengths: John Rowarth was one. After several convictions for absence he feigned madness to avoid duty in the trenches. When it seemed that his tricks were about to be exposed, he walked into the path of a truck so that it ran over his foot. His view was: 'I admit I am a coward, a bloody, bleeding coward, and I want to be a live Coward [rather] than a dead blasted Hero.'[3] No wonder that it seems to the relatives of some executed men, who had served well before their lapse, a great injustice that such shirkers were awarded their medals, while the executed men were not.

The doctors were also products of their time and background. Medicine may have been making progress in leaps and bounds, but many doctors in the field were not aware of new developments. An MO at the front was largely deprived of his medical journals and the normal interaction with colleagues which is the cornerstone of medical education – there was no continuing medical education programme for doctors in 1914. As late as 1945 Moran wrote, somewhat simplistically, that men could be divided into four categories: 'men who did not feel fear; men who felt fear but did not show it; men who felt fear and showed it but did their job and men who felt fear, showed it and shirked'.[4] This was very much the prevailing view during the war. Fear could be conquered and giving in to it was unmanly and was shirking your duty, and Imperial Man did not give in to such impulses. Such a rigid definition makes no allowance for the genuinely traumatized individual who had tried and was unable to conquer his personal demons or just needed a respite before going back to the war.

Given the limitations of the system and of the men who did their best to administer it, it is not surprising that the doctors sometimes got it wrong. The situation was actually made worse rather than better when the existence of shell shock was recognized. The army was slow to accept that shell shock could occur unrelated to a physical wound and as late as December 1916 instructions sent to field ambulances said:

> The diagnosis of shell shock must only be made when there is sufficient corroborative evidence, such as perforation of the tympanic membrane

[the eardrum] or obvious lesions due to shell. Other cases should be marked 'shell shock query'. In neither case should the patient be told that his diagnosis is shell shock.[5]

There was genuine concern that by giving such cases a label, shell shock would become respectable and that such cases would increase. Moran described the situation:

When the name shell-shock was coined the number of men leaving the trenches with no bodily wound leapt up. The pressure of opinion in the battalion ... was eased by giving fear a respectable name ... the hospitals at base were said to be choked with these people though the doctors could find nothing wrong with them.[6]

The men in the front line lived with one sort of fear, their commanders lived with different fears – fears that their unit would cease to function, through either disobedience, mutiny or fear. One of the worst scenarios for a unit commander was to have to admit to his superior that he could not rely on his men to hold the line – as happened in 1916 to the 16th Cheshires.[7] This was a disgrace from which he and the men concerned would not recover. For this reason no commander could risk an epidemic of shell shock in his battalion. If his unit was sound and discipline good, he could afford to be magnanimous about the occasional shell-shocked deserter, but if discipline was bad and the collective nerve shaky, then, shell-shocked or not, an example was called for and a man sacrificed to ensure the future courage of the battalion.

To execute a shell-shocked, traumatized man seems by our standards to be horrific. But war is brutal: this is its nature. The war had to be won; in order to win it was necessary to keep as many men as possible in the field. There was no time in this war to end all wars to worry about the deeper recesses of men's minds; their job was to do their duty, and if one man's death could encourage others to do their soldierly duty, then his death was an unfortunate consequence of war.

The contemporary situation regarding insanity and mental illness can be illustrated by reference to a trial for murder which took place in 1919. Frederick ('Eric') Holt was a Territorial officer in 1914 and fought in the war before being invalided out of the army. He then went to Malaya, but returned to the UK in 1918, when he met Kitty Breaks, a married woman living apart from her husband. An affair resulted, but on Christmas Eve 1919 Mrs Breaks was found dead in the sand dunes at St Annes. Holt was arrested and Sir

Edward Marshall Hall, the famous barrister, was instructed for the defence.

Marshall Hall thought that Holt was 'unfit to plead' and laid this before the court, with supporting medical evidence. Under the law which pertained at the time, either the prosecution or the defence could raise the issue of 'unfit to plead', on the basis that the accused was either unable to give instructions for his defence, or unable to follow the evidence given. However, a man found 'unfit to plead' was not acquitted, but sent to a criminal lunatic asylum to be detained 'during His Majesty's pleasure'. The fundamental legal rules pertaining to insanity at the time were the McNaghten rules, formulated in 1843, of which Edward Marjoribanks wrote in 1929:

> The judges in 1843 had not at their disposal the knowledge of insanity
> which is now available for every medical student ... The rules in
> Macnaughton's case were a step in the right direction. But should there
> not perhaps be a further step in the light of modern scientific research?[8]

In the Holt case evidence was given that his grandfather and first cousin had been insane, but the court decided that the accused man was fit to plead, and the trial then hinged on whether this man, with a family history of insanity and whose brain may have been unhinged by his war experiences, murdered, in a fit of madness, the woman he clearly adored. Marshall Hall pleaded: 'A man like the prisoner who has been in France and subjected to the nerve-wracking experience of the Festubert bombardment – a man who is neurasthenic, and has suffered from loss of memory and depression – is the very man who might at any moment go mad.' Marjoribanks gives an insight into the mind of the day: 'There must be tens of thousands of men who, had they been present, would have responded in their hearts to that appeal.'[9] Holt was found guilty and sentenced to death, crucial evidence being presented that he had persuaded his mistress to take out a life insurance policy shortly before her death.

The case went to appeal, and Marshall Hall summarized the argument:

> Will is different from reason. A man may know the difference between
> right and wrong and may appreciate the nature and quality of his acts
> and the consequences thereof, and yet be deprived of that instinctive
> choice between right and wrong which is characteristic of a sane person.
> Hitherto, intellectual insanity, defective reason, has been the only insanity
> recognised by the law, but our contention is that a man's reason may be
> clear, even his judgement may be clear, yet his will-power is absent or

impaired or suspended, so as to deprive the person affected of the power to control his actions or exercise his will power.[10]

This statement describes with great clarity the situation in which some shell-shocked men found themselves. Harry Farr knew that it was wrong not to obey orders but his will power had been destroyed by his experience of battle. However, the law of England only recognized insanity within the parameters laid down by the McNaghten rules, and as these stood, men who claimed shell shock or battle fatigue fell outside the legal definition of insanity. The same rules applied to a military court. With this knowledge, we cannot therefore be surprised that men with their minds ravaged by their experience of war were sentenced to death and executed: there was no precedent for any other recourse.

From the evidence presented at the capital courts martial it is difficult – if not impossible – to assess how many of the men might have been suffering from a mental breakdown in consequence of their war experience. With hindsight it seems probable that virtually every man who served for any time at the front – both officers and men – suffered from what we would now call post-traumatic stress disorder. Men buried these memories deep inside their subconscious and did their best to get on with post-war life, often plagued by nightmares and flashbacks. The clue to the mental trauma is in the phrase 'but he never talked about the war'. The psychological wounds of a whole generation went largely unrecognized and untreated.

In this respect the majority of men executed for various offences were probably no worse affected than their comrades. It is only in a few cases that it is clear that a man had reached his breaking strain and this led him to take actions that he would not have otherwise considered. Lord Moran wrote:

How is courage spent in war? Courage is will-power, whereof no man has unlimited stock; and when in war it is used up, he is finished. A man's courage is his capital and he is always spending. The call on the bank may be only the daily drain of the front line or it may be a sudden draft which threatens to close the account.[11]

It is easier to identify the men who have emptied their bank account of courage amongst the cowardice cases than among the deserters. Nonetheless, there are amongst the latter group a handful of cases where psychologically damaged men faced a firing squad.

Desertion, in military terms, is fairly straightforward to prove: all that concerned the army was whether a man was where he should be. If he was not in the correct place he had either gone absent without leave or deserted. It was immaterial to the army *why* someone had gone absent. All that concerned them was his intention: if he intended to absent himself permanently this was desertion, or if he intended to miss a particularly onerous or dangerous duty, that too was desertion. It is the word 'intention' that is crucial in military law. If intention could not be proved, then the man could only be found guilty of absence. Equally, if a man could be shown to be not responsible for his actions, he could not form the intention to desert and was not guilty of this offence, but crucially the onus was always on the defendant to prove that he was not capable of forming the intention to commit an offence.

One of the earliest cases of the war where a man who was subsequently executed appears to have deserted as a result of psychological trauma is that of Pte Edward Tanner. Pte Tanner was a regular soldier serving with the 1st Battalion, Wiltshire Regiment, which had fought at Mons, Le Câteau, on the Marne and on the Aisne. This unit was involved in more or less continual action between 23 August and 24 September 1914.[12] In the middle of October Tanner deserted.

He was tried at Richebourg St Vaast on 23 October 1914, with a charge of 'when on active service deserting His Majesty's Service in that he at Helpegabe on 18th October 1914 absented himself from the 1st Battalion Wiltshire Regiment until apprehended in civilian clothing at Helpegabe about 9.15 a.m. on the 19th October 1914'.[13] The fact of his being in plain clothes would count very heavily against an accused man, as this would be taken as proof that he did not intend to return to his unit.

Three witnesses gave evidence at the trial. Pte Tanner did not have a prisoner's friend and he does not appear to have cross-examined any of the witnesses.

Pte Jones told the court that on 18 October he had been one of a party of men, which had included Tanner, who were rejoining their unit. They had stopped at a village on their line of march, and when they left, at 8.30 p.m., Tanner, who was in uniform, was missing. Lt Clemens, Adjutant of the 2nd South Lancashires, gave evidence that at 9.15 a.m. on 19 October he saw Pte Tanner dressed in plain clothes enter the village from the direction of the German lines. The officer, believing him to be a local inhabitant, spoke to him and, when he discovered that he was English and noticed that he was wearing army boots, arrested him. Sgt Sweeney of the 1st Wiltshires described how he had taken over custody of the accused, who was in plain clothes, from the South Lancashires and how, on the way back to their battalion, Tanner had pointed out the house where he had left his equipment. There the sergeant found a rifle and equipment hidden under some straw.

Pte Tanner gave evidence on oath, stating:

> I lost my party at the village on the night of 18th October and after they had left I went off on my own in the direction where I thought my regiment was, when I walked into a firing line of some troops, so I turned round and came back to the village and slept there until daylight. I was terribly overcome by nervousness from heavy firing and do not know what I was doing at the time. I had left hospital suffering from dysentery and my nerves were shattered by the Battle of the Aisne.

No character evidence was given, nor any as to his previous service, and he does not seem to have been medically examined. Gen. Smith-Dorrien, commanding II Corps, recommended that sentence be carried out and this was confirmed by the Commander-in-Chief, John French, on 26 October. Pte Tanner was shot shortly after 7 a.m. on 29 October 1914. His grave was lost in the subsequent fighting and he is commemorated on the Le Touret memorial.

Tanner was a regular, and was tried by the standards of the regular army. To the army, being found in civilian clothing was a clear indication – as in the case of Thomas Highgate – that he had no intention of returning to his unit. Also, in the eyes of the pre-war army, his admission of shattered nerves was a danger signal. At that stage of the war there was a real danger that if soldiers who were afraid could slope off and escape punishment, this would become an epidemic. Discipline had to be reinforced to demonstrate that being afraid and failing to do your duty was not an acceptable attribute in a soldier. Also, in 1914, before the Suspension of Sentences Act came into being, a man whose sentence was commuted was as lost to the army as if he had been shot. There was therefore a ruthless logic that a man shot as an example to others was more useful to the army than a man languishing in jail far behind the firing line.

Shortly after Tanner's execution another soldier went missing. L Sgt William Walton was a reservist serving with the 2nd Battalion, King's Royal Rifle Corps, which had been in action on and off since the beginning of the war. On 1 November 1914 this unit was near Ypres when it was suddenly called on to reinforce the regiment's first battalion, which had been overrun near Herenthage Château. When his company fell in Walton was present, but he was not seen again for several months. Sgt Murdy gave evidence that at the time Walton disappeared the battalion was under heavy fire and it had been thought that he had been wounded and admitted to hospital.

L Sgt Walton remained missing until 3 March 1915 when, acting on information given to him, a French gendarme went to the house of Eugénie Ducâtel in Arques. There he found a British soldier wearing khaki trousers and a jersey and arrested him. Ernest Ducâtel told the court that on about 18 December 1914 Walton had arrived at his house asking for a bed for the night. He was wet through, tired, with a bad cold and traces of wounds on his left arm and hand and had no rifle or equipment. He stayed in the house for some time, and Monsieur Ducâtel had reported his presence to the gendarmerie on 23 December, but no action was taken. Other British soldiers, for whom Madame Ducâtel did washing, gave Walton cigarettes and newspapers, and must have recognized him as a deserter.

Walton elected to give evidence on oath and made a long statement about events on 1 November. He told the court that he had led his company forward under heavy fire, and that he had then been given charge of some stragglers by an officer. He had subsequently been wounded and spent some days in a trench before trying to rejoin his battalion. He described his movements to Cassel, Arques and Hazebrouck looking for his unit, before returning to Arques. He insisted that all the time he was at Monsieur Ducâtel's house he was trying to find his battalion. He then underwent a detailed cross-examination about his movements during his absence.

After his arrest on 3 March Walton was handed over to the APM, who questioned him and Monsieur Ducâtel, and then wrote a letter to the CO of 2nd Battalion, KRRC, which was sent back with the prisoner. In it he noted that Monsieur Ducâtel had a bad reputation and that his statements might not be reliable. He also wrote: 'Neither can I get much out of Sergeant Walton, who seems half-dazed and to be either unwilling to, or incapable of, giving straightforward answers to the simplest questions.' On the same day, Walton made a statement to the APM, and in it he said: 'I have been suffering from a nervous breakdown ever since I was wounded.'

Given his long absence, and the fact that he could have reported himself to someone in the army if he had genuinely become separated from his unit, the court found Walton guilty of desertion. No evidence was presented at the trial as to his state of mind, and Walton himself did not raise it.

On 15 March, after sentence but before confirmation, when Walton would have been unaware of his fate, Brig. Gen. Oxley of GHQ Troops wrote to the DJAG expressing concern as to Walton's mental state. He said:

> The Chaplain, the Revd. R. Hack, has been to see me this morning; he tells me that, in his opinion, there are signs that Lance Sgt Walton's mind is unhinged and that he seems incapable of grasping what has happened or his position; that there is a wild look about his eyes and that he seems to forget things. He further says that the men on guard think that he is 'not right'. He informs me that L. Sgt Walton spent 2 years in India and came out from the reserve with a draft about a fortnight after the Battalion at the commencement of the War. These papers have not been before the Court.

In consequence of this, Col. Wyndham Childs wrote on behalf of the AG and asked that Walton be kept under medical observation until the doctor could reach a definite opinion as to the state of his mind.

On 20 March a medical certificate was prepared, saying: 'Certified that the undermentioned have examined this day No. 7552 L. Sergeant Walton W. 2nd Kings Royal Rifles and are of opinion that he is of sound mind.' This was signed by three officers of the RAMC, the clear implication being that the prisoner was seen by a medical board, rather than being kept under observation, but early in 1915 doctors often failed to recognize purely psychological breakdown from battle stress. It is not possible to tell at this distance of time whether William Walton was suffering from battle stress and whether this contributed to his attempt to desert, or whether a sympathetic padre did his best to get a condemned man another chance. If so, his attempts were in vain, and L Sgt Walton was shot on 23 March 1915.

Both Tanner and Walton appear, with the benefit of hindsight, to have been mentally traumatized, but fell into the category of men with subjective disorders, with only minor physical manifestations of their psychological trauma. It was of this group of disorders that Elliot Smith and Pear wrote that they were frequently more serious than the objective disorders, but were apt to go unrecognized.[14]

A year later, in March 1916, a young volunteer found that soldiering on the Western Front was not quite what he had envisaged. Abraham Harris (whose real name was Abraham Beverstein) enlisted into the 11th Battalion, Middlesex Regiment in September 1914 and went to France in May 1915.[15] All seemed to go well until just before Christmas, when the battalion was at Givenchy.[16] A German mine was exploded and this was followed up by a heavy bombardment, culminating in the firing of another mine a few days later. At some point in the concentrated warfare Pte Harris was wounded in the back and admitted to hospital. The telegram to his family told them that he had been admitted to No. 38 Field Ambulance 'suffering from wounds and shock (mine explosion)'.[17]

He left hospital on 19 January 1916 and returned to his unit, but was soon to be in trouble. Less than four weeks later they were back in the front line near the Hohenzollern Redoubt.[18] At his trial the events emerged.[19] Harris was charged with desertion 'in that he, at Sailly La Bourse, on the 13th February 1916 when ordered to return to the trenches absented himself from the 11th (Service) Battalion Middlesex Regiment, until apprehended at La Flanderie on the same day'.

CQMS Simpson gave evidence that at 8.30 a.m. on 13 February he was at Sailly La Bourse when Harris, in full trench order and with his rifle, reported to him, saying that about 6 p.m. the previous evening he had been sent to the dressing station but could not find it and stayed overnight in Vermelles. The NCO took Harris to the doctor, who said that he was fit for duty. The CQMS then took Harris back to the quartermaster, who – clearly trying to give the soldier another chance – gave him a note and ordered him to go to the trenches and report to the adjutant. He also warned Harris that it was a serious offence if he failed to report himself. At about 10 to 10.30 a.m. Harris then went off in the direction of the trenches. In his evidence CQMS Simpson commented that when Harris reported to him he had said that he had been sent from the trenches suffering from shock from a rifle grenade. He added: 'He seemed in a nervous condition.'

The second witness was the medical officer who had examined Harris. He told the court: 'I examined the accused … I found him suffering from no appreciable disease and marked him "duty". I told him he was fit for duty in the trenches. He did not strike me as suffering from nerves at the time.' Under cross-examination by the court he said: 'When he came to me the accused said he was suffering from deafness caused by the explosion of a rifle grenade.'

Cpl Lafont of the Buffs gave evidence about Harris's capture. He told the court that on 13 February at about 11 a.m. at La Flanderie he saw Harris at the farm where he was billeted. 'He told me that he had just come out of hospital. He had no greatcoat or hat and was covered with mud. He stayed in the farm all afternoon sitting by the fire warming himself.' At 7.30 p.m. the corporal again asked Harris where his regiment was, and when told 'in the trenches' Lafont arrested him.

The next witness had not appeared on the summary of evidence, and Harris was asked if he objected to her being called. Perhaps unwisely, he made no objection. Madame Cordionne said that she recognized Harris as he had been billeted at her farm previously, and on this occasion had arrived there between 3 and 4 p.m. She then made a damning statement: 'He said that the Germans had been bombing our trenches and he had left them and was going to England.' She told the court that she was quite clear about what had been said, and had not misunderstood.

Pte Abraham Harris made a statement on oath:

I left the trenches because three rifle grenades exploded near me. I was deafened and my nerves had gone a bit. The quarter-master sent me to Capt. Ward RAMC and he passed me as fit for duty and told me I was fit for the trenches. The quarter-master told me to report to the Adjutant and gave me a note for him. He told me to return to the trenches and warned me it was a serious thing not to go back. I felt nervous and lost my head. I wandered around the town towards Bethune into La Flanderie, thinking to stop there a few days and then return to my regiment.

Under cross-examination he said that he had understood the orders to return to the trenches and knew that he was going in the opposite direction. 'I meant to go to the farm at La Flanderie and stay there a few days.' He then made a fatal statement: 'I did not intend to return until the company came out of the trenches.' He denied telling Madame Cordionne that he intended to return to England.

Second Lt Redford gave evidence as to character, telling the court that the soldier's AFB122 (regimental conduct sheet) was locked away with the other papers whilst the unit was in the trenches. He said: 'He bears a good character. When the Battalion came out [to France] the accused begged to be allowed to come with it. It was intended to leave him behind but he was very anxious to come out.'

The court decided that Harris had intended to desert, and by his own admission, even if Madame Cordionne's statement was discounted, he did not intend to return until the battalion came out of the trenches, and therefore intended to miss a dangerous duty. The Commander-in-Chief confirmed sentence of death and Abraham Harris was shot at Sailly La Bourse on 20 March 1916. His parents, who had received a letter from their son saying that he was in trouble, heard of his death by means of a War Office letter telling them that their son had been executed for desertion.[20]

The soldier's distraught family contacted Sylvia Pankhurst and she went to meet them. They showed her their son's letters and told her that he had joined up at the age of 18 years and 3 months without their permission. At first he seemed enthusiastic but after his first spell of front line duty he wrote: 'I have been in the trenches four times and come out safe ... We go into the trenches for six days, and then we get relieved for six days rest ... Dear Mother, I do not like the trenches.'[21] This young soldier was probably regretting his impulse to rush to the colours. In January, when in hospital, he wrote home many times, but in none of his letters does he mention the mine explosion or shell shock, only that his back was hurt and that he had developed a sore heel. On 20 January he wrote: 'I am quite well and came out of hospital on Wednesday (19th).'[22] His last letter home was to tell his mother that he was in trouble – after that they heard nothing until the War Office letter arrived.

It is perhaps surprising that a soldier with a good record, missing for such a short period and found only a few miles in the rear, making no attempt to hide, should have been shot. There are probably two reasons for this: the evidence of Madame Cordionne that he intended to return to England, and his own evidence confessing that he intended to go back to his battalion only when they came out of the line. Had Harris been defended by an able prisoner's friend, perhaps Madame Cordionne's evidence would not have been permitted and the outcome might have been different, but from his own admission his intention to miss duty in the front line was clear.

It is impossible to say how much this young man's nerves were affected by the fighting and his injuries in December. With hindsight and the knowledge that this enthusiastic volunteer had pleaded to go to the front with the rest of his battalion it is easy to say that he had been affected by his experiences in December and that he should have been given a second chance. However, by the army's rules, Harris/Beverstein was guilty of the offence with which he was charged. Pte Harris paid for his enthusiasm for soldiering with his life.

Another 1916 case makes chilling reading. William Moon was a Kitchener volunteer who had joined the army in November 1914 and who went to France with the 11th Cheshires on 25 September 1915 and proved to be a good soldier, earning his lance corporal's stripe. However, in May 1916 he went absent and it was five months before he was arrested at St Pol. The evidence at the trial provided the full picture of events.[23]

At the end of December 1915 an event took place which deeply affected L Cpl Moon. It was described at the trial by CSM Love:

The shock was caused by an incident that occurred on 31st December 1915 when a shell burst close to him and blew part of a comrades head and brains into his face. The accused went into hospital and after coming out was continually going sick until we went into rest for about ten weeks. He seemed to be all right when we went back into the line until admitted to hospital on 1st May 1916.

Moon spent two weeks in hospital from 1 May until the 14th and was then readmitted on the 15th and finally discharged on 26 May.

CSM Love told the court: 'On 28th May I saw the accused at Ecoivres, he was then in a nervous condition.' On the 29th when the evening roll call was taken Moon was found to be missing, and was not seen again by his battalion until he was brought back under escort over four months later, on 6 October 1916.

Cpl Elford, Royal Engineers, told the court that at the beginning of July 1916 he had been stationed at St Pol and had met Moon at Mechal, just outside the town. He then saw him from time to time and on one occasion had lent him 20 francs to buy new boots; Moon had given him an IOU in the name of Welsby. Elford said that Moon/Welsby wore no cap badge or numerals and he commented that his health seemed to be all right.

Moon's luck ran out on 3 October when L Cpl James, a military police detective, saw him in a YMCA hut at St Pol. As he was wearing no badges, James questioned him and then arrested him. He gave evidence that, 'The accused's appearance was quite normal and he seemed to be in good health. His manner in speaking was quite rational.'

Moon made a statement, not on oath: 'I say I am not responsible for my actions. Ever since I was with the Battalion at the end of 1915 I have been in a queer state and have often been in a condition in which I have not known what I am doing.' He handed in to the court a letter which he said had been written to his mother by Lt Col. Aspinall on 23 June. It read:

As there is a considerable accumulation of letters for your son No. 17790 L Corpl W. G. Moon it is evident that you have not heard from him for some time. In consequence I feel it my duty to inform you that L Corpl Moon left his Billet without permission while the Battalion was resting from the trenches, on 29th May. Every step has been taken to trace him, but no news of him has been received, and I have been hoping every day he would reappear, as it sometimes happens out here that men take 'French leave' in this fashion for some unaccountable reason, and eventually report themselves to their Battalion.

Your son had twice suffered from shell shock during this campaign, and it is quite possible that he may be housed in some village far away from where there are troops and may be suffering from loss of memory.

I am afraid that this news will be a great worry to you, and give you much anxiety but I think you have reason to hope that your Son will reappear sooner or later.

Assuring you of my sympathy, & trusting that I may soon be in a position to give you better news.

Believe me

Yrs faithfully

R.L. Aspinall Lt Col

Comg 11th Batt Cheshire Regt.

The court then called the battalion medical officer to give evidence:

I have seen the accused on one occasion only when he was suffering from acute laryngitis. That was about a month ago. I have no knowledge of the accused's medical history and I have never made any examination of him to ascertain his mental condition and I am unable to make any statement on the subject.

The court did not attempt to obtain evidence from the doctors who had treated Moon during May 1916.

The court closed to consider its verdict and then heard evidence as to character. CSM Love said: 'I have known the accused for two years during which he was a member of my company. I have always found him to be one of the best soldiers and I have never had any trouble with him.' Moon's conduct sheet had no entries but despite this, he was sentenced to death for desertion, his long absence undoubtedly counting against him.

After the trial Lt Col. Evans, CO of 11th Cheshires, wrote that Moon had served with the BEF since 25 September 1915 and that he bore a very good character. He said that he could not say whether he thought that the crime was deliberate as there were no officers currently serving with the battalion who had been with them in May. He wrote: 'I do not consider that the existing state of discipline in this unit makes necessary the carrying out of the extreme penalty in this case.' This view was supported by the commander of 75th Infantry Brigade, Lt Col. Bond:

I am of the opinion that the accused ... was not in a good state of health at the time of his absence on 29th May 1916 and that he was not then responsible for his actions. The state of discipline in this battalion is satisfactory. I do not in consequence consider it necessary for the extreme penalty to be carried out.

Brig. Gen. Pratt, GOC 25th Division, disagreed: 'I am of the opinion that this is a clear case of desertion and that there is no reason why sentence should not be carried out.' Lt Gen. Gordon, temporarily in command of Second Army, concurred and L Cpl William Moon was shot by firing squad on 18 November 1916, undoubtedly a victim of one of the harshest decisions of the war.

There seems to be no doubt that Moon had been a good soldier until the fateful day in December when his comrade's brains were spattered in his face, an experience so horrific that it would unman many, although far from unique in the slaughterhouse conditions of the Western Front. From then until his desertion he appears to have either been in hospital or at rest with the battalion, and at the point when it seemed inevitable that he would have to return to the firing line he deserted, unable to face once again the horrors he had experienced so vividly.

From the way the evidence was given, especially from CSM Love, it appears that there was genuine sympathy for this deeply traumatized man. The court however chose to ignore Moon's medical history and placed their reliance on Cpl Elford's statement that 'his health seemed all right' and L Cpl James's 'the accused's appearance was quite normal'. The doctor called to give evidence could not give the court the information they required, but they did not seek specialist advice. This could have been requested during the confirmation process, but it may be that the battalion and brigade commanders were confident that sentence would be commuted and did not press the medical point.

The army charged L Cpl Moon with desertion. He was not where he should have been and, having proved that, they were not concerned about why he was absent. He was behind the lines at St Pol, he had been absent for five months – a long time in the BEF – and his intention to remain permanently absent was proved. This volunteer soldier was failed by the system, both military and medical. Had he been fortunate enough to have been examined by one of the new specialists in shell shock, he might have become a model case in a textbook. He had been traumatized beyond endurance and his bank account of courage had been drained, and he was shot. In July 1916 instructions had been issued under the heading 'Courts Martial. Mental condition of accused', saying:

When it appears from perusal of the proceedings that the mental condition or fitness for service of the accused is open to doubt, the Confirming Officer will, after confirmation, take steps to insure that the Commandant of the detention barracks or the Governor of the prison to which the soldier is committed to undergo his sentence is informed of the circumstances with a view to the soldier so committed being placed under medical observation.[24]

Unfortunately, if a man had been shot he could not be placed under such supervision and L Cpl Moon's mental state remained uninvestigated.

Another potentially shell-shocked soldier faced a firing squad in October 1917. Pte Frederick Coutts Gore had volunteered in December 1914 and was serving with the 7th Battalion, East Kent Regiment (the Buffs) when he committed his offence. It has been said that this soldier had enlisted at the age of 16 and was serving under two suspended sentences of death, but it would appear that Gore has been confused with another man.[25]

The evidence presented at his trial indicated that Pte Gore was one of a party going from Dickebusch Huts to Railway Dugouts on 10 August 1917.[26] At 6 p.m. the men were warned that they were to parade at 8 p.m., and shortly after this Gore went missing. Nothing further was seen of him until 19 August 1917 in Boulogne when at about 10 a.m. he presented himself to Pte Tonks, who was on police duty at Ostrohove Camp. Gore said that he was a deserter from Etaples; he was wearing uniform and gave his name and regiment. Tonks put him in the guardroom, where he remained until collected by an escort.

Pte Gore gave in a written statement in his defence:

The reason why I deserted my battalion because I cannot stand the strain of the shell fire owning [sic] to the very bad state of my nerves. I have been to the Medical Officer and he said nothing could be done for me and I have always tryed [sic] to do my best to carry out my duty. Before I came to France, where I have been for 15 months, I was rejected for service abroad owing to my nerves. I am very sorry to think that this has happened after my three years in the service.

The word 'deserted' has been heavily underlined in pencil.

Under cross-examination he confused the issue somewhat by stating:

I have never reported to the battalion M.O. that my nerves would not stand shell fire. The doctor did ask me 'what was the matter with me?' and I told him I could not stand shell fire but he did not examine me or say anything further.

Under further questioning he said:

> I have suffered from shell shock before this. I was on that occasion
> examined by an M.O. in hospital at Frevent ... This was in May 1917.
> I was 5 weeks in hospital and returned to the Bn about the middle of June
> 1917. I had another shaking-up when we were holding the line at the end
> of July. On that occasion I was not examined by an M.O. but by a
> stretcher bearer who sent me back to my Company.

Gore's only medical examination was just prior to the trial, when he was
found fit for trial and to undergo imprisonment.

His 'crime sheet' showed that Gore had a few entries: March 1916 insubordination (in the UK), January 1917 attempting to remove government property, April 1917 absence, for which he lost his lance corporal's stripe; although
this offence seems to have occurred in April his punishment was dated June,
which suggests that it was not dealt with until after his discharge from hospital. Shortly after this, in July 1917, he was charged with 'leaving his company
trench without permission until found on steps of dugout in another trench.'

Shell-shocked or not, Pte Frederick Gore was shot at Poperinge at 6 a.m. on
16 October 1917 and was the last of seventeen executed British servicemen to
be buried there.

A SHELL-SHOCKED OFFICER

War puts such stress on men as they know not elsewhere.

S. L. A. MARSHALL, 1950

In total, forty-six officers were tried for desertion during the war.[1] As a result of these trials four death sentences were awarded, with two executions being carried out.[2] In comparison, 38,584 soldiers were tried for the same offence, with just over 2,000 death sentences being awarded, of which 266 were carried out.[3]

These figures show that if an officer was tried for desertion there was a much greater probability of a death sentence and subsequent execution, with 7.7 per cent of the officers' trials for this offence ending in execution. On the other hand, amongst soldiers, only seven of every thousand men tried for desertion came before a firing squad.

Officers were not immune to fear, neither were they immune to shell shock, and the first officer to be executed in the war had a history of shell shock. Eric Skeffington Poole was a Second Lieutenant serving in the 11th Battalion of the West Yorkshire Regiment on the Somme in October 1916. He had been born in 1885 in Nova Scotia where his father (a Canadian by birth) was a mining engineer, but in 1914 the family was living in Guildford. In August 1914 he applied for a commission in the regular army, and on 17 August he passed the necessary medical and was approved for a temporary commission.[4] His application was supported by an ex-commander of the Canadian Militia, who wrote:

> This is to certify that Mr Eric Skeffington Poole of Spreyton, Guildford served as a Lieutenant for two years in the 63rd Regiment Halifax Rifles – Canadian Militia and was for some little time attached to the Royal Canadian Regiment stationed at Frederickford, New Brunswick for training and I believe that he is a suitable person for a commission in the Territorial Force.

In October 1914, whilst awaiting the outcome of his application, Poole joined the Honourable Artillery Company and then in April 1915 the War Office appointed him a temporary second lieutenant in the 14th (Service) Battalion, West Yorkshire Regiment. When he left the HAC in May, his character was described as very good.[5]

On 5 October 1916 the battalion carried out a relief of the front line trenches at Flers. Second Lt Poole had been present when his company commander issued orders about the relief, but was missing by the time his platoon arrived in the front line. He remained missing for two days, until on the morning of the 7th he was found near Henencourt, and was returned to his unit.

On 10 October his commanding officer, Lt Col. Barker, ordered a regimental court of inquiry to be convened to investigate the incident. In consequence of the facts which emerged a charge sheet was drawn up, and signed by the president of the court of inquiry, Captain Crabtree.[6] The charge read:

The accused 2nd Lt E.S. Poole 11th West Yorkshire Regiment, an officer of the Regular Forces, is charged with 'when on Active Service deserting His Majesty's Service' in that he near Martinpuich on 5th October 1916 absented himself from the neighbourhood of the front line trenches and remained so absent until apprehended at Henencourt Wood by the Military Police on 7th October 1916 with intent to avoid duty in the said trenches.

A week later, on 17 October, the court of inquiry findings were forwarded to 23rd Division by Brig. Gen. Lambert, GOC 69th Brigade. He wrote:

The attached proceedings of a Court of Inquiry held on the absence of 2nd Lieut. E.S. Poole, 11th West Yorkshire Regiment are forwarded for favour of instructions by G.O.C. 23rd Division.

I do not think it will be satisfactory to try this Officer by Court Martial. He was once before, on 7th July after the action at Horseshoe Trench on 5th July, admitted to Hospital suffering from shell shock and I doubt if he is really accountable for his actions. He is of nervous temperament, useless in action, and dangerous as an example to the men. The Battalion is, in my opinion, in an excellent state of discipline and has never failed to carry out in action any duty that has been given it.

At Le Sars on 7th October the Battalion maintained its reputation and did very fine work in spite of heavy casualties. I recommend that 2nd Lieut. E.S. Poole be sent home away from the firing line as soon as possible.

Before the War he was employed on engineering work in Canada. He could be usefully employed at home in instructional duties or in any minor administrative work, not involving a severe strain on the nerves.[7]

Two days later the ADMS was asked to arrange a medical examination to establish Poole's state of health and whether he was responsible for his actions. The RAMC lieutenant colonel who examined him wrote:

> I have examined 2/Lieut. E.S. Poole, 11th West Yorks Regt. and find that physically he is in a good state of health, but he is of a high-strung, neurotic temperament, and I am of the opinion that it is possible that excitement may bring on a condition of mental aberration which would make him not responsible for his actions at that time.

On 22 October a letter was sent from 23rd Division to Second Army HQ to establish whether there was sufficient evidence for a court martial. The DAAG, Second Army wrote back on 25 October to say that 'The Army Commander wishes this officer to be tried by Court Martial and charged with Desertion.' A new charge sheet was then prepared, and signed by Lt Col. Barker, CO of the 11th West Yorks, on 8 November. Poole must have been told of the charge on the same day, as he wrote to the adjutant of his battalion to request a prisoner's friend. The mechanism of court martial was now well under way. Three days later Lt Col. Gilbert Mellor, the DJAG, wrote commenting on the summary of evidence, and on 19 November a letter from the DAA & QMG 23rd Division said that the officer it had been hoped would be able to act as prisoner's friend was not available, and commented: 'This duty will therefore devolve to 2nd Lt M. Dawson.'

Before the trial, Second Lt Dawson of 69th MG Company wrote asking for a medical board to be convened to examine Poole, to assess his mental state. The reply from the DAA & QMG 23rd Division read:

> In the absence of strong grounds for supposing that the accused was insane on 1st October or that he is now so, it is regretted that a Medical Board cannot be assembled to enquire into the mental condition of 2nd Lt. Poole. It should be noted that the proceedings of such a Board are not admissible in evidence and that it is open to the accused to call any medical or other evidence in his defence to testify as to his state of mind.

Second Lt Eric Poole was tried by a GCM at Poperinge near Ypres on 24 November 1916 with Brig. Gen. H. Gordon, DSO, GOC 70th Infantry

Brigade, presiding over a panel of four officers. Second Lt O. F. Dowson was appointed as the Judge Advocate to ensure that the correct legal procedures were adhered to.[8]

The first witness was Capt. Armstrong of 'C' Company, 11th West Yorks. He told the court that on 5 October he carried out preparations to relieve the front line and led his company forward, Poole having been told to follow with his platoon. Capt. Armstrong set off at about 4.30 p.m. and arrived at the front line about 11.30 p.m.

Lt Col. Barker, CO of 11th West Yorks, then gave evidence that he had not given Poole permission to leave the trenches. Under cross-examination he added: 'I knew the accused had been in hospital. I should say he is below the average in intellect. He is rather stupid.' Lt Whitby of Poole's battalion reported to the court that in conversation with Poole on the morning of 5 October, Poole had said that he felt 'damned bad' and thought of seeing a doctor. He also said that he had a touch of rheumatism.

Other witnesses then described Poole's discovery on 7 October. L Cpl Homewood, of the Military Foot Police, told the court that at noon on the 7th he was on the Millencourt to Albert Road when the water tank police asked him to 'see an officer near the water tanks'. L Cpl Homewood found Poole there, wearing a private's tunic with a star on each shoulder strap and a leather jacket over the tunic. (This last piece of evidence is underlined in the papers.)

Lt Berry of the RAMC gave evidence that on 6 October at about 10 a.m. he saw an officer at his aid post near Martinpuich who had asked him for tablets for rheumatism, but that he could not identify this man as the accused.

The 11th West Yorks quartermaster Lt Cooper then said that on 7 October he had sent the mess cart to Henencourt to collect Poole.

> He seemed to me to be in a very dazed condition and from conversation which I had with him I came to the conclusion that he was not responsible for his actions. He was very confused indeed. I attributed his condition to exposure since he had left the battalion. The accused seemed much better after a night's rest.

Cross-examined, he said: 'I remember seeing the accused one day about the end of August 1916 in the same sort of condition that he was in 7th October.'

Lt Col. Barker then gave additional evidence to say that he had placed Poole under arrest on 10 October (i.e. after the court of inquiry had sat).

Second Lt Eric Poole gave evidence in his own defence. He told the court that he had joined the 11th West Yorks in May 1916, and that on about 9 July he had been sent to hospital with shell shock. He had rejoined his unit on about 1 September, but 'since I have had shell-shock I at times get confused and I have great difficulty in making up my mind. I was in this condition on 5 October. I went to an aid post as I had a slight touch of rheumatism.' When the court cross-examined him, he added: 'I went away about 5 p.m. I did not leave anyone in charge of the platoon and I did not tell anyone I was going away.'

Evidence for the defence was given by Lt Alnwick, who told the court that he had known Poole in England and then said: 'When he first came he was eccentric. This I put down to nervousness at first, but at the end of four months he was just the same.' He went on: 'I should say he was not fit to have charge of a platoon. He is, in my opinion, more than eccentric. When talking he is apt to wander and not keep to his subject.'

Capt. Riddell, RAMC, DSO, MO of the 11th West Yorks, said that he had known Poole since May 1916 and added:

I have always noticed something peculiar in his manner. He is somewhat eccentric and markedly lacking in decision. I think that in times of stress or while under shell fire the accused's mental condition is such that he might very well have great difficulty in coming to any decision and might become so mentally confused that he would not be responsible for his actions.

Under cross-examination he said: 'The accused is in my opinion more liable to shell shock than a normal man.'

Lt Dawson, the prisoner's friend, addressed the court. He submitted that there was something more abnormal in Poole's condition than could be produced by shell shock, and that the court had heard that he was 'more than eccentric'. Lt Dawson told them: 'With his poor mental equipment the effect of shell shock on him is very great', and then: 'I submit that under these circumstances you cannot find the accused capable of framing the intention necessary to prove desertion.' In respect of Lt Alnwick's evidence, he said that Poole was 'super-eccentric and that this is only a kind word for a graver mental defect'.

The Judge Advocate, Second Lt Dowson, summed up, the salient points of the case being that the material facts had not been challenged by the defence, and that the question was whether intention had been proven, the defence being that 'when he absented himself, [he was] in such a condition of collapse and weakness that he was incapable of forming the intention to desert'. He made the point: 'A man is not, of course, unable to form an intention to go away or to shirk a duty because he has a feeble type of intelligence.' He completed his summing up by reminding the court that Poole had joined the battalion in May 1916 and 'has served in France for six months and has taken part in the ordinary trench warfare. He has taken part in no actions.' Finally, the prisoner's friend said: 'The accused was a 1914 volunteer and came forward to do his best for his country.'

After the court had found Second Lt Poole guilty and sentenced him to death, the papers went up through the various unit commanders for them to add their views. Lt Col. Barker, CO of 11th West Yorks, wrote: 'I beg to state that I consider that the crime was deliberately committed, but that I do not consider the mental capacity of the officer is sufficient for him to have realised the seriousness of his action.' Brig. Gen. Lambert, commanding 69th Brigade, wrote that Poole had been present at the action of Horseshoe Trench on 4–5 July, but his company was in support and not actively engaged. On 7 July when his unit moved to Fricourt he was found to be missing, but it was later discovered that he had been admitted to hospital with shell shock. Of the incident which led to the court martial, Brig. Gen. Lambert wrote: 'Though 2nd Lt Poole must have known he was avoiding the action, I think his mental balance was upset and he wandered away aimlessly rather than with any deliberate intention.'

The divisional commander, Maj. Gen. Babington, also recommended leniency:

> I recommend the punishment awarded be commuted, but am of opinion that the gravity of the offence should be marked by a more serious sentence than cashiering … While I consider the responsibility of an Officer is greater than that of a N.C.O. or private soldier and that he should suffer for any offence committed equally with them, yet it appears a question whether 2/Lt. Poole's mental capacity was such as to enable him to fully realise the gravity of his Act.

The corps commander, Lt Gen. Morland, agreed, writing:

> While I consider the offence of desertion by an officer to be much more serious than that of an N.C.O. or Private, in view of the evidence as to this officer's mental condition previous to and at the time of the offence, I recommend that the sentence be commuted to one of penal servitude.

Unusually, Gen. Herbert Plumer, GOC Second Army, a man widely respected for his humanity and compassion for the welfare of his soldiers, did not agree. 'I have considered the case very carefully,' he wrote. 'Despite the evidence as to the accused's mental condition I should, if he had been a Private, have recommended that the sentence should be carried out ... in view of the inherent seriousness of the offence when committed by an officer I recommend that it be inflicted.' This was a damning indictment.

However, before sentence was confirmed by the Commander-in-Chief it was arranged for Poole to be examined by a medical board. This met on 3 December 1916, and was composed of Lt Col. Martin (president) of the Standing Medical Board, Base Depot, Etaples, with Maj. Sheehan and Capt. Crookshank. The board was asked to establish whether Second Lt Poole was of sound mind and capable of 'appreciating the nature and quality of his action in absenting himself without leave from his unit on 5th October 1916' and whether he was now of sound mind or not.

The board had access to Poole's medical history and this revealed that he had met Lt Col. Martin and Capt. Crookshank before. On 7 July 1916 Second Lt Poole had been admitted to No. 58 Field Ambulance, classified as 'shell shock (wounded)'. This was important, as the designation meant that he was suffering obvious physical signs of being in contact with shell blast. He was evacuated to No. 38 CCS at Heilly, as 'shell shock (W)', and on 8 July sent to No. 20 General Hospital at the Base. He was there for seventeen days before being transferred to the Canadian Convalescent Home at Dieppe. A summary of his case was made on 9 August (this may be a typing error for 9 July) by Dr Crookshank: 'At Contalmaison (7/7/16) was knocked out by clods of earth distributed by H.E. Shell. Did not lose consciousness. Now: cerebration slow; pain in back.'

A summary of his stay in the Canadian Convalescent Home said that although his condition improved, he did not look well. On 19 August 1916 he was seen by Sir James Fowler, who found 'an irregular action of the heart and tachycardia' (that is, fast heartbeat) but 'no signs of any nervous lesion'. This eminent physician agreed with Lt Col. Foster, commanding the Convalescent Home, that Poole was unfit for duty and that he should be sent to temporary base duty.

However, when Poole arrived at No. 33 Infantry Base Depot, classified as 'Temporary Base', he was seen by the Standing Medical Board at No. 6 Convalescent Camp and classified as 'A' (fit for duty). The president of this board was Lt Col. Martin, who was subsequently president of the board which was assembled to assess Poole's mental state after his court martial.

This medical board reported:

> The Board is of the opinion that he
> (a) was of sound mind and capable of appreciating the nature and quality of his action in absenting himself without leave from his unit on 5th October 1916 and that such an act was wrong.
> (b) is now of sound mind. The Board is also of the opinion that his mental powers are less than average.

There are cases where private soldiers were shot when perhaps shell-shocked, who were not given the opportunity of being examined by a medical board. – Harry Farr being an obvious case. However, it is clear from reading these comments on Eric Poole that it is unlikely that a medical board would have altered the outcome of many cases. In mid 1916 'shell shock' was not a defence; the only possible defence was that a soldier was unable to appreciate the nature of his actions – effectively was unable to tell right from wrong; this was the standard applied in English criminal law, and in military law. If a man could tell right from wrong, he was culpable and could be sentenced to death. Legally, by the standards of 1916, Second Lt Poole knew exactly what he was doing and the likely consequences.

Field Marshal Haig confirmed the sentence on 6 December 1916, and wrote in his diary:

> This morning the Adjutant General brought me Court-Martial proceedings on an officer charged with desertion and sentenced by the Court to be shot. After careful consideration I confirmed the proceedings. This is the first sentence of death on an officer to be put into execution since I became C-in-C. Such a crime is more serious in the case of an officer than of a man, and also it is highly important that all ranks should realize that the law is the same for an officer as a private.[9]

The Adjutant General wrote to Second Army on the following day to say:

> It should be noted that under the Army Act an officer does not cease to be an officer by reason of sentence of death being promulgated. 2nd Lt Poole should not therefore be deprived of his badges of rank before the sentence is carried out.

Second Lt Eric Skeffington Poole became the first British officer to face a firing squad during the war, and was executed at Poperinge at 7.25 a.m. on 10 December 1916.

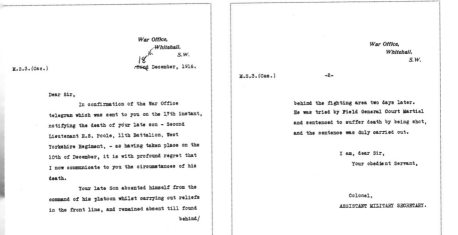

The letter sent to the family of Second Lt Eric Poole, informing them of the means by which he met his death

The execution of an officer was no less tragic for his family than the execution of any other soldier. Eric Poole's family was no exception. They first heard of his death on 17 December, by telegram:[10] 'Deeply regret to inform you that 2 Lieut. E S Poole 11th Battalion West Yorks Regt. died 10 December. The Army Council express their sympathy.'

The following day a letter was sent to the family from the War Office:

Dear Sir,

In confirmation of the War Office telegram which was sent to you on the 17th instant, notifying [you of] the death of your late son … as having taken place on the 10th of December, it is with profound regret that I now communicate to you the circumstances of his death.

Your late son absented himself from the command of his platoon whilst carrying out reliefs in the front line, and remained absent till found behind the fighting area two days later. He was tried by Field General Court Martial and sentenced to suffer death by being shot, and the sentence was duly carried out.[11]

This letter was clearly a dreadful shock for the family, and Eric Poole's sister wrote to the War Office:

Dear Sir,

Your letter just received, my Mother is prostrated, my Father is away from home, he is old and very ill, & we do not want him to know. Could you write again simply stating the place where my brother died, a letter we could shew my Father, and can we hope it is kept from the world? It is so short a time since he was shell shocked, that we feel sure that accounted for it.

Yrs. truly

M. E. Poole.[12]

Letter from Eric Poole's sister to the War Office, asking that his execution be kept from her father, and asking that it should be 'kept from the world'

A humane Col. Graham of the War Office acceded to Miss Poole's request, and wrote directly to her father:

> Dear Sir,
> In confirmation of my telegram of yesterday's date, I beg to inform you with very great regret, that I have not been able to ascertain the station in France at which your son died. I am making enquiries and will advise you in due course.[13]

Col. Graham also wrote to Miss Poole, telling her that he had written to her father; he also wrote:

> I need hardly assure you that no notification will appear in the Casualty Lists and that no information as to the circumstances of death will be released to the public by the War Office.[14]

He again wrote a few days later to Mr Poole, explaining that his son's death had occurred at Poperinge.

Eric Poole's father died sometime in early in 1917 and a lawyer, Mr Nicholls, was concerned with the winding up of his estate. At this time Miss Poole again wrote to the War Office: 'Sir, I shall be obliged if you will not mention the cause of Lt E. S. Poole's death when writing to Mr G. Nicholls.'[15]

The Graves Registration Unit also wrote to Miss Poole on 6 January 1917 to tell her that her brother was buried in Poperinge New Military Cemetery,[16] and that his grave was 'marked by a durable wooden cross, bearing full particulars'.

After the war, when details were obtained from relatives for entry in the cemetery register, Miss Poole chose 'Died of wounds 10 December 1916. Age 31. Son of Henry Skeffington Poole and Florence Hope Gibsone Poole, of 2, Rectory Place, Guildford, Surrey. Born Nova Scotia.' For the grave marker she selected the inscription: 'Grant him eternal rest O Lord Jesu Mercy.' For many years Second Lt Eric Poole's original grave marker carried the badge of the Yorkshire Regiment, but his replacement stone bears the correct badge of the West Yorkshire Regiment.

In a television programme in 1998 it was implied that there was a need for an officer to be shot, to appease the other ranks in the army, and that the officer chosen was Poole, who was not a public schoolboy and was not a member of the old boy network.[17] In fact, Eric Poole most certainly came from the 'officer class'. Until 1916 the army selected as officers men from a certain background, e.g. public school or experience in an Officers' Training Corps, to reduce the amount of training required. As Poole came from a professional, middle class background and had experience with the Canadian Militia this made him, in the army's eyes, suitable for a commission. Poole was no young soldier plucked from the ranks to be turned into an ersatz officer, later to be used as a sacrifice to encourage other officers. Eric Poole came from a family that was absolutely typical of the 1914–18 volunteer officer class. In addition his elder brother, Henry Reynolds Poole, was already an officer in the regular army; he had been commissioned into the Royal Artillery in 1899 and had served through the Boer War, and by 1914 held the rank of major. In January 1916 he had been awarded the DSO, and eventually retired from the army in 1921.[18]

Any family who had a son, brother or husband executed by firing squad must have suffered agonies of shame and anger, but for Poole's family, with his military background, the shame would have been intolerable – one son and brother a hero, the other a coward. It is also possible that Eric Poole's execution affected his brother's army career: Henry Poole was a major in 1914 and retired at the same rank seven years later, when he might have expected accelerated promotion as a result of the casualties suffered by his regiment.

CHAPTER 27

REPEAT OFFENDERS

He that knows little often repeats it.

OLD PROVERB

As the war continued past Christmas 1914 and into the New Year of 1915 the number of deserters and absentees rose, and it became apparent that for some men, serving a jail sentence was preferable to front line service. Soldiers sentenced to imprisonment with hard labour generally served their time in a prison in the field, such as the one at Blargies, near Rouen, but others, sentenced to penal servitude, were returned to the UK. These prisons were not a 'soft' option but were, for many, better than the trenches.

Early in 1915 Maj. Wyndham Childs, assistant to the adjutant general, and the man responsible for ensuring that capital sentences were reviewed by the Commander-in-Chief, was in St Omer. He had already held discussions with the AG, Sir Nevil Macready, about a form of 'probation' for soldiers, but nothing had come of this. Then, in St Omer, he saw a group of 120 men under armed escort: 'they were singing and whistling and in very good humour'. When he asked why the men were so cheerful he was told that they were on their way to a prison at the base, away from the firing line. 'It was pretty obvious, at once, that such a state of affairs could not continue, as it was evident that certain types of men would commit crime solely to avoid duty at the front.'[1]

Childs thought about this, and that same night drafted a proposal that would allow for a prison sentence to be suspended for the duration of the war, so that the man could be returned to front line duties. He said: 'It is a fundamental principle that any penalty inflicted on the troops must be one that will not cause a shortage of men.'[2] This proposal was put to Parliament, and within fourteen days became the Army (Suspension of Sentences) Act in April 1915. The final arbiter as to whether a death sentence should stand or be commuted remained with the Commander-in-Chief, but an army commander could order the suspension of a non-capital sentence.

Once the Act became law, many men already serving sentences were released under its provisions. The sentence was periodically reviewed and if a man served well or showed particular gallantry then it could be remitted completely.

As the war progressed, the numbers of men serving under a suspended sentence obviously rose, and many of the capital sentences carried out in the second half of the war were on men serving under an earlier sentence. Some men reoffended shortly after the suspension of their original sentence. One such man was Pte Evan Fraser, who had been convicted of attempted desertion by FGCM on 21 April 1915 and sentenced to death. Under the new Act this had been commuted to ten years' penal servitude and suspended. On 27 April Fraser returned to his unit, 2nd Battalion, Royal Scots, but less than a month later he made another bid for freedom. He was soon caught, but escaped, went missing again, was then recaptured and, on 19 June, whilst serving with his unit in the trenches awaiting trial, he absented himself for the third time.[3]

In consequence Fraser faced an FGCM on 13 July 1915 on four charges, three of desertion and one of 'when on Active Service and to the prejudice of good order and military discipline'. In many cases this is the charge used to cover self-inflicted wounds, which may be why it has been said that this soldier was tried for a self-inflicted wound.[4] In fact, in this case, the charge related to a forged pass.

The court martial took place at Brandhoek. The panel was composed of three regular army captains, a pencilled note on the trial documents saying that no field officer (major or above) was available. They heard evidence that on 24 May 1915, whilst the battalion was at La Clytte, sudden orders were received to move. When the roll was called, Fraser was missing.

Only the sergeant who had found the soldier missing gave evidence of Fraser's absence. Admitted into evidence was a written statement relating to Fraser's arrest, made by Maj. Fraser, APM of the Cavalry Corps. This said that Pte Fraser had been found at Motte au Bois and that he had claimed that he was going to St Omer to see his brother and had produced a piece of paper, purporting to be a pass, giving him leave of absence from 9 a.m. to 9 p.m. on 25 May for this purpose.

However, such a written statement was inadmissible in evidence – this particular error seems to be one of the commonest made at trials in the field. The court therefore decided that this charge had not been adequately proven, and Fraser was found not guilty on this charge of desertion. In some ways this does demonstrate how officers on courts martial panels did do their – albeit limited – best to administer justice in the field. The second charge related to the forged pass, and Fraser pleaded guilty.

The court then proceeded to hear the evidence on the remaining two charges of desertion. Evidence was given that when Pte Fraser was in the charge of Cpl Woodard on the Vlamertinghe Road, on the night of 3–4 June 1915, the prisoner escaped. On 5 June he was seen at an ammunition park behind the lines at St Sylvestre Cappel, where he was questioned. He could give no adequate explanation for his presence there and he had no rifle or equipment with him so was arrested. Fraser, who was not defended, did not cross-examine any of the witnesses and made no statement in his own defence – either because he could not contest the evidence, or because he was resigned to his fate.

The notes of evidence on the final charge are rather muddled and show signs that some inadmissible evidence was introduced and later struck out. Cpl Woodard told the court that on the morning of 19 June, when the battalion was in the trenches on the Vlamertinghe Road, he had handed Pte Fraser over to Sgt Evans to perform his fatigues, whilst he himself carried out his police duties. When Woodard returned, his prisoner was again missing.

On the following day Fraser was seen in a farmhouse by two men of the 48th South Midland ammunition park. When asked about his unit he replied that he was from the RFA, and a little later he left the house. The two soldiers were suspicious and followed him to a cottage, where Fraser said to them: 'You have no authority to arrest me.' Being suspicious, the two soldiers demonstrated their authority and arrested him. On his way back with them to Flêtre, Fraser retrieved his cap, with a Royal Scots badge, from a field. He was then returned to his unit under escort.

Fraser again made no attempt to defend himself on this charge, and made no plea in mitigation of punishment. The court found him guilty on both charges of desertion. His conduct sheet showed that Fraser had enlisted just before the start of the war, in June 1914. There was only one entry, the previous conviction of desertion. Character evidence was then given by the adjutant of the battalion: 'The accused has, since he joined, been a continual source of annoyance to the Regiment. He always tries to shirk his work and have several times [*sic*] and refuses to soldier by continually deserting.' This bad character reference is most unusual, and should not have been given, as was later pointed out in a marginal note: 'II Army Routine Order 116 R.P. [Rules of Procedure] and custom of service not to give this.' This note was probably added by the DAA & QMG of V Corps, who wrote on 21 July: 'The Divisional Commander directs that the Court be reassembled for the revision of the finding in the cases of the 3rd and 4th charges. He considers that in neither of these charges is there enough evidence to prove desertion.'

Again, the army system was operating as it was designed to do, and the commanders were attempting to deliver justice. The court martial panel reconvened to consider their verdicts again, and decided that on the third charge, Fraser was not guilty of desertion but was guilty of the lesser charge of absence without leave, and on the fourth charge was not guilty of desertion but guilty of attempted desertion. However, the court chose to leave the death sentence unchanged.

The comments by the formation commanders were brief and to the point: all recommended that sentence be carried out. No doubt these generals, possibly suspicious of the efficacy of the Suspension of Sentences Act, had no intention of treating such a repeat offender leniently. Pte Evan Fraser became the first man under a commuted and suspended sentence to be executed for a reoffence. As it was high summer and dawn came early, he met his death by firing squad at 4 a.m. on 2 August 1915.

No reason ever came to light to explain Fraser's attempts to get away from his unit. He was not defended at his trial and made no attempt either to defend himself or to explain his actions. There is no evidence that he was shell-shocked and his case remains a mystery. At the time of his trial he was 19 years 7 months old, according to his attestation age. It would therefore appear that he joined up at 18½, and was sent to France in December 1914, after his 19th birthday.

At the end of 1915 another soldier under a suspended sentence deserted. Pte John Dennis, of 1st Battalion, Northamptonshire Regiment, was a re-enlisted man with about thirteen years' previous service. This battalion had formed part of the original BEF, fighting at Mons, on the Marne and on the Aisne before moving north to the line around Ypres, where Pte Dennis joined it. Soon afterwards Dennis had absented himself from his battalion and on 28 December 1914 had been sentenced to two years' imprisonment with hard labour for desertion. When the Suspension of Sentences Act came into force his case was reconsidered and on 4 June 1915 the commander of First Army, Gen. Haig, suspended the sentence.[5]

On 18 September Pte Dennis's unit was at Burbure and the soldier was present at a kit inspection when the men were told to make good any deficiencies, ready to move to the trenches in a few days' time. On

20 September when the roll was called, Dennis was found to be missing. He remained absent until 11 November 1915 when he was found in the kitchen of a farmhouse at Bas Rieux. He was arrested and returned to his unit.

The prisoner did not contest any of the evidence. He made a statement on oath to say that on the morning of 20 September he had reported sick. He said he had then gone for a walk and got lost, before finding himself about 3km from Burbure. He admitted that he had then stayed there until about 10 November, when he enquired after his regiment. He was told it was at Lillers, but on his way there found himself near his brother's unit of the Royal Engineers so went to see him. He had then been arrested.

Under cross-examination he said that he did not know that his battalion was due to move to the trenches when he left it, but admitted being at the kit inspection on 18 September. He told the court that when he became lost he tried to find his regiment, but there were no troops to ask, and admitted that it was not until 10 November that he got in touch with some soldiers at Auchel.

Although Pte Dennis is described in *Shot at Dawn* as being aged 19 and as having said in his defence that heavy shelling had affected his mind, this is nowhere confirmed by the trial transcript.[6]

After finding him guilty the court heard of Dennis's previous offence and suspended sentence. Unsurprisingly, given his previous absence and the length of his desertion, he was sentenced to death.

After the trial, during the process of confirmation, Maj. Bethell, commanding 1st Northamptons, wrote:

> The accused has served only three months with the battalion and is useless from a military point of view. He joined the battalion in Ypres about 15 months ago and continually absented himself from the trenches on various excuses. He very shortly proceeded sick to Havre. He rejoined in December 1914 and deserted a few days afterwards. He rejoined under escort during May 1915 and again deserted in September.

This letter also mentions that discipline in the battalion was good, with only two other cases of desertion since 12 August 1914 (these two men were Pte Stone, who had deserted on 15 December 1915, and Pte Jones, who had gone missing on 14 December 1915. Both were still absent when the letter was written, on 18 January 1916.)

Pte Dennis's previous absence militated against any recommendation to mercy and he became the first man to have his death sentence confirmed by the new Commander-in-Chief, the same Gen. Haig who had approved the suspension of his earlier sentence. The execution took place at Lillers and Pte Dennis is buried in the communal cemetery there.

No explanation for Dennis's absence became apparent at his trial. From the CO's letter and his records, it would appear that the first desertion occurred whilst the battalion was engaged at Ypres and that the second episode took place after a period of rest. The soldier himself put up no defence, so the real reasons remain a mystery. Pte Dennis was an old soldier who knew the rules. On enlistment he would have received *The Soldiers' Small Book*, which contained a list of the offences punishable by death, and he must have been aware of the risks he ran in going absent a second time.

Pte John Docherty had enlisted in the Black Watch on 21 June 1915 and had been posted to the 9th Battalion. Three months later he found himself at the battle of Loos, where his battalion lost 252 men killed and the division took over 4,000 casualties.[7] On 14 December 1915 he deserted from his unit, and on 4 January 1916 was tried by FGCM for desertion and for disobeying a lawful command. For these offences he was sentenced to death. This was subsequently commuted to five years' penal servitude, sentence being promulgated on 29 January 1916, but by then Docherty had gone missing again.[8]

On 24 January 1916 Pte Docherty had been in the trenches with his company for nine days. At some point around midday he and another man, Pte McCabe, made off and by the following day were in Béthune, about 7 miles behind the lines. There they approached Cpl Groom of the Military Police and, according to his evidence, asked if he could find them a billet for the night. As neither man could produce a pass and they were not properly dressed he questioned the men further, when they admitted that they had deserted from the trenches at Loos. Cpl Groom then arrested both men and took them to the police station at Béthune, where they were handed over to L Cpl Preece. In his evidence he said that he had cautioned Docherty: 'You need not tell me unless you like, but anything you say I shall make a note of, and it may be used in evidence against you.'

Neither Docherty or McCabe (who were tried separately by the same court martial panel on the same day) had a prisoner's friend, and neither made any defence to the charge of desertion.

After the court had considered its finding, the character evidence was presented. Both men had some minor charges against them (McCabe had committed the offence of 'being in unlawful possession of a kilt' whereas the more usual crime in a Highland regiment was 'by neglect losing a kilt'). Both men had joined up within a few days of each other in June 1915. The main, and crucial, difference between them was that Docherty was already serving under a very recent suspended sentence. In consequence, the court sentenced him to death, and McCabe to ten years' penal servitude.

GOC 15th Division recommended, in view of Docherty's previous record, that sentence of death be carried out, and that McCabe's sentence should not be suspended. He wrote: 'The present constitute the Fourth and Fifth cases of desertion in the 9th (S) Battalion The Black Watch since arrival in this Country, and I consider that these sentences should be put into effect in order to act as a deterrent.' Lt Gen. Wilson, commanding IV Corps, and Gen. Monro, the First Army commander, both recommended that sentence be carried out on Docherty. After this, on 10 February, GOC 15th Division wrote to the DAAG First Army in response to a telegram now missing from the file. In it he wrote: 'The Battalion Commander states that Private Docherty's conduct up to 25 September (Loos) was good, after that date bad.' There must have been some question about Docherty's mental state, as the letter continued:

> Private Docherty has been examined this morning by two medical
> officers who state – 'Although not of unsound mind, he is suffering from a
> marked degree of neurasthenia. Whether this is the result of shell shock
> or of recent onset, we are unable to state'.

Two days later the Commander-in-Chief confirmed the sentence on Docherty, and at 7.11 a.m. on 15 February 1916 he became one of the eleven men who were shot in the abattoir at Mazingarbe.

From our modern perspective it is easy to say that Docherty, turned from civilian to soldier in three months, faced with the carnage of the battle of Loos, was not mentally robust enough to cope with his experiences. A good soldier, faced with the reality of modern warfare, gave way and tried to terminate his contract with the army – but this was not an option with his country at war, and he paid the ultimate price. We can accept that his 'marked degree of neurasthenia' showed that he was traumatized and shell-shocked, but it was less easy for the old regular army to accept failure by one of the new 'citizen army'. Neither was it easy for the doctors – able to recognize the signs of mental trauma but unable to recognize these as markers of battle shock. Docherty repeated his offence because the terrors of the battlefield affected his thinking and led him to commit a second, fatal offence.

Another man with a bad record was shot in August 1916. Pte William (Billy) Nelson had joined 14th Battalion, Durham Light Infantry on 7 September 1914 and had sailed to France a year later on 11 September 1915.

This battalion formed part of the 21st Division, which was a 'K3' unit, raised from the 'third hundred thousand' volunteers who rallied to Kitchener's call. The officers and men had little experience:

All the battalion commanders were ex-Regular officers, mostly retired officers of the Indian Army; besides these there were only 14 Regular and ex-Regular officers in the 13 battalions. Other officers of the infantry were newly commissioned, mostly without special training. In the ranks were a few old soldiers, and some ex-N.C.O.'s were attached as instructors, but of these the earlier divisions had got the pick.[9]

Speaking of 21st and 24th Divisions, the official historian summed up: 'In general, the two divisions were thought to be better trained than they were, and were sent into action after being three weeks in France in back areas, without any period of initiation.'[10] The battle of Loos exposed their inexperience.

The 14th DLI were part of 64th Brigade, attacking to the north of the village of Loos. To move into position, they had a difficult overnight march on 25–26 September; traffic control was bad, there was no hot food available and water was short. From this developed the legend that 'worn out by continuous night marching and unfed, they disgraced themselves and the New Army by retiring before the enemy'.[11] In fact, as Brig. Edmonds, the official historian, says: 'It was as "old campaigners" that the divisions failed, and this, seeing how few experienced men they contained, can be no reproach to them.'[12]

The 14th DLI had a particularly bad time. Having reached their position on 26 September, they were sent to support 63rd Brigade. Their arrival coincided with a withdrawal by British troops, and 14th DLI, thinking that these were Germans, opened fire. They then had to move forward, through the retreating troops, to try to hold a position near Bois Hugo, but in turn were forced to retreat. The battalion lost 220 other ranks, killed or wounded, and seventeen officers.[13]

This, then, was Pte Billy Nelson's first exposure to the reality of war: far from the picture painted by the recruiting posters and patriotic fervour in the UK. According to his CO, Nelson had been wounded at the battle of Loos and this wound kept him at base until 1 December 1915, when he rejoined his battalion, which had now been transferred to 6th Division.

Three weeks after returning to duty, on Christmas Eve 1915, Pte Nelson went absent and remained missing until 15 January 1916. He was tried by FGCM and found guilty of absence without leave and sentenced to twelve months' imprisonment with hard labour. On 6 February he was released under the Suspension of Sentences Act and returned to his unit but it would appear that this soldier had no intention of serving honourably as he deserted his unit again after only a week. He was recaptured six days later, on 21 February 1916, and on 28 February faced his second FGCM within a month, charged with desertion. As the records of this trial have not survived we do not know the details of the case, nor what mitigating circumstances were presented by Pte Nelson. He was found guilty of desertion but escaped the death penalty, being sentenced to penal servitude for life. This was subsequently commuted to ten years' penal servitude and, on 10 March 1916 the sentence, was suspended.

Pte Nelson went back to his unit and appears to have avoided further trouble until July 1916 at which time his battalion was serving in the Ypres sector, awaiting a move to the Somme. On 8 July Nelson stole 'a pair of puttees the property of an officer' and on the 13th he was given punishment of twenty-one days' FP No. 1 by his CO. Two days later he deserted his regiment yet again.

His subsequent trial took place at Wormhoudt on 1 August 1916, in front of a court martial panel comprising Maj. Taylor of 2nd DLI, Capt. Rosher of 14th DLI (his own unit) and Second Lt MacMichael of 11th Essex.[14] Pte Nelson elected not to have a prisoner's friend.

The court heard from Sgt Gingell that at 6 p.m. on 15 July 1916, at 'K' camp, Pte Nelson, who was undergoing FP No. 1, was handed over to him by the battalion's provost sergeant. At 6.30 p.m. Sgt Gingell told Pte Nelson that he was to parade for the trenches at 8 p.m. that night, but at 7.30 p.m. it was reported to him that Nelson had gone missing. Pte Milburn gave evidence that Nelson had been given into his custody at 6 p.m. and that he had then asked permission to go to the canteen. Pte Hornsley had escorted the prisoner to the canteen, and he told the court that when they arrived there, a crowd was around the door and he became separated from his prisoner. By the time Hornsley got through the crowd Nelson had disappeared. He and Pte Milburn searched for him, but gave up at 8 p.m. when they paraded for the trenches.

Cpl Jones of 1st KSLI gave evidence that at 10 p.m. on 18 July 1916 he had been on duty at the 6th Division stores when Pte Nelson had gone in and asked him for a night's sleep. The NCO had questioned Nelson, who then admitted he was an absentee, and arrested him. Cpl Morrant, of 11th Essex, on duty with Cpl Jones, corroborated this evidence.

Pte Billy Nelson made a statement on oath:

I have had a bit of trouble at home, and my nerves are badly upset. My father is a prisoner in Germany and is losing his eyesight there through bad treatment. My mother died while I was still in England, leaving my sister aged 13 and my brother aged 10. I am the only one left. I had to leave them in charge of a neighbour. I had no intention of deserting. I did not realise what I was doing when I left the camp. When I did so I went and gave myself up. When I went to the store my object was to get a night's sleep and then go and surrender in the morning. I thought it was too late to do so that night. I did not know when the battalion was coming out of the trenches.

Not surprisingly, Pte Nelson was found guilty. Character evidence was given by Lt Liddell, who told the court of the accused man's previous convictions, and said: 'He was wounded on 26 September at Loos in the hand.' The words 'in the hand' have been heavily underlined, presumably during the confirmation process, the clear implication being that this was self-inflicted, although there is no evidence for this in the soldier's record.[15] However, it is unlikely that this influenced the eventual outcome, given the soldier's bad record.

After the trial the CO of 14th DLI, Lt Col. Menzies, wrote that the man had a bad character and noted three episodes of desertion; the first (December 1915) is again heavily underlined, with '?' in the margin – someone in the chain of command confirming sentence noting that the conviction had, in fact, been for absence, not desertion. Lt Col. Menzies also commented that in his opinion, the absence was deliberate, to avoid duty in the trenches.

Brig. Gen. Tew, commanding 18th Brigade, agreed that the absence was deliberate, and wrote: 'As he has already twice previously absented himself, I recommend that the sentence of death be carried out.' Maj. Gen. Ross, GOC 6th Division, noted that discipline in 14th DLI was good, although there had been a few cases of desertion. He noted: 'On the other hand this is a bad case of deliberate desertion to avoid duty in the trenches by an old offender. Pte Nelson is not a good fighting soldier. I recommend that the sentence of death be carried out; because if the sentence is commuted in so grave a case as this, it will encourage others to chance it.' Lord Cavan, the corps commander, and Gen. Hubert Gough agreed, saying: 'I recommend that the sentence be put into execution owing to the seriousness of the offence and the man's previous character.'

Sentence was confirmed by the Commander-in-Chief on 7 August, by which time the battalion had moved to the Somme. The execution of Pte

Billy Nelson was planned for 4 a.m. but actually took place at Acheux at 5.15 a.m. The reason for the delay was explained in a note from the APM 6th Division to APM XIV Corps: 'I certify that No. 14387 Pte William Nelson 14th D.L.I. was executed by shooting at 5.15 a.m. this morning death being instantaneous, there was no hitch. The time had to be altered owing to thick fog at 4 a.m.'

In recent years more has emerged about this case. From information given by Mrs Nora High, Pte Nelson's niece, it appears that Nelson's first absence from his battalion coincided with the anniversary of his mother's death.[16] It is quite possible that this was taken into account at his subsequent trial, hence his being found guilty of absence rather than desertion. The information on the Pardons Campaign web site suggests that the second episode of desertion was prompted by Nelson's discovery that his pay would have been stopped.[17] However, as his sentence was suspended, he would have been paid whilst he was on active service. Even if his pay had been stopped, it is difficult to understand what this soldier might have hoped to gain from deserting his unit. As regards the third absence, the web site suggests that this was the consequence of the conditions under which FP No. 1 was carried out. However, this is an unsubstantiated statement. Thousands of men were given sentences of field punishment during the war, and unpleasant though it was (and was meant to be, to deter future crime), these men did not desert in consequence. At the time of his fatal desertion Billy Nelson had undergone at most two days of FP No. 1; many men served sentences of twenty-eight or more days.

Between 1914 and 1918 the army had a job to do: the Germans had to be driven back from France and Belgium. Like any court of the day, a court martial panel was interested only in the facts: was a man where he should be, or not? If not, then he was absent without leave. If evidence indicated either that he intended to desert permanently, or that he was avoiding a specific dangerous duty, then he was guilty of desertion. The reasons for his desertion were immaterial, in the same way that in a criminal court the reasons a robbery or murder were committed were irrelevant. Billy Nelson had home troubles on his mind, and in that one has sympathy for him as a man, but in the midst of war one man's personal problems count for little. One absence – such as his first – might be treated leniently, but Pte William Nelson ran away from his battalion on three occasions, and there are clear limits to what an army at war can tolerate.

A young soldier with a bad record paid the ultimate price for desertion in front of a firing squad at dawn on 15 June 1917.[18] Rifleman Arthur Allsop had been conscripted into the army on 21 June 1916 and appears to have been a reluctant soldier. Two months after joining 6th Battalion, King's Royal Rifle Corps he absented himself from camp in the UK, remaining away for three days, until 15 August. He was confined to camp but broke out again on the 17th, being arrested later the same day. He managed to stay out of trouble for the next six weeks, but on 4 October 1916, still in the UK, he went absent again, apparently for a few weeks, as he was not tried until 14 November. A DCM found him guilty of desertion, and 'losing by neglect his equipment, clothing and regimental necessaries' (implying that he was arrested in plain clothes); he was sentenced to 112 days' detention and stopped 33/- in pay.

Allsop subsequently went to France with the 12th Battalion, KRRC, but on 19 February when his unit was moving from Avuley to the front line at Les Boeufs he fell out on the line of march. He remained absent until arrested by the Military Police in Albert on 4 March 1917. For this act of desertion he was sentenced to death by FGCM, the court taking the view that the soldier was intending to avoid front line duty. By this stage of the war the old regular army was beginning to realize that pre-war standards could not easily be applied to a conscript force, and Allsop's sentence was commuted to five years' penal servitude and suspended. Although *For the Sake of Example* suggests that sentence was commuted because the desertion occurred from a base camp,[19] this is incorrect.

A few weeks later, on 31 May 1917, Rifleman Allsop again found himself facing an FGCM. This time the 19-year-old soldier was supported by a prisoner's friend, Capt. A. M. Bertie of the 11th Battalion, KRRC. The court was told that on the night of 24 April 1917 Allsop's platoon was in dugouts at Metz-en-Couture preparing for an attack. At 8 p.m. the platoon sergeant, Sgt Pease, went round his men to explain the arrangements for the attack. Allsop was present at this briefing and was also present five minutes later when the sergeant issued bombs and ammunition. However, at 8.20 p.m. when the platoon fell in and the roll was called Allsop was absent, and the unit went into the attack without him. Under cross-examination, Sgt Pease was absolutely clear that he had seen Allsop and told him his orders, but admitted that there were no written orders.

Allsop remained undetected until the evening of 30 April 1917 when he was seen in Meaulte by two NCOs of the Military Foot Police. These men asked him where he was going, to which he replied: 'I am going to the hospital at Grove Town to report sick.' This did not satisfy the police and Allsop was arrested.

In his defence he made a brief statement: 'At the time I absented myself from the Battalion I had home troubles. My brother died and my mother was ill. My brother was killed in action about four months ago. I have just turned 19 years of age.' Cross-examined by the court, he added: 'The worry had told on me and I was in a weak state of health at the time, but I had not been to the Doctor. I had had no letter from home for six weeks and this fact had worried me.' The implication of this was that his brother had been killed in late 1916 or early 1917, but a search shows no one of the name Allsop dying between October 1916 and February 1917.[20]

The prisoner's friend addressed the court to say that only one witness had given evidence that warning had been given that the unit was going to the trenches, and that no written orders had been posted to this effect. He also asked the court to take into account the accused man's extreme youth and his home troubles. The court considered their verdict and then heard the character evidence from the adjutant of the battalion, who gave details of Allsop's previous convictions. He also told the court that the accused man was 19 years and 11 months old. Under cross-examination the adjutant made a rather enigmatic statement: 'I have known the accused for five months during which time he has never been in the front line but I think if he did get into there he might do something.' Allsop said in mitigation of punishment: 'I should like a chance to go into the line. I think if it were given me I should make up for lost time.'

The court was not convinced and Rifleman Arthur Allsop was sentenced to death. The unit commanders' recommendations are no longer among the court martial documents, but it would seem unlikely that they would have suggested leniency in view of the soldier's previous record. Sentence was confirmed on 11 June and Rifleman Allsop was executed by a firing squad composed of the battalion snipers, at 4.15 a.m. on 15 June 1917.[21]

The case of another repeat offender, Pte John Taylor of the 2nd Staffordshires, executed in November 1917, is a strange one. Pte Taylor was a regular who had joined up for six years, or seven in case of war, and who, by his reckoning, became time-expired on 9 August 1916. He had gone to France with his battalion on 27 November 1914.

In September 1915 he had deserted from his unit, and had been tried by FGCM and sentenced to five years' penal servitude, commuted to two years' imprisonment with hard labour. This sentence was suspended and Taylor returned to his battalion, but on 2 June 1916 he faced another FGCM, this time charged with leaving his post without orders and with disobeying a lawful command. For these crimes he was again sentenced to five years' penal servitude, and again this was commuted to two years' imprisonment with hard labour. This time he was sent to the military prison at Rouen to serve both sentences concurrently.

On 11 June 1917 his sentence was again suspended and he was returned to his battalion. He had only been back with his unit for three months when he went absent again. On 24 September 1917 the 2nd South Staffordshires were at Gorre and were under orders to prepare to move into the Givenchy right subsector to relieve the 1st King's (Liverpool) Regiment. At 6 p.m. when the unit fell in, Pte Taylor was found to be missing. Evidence was presented at his subsequent trial to show that he had been present when the order was given.[22]

Two days later, at 10.45 p.m. on 26 September, Taylor was found asleep at the Band and Drums billet, in Gorre. He was arrested and sent back to his battalion under escort.

On 28 September the battalion was still in the line at Givenchy and Taylor was one of a working party, working from 9 a.m. to 1 p.m. At about 10.30 a.m. he was given permission to visit the latrine, but did not return and could not be found. He remained absent until found in a disused dugout at Le Plantin by the regimental police on 2 October 1917. At that time, although he was in uniform, he had no arms or equipment.

As a consequence of these two absences Pte Taylor faced his third FGCM on two counts of desertion and on one of losing by neglect his arms and equipment. The trial took place on 16 October 1917.

Taylor was not defended. In his defence he stated details of his previous service, and said that he had been time-expired since 9 August 1916: 'I thought I was entitled to a month's leave – same as other men. I felt I was unjustly dealt with. That is why I ran away.' Under cross-examination he admitted to hearing the order to prepare to move to the front line, given on 23 September.

Taylor was found guilty on both charges of desertion, but was acquitted on the charge of losing his equipment. After hearing evidence about his previous record the court sentenced him to death. In common with many other 1917 cases, the court martial file has been weeded and the letters from the different formation commanders are no longer in the file. The only character reference on file is that given at the trial by Second Lt Wright of 2nd South Staffordshires, his platoon commander for the period June to September. He told the court: 'I have always found accused a very good soldier in and out of the trenches, cheerfully carrying out any order given. Had under consideration the giving of lance-stripe to him.'

It is difficult to understand Taylor's reason for his fatal crime. He had already two experiences of courts martial and must have realized the risks he ran in going absent. He does not appear to have been frightened or shell-shocked, but was simply nursing a perceived grievance about his entitlement to leave – but a moment's reflection would surely have told him that as he had only recently been released from prison it would be most unlikely that he would be considered for leave. It also seems unlikely that an old regular had not discussed this issue of leave with a senior NCO. Taylor came close to being a reformed character with his sentence served and a lance corporal's stripe in the offing – instead he faced a firing squad in the early morning of 6 November 1917.

One of the most prolific repeat offenders appears to be Pte David Stevenson who enlisted into the Lowland Field Artillery on 17 August 1915 and the first of many entries onto his field conduct sheet followed almost immediately. His record is one of the longest amongst all the surviving records of courts martial: it is summarized below.[23]

In the UK:

1/9/15	Absent for six days
13/9/15	Absent for one day
18/9/15	Absent for four days
30/9/15	Absent for five days
5/10/15	Absent for one day
7/10/15	Absent for one day
11/10/15	Absent for seven days
20/10/15	Malingering
15/1/16	Absent for twenty-eight days
17/3/16	Drunk, creating a disturbance
2/4/16	Drunk, creating a disturbance
24/4/16	Breaking out of hospital
14/5/16	Absent for nine days
28/5/16	Creating a disturbance; damaging public property
30/5/16	Not complying with an order
31/5/16	Creating a disturbance; damaging public property
7/6/16	Absent for two days
14/6/16	Absent for three days
15/7/16	Absent for eighteen days
19/8/16	Absent for seventy-four days

18/11/16	Absent for one day
21/11/16	Insolence to an NCO
1/12/16	Absent for seven days
18/12/16	Absent for eighteen days

It would then seem that Pte Stevenson was sent out to France, as his next offence was 'in the field'.

18/8/17	Telling a lie to an NCO. Hesitating to obey an order.
27/8/17	Losing a folding saw by neglect
22/10/17	Desertion: tried by FGCM on 9 November 1916 and sentenced to five years' penal servitude
20/12/17	Drunk in camp; entering guard tent without permission; resisting escort.

Then on 8 March 1918 Pte Stevenson went missing again and managed to remain absent for almost three months but in June found himself facing another FGCM.[24] At the trial Sgt Colland gave evidence that at Bernes on 8 March 1918 he called the roll at tattoo and found that Stevenson was missing. The next witness, Maj. Brownilow, was the acting APM at Hallencourt, and gave evidence that he had seen Stevenson leading a civilian pony on 29 April 1918. Stevenson had told him that he was employed by the Town Major, but Maj. Brownilow disbelieved him and took him to the Town Major's office. On the way there Stevenson ran away but he later appeared at Maj. Brownilow's office and told this officer his correct name and regiment. As he had no identity disc or pay book the APM arrested him. On 3 May 1918 the prisoner was sent under escort to army HQ.

On 5 May, whilst a prisoner, Stevenson was admitted to No. 55 Casualty Clearing Station but his escort did not stay with him. Pte Naylor of No. 55 CCS told the court: 'The usual treatments were carried out, bath and change, clothing fumigated and accused was ready for returning to Fourth Army HQ the next day. After tea he disappeared and I did not see him again.' Three days later, on 8 May, Sgt Lambert of the Ox and Bucks LI saw Stevenson 'loitering about' in Saleux and arrested him.

Stevenson, who was defended at his trial, made a long statement on oath in his defence. He alleged that on 8 March Sgt Collard had told him that he was for leave, but a few minutes later returned and said that the leave was cancelled. Stevenson said: 'This worried me a bit as I had some trouble at home and was very anxious to get back.' He explained that he had no intention of going away, but just went for a walk.

I do not know what came over me for the moment but I went too far from my unit so I went on and got to Mons. When the fighting began on 21st March the police turned me back and told me to get equipment and rifle and go up the line at once as they were stopping all stragglers. I went up the line and found an [*sic*] equipment and was in the trenches with some Irish Division. I believe the 16th.

During this time he did not report to anyone, although he said that he later tried to find his unit, but was afraid of getting into trouble, so 'just loitered about' until he was arrested by the APM.

As for escaping from hospital, he told the court that he had thought that he was free to go out for a walk when he liked. He added that he had not had leave since arriving in France in July 1917.

The court found Stevenson guilty of both charges. A copy of his conduct sheet was produced and the prisoner made a brief plea in mitigation of sentence:

I have had one crime in the Regiment since which I have never had a chance. If I could get a transfer to another regiment, I could prove myself a soldier. I am 23 years old and was in the RFA 2 years and if I could get back to them I could soldier with them because I know my work there.

The court, having seen his long record, did not believe this assertion, and sentenced him to death. The unit commanders all recommended that the sentence be put into execution. His brigade commander wrote: 'To my mind there are no redeeming points in this case. There are many young men now serving in the Battalion. Such an example as this is a bad one for them.' Maj. Gen. Daly, GOC 24th Division, whilst agreeing: '... the sentence is well-merited and in my opinion should be put into execution', went on: 'The only possible explanation is that Pte. Stevenson may not be responsible for his actions' and proposed that a medical examination should be considered. However, Lt Gen. Hunter-Weston did not agree, saying that the man appeared to be in full possession of his mental faculties, and that: 'I think his conduct can be explained by his obvious and habitual tendency to avoid all authority.' Gen. Horne, commanding First Army, agreed, and sentence was confirmed by the commander-in-chief. Pte Stevenson was shot at Bully-Grenay on 13 July 1918.

This is another strange case: with his bad record, Stevenson must have known that he was heading for a death sentence, and yet persisted with the behaviour which would inevitably lead to his execution.

CHAPTER 28

PHYSICAL VIOLENCE

Self-control is the chief element in self respect; and self respect is the key to courage.

THUCYDIDES, 404 BC

In the hierarchy of military disobedience, one step up from disobeying an order and wilful defiance of authority is the striking of a superior officer. During the Great War three British soldiers were executed for this offence, all on the Western Front and all in 1916. The first man to face a firing squad for a physical attack on a superior officer was Pte J. Fox of the 2nd Battalion, Highland Light Infantry.[1]

The incident which led to the charge occurred at 8.30 a.m. on 8 April 1916 at Thérouanne. Second Lt O'Halloran had paraded his platoon for inspection and found that Pte Fox had a dirty rifle and boots. After ordering the sergeant to take the dirty soldier to the orderly room, O'Halloran carried on with the inspection. Fox suddenly moved forwards, swore at the officer and kicked him twice on the knee. The sergeant, seeing that Fox's rifle was raised, thought that Fox was about to attack the officer with it, so disarmed him. Three witnesses, Second Lt O'Halloran, L Sgt Stewart and Cpl McKay, all confirmed the series of events. Sgt Stewart alleged that Fox had said: 'The rifle is not dirty ... You're no fucking officer.' All three witnesses said that in their opinion Fox was sober at the time of the attack, although Cpl McKay told the court that he had seen Fox go into an estaminet earlier that morning.

Fox gave evidence on oath in his own defence, saying he had been in France since November 1914. He said his mother had died two months previously and he was worried about his paralysed sister. He admitted to being drunk the night before he attacked Second Lt O'Halloran, and said, in addition, that he had drunk two glasses of rum that morning. He told the court: 'I had no intention of doing what I did ... I feel very sorry for what I have done.'

The court took a dim view of this apparently unprovoked attack on an officer, and found Fox guilty. Under other circumstances this unruly soldier might have been given a spell of FP No. 1, or a prison sentence, but unfortunately Fox had a bad record and it transpired that he had been released from prison only two months earlier. His conduct sheet showed three entries for crimes committed in the UK and eight more since his arrival in France. On 7 April 1915 he had refused to obey an order and had been insolent to an NCO, then two days later had used insubordinate language to his superior officer. This had led to a court martial and a sentence of eighteen months' imprisonment with hard labour. Fox served eight and a half months of his sentence before the remainder was suspended on 31 January 1916. Within five days of leaving prison he was in trouble again, and then on 2 March had been charged with insolence to Second Lt O'Halloran and not complying with an order. Unwilling or unable to control his behaviour, on 18 March Fox was in trouble again, for stating a falsehood to Lance Sgt Stewart.

In the light of this string of offences, his commanding officer's comments are interesting. Lt Col. Prentice wrote: 'He is a naturally insubordinate fellow, and gives trouble in his company. On the other hand his company commander reports that he does his work quite well when he is in the trenches.' However, Lt Col. Prentice added: 'he has never taken part in an engagement', and continued:

> I am of the opinion that his naturally insubordinate characteristics led him to commit the crime in anger and that it was not deliberately premeditated. During my 23 years of service with this battalion I can never recollect a previous case of an officer of the Battalion being assaulted by one of the rank and file and I submit that the extreme penalty is not necessary as an example.

The brigade commander of 51st Infantry Brigade, Charles Corkran, disagreed:

> In spite of what Col. Prentice says, I recommend that the extreme penalty be inflicted. Col. Prentice in my opinion is a fine disciplinarian, but he has a good rough lot to deal with, and an iron hand is necessary for the maintenance of discipline in this battalion.

Whilst the divisional commander agreed with Corkran, Henry Wilson, GOC of IV Corps, did not – for very shrewd reasons. In his opinion, as the incident happened during training and not when in contact with the enemy, this lessened the severity of the offence. Also, the offence was so rare that punishment would not affect future cases of this type and, although Fox was hot-headed, he had behaved well in the face of the enemy and there was no question of cowardice being involved. However, subsequent to the trial, someone apparently quoting Lt Col. Prentice has appended a note in the margin of the papers: 'Has never taken part in an engagement but has behaved quite well in the trenches.'

Had the army commander supported Wilson's recommendation, Fox might have been reprieved, but Fox was serving in First Army, under Gen. Monro, who wrote: 'I recommend the execution of the sentence in this case. I cannot conceive a more disgraceful violation of the principles of discipline than the evidence discloses.' These comments sealed Fox's fate and he was shot at Bully-Grenay on 12 May 1916.

The men of the HLI were a rough tough, lot, many from the Glasgow tenements, and they were hard-drinking, hard-living, hard-fighting men. When their efforts were directed against the enemy they were doughty fighters. Col. Prentice clearly knew his men and was tolerant – but firm – with even such an insubordinate character as Fox, because he recognized his fighting attributes. Prentice knew his men and Henry Wilson could be impartial from a distance and gave a fair and balanced view on the case. But the death warrant was, effectively, yet again signed by Monro, who was not prepared to accept any overstepping of the bounds of discipline, particularly by the HLI

The other two instances of a soldier striking a superior both occurred in September 1916 and both men were serving in the same unit, 72nd Battery, RFA, although the offences were unrelated. Like Pte Fox, Driver Thomas Hamilton also hit an officer, Second Lt Oates.[2] This officer noticed that Hamilton was smoking on a stable parade and ordered the sergeant major to take his name. Hamilton told this NCO that he wanted to talk to the officer, to explain that he had not been smoking but had picked up the butt of a cigarette, which had fallen from behind his ear, and 'had put it in his mouth while feeding the horses'. The sergeant major talked to the officer but received no reply and told Hamilton that the officer would not see him. Not satisfied, Hamilton intercepted Second Lt Oates as he left the officers' urinal, saying: 'Beg pardon, Sir …' The young officer made it clear that he was not prepared to listen to Hamilton, who, incensed by the apparent injustice, hit Oates on the face and body with his fists.

Hamilton defended himself, fairly ably, and managed to demonstrate to the court that Second Lt Oates had not given the complete story in his version of the evidence. A bombardier who gave evidence for the prosecution said he had not seen Oates struck but had had his attention drawn to the mark left on Oates's face, which did not look as though it had been caused by a blow.

In his defence Hamilton said he felt he had been unjustly accused by the officer and had tried to speak to him about it. He told the court that Second Lt Oates had stumbled on the sloping ground, and that, at first, he did not realize why he had been arrested. The character evidence showed that Hamilton was a pre-war regular, having joined up in 1911. He had four entries on his 'crime sheet', all fairly minor, the most serious being hesitating to obey an order in December 1914.

As in Fox's case, this offence happened in a rear area. The Commander, Royal Artillery 6th Division, wrote: 'I recommend that sentence ... be carried into effect. There are no extenuating circumstances and the state of discipline in this unit requires an example.' Division and corps commanders supported this recommendation, but Rawlinson, Fourth Army commander, disagreed, making an important point: 'I am doubtful if in this case it is desirable to carry out the sentence as the officer refused to allow the prisoner to speak. But in view of the state of discipline in the battery a sentence of 7 years' penal servitude might meet the case.' Rawlinson's argument appears sound – Second Lt Oates does not seem to have handled the matter well and should have at least indicated that he would talk to Hamilton later. However, for once, the Commander-in-Chief disagreed with his army commander and Driver Hamilton was shot on 3 October 1916.

On the same day that Hamilton was tried, Driver James Mullaney from the same battery also faced a court martial. He was charged with 'Striking his superior officer in that he in the field on 16th September 1916 when ordered in close arrest by Battery Sergeant Major Hughes, struck the said Sergeant Major with his fist knocking him down.' The dispute had started because Driver Mullany wanted his tea.[3]

Battery Sergeant Major Hughes explained to the court that on the afternoon of 16 September he had ordered that six teams be harnessed up. Mullany's response was to shout: 'What about some fucking tea.' Placed under open arrest, Mullany asked to be put under close arrest (as this would mean he would get his tea). The NCO, being wise to this ploy, told him to get on with the harnessing up, whereupon Mullany swore at the sergeant major, who ordered him to be put in the guardroom. Mullany then knocked over the NCO, punching him while he was on the ground. Bombardier Trueman pulled Mullany off and the sergeant major got to his feet, only to be attacked and knocked down again by Mullany.

In his defence Mullany said that he had been cleaning his harness when the order to harness up was given. He said that as it would be late when they returned from replenishing the ammunition, he had expected to get his tea before turning out. He alleged, despite the evidence of the prosecution witnesses, that he did not hit the NCO. His version of events was that he went up to Sgt Major Hughes with his fists raised, the NCO had taken up a defensive stance, 'and somehow we ran into each other and fell to the ground'. When asked why he had wanted to be put under close arrest Mullany replied: 'Simply because I was fed up with the unit I was in and also because it is absolute torture to serve in the battery.' No doubt many of the front line infantry serving on the Somme would have been more than happy to change places with him.

The accused's conduct sheet showed only one entry, from 25 June 1916, for 'making an improper reply to an officer'. Mullany had asked for a character witness to be called but he was not available and Capt. Cory, the court martial president, wrote:

> I have to report that the accused, Driver Mullany, on being asked if he
> had any witness to call as to character said that he was desirous of calling
> Second Lt Taylor, 72 Battery RFA. This officer was not available, being
> up at the guns and unable to get away. No evidence as to character that
> this officer could have given would have affected the sentence of the court.

Nonetheless, the army, ever meticulous, obtained a written statement from Second Lt Taylor. This young officer wrote that Mullany had been an acting bombardier in April but had given up his stripe when passed over for promotion. He also said that whenever Mullany asked for permission of any sort he used an insolent tone but was never openly insolent. He added that Mullany had kept his horses and harness fairly well.

Maj. Barnwell, commanding the battery, said that Mullany had been insolent on two occasions, first when he gave up his stripe and secondly when ordered to stop kicking a football around amongst the horses. However, the commander of 38th Brigade of the RFA was more forthright. Speaking of Hamilton and Mullany he wrote:

> Having seen these men and heard the evidence in their respective cases
> I am of the opinion that both are of a type that under pre-war conditions
> should not have been retained in the service. Driver Hamilton, who has
> some knowledge of boxing, is an ill-conditioned bully. Driver Mullany was

not appointed Acting Bombardier under my command but joined with such a stripe on his arm. He is quite unfitted for any such appointment. I consider him an insubordinate man of low class.

All the commanders recommended that the sentence be carried out. Lt Gen. Lord Cavan, the Corps commander, wrote: 'I recommend that the death sentence be carried out as the discipline in this battery is bad.'

Mullany and Hamilton were executed together on 3 October 1916. As a result of these cases, the DA & QMG of XIV Corps wrote to the CRA 6th Division to enquire whether there was any reason for these offences – for example, was the battery commander unduly severe? The reply was that as only one officer could be spared from the gun lines to look after the wagon lines, discipline had become lax and the CRA had given orders that all serious offences were to be dealt with in accordance with King's Regulations and military law. It may be suspected that the CRA was reminded he had now had his examples and no more were required.

Neither Hamilton nor Mullany had bad records. It would seem that they – and no doubt others in the unit – had become accustomed to grousing and seeing what they could get away with when the officers were not around. However, the new orders from the CRA that a firmer line be taken meant that the days of such insubordination were numbered. These two drivers' violence was ill-considered and their punishment was to be an example to others in their battery and in other units with similar problems. There were no further executions of British servicemen for this offence during the war.

It is tempting to allege that, in effect, Hamilton was shot for smoking on parade and Mullany was shot for wanting his tea. However, such an argument is flawed. In both cases, had the men simply groused in the usual way of soldiers they would probably, at worst, have been given FP No. 1, but an army cannot function if the 'rank and file' physically attack their NCOs and officers. Hamilton and Mullany died to remind other soldiers of that stark and simple fact.

CHAPTER 29

THE MILITARY MURDERERS

From battle and from murder, and from sudden death, good Lord deliver us.

THE LITANY, 1549

The figures compiled after the Great War show a total of thirty-seven executions for murder.[1] This number includes:

10 men of the Chinese Labour Corps, for the murder of civilians or
fellow Chinese
3 men of the Cape Coloured Regiment for murder of civilians or fellow-soldiers
2 men of the British West Indies Regiment, one in Italy and one in Palestine
1 West African
1 South African
2 Canadians
5 muleteers of the Mediterranean Force
13 British servicemen

The authors of *Shot at Dawn* also found evidence that two further British soldiers, L Cpl William Price and Pte Richard Morgan of the 2nd Battalion of the Welsh Regiment, had been executed in February 1915 for the murder of their sergeant major, CSM Hayes.[2] Although there is no record of this trial or sentence in the Registers of Courts Martial,[3] nor is the case included in the postwar statistics (implying that no records existed of the trial), there appears little doubt that the murder and executions took place.

It is inevitable in war that men issued with firearms sometimes used them in ways not intended by the War Office. There have always been anecdotal reports of unpopular officers and NCOs being shot by disgruntled soldiers during an attack, and there is little doubt that some old scores have been settled in this way.

It has also been alleged that when a company 'went over the top', officers and military police lined the trenches, revolvers at the ready, to shoot those who did not leave the trenches. Most of this is anecdotal and actually casts an unnecessary slur on the average Tommy, who went into an attack with his mates because it was his duty and not because he was afraid of retribution. 'Battle police' were indeed stationed at key points well to the rear of communications trenches to control movements into and out of the battle area but their main role was to act as traffic controls. Stragglers and those trying to 'slope off' away from the action were generally rounded up and sent back to the firing line with an NCO or officer.

Brig. Gen. Crozier describes shooting an officer to stop a panic-stricken retreat, remarking: 'I believe I am right in saying that only one officer was shot for cowardice by sentence of a Court Martial in France; although, of course, a good many were shot out of hand in order to stem the tide when running away.' He then describes how he shot a fleeing subaltern and the German chasing him, on the Strazeele Road in 1918, after the Portuguese holding the line broke. In explanation he said: 'My duty was to hold the line *at all costs* ... Even if the effort did mean murder, the line had to be held.'[4]

War provides ample opportunities for the would-be murderer and it is almost certain that the vast majority of murders in the field went undetected. Brig. Gen. Crozier quotes one such case:

A British NCO had been bullying some of his subordinates. As there appeared to be no way of dealing with the case there, aggrieved men decided to deal with the matter in their own way ... A Mills bomb has a local but very violent explosive effect. They decided that the Mills bomb should therefore be their agent. They caught their victim bending, so to speak. Pulling out the pin from the bomb ... one of them – they had previously drawn lots for the job – pushed the bomb down the back of the NCO's trousers after which they made off at lightning speed to avoid the explosion ... There was no trace whatsoever left of this NCO.[5]

'Fragging', to use the American term in Vietnam, is by no means a new phenomenon.

Chesterton wrote: 'Where would a wise man hide a leaf? In the forest', and went on to say that the place to hide a body was on the field of battle.[6] Any wise soldier planning murder would pick his time and place, hiding the body amongst the carnage of no-man's-land. With such opportunities, it was probably only those who acted on a sudden impulse who were caught and who suffered the full consequences of the law. Drink was often at the bottom of the problem, as with the case of Pte Charles William Knight, serving with the 10th Battalion, Royal Welch Fusiliers.[7]

On 3 November 1915 at about 8.15 p.m. Pte Knight appeared in his billet in a barn, staggering and apparently drunk; he then picked up his rifle and started to parry at the wall. Pte Richardson asked him to put the rifle down, and tried to disarm him, but Knight evaded him and started to load the rifle. As Richardson ran for help, he heard a shot. Sgt Grundy, as he left the guard-room to go to the barn, also heard a shot and heard Pte Poffley call out: 'Oh my leg.'

CSM Fisher, summoned by Richardson, then arrived and Sgt Grundy warned him not to stand in the doorway as some shots had come through. Grundy later told the court that he thought he had heard thirty to thirty-five shots fired altogether.

CSM Fisher, on orders from Maj. Freeman, the company commander, charged the barn and managed to get inside. He spotted Knight by seeing the rifle flashes and managed to leap on him from behind, disarming him. In the meantime, Sgt Grundy had found Pte Edwards dead in the guard-room.

Maj. Freeman gave evidence at the trial that when Knight was finally captured his rifle was red-hot. There were twenty-five empty cartridge cases on the straw where he had been standing, five rounds in the magazine and a further 125 live rounds nearby. A post-mortem examination showed that Pte Edwards was dead from a chest wound and that Pte Poffley had four wounds.

Several of the witnesses at the trial thought that Knight had been drunk, although Maj. Freeman, who finally arrested him, said: 'In my opinion he had been drinking but I do not consider that he was drunk.' The doctor saw Knight in the guardroom at about 10.45 p.m. and described him as semi-conscious, 'his speech was of the alcoholic type and his breath was slightly tainted with liquor'. He added: 'I do not consider his mental condition was normal at that time and I consider that it was due to drink. I saw him again next morning ... and found him quite sensible.'

Pte Knight, surprisingly for a capital charge, had no prisoner's friend. He made a statement saying that he had 'gone out just before tea-time to take some washing to a nearby house'. On his way back he had stopped for coffee, when he felt strange and heard a rattling noise in his head. He returned to the barn, had his tea and tried to sleep, then later went for a walk, met some friends and had a few drinks. But his head got worse and after sitting down for a while he went back to his billet and lay down. About ten to fifteen minutes later he saw shadows on the wall, grabbed something and attacked the wall, then remembered almost nothing until the next morning.

The question was whether the crime was committed as a direct consequence of drunkenness, rendering Knight incapable of appreciating the nature of his actions in firing off his rifle at random. This was a permissible line of defence, but it was up to the defendant to demonstrate that he was not responsible for his actions. The court did not believe that Knight had proved this, and found him guilty. After the finding his conduct sheet was produced and showed that Knight's character was regarded as 'indifferent' and that he already had five charges of drunkenness in his fourteen months' service.

Lt Col. Beresford-Ask, CO of the 10th Royal Welch Fusiliers, wrote:

No. 15437 Private Charles William Knight of the battalion under my command is a man of apparently very low origin, though of considerable personality. He had great influence amongst the other men, and was on more than one occasion recommended to me for promotion. He is a man who is addicted to drink, and when under its influence appears to lose control over his actions. He joined the BEF on 28th September last.

The commander of 76th Brigade wrote: 'In my opinion it is a clear case of murder and owing to the ease with which men can obtain ammunition on active service it is necessary in such cases to carry out the extreme penalty of the law.' Maj. Gen. Haldane, commanding 3rd Division, had some concerns about the trial, asking 'whether anyone else fired at all, or whether all the other rifles, being examined, showed no traces of having been fired'. He gave a possible course of action: 'the finding, not having been confirmed, it is possible to try the man again and bring out evidence on these points, should such a course be considered necessary'. He went on: 'There appears, however, to be no doubt that the accused's conduct was such that any "reasonable man" must have known it was likely to cause grievous bodily harm, and that the charge is correct. I recommend that Private C Knight's offence be treated as murder and not manslaughter.'

In forwarding the proceedings to the adjutant general, Maj. Gilbert Mellor, the DJAG, made the important point that

The substantial question for the Court to decide was whether the accused was in a state of mind to intend to kill or to inflict grievous bodily harm or to know that what he was doing would reasonably and probably cause that result, and in law it rested, in this case, upon the accused to show that he was not legally responsible for his actions.

This was a crucial statement: although a man is innocent until proven guilty, it was up to the defendant to demonstrate that he was not responsible for his actions. This, of course, was true in all such WW1 courts martial defence claims, be they for murder, desertion or cowardice. This was the burden of proof – under criminal as well as military law – which the executed men frequently failed to meet. Maj. Gilbert Mellor added: 'There is no reason to suppose that the accused had he been sober, would have committed this or any other serious crime.'

Gen. Plumer recommended the sentence be carried out, and Sir John French confirmed the sentence on 13 November 1915. Pte Charles Knight was executed at dawn on 15 November 1915.

In February 1916 another drunken soldier committed murder. Pte Arthur Dale of 13th Battalion, Royal Scots shot his friend L Cpl Snedden for no apparent reason.[8]

At 11.10 a.m. on 7 February 1916 Pte Arthur Dale and Pte Robert Hutchinson went into an estaminet near their billet and had 'two glasses of stout'. Dale was already drunk and L Cpl Snedden, who was in the estaminet, told Dale to get his equipment and go to his billet at Philosophe. Dale swore at Snedden, whereupon the NCO took the drunken soldier by the coat and led him to the ladder up to his billet. Dale, having climbed up the ladder without assistance, shouted: 'Here you are Corporal', and men in the yard, including Hutchinson, then looked up and saw Dale with his rifle aimed at Snedden. A shot rang out and the NCO fell to the ground. A doctor was summoned and the wounded man was taken to No. 1 Casualty Clearing Station, with a serious abdominal wound from which he later died.

Hutchinson and another man ran up the ladder and found Dale lying behind the door crying; Hutchinson told the court: 'I think he was delirious.' Two military policemen arrived and described Dale as '… lying on the floor behind the door. He was very drunk and crying, and mumbling in a stupid way.' His rifle was leaning against the wall about 2 feet away and was found to have one discharged round in the breech. One of the MPs told Dale that he was being arrested for shooting Cpl Snedden, but he appeared not to understand what was being said to him, and was unable to get down the ladder unaided. The MP added: 'I lifted him down the ladder by his coat collar. He walked with a stagger, one man on each side of him.'

Dale did not make a statement in his own defence, but two other witnesses gave evidence on his behalf. Cpl Bain said that Snedden and Dale were friendly with each other and he had never known them quarrel. RSM Price told the court that he had known Dale for twenty-six years, since 1890, and that he was a good soldier with a good character. Capt. Yule, defending Dale, told the court that the evidence showed no malice aforethought and that Snedden himself had said it was an accident. However, as in the previous case, onus of proof that Dale was too drunk to be responsible for his actions rested solely with the defence. The *Manual of Military Law* is quite clear on this point: 'If one person is proved to have killed another, the law presumes *prima facie* that he is guilty of murder. It will be on the accused to prove such facts as may reduce the offence to manslaughter, or excuse him from all criminal responsibility.'[9]

Dale's records showed him to be 46 years old, probably a re-enlisted man, with a good character.

Neither his CO nor the brigade commander made recommendations to sentence, the latter simply pointing out that Pte Dale was drunk. Lt Gen. Henry Wilson, commanding IV Corps, wrote a carefully considered recommendation pointing out that Dale was drunk, that there was no motive for murder and that Dale had a good character. He concluded: 'I do not think this is a case for the extreme penalty.'

However, Gen. Monro, commanding First Army, taking a tougher line, disagreed: 'I recommend the execution of sentence in this case. Enquiry is being made as to the rules in place concerning Inspection of Arms in billets so as to ensure that magazines do not remain charged in these circumstances.'

Sentence was confirmed by the Commander-in-Chief, and Pte Arthur Dale was executed in the abattoir at Mazingarbe on 28 February 1916.

Drink was probably at the root of another military murder in early 1916, when Driver Thomas Moore of the Army Service Corps shot and killed his friend Staff Sgt Pick.[10] On the night of 11 February 1916 Moore was in his billet, a hut at Busseboom in Belgium. After the men in the hut had been told by an officer to quieten down, Moore picked up a rifle, loaded it and fired a shot through the roof. When two senior NCOs arrived to investigate, Moore threatened them and an officer. He then left the hut and several witnesses heard Staff Sgt Pick shout: 'Chuck it Darky' (Moore's nickname). One witness heard Moore say: '… it's Ginger, the Bastard I want.' ('Ginger' was Sgt Maj. Bagshawe.) A shot was fired and Pick called out. Moore was then alleged to have said: 'Is that you, Pick?' or 'It is you Pick, is it?', then 'Speak. Won't you speak. I will make you speak' and another shot was fired. Pick was found to be badly wounded and died shortly afterwards. After examining the body, the battalion medical officer thought that the second, fatal, wound had been fired from above while the victim was on the ground.

Lt Col. Lord, the commanding officer of the 24th Divisional Train troops, arrived on the scene at 11.40 p.m., by which time Moore had been secured. He told the court that Moore had then said: 'Put a bullet through me. This is purgatory. It was Ginger I wanted. It was Ginger Bagshawe I wanted. I had nothing against Pick.'

The MO saw Moore at about 12.15 a.m. when he was heavily asleep, and could only wake him by violent shaking. His pupils were dilated and did not react to light, and he was only semi-conscious. The MO found nothing to indicate whether he was sane or insane, but said: 'He gave me the impression of a man recovering from drunkenness. I do not consider that his condition could have been the result of shock.' About an hour later, Moore was speaking rationally, but with slurred speech. The doctor said at the trial: 'I have not seen any signs in the accused which I could recognise as signs of insanity.'

Driver Thomas Moore, who had a prisoner's friend at his trial, handed in a written statement in his defence. In it he said that at about 6 p.m. he had been to an estaminet with friends and had been joined by Pick. At closing time he and Pick left together, and as they walked back to the camp Pick gave him a drink from a bottle. After that, Moore remembered nothing until he found himself wrestling with someone in the doorway of his hut.

Two other drivers gave evidence in Moore's defence. Driver Kenny had been drinking with Moore and Pick in the estaminet, and described Moore's condition: 'The accused was neither drunk nor sober when I left him but between the two. He had a good few drinks.' He said: 'When Pick and the accused left the estaminet they were the best of friends.' Driver Lee told the court that he knew Moore and his family well, and said: 'His mother is in the asylum, the Durham County asylum – if she is still alive; his father is an eccentric sort of chap who knocks around the racecourses. His brother is a wild sort of chap.' Of Moore, he said: 'He is a very strange sort of chap if he gets a glass of beer.'

The court found Moore guilty. His 'crime sheet' was then presented, showing some minor offences in 1915, drunk in July 1915, drunk and resisting escort in September, and in November 1915 he had been given twenty-one days' FP No. 1 for recklessly firing off a rifle and threatening to take his life (suicide was still a criminal offence in 1916). In mitigation Moore said that he was 'out of his mind at the time' and 'didn't know what happened', the common defence of the private soldier in the First World War One.

All the unit commanders recommended that sentence of death be carried out, and it was confirmed by Field Marshal Haig on 23 February 1916. Driver

Thomas Moore was shot at Busseboom by men from his own company and buried there,[11] but the grave was not found after the war, and he is today commemorated on the memorial at the Menin Gate. His victim, Sgt Pick, lies buried at Poperinge New Military Cemetery, ironically close to the graves of several soldiers executed for military offences.

Although the evidence presented at the trial dealt solely with Moore's offence, it appears from the unit war diary [12] that there was a discipline problem with 197th Company, and Lt Col. Lord was ordered to make arrangements for Maj. Gen. Capper, commander of 24th Division, to speak to the men. On 15 February the whole of 197th Company, officers as well as men, were paraded for public rebuke by Maj. Gen. Capper, a highly unusual proceeding.

Thomas Moore had shot the wrong NCO by mistake, but in July 1917 another rear-echelon soldier, Sapper Philip Oyns, deliberately selected an NCO, CSM McCain, against whom he had a grudge and shot him. Yet again, drink was involved.

On 13 July the men of 50th Field Searchlight Company, Royal Engineers were going about their business in camp at Brie.[13] At about 9 p.m. Sapper Lawlor was chopping wood near the huts in which the men were living, and Sgt Majors McCain and Finniston were sitting nearby, talking. Sapper Oyns came out of his hut shouting and CSM McCain went over and spoke to him. A few minutes later two shots rang out: CSM McCain fell to the ground and Sgt Maj. Finniston was hit between the shoulder blades. Sapper Anson then managed to get the rifle away from Oyns and wrestle him to the ground.

Several witnesses gave evidence about Oyns's behaviour. Sapper Anson said that about an hour before the incident Oyns had been excited and quarrelsome. He also had bottles of beer in his pocket, and Anson said that when drunk on a previous occasion, Oyns had been violent. He also told the court that Sgt Maj. McCain was popular and had seemed like a father to Oyns. L Cpl Boyce had seen Oyns in an excited condition between 9 and 9.20 p.m. and that this was not his normal state; 'he was like it only when he had had some beer'. He told the court: 'CSM McCain was always very nice to me. I have heard the accused had a grudge against CSM McCain.' He later said that he had been told this by Oyns, who about a month previously had said: 'I will go up against the wall for one bloody man.' Sapper Lawlor, who had seen Oyns drinking in the canteen earlier, said: 'Accused was a man who always had a grievance, imaginary or otherwise.' He added: 'I say he was not friendly with the Sgt. Major because he (accused) told me the Sgt. Major was responsible for getting him 14 days.' Sapper Hathaway said that the accused did not seem to be the worse for drink and that on previous occasions when drunk, Oyns had been noisy and violent.

After Oyns had been subdued, Bombardier Windebank had taken charge of him, and gave evidence that 'The accused was the worse for drink. He did not appear to have a clear idea of what he had done.' According to this witness, during the night Oyns said: 'I think something serious has happened. Is anyone dead?' He was also alleged to have said: 'No, not you, Finn, you're one of the best – but that Bugger – if I had a Lewis Gun I'd wipe the whole lot out.' Under cross-examination Windebank said: 'I consider accused was drunk … He smelt strongly of drink.'

CSM McCain died later in the casualty clearing station, of a wound to his neck and chest, and was buried at La Chapelette Cemetery, Peronne. CSM Finniston did not give evidence at the trial as he was still in hospital under treatment for his wound.

Oyns, who was defended, pleaded that he had been affected by drink. He said that he had several drinks after tea and added: 'Drink always affects me in this way. About 7 months ago I got 14 days No. 1 for being drunk. This had nothing to do with CSM McCain. Sgt. Major McCain has always got me out of scrapes. I never bore him any grudge for the simple reason he never did me any harm.'

He told the court that before the war he had been an electrical worker and had lost jobs through drink. He also said that his defence to his charge of drunkenness seven months previously had been that he remembered nothing. He explained that he had received a blow on the head during the Liverpool Riots twelve years previously and since, whenever he got drunk, he remembered nothing of what had happened.

His character reference from Capt. French Mullen said that Oyns was 'hard-working and good at his trade, but that he did not get on well with the NCOs or other men'. He told the court that McCain did his best to help Oyns, trying to settle any difficulties without going to an officer, and that on a previous occasion had arranged for Oyns to be charged with a more minor offence than might otherwise have been the case.

The prisoner's friend, Lt Pilcher, said the facts of the case were not contested, but that Oyns was not guilty of murder, that he was drunk 'and in that condition, he was not capable of forming the intention of shooting to kill'.

Despite Oyns's protestation that he had no grudge against McCain, his AFB122 suggested differently: on 20 April 1916 he had been charged with hesitating to obey an order, the witness being Sgt Maj. McCain, and on 9 March 1917 McCain was again a witness when Oyns was charged with being drunk and causing a disturbance.

The court martial panel found Oyns guilty and sentenced him to death, and this was confirmed by the Commander-in-Chief on 17 October 1917. There is no indication as to why there was such a delay (three months) between the crime and the trial, although it is clear that Oyns was kept under arrest for twelve weeks before trial. There are two possible reasons: the trial may have been a retrial, the earlier papers now being lost, or proceedings may have been delayed in the hope that Sgt Maj. Finniston could recover sufficiently to give evidence. Oyns was shot at Coxyde, near the coast at Dunkirk, on 20 October 1917.

In 1918 another Royal Engineer, Sapper Robert Bell, went even further, and shot and killed an officer, Second Lt Wynell Lloyd.[14]

Robert Bell belonged to 123rd Field Company of the Royal Engineers. After lunch on 17 April 1918 he was given permission by his corporal to go out for a walk, and he went out to see if he could find a hare or partridge to supplement the rations. He arrived back at the camp ready for a parade at 4 p.m. His section fell in, in two ranks, with Bell in the front rank; when Second Lt Lloyd arrived he noticed that Bell was not wearing his puttees and sent him off to find them. In the meantime, the officer inspected the men's rifles and iron rations. He then moved away from the front rank, towards the covered-in trenches that Bell had gone to, whilst Cpl Prior inspected the rear rank of the platoon and the gas NCO inspected the front row. Suddenly there was a shot and Lt Lloyd fell to the ground with a bullet through his temple. Hardly surprisingly, the parade broke up in disorder.

At Bell's subsequent trial, Sapper Pears gave evidence that he had seen the muzzle of a rifle sticking up out of the trench in front of the parade. Another witness, L Cpl Ordish, said that when he was shot Lt Lloyd was about 4 yards in front of the trench and Bell was standing in the trench. He did not see a rifle in Bell's hands, but had seen one in the trench about 2 feet away, leaning against the parapet. Ordish was very clear in his evidence that when he saw it, the rifle was not pointing towards Lt Lloyd.

Cpl Prior, who had earlier given Bell permission to go shooting for game, was sure that the shot had come from the direction of the trench, and arrested Bell. He told the court that the other men's rifles had been examined after Bell had been sent off parade and as Bell had taken his rifle into the trench with him it had not been inspected. The men had all been told to clean their rifles before the inspection, but Prior admitted that Bell was not present when this order had been given earlier in the afternoon. Asked about Bell's demeanour after his arrest, Prior said: 'The accused was not upset so far as I noticed when I got to him at the trench.'

CSM Foster was in a dugout with Sgt Ferris about 60 yards away when the shot was fired. He saw Lt Lloyd fall down but by the time he reached the officer he was clearly dead and Bell had been arrested. The CSM searched Bell and found two clips of five rounds in his pocket. The rifle had an empty case in the breech and two live rounds in the magazine. As CSM Foster went towards the officers' tent, Bell said to him: 'You know me Sergeant Major', and 'when I set out to accomplish a thing I do it – there it is'. Foster also told the court: 'so far as I knew the accused had no ill-feeling towards Lt Lloyd'.

Sgt Ferris, who had been in the dugout with CSM Foster, told the court that he had held Bell's hands whilst he was searched by CSM Foster, and alleged that after Foster had walked away, and he himself was standing behind the prisoner, Bell said: 'I've done the section a good turn and you'll think of Bob Bell in years to come.'

Sapper Robert Bell, who had taken advantage of his rights to a prisoner's friend, made a statement, not on oath, in his defence. He said that at 12.30 p.m. he had been given permission by Cpl Prior to go for a walk and had taken his rifle with him in the hope of finding a hare or partridge, but 'I failed to get a shot at a hare and returned to camp'. He went on parade with the rest of his section, but was sent to put on his puttees and went into the covered trench-cum-shelter. He couldn't find them and after looking for about ten minutes got out of the trench. 'In jumping up I slipped the rifle flying forward and exploding accidentally. I had forgotten to abstract the round which I had put in, in the earlier part of the afternoon and that was the cause of the unfortunate result.'

However, Sapper Short then gave evidence which contradicted Bell's statement that he had shot nothing that afternoon. He said: 'I saw accused come back on 17 April. He had with him a small black rabbit. The rabbit had been shot.'

The prisoner's friend made a spirited defence. He pointed out that no one had seen the fatal shot fired, that no one could give evidence of any argument between Bell and Second Lt Lloyd and that there was no motive. He suggested to the court that the officer's death had been an accident and pointed out that the court must be convinced that this was a case of such gross negligence, or that there was an intention to shoot Second Lt Lloyd, before they could find Bell guilty of murder. At worst, it could only be considered manslaughter.

Maj. Wood, who was also the prosecutor in the case, gave character evidence to say that Bell had always worked well. His disciplinary records showed two minor offences, and that he had joined up in January 1915.

The court found Sapper Bell guilty of the murder of Lt Lloyd and sentence was duly confirmed. There appears to be little doubt that Bell shot his officer. Although the evidence was circumstantial, no motive emerged. Unlike the previous cases discussed, drink did not appear to be an issue and it would seem that Bell's level of resentment against Lt Lloyd had finally pushed him to commit murder.

In none of the cases discussed above did the men deny that they had been responsible for the death of another soldier. The *Manual of Military Law* makes it clear that under these circumstances it was up to the accused to prove why the charge of murder was not justified. If we review the trial transcripts of the men executed for murder, there seems little doubt that they received a fair trial and were guilty of the offence as charged. Had they been civilians they would undoubtedly have hanged, the standard penalty for convicted murderers at the time. In army service and under military jurisdiction they were shot as military law prescribed. It would be hard to discern any logic in a campaign to pardon the military murderers of the First World War. To retrospectively change legally binding decisions taken by a competent authority over eighty years ago would set an undesirable precedent for every case of a civilian hanged for murder at the time.

CHAPTER 30

A VERY TEMPORARY GENTLEMAN

The military officer is considered a gentleman ... specifically because nothing
less than a gentleman is truly suited for his unique responsibilities.

S.L.A. MARSHAL, 1950

O nly one officer was executed during the war for murder in the field.
Second Lt John Paterson had deserted his regiment and was a man on
the run. Faced with arrest, he chanced his luck and tried to shoot his way out
of trouble, killing the military policeman who had tried to arrest him. The
case is a strange one and elements of it were never explained at the trial.

On 6 April 1915 a 25-year-old storekeeper, John Henry Paterson, walked
into the recruiting office in Kingsway, Holborn, and signed on to join the
17th Battalion of the Middlesex Regiment, known as the Footballers' Battalion.[1] His papers show that he had been born in Bow, that he was single and that
his physical condition was good. After training, Paterson arrived in France
with the battalion on 17 November 1915.

In February 1916 Pte Paterson spent two weeks in hospital but by the time
that they moved to the Somme in July he had rejoined his unit. The 17th
Middlesex were not engaged in the 1st July attacks, but towards the end of
that month were involved in the heavy fighting for Delville Wood. On 29 July
the battalion war diarist wrote:

> Terrific artillery fire continued all day, we were relieved by 13th Essex at
> 9 p.m. took over our support line in Montauban Alley ... All ranks behaved
> with great gallantry. The devotion to duty was magnificent. The Division
> has been thanked for capturing the wood.[2]

Paterson's military history sheet shows that he was evacuated with shell shock
on that day, although his medical notes show that he was admitted to the XIII
Corps main dressing station with a gunshot wound to his neck. He was
evacuated to a base hospital and returned to his unit on 1 September. On

13 November in the attack on Beaumont Hamel he was wounded again: his medical notes describe this as a head wound, but his military history sheet describes him as suffering from that suspicious injury 'Gunshot wound left hand'. There is no explanation for this discrepancy in his records. On recovery he was sent to No. 41 Infantry Base Depot. Whilst there he applied for a commission, and whilst the War Office considered his application he was sent to training camp, and then in March returned to England to go to an officer cadet unit.[3]

His application for a commission was accepted in June 1917 and he was posted to the 3rd Battalion, Essex Regiment as a Second Lieutenant, but was sent to France to serve with the 1st Battalion. He served with this unit through the winter of 1917, but on 26 March 1918, when his unit was near Zillebeke, he disappeared. At first it was thought that he had been killed or wounded in the chaos of the Kaiser's offensives and his wife was sent a telegram to say that he was missing. Later it became apparent that he had deserted from his battalion.

In due course Paterson was found, and in trying to avoid arrest shot a military policeman. He was eventually captured and faced a GCM on 11 September 1918 on seven separate charges: murder, desertion and five charges of forgery. He was tried by a panel of five officers, with Brig. Gen. Lumley as president and Maj. Green of the Welch Regiment as Judge Advocate. Lt E. P. Walsh, a barrister in civilian life, defended Paterson.[4]

Lt Walsh applied to the court to have the murder charge tried separately, and for this charge to be taken first; the court acceded to this request.

The main prosecution witness was L Cpl Stockton of the Military Foot Police, who on 3 July 1918 was working with Detective Sgt Collison. It never became clear in the evidence whether the two policemen were specifically searching for Paterson (in which case their subsequent actions were bizarre) or whether they simply spotted him by chance. Both men were wearing artillery badges to disguise the fact that they were police and Stockton was not armed. During the trial he was asked about this and replied that although he normally carried a revolver, 'I was not carrying one that day as I was on a duty which made it dangerous to carry a revolver.' He added: 'It did not seem to me that the arresting of an absentee officer would be a particularly dangerous duty.'

Stockton gave evidence that at 6.30 p.m. on 3 July 1918 he saw a British officer with a woman at the wooden footbridge at Pont Coulogne, not far from Calais, and that he and Sgt Collison followed them towards Coulogne

Village. Collison had then gone up to the officer and told him that he matched the description of a wanted officer. On being asked his name, the officer said that he was Second Lt Barford of 1st Essex, but he could not prove his identity. The two policemen, Paterson and the woman then all set off for Beaumarais Camp but on the way the officer said to Collison: 'See here sergeant, I am Second Lt. Paterson; I think I am the officer whom you are looking for. I just want to go and have tea with this young lady in that house over there. Do you mind waiting about half-an-hour?' Amazingly, Collison agreed to wait. It was now about 7.30 p.m.

He kept watch on one corner of the house, whilst Stockton watched from the opposite side. About 8.45 p.m. Paterson came out, spoke to Stockton and then returned to the house. Then, at 9.20 p.m., Stockton saw Paterson and Collison talking together, and Collison called him to join them. As he was on his way over he heard a shot, and Collison said: 'What's that?' Stockton told the court that Paterson then pointed a revolver at Collison and fired. What happened next was disputed at the trial. Stockton's version of events was that he started to run for help and as he did so, Paterson fired at him. The NCO then called to two passing soldiers for help, and himself ran to Beaumarais to fetch a doctor.

Mademoiselle Duquenoy was the young lady who had been with Paterson. She confirmed most of the evidence given by Stockton, adding that the house where the incident occurred belonged to her father. She said that during the evening, Paterson had said: 'If they do not leave I will fire at them.' She had seen Paterson talking to the sergeant and heard a shot, and she saw that the officer had his revolver in his hand. She said that Paterson then dragged her away and that they went to Calais and spent the night in a hotel, when she 'then noticed that the accused was wounded in the leg near the private parts'. She was certain that Paterson had not fired at Cpl Stockton. Under cross-examination by the court she said that Paterson's trousers and pocket had a hole in them, and that his leg wound was quite deep.

Mademoiselle Duquenoy's sister gave evidence that she had seen Paterson talking to Sgt Collison, then heard an indistinct shot followed by a clearer second shot. Her father gave similar evidence, adding that he rushed outside to see to Collison. Paterson and Mlle Augustine Duquenoy spent two days at the hotel in Calais, after which they parted, and he went into hiding.

By the time that help arrived, Sgt Collison, DCM, was dead from a bullet which had passed through his lungs and heart.

On 22nd July 1918, 'acting on information received' (from where was not explained), the Chef de Service du Sûreté went to a house owned by a woman in St Omer and kept watch there. Just after 11 p.m. a British officer arrived and the translation in the summary of evidence provides a graphic description: 'Our three inspectors and ourselves jumped on him and mastered him quickly.'

The court then questioned Cpl Stockton further. The evidence now seemed to point to the fact that Paterson had accidentally fired his revolver when it was in his tunic pocket, wounding himself, and had then deliberately fired a second shot at Collison. Stockton alone alleged that he had heard a third shot fired. The implication was that after seeing Collison shot, Stockton ran away and later could only justify such an action by saying that he had also been fired at.

Paterson gave evidence in his own defence. He told the court that he had returned to England in February 1914 after a spell as a trader in West Africa. He said he had got into the habit of carrying a revolver whilst in Africa. He agreed that Cpl Stockton's statement was substantially correct, and said: 'I had told the sergeant who I was. I was under the impression that I was being arrested for desertion.' He explained that his revolver was prone to go off easily and that as he put his hand in his pocket the gun went off, wounding him. He then pulled it out of his pocket, and it went off again, hitting Collison. The unspoken implication was that both shots were accidental. If only two shots had been fired that night this defence was just about tenable; if, however, Stockton was right about the third shot, this destroyed Paterson's defence. It is possible that Paterson and Mlle Duquenoy worked out this story whilst in hiding at Calais and she persuaded her family to back up the idea that only two shots were fired. We shall now never know whether Stockton was mistaken, or whether the Duquenoy family committed perjury.

Paterson alleged that he only intended to frighten the policemen off with the revolver, and said: 'I did not wish to be taken that night.' He insisted that he did not fire at Stockton. Under cross-examination he admitted that 'Sgt Collison met his death as the result of a revolver shot fired by me', and emphasized that the shot was accidental, but said: 'I did not intend to give myself up that night.'

The prosecutor told the court: 'There is only one question for decision of the Court. The presumption is exceedingly strong that the shooting was committed with the intent of escaping arrest … from his own statement, he did not mean to be arrested that night.' In relation to Stockton's evidence, he said: 'The fact that Stockton may have been wrong about the third shot does not mean that his other evidence is at fault.'

Counsel for the accused told the court martial panel that there were three possible verdicts: murder, manslaughter or not guilty, and attempted to discredit Stockton's crucial evidence. The Judge Advocate then summed up: 'It having been admitted by the accused that Detective Sergeant Collison died as the result of a revolver shot fired by accused then the Court has to consider the circumstances under which that shot was fired. L. Cpl. Stockton was the only witness who saw the shot fired, but Mlle. Duquenoy saw him with the revolver in his hand immediately after the shot was fired.' After directing the court to the appropriate page of the *Manual of Military Law*, he pointed out that if the court had any doubt, the accused must have the benefit of it.

The court found Paterson guilty of murder, and then proceeded with the other six charges; Paterson pleaded guilty to the charge of desertion and the five charges of forgery. As a result of an amendment to Rules of Procedure, in consequence of Gen. Smith-Dorrien's concerns after the Byers case, despite the guilty plea the court proceeded to hear the evidence on the desertion charge.

Sgt Appleton of 1st Essex told the court that on 26 March 1918, Second Lt Paterson had been in charge of a working party on the Ypres front. They had left camp at about 5.30 p.m., and about half a mile beyond Shrapnel Corner, Paterson told the men to fall out as they were too early. At about 7 p.m. they moved off again, but shortly after this Paterson told the sergeant that he had lost his pocketbook and told him to wait with the men whilst he returned to find it. After about an hour the NCO sent back a runner, who found no sign of the officer; Sgt Appleton then went back again, thinking that the officer must have been wounded. Still finding no trace, the NCO phoned to the adjutant for advice. Another witness corroborated this evidence.

When asked about a defence, Paterson's counsel replied:

> The Court would realise that as both he (Counsel) and accused wished to enter a plea of guilty on this charge (but the Court refused to accept such a plea) it was impossible for him to deny the facts as proved by the prosecution.

Paterson was, unsurprisingly, sentenced to death and sentence was confirmed by Sir Douglas Haig on 20 September. Paterson faced a firing squad on 24 September 1918 and was buried at Terlichthun British Military Cemetery, whilst his victim, Sgt Harold Collison, is interred at Les Baraques Military Cemetery, Calais. Collison had joined the army in 1896, and re-enlisted during the war. He was an experienced policeman who had won the DCM under unusual circumstances earlier in 1918; the citation reads: 'for conspicuous gallantry and devotion to duty. He has served at the front during many engagements. His duties, which mainly consisted in making enquiries into alleged looting of the dead, took him frequently into positions of great personal danger.'[5] This brave police officer made a fatal mistake in allowing Paterson the chance of a last meal with his girlfriend.

From correspondence in Paterson's army records it appears that he married sometime between his enlistment and his desertion, and that his wife heard nothing of him between 26 March 1918 and his death.[6] After his arrest she must have been informed that he was no longer missing, as on 5 August she wrote to the Military Secretary to ask where she might write to her husband. The brief reply suggested that she should write c/o 1st Essex. However, in the chaos of war, different branches of the army organization failed to communicate. On 29 September, five days after his execution, Paterson's wife wrote both to the Essex Regiment at Warley and to the War Office, saying that her letters were still being returned 'not known' and that she was extremely anxious, not having heard from her husband for seven months. A few days later the Military Secretary wrote back to say that they had no further information, but he would instigate a special enquiry, and that her request for maintenance had been forwarded. By 23 October she had still not received any information and her brother wrote to the War Office to say that her letters were still being returned 'not known' and that she was desperate for information. A reply was sent on 27 October to say that 'everything that is possible is being done to trace Second Lieutenant Paterson, and immediately any news is received, Mrs Paterson will be at once informed'. The following day another letter followed: 'It is my painful duty ... to inform you that ... Second Lieutenant J H Paterson, Essex Regiment, has died on service in France on the 24th September 1918.'

If only Mrs Paterson had let sleeping dogs lie, she would have been spared the knowledge that her husband had been shot. She wrote, on black-bordered paper, to the Military Secretary on 20 November: 'I feel that I must ask if you can convey to me the principles by which he met his death and to whether he left any message for me as I am in the unfortunate position of knowing nothing whatever.' The army replied '... it was hoped that, as you had not ere this referred to this Office letter which conveyed to you the news that he died in France upon September 24 1918, you would not ask for any details'. The letter continued: 'However, as you do now ask it is with extreme grief that I am directed to tell you that he was shot at 6.27 a.m. upon that date consequent upon a sentence of death ...' Even now, the army did its best to conceal from her that her husband was a murderer, saying: 'He was found guilty of desertion, and other crimes.'

The final items in Paterson's file provide a coda: there is a press cutting from the *Daily Mail* of 28 January 1919 announcing the murder of Sgt Collison and stating that he had been 'murdered by a commissioned officer, who has since been dealt with in accordance with military law'. Finally, there is a bill from Paterson's tailors, dated 27 May 1919, relating to items he ordered when a cadet in 1917 and for which they were still awaiting payment.

The single most pressing question in this case is why Paterson was given a commission. He had a reasonable education and may have had some experience of handling men when in Africa but he had seen only brief active service as a private soldier and does not seem to have distinguished himself; in addition, he may have suffered from shell shock. Perhaps an army desperately short of junior officers after the death toll of the Somme was prepared to try almost any apparently suitable applicant or perhaps the checking procedures simply failed under wartime conditions.

CHAPTER 31

MUTINY!

Why does Colonel Grigsby refer to me to learn how to deal with mutineers? He should shoot them down where they stand.

LT GEN. THOMAS 'STONEWALL' JACKSON, 1862

If disobedience strikes at the very heart of an army's discipline, then mutiny is the gravest offence of all. Every experienced officer or NCO understands only too well the need to carry his men with him, and has done since time immemorial. Leadership, after all, implies 'followership'. Even the most professional specialist units like the British SAS are renowned for their open debates or 'Chinese Parliaments' to discuss the practicalities of any operation. Half-baked ideas from on high tend to get short shrift before experienced men will risk their lives; and always have, as any reading of Alexander the Great's campaigns proves. Fear of disobedience, particularly 'collective disobedience' (the official definition of mutiny), lies deeply buried in even the most successful warrior's psyche and sometimes haunts his nightmares.

Given the sheer scale of the killing in the period 1914–18 it is therefore astonishing just how little mutiny figures in the British Army during the First World War. The authoritarian nature of pre 1914 society, the common cause to throw the Hun off French soil and the shared acceptance of a code of national social values go a long way to explain this, but still do not fully account for the rarity of collective disobedience given the dangers and strains placed on men's lives in the front line. Such mutinies as there were tended to be found in the rear areas, not the combat units.

A comparison with other armies reinforces this view. Collective disobedience and mutiny crippled the French, German, Russian and Austro-Hungarian armies at one time or another during the Great War. Britain's army alone seems to have been strangely immune. According to the official records, only 1,800 men were charged with mutiny between 1914 and 1920.[1] When a comparison is made with, for example, Britain's French ally, the difference is

379

striking. The smallest estimate of French mutineers is 25,000.[2] Other French estimates are more damning. According to experts who have trawled all through the French sources, the true figure of French mutineers is nearer 40,000 in just one year, 1917.[3] More importantly, the French Army put down its mutinies with calculated ferocity. Over 400 soldiers – not always the ringleaders – were condemned to death, and over fifty executed in the summer of 1917 alone. During the 'Battles of the Frontiers' in August 1914 the French did not even keep a record of those they executed, and the willingness of Joffre, the French Commander-in-Chief, to enforce discipline by executing recalcitrant *poilus* at that time of crisis was legendary.

By comparison with this repression of mass indiscipline, the British Army charged only forty-two men with mutiny on the Western Front between 1914 and the beginning of 1918, and only three soldiers were actually executed for mutiny. Taken in context with the other armies engaged in the struggle this is a remarkable endorsement of the British Army's discipline and cohesion. Although there were numerous incidents of 'collective indiscipline' from summer 1918 onwards, these on examination were much more in the nature of 'strikes' than 'mutinies', and were (like the widespread soldiers' strikes in early 1919 and the Canadian mutiny at Kimmel, in Wales, in March 1919) more concerned with demobilization grievances than with refusing to fight. These grievances about living conditions and terms of service were very real, but can be found from the earliest days of the war, when several examples are recorded of soldiers effectively going 'on strike' over rotten food, poor accommodation or general administrative incompetence.[4]

For example, in late November 1914 five reservists of 3rd Battalion, the Dorsetshire Regiment were charged with mutiny after what appears to have been a drunken brawl near Upwey.[5] At Tidworth – then a hastily built collection of spartan wooden huts on Salisbury Plain – the sappers of 152nd Field Company Royal Engineers carried out a silent protest over bad rations in May 1915 that was effectively a mini-mutiny.[6]

By far the most serious mutiny was that of the 5th (Native) Light Infantry at Singapore in February 1915. Thirty-seven convicted mutineers were publicly shot, following a 'riot' which caused thirty-two European and fifty native deaths. The 5th Light Infantry suddenly erupted on the day of the Chinese New Year. Fuelled by a potent cocktail of fear of being posted, distrust of British intentions and nationalist fervour, the Indian soldiers broke out of their lines and ran amok. Bewildered German prisoners of war were set free and British and local Malays gunned down at random.[7]

The British authorities reacted swiftly and savagely. The Indian Mutiny was still a not too distant memory in 1915, and colonial citizens, armed sailors and British units slowly rounded up the mutineers. At least fifty-six were killed in the process. Eventually no fewer than 202 men of the 5th Light Infantry were court-martialled and given a remarkably impartial trial considering the circumstances and nervousness in the colony. Forty-seven men were sentenced to death of which ten sentences were later commuted. The two ringleaders were executed by firing squad on 23 February 1915, and a second firing party of 105 British infantry dispatched twenty-one mutineers in full public gaze.[8]

A subsequent board of inquiry found that there had been no complicity between the German prisoners of war or internees and the 5th Light Infantry. The true cause appears to have been fears and rumours that the regiment was being shipped far from home to fight for the Raj, fuelled by internal dissension, rivalries and religious tensions. Although an entirely Muslim regiment, the 5th Light Infantry was an unusually mixed regiment in terms of tribe and class, with the Musselmans, Jats, Pathans and much despised Ranghars (considered by the Pathans as little better than gypsy horse thieves) all fighting amongst themselves over domestic class issues, even down to the appointment of the senior Indian 'Subadar Major'.

Over this potent brew of nationalistic tribal rivalries presided a weak team of British officers. The CO had been described as a 'sleepy easy going fellow' and after the mutiny it became apparent that the officers' mess was also riddled with faction and intrigue and that officers were arguing amongst themselves in public. Eventually the 5th Light Infantry was split up and its officers posted, but they had presided over the worst mutiny in the British services in the First World War.[9]

There were effectively only three major mutinies recorded among front line British units of the BEF on the Western Front: 12th Battalion, South Wales Borderers in January 1916; a specialist mortar unit from 38th (Welsh) Division in September 1917; and the well-known uprising at the notorious 'Bull Ring' complex of training camps near Etaples in September 1917. To these three incidents must be added a serious case of collective refusal to obey orders at the Blargies Military Prison Camp near Rouen in 1916 and the well-known mass mutiny in October 1918 of 1st Battalion, Australian Expeditionary Force, who were protesting about always being used as the BEF's shock troops.

The three soldiers executed for mutiny were a New Zealander, Pte John Braithwaite, Gunner Lewis of the Royal Field Artillery, like Braithwaite found guilty of mutiny in 1916 in separate incidents at the Blargies Military Prison, and Cpl Jesse Short of the Northumberland Fusiliers, who was part of the drunken rioting mob that took over part of the Etaples Base Camp during the famous 'Bull Ring Mutiny' in September 1917, later popularized in TV's *The Monocled Mutineer*, which owed more to fiction than to truth.[10]

There can be little doubt that No. 1 Military Prison, Blargies North Camp, Abancourt was a grim place in summer 1916. Behind belts of barbed wire was a small stockade of corrugated iron housing twenty-five bell tents, a punishment cell block and up to 300 disaffected prisoners, all condemned by court martial to varying terms of hard labour. They had all been transferred from the proper military prison at Rouen to the tented stockade, and conditions were extremely poor. This was, to some extent, deliberate policy by the BEF 'A' Staff, to deter men from thinking that prison was a soft option compared with the front line.

The convicted soldiers' main task was to provide labouring parties for the Royal Engineers and to help move ammunition at the nearby railway junction. As the hot summer of 1916 wore on, trouble began to brew. Water and washing facilities were few and even latrines were restricted, with only twelve to fourteen seats for up to 300 men, many suffering from acute diarrhoea.[11]

The arrival of a group of thirty-five unruly Australian prisoners earlier in August was the catalyst for trouble. In typical Anzac fashion they were surly and truculent and had, on 12 August, refused to obey orders, forcing the camp commandant, Capt. Barker, to make a number of concessions over razors, washing facilities and living conditions. The British prisoners saw a precedent being established. However, there was a difference: Australians were not subject to the ultimate sanction, the death penalty.

After lunch on 14 August 1916, sixty-seven men of the British contingent refused to march off to work. The protest swelled and the deputy governor and camp commandant was sent for. He ordered the recalcitrant prisoners to be handcuffed as a punishment, and further troubles erupted. One Staff Sgt Aves of the guard force began handcuffing a private with unnecessary force, and as the soldier screamed and fainted, Aves was surrounded, abused and intimidated by prisoners, including Gunner Lewis. With the compound on the verge of riot, the alarmed guards drew their revolvers and levelled rifles at the prisoners. Capt. Barker stopped the handcuffing and ordered the rioters to move to another part of the camp. Jeering, the sixty men shambled off to six segregated bell tents to spend the afternoon lolling about in the sun.

Next morning the camp was paraded for work. After a period of hesitancy, none marched off. More guards were called, arrests made and on 5 October 1916 seven men stood trial for mutiny. Such was the bare story of the mutiny.[12]

At the GCM held at Rouen from 5 to 9 October 1916, seven men were collectively tried on a charge of

> Joining in a mutiny in Forces belonging to His Majesty's Regular Forces, in that they at Blargies, on August 14th 1916, joined in a mutiny by combining amongst themselves and with other soldiers to refuse to work, to resist arrest and to threaten violence to Captain A Barker, Sergeant Major G Gill and Staff Sergeant SV Aves, their superior officers in the execution of their office.

The charge sheet was drawn up by none other than the Director of Military Prisons and the court was convened by the Inspector General of Communications for the BEF, a full lieutenant general. The BEF clearly took the Blargies mutiny very seriously indeed. The court martial of the Blargies mutineers was certainly no drumhead court. From the court martial papers it is quite clear that the accused were represented by a specified 'defence counsel'.[13]

First to testify was Sgt Maj. Gill of the Military Provost Staff Corps. He swore that the mutineers had 'deliberately gathered in the rear of the parade' as a separate group, after the lunch meal on 14 August. He said that they had refused to obey orders and march off to work, and after the biddable prisoners had marched away, he 'went to the party in the rear and asked them what was the matter'. They began shouting and demanding that 'the chains were taken off', a reference to the restrictions placed on those prisoners who were undergoing extra punishment for attempting to escape. Gill, an experienced provost sergeant major, then drew a clear legal line, ordering 'any man refusing to work to take one pace forward'. He testified: 'They all did so.' The die was cast – the sixty-seven had now refused to obey a direct and legal order to work. Collectively they had disobeyed a lawful command.

Recognizing the seriousness of the situation, Gill sent for the officer in charge, Capt. Barker. Barker told the assembly to parade at 7.00 a.m, next morning 'at the office' if they had any complaints, and to get back to work. According to Gill's evidence 'Gunner Lewis ... stepped forward and demanded in an insubordinate way that the chains be taken off ...' Supported by another of the accused, Driver Peden, the men continued to argue with the captain. Barker then ordered 'those men willing to work take one pace forward'. None of the mutineers complied, and Gunner Lewis shouted to his fellow mutineers to stand still. Capt. Barker then ordered *all* sixty-seven to be placed in irons, ordered up an armed escort with bayonets fixed and directed the whole group to be handcuffed, one at a time. There was then a violent struggle as the angry soldiers refused to be handcuffed. One in particular, Trooper Thom, appears to have been handcuffed so tightly by Staff Sgt Aves as to make his wrists bleed and the situation deteriorated as he screamed and fainted. The guards were rushed as another of the seven accused, Pte Delaney, shouted: 'Let's do the buggers in!' and 'I am here for fuck all!', according to Gill's evidence.

Sgt Maj. Gill's testimony was damning. Although he was cross-examined by several of the accused, his story remained both clear-cut and unshaken. Moreover, his basic narrative about the facts was unchallenged and broadly supported by the other witnesses. Most damaging of all, he identified Lewis as the ringleader or spokesman of the group.

In his defence, Lewis challenged this interpretation of events, claiming that he had actually been asked to speak up on behalf of the group by Sgt Maj. Gill. Reading between the lines of the court martial evidence, the most likely explanation is that the group were shouting at the captain and human nature and common sense led the sergeant major to tell them to shut up, and then invite the most vociferous, Lewis, to state his grievances. On his own admission, Lewis was no reluctant spokesman.

Capt. Barker's testimony confirmed Gill's story, adding only that when he ordered the first of the group handcuffed they began '... booing and hissing ... and shouting, "release him!" I ordered the staff to draw their revolvers ...' He also added that when the provost sergeant did so, the mutineers shouted: 'Shoot! We are not bloody well afraid.' He went on: 'To save bloodshed I ordered that the handcuffing should be stopped.' On that hot August afternoon in 1916 it must have been an ugly scene in the Blargies compound. Significantly, Capt. Barker singled out Gunner Lewis and Pte McCorkindale as the most prominent, adding: 'Gunner Lewis in particular was very insubordinate ...' Under cross-examination by the accused, Barker testified that he 'considered Pte McCorkindale and Gunner Lewis were self-elected spokesmen'.

The next witness was the guard NCO, Staff Sgt Aves, who actually began the handcuffing of the group and whose role appears to have been provocative. After confirming the facts of the parade he went into some detail about the handcuffing: 'On proceeding to start handcuffing ... McCorkindale, Lewis and Garden demanded in an insubordinate manner that the handcuffs be taken off ...', which as he had just handcuffed Thom so tightly that his wrists were bleeding is hardly surprising. When Aves refused to comply, he told the court, these three had shouted at him: 'Fuck Captain Barker's orders, he is fuck all now, you'll take your orders or we'll murder you, you fucking bastard!' or words to that effect.

Aves was cross-examined closely by the accused men personally. Lewis asked the staff sergeant if he, Aves, had invited Lewis to 'continue being the spokesman'. Aves, unsurprisingly, claimed to have no memory of such a request, although other prisoners testified that Aves had effectively encouraged the mutineers to keep their protest going later in the afternoon. Trooper Thom, the soldier who was handcuffed so tightly 'that his hands were covered in blood', which caused the men to riot, asked no questions of the prosecution witnesses and, if we read between the lines of the court martial, appears to have been a quiet and frightened man.

Other witnesses confirmed Lewis's role in the events of 14 August. In particular he was specifically identified as the one who extended his arms and shouted: 'Stand fast!' when Capt. Barker invited those willing to work to take a pace forward.

Lewis, however, was not alone. In particular, another of the accused, Pte Murphy, had also been identified as a ringleader once the group had been put into the separate bell tents, going round the group saying: 'Stick together boys.' More damning was a claim made by one of the prosecution witnesses that it had been Lewis and McCorkindale who had led the concerted rush on the guards when the latter drew their revolvers. An unequivocal pattern of Lewis's involvement at virtually every stage clearly emerged from the prosecution's case.

The next day, 6 October, the court heard the defence. Lewis, on oath, was taken through his evidence by his defence counsel, or prisoner's friend. Lewis's defence was simple. He claimed to have been invited by the captain and sergeant major to speak up on behalf of the group. 'He (Captain Barker) said he could not understand all the people shouting at once and he would like to have one spokesman … Sergeant Major Gill picked me out.'

Lewis further testified that Staff Sgt Aves had pleaded with him later that afternoon in the bell tent area to go back to work, and that he, Lewis, had told Aves that he did not really want to be spokesman for the group. Lewis also spelled out the very real grievances of the men: 'Filthy, lousy clothing, no soap to wash, lousy blankets, dirty mess tins, filthy tents …' plus excessive and harsh punishment. He also complained that there was not enough time even to use the latrines. These conditions, whilst undoubtedly appalling, would not have been unfamiliar to any occupant of a front line trench in August 1916 – a fact of which the court would have been only too well aware in considering the merits of the prisoners' case.

In the defence testimonies of the other accused, one in particular pushed

Lewis even further into the limelight. Pte Garden swore on oath that Sgt Maj. Gill had said to Capt. Barker: 'This is a man who seems to have something to say …', indicating Lewis. Garden also swore that Staff Sgt Aves had walked round the tents in the afternoon 'inciting the men to stick together' and to hold out for their grievances. The court martial transcript has been heavily underlined under both Lewis's and Aves's names. In evidence corroborated by other defence witnesses Delaney, one of the accused, testified that 'Lewis was selected by the men on parade as their spokesman.' Remembering that the traditional sergeant major's challenge to a 'mouthy' and insubordinate soldier has always been: 'You've got a lot to say for yourself, lad,' the evidence of the court martial papers seems clear: Lewis was one of the ringleaders and a far from reluctant spokesman for the group. His principal partner in crime seems to have been McCorkindale. Authority was unlikely to warm to such individuals.

The counsel for the accused, Capt. J. W. Lees of the South Staffords, summoned all four principal prosecution witnesses back to the stand and, from the trial proceedings, clearly gave them a hard time. From the cross-examination, however, it is apparent that the facts of the basic story remained unchanged.

The Judge Advocate then summed up, pointing out (doubtless with one eye on the inevitable inquiry into the harsh treatment of Pte Thom and the generally appalling conditions at the camp revealed at the court martial) that 'provocation by a superior, or the existence of a grievance is no justification for mutiny'. Perhaps because of this tacit judicial admission of extenuating circumstances he stressed the seriousness of the charge and emphasized the role of the ringleaders, i.e. all the accused, with the exception of Pte Thom.

Counsel for the prisoners then addressed the court. He laid great emphasis on the hellhole that was Blargies, stating: 'the story makes me earnestly hope that there are few places like Abancourt prison camp'. He stressed that some of the accused had been 'deliberately picked out by certain prison staff to act as spokesmen, thus at once constituting them as ringleaders …'

Ominously, the prisoner's friend singled out Thom and Murphy as being effectively blameless, leaving the court to draw its own conclusions on Delaney, McCorkindale and Lewis, merely adding that 'the case that they were ringleaders was not established'. Finally, the defending officer made a revealing peroration:

> I would say that all the accused have been in the trenches and that they are all, in the eyes of the service, young men. They are all volunteers.

I ask the Court to take into consideration these facts and to make every allowance for the somewhat doubtful benefit of a soldiers' friend.

I further ask the Court to seriously consider, as I believe myself, that this unfortunate affair was a stupid mistake and a technical offence which the conduct of the Australians was responsible for.

The court was having none of it. By October 1916 as the 'big push' on the Somme ground to a standstill in the mud and disillusion of yet another winter coming, Haig and GHQ were nervous: nervous of failure, nervous of a breakdown. Dissent was to be punished ruthlessly, a view understood by every subordinate in the vast machine that was now the BEF. All seven defendants were found guilty of mutiny and sentenced to death, with the exception of the hapless Thom (whose only 'crime' appeared to have been resisting the lacerations of too-small handcuffs), who received five years' penal servitude, later reduced to two years, by the commander-in-chief.

Lt Col. Gilbert Mellor, DJAG at GHQ, submitted the court martial papers to the C.-in-C. on 19 October, with a clear recommendation that all the death sentences be commuted to ten years' penal servitude. He also urged Haig to reflect on Staff Sgt Aves's dubious conduct in encouraging the soldiers' grievances and the soldiers' complaints about excessive punishment, although he pointed out that the latter had been 'authorised by the Director of Prisons'.

Within a week the C.-in-C. had replied. Lewis's record of service showed that he had been court-martialled twice before: once in June 1915, when he had been given a suspended sentence of six months' hard labour for absence, and once earlier in 1916, when he had been given a year's imprisonment for theft. Haig confirmed Lewis's sentence but reprieved all the others, who were shipped to England to begin varying terms of prison sentence ranging from fifteen years' penal servitude downwards.

Gunner Lewis was shot at Rouen on 29 October 1916. His fault appears to have been that he undoubtedly was one of the ringleaders and that his record – of two previous convictions by courts martial – was bad. His guilt as a mutineer seems beyond doubt, so his sentence, by the standards of 1916, would appear to be justified. McCorkindale, Delaney and Murphy would probably have counted themselves lucky to be pardoned by Haig – they were equally guilty and nearly as implicated. The hapless Thom appears to have been particularly hard done by. Today Lewis lies buried in the CWGC plot of the vast French cemetery, St Sever, at Rouen alongside thousands of his comrades who died as a result of wounds received in battle.

A curious fictional parallel exists for the Blargies riot. In 1965 Sean Connery made one of his finest and least-known films, *The Hill*, a grim *film noir* about a British military prison camp in the Second World War. Its story strikes an eerie resonance with the camp at Blargies revealed by the Rouen court martial of October 1916 and gives a good representation of what life must have been like in a British military prison in the first half of the twentieth century.[14]

Close to Lewis's grave lies that of another soldier shot for mutiny in a separate incident at Blargies. Pte John (Jack) Braithwaite of the New Zealand division was a 35-year-old journalist from Dunedin, shot on the same day as Lewis, the only one of the thirty-four New Zealanders charged with mutiny to be executed. Braithwaite was in Blargies jail because he had been convicted three times by court martial since he arrived in Egypt in February 1916. On 12 June 1916 a court martial found him guilty of three charges: absence, lying to an officer and forging a leave pass. For these offences he was awarded the relatively mild sentence of sixty days' FP No. 2.

By 7 July the ex-journalist had reoffended and was again court-martialled. This time the court martial was less lenient and sentenced him to two years' hard labour and to be deported back to New Zealand – the ultimate public disgrace for any robust NZ soldier in the Great War. This time, Braithwaite deserted and went on the run. Caught and tried, he was sentenced to a further two years on 19 July and sent to Blargies.[15]

The crime that brought Braithwaite to a firing squad had nothing to do with Gunner Lewis and the British mutiny of 14 August. On 28 August, two weeks after the British mutiny, an Australian, Pte Little, was showering in the Anzac compound at Blargies when the water stopped. Turning to the provost staff NCO he shouted: 'Do you call this a fucking hot bath?' The NCO, Sgt Shearing, told Little to behave himself and was treated to a torrent of abuse. As a result, the provost NCO ordered Little to be arrested.

In true Anzac fashion Little went to the guard tent cursing the NCO and demanding justice, plus, more importantly, 'his dinner'. In his evidence at the court martial the company sergeant major testified that he saw Braithwaite drag Little away from Staff Sgt Shearing, who was trying to make an arrest. The CSM also said:

> Pte Little was taken by Pte Braithwaite to his tent ... The Australian and New Zealand section was in an unruly state. It would not have been possible for the Staff NCOs to have gone among the Australians without risking bloodshed.

The sergeant major's words understate the gravity of the incident, which was now assuming the proportions of a riot, with the Anzac prisoners about to attack the British guards. Three other Australians now moved in and stood around Shearing, defying him and preventing his getting to Little.

At his court martial Braithwaite claimed he had in fact been shielding Little from more trouble and was trying to calm him down. However, the five British officers at the court martial were unconvinced and had little patience with riots and disturbances amongst convicted criminals at Blargies prison while their colleagues were fighting and dying on the Somme. They found all four defendants guilty of mutiny and sentenced them to death.

Despite a moving and evidently sincere plea in mitigation from Braithwaite:

> I am not a born soldier, just a Bohemian journalist ... who answered the
> call ... Unfortunately I have made a serious mess of things, and where
> I came to win honour and glory, I have won only shame, dishonour and
> everlasting disgrace ...[16]

the Inspector General of Communications, Lt Gen. Clayton, forwarded the findings for confirmation to Haig's GHQ though with a recommendation for mercy, adding: 'As regards Pte Braithwaite I think that you may like me to draw your attention to the fact that the evidence in this case might be considered to bear out the accused's version ...'[17]

Haig disregarded the recommendation. Whilst the three Australians' sentences were commuted to two years' hard labour, in accordance with what seems to have been a deliberate policy of 'pardoning all except one', Braithwaite's sentence was confirmed.[18] The New Zealander was shot at 6 a.m. on 29 October 1916 at Rouen and he too lies in the CWGC plot at St Sever, not far from Lewis.

The second British soldier to be executed for mutiny was, in many ways, a much more clear-cut case. By 1917 the British Army in France had, like all bureaucracies, institutionalized its various administrative systems. Far behind the lines, near Boulogne, the BEF's principal entrepôt, a vast network of camps, dumps, depots and hospitals had been established amongst the sand dunes on the northern edge of Etaples. This conglomeration of tents, huts, training grounds and railways was home to no fewer than 50,000 men in transit. It was the British Army's biggest base depot in France.

At the heart of the complex was a vast, flat, sandy beach area known as the 'Bull Ring'. This was used as an infantry training area to put soldiers arriving in France through their paces before sending them up to the front. Even old soldiers, wounded and returning from England, or decorated for valour, had to undergo 'refresher training' at one of the Etaples Infantry Base Depots before rejoining their regiments. This was not as unreasonable as it may seem. The technology of war accelerates change more than any other, and so new techniques had to be taught, returning soldiers had to be brought up to date with the latest German weapons (such as improved poison gases), and newcomers to France had to be given some awareness of the realities of trench warfare before being sent up the line. However, as most of the NCO instructors seemed obsessed by spit and polish and the impracticalities of bayonet fighting, even their training was treated with derision by experienced hands.

The main problem at Etaples appears to have been that the conditions for the thousands of soldiers marching off to train at 6 a.m. every morning in field service marching order were worse than either barrack or even trench life. Their instructors, a group of NCOs with yellow armbands – and therefore known as canaries – were universally detested. They in their turn were over-zealous in pursuit of their duties, treating experienced and be-medalled veterans 'out since 14' and newcomers to France alike, as raw recruits to be shouted at, chased and worked hard. To make matters worse, many of the 'canaries' had never been in the front line themselves or seen any real action and were seen as clinging onto 'cushy billets' as a way of avoiding the dangers of the real trenches. For a decorated veteran returning from hospital, to be abused by such a creature must have been hard to take, to say the least. Add to this bad food, no recreational facilities after work (and the out-of-bounds town of Etaples with its bright lights, bars and girls just the other side of the river), plus an officious and heavy-handed force of military policemen who had never seen any front line action – and any experienced provost marshal would have advised his base commander that he was sitting on a potential powder keg should anything go wrong.

It did. Once again Anzac troops were involved, albeit indirectly. Australian troops had a curious reputation on the Western Front. Whilst no one doubted their ferocity in action or their fighting ability, they were, by British Army standards, woefully undisciplined. Australian bloodlust in the attack was legendary and they frequently took no prisoners, as at Polygon Wood near Ypres in the final assault towards Passchendaele. Here they encountered the Prussian Guard, whom they had fought before on the Somme at Pozières the year before. Even the official communiqué admitted: 'this ANZAC Corps took no prisoners'. In his well-known account in *Goodbye to All That* Robert Graves claimed that an Australian had boasted of robbing a dozen German prisoners and then killing them all in cold blood with grenades.

These excesses were not just confined to the battlefield. Stories of Australian lawlessness and misconduct abound and a host of first-hand contemporary references detail the lengthy list of their misdeeds – which were not limited to drunken sprees in estaminet behind the lines, either.[19]

This cavalier attitude to formal discipline was reflected in their remarkable record of disciplinary infringements and imprisonment. By 1918 nine Australians per thousand were in prison for military crimes, some of them extremely serious; for the rest of the Dominion troops (New Zealanders, South Africans and Canadians) the figure was only 1.6 per thousand. Australians were even bold enough to cut down British prisoners undergoing field punishment and dare the military police to try to re-imprison them. The Australians were not just tough and resourceful; they were also brazen in their defiance of authority, flaunting their own casual discipline.

One of the big differences appears to have been the absence of the death penalty. Alone of the troops under the command of the BEF, Australians were effectively exempt from capital punishment. Although 129 Australians were sentenced to death in the war, including 119 deserters, none was executed. The confirming authority for sentence was the Governor General of Australia under the 1903 Australian Defence Act, and although the British C.-in-C. Haig, made several strenuous pleas for the death sentence to be enforced on the bolshy Australians, for domestic Australian political reasons the penalty was never enforced. Whatever the reasons, wherever Anzac troops gathered in a gang out of the line there was usually crime, disorder and trouble.[20]

On 9 September 1917 a New Zealand gunner called Healey was arrested by the military police as he tried to slip back into the Etaples camp base after overstaying his local leave. The MPs marched him off, and a jeering crowd of bored, off-duty soldiers soon formed outside the makeshift guardroom. The situation began to get ugly, with soldiers jostling the policemen. One of the regimental police fired a revolver to scare off the crowd, accidentally hitting and killing a Cpl Wood of the Gordon Highlanders. Infuriated, the assembled soldiers went for the MPs. Faced with an angry crowd of young men, mainly Scots and Anzac soldiers with their blood up and quite clearly determined to lynch them on the spot, the MPs fled. Order broke down and the mob surged towards the town, looking for revenge, female company, or a run ashore in one of the off-limits bars. As night fell the soldiers dispersed and it appeared that the disturbances were over.

Next day, however, after work, the crowd gathered again at the three-arched bridge leading to the town and, led by Scots soldiers seeking revenge, forced their way across into the town by sheer weight of numbers. The base area commander, Brig. Andrew Thompson, later remonstrated with the crowds of cheerful, drunken soldiers, who were looking for a bottle of wine, or an MP to kick, and managed to persuade them to disperse.[21]

Unfortunately, a 'pattern of leisure activity' appears to have now been established. On 11 September 1917, the third day of the troubles, the usual crowd of soldiers, again with many Scots well to the fore, assembled at about four in the afternoon and rushed the bridge over the River Canche. The picket guarding the crossing was simply brushed aside by a cheering crowd calling on the assembled throng 'to release the MPs' prisoners' and storming off towards the fleshpots of Etaples. One of the picket later claimed in a newspaper story after the war that the mob was essentially good-humoured.[22]

Good-humoured or not, the military authorities were by now seriously alarmed by the momentum of events and the breakdown of discipline and order. Extra troops were called in, live ammunition issued to guards, and 'officer patrols' were established in an attempt to contain the disorder.

Cpl Jesse Short of 24th Battalion Northumberland Fusiliers was one of those involved in the collective disorder of 11 September. After a scuffle on the Canche bridge during one of the evening disturbances he was arrested by the guard picket and charged with mutiny. The very next day he faced an FGCM. The court martial was convened by Brig. Gen. Thompson, Commandant, Etaples Base, and consisted of two experienced majors and a captain, all from the staffs of the various infantry base depots in the area. The charge sheet states that Cpl Short was charged with

> Endeavouring to persuade persons in His Majesty's Forces to join in a mutiny, in that he at Etaples on 11th September 1917, endeavoured to persuade a picquet not to listen to their officers but to lay down their arms and go with him, referring to the officer in charge of the picquet, said to the picquet, 'You ought to get a rope tie it round his neck with a stone and throw him into the river,' or words to that effect.[23]

The case against Short was fairly straightforward and graphically narrated by the evidence of the picket commander on that fateful evening, Capt. E. F. Wilkinson of the West Yorkshire Regiment. He had been posted on the Canche bridge with a mixed picket or guard force of soldiers from the West Yorkshires, the Manchester Regiment and some Canadians. In his own testimony:

At about 9.10 p.m. about 70 or 80 men with notice boards torn up from the camps and waving flags which were handkerchiefs of all colours including red attached to sticks approached me. These men pushed through – the picquet practically standing to one side. But 4 officers who stood out were also pushed aside. The picquet was absolutely unreliable at that moment, so I called the officers together and made them fall their men in by regiments, then addressed the picquets and whilst I was doing so … the accused came back from the crowd of men and told (the picquet) not to listen to me, and said, 'what you want to do to that bugger is to put a stone round his neck and throw him in the river …'

Wilkinson said that Short then moved on, giving the captain 'time to get the men in hand' and detailing an NCO and four men to arrest Short if he came back.

Foolishly Short did come back and was, in Capt. Wilkinson's words, 'quickly and quietly arrested'. despite evidence from another officer that Short resisted arrest and gave a false name, Davidson.

Wilkinson's testimony was supported by four other witnesses, including Pte Bielby of the West Yorks, a sentry on the bridge, who added:

I was one of the picquet … The accused came to the bridge and started using abusive language. He said to the officer in charge of the picquet 'fuck him – if we want to rush the Bridge Picquet, we will rush it!'

Faced with this barrage of evidence, Short's defence was essentially that he had been drunk at the time and presumably therefore not responsible for the gravity of his actions. It was to no avail. Several of the witnesses believed he was lucid and not drunk, and there can be little doubt, reading the contemporary record, that the mutiny at Etaples severely rattled some officers at GHQ.[24]

Haig himself may have felt the need for exemplary action, fresh in the knowledge that both the French and Russian Armies had recently suffered serious mutinies. On 30 September 1917 he confirmed the death sentence on Short and on 4 October the soldier was executed. He lies buried in the large Boulogne Eastern CWGC cemetery, the last British mutineer to be executed in the Great War. Of the fifty-odd men court-martialled at Etaples during the weeks of rioting (which was finally solved by posting most of the men away from Etaples and on to their units), only four were charged with mutiny, and Cpl Short was the only man to be executed.

Although the Etaples mutiny was undoubtedly a 'collective disobedience', it was never a serious or rebellious threat to the BEF's fighting capability:

> Though crowds of soldiers chased military policemen and regularly broke out of camp, guns were not deployed by the rioters, no general harassment of officers was reported, routine training continued, trains continued to operate ... And absenteeism was minimal ... Haig attached great significance to the testimony of a couple of junior officers who claimed ... that Red Flags were trailed by rioters and dignified Short's drunken abuse as 'Socialist rhetoric'.[25]

This seems a fair assessment of the facts, and Short may have been unfortunate and the victim of a rushed court martial by nervous senior officers anxious to restore order and stop trouble spreading. It is important to remember that the French Army had mutinied *en masse* in the spring and summer of 1917. The facts of the French mutinies were the biggest single secret known to the British senior commanders, who were terrified that the Germans might learn of them. With this background, the British generals may have had good cause to be worried about an outbreak of the French troubles in their own ranks. In this climate – given the mass of men rioting in Etaples during those chaotic days in September 1917 – Short may have been just plain unlucky to have been arrested on the Canche bridge that September night. That he was guilty of mutinous conduct there can be no doubt. The fact is, however, that the British Army appears to have been remarkably free from any serious mutiny during the fighting on the Western Front and seems to have shown unusual clemency compared with the other warring armies.

However, this clemency did not extend to the various colonial labour corps. Throughout the war there were various incidents involving native workers recruited from the British Empire and from China and brought to France to carry out basic pioneer and labouring duties.

In particular, throughout 1917 there was a series of incidents amounting to withdrawal of labour, mutinous conduct and strikes by the disaffected 'native' contingents. The South African Native Labour Corps rioted in spring 1917, and in their turn the Chinese Coolies and Egyptian Labour Corps rebelled against officious and insensitive white officers and NCOs, or even their own compatriots. The army's insensitive imperialist attitudes, common at the time, cannot have helped. For example, at Camp Fournier near Marseilles on 16 September 1917 the men of the Egyptian Labour Corps No. 71 unit rose up against their British officers in a dispute over an unauthorized extension of their contracts and what appears to have been religious animosity. At the high point of the riot, Mahmoud Mahomed Ahmed hit an officer with a stick, shouting: 'Take that, you dog of a Christian!' This was a fatal mistake. Ahmed was subject to British military law.[26]

Eventually the disturbances were put down by Indian and British units. No. 385 Labourer Ahmed was subsequently charged with 'striking his superior officer', 'intent to murder' and 'joining in a disturbance of a mutinous nature'. Ahmed made a spirited defence and claimed:

My Pasha said that my [work] agreement would only be for seven months … (we) had completed our agreements. The reply [we] got was, 'you sons of dogs will be kept here by force'.

Unsurprisingly, this remark (by Foreman Sergeant Sellek) was the spark that started the riot. However, the court was unimpressed and found Ahmed guilty of striking his superior officer and mutinous conduct, both of which he effectively admitted. The sentence was confirmed by the Commander-in-Chief, far to the north at Montreuil, on 5 October 1917 – the day after Jesse Short's execution – and Ahmed was executed by firing squad on 10 October.

Ahmed's judicial execution was not the last death amongst mutinous native labourers. The army seems to have exercised authority over non-white mutineers with naked force, and before the Director of Labour was replaced in February 1918 there were at least ten 'fatal incidents' involving native workers. In one particularly unpleasant affair near Locre in Belgium, men of the Royal Welch Fusiliers were ordered to round up 'escaped' Chinese labourers and shot and killed between three and eight of them.[27]

That we find such behaviour and attitudes shocking nowadays is indicative of just how far society has changed in the last eighty years. But to Imperial Man the native labour force was regarded as almost a subspecies of humanity, 'lesser breeds without the law'. Whilst mutiny from a British soldier was never tolerated, at least he got a fair trial by the standards of the day.

Considering that 5,363,352 men served in the British Army during the First World War, it is astonishing just how few mutinies appear to have taken place, and equally astonishing that only 1,132 men were charged with mutiny on active service.[28] That speaks volumes for the army's discipline. That only three soldiers were executed for this most serious of military crimes speaks volumes for its humanity by the standards of the day.[29]

CHAPTER 32

THE LAST EXECUTIONS

Law cannot persuade where it cannot punish.

THOMAS FULLER, 1732

Two men were shot for desertion during the very last days of the war: Pte Louis Harris of the West Yorkshire Regiment and Pte Ernest Jackson of the Royal Fusiliers were both shot on 7 November 1918, as the war drew to a close.

Pte Jackson, serving with the 24th Battalion Royal Fusiliers, was a 32-year-old conscript who was possibly serving his country reluctantly. He had joined the army in July 1916 and had gone to France in November that year. Apart from two entries on his conduct sheet for minor offences, he seems to have served adequately until 13 April 1917, when he went missing from his unit and was arrested in St Pol twenty-eight hours later. For this apparently brief absence he was sentenced to two years' imprisonment with hard labour. Unusually, for reasons which are not now apparent, the sentence was not immediately suspended and Jackson served sixteen months in prison before he was released under the Suspension of Sentences Act and returned to his battalion on 19 August 1918.[1]

Only a few weeks later Pte Jackson went missing again. On 29 September 1918 he was at his battalion transport lines near Flesquières, sick. Although he was seen during the morning, when Sgt Knappett, the orderly sergeant, called the roll during the afternoon Jackson was found to be missing. Sgt Knappett subsequently told the court martial that Jackson had not reported sick but was at the transport lines by order of the MO, implying that he would have been sent, with other sick men, to the field ambulance on the following day.

The NCO told the court that he did not see Jackson again until he was handed over, under arrest, on 3 October. Later the same day the prisoner was put into the charge of Cpl Baker, who took him back to his company at Noyelles and handed him over to Sgt Fielden. At the trial no evidence was given to show when or how Jackson was arrested, a surprising omission on a capital charge so late in the war.

On 4 October 1918 the battalion was in support, about 3,000 yards behind the front line, at Noyelles. At 1.45 p.m. Sgt Fielden looked for his prisoner but could not find him. On 8 October the NCO found Jackson's arms and equipment in a nearby shelter.

L Cpl Cox of the military police had been on duty at Doullens on 5 October 1918 when he saw Jackson and asked him what he was doing. As he was not satisfied with the answer he arrested him. He told the court: 'Accused seemed to be confused but otherwise quite ordinary. He did not ask for the aid post. He was wearing a Royal Fusiliers badge.'

As a result of his actions, Jackson faced an FGCM, on three charges:

1. When on Active Service absenting himself without leave in that he on 29th September 1918, absented himself without leave from Transport Lines near Flesquieres until reporting to the APM 2nd Division on 1st October 1918.
2. 4th October 1918. When on Active Service, deserting His Majesty's Service.
3. When on Active Service, on 4th October 1918, shamefully casting away his arms, ammunition and equipment in the presence of the enemy.

In his defence Jackson told the court that on the 29th he had been sick with rheumatism and that his leg had become bad. He had been unable to find the sergeant, so he had gone to an aid post where the MO gave him 'medicine and duty'. On 1 October the doctor, who must have had suspicions about Jackson's 'illness', handed him over to the APM, who sent him back to his battalion transport lines. Jackson said: 'I was then placed under arrest which upset me and I was determined to get away.' Later he told the court: 'I left because I could not stand the treatment I was receiving. I wanted to get away from everything.' He added: 'On joining the battalion after doing imprisonment the CSM, in front of everyone, called me a "gaol bird" and said he would make my life a misery. I have been looked down on by everyone and that is the cause of my being here today.' He hinted at mental problems: 'Both my father and mother died in an asylum. I suffer from the same mental trouble caused by worries.' Jackson then handed in to the court a Return of Stragglers form, which implied that he had reported to the APM on 1 October, but this had little bearing on his second desertion on 4 October.

After the prisoner had been found guilty and sentenced to death the trial proceedings were forwarded up the chain of command for comment and confirmation. His commanding officer wrote: 'No experience of the man's conduct in action owing to his having shirked or having been undergoing punishment.' He recommended sentence should be carried out, saying: 'My opinion is that the crime was deliberately committed. The opinion is based on the fact that this man has on more than one occasion absented himself from active operations ...'

The brigade commander wrote:

I know Pte. Jackson personally and I have investigated two previous charges of a similar nature whilst commanding his battalion. In the first case, he pleaded as now, that he was mentally deranged. He was sent down to base under medical observation and was to be declared of sound mind. On that occasion he was convicted and sentenced. On the second occasion last month there was no clear evidence on which to send Pte. Jackson to trial and I dismissed the case after talking very seriously to him.

Division, corps and army commanders all recommended execution of sentence. However, when the trial papers were scrutinized by Brig. Gen. Gilbert Mellor, DJAG Third Army, he wrote to the Adjutant General to say that the sentence on the first charge should not be confirmed, as no evidence was given as to 'termination of absence'. In reference to the second charge, he wrote that Jackson had received no special warning for the front line and his battalion had been in support, and 'In these circumstances there may be some doubt whether the accused really intended to evade the "important particular service" in the front line' (which would constitute desertion). However, he added: 'I am of the opinion that the conviction can be confirmed.'

In another note to the AG, it was pointed out:

We have not carried out a sentence in similar circumstances. The DJAG agrees that we are carrying the doctrine of 'constructive' desertion much further than we ever have ... I strongly recommend that the sentence be commuted and suspended. If he does this again he could be shot.

Field Marshal Haig did not confirm the sentence on the first charge, but did confirm sentence on the second charge, no doubt feeling that by making his way from Noyelles to St Pol Jackson made his intentions plain. Pte Jackson was shot by firing squad at 6.10 a.m. on 7 November 1918 at St Python. Although he could argue that he had, perhaps, been treated harshly by an army which had by 1918 had modified its disciplinary process to deal with a

A.G. 3000+ behind

The man got a long way back but his Bn was in _support_ & he was in close arrest & that we have not carried out a sentence in similar circumstances. The D.J.A.G. agrees that we are carrying the doctrine of "constructive" desertion much further than we ever have but as he points out he cannot say there was "no evidence" I strongly recommend that the sentence be commuted & suspended. If he does this again he could be shot

26/10 JHW

A note attached to the court martial documents in the case of Pte Ernest Jackson, one of the last two men to be executed for desertion, recommending that sentence should be commuted.

citizen, now conscript, army, his record of previous absences counted heavily against him.

Nineteen minutes after Jackson's execution Pte Louis Harris became the last British soldier to be shot for a military offence during the war, all the subsequent executions being for murder.

According to the evidence he gave in his defence at his trial, Louis Harris had joined the army as a Kitchener volunteer in early 1915, but had been discharged as unfit. He subsequently rejoined in April 1916, probably as a conscript, and went to France in July of that year serving with the 10th Battalion, West Yorks Regiment.[2]

On 2 September 1918 the 10th West Yorks were preparing for an attack at Rocquigny. Harris was present when his unit formed up at the assembly point but he was missing when they reached their objective. Pte Helliwell told the court that he and Harris belonged to the same Lewis gun team and that during the attack the team had halted briefly. Harris had then dumped his kit and hung back when the others moved on. When the team reached their final objective Harris was found to be missing. Helliwell added that during the attack there was no firing and practically no opposition.

Lt Gill of 10th West Yorks gave evidence that at 11 a.m. on 3 September he was with 'B' echelon at Martinpuich, when he saw the accused. After talking to Harris, Lt Gill arrested him.

On 19 October Pte Louis Harris faced an FGCM. The president, Maj. Anderson, was a member of Harris's battalion. The prisoner was charged with 'misbehaving before the enemy in such a manner as to show cowardice' with an alternative charge of 'Deserting His Majesty's Service'.

Harris – surprisingly at this stage of the war – was not defended at his trial and made no attempt to cross-examine any of the witnesses, nor did he make any statement in his own defence. It would appear that the 23-year-old soldier either did not understand the seriousness of his position, or was resigned to his fate.

The court found Harris not guilty of the charge of cowardice, but guilty of the charge of desertion, and sentenced him to death. It emerged that Harris had a bad record. His regimental 'crime sheet' showed the following charges on active service:

10/9/16	Improper conduct	4 days' CC
18/9/16	Not complying with an order	14 days' FP No. 1
13/10/16	Refusing to obey an order	7 days' CC

29/10/16	Absent from the trenches	5 days' FP No. 1
14/11/16	Refusing to obey an order	5 days' CC
15/11/16	Disobeying a lawful command given by his superior officer (tried by FGCM)	3 months' FP No. 1
25/12/16	Losing by neglect his trench waders	5 days' FP No. 1
11/9/17	Unshaven on parade	3 days' CC
25–26/1/18	Not alert at his post when Brigade HQ guard	28 days' FP No. 1
4/6/18	Absent 3.30 p.m. 4/6/18 to 8.10 p.m. 4/6/18; surrendered himself	25 days' FP No. 1

After the trial Lt Col. Gibson, CO of 10th West Yorks, wrote: 'Pte Harris L. has not got a good record in this Battalion. His fighting value is NIL.' He also regarded the desertion as deliberate and in a second note explained his reasons: 'This was the second occasion within three days that Pte Harris L. had come away from the line without permission. Two days prior to the date on which he was charged he had made his way back to B echelon without permission.'

The Brigade Commander wrote:

I recommend that the extreme penalty be carried out for the
following reasons:

a. Pte Harris' action was deliberate.

b. He has previously attempted to desert unsuccessfully.

c. He is worthless as a soldier.

d. During an action he deliberately abandoned his comrades.

e. His example is a disgraceful one.

Division, corps and army commanders all agreed and the commander-in-chief confirmed the sentence. As the firing squad volley rang out at 6.29 a.m. on 7 November at Locquignol, Pte Louis Harris became the last man to be executed by a British Army firing squad for desertion. After 11 November all outstanding death sentences for military offences were commuted to penal servitude and in 1929 the death penalty was abolished for desertion and other purely military crimes.

PART THREE

CHAPTER 33

THE PARLIAMENTARY DEBATE
AND CONSEQUENCES

War cannot be separated for a single second from politics.

MAO TSETUNG, *c.* 1950

In the early days of the war, military law and its execution were far from the parliamentary mind, but by 1915 some members of the House were beginning to ask difficult questions. In response to a question, on 9 June 1915, as to whether any soldiers had been executed after sentence by court martial, the Undersecretary of State for War confirmed that executions had taken place. He did not identify the offences involved, referring his questioner to the Army Act for the offences punishable by death.[1]

The House became curious about these matters, and a week later the issue was taken up again. This time the questioner wanted to know whether the convicted man had the right to make representation to the confirming authority regarding trial or sentence.[2] On 1 July 1915 the Undersecretary, Mr Tennant, was asked how many courts martial had been held and the number of death sentences passed. However, the Undersecretary refused to supply this information, on the basis that it was not in the public interest so to do.[3] A few days later he had to field another difficult question when he was asked how relatives of executed men were informed of their deaths. The reply was that next of kin were informed of the execution as soon as the Army Record Office received the official report.[4]

The matter fermented quietly until January 1916 when an Irish MP asked for details about the trial and execution of Pte Thomas Hope of the Leinster Regiment, executed on 2 March 1915. He wanted to know whether this young volunteer had been defended by an advocate, and also whether it was true that he only learned that he was to be shot half an hour before his execution. Mr Tennant explained – as he was to do several more times during the war – that it was impractical to employ legal counsel in the field, and that

Hope's sentence had been reviewed in the normal way, the soldier being told of his execution at least twelve hours before it was carried out.[5]

A few days later (26 January 1916), Philip Snowden, the leader of the Independent Labour Party, followed this up. He asked how many men had been shot for desertion and other military offences since the war had started. Mr Tennant phrased his reply carefully, saying that no British soldier had been shot in the UK. So far as overseas forces were concerned he said: 'I will ask my honourable friend if he will be good enough not to believe that the number has been considerable.' He was again evasive a month later. When asked about the delay between dismissal of an appeal by the Court of Criminal Appeal and the execution, he chose to overlook the fact that such cases did not go to the Court of Criminal Appeal, simply replying that the average was five days.

Over the next weeks, several of these issues were raised again. In March Mr Thomas Lundon asked whether it was true that relatives of executed men received notification of their relative's execution by postcard.[6] Mr Tennant replied that a standard form was used for such purposes, and that it was best that relatives were informed as soon as possible, so that they did not discover the true facts by rumour. In April Mr Tennant again refused to tell the House how many executions had been carried out, and reiterated that it was not practical, at an FGCM, for a man to be represented by counsel.

Specific cases came to the attention of the House. On 4 May Mr Jowett asked about the case of Abraham Beverstein (who served as Abraham Harris, and had been shot on 20 March 1916 for desertion; see Chapter 25. His family had been in contact with the formidable social reformer Sylvia Pankhurst, who had mobilized her Socialist contacts in Parliament.) The Undersecretary was asked about the case, and to comment on the fact that this 19-year-old boy had suffered from shell shock shortly before his execution. Mr Jowett asked the government to undertake that no soldier under the age of 21 would be executed, nor any man who had been wounded in action.[7]

Shortly after this the battle of the Somme intervened and the parliamentary debate on the matter of capital courts martial subsided for nearly a year, until after the battle of Passchendaele. It was Philip Snowden who again took up the cudgels. On 31 October he asked the Undersecretary of State for War (now Mr Macpherson) whether, amongst other things, he would allow the relatives of executed men to examine the records of the court martial.[8] Mr Macpherson's reply was a clear negative.

Philip Snowden then raised the matter of shell shock, and asked the

Minister to look into the case of Stanley Stewart, a 21-year-old private in the Scots Fusiliers who had been shot for desertion after previously having been invalided home to the UK with shell shock. Mr Macpherson declined, saying that the Commander-in-Chief only confirmed sentence after a full review of the facts, and that he would not interfere with the process.

Throughout early November the House persisted with its questions. In particular a Labour member, Mr King, raised the question again of how relatives were informed of the deaths of executed men. Mr Macpherson was asked that, in future, the names of these men should be published in routine casualty lists, but he demurred. However, on 26 November 1917 the Chancellor, Mr Bonar Law, made a statement: 'It has been arranged that in the future the communications made to dependants of the soldiers shot at the front should merely state they have died on service', and added that the matter of pensions was still under consideration.[9]

The debate rumbled on through the winter. The House continued to express concern that a man with shell shock could be executed. A question by Gen. McCalmont asked whether or not it was universal practice for a complete report to be called for after a death sentence had been awarded, and therefore, as this would contain details of any shell shock, whether this would be taken into account. Macpherson's reply was evasive: 'I am assured of all these facts, and in the cases personally brought to my notice the Court had given them most careful consideration.'

Although the families were no longer directly informed that their relative had been executed, it became apparent that the procedure used by the army to publicize such executions would lead to relatives discovering the true fate of an executed man. Just before Christmas 1917 Mr Macpherson was asked to discontinue the practice of including the men's names and details in Routine Orders. As the principal reason for this practice was its deterrent effect, Mr Macpherson refused to discontinue it.[10] In response to further questions he gave reassurance regarding shell-shocked men, saying that he had never come across a single case where any soldier had been executed without being examined, before trial and before sentence, by a medical officer. Either Mr Macpherson was stretching the truth, or his advisers had misled him.

In February Philip Snowden brought up the matter of shell shock again, asking whether the medical evidence that a man was not suffering from shell shock was given on oath, and was subject to cross-examination.[11] The Undersecretary was less than completely truthful in his reply, which stated that all evidence at a court martial was given on oath and could be cross-examined.

What he omitted to say, however, was that a convicted man was frequently examined only *after* sentence had been awarded, and the convicted man remained unaware of the results of this examination, the report going, with the other papers, up through the confirming process.

Mr Macpherson became somewhat agitated, and when a Labour back-bencher, Mr Whitehouse, suggested that some shell-shocked men had been shot, he demanded that this allegation be withdrawn.[12] Later the same day, Macpherson again denied that any of the men executed had either been wounded or suffered from shell shock, saying: 'I have made, and shall continue to make, investigations with regard to the facts stated in the various questions, and I have not yet been able to come across a single case where a man who was proved in the past to have suffered from shell shock, or was proved to have been wounded, has suffered the death penalty after being sentenced to death.'

A few days later, on 23 February, *John Bull* published an account of the trial and execution of Sub Lt Edwin Dyett, leading to more questions in the House.[13] Mr Macpherson said that before he could express an opinion he would have to investigate the facts of the case. Mr J. H. Thomas, the Member for Derby, asked if it might be possible for the court martial documents to be seen by some Members of the House, but this was refused – the only person entitled to see the documents, said Mr Macpherson, was the accused man. He did, however, undertake to examine the papers himself and to disclose to the House the relevant facts.[14]

The facts presented in *John Bull* were not entirely correct – its founder Horatio Bottomley was, as ever, more interested in a good story and an excuse to stir up debate than the truth. His version of events was that Dyett had taken part in the defence of Antwerp and served in Gallipoli, before going to the Somme. Bottomley also alleged that Dyett had not met his defending officer until half an hour before his trial. The article was followed up, on 2 March, by a ferocious attack on the court martial system, asserting that 'the whole proceedings preliminary to and after the trial should form the subject of a special enquiry'.[15] In the House of Commons, on 6 March, Mr Macpherson stated that the facts published were not substantially correct, but the debate continued.

The argument rumbled on, both in *John Bull* and in the House. Horatio Bottomley had achieved his aim of making the Members of Parliament discontented with the court martial process.

At the same time as the Dyett debate was going on, the question of men with shell shock being executed came up again on 14 March.[16] Mr Macpherson read part of a letter from Sir Douglas Haig to put the matter to rest:

> When a man has been sentenced to death if at any time any doubts have been raised as to his responsibility for his actions, or if the suggestion had been advanced that he has suffered from neurasthenia or shell shock, orders are issued for him to be examined by a Medical Board which expresses an opinion as to his sanity, and as to whether he should be held responsible for his actions. On the members of this Board is always a Medical officer of neurological experience. The sentence of death is not carried out in the case of such a man unless the Medical Board expresses the positive opinion that he is to be responsible for his actions.[17]

Mr Macpherson then pointed out that in the case of Sub Lt Dyett, the military commanders had only administered justice under an Act given to them by Parliament.

The debates then wound down somewhat after the German spring offensives and the subsequent Allied attacks and ultimate victory, but these issues raised were not forgotten and in 1919 a committee was established to inquire into 'the laws and rules of procedure regulating Courts Martial' under the chairmanship of Mr Justice Darling.

The official statistics of the war were first made public in April 1920, informing the public that 3,076 death sentences had been passed, resulting in 346 executions.[18] This provoked various responses. Sylvia Pankhurst wrote:

> Men often told us sadly that they had been in firing parties which had been ordered out at dawn to shoot six or seven poor fellows. Such reports were so general, that on April 28th 1920, the Under Secretary of State for War was put up in the House of Lords to contradict them. He declared, as I still believe most falsely, though whether by misinformation, or deliberate intent on his part, I cannot tell, that the number of officers and men sentenced to death from August 1914, to December 31st 1919, was 3076, and the total death sentences actually carried out numbered on 343 [sic].[19]

After publication of the statistics a Mr H. V. Clarke wrote to various newspapers, informing them of the 'true' facts. A prominent Socialist, Clarke had worked at GHQ during the war and said that he had extracted from General Routine Orders data relating to executions for disciplinary offences. His figures were:

Year	No. of executions
1914	528
1915	10,488
1916	12,689
1917	13,165
1918	1,035

Although the newspapers refused to publish these figures, Sylvia Pankhurst's publication *Dreadnought* did so. In consequence, detectives called on Mr Clarke, but found him out. When he learned of their visit he destroyed all of his 'evidence' – the names he had allegedly copied from General Routine Orders. This mystery was never resolved, and Sylvia Pankhurst wrote: 'Clarke was undoubtedly a sincere man, passionately in earnest. If his figures were incorrect, then he was suffering from delusions.'[20]

No evidence has ever been found to substantiate Clark's extraordinary claim that the British Army executed 37,905 of its men during the 1914–18 War

CHAPTER 34

THE DARLING COMMITTEE

Military leaders who lack the courage to offer their opinions ...
[on matters of military importance] ... are just as accountable to the
peoples as the politicians who have secured their silence.

JAMES H. WEBB JR

The political, legal and medical debates went on after the war and concerns about military justice and courts martial in the field continued to
be raised. In April 1919 the Army Council constituted a committee under
the chairmanship of Sir Charles Darling, a senior High Court judge. This
committee was asked 'to enquire into the law and rules of procedure
regulating military Courts-martial in both peace and war and to make
recommendations'.

The committee comprised:

Five members of Parliament, including Horatio Bottomley
The Judge Advocate General, Mr F. Cassel
The DJAG, Brig. Gen. Gilbert Mellor
The DAG, Maj. Gen. Wyndham Childs
The Chief of the Imperial General Staff, Lt Gen. the Earl of Cavan

It sat for twenty-two days and heard evidence from a variety of witnesses. On
26 November 1919 it delivered to Parliament two reports, a majority report
and a minority report, this latter being signed by three of the MPs: Horatio
Bottomley, Christopher Lowther and Stephen Walsh.

Although the recommendations of the committee were published it advised
that the evidence presented to it should not be published, and this advice was
followed.[1]

In most of its substance, the majority report was accepted by the signatories of the minority report, with a few notable exceptions.

The report first highlighted the scale of courts martial held during the war, comparing 1913 with 1918:

	1913	1918
GCMs	7	1,685
FGCMs	0	32,977
DCMs	3,683	40,646

On average, through the war, there were 1,047 GCMs per year, and in total (excluding RCMs) there were 252,773 courts martial held.

The problems associated with such an expansion in courts martial were exacerbated by the fact that many experienced regimental officers were lost during the early part of the war, their replacements not being fully trained in military law.

The report stated:

> The results of our investigations into a limited number of cases put
> before us as typical lead us to the conclusion that, having regard to all the
> circumstances, the work of Courts-Martial during the war has been well
> done. We are satisfied not only that members of Courts-Martial intend to
> be absolutely fair to those who come before them, but also that the rank
> and file have confidence in their fairness.

Significantly, the signatories of the minority report did not disagree with this statement.

Having said this, the committee felt that there was room for improvement on certain points. They believed that the Army Acts, King's Regulations and the Rules of Procedure were unnecessarily complicated and recommended that the *Manual of Military Law* be rearranged and condensed. In fact, although this volume was revised and reissued in 1929 after changes to the Army Act, it remained in substantially the same form as it had been in 1914. The other matter which the committee commented on before proceeding to its report was the legal knowledge of officers. Its members felt that officers concerned with administering the code of discipline must be familiar with normal legal processes, and they suggested that the court martial officers introduced during the war should become a permanent feature. These CMOs should be solicitors or barristers, holding a commission, working under the JAG. Their duties would include training of officers in legal matters, advising and assisting in convening courts martial and in the confirmation process, and acting as judge advocates when required.

The committee also recommended that inducements should be offered to officers who took and passed a course on military law, and that such officers could then act as court martial presidents.

The report then goes on to consider the main thrust of the tasks allocated to the committee.

Under 'arrest', it noted that the whole section of 'arrest and custody' should be revised and simplified in King's Regulations.

As to delays between arrest and trial, and trial and confirmation, the committee felt that although these may sometimes have caused hardship and were regrettable, these delays were due to the exigencies of active service. They also drew attention to the fact that there were similar delays in the civil courts, and pointed out that some delays were caused by the confirmation process when enquiries were instituted which led to a reduction in sentence.

The 'summary of evidence' was discussed in some detail. Although it had been suggested that this should not be available to the court, as it might contain inadmissible evidence or admissions by the accused, the committee were not in agreement with this. However, they did advise that the summary should be taken on oath and that if a witness was not readily available the abstract of evidence be accepted unless the accused objected.

Another major issue was the accused's right to a defence. They were agreed that soldiers usually, but not invariably, were aware of their rights and suggested that a notice containing details of an accused man's rights (in simple language) be put on the wall of every guardroom. He should also be told of his right to a prisoner's friend and that if he declined this, it should be put in writing.

There had been a proposal that a defendant should be able to choose as his prisoner's friend any member of His Majesty's forces, but the committee advised against this, feeling that it was not in the accused's best interest, as 'a poor advocate is worse than useless, and frequently injures his client's case'.

Concern was expressed that the committee had heard evidence that, on occasion, officers had been discouraged from appearing on behalf of an accused. In their view, 'an officer should feel himself at perfect liberty to defend any man of his unit or company if asked to do so'. At the same time, however, no one officer should regularly act as a prisoner's friend.

The fact that courts martial are public courts was reiterated – clearly many men had felt that these were closed courts. On the other hand, it was felt that public notice of such trials should not be given, beyond the information supplied in Routine Orders.

As to the courts and their composition, the committee believed that RCMs should be abolished. The signatories of the minority report thought that DCMs should also be abolished. The authors of this report felt that holding over a quarter of a million courts martial during the war (excluding regimental courts) had been time-consuming and taken the people involved away from their primary duty of fighting. The main report observed that in many cases the officers sitting on a court martial panel had been too young, and that no one under the age of 25 should sit on a panel, as was the case in French military law.

The importance of the independence of courts martial was emphasized. Whilst sentence may be influenced by the prevalence of an offence, circulars had been wrongly issued regarding sentences. It was recommended that King's Regulations be modified, and that 'the Army Council deal severely with any attempted interference with the judicial discretion of the courts'.

The system of recording evidence during trials had been criticized. It was time-consuming, and sometimes confusing, as a witness's evidence was interrupted whilst the president tried to capture, in longhand, the facts. The Darling Committee considered this, and advised that when possible, the recording should be done by the Judge Advocate and not the President, and that in cases not on active service a shorthand writer be used. In fact, in some trials during the war it is clear that a court martial officer has taken the notes. The committee advised that a complete transcript of evidence should be taken to ensure capture of the material facts.

There was concern as to the delays which sometimes occurred between the finding and sentence, and it was recommended that the sentence should be announced either in open court or in private to the accused man. However, it was agreed the confirmation process should be retained, as this was desirable from the point of view of discipline and of the man concerned. The report pointed out that the existence of a confirming authority did not lessen the responsibility of the panel in determining either sentence or finding.

Sentence of a court martial had, historically, been promulgated on parade, and the committee recommended that this practice be discontinued. The outcome of all courts martial – acquittals as well as convictions – should continue to be published in Routine Orders.

The members of the committee agreed that the Suspension of Sentences Act had worked well, and should continue.

As to the issue of only the accused being allowed access to the trial documents, which had caused so much debate in the House, the committee thought that this right should be extended to his legal representatives or next of kin, unless the trial had been held *in camera*.

The members of the committee considered the matter of right to appeal in some detail. They pointed out that there was no automatic right of appeal in a criminal case – there had to be demonstrable grounds for such an appeal, and this only took place if a convicted person requested it. The soldier, they decided, was in a better position then civilians as the confirming authority reviewed every case and the JAG's office scrutinized the legality of the finding.

The committee wrote:

> We are of the opinion that it is undesirable to set up any formal court of appeal from the decisions of Courts-Martial, since these Courts sit and adjudicate in circumstances wholly different from those in which Civil Courts exercise their powers.

They did not think that an exception to this should be made in the case of death sentences:

> During the last war not a single officer or soldier was executed under sentence of Court-Martial in the United Kingdom. Abroad a certain number of death sentences were carried out. In each case they were only carried out after personal consideration by, and upon the orders of, the Commander-in-Chief, and after the Judge Advocate General, or his deputy, had advised on their legality. Moreover, when considering them, the Commander-in-Chief almost invariably had before him recommendations from the Officers commanding the Unit to which the accused belonged, the Brigade, the Division, the Corps and the Army.

It was also noted that

> no fewer than 89 per cent of the death sentences were commuted by the Commander-in-Chief. We doubt very much whether any Court, necessarily not possessing the information which he possessed as to the discipline and morale of the Army, would have ventured to exercise clemency to such an extent. The Commander-in-Chief, of course, commuted sentences in many cases where the Court of Criminal Appeal would have had no legal grounds for interfering, and must therefore have dismissed an appeal.

The authors of the minority report disagreed with this, recommending that the confirming process be abolished, and that a Court of Appeal be established. This would not, however, operate 'in the field', except that death sentences 'in the field' should be referred to the Court of Criminal Appeal, perhaps assisted by military assessors.

This particular hare was raised by Maj. Lowther, a signatory to the minority report, in the House in April 1920. He proposed an amendment to the Army Act giving a right of appeal to the Court of Criminal Appeal in cases where the death penalty had been awarded. This motion was lost, after a short debate.[2]

If the Darling Committee had been intended to defuse the parliamentary pressure for reform, it had failed. The minority report, and the new ideas of shell shock, had given the military law reformers a clear agenda with which to work. The 'Courts Martial Problem' was not to be wished away by a single, divided, Parliamentary Committee.

CHAPTER 35

POST-WAR VIEWS ON SHELL SHOCK –THE SOUTHBOROUGH COMMITTEE

One can no longer imagine a battlefield without psychiatrists and psychologists.

HANS BINNEVELD, 1997

By the end of the war neither the army nor the medical establishment could ignore the scale of psychiatric casualties. The medical statistics of the war showed that in a total of just over 1 million casualties, 4,692 officers and 16,857 other ranks had been classed as suffering from 'functional diseases of the nervous system (including neurasthenia and shell shock)'.[1] Of these, over 17,000 returned to duty and 3,325 were invalided out of the service. In addition, a further 6,877 officers and men had suffered from other nervous or mental diseases.

During the war the army had been reluctant to allow its doctors to write on the subject of shell shock or war neurosis, but after the war many doctors rushed into print to give their views on the subject and to describe their treatments and lessons for the future. Some of these made a valuable contribution to medical knowledge, and the concept of 'military psychiatry' became acknowledged. The war also changed the nature of thinking about mental illness; both psychiatry and neurology were moved forward by the events and tragedies of the war. Such books as Stanford Read's *Military Psychiatry in Peace and War* laid the foundations of future practice.[2] Others were less rigorous: an American book containing case histories from all nations involved in the conflict persisted with misleading categorization, still confusing pre-existing mental conditions, such as syphilis, mental deficiency, thyroid disease and other organically based disorders, with war neurosis and nervous damage from shell explosion.[3] Elliot Smith and Pear, as early as 1917, had thrown down the gauntlet:

Excuses for inertia, brought forward before August 1914, can be accepted no longer. The thousands of cases of shell-shock which have been seen in our hospitals since that time have proved, beyond any possibility of doubt, that the early treatment of mental disorder is successful from the humanitarian, medical and financial standpoints. It is for us, not for our children, to act in the light of this great lesson.[4]

After the war, Parliament and public alike continued to debate the issues of shell shock and the capital courts martial. On 28 April 1920, during a post-Darling committee debate in the House of Lords, Lord Southborough asked the government to establish a committee to inquire into shell shock during the war, particularly in relation to death penalties imposed for cowardice. Four months later a War Office committee of inquiry was established under Lord Southborough's chairmanship. The committee consisted of eleven doctors with wartime experience, two Members of Parliament and Col. Gilbert Mellor, the wartime DJAG of the BEF.

The terms of reference of the committee, as laid down by the Army Council, were:

To consider the different types of hysteria and traumatic neurosis, commonly called 'shell-shock'; to collect the expert knowledge derived by the service medical authorities and the medical profession from the experience of the war, with a view to recording for future use the ascertained facts as to its origins, nature and remedial treatment, and to advise whether by military training or education, some scientific method of guarding against its occurrence can be devised.[5]

The 'Shell Shock Committee', as it became known, heard evidence from fifty-nine witnesses over a period of nearly two years from September 1920 to summer 1922. It started by considering the term 'shell shock', the report noting:

... it became abundantly plain to the medical profession that in very many cases the change from civil life brought about by enlistment and physical training was sufficient to cause neurasthenic and hysterical symptoms, and that the wear and tear of a prolonged campaign of trench warfare with its terrible hardships and anxieties ... produced a condition of mind and body properly falling under the term 'war neurosis', practically indistinguishable from the forms of neurosis known to every doctor under the ordinary conditions of civil life.

It continued:

> The Committee recognised, therefore, from the outset of the enquiry
> that the term 'shell-shock' is wholly misleading, but unfortunately its use
> had been established and the harm was already done. The alliteration
> and dramatic significance of the term had caught the public imagination,
> and thenceforward there was no escape from its use.

Finally:

> Without exception our witnesses condemned the term 'shell-shock' and
> held that it should be totally eliminated from medical nomenclature.[6]

To ensure a standard approach to the way that evidence was collected from
the witnesses the committee drew up a list of thirty-eight comprehensive
questions to be asked of most or all of the witnesses. These covered such
topics as:

> How should recruits be classified for modern warfare having due regard
> to their physical, mental and nervous condition?
>
> Do you consider that a nervously unstable man/a man who has been
> insane/a mental defective can be trained into an efficient soldier?
>
> Was there any general characteristic common to the individuals so
> affected?
>
> Under what conditions have you seen shell shock and mental breakdown
> arise?
>
> Was the incidence of shell shock greater amongst troops who were fresh
> in the line or in those troops who had been in the line for some time?
>
> Do you consider that responsibility increased or lessened the incidence
> of shell shock?
>
> Do you consider shell shock is more likely to arise in single or married
> men?
>
> Was the incidence in any way related to age?
>
> Does good morale in troops tend to lessen the incidence of shell shock?
>
> What mode of treatment did you find most valuable?
>
> Do you consider that a soldier who has once suffered from shell shock is

capable of further active service?

Have you any evidence of the part played by mental failure as a cause of desertion?

Have you any experience of courts martial for cowardice and other military crimes?

The committee was, to some extent, hampered by the lack of accurate statistics (some of which became available subsequently with the publication of the *Official History*).[7] Although some figures were available (for example, in seventy-eight cases of 'concussion', 30.7 per cent were married, compared to 37.8 per cent of ninety-four 'nervous breakdown' cases), no statistical analysis was carried out and no figures are given for the marital status of men suffering from other illnesses or wounds.

To establish the background to 'shell shock', Sir John Fortescue, the eminent historian of the British Army, was invited to present information on war neurosis in previous wars. The information which he provided was fairly brief, and omitted any reference to the American Civil War or the Russo-Japanese War. He confirmed his comments to anecdotal evidence from British experience. The committee did, however, refer to a book by Sir Frederick Mott, which quoted examples of war neurosis in Lucretius and Shakespeare.

Evidence was given by Gen. Horne, who had been in command of First Army at the end of the war. In his view, men who lived an open-air life were less susceptible to shell shock than the 'clerk or artisan'. As a commander he had looked with disfavour on units with a high incidence of mental breakdown, as this was a reflection of poor morale, and felt that everything possible should be done to raise morale. He also considered that shell shock had become a serious factor owing to the peculiar character of this war, with its high explosives and bombardments.[8] Lord Gort of the Grenadier Guards, who had won the Victoria Cross in September 1918 leading his men under heavy fire and who also held the Military Cross and DSO with two bars and was therefore no stranger to front line warfare, was less sympathetic. He felt that 'Among the regular battalions with a good class of men the circumstances were rather different to those in the New Army units, and there were very few cases of real "shell shock".' He also emphasized the role of morale: '... that in the face of strong morale and *esprit de corps* "shell shock" would be practically non-existent,' adding: 'I think shell-shock, like measles, is so infectious that you cannot afford to run risks with it at all and in war the individual is of small account. If one or two go by the board it is extremely unfortunate and sad but it cannot be helped. A large proportion must be wounded or killed. It must be looked on as a form of disgrace to the soldier.' Lord Gort's views were to find an echo in 1940.[9]

Lt Col. Jackson, who had commanded a battalion of the Northumberland Fusiliers, thought that it was trench warfare and the effect of the trench mortar which was responsible for most shell shock, and the feeling of being tied down in the trenches.[10] Col. Burnett, of the Gordon Highlanders, when asked whether it was a disgrace to a man to lose control of his actions or a disgrace to the army, replied: 'A disgrace to the man. Although a man's nerve may break down we must look upon it as a disgrace, otherwise you would have everyone breaking down as soon as they wanted to go home.'[11] A senior commander, Maj. Gen. Jeudwine, considered that the incidence of shell shock was greater in the middle of the war than at the end because at the end of the war troops were advancing and the army was more successful. In his opinion it was the sitting, watching people on either side being killed, not knowing when it would be their turn, which led to men breaking down.[12] Lt Col. Jervis of the 5th Lancers and the Machine Gun Corps was not sympathetic to the idea of shell shock. In his opinion loss of nerve was not shell shock and should never have been called by that name, but for the purpose of answering questions from the committee he regarded shell shock as loss of nerve and said that he was inclined to think that 'emotional shell shock was a disgrace to a regiment'.[13]

Another witness, Squadron Leader Tyrell (who had himself suffered from shell shock and subsequently returned to duty), said: 'Shell shock is born of fear. Its grandparents are self preservation and the fear of being found afraid.'[14] He believed that the main cause of the condition was loss of sleep and inadequate rest, in conjunction with the bursting of high explosives. 'Severe mental stress grouped with fatigue and blood, wet and cold, misery and monotony, unsavoury cooking and feeding, nauseating environment etc' all exacerbated the problem. In his own experience 'he had seen cases of an emotive state in the form of irresistible fear of danger, associated with crises of terror and anxiety at the front, leading up to desertion from post of duty or reckless behaviour; one of whom, a regular serving non-commissioned officer, with an excellent pre-war character, was eventually shot as a persistent deserter.'[15]

An interesting view came from Maj. Gen. Wyndham Childs, DAG during the war. He said that in any court martial case where there was a plea of war neurosis the accused was thoroughly examined under expert advice before a capital sentence by courts martial was confirmed, and assured the committee that the greatest care was taken by the Commander-in-Chief not to confirm any such sentence until the prisoner's case had been fully examined by experts in nervous disorders. He added that the protocol controlling this court martial procedure had been put in force as early as the autumn of 1914. Childs gave the impression that he did not entirely believe in war neurosis, as he said that he did not believe that there was much cowardice but there were certain kinds of men who could not control their nerves and under certain conditions they became deserters. 'Where discipline is bad you get desertion; where there is no *esprit de corps* you get cowardice; where you get *esprit de corps* plus discipline you will not get that type of thing at all. It was all a question of morale.'[16]

The first medical witness was Lt Gen. Sir John Goodwin, Director General Army Medical Services. In his opinion shell shock should be looked upon as a genuine affliction. He observed that at the start of the war he saw very little shell shock, and was certain that well-trained and disciplined troops were less liable to suffer from mental breakdown, and observed that an important part of training was for a man to develop *esprit de corps*, pride in himself and pride in his unit and the history of his regiment. He also recommended that troops be properly looked after, that attention should be paid to cleanliness, baths, food, clothing, meals and recreation and that when out of the line they should be given proper opportunity for rest, both physical and mental.[17]

Dr Hurst, of Guy's Hospital, observed that 'Prolonged responsibility was a common cause of breakdown, with the development of psychasthaenic symptoms, in officers. The fatigue, strain and responsibility of long service eventually led to breakdown in many men who appeared to be constitutionally absolutely normal, and who stood the stress of battle and responsibility without any difficulty at first.' Dr Hurst had been at Lemnos during the withdrawal from Gallipoli and observed: '... practically every man coming out of the peninsula was neurasthenic ... Very few could hold their hands out without shaking, and they were all in a condition of profound neurasthenia.'[18]

Dr Mapother, Medical Superintendent of the Maudsley Hospital, told the committee that intellectually defective men often developed a psychosis, as 'far from receiving help in times of trouble, which others did from comradeship, he usually suffered continuously from his sense of the contempt of others'. In his opinion, regarding men defective in social or moral sense, 'The importance of the latter factor in the genesis of admissions to shell shock hospitals has been greatly underestimated … The most important document received with the patient was generally the conduct sheet.'[19]

William Rivers, famous for his treatment of Siegfried Sassoon and a highly respected neurologist, objected to the term shell shock 'root and branch'. Nor did he use the term 'neurasthenia'; he used 'anxiety neurosis' to describe this condition. He spoke of two types of psychological casualties amongst officers: those who broke down soon after going to the front, because they were unfitted for the job (who could not be said to be suffering from a true neurosis) and those who broke down after continued strain. He reiterated that good training, good morale and *esprit de corps* reduced casualties from neurosis and again made the point that inaction under fire was a cause of breakdown.[20]

Gordon Holmes, who had replaced Charles Myers as Consulting Neurologist to the British Armies in France, provided much information to the committee. In his view, early in the war, whilst a considerable number of men had been admitted to the base hospitals with hysterical symptoms, such as paralysis or loss of speech, there were few cases of war neurosis, which he ascribed to the better morale and discipline of the troops and the less severe form of fighting. He also believed that the idea of shell shock had then not been common amongst the troops and so had not spread by suggestion. The most potent causes of shell shock, he thought, were the stress of battle, exposure to high explosive, prolonged mental stress and prolonged service. In many cases, he felt that men simply needed a good rest.[21]

Another doctor with considerable experience in France was William Brown, neurologist to the Fourth and Fifth Armies in France. He observed that there were considerable differences between the cases of shell shock from different units: 'The doctors could not help being struck by the fact that men from certain regiments came up again and again. They also noticed that in certain units there were many more court martial cases. Where there was more shell shock there was more scrim-shanking.'[22] He told the committee that he had considerable experience of seeing men charged with military offences such as desertion and frequently gave evidence at courts martial, confessing that he found this a difficult and distasteful task. He said: 'After my first two or three courts martial I found I was practically in every case giving evidence in favour of the man … I felt that his state of mind in the line, when he was under heavy shell fire, was not the same as his state of mind when he was at the Base, or somewhere between the Base and the line.'[23]

The committee collated the evidence and came to its conclusions in a unanimous report. The main issues, it felt, were as follows: first, that the term 'shell shock' was a gross and costly misnomer. Secondly, that the war had produced no new nervous disorders; those which occurred had been recognized in civilian practice and fell into three groups: genuine concussion with no visible wound (which was rare); emotional shock; and nervous and mental exhaustion. Thirdly, the committee regarded medical examination of recruits early in the war as inadequate. Finally, training, morale and discipline were important in reducing the level of battle shock.

They went on to summarize the conditions which contributed to the development of war neurosis. They identified four key issues: first, some men were given responsibilities for which they were unsuited, which caused stress and exacerbated any tendency to neurosis. Secondly, inaction under fire increased men's feelings of helplessness, which led to the development of neurosis. Thirdly, exhaustion, fatigue and sleeplessness all operated to lower troops' resistance and increased the likelihood of shell shock. Finally, men suffering from other diseases were more likely to develop the condition.

The members of the committee reviewed the best methods of dealing with psychological casualties and referred to a note sent them by Charles Myers, which defined the key elements as promptness of action, suitable environment and psychotherapeutic measures. Another debate was as to whether men once treated could be returned to the firing line. Several medical witnesses told the committee that men with psychological trauma could be returned to active service, but that this did depend on the individual and the type of neurosis. Men who broke down through exhaustion and were simply tired out often did quite well on their return to the line.

Cowardice and shell shock seemed to be less clear-cut. The committee noted that some of the witnesses refused to define cowardice and others did so only with reservation. Capt. Dowson, a barrister with considerable court martial experience, defined it as 'showing fear in the face of the enemy', but the committee regarded this as unhelpful in determining the relationship between shell shock and cowardice, and observed that fear was an emotion common to all and that some very brave men had frankly acknowledged feeling it.[24] They did comment that the witnesses (presumably including the medical witnesses) agreed that cowardice should be regarded as a military crime to be punished when necessary by death. Opinions varied. One doctor said: 'Fear is really an unconscious thing and has a very definite physical manifestation … Cowardice is a voluntary attitude taken up by an individual …'[25] Professor Roussy, consultant to the French Army, said: 'Cowardice is lack of self-control of an individual over himself. In the presence of a situation in which there is an element of danger ... any man who can control himself is a courageous man, but he who gives way, runs away or does certain other actions not esteemed worthy is a coward.'[26]

The committee defined the problem:

> If the individual exercises his self-control in facing the danger he is not guilty of cowardice, if however, being capable of doing so, he will not face the situation, he is then a coward. It is here that the difficulty arises in cases of war neurosis for it becomes necessary to decide whether the individual has or has not crossed that indefinite line which divides normal reaction from neurosis with impairment of volitional control.[27]

They also commented that the system followed in courts martial during the war as regards medical evidence seemed to have been satisfactory and that in the light of the Darling Report they expected that in any future war, justice would be administered in a thoroughly satisfactory manner.[28] Lord Southborough's committee concluded:

> That the military aspect of cowardice was justified
> That seeming cowardice might be beyond an individual's control
> That experienced and specialized medical opinion is required to decide
>   in possible cases of war neurosis of doubtful character
> That a man who has already proved his courage should receive special
>   consideration on case of subsequent lapse.

Finally, the committee reviewed recruiting procedures, proposing that these be made much more rigorous, to exclude men mentally and nervously unsuited to fighting. Men with epilepsy or who had a definite history of insanity were not suitable for military service. Training should be sufficient not only to ensure that a man was physically fit, but also to ensure that morale, *esprit de corps* and discipline were developed, to enable a man to put the welfare of his unit before his own personal safety.

As to the terminology used, the committee were adamant:

> The term shell shock should be eliminated from official nomenclature, the disorders hitherto included under this heading being designated by the recognised medical terms for such conditions. Abbreviations such as N.Y.D. Nervous and Mental, or N.Y.D.N., D.A.H., etc should be avoided

as they are liable to become catchwords, and so react unfavourably on the patients themselves and on others.[29]

As to the classification of casualties, the committee was equally clear:

> No case of psychoneurosis or of mental breakdown, even when attributed to shell explosion or the effects thereof, should be classified as a battle casualty any more than sickness or disease is so regarded.[30]

The Southborough Committee had done its job thoroughly and had produced an excellent report summarizing the state of medical and military knowledge at the time. The key elements contributing to war neurosis and battle shock had been itemized and the most appropriate methods of treating these conditions identified. Some of the lessons learned were taken into account in the recruitment and training of troops, and in planning medical services, so that when war broke out in 1939 the Army was, to some extent, prepared for psychiatric casualties, but was confident that the new procedures which had been put into place would mean that mass breakdown was unlikely. In 1940, as the BEF was driven back to Dunkirk, it became apparent that this confidence had been misplaced: of the 13,000 cases needing medical attention, between 10 and 15 per cent were psychiatric casualties.[31] This was a serious blow and caused much soul-searching in the War Office.

It took time for the subject of shell shock to move from the province of the psychiatrists, and the idea that the condition was related to a form of insanity, to the psychologists, who formulated the concept of post-traumatic stress disorder. It was to take a further world war and numerous other conflicts before the psychological impact of traumatic experience was to be fully recognized. Hans Binneveld summed up the situation in 1997, when he wrote: 'One can no longer imagine a battlefield without psychiatrists and psychologists. Their presence is due to the fact that participation in a war, for many of those involved, is an extremely traumatic experience.'[32]

CHAPTER 36

PROGRESS?

Run away? Run away? Damn me Sir, of course soldiers run away!
Every soldier runs away. But the good ones always come back.
They're the fellows.

THE DUKE OF WELLINGTON

By the mid 1920s, despite the various committees set up to defuse the issue, there were three pressures working directly on the government to change the law and abolish the death penalty for specifically military offences such as cowardice, desertion, etc. The Darling Committee, with its minority report of MPs, still lay unanswered and Lord Southborough's 'Shell Shock Committee' had increased the impetus to act. The third pressure was the tenacious campaign still being waged in Parliament by a small but determined group of MPs who were reflecting a widely felt public unease. They were greatly helped by the general anti-military mood for peace at any price that was eventually to become one of the pillars of appeasement in the 1930s. The 'war to end wars' had convinced everyone that modern war was now just too dreadful to contemplate.

The principal campaigner against the death penalty was Ernest Thurtle, an MP who had volunteered to join the army as a private soldier in the Great War, risen to the rank of captain and been wounded in the trenches. Driven by his experiences and his marked radical political views, Thurtle worked tirelessly to get the death sentence removed from the military's jurisdiction. As well as writing various books and articles, he was an unflagging campaigner in the House of Commons, using the annual debates over the Army Act to press his case. He acted as the catalyst and focus for the anti-abolitionists and pulled the work of the various committees together in his demands for changes in legislation.[1]

He was supported by the radical Socialist George Lansbury, who wrote in his foreword to Thurtle's book *Military Discipline and Democracy*:

If there must be an Army, then I want it to be an Army controlled by the workers, made up of the workers and enlisted under conditions consistent with the workers' ideas of justice: and I want this because I am quite confident that with the growth of intelligence and knowledge and what is of far greater importance, of understanding, those working people will hesitate to plunge themselves into war against their fellows in other countries.[2]

With a political agenda like this, and given the climate of war weariness, pacifism and disillusion at the time, Thurtle and his allies were a powerful force for change. The War Office reflected this broad desire for change after the 'war to end wars'. During the 1919 debate on the Army Act the Secretary of State for War stated:

> let us see if we can apply all this new knowledge and opinion to make an ... improvement of our CM procedure; ... and see in what way CMs can be carried out to a greater degree of equity and tolerance with greater securities for prisoners without hampering that rough and ready justice that is a vital component of the operations for life and death in the field ...

The Darling Committee, set up to review all aspects of the system after 1918, gave these ideas broad support. Its main conclusions had been that the process could be improved in three main areas: first, greater efforts to ensure that accused soldiers were made fully aware of their legal rights and given every opportunity to exercise those rights; secondly, there should be a more formalized and public 'appeals system'; and lastly, any soldier convicted of a capital crime should have a formal right of 'petition' against a death sentence.

These points were disputed by the various military authorities, who pointed out (with some justice) that convicted soldiers were in fact better provided for in terms of levels of legal scrutiny after conviction than any comparable civilian. Nevertheless, the three MPs on the committee had not been able to agree with the majority, and produced a minority report demanding that in the case of death sentences there should be a right of appeal to the Court of Criminal Appeal, and that the power of life and death be effectively removed from commanders-in-chief and the military. In the words of the minority report:

> No man on joining the Army should forfeit the right of appeal for his life to a competent judicial tribunal. No inconvenience could in our opinion be caused to the Army by this reform, whilst the JAG and others would be relieved of a grave responsibility, which, in our view, ought not to rest upon them.[3]

This pressure by the abolitionists did not abate and when, in 1920, Lord Southborough raised the matter in Parliament again, stressing the dangers of convictions for cowardice in connection with possible shell shock, he was invited to form a committee to review the whole matter of 'shell shock'.

In 1922 Southborough's committee reported, (see Chapter 35) concluding that only 11 per cent of men sentenced to death had actually suffered the penalty and, significantly, the reprieved 89 per cent were mainly spared as a result of medical experience. They were almost entirely cases of chronic and acute nervous exhaustion with a history of sickness and wounds, who had suffered an acute breakdown at the time of their action. A few were genuine 'fugues' (the psychological term for a dazed incoherence where individuals have lost mental control of their actions) and had wandered away in a dazed condition. Only a few of the cases were caused by mental deficiency. This was an important point as Southborough's committee saw evidence from all sources and had access to information lost to us today, in particular the original court martial papers of the courts martial where capital sentences were commuted. They saw more and knew more than we know today. They were therefore far better qualified to rule on the subject not only by the values of the day but also by the evidence before them. To question Southborough is legitimate, but only on points of opinion and interpretation, not of contemporary facts, to which they had far better access. Even more important, there was no minority report, even from the MPs on the committee, one of whom had earlier been a member of the Darling Committee: the findings were unanimous.

Despite the Southborough findings and proposals, the abolitionists were still not satisfied and in 1924 yet another committee was formed specifically to examine the single issue of the death penalty. The committee concluded that the death penalty should be retained for certain military offences; but the abolitionists still kept up their pressure, mainly through the annual Army Act debates. As a result, in 1928 major changes were proposed, retaining the death penalty on active service for only the five most serious military offences: mutiny, desertion, cowardice, quitting post without orders and treason/treachery. Even this was not enough. The abolitionists were determined to remove the power of life or death from military commanders-in-chief. By 1929 events favoured Thurtle and his fellow campaigners as Ramsay MacDonald's new Labour government came to power. On a free vote Thurtle's amendment to the government's proposed legislation was carried by 219 votes to 135, leaving only mutiny and treason as capital offences in military law.

Significantly, a portion of Thurtle's support came from several experienced ex-soldiers. For example, a Maj. Gen. Hutchinson MP spoke up welcoming the changes:

> anyone who has had service in the field knows the extraordinary strain under which men and especially private soldiers suffer. I look upon a man whose brain has gone under that stress as being a wounded man – a mentally wounded man …[4]

Thurtle's parliamentary victory was challenged in the Lords and the argument thrown open when the Upper House reinstated execution for desertion, cowardice and quitting post. The older peers who had started their careers in Queen Victoria's day had genuine difficulties in comprehending that their world had passed and that their time-honoured values and nineteenth-century military laws, rooted in ensuring that the 'scum of the earth, enlisted for drink' did not run amok, had little place in Britain's modern services.

Thurtle however was brooking no more opposition and in an impassioned plea on a motion rejecting the Lords' changes to the Bill, he carried the day by 194 to 50. After a decade of campaigning, Thurtle had won his parliamentary campaign to change the law. From 1929 onwards execution was possible only for offences that were capital charges against the citizen in civil law and for mutiny. The Army Act was changed and the second BEF that went off to France in 1939 to fight Hitler did so without having to face the draconian penalties their fathers had lived under in 1914. The Second World War was to be fought without the threat of execution hanging over unwilling or traumatized soldiers. It was to be left to the Wehrmacht and Luftwaffe to teach the harsh realities of war to the British Army.

The sense of unease about courts martial continued however, and in March 1938 yet another committee was convened under the chairmanship of a distinguished lawyer, Sir Roland Oliver, who had himself won an MC during the Great War. The Oliver committee was charged with examining 'the existing system of trial by CM'. It was also tasked with looking closely at the right of a convicted serviceman to appeal against sentence. By early 1939 the Oliver report was being studied by Cabinet committees. The report noted a marked lack of interest from servicemen in military legal matters, and considered that the post-Darling and Southborough arrangements were therefore satisfactory. It found that the numbers of courts martial were declining rapidly (from 10,000 in 1909 to 2,000 in 1937) and found no evidence of miscarriages of justice in previous convictions. However, the committee recommended that the JAGs should be seen to be independent of the Service hierarchies and that there was still a need for more trained lawyers and legal education in the services. Oliver's final recommendation was for increased access to professional legal assistance for accused servicemen. However, the typically ponderous Whitehall deliberations over such weighty matters as who would pay for the newly independent JAGs were cut short on 1 September 1939 when Hitler invaded Poland and the armed forces were called on, yet again, to confront the armed might of Germany.[5]

But the 1939–45 war, like the conflict only twenty years before, was going to impart its own brutal lessons, and not all senior officers in every army agreed with the British liberals' agenda. Several experienced campaigners who had seen both wars advocated tough, old-fashioned measures on the treatment of 'cowards and shirkers'. In August 1943 Gen. George Patton, commander of Seventh US Army in Sicily, visited hospitals to meet the wounded men and distribute Purple Heart medals. Encountering two 'shell-shocked' soldiers, Patton's self-control snapped and he smacked them across the face with his gloves, calling them 'yellow bastards'. For good measure he added: 'You ought to be lined up against a wall and shot. In fact I ought to convene a Court Martial and shoot you myself right now ...!'[6]

Patton's fury – presumably based on a mixture of martial pride, compassion for his 'genuinely' (i.e. physically) wounded soldiers and sheer plain ignorance, which nearly cost him his job – stands in stark contrast to the attitudes of most British officers during the Second World War, many of whom had learned from their experiences of 1914–18. But even in the British Army these memories still did not entirely expunge the basic responses of some very senior soldiers to the problems of discipline in war. Thus as early as March 1940 Lord Gort (C.-in-C. of the BEF in 1939–40) was pushing at Cabinet level for the reintroduction of the death penalty for desertion on active service as he felt that 'penal servitude was an insufficient deterrent'.[7] It is highly unlikely that the C.-in-C. of the BEF was acting alone and not also reflecting the views of his corps commanders and the AG of the BEF. What is significant is that Gort and his senior subordinates were all experienced front line commanders from the First World War (Gort had won the VC in the trenches) and might have been considered relatively 'enlightened' in their views.

Even the victor of Cyrenaica, Gen. Sir Richard O'Connor, whose stunning victories over a massive Italian army in the Western Desert in 1940 (Operation Compass) are now long forgotten but who is remembered as an outstanding and humane leader in the Nelson and Rommel style, felt the same. After he was released from an Italian prisoner of war camp in 1943 he commanded a corps in north-west Europe. During stalemate in Normandy he saw the effects of war close up and wrote long afterwards:

> there were (some) genuine cases of shell shock but the great majority were merely frightened of shelling and wanted an excuse to get out of it. The shelling was horrible and most frightening, but if people were allowed to leave the battlefield every time they were frightened the army would have disintegrated in no time. [8]

O'Connor's views went to the heart of the debate. In the overwhelmingly conscript British Army of the 1940s it would appear that many experienced and highly intelligent senior officers did not entirely trust the cutting edge of the weapon given to them by the nation. For example, as the Western Desert campaign disintegrated into the shambles of the 'Gazala Stakes' and the rout after the fall of Tobruk to Rommel's Panzer Armee Afrika in summer 1942, a despairing C.-in-C. Middle East, Sir Claude Auchinleck, cabled the War Office requesting

> in strongest possible terms for earliest possible agreement to re-introduce death penalty for specified offences. Recent desertions show alarming increase even amongst troops of highest category. Present punishments are insufficient deterrent.

Interestingly, Auchinleck added a significant example, making an important comparison between the First and Second Wars:

> Would stress that cases where deserter takes truck containing food and water and means of transport of his comrades are far more serious than similar cases in last war ...[9]

Auchinleck – and his army and corps commanders – were concerned at the alarming increase in desertion from the front line. In late July 1942, for example, there were no fewer than 120 prisoners in Cairo awaiting court martial for desertion and over 1,700 deserters on the run from Eighth Army in the desert. The fact that Royal Military Policemen at traffic control checkpoints had had to fire their revolvers to control the Gadarene-like rush of rear area troops attempting to flee Rommel's advancing tanks may have coloured Auchinleck's views. Despite his entreaties, Churchill and the War Cabinet ignored this request from the C.-in-C. Middle East Forces. There would be no death penalty for desertion.[10]

Eighteen months later desertions had reached such a state in Italy that both the C.-in-C. Mediterranean Forces (Gen. Maitland Wilson) and the commander in Italy (Gen. Alexander) pleaded jointly for the right to take tougher disciplinary measures. Although Alexander wrote that 'it was a great mistake to have done away with the death penalty for desertion' he acknowledged that 'it will be a difficult thing to get through [Parliament] because it is essentially a political thing'.[11] His concerns were based on the chaos and indiscipline, looting and corruption endemic in some areas behind the lines in Italy, where over 2,200 soldiers had been court-martialled for desertion in 1944 and another 840 for absence.

The Army Council looked hard at all these requests but in every case rejected them for the same basic reasons. In the first place, the incidence of desertion in Britain's conscript army in the Second World War was demonstrably lower than in the 1914–18 war. Secondly, it was proving difficult to sort out the cowards and deserters from the genuinely shell-shocked or battle-stressed; and lastly, the politics of the day could not openly admit that, at times, British Army morale was disastrous.

The background to these three factors is well documented. However, whilst there were occasional serious concerns and setbacks, even at the worst moments of the Second World War desertion never rose above 0.088 per cent of the army's strength; hardly a significant drain of manpower.[12] Compared with the 10.26 deserters per 1,000 men of 1914–18 (with the death penalty), the figure for WW2 was only 6.89 per 1,000. The truth was that the death penalty appeared to make little difference.[13]

The problem of separating battle-fatigued men – i.e. genuine combat-shocked casualties – from the cowards, deserters and just normally frightened was compounded by the army's own extensive reliance on psychiatrists and psychologists as professional advisers. From the earliest days of the second war, unlike that of 1914–18, the British Army had openly embraced the existence of fear, battle stress and the possibility of human breakdown. Not only had the authorities taken the concept on board, by 1942 they had institutionalized it into a series of psychological screening tests designed to weed out the unsuitable recruits from front line units. So for example, of the 203,000 men who joined the army between July 1942 and January 1943, 8,000 were weeded out as 'psychiatrically unsuitable' and 3,200 were graded as 'unfit for front line service on psychiatric grounds'.[14]

Despite this, many still doubtless slipped through the net to experience what the Adjutant General of the day called 'the universal emotion [of the battlefield] – fear'. He added for good measure: 'the brave man and the coward have this in common. They both feel fear – one controls it, the other collapses under it.'[15]

The problem was that in the casualty clearing stations and hospitals those very doctors who had advised the generals were now having difficulty distinguishing the brave man at the limit of his endurance from the cowardly malingerer. Even the doctors could not sort out those who were feigning 'shell shock' from those men who were genuinely traumatized by battle. In Normandy in 1944 No. 21 Field Ambulance admitted 280 cases of 'battle exhaustion' in one three-day period. Of these, the senior RAMC doctor estimated that '70% were no more exhausted than the walking (physically) wounded ...' He added for good measure that 'the majority should never have been allowed to quit their front line units, let alone be evacuated as casualties by the Regimental Medical Officers'.[16]

The pendulum had now swung too far the other way and some soldiers not unnaturally elected for the safety of a medical tent well behind the lines rather than the terror of being incessantly 'stonked' in their trenches by well-handled German *Minenwerfers* and mortars.

But the third and most telling reason why the Cabinet and Army Council never agreed to requests from commanders-in-chief, however impassioned, to reintroduce the death penalty was the political dimension. As the Army Minister informed Churchill in mid 1942:

> Directly we introduce legislation, we are at once in a serious dilemma.
> If legislation is necessary, then the facts and figures must be serious. But,
> if they are so serious, then we can't afford to [publish] them to our friends
> or to our enemies.[17]

The bottom line was that if the situation was really as bad as commanders-in-chief claimed, then advertising the army's problems would only make it worse and give Britain's enemies – and even its allies – a deeply damaging propaganda coup. Churchill said 'no' and there the matter rested, to the frustration of the army commanders-in-chief, who, the AG reported, were still 'obsessed' with the subject of desertion when he made a flying tour of the commands just before the end of the war.[18]

In this they were not alone by the end of the Second World War. The American Army had wrestled with a tide of desertion and theft at various times in the European theatre. The final straw came when thousands of American troops fled from the mist-shrouded forests of the snowy Ardennes as the Germans launched their final offensive at Christmas 1944. Even the

Supreme Allied Commander and his fellow generals in Paris were alarmed and began to prepare for their own withdrawal as some of the fleeing men made it a long way back from the line, speading panic and confusion as they ran. When the scare was over, hundreds of the deserters were arrested and court-martialled. Eventually an exasperated Eisenhower confirmed one death sentence 'as an example' and to make a point to the US Army in Europe and its *40,000* deserters that military discipline meant what it said. On 31 January 1945 Pte Eddie Slovik of 28 Infantry Division was executed by a firing squad of his fellow US soldiers for cowardice and desertion in the face of the enemy; the only US – or British – soldier to be executed in the Second World War for specifically military offences. The British Army was not unique in its struggle to balance compulsion with motivation.

But the truth was, whatever the problems of the British Army between 1940 and 1945, and they were many, the death penalty would probably not have made things any better and would even have risked making the control, discipline and morale of a mass group of civilian conscripts worse.[19] Reported cases of genuine cowardice appear to have been few, and the army of 1940–45 was undoubtedly more understanding and tolerant of normal human reaction to the terrors of battle than that of 1914–18. Given the dire straits the army – and particularly the infantry – were in by the end of the war, this tolerance is all the more remarkable. For example, one general wrote:

> their stock of courage could soon be exhausted leaving them bankrupt and bereft of bravery. After the first few weeks in Normandy about 10% of 2nd Army casualties in Jun 1944, and nearly 50% of one of the veteran divisions were classified as battle exhaustion.[20]

This reluctance to fight, and specifically to avoid casualties (what one general who had fought in the trenches in WW1 dryly called 'the "keep a whole skin" brigade'), went deep and was, hardly surprisingly, noted by the enemy. In July 1944 an intelligence report from the Wehrmacht's Panzer Lehr Division in Normandy noted that

> the enemy (i.e. the British Infantry) is extraordinarily nervous of close combat. Whenever (the British Infantry) is energetically engaged [by German attackers] they usually retreat – or surrender.[21]

Even that well-known enthusiast Gen. Sir Brian Horrocks gloomily concluded that the British Army 'seems to have lost the sharp edge of its offensive spirit'.

After four years of reverses, defeats, retreats and bloodshed, even in victory Britain's citizen army was an extraordinarily fragile instrument, and all the senior officers and politicians knew it. The army of 1939–45 was not the volunteer force of 1914, and the damage of the Somme and Passchendaele went deep in the collective national psyche. To put it bluntly, in Gen. Essame's words, 'compared with the Great War veterans, there was a lack of moral fibre in the younger generation of soldiers'. The army of 1939–45 needed sensitive handling, not brutal threats, to get it to do anything. The following brief extract from 21 Army Group's after-action report on operations in North-west Europe rams the point home that the lessons of 1914–18 had been learned only too well:

> The chief task of psychiatry during the campaign was the treatment of acute psychiatric battle casualties ... rising to 20% of all casualties in July '44 ... [Battle] "exhaustion" rose to over two thousand per week ... The ratio of men leaving the battlefield unwounded rose to ... one in three (in newly committed units).
>
> Three weekly courses in clinical psychiatry were run for RMOs. Valuable training films were made, 'Field Psychiatry for RMOs' ...
>
> The use of psychiatric reports in disciplinary cases was extended in two directions ... The function of the Psychiatric Report was to assist the Commanding Officer or Convening Officer [ie, of a court martial] in coming to a decision whether it was in the best interest of the service and the man that he should be dealt with by a summary trial, court martial or on a purely psychiatric case.[22]

From the above it is clear that not only did psychiatry play an important part in helping the British Army to get through the struggle of the Second World War, it also frustrated several senior officers (who would have preferred more stick and less carrot to stiffen their soldiers' resolve). The psychologists and modern notions of battle strain also appear to have offered a tempting escape route for the frightened front line soldier. To what extent this balance helped or hampered the army in its primary mission, to kill the enemy, must ever remain a matter of debate. Although the greatest number of deserters and the greatest number of psychiatric cases came from the infantry, the inescapable fact is that the army fought on in defeat and victory, without breaking. Just as in the First World War the number of men who broke was a tiny percentage of the whole. For officers and men alike, most regimental soldiers would have gone to almost any lengths to stay with their mates and comrades-in-arms in that most intimate and impenetrable élite: a fighting unit.

But the stress of combat in the Second World War was not confined to the army, however protracted ground operations became.

The RAF's Bomber Command fought a battle virtually every night, and often with the same warriors in the front line, week in week out. In many ways the battle stress of bomber crews between 1942 and 1945 is the nearest comparison we have to the strain of constant trench warfare experienced by their fathers a generation before in France. Inevitably that strain told: and its effects – and its disciplinary consequences – had some uncomfortable parallels with the 1914–18 experience.

Like Kitchener's volunteers, the RAF creamed off an almost entirely volunteer force of British and Commonwealth manpower in 1939–41 to fight Hitler's Germany. It effectively took in the equivalent of two army divisions' manpower, all of it educationally qualified as army NCOs or even officer material. The average RAF recruit was 'high quality, skilled and self-reliant' compared to his army counterpart.

Over 50,000 Bomber Command aircrew perished during the war, and by 1942 the Air Ministry had calculated that an average bomber crew had only a 33 per cent chance of surviving one tour of thirty 'Ops' and only a 16 per cent chance of surviving a second. Yet despite this, Bomber Command fought on night after night.[23]

There were, inevitably, psychiatric casualties, stressed beyond endurance by fear of operations and by fear of flying; at least another 8,000 aircrew died in flying accidents. As soldiers in the 1914–18 trenches had discovered, it was the constant daily – or in Bomber Command's case, nightly – grind of fear, and the need to overcome that fear on a routine basis, that sapped even the bravest man's courage over the months. Even the hardest-nosed crew, secure behind the comforting personal fiction, 'it can't happen to me', must have experienced some doubts when they saw their friends frying in their own fat as a stricken bomber plunged to its doom, leaving them alone to be stalked as the next victim by some deadly invisible predator high in the dark sky above Germany. Such nightly terrors act like an acid on the soul.

Inevitably some men cracked. 'Loss of keenness for flying duties' became the precursor to the dreaded 'Lack of Moral Fibre', or LMF (first spelled out in Air Ministry Memorandum S. 61141/S. 7 of 1940). By mid 1942 the situation had become serious enough for Bomber Command to set up its own informal inquiry, 'An Investigation into Psychological Disorders in Flying

Personnel'. The report's findings unsurprisingly chronicled Bomber Command's own version of 'shell shock' – 'combat stress'.[24]

Just as with the infantry of 1914–18 all sorts of reactions to battle stress were uncovered. Some men went sick with trivial complaints, some became reckless, others drank; pilots admitted losing weight, listlessness, fatigue and fear. The aircrew of Bomber Command were, like the infantry of 1914–18, a group of young men frightened and stressed almost beyond endurance. Sometimes 'the RAF treated such men with considerable harshness', in Max Hastings's phrase. To ram the point home, one of Hastings's RAF sources claimed: 'I made certain that every case before me was punished by Court Martial, and where applicable by an exemplary prison sentence, whatever the psychiatrists said …'[25] Gen. Monro of the MEF and First Army in 1914–18 would have been proud of such a hardened disciplinarian.

This attitude was unusual. In a self-disciplining organization like a bomber crew it was more normal to remove aircrew who refused to fly (or asked to be transferred out) immediately to the Central RAF Depot, with their documents stamped 'LMF'. Loss of rank (to the lowest of the low, Aircraftsman 2nd Class), withdrawal of flying pay and loss of the coveted aircrew brevet or 'wings' accompanied such a move. This degradation and humiliation was precisely intended to publicly stigmatize and punish reluctant airborne warriors. Such aircrew were not shot for 'cowardice' or 'desertion': they were instead held up in disgrace as examples to the others.[26]

Despite the fear that these 'LMF' cases might infect aircrew, the incidence of 'cowardice' in Bomber Command was astonishingly low given its grinding task and bitter losses. Much of this is attributable to self-discipline and the *esprit de corps* of a volunteer élite: but it was remarkable nonetheless. Out of a total Bomber Command force that peaked at 155,000 personnel, only 2,726 sets of documents were stamped 'LMF' in the whole war, of which 389 were officers and 2,337 were NCO aircrew.[27] For a force that offered only a one in five chance of living through two operational tours, Bomber Command's human failures accounted for only 0.3 per cent of their total combat aircrew. Despite the shame and humiliations of the 'LMF' system it was a remarkable achievement.

The legacy of that fear and strain can still be seen today. Late at night surviving Lancaster aircrew can still find the terror that haunted them over fifty years ago: old men's eyes bear potent testimony to the perennial effects of battle on the human psyche as did doubtless Hector's, Falstaff's and Sir Thomas Picton's long before.

The RAF was in a minority. In modern warfare, psychiatric support was – and now is – seen as essential for dealing with wounds of the mind every bit as much as surgeons are called upon to deal with gaping bloody rips in flesh. By the end of the Second World War, army psychiatrists had recognized that the first few hours of fighting disabled 10 per cent of the fighting force.[28]

After the Vietnam War the Americans came to realize that psychological breakdown did not always occur in the battle zone. In that conflict, few soldiers broke down during combat (only 6 per cent of medical evacuations had taken place for combat stress, compared with 23 per cent during the Second World War), but the real problem emerged later, after the war, when many of the veterans started to suffer from psychological disorders.[29] In consequence a new chapter had to be written in the history of military psychiatry with the birth of the concept of 'post-traumatic stress disorder'. But all these views – and the new policies they engendered – owed much to the ground-breaking work of Lord Southborough's 'Shell Shock Committee' back in 1920.

Even so, the British Army's record of treating psychological combat stress has not been especially good by modern standards. For the Falklands War in 1982 no specialist RAMC officers accompanied the Task Force south, although the Royal Navy sent two doctors qualified in psychiatry. They recorded later that they had had plenty to do, from dealing with anxious NCOs before going into action (worried about letting their men down), to a classic self-inflicted wound to avoid the battlefield that could have come straight out of the 1914–18 war.

One of the most poignant stories of the war was that of a guardsman who ran away during the attack on Mount Tumbledown. In June 1982 the Scots Guards had closed with the Argentinian defenders and driven them off the hill in an old-fashioned battle 'fighting through the objective', using bayonet, grenade, butt and boot. It was a savage night characterized by the kind of close-quarter fighting that many armchair theorists fondly believed was a thing of the past. The Tumbledown battle could have come straight out of the trenches of the Somme or the slopes of Cassino. Casualties were bad on both sides. As dawn broke over the exhausted but victorious guardsmen, one man was missing.

Two months later he reappeared, having been on the run and sheltering with a Falkland family. The mood in HQ Land Forces Falkland Islands was uncompromising, with demands for a court martial for an obvious desertion, just as in the Great War. But nothing was to be allowed to tarnish the political laurels of the Falklands. To the astonishment of some of the LFFI staff advocating a hard line, the guardsman was whisked back to the UK and the problem handed over to the commanding officer of the Scots Guards. It was to be 'his problem' By subtle winks and nods it was made plain that although the final responsibility was his, any suggestion of an automatic court martial even for such a blatant act of indiscipline 'might not be in the public interest'. Thanks to a merciful CO and the MOD's pressure not to cause undue PR or media embarrassment, the matter was allowed to slide until the wretched soldier could eventually be quietly discharged. He was lucky, and the case symbolizes just how far we have progressed since the generation of 1914. In the Great War the individual concerned would almost certainly have been charged with either cowardice or desertion and dealt with harshly. Nowadays we realize that it is group bonding and peer pressure that enable men to fight and overcome their fear and not the threat of discipline, however draconian.

The tragedy was that the Falklands, like the long haul of the counter-terrorist campaign in Ulster, has left many modern psychological casualties. By the 1970s and 1980s PTSD was beginning to be recognized and acknowledged as a medical condition requiring treatment. Even policemen (who presumably joined the constabulary in the clear knowledge that a policeman's lot will not invariably be a happy one) felt so stressed and injured by the sights they had witnessed in the execution of their duty that they felt impelled to sue their superiors for causing them unnecessary suffering. For a fighting force or an army such modern legalistic solutions may be inappropriate. Although the whole nature of battle is stressful, in an élite fighting force *any* sign of weakness by a strong leader is always seen as an admission of failure. Few self-respecting officers or NCOs would dare to admit to feeling inadequate or frightened by their job unless they were at their wits' end. Careers can be ruined and promotions lost. After the Falklands, Northern Ireland and the Gulf many veterans took to the bottle, argued with their wives or got divorced. A disproportionate number (one 1980s estimate was that 7 per cent of the adult prison population were ex-soldiers) ended up in jail or even on the streets, where their problems became even worse.

In a strange echo of the problems of Bomber Command during the Second World War, combat stress problems affected even élite undercover special forces units. It was widely understood that Capt. Nairac, the Special Forces liaison officer tortured and shot by the IRA after being caught in an unauthorized reconnaissance on his own, was overtired and overconfident and should not have been allowed to extend his tour of duty in Northern Ireland.

However, like so many of the special operators, Nairac's critical faculty had gone, to be replaced by an unfounded belief in his own ability to cope. He begged to be allowed to continue, even though his judgement of risk had been clouded and he had become a danger to himself and his comrades through combat stress. Capt. Robert Nairac, George Cross, paid the ultimate price.

Nairac's death did have some good side effects. Not long afterwards an experienced senior NCO, who had been carrying out the most sensitive and dangerous missions during two undercover tours in Ulster, came to his depot in England and, almost in tears, said that he couldn't face another operational tour in the province. He was happy to train new special operators and monitor operations, but a third tour in the front line, on his own, was too much for a married man in his mid thirties with a young family.

It was the classic Bomber Command 'LMF' problem. Fortunately his OC knew about combat stress and the problems of operational tours. The NCO was quietly transferred to training duties and even given a gallantry award for his past exploits. Even the bravest man can only do so much.

The fact is that battle stress cannot be dealt with by rules, regulations and the Law. War and its long-term effects on the human psyche will remain a permanent challenge to humanity's progress towards some future risk free Utopia

This raises an important contradiction for progressive liberal societies. War is nasty, brutal and unfair and does not lend itself to 'individuals' rights' over stress. War is intended to be stressful and is specifically sets out to destroy the most basic human right of all – the right to life. No amount of progressive theorising or waving legal 'group compensation claims' for soldiers can undo that savage truth. The point of battle is intended to be the very negation of civilisation. As George Patton put it with brutally simple clarity: *"The aim is NOT to die for your country – it's to make the other son of a bitch to die for his"*. Battle shock exists because battle is, and always will be, shocking.

The real danger to progress may in fact lie in the contradiction between lawers' ideas of peacetime human rights and bloody truth of the battlefield. The gravest danger may well be that our new concerns for the rights of the individual might one day risk rendering our armed forces ineffective in the test of war. That will not be progress. But of one thing we may be sure, just as in the 1914 trenches there will be no legal representatives in the front line and, should they ever get to the real fighting, the enemy will try to kill the lawyers with everyone else.

It is stressful, shocking and unfair: but it is war.

CHAPTER 37

PARDONS FOR ALL?

None but a child would complain that our teachers have not yet eradicated the errors and superstitions of the past.

PROFESSOR WILL DURANT, *THE LESSONS OF HISTORY*

One of the more remarkable features of the whole subject of soldiers 'shot at dawn' in the Great War has been the growth of a campaign to posthumously pardon the convicted men. The motives behind the campaign, which is a loose alliance of individuals and organizations, cover a wide spectrum ranging from sometimes the ill-informed, ignorant or indignant on the one hand, to genuinely high-minded parliamentary campaigners in the long and honourable tradition of Ernest Thurtle MP on the other. Broadly the actual impetus for pardoning the convicted comes from two other streams: the relatives and the 'reformers'. Compassion for past wrongs is often mixed with a campaigning zeal.

Public unease about the whole subject of military executions started early and was voiced in Parliament during the Great War. The subsequent – and eventually successful – post 1918 parliamentary campaign to abolish capital punishment for 'military' crimes over what one author has called 'one of the shabbiest episodes in British history' fuelled the fears of the relatives of the convicted men, who wanted to know more, but were reluctant to ask. For a relative to have been shot for desertion or cowardice was a social stigma in the 1920s and 1930s. Whitehall's files stayed firmly shut.

Excessive bureaucratic secrecy did little to dispel dark myths and stories that circulated in the post-war press. Newspaper articles after the war often gave supposedly first-hand accounts of firing squads and trials 'hushed up' by the military authorities. However, they could not be checked by an interested public, or even denied by the War Office at the time, because a decision had been taken in 1919 to keep the details of the trials confidential under the 'hundred year rule'. Allegations that the intention was to protect the officers who sat on the various courts martial are demonstrably wrong. The principal reason behind this decision appears to have been to spare the relatives' feelings and to protect their interests. For example, after the war the Director of Records of the Imperial War Graves Commission wrote to the JAG to ask him for details about the executed men so that they could be commemorated in the same way as others killed in the war. A further letter from the IWGC noted: 'the greatest care will be taken to prevent any leakage of the information'.[1] It appears that, in the main, this policy worked and the 'shame' of the relatives quietly slipped away with the years, the impact of the Second World War, and a decline in public interest.

Whitehall's legal obligation to protect sensitive personnel files for one hundred years conspired, not for the first time, against an open discussion of the truth. Excessive bureaucratic secrecy and mysteries, however laudable the motives, invariably inspired dark theories of conspiracy, as any reader of the standard works on aliens, flying saucers or Kennedy's assassination knows only too well. The closed files in the PRO, most of them barred until well into the twenty-first century, drew the attention of academic historians and conspiracy theorists alike. Rumour and speculation took the place of fact, and public interest began to regenerate, led by academics, such as Douglas Gill, keen to unravel the mystery.

In May 1972 Don Concannon MP, who had served in the infantry during the 1939–45 war, rose in the House and asked if the surviving records could be destroyed, 'to prevent the names ever being released ...' (and becoming public). The Minister's answer sums up the whole bureaucratic position and the motives behind it:

> The present policy ... attempts to strike a balance between the protection
> of the innocent from unnecessary pain and the preservation of material
> that is part of our history.[2]

The Minister, Geoffrey Johnson Smith, therefore refused to recommend destruction of the surviving CM papers. Subsequent ministers may have wished he had.

From then on both public and parliamentary interest increased, encouraged by the journalist William Moore's *The Thin Yellow Line*.[3] Moore's 1974 book was a tour de force of investigative research. Denied any access to official documents he nevertheless dug up sufficient references to support a powerful narrative and to voice an equally indignant critique of successive governments' policy. He was repelled by what he felt was the excessive secrecy that had surrounded the trials for over fifty years. In his peroration he voiced the principal claims of what was to become the origins of the 'Pardons Campaign':

> The same yellow line which runs through us all shows in different ways at different times. To abandon the quest for truth under the smokescreen of false sentiment and before the parapets of bureaucracy is infinitely worse than desertion in the face of the enemy.

The cause now had a rallying cry and a preliminary list of cases, albeit speculative and unnamed.

In what appears to have been a belated attempt to put Whitehall's view, the Lord Chancellor's department allowed an experienced lawyer with a distinguished record in WW2, Judge Anthony Babington, to see the surviving court martial documents. Babington's book *For the Sake of Example* was published in 1983 and, like Moore's, became a steady seller. Babington was allowed to publish comments on the cases, but he did not name the individuals executed. He took a generally critical tone against the legal establishment's desire for secrecy, mainly driven by his unease, as a lawyer, with the conduct of the Field General Courts Martial. Babington's book further demonstrated not only that there was a growing public interest in the subject but that it was now becoming possible to link cases to names. By 1985 even the British Legion was calling for an inquiry. The pressure for more information became irresistible to two researchers.

In 1989 Julian Sykes and Julian Putkowski published *Shot at Dawn*, the first ever book naming the 309 men executed for military offences under the authority of the British Army Act between 1914 and 1920.[4] The authors attempted to take the moral high ground, possibly as a justification for their publicly identifying the men, a move that could have been calculated would guarantee publicity, sales and commercial success. They dismissed any possible embarrassment to the families and surviving relatives by claiming that they were uncovering a great scandal and revealing: 'the ineptness, ignorance and unfairness of the British Courts Martial at the time ...', and that 'the next of kin of executed men were hoodwinked into believing that their men had died in action', 'a system of cover up that exists to this day.'[5] Even the soldiers' offences were categorized as 'crimes', in inverted commas, implying that in some way they were not.

These authors also set out their personal agenda in a 'Statement' in the book:

We believe that few will read *Shot at Dawn* and conclude that these men deserved their fate, or that their shamed relatives should continue to suffer and endure the associated disgrace. Accordingly we repeat our call for the MOD to have the courage to admit these injustices and to initiate procedures for exonerating all 351 men who were executed by the British Army in the First World War.[6]

The 'Pardons Campaign' now had not only a cause, but a rallying call, plus a text to quote. However, the authors' statement skated over some unpalatable truths. In the first place, many of the surviving families had no knowledge of their long-dead relatives' fate until Putkowski and Sykes brought their 'shame' to public attention. Secondly, neither of the authors had originally had the benefit of reading the courts martial papers but had deduced and inferred much detail from various summaries and secondary sources, especially Babington. Finally, and most remarkable of all, the authors were in fact calling for the legally convicted military murderers to be 'exonerated' (thirty-seven of the 346 cases were executed for murder), without any comparable call for civilians convicted for murder at the same time to be 'pardoned'. This unprecedented demand continued to be repeated in later editions.

The regular sales of *Shot at Dawn* fuelled a full-scale Pardons Campaign. Much of the impetus has come from the North-East, where, from 1990, an activist, John Hipkin, became a tireless campaigner. Hipkin, taken prisoner during the Second World War as a 15-year-old merchant seaman, took up the cause and he began to picket and demonstrate with sandwich boards at various military events to draw attention to the executions of under-age soldiers seventy-five years before. Hipkin founded the 'Shot at Dawn Pressure Group' and quickly found allies, most notably from the families of the 19th DLI Bantams Willie Stones, Peter Goggins and John McDonald. The Pardons Campaign began to attract public attention and, despite official attempts to play down the matter, by 1992 had become a full-blown single-issue pressure group drawing broad support from a variety of individuals whose main source of information appears to have been Putkowski and Sykes's *Shot at Dawn* and various newspaper articles.

In 1992 the Labour MP for Thurrock, Andrew MacKinley, was taking an interest in the public campaign and began a correspondence with the then Prime Minister, John Major. In 1993 MacKinley moved a Private Member's Bill in the House, and in 1995 drew a statement from the office of the Leader of the Opposition, Tony Blair, that any future Labour government would look 'sympathetically' at the various cases and 'review the subject'. This statement followed publication of a Bill sponsored by Andrew MacKinley MP calling on Parliament to pass a measure to

> provide for the granting of pardons to soldiers of the British Empire forces executed during the Great War of 1914 to 1919 following convictions for offences of cowardice, desertion, or attempted desertion, disobedience, quitting post, violence, sleeping at post, throwing away arms or striking a superior officer …[7]

Significantly, MacKinley's Bill stopped short at calling for pardons for the murderers executed by military authorities in 1914–19. The precedent for pardoning military murderers eighty years on without fresh evidence would have major civilian legal implications. MacKinley's Bill was a legal embodiment of a 25,000-name petition collected in 1994.

The Bill provided for the establishment of a 'Pardons Tribunal' of three High Court judges to examine and report on every case and recommend the grant of a pardon where appropriate, using the power of the royal prerogative. More controversially, the Bill went on to provide compensation at the discretion of the Secretary of State, who would specifically 'make such payments as he considers reasonable in all the circumstances to any dependant of any such person'.

The Bill failed to make Parliamentary progress, but when the Labour government was elected in 1997 many observers, including seasoned 'Pardons Campaigners', felt that their claims would at last receive a more sympathetic hearing. In accordance with pre-election promises the new administration promptly undertook a review of the capital courts martial. The minister responsible was initially suspicious of his officials' advice but as he began to read the detailed transcripts he began to realize just why successive administrations had refused to make the cases public or to make political gestures with the courts martial. Many of those convicted had been only too guilty by the standards of the day.

The findings of that review were announced by the Minister for the Armed Forces, Dr John Reid, in July 1998. To the surprise of many he flatly refused any pardons, although he expressed 'a deep sense of regret at the loss of life … both those who died at the hands of the enemy and those who were executed'. His refusal was based on a well-argued case following a comprehensive review of every aspect of the subject, plus his own detailed study of over 100 of the original courts martial papers.

The Minister made two key arguments. First, the passage of time meant that the grounds for any 'blanket pardon' on the basis of unsafe conviction just did not exist. So no 'blanket pardon' was feasible. Any review would therefore have to examine individual cases. Secondly, any individual pardons had to be based on some new, concrete, evidence – and none existed. In his own words:

So if we were to pursue the option of formal legal pardons, the vast majority, if not all, of the cases would be left condemned ... by a lack of evidence to overturn the original verdicts. In short, most would be left condemned, or in some cases, re-condemned 80 years after the event.

He went on to say that he wished to be fair to all, and that 'we did not wish, by addressing one perceived injustice, to create another ...' Dr Reid summed up his position (as a sympathetic Labour Minister who had conscientiously read all the available evidence and personally reviewed over a hundred of the cases in some detail) thus:

The point is that now 80 years later and on the basis of the evidence, we cannot distinguish between those who deliberately let down their country and those who were NOT guilty of desertion or cowardice.

In response to questioning he clarified the point even further: he could not throw aside all legal precedent and '... make a judgment on what he believed rather than on the evidence ...'[8]

In his response for the Opposition, the MP for Mid-Norfolk, Keith Simpson, welcomed the statement by the Minister. Simpson's remarks were given extra weight by his background as a respected and thoughtful military historian. He made two key points. First, Dr Reid's statement would not satisfy the Pardons Campaign lobby; secondly, the Minister's 'expression of regret' was a dangerous precedent, and he enquired whether 'expressions of regret' were now to be offered to victims of Bloody Cumberland after Culloden, or the captured Indian Mutineers? He closed by saying that these were questions that involved looking back into history and making value judgements. This view was echoed by many subsequent political commentators, who although expressing compassion for those executed, agreed with the debate in the House that it was 'jejeune to make historical judgements through the prism of modern sensibilities'.

Predictably, the government's decision engendered headlines in the North-East such as 'Pardons for Executed Soldiers will be Denied Sparks Outcry' and considerable correspondence in both local and national press. Significantly, both the Western Front Association and the Royal British Legion refrained from joining the outcry.

But despite the political setback the Pardons Campaign continued its efforts. As the twentieth century drew to a close, for the first time a wreath was placed by the families at the Cenotaph as part of the Remembrance Day events and the activists began a widespread publicity and lobbying campaign to draw attention to their 'grievance'. Local councils were encouraged to pass votes calling for a pardon, and a special web site was established.[9] This helpfully included key spin-doctor-like 'lines' to take in response to various questions (e.g. Objection: 'You should not use today's standards to judge the past.' Response: 'This assertion is invalid because …' etc.)

The principal and most vocal activist appeared to be Julian Putkowski, one of the authors of *Shot at Dawn* and a tireless organizer and proselytizer for 'the cause'. In his own writings and speeches he frequently represented the issue in terms of 'class', laying great stress on the role at courts martial of officers and 'their public school origins'. Quite how 1914–18 courts martial should have been staffed and set up other than by officers remained broadly unanswered. It can only be inferred that some kind of civilian legal court or a Marxist revolutionary tribunal composed of like-minded and sympathetic soldiers was seriously being proposed as some kind of alternative to the legally constituted courts martial, established by Parliament. The Pardons Campaigners are unclear on such questions, and most of the families of executed men do not care about class-based political agendas, only their long-dead relative.

It is genuinely difficult to understand the aims and motives of the Pardons Campaign, which effectively took on a life of its own in the 1990s. Part of the problem, as the government, like its predecessors, had spelled out, was the sheer variety and range of the cases, the lack of remaining evidence and the varying degrees of guilt. For example, the relatives of Harry Farr undoubtedly have a point when they claim that their dead relative was 'shell-shocked'. No reasonable and compassionate reading of the court martial papers supports any other conclusion. But men like Rose, Mills or Lawrence were manifestly guilty as charged. Even the two 'Pals', Ingham and Longshaw, were demonstrably guilty and deserved the full rigour of the law by the standards of their time. It is deeply invidious to have to single out such individuals across the gulf of the years, but the claims of the Pardons Campaign force such 'naming and shaming' if only to emphasize and reinforce the injustice of Harry Farr's case or the genuine claims of the late Tom Stones for a re-examination of his great-uncle Willie Stones's trial. But the whole point of justice is to discriminate between the innocent and the guilty. As presently constituted the Pardons Campaign fails to address this essential requirement.

Instead it tends to concentrate on a broad-brush approach of what Americans call 'shroud waving' and a shared sense of injustice. This has fuelled such initiatives as the memorial to the executed men at the National Memorial Arboretum in Staffordshire, effectively a shrine to the unlucky, the shell-shocked and the rogues alike, centred around a statue of the under-age Herbert Burden. The legal and practical difficulties – if not the illegality – of 'pardoning' the guilty men along with those who genuinely may have had mitigating circumstances unknown at the time appears to have been ignored. The truth is that the Pardons Campaign by the turn of the century had become a highly vocal protest group, a loose alliance about the alleged grievances of a small group of men legally executed over eighty years ago. It had become a matter of radical and regional politics driven principally by emotion and a sense of grievance or some hope of financial compensation, rather than hard fact.

In particular, its claim to a monopoly of compassion is deeply unfair both to the soldiers who did their duty and to the commanders of the Great War. The generals of 1914 may have been misguided and stubborn but they were engaged in what they genuinely believed to be the final clash of Empires and to stigmatize them as some species of unfeeling class warriors, totally indifferent to the casualties and the suffering of their soldiers, is a serious slur. As the German general Hans von Seekt, founder of Germany's post 1918 Reichswehr, pointed out in 1930, 'The figure of the sabre-rattling, fire-eating general is an invention of poisoned and unscrupulous political activists … the soldier, having some experience of war, fears it far more than doctrinaire academics ignorant of war …'

There seems little doubt however that, whatever the political decisions, the Pardons Campaign, like so many protest movements, has a life of its own, impelled by the zeal of its members. Fuelled by the decision of the New Zealand government to issue a "Pardon" and by increasing pressure on the Canadian authorities, the alleged grievances of a tiny group of long dead men were still being forced onto the political agenda of the twenty first century. It is a sad postscript to a complex issue.

Saddest of all perhaps was the insistence of the Pardons Campaign on focusing attention on the the cases of the tiny minority of 306 men legally executed, and the apparent lack of compassion or equal concern for their 750,000 comrades who did their duty, and fought on until they paid the final price. In the Minister's words in Parliament in 1998, 'they were all victims of war'. Whatever our motives we cannot re-invent the past.

CHAPTER 38

FINAL THOUGHTS

But the Past is more readily lamented than corrected.

HANNIBAL TO SCIPIO AFRICANUS, 202 BC

The events of the First World War still exert a powerful hold on our imaginations. From the horrors of the trenches to the sheer numbers of men killed, our emotions are stretched unbearably, and never more than in the shadowy cases of those men executed for military offences.

The official policy of keeping the cases confidential after the war (under the 'hundred year rule', in common with all other controversial civil service personal documents which could impact on those still alive) further exacerbates the apparent mystery and sense of a cover-up. This quite naturally arouses even stronger feelings, but these are also mixed with considerable misunderstanding and confusion over the concept of military justice, the court martial process, and the individual cases themselves. It is also, in some cases, tied into an incomprehension of the realities of war or even the nature of war itself. As long ago as 50 BC Cicero noted: '*Silent enim leges inter arma*', which translates loosely as 'Laws are dumb in time of war', a frank admission that war is often a brutal and largely unregulated human activity. One of the problems with the modern debate about justice in war and pardons for judicial decisions which we do not like is the almost unbridgeable gap of comprehension between those who have been in action and those who have been spared that experience. In a world that is travelling ever further from any collective memory of battle, the attempt to apply modern civilian peacetime values to a primeval institution whose members exist to kill and destroy becomes both politically easier and potentially more disabling in the fierce test of war. Soldiering is not 'just a job', and never will be. The challenge is to keep the citizen's and the soldier's 'rights' in an equable balance.

Whilst the historic 'Mutiny Act' and the 'Articles of War' recognized that even as a soldier, a British citizen retained certain basic rights, the law has always acknowledged that these were modified on enlistment to meet the special needs of the armed services for enforcing discipline. In time of war these were even further changed to meet the particular demands of the battlefield, as the preamble to the 1913 Army Act clearly spelled out:

> ... and whereas no man can be forejudged of life or limb, or subjected in time of peace to any kind of punishment within this realm, by martial law, or in any other manner than by the judgment of his peers and according to the known and established laws of this realm, yet nevertheless, it being requisite, for the retaining of all the before-mentioned forces, and other persons subject to military law, in their duty, that an exact discipline be observed and that persons belonging to the said forces who mutiny or stir up sedition, or desert HM's service, or are guilty of crimes and offences to the prejudice of good order and military discipline, be brought to a more exemplary and speedy punishment than the usual forms of the law will allow.

This basic principle was not only legally authoritative in 1914 but its effects were well understood by every officer and soldier who had stood on a parade ground. All concerned – even the later generation of volunteers and wartime conscripts – knew that if you didn't obey lawful orders without a good excuse there would be trouble and if you failed in your duty on active service you might be shot. It was a straightforward and well-understood contract known to officers and soldiers alike. The *Soldier's Small Book*, issued on enlistment, actually contained an abbreviated list of the capital offences as a warning to the soldier going on active service.

Part of the problem in the Great War lay in the philosophy behind British military law, which had evolved during the nineteenth century to control the 'drink-sodden scum' of Wellington's day. But the army that went to war in 1914 was a well-disciplined and professional force whose main disciplinary problems – like those of the rest of the Edwardian workforce – were recreational boozing and occasional absenteeism. Serious charges against the well-regulated volunteers of the old regular army were rare, and behaviour patterns a far cry from the brutal and licentious soldiery so feared by legislators in the past. Perhaps because of this, the rigid Victorian codes spelled out in the various editions of the *Manuals of Military Law* between 1881 and 1913 were rarely tested or applied. This very lack of use (very few soldiers were executed for military offences in the long period of peace before 1914) caused many military laws to be unquestioned, by soldier and civilian alike. Old forms stayed on the Statute Book because they were there and had never been tested.

Most of the military law enacted by Parliament was genuinely intended to help the armed forces perform their brutal task on behalf of the rest of society, often in bad conditions and a long way from home. Where there were procedural differences between courts martial and civil courts – such as dispensing with procedures in the needs of active service – these were essentially to meet the special needs of military justice in war. Notwithstanding this, courts martial were required to follow the procedures and practices of English law of the period, even down to precisely the same standards of evidence and strictly enforced Rules of Procedure. On active service the whole procedure could be accelerated by the use of the Field General Court Martial (FGCM). The whole purpose of these proceedings was to speed up the military legal process, enforce discipline and provide an element of exemplary punishment if required and without delay.

It is significant that in not one of the surviving sets of court martial papers is there any argument that the wrong man had been convicted, or that a completely innocent man had been executed. What does come through, however, is – in a very limited number of cases – a failure by the court to recognize extenuating circumstances which we would admit today that could have mitigated punishment. Even this harsh sentencing policy was tempered in the paternalistic society of 1914 by the desire to punish only in the interests of group discipline and, wherever possible, by Haig's desire to give a man another chance. The various c-in-cs' refusal to confirm 89 per cent of the death sentences strongly supports that view, and undermines allegations that he was a ruthless, unsympathetic commander-in-chief. This view is further supported by the sheer scale and number of men whose capital sentences were suspended or commuted to a lesser penalty. This desire *not* to punish unduly in most of the cases is even further reinforced by the large number of men who were on their second or even third capital conviction before they finally came face to face with the ultimate sanction of the law of the day. The military justice system, from the numbers alone, seems to have been fairly reluctant to enforce capital punishment, notwithstanding the potentially large number of military capital offences available.

Nonetheless, there remains a genuine unease about a small percentage of the 306 men executed for specifically military offences. Although in every case the individual appears to be guilty of the offence with which he was charged, there are a number of cases where the man's explanation for his actions seems to require more sympathetic understanding than was given by the court at the time. By 1917 this was acknowledged both in the field and in Parliament, with at least one MP calling for the death sentence for cowardice to be suspended in the case of any soldier previously wounded or invalided for shell shock. As only a small number of men (eighteen out of 306) were executed for 'cowardice', even this would have had little effect. The truth is that in 1914 no one really understood the effects of shell shock (or battle stress), and knowledge of its existence and effects percolated slowly through the vast (over 5 million strong) civil–military bureaucracy that was the British Army between 1914 and 1918.

Today it is well recognized that combat stress reaction (CSR) and longer-term post-traumatic stress disorder (PTSD) can affect soldiers – and others – doing difficult jobs in dangerous conditions. Because of our longer experience of war and wider medical and psychiatric knowledge it is often automatically assumed that there must have been deliberate injustice in the treatment of accused soldiers in the First World War because 'shell shock' was ignored deliberately, and that the men who were shot were treated unfairly. The evidence very rarely supports this view.

However, the level of medical knowledge in 1914, whilst crude by modern standards, developed surprisingly rapidly in the pressure cooker of war. Whilst there was no standard diagnosis, and (inevitably) doctors' professional opinions varied as much as they do today, the medical profession did not ignore the evidence of shell shock before its eyes. For example, as early as the period from August to December 1914 (that is during the first months of the war, fought by the old regular army) there were 520 men whose diagnoses were categorized as 'functional nervous diseases' according to *The Official History of the War Medical Services*. This also also notes that, as in former campaigns, such cases were listed frequently with 'mental disability' or 'mental exhaustion' rendering the soldier unfit for battle right from the start. The difficulty was that there was no real policy for dealing with this type of casualty in an army that admitted no question of fear and did not understand the nature of stress trauma any more than did the German, French or any other army in 1914.

'Shell shock' casualties became serious for the BEF after the opening phase of the battle of the Somme in July 1916, when in just a few weeks thousands of soldiers were evacuated away from the firing line with nervous disorders. On being taken to the doctors men increasingly complained of 'shell shock, Sir'. The difficulty confronting the RMOs was very clearly spelled out by Lt Col. Charles Myers RAMC, one of the first physicians to recognize and deal with psychiatric trauma amongst soldiers, who said, in response to a query about the misuse of the term 'shell shock':

… I was in hearty agreement: I also had seen too many men at Base
Hospitals and Casualty Clearing Stations boasting that they were
'suffering from shell shock, Sir' when there was nothing appreciably
amiss with them save 'funk'…

To help deal with this problem, specialist 'shell shock' centres were established towards the end of the war, where attempts were made to grapple with
one of the most serious and least understood medical, military and legal problems of the war, the need, in Dr Myers's own words, 'to separate the blame
worthy weaklings from the rest'. They also helped to balance the views of
Myers and many other doctors beginning to specialize in the newly emerging science of 'neurology' who were struggling to reconcile their experiences
with the law of the day which effectively said that '… from a military standpoint a deserter was either insane and destined for the madhouse or legally
responsible for his actions and therefore capable of standing trial and liable to
be punished accordingly'. Myers's version of the doctor's dilemma in war
remained throughout the Second World War as an intractable difficulty and
may indeed be a perennial problem for medicine in wartime. By 1939 the
Army had even reached the stage of putting doctors effectively in the position of judges, ruling whether a man was sick and to be evacuated, or a coward
to be disciplined with the full rigour of the law.

As the war went on, Myers himself and many other doctors frequently
gave evidence to courts martial, either trying to save soldiers who were not
wholly responsible for their actions or, in some cases, actually insisting that
soldiers should not escape the consequences of their actions as there were no
extenuating 'mental' circumstances. These increasingly sophisticated medical arrangements had an impact. The 'Shell Shock Committee' after the war
recorded that by the end of 1917, after improved methods of treatment had
been introduced, 'battle shock' casualties showed a 66 per cent reduction
from mid 1916 levels.

These medical advances were reflected in corresponding legal developments during the war. From the crude, almost Wellingtonian, discipline of
September 1914 the system evolved, until by 1918 it is clear that a military
disciplinary system that believed in making an occasional example was also
well aware of the need for a scrupulously fair trial with a clearly and appro-
priately framed charge, plus the fullest consideration of any mitigating circumstances for what had become by 1918 standing semi-professional courts
martial.

These changes to pre-war military law procedures began soon after the start of the war. As early as the spring of 1915 the process of reviewing a soldier's overall performance and the needs of the unit or formation began to be a consideration during the process of confirmation of sentence. Idiosyncratic and lacking compassion as many of the surviving senior officers' comments in the CM papers are, the fact is that in the great majority of the cases humane or medical considerations far overshadowed any need for exemplary punishment. The tragedy is that, because we can no longer examine the cases which were commuted to see just what medical or other mitigating evidence was given, we cannot tell to what extent senior officers heeded this advice. All we can tell is that nine out of ten 'appeals' – which is what the confirmations process effectively was – against the death sentence were successful. Nine out of ten convicted men were *not* shot.

The changes in the army in France were matched by growing parliamentary unease, particularly among radical MPs who wanted to modernize the military law procedures and make them more akin to civilian practice. The wartime government, advised by the army authorities, rejected these proposals, pointing out that the vicissitudes of active service and the realities of warfare made many of the proposals impractical. Ministers drew attention to the special requirements of military law in war, and to the existing statutory powers of the Army Act, and cited the lengthy confirmation and review process as part of the system of checks and balances.

Such assurances did not satisfy the radical and 'reformist' MPs, who argued strongly for soldiers' right to legal counsel to defend them at courts martial. They were also concerned about soldiers who might be under-age, or who had 'given way under stress', and the possibility of unusually harsh and severe punishments. Under these pressures, from 1915 onwards the War Office issued a steady stream of guidance memoranda designed to ensure a consistent military legal system and brought more and more legally qualified officers into that system to ensure judicial competence. One of these memoranda, issued by the Legal Branch at GHQ at the mid point of the war in 1916, and used by the Minister for the Armed Forces in his statement to the House of Commons in July 1998, demonstrates clearly the guidance being given for fairness:

> Cowardice: Charges of Cowardice, in the absence of specific evidence of an exceptional nature, can only be sustained when the occurrence takes place under fire. The fact of absence is not, by itself, sufficient to support a charge of Cowardice.

Desertion: It is to be remembered that desertion involves a question of special intention, and that there can be no intention without knowledge; where, therefore, the accused has been absent for a short time only, the prosecutor must be prepared to prove that the offender knew, with reasonable certainty, that he would be required for some special duty. If the only evidence is that the man absented himself and no evidence whatever is produced (eg, special warning, usual routine, length of absence) to show the probable state of his mind, THE COURT CANNOT MAKE ANY ASSUMPTION AS TO HIS INTENTION, [capitals in the original] and they can convict the accused of absence only [a non-capital offence].

Mental Deficiency, Shock, etc: Where a Medical Board has been held and the accused found sane, or where the question of insanity has not arisen at all, the prosecution or the defence may call evidence to show that the accused is lacking in intelligence, or is suffering from mental shock, etc. This class of evidence should usually be given AFTER THE FINDING, unless the accused calls it in his defence to prove that he was not responsible for his actions at the time of the occurrence, when it may be given before the Finding. It is similar to statements made by the accused in mitigation of punishment, and must be considered by Courts in estimating the sentence.

Procedure At Trial WHEN A SOLDIER IN HIS DEFENCE, OR IN MITIGATION OF PUNISHMENT, URGES A SUBSTANTIAL PLEA RESTING ON MEDICAL GROUNDS, A MEDICAL WITNESS SHOULD INVARIABLY BE CALLED TO EITHER SUBSTANTIATE OR REBUT THIS, BEFORE THE FINDING IF IT IS IN HIS DEFENCE, AND AFTER, IF IT IS URGED IN MITIGATION OF PUNISHMENT. [All in capitals in original]

As a general rule, no evidence of BAD character should be produced before the Court, except the Field Conduct Sheet which must be produced by a Witness on Oath after the Finding, to guide the Court as to sentence. ANY evidence of good character is admissible and will be recorded.

Rules of Evidence: Great latitude should be given to the defence both in cross-examination of witnesses for the prosecution and in the evidence produced by it, eg, written statements, letters and hearsay can be considered by the Court, if tendered for the defence.

Procedure After Trial: Death Sentences for Constructive Desertion:
In particular the fullest information on the following four points is to be
forwarded with the proceedings in all cases where it is considered that the
extreme penalty should be inflicted for 'Constructive Desertion'.

(i) The character (from a fighting point of view as well as from that of
behaviour) of the soldier concerned, his previous conduct in action,
and the period of his service with the Expeditionary Force.

(ii) The state of discipline of the regiment, battalion or unit concerned.

(iii) The Commanding Officer's opinion (based on his personal
knowledge, or that of his officers, of the man's characteristics), as to
whether the crime was DELIBERATELY committed with the sole
object of avoiding the service involved.

(iv) The reasons WHY the various reviewing authorities recommend
that the extreme penalty be inflicted, or otherwise.

By these reports the Commander-in-Chief hopes to assure himself that a
good fighting man is not shot for absence arising from, for example,
accident or a drunken spree.

The memorandum, approved by Douglas Haig, also included a note on the
Army (Suspension of Sentences) Act 1915, which aimed to avoid men being
lost from the firing line to serve lengthy terms of imprisonment.

To prevent wastage of troops by the withdrawal from the front of men
sentenced to penal servitude or punishment; to ensure that men who
deliberately commit crime in order to avoid duty shall not attain their
object; to give men who have committed serious military offences
through exhaustion or temporary loss of nerve an opportunity of
redeeming their character and earning the remission of their sentence.

From this one example of detailed guidance given by the Judge Advocate's
Branch in the middle of a major war, it is clear that military and civil authorities took their legal responsibilities and procedures very seriously indeed.

After the war the MPs who had pressed for reform during the war continued their campaign, demanding radical changes to the court martial system
and in particular the abolition of the death penalty. Reading the debates of
the period makes it clear that some of the reformers were primarily driven
by an essentially 'left wing' or 'radical' agenda dictated by a philosophical
view of politics and not for primarily 'humane' reasons. That industrious
reformer Ernest Thurtle specifically stressed this point, arguing strongly that

his mission was in fact to 'reform' (in his view) the army and to abolish war. Thurtle had enlisted as a private soldier, and had robust views:

This book which is the result of the author's war experience seeks to establish two points, each of which is of vital interest to the democracies of the world.

The first of these points is that military law as it exists throughout the civilised world today is the complete negation of all that is best in democracy. In consequence, it is the urgent and imperative duty of the civilised peoples to make drastic alterations in this law.

Eventually, in 1929, Ernest Thurtle and his political allies won the day on a free vote in the House of Commons. From 1930 only mutiny and treason were punishable by death, a situation that remained until recently, and since 1922 no British soldier has been executed for a specifically military offence.

Thurtle was right in one key respect, even if his motivation was political and not compassion for the soldiers executed: it is not fear of being shot by their own side that induces soldiers to fight. The death penalty is pointless in battle. Any infantry officer knows that in the final analysis discipline comes from working in a tightly knit group whose members hang together in the face of a life-threatening crisis. The idea of saying 'Charge that machine gun, Private Smith, or I will charge you under Section 69 of the Army Act!' is frankly ludicrous, and exists only in the dialogue of the worst kind of 'socially aware' television programmes. In the real world fighting men are driven by other demons.

Although the generals of 1914, as in all armies, applied savage laws to compel their troops to fight, in reality few soldiers think that they may be shot by their own side in battle. The death penalty can only rarely have been a real deterrent in the trenches or, more dangerously, going 'over the top'. Soldiers are just too busy, too bored or too frightened. It is the identity of the 'tribe' that keeps men fighting, not some shameful legal ritual imposed by those far away. Regimental officers were aware of this elemental truth and dealt with their soldiers accordingly, depending on their assessment of the men.

No one has expressed this more clearly and accurately than Hugh McManners, a one-time commando gunner who saw action in the Falklands and went on to become a respected defence correspondent and writer on military affairs:

For individual soldiers in combat, military law gives a foundation to their determination to stick it out ... Military law can be a subconscious source

of stability and therefore a comfort when things get really grim ... In a
hostile and dangerous environment, rejection by the group is the worst
fate of all ... For each lonely individual, earning and retaining the
approval of their comrades is the single most important motivating factor
... At this level military law has no significance unless the leader needs to
invoke it ...[1]

McManners's experienced, perceptive but, above all, modern eye has told us
precisely what was the problem with the military executions in the Great War:
they encouraged no one and probably deterred very few. They were, tragi-
cally, merely legal symbolism, voted into law by society in Parliament and
accepted by society at large as part of life and culture long ago. With our
more modern and enlightened views it is hard not to feel compassion for those
who died as a result of such laws. The fact that many today *now* feel it is wrong,
however, does not make it wrong by the standards of its day, any more than we
can do anything but deplore the inability of doctors in the Great War to carry
out blood transfusions or their attempts made in good faith, to solve psychiatric
trauma by applying electric shocks which amounted to sheer physical torture.
We cannot undo the deeds of the past.

It is against this background that we must view the ideas of pardoning
those who suffered under other laws long ago. The pressure to 'pardon' those
soldiers legally executed during the First World War is a relatively modern
(1972) phenomenon and seems to stem from a variety of motives: genuine
compassion and a belief that injustices have occurred; a dislike of the establishment or the army; the belief that the trials were illegal; even a desire to
exact compensation for a perceived wrong, or some infringement of human
rights. Perhaps most pernicious of all is the canard that the executions were
some deliberate policy of class warfare or 'ethnic cleansing' by the 'ruling
class' to enforce early twentieth-century scientific theories of eugenics. None
of these assertions, save compassion, survives contact with the facts. More
importantly, these ideas suffer from two crippling weaknesses.

In the first place, by definition any pardon or quashing of sentences as
demanded by the pardons campaigners must be a selective judgement. Given
political will, there would be no insuperable obstacle were there to be sufficient evidence on which to make a judgement. However, the files today are
not merely incomplete: only those relating to the men who were actually executed survive. Unlike Southborough in 1922 we have no way to compare the
records of those confirmed for execution and those reprieved. How then can

we re-judge cases from the past with any pretence to impartiality or natural justice? As successive governments have discovered, selective judgements would risk being mere arbitrary opinions.

Any demand for a 'blanket pardon', citing natural justice, is equally flawed. It would be a judgement that chooses to ignore unpalatable facts. It also conveniently ignores those murderers, for example, who were legally executed after conviction in civilian courts between 1914 and 1918. Any attempt to equate a thrice-convicted absentee, a long-term deserter who killed the policeman sent to arrest him, or a mutineer, with a genuinely shell-shocked and confused man who ran away from the line is perverse. It conflates two widely different moral standards and discriminates in favour of the criminal at the expense of those who may have had genuinely extenuating circumstances. It is most emphatically *not* natural justice. Moreover, by ignoring contemporary views and attitudes and by arrogating justice and morality to later generations in defiance of the facts, it establishes an unwise precedent. Today's generations cannot be responsible for past deeds or even misdeeds. We can only regret the past, not change it.

The options open to society today are clear: a free, or conditional, pardon can be given by the Crown using the prerogative of mercy. The Sovereign normally pardons cases only where there is clear evidence that the finding and sentence were illegal. Secondly, there could be a new political solution to create a 'statutory pardon' using a review tribunal. Any review under such a scheme would almost inevitably founder for lack of evidence should cases be re-examined today.

It is genuinely impracticable and impossible for us to properly re-judge all the cases today. The truth is that most of the men would be left condemned or even, and most troubling to some relatives nearly a century later, *re-condemned.* Even the most cursory examination of the surviving court martial papers clearly demonstrates the guilt of many of those who were executed. For example, many of those executed for 'desertion' had already received a commuted and suspended death sentence for the same offence; others had never seen front line service. Fresh revelations of this sort will not help the families of those convicted, but only revive old pains or create new grievances.

If we are to assuage our modern consciences for the deeds of our forefathers then we have to readdress the balance of historical fact against modern sensibilities. For as a Judge Advocate General pointed out when reviewing the cases in 1984, this issue is far from unique:

… history abounds in trials and sentences capable of being seen through later generations as harsh and patently unjust. The view traditionally taken has always been that they must be accepted as part of history and that it is not the business of ONE generation to sit in judgment on the legal process of its forebears, whatever compassion they may feel …[2]

There is a possible precedent for overcoming such a judgement, as Professor G. R. Rubin of the University of Kent at Canterbury has argued. One solution could be a review of individual cases conducted along the lines of the cases of Timothy Evans and Derek Bentley whose convictions were subsequently quashed. Both Evans and Bently were hanged for murder but were given posthumous pardons. A statutory review body set up by Parliament, as proposed by Andrew MacKinley, could examine the surviving case files. Where, in their view, they found prima facie evidence of exonerating circumstances they could recommend that those cases be put forward either for 'questioning' on technical grounds or for 'pardoning' by the Sovereign, acting on the advice of the Lord Chancellor and Defence Council, using the various legal powers available.

Any such review would by its very nature be highly controversial, using scanty evidence to overturn old judgements arrived at by the competent legal authorities of the day with greater access to all the facts. It stands in stark contradiction to the Evans and Bentley cases, which hinged on new facts emerging long after they were hanged. But there are no new facts to be added to the court martial papers; only new interpretations of long gone truths.

Furthermore, such a review process would be selective. Not all those executed were shell-shocked, or at the end of their tether. The court martial papers reveal many of those executed to have been calculating rogues, some never having seen action, looking for a soft option while their comrades fought on. They were not 'exploring the theoretical boundaries of consent between citizen soldier and the State' (in the jargon of one young American professor of social science chairing a conference on the issue); they were deliberately breaking the law of the day for their own ends and to save their skin.

This does not mean that the dead should be left to moulder and that we should not disturb their rest; we should keep the question alive if only to remind ourselves that, in the words of the government's 1998 review: 'All those who were executed were themselves victims of the war …' The real truth is that every soldier knows that military law is the foundation of discipline; and discipline is essential for the unit or small fighting group to survive.

Military law is really only of use when things go wrong in the group, which is self-motivating and self-policing in its conquest of fear. It is of note that a substantial number of those shot had been plucked from their own units and were no longer serving amongst safe, familiar faces. Just like the Highlanders who rebelled at Salerno in 1943 and who refused to soldier with other regiments, many of the men executed in 1914–18 were frightened, trapped amongst strangers, and far from the comrades with whom they had trained and fought and on whom they could rely. For soldiers, just like anyone else, comfort and reassurance comes from the familiar: the group, the battalion, your chums or your mates.

The Great War happened. We cannot remake broken worlds and reconstruct them in our own image. Old ideas were torn apart and old empires destroyed. Amongst the casualties was the dusty Victorian concept of military law, with its savage penalties and obsolete forms, imposed on regular, volunteer and conscript alike with equal severity.

In many cases, were the men to be tried for their military crimes today, they would be found guilty. Some might be given relatively light sentences and others would be treated as medical cases, but the truth is that the majority of those executed for military crimes in the First World War were guilty of the charges against them and, by the standards of their time, their sentence was not regarded as inappropriate. Today we may well recognize factors that we would admit as 'mitigating circumstances' and would doubtless sentence *all* the cases differently: for example, most obviously, we have no death penalty nowadays. The truth is, as an 'enlightened liberal democracy' we are repelled by many aspects of the past.

One of the saddest parts of the whole saga, and one which is frequently overlooked today, is the depressing but unavailable fact that many of those who were executed were not the brightest of men. The really cunning rogues and the clever deserters usually got away with it. Men like Lawrence, 're-enlisting' himself into the RFC, rarely got caught and the clever, cunning and unscrupulous planned their getaways carefully and frequently made it, to emerged unscathed several years after the war. Only the foolish, simple or unlucky deserter was caught hanging aimlessly about the brigade transport lines or shivering in the medical tent of a neighbouring battalion. We know from the diaries that the sight of a frightened boy who couldn't take any more was a common one and many a sergeant major or officer gave the lad a meal and made sure he got back to where he was meant to be. The matter would usually be hushed up and no formal action taken. A large number of those executed were just plain simple or unlucky, a thought that must have haunted the memories of the firing squads themselves as for years afterwards they stared down the rifle sight in their nightmares: for the blindfold was not just to protect the convicted man from the last mortal terror. We know that it was also a blessing that protected the men with the grisly duty of a firing squad from staring point-blank into their victim's eyes.

In particular the firing squads haunt our imagination. They were squalid little affairs that sickened all concerned, but they are really only a detail at a time of much greater tragedy. We must never forget that in every case, not far from the drab little barns, abattoirs, fields and quarries that were used as the execution sites for 306 frightened military offenders between 1914 and 1918, for four long years 400 equally frightened men were being slaughtered *every day* for doing their duty without running foul of military law. The Great War devoured them all, hero and coward, shell-shocked and rogue alike.

The sad fact is that we cannot undo the past – we can only learn from it. Perhaps the best way of understanding what happened is to let the men who were there at the time speak for themselves.

> When Miller disappeared just before the Hun attack, many of the men said he ... must have gone over to the enemy lines. They were bitter and summary in their judgement of him. The fact that he had deserted his commanding officer ... was as nothing to the fact that he had deserted them. They were to go through it while he saved his skin. It was about as bad as could be, and if one were to ask any man who had been through that spell of fighting what ought to have been done in the case of Miller there would only have been one answer. Shoot the bugger![3]

A slightly more thoughtful view came from a young private of the Leicesters who wrote at the time about what it was really like to be shell-shocked, afraid and still fight on. He had been nearly blinded five months before on the Somme. After coming out of hospital, and nearly being hit by a gas shell on Christmas Eve 1916, he wrote:

> I had nerves of steel before all this happened. But now when the guns were firing and a shell burst anywhere near I shivered and trembled with unknown fear. My nerves had gone. At night I was out with a wiring party repairing the wire and I stood holding the spade petrified and shaking with fear. The Lieutenant asked me if I was all right. I explained to him

that I'd been in the 8th Battalion for about ten months and had been wounded in the Somme battle and that I was the man who had been nearly hit by the gas shell that morning and that had shaken my nerves. He asked me if I would like to go back to the dugout but I said 'No – I can't let the lads down' and he understood that I was trying to hold on, for my nerves were at breaking point and I must not give in but fight it off.

Soon it was my turn for sentry and in the blackness of the night all the fears came crowding in. I was in the grip of an unreasoning fear that would make me want to go screaming, anywhere, to get away from the noise of the guns, the horror, the degradation, the filth and the lice, anything [to get] away from it all.

But there was no way of escape – go forward onto the wire and I'd be shot – go back to the support trenches, not possible. 'Johnny Redcap' [the military police] would soon be hunting for you and quickly get you. Then there would be a court martial by men who could never know what it was like to be afraid of even life itself; who would, and did, order a man – no a boy – to be shot for cowardice. I know. I saw it happen and no man who had served in the trenches could ever be called a coward. So … cold logic and reasoning with myself made way for a reasonable frame of mind.

Some people called it 'shell shock' and if you've ever seen young lads with shattered nerves trembling and shivering … however … I managed to escape it by calm reasoning …"[4]

This remarkable and undeniably accurate revelation of what it must have been like to be frightened, alone and on the edge of a breakdown gives the authentic voice of the experience which many thousands of officers, NCOs and soldiers must have experienced over and over again on the Western Front. The sheer humanity reaches across the years, far more than the pleadings of any present-day campaigners on behalf of the tiny minority who did crack under the strain of battle. Pte Horner of the Leicesters did not run away, nor did he break: but in him we hear the honest voice of the 1914–18 soldier, and, it must be said, not a little genuine heroism.

On reading this voice from the trenches it is clear that, like life itself, all human experience was there on the Western Front between 1914 and 1918. If there were injustices done, then let us identify them and give credit and honour back to those who deserve it; but let us draw a gentle veil over those less deserving of our pity. In the words of another distinguished soldier who fought in the trenches, Col. Lambert Ward, DSO, who in the 1919 parliamentary debate appealed to his fellow MPs with words that spoke for Pte Horner's and Frederick Manning's generation and carry down to us over the years :

> [I appeal] to the House of Commons against any differentiation between the graves of those who had been killed in action or had died of wounds or sickness, and those unfortunate men who had been shot for cowardice or desertion.

He added:

> I ask the House not to dismiss this petition with the remark that these men were cowards and deserved their fate. They were not cowards in the accepted meaning of the word. At any rate they did not display one-tenth part of the cowardice that was displayed by the [civilian] cowards in London who went flocking to the Tube stations on the first alarm of an air-raid. These men, many of them, volunteered in the early days of the war to serve their country. They tried and they failed.

The tragic irony is that so many of the men executed found at the end, blindfold and alone, the very courage which had earlier failed them.

Like Pte Horner and Col. Ward, let us leave the courage – and the cowardice – of the Western Front and the lost world of our grandparents' where it belongs: long, long ago.

APPENDIX 1

The House of Commons statement and debate July 1998.

In July 1998 the Minister for the Armed Forces in the new Labour government made a statement in the House of Commons rejecting any pardons for military offences in WW1. Dr John Reid had made a personal study of all the files as part of a ministerial review in response to the campaigning of Andrew MacKinlay MP. In his statement the Minister identified all the key elements of the debate and highlighted the need for the rule of law to be supreme, not personal political opinions. He particularly cautioned the House against the dangers of setting any precedent for retrospective legal 'pardons' based on no new evidence

First World War (Executions)   *11am*

The Minister for the Armed Forces (Dr. John Reid): With permission, I will make a statement about executions of soldiers and others in the First World War.

I doubt that anyone who has not gone through the awesome experience of war can ever truly imagine its effects on the emotions of human beings. Some 9 million troops from all sides died during the Great War. Almost 1 million British and Empire soldiers fell, heroes to their nations and a testimony to the awfulness of war.

We rightly remember them still, not only on the 11th of November, but also in ceremonies throughout the year and throughout the globe. Today, I am sure that I am joined by the whole House in once again paying tribute to the courage and fortitude of all who served from throughout Britain and the Empire.

For some of our soldiers and their families, however, there has been neither glory nor remembrance. Just over 300 of them died at the hands not of the enemy, but of firing squads from their own side. They were shot at dawn, stigmatised and condemned – a few as cowards, most as deserters. The nature of those deaths and the circumstances surrounding them have long been a matter of contention. Therefore, last May, I said that we would look again at their cases.

The review has been a long and complicated process, and I have today placed a summary in the Library of the House. I will outline some salient features.

Between 4 August 1914 and 31 March 1920, approximately 20,000 personnel were convicted of military offences under the British Army Act for which the death penalty could have been awarded. That does not include civilian capital offences such as murder. Of those 20,000, something over 3,000 were actually sentenced to death. Approximately 90 per cent. of them escaped execution. They had their sentences commuted by their commanders in chief.

The remainder, those executed for a military offence, number some 306 cases in all. That is just 1 per cent. of those tried for a capital offence, and 10 per cent .of those actually sentenced to death. Those 300 or so cases can be examined, because the records were preserved. In virtually all other cases, the records were destroyed. It is the cases of those 300 that many hon. Members, notably my hon. Friend the Member for Thurrock (Mr. Mackinlay), and others outside the House, including the Royal British Legion, have asked us to reconsider with a view to some form of blanket pardon.

Let me make it plain that we cannot and do not condone cowardice, desertion, mutiny or assisting the enemy – then or now. They are all absolutely inimical to the very foundation of our armed forces. Without military discipline, the country could not be defended, and that is never more important than in times of war.

However, the circumstances of the first world war, and the long-standing controversy about the executions, justify particular consideration. We have therefore reviewed every aspect of the cases. We have considered the legal basis for the trials – field general courts martial. The review has confirmed that procedures for the courts martial were correct, given the law as it stood at the time.

The review also considered medical evidence. Clearly, if those who were executed could be medically examined now, it might be judged that the effects of their trauma meant that some should not have been considered culpable; but we cannot examine them now. We are left with only the records, and in most cases there is no implicit or explicit reference in the records to nervous, or other psychological or medical, disorders. Moreover, while it seems reasonable to assume that medical considerations may have been taken into account in the 90 per cent. of cases where sentences were commuted, there is no direct evidence of that, either, as almost all the records of those commuted cases have long since been destroyed.

However frustrating, the passage of time means that the grounds for a blanket legal pardon on the basis of unsafe conviction just do not exist. We have therefore considered the cases individually.

A legal pardon, as envisaged by some, could take one of three forms: a free pardon, a conditional pardon, or a statutory pardon. We have given very serious consideration to this matter. However, the three types of pardon have one thing in common – for each individual case, there must be some concrete evidence for overturning the decision of a legally constituted court, which was charged with examining the evidence in those serious offences.

I have personally examined one third of the records – approximately 100 personal case files. It was a deeply moving experience. Regrettably, many of the records contain little more than the minimum prescribed for this type of court martial – a form recording administrative details and a summary – not a transcript – of the evidence. Sometimes it amounts only to one or two handwritten pages.

I have accepted legal advice that, in the vast majority of cases, there is little to be gleaned from the fragments of the stories that would provide serious grounds for a legal pardon. Eighty years ago, when witnesses were available and the events were fresh in their memories, that might have been a possibility, but the passage of time has rendered it well-nigh impossible in most cases.

So, if we were to pursue the option of formal, legal pardons, the vast majority, if not all, of the cases would be left condemned either by an accident of history which has left us with insufficient evidence to make a judgment, or, even where the evidence is more extensive, by a lack of sufficient evidence to overturn the original verdicts. In short, most would be left condemned, or in some cases re-condemned, 80 years after the event.

I repeat here what I said last May when I announced the review – that we did not wish, by addressing one perceived injustice, to create another. I wish to be fair to all, and for that reason that [sic] I do not believe that pursuing possible individual formal legal pardons for a small number, on the basis of impressions from the surviving evidence, will best serve the purpose of justice or the sentiment of Parliament. The point is that now, 80 years after the events and on the basis of the evidence, we cannot distinguish between those who deliberately let down their country and their comrades in arms and those who were not guilty of desertion or cowardice.

Current knowledge of the psychological effects of war, for example, means that we now accept that some injustices may have occurred. Suspicions cannot be completely allayed by examination of the sparse records. We have therefore decided also to reject the option of those who have urged us to leave well alone and to say nothing. To do nothing, in the circumstances, would be neither compassionate nor humane.

Today, there are four things that we can do in this House, which sanctioned and passed the laws under which these men were executed. First, with the knowledge now available to us, we can express our deep sense of regret at the loss of life. There remain only a very few of our fellow countrymen who have any real understanding or memory of life and death in the trenches and on the battlefields of the first world war. This year

(19**7**8) marks the 80th anniversary of the end of the war, and we are recalling and remembering the conditions of that war, and all those who endured them, both those who died at the hands of the enemy, and those who were executed. We remember, too, those who did their awful duty in the firing squads.

Secondly, in our regret, and as we approach a new century, let us remember that pardon implies more than legality and legal formality. Pardon involves understanding, forgiveness, tolerance and wisdom. I trust that hon. Members will agree that, while the passage of time has distanced us from the evidence and the possibility of distinguishing guilt from innocence, and has rendered the formality of pardon impossible, it has also cast great doubt on the stigma of condemnation.

If some men were found wanting, it was not because they all lacked courage, backbone or moral fibre. Among those executed were men who had bravely volunteered to serve their country. Many had given good and loyal service. In a sense, those who were executed were as much victims of the war as the soldiers and airmen who were killed in action, or who died of wounds or disease, like the civilians killed by aerial or naval bombardment, or like those who were lost at sea. As the 20th century draws to a close, they all deserve to have their sacrifice acknowledged afresh. I ask hon. Members to join me in recognising those who were executed for what they were – the victims, with millions of others, of a cataclysmic and ghastly war.

Thirdly, we hope that others outside the House will recognise all that, and that they will consider allowing the missing names to be added to books of remembrance and war memorials throughout the land.

Finally, there is one other thing that we can do as we look forward to a new millennium. The death penalty is still enshrined in our military law for five offences, including misconduct in action and mutiny. I can tell the House that Defence Ministers will invite Parliament to abolish the death penalty for military offences in the British armed forces in peace and in war. [HON. MEMBERS: "Hear, hear."]

There are deeply held feelings about the executions. Eighty years after those terrible events, we have tried to deal with a sensitive issue as fairly as possible for all those involved. In remembrance of those who died in the war, the poppy fields of Flanders became a symbol for the shattered innocence and the shattered lives of a lost generation. May those who were executed, with the many, many others who were victims of war, finally rest in peace. Let all of us who have inherited the world that followed remember with solemn gratitude, the sacrifices of those who served that we might live in peace.

Mr. Keith Simpson (Mid-Norfolk): I thank the Minister for generously allowing me a copy of his statement and the background information well in advance. He spoke with great understanding and sensitivity about a war that took place 80 years ago. There is probably no man or woman in the House whose father, grandfather or great-grandfather did not serve in the first world war. Many will have been wounded or killed. I was in the minority; both my grandfathers came back from the war. We should remember that a generation of Members of Parliament also served in that war, with great suffering. I think in particular of both the Labour Prime Minister Clement Attlee and the Conservative Prime Minister Harold Macmillan.

The British soldiers who were executed during that war have been subject to great debate over the past 80 years. The Minister rightly pointed out that there have been numerous internal and external Government inquiries. Before 1994, all Governments refused to release the case files and other documentation for public access, thereby creating a suspicion in some people's minds of a cover-up. I hope that the Minister's statement will leave no suspicion of a conspiracy or cover-up on a highly sensitive issue.

The matter has recently been brought to a head by the hon. Member for Thurrock (Mr. Mackinlay), who has pursued it since 1992 with early-day motions and a private Member's Bill. All hon. Members recognise the hon. Gentleman's great interest in the matter. In February 1993, when he was Prime Minister, my right hon. Friend the Member for Huntingdon (Mr. Major) rejected the hon. Gentleman's call for a pardon for those who were executed. Members who were here will recall that my right hon. Friend spoke with a great deal of sensitivity, advancing arguments similar to those of the Minster for the Armed Forces.

My right hon. Friend's Government's decision was based on a detailed, two-stage study of the files – first selective, then comprehensive – between 1992 and 1994 by the Army Historical Branch of the Ministry of Defence. I pay tribute to the men and women of that branch for their hard work in difficult circumstances. Their studies reached basically the same conclusions on legal and medical evidence that the Minister has outlined today.

On 16 September 1995, the office of the then Leader of the Opposition – now Prime Minister – announced that a future Labour Government would consider the matter sympathetically. The Minister, when in opposition, signed an early-day motion calling for a review. In May 1997, the Minister announced his review, and he has taken a personal interest in the matter, considering the cases himself and holding discussions with many legal and medical experts and historians.

The Minister's conclusions are virtually the same as those of the previous Government, but there are two differences. First, he has pushed for greater transparency. The previous Government began to move towards that, but he has continued it, and we should all welcome the move. Secondly, he has concluded, as he put to the House today, that, having reviewed the evidence, he faced three options. The first was a legal pardon, the second was the status quo and the third was an expression of regret.

Like previous Governments, the Minister has rejected the legal pardon. He finds the status quo unacceptable, and has opted for an expression of regret. I fear that the Minister may not satisfy two perhaps large groups of opinion. I may be assuming in advance the views of the hon. Member for Thurrock, who I hope, Mr. Deputy Speaker, will be lucky enough to catch your eye, but he has, of course, always argued for a pardon. Equally, there are those, including me and others, who believe that the status quo – leave history alone – is perhaps the option that we should still consider.

The status quo is not about indifference or callousness; I do not think that anyone who has looked at these questions can believe that. I have to declare a personal interest here: as a military historian 20 years ago, I interviewed dozens of surviving soldiers of the first world war on this issue and many others. There is recognition of the impossibility of rewriting history. Among British soldiers at the time – I know that the Minister found this when he interviewed some of the very few surviving veterans – to say the least, there was an ambivalent attitude to the whole question of executing soldiers for desertion or mutiny.

Expressions of regret can become so generalised as to appear meaningless. I am not by any means implying that the Minister is trying to do that, but my fear is that we will end up setting a precedent. Last year, the Prime Minister expressed regret over the Irish potato famine, an action that many people agreed with. However, we have to consider: where does this begin and end?

I say in all seriousness: are we to consider giving expressions of regret for those people who were executed in the highlands after the battle of Culloden by forces of the Crown? Are we to express regret for those people who were executed by forces of the Crown after the Indian mutiny? Those are questions that involve us looking back into history and making value judgments. My fear is that the Minister's statement has not drawn a line under this issue.

Every hon. Member will stand in awe of those men and women who endured so much, so that we today can debate this issue. In particular, I stand in awe of all those hundreds of thousands of men and women who, in the face of the most appalling circumstances, controlled and conquered their fear and did their duty, so that we might live in a democracy, as we do today.

Dr. Reid: I thank the hon. Member for Mid-Norfolk (Mr. Simpson) for what I think was a cautious, though at times cynical, welcome of the statement; perhaps I misinterpreted it. I join him in thanking the Army Historical Branch and the services for all their work. I want to put it on record that, despite the rumours that accompany such reviews from time to time, there was no resistance whatever to a full and transparent, academic and compassionate review of these cases from the forces, which have been of immeasurable assistance to me in attempting, after all these years, to do justice to a complicated issue.

Of course I join the hon. Gentleman in recognising the sacrifices of all those who died, which I recognised at the top of my statement. We in the House owe an immeasurable dept of gratitude to those who went over the top, fought in the battlefields and made the ultimate sacrifice for their country. We promised at the end of that awful war that, through the generations, we would not forget them, and we have not done so. Today we pay tribute to them as well.

However, I did point out that there were certain people – 306 people – whose families had suffered a stigma for eight decades. I feel that, in the light of what we know, it was the view of the House as a whole that I was expressing when I said that that stigma should be lifted, and that those people should be recognised as victims. [HON. MEMBERS: "Hear, hear."]

May I deal with the point that the hon. Gentleman raised about not rewriting history? I did not use that expression – it was used by the previous Government – because I do not believe it. History has two meanings. One is what actually happened. Of course we cannot help what actually happened, or change it, but history has another meaning, which, as a historian, I recognise and which I thought that he, as a historian, would recognise as well. It is the interpretation of what happened.

In all fields of life, we constantly revise our interpretation of what happened. I argue, as a human being as well as a politician, and partly as a historian, that not only is it open to us to reinterpret the events, but, in a decent civilised society, we have an obligation to reinterpret those events. That is what have I tried to do.

The hon. Gentleman mentioned various other executions throughout history. I think that there is a difference. These events occurred within living memory – this century. I think that I am right in saying that, in the period before 1914, as far back as the Napoleonic wars, there were no more than two executions under these same Acts. From 1918 until today, I do not think that there have been any more than three. In the whole of the second world war, I think that there were three executions for mutiny and one for a capital offence which was not a military offence. Therefore, these events are specific – I think that they are ring-fenced. The conditions and nature of the first world war distinguish it from all other wars.

I am sure that the hon. Gentleman has read of the awful conditions, the extremes of cold and heat, the mud, the vermin, the lice, the cacophony of shellfire, the amazing barrage under which human beings were put, whose batteries of courage were constantly being tested to the limit. The conditions of that war do make it somewhat different.

On the question of the individuals versus the group, I was asked to review these cases as a whole, and I have done so. I said, not only last May but in the debate in the House, which I have here, that that would not necessarily mean a legal formal pardon, but, where there are apparent or possible injustices within living memory, it is the obligation of Government, particularly when people were involved in a life-and-death struggle, to do their best to express the sentiment of the House and the will of the nation.

If I have one wish, it is that, whatever the legal formality today, we do indeed create the conditions in which, as a nation, we can say to all those who died, including the executed soldiers and others, "May you rest in peace now." May this case also rest in peace: after all these decades, I believe that we have now finally done justice to the obligation to examine it and to dispense our view, and the public view, as fully as we possibly could.

Mr. Andrew Mackinlay (Thurrock) *rose* –

Hon. Members: Hear, hear.

Mr. Mackinlay: I sincerely thank the Minister for all his efforts in this regard, the attention that he has given to this matter, and his statement today. I couple that with thanks for the work of many people, but particularly His Honour Judge Anthony Babington, Julian Putkowski, who did research work in this regard, which has assisted all of us and promoted our interest in this issue, and, last but not least, Ernest Thurtle, who was a Labour Member of Parliament in the 1920s and 1930s and who alone raised this issue. We should remember him today, because he did a great deal in exposing the fact that the British establishment suppressed these documents for three quarters of a century.

I hope that the Minister will understand if I reserve my position in one regard. I think that there could have been a formal legal pardon, but there may be a legislative opportunity for me or others to raise the matter in future. However, it would be churlish and unrealistic not to acknowledge that what the Minister has said is a major statement by the Government, which I deeply appreciate and which I know will be appreciated by the families of the men involved, the people who have campaigned for them and the few remaining veterans of the great war. They, late in the evening of life, will know that not only do the people support the pardons – I think that they have done so all along – but that Parliament has now reflected the fact that they should be acknowledged as victims of the great war along with the many other millions.

In response to the hon. Member for Mid-Norfolk (Mr. Simpson), there was not an option to leave the matter alone. That is precisely what the British establishment wanted to do for 75 years. History needs to be written with clarity and precision, and I hope that the Minister feels that, with his statement, he has written a chapter of history with clarity and precision this morning.

With your indulgence, Mr. Deputy Speaker, I should like to point out that my hon. Friend the Member for Bolsover (Mr. Skinner) nudged me to draw attention to the fact that, at the very moment when the Minister was expressing regret, it was 11 minutes past 11. I thought that that added to a profoundly moving statement.

This certainly closes a chapter on a very unhappy episode. As we come to the end of a troubled century, when we teach our schoolchildren about the miscalculations and selfishness of politicians in general, we can at least take some pride this morning in the fact that the ordinary British soldier and the other victims of the great war have been given the long overdue acknowledgment that they were victims of the decisions of selfish people. I hope that we can salute them this morning.

Dr. Reid: I thank my hon. Friend for his welcome and his kind words. I take this opportunity to thank Judge Anthony Babington, not only for his pioneering work in this generation but for the assistance that he gave me when I met him. I also thank others, including Julian Putkowski for assisting me to clarify my own thoughts on this matter. Of course, I did not meet Ernest Thurtle, but I became very familiar with his thoughts and works as I worked through the review. To that list I would add my hon. Friend himself, who has played a pioneering role in the last decade. He has taken an interest in all things military in the House, as well as in the soldiers and others who were executed.

There is not much that I can add, other than to say that, as I read the case files, I appreciated the nature of war. No one could remain unmoved who reads about the conditions endured by the soldiers who died in the first world war, who went over the top and made the sacrifice, and who had what Napoleon regarded as the main characteristic of a good soldier – not courage, but endurance. I certainly did not. Some of the words come back to haunt me. The last words of one young man who was executed were, "What will my mother say?" Such instances cannot leave us unmarked.

I do not believe that it is a sign of fortitude or strength to ignore compassion. Compassion, as exemplified by millions of soldiers throughout the centuries and throughout this nation, is an integral part of fortitude. We are all the stronger for having compassion – defiance in defeat, certainly, but as Churchill once said, magnanimity in victory. Those of us who have been fortunate enough to have the victory of life, and those who were fortunate enough, despite all their sacrifices, to come back, will share with the House the magnanimity and understanding of those who were executed during that terrible war.

Mr. Mike Hancock (Portsmouth, South): I echo the sentiments of the hon. Member for Mid-Norfolk (Mr. Simpson), and thank the Minister for his courtesy in making this statement. I doubt that a single hon. Member who heard the Minister's words could fail to be moved by what he had to say and the sincerity with which he said it. From the tone he used, I suspect that he was greatly disappointed in the words that he had to utter.

The statement contained the phrase that "formality of pardon" was impossible. I am sure that the Minister will agree that, when he replied to the hon. Member for Thurrock (Mr. Mackinlay), he used the words of compassion. I am sure that most men, women and children will think that compassion could have been shown to the 300 men and their families, and that the formality of pardon was not an impossibility. They will think that a society which, with the ability to look back and say that things would have been so different today, could have shown the compassion necessary to ensure that the pardon was not an impossibility. I am sure the Minister will agree that countless millions of people will not understand why it is impossible for the House to grant the pardon.

I am sure that every voice in the land will echo the sentiments that the Minister expressed in going over what these men went through. He recognised that the majority of them were volunteers and had been in action for a long time. He eloquently exposed the fear experienced by anyone placed in real danger, but these men were in danger day in and day out, week in and week out, for years in some instances.

The nation owes it to those men to show the compassion that is needed. Perhaps, just perhaps, some were guilty of the offences in question, but pardoning them in order to pardon them all is a price that the nation would willingly pay in order, once and for all, to lift this stain from our nation's military history. I hope that, even now, the words of the hon. Member for Thurrock will be taken up by other hon. Members, and that we shall introduce legislation that will finally remove this stain from our history.

It gives me great pleasure on behalf of my party to thank the Minister for his honest endeavours and determination in bringing us to this stage today, but please do not let this be the end of the story.

Dr. Reid: The hon. Gentleman raised three points to which I shall respond. To pardon a few, or one or two – I have not said that, in my view, the evidence would have been sufficient for such a pardon; it might have been sufficient to consider it – thus in effect condemning 300, or 290, would not have been the compassionate response.

Mr. Menzies Campbell (North-East Fife): All or none.

Dr. Reid: As the hon. Gentleman's hon. and learned Friend says, it is all or none.

Secondly, the hon. Member for Portsmouth, South (Mr. Hancock) believes that some people will not understand. I think that they will understand perfectly, and I shall explain it in simple terms to the hon. Gentleman.

The people who died throughout this century in the British armed forces died fighting to preserve democracy. The basis of democracy is the rule of law. If any politician was to overturn not only several hundred years of precedent but the basis of that democracy by setting aside the belief that there has to be evidence for a conviction; or if he did so on a political whim or prejudice or on a suspicion, no matter how sincere, it would undermine the very basis of law and democracy for which so many millions have fought and died.

Therefore, I do not believe that it would have been open to me, without transgressing the very values for which so many service men have fought and died, to throw aside all legal precedent and make a judgment on the basis of what I believed rather than on the evidence. I think that that will be understood – it is understood in the House, and I think that it is understood across the country. But, short of that, I believe that I have done what the House would think is right.

The Government have not taken action and said what we said only because we thought that the House would think that it right to do so or because of this or that pressure group, but because we think it is the right thing to do. We have expressed regret and the view that – like all those who died – those people were victims of that terrible, terrible war. We have asked that the stigma of the executions be lifted and that those names be added to books of remembrance and memorials. We have also on this day announced that we will be inviting the House to abolish the death penalty. I think that those measures will be warmly welcomed by hon. Members and by the public.

I hope – for the benefit of the families and those who were executed – that we can now genuinely say, "Let them rest in peace". If individuals wish to petition on individual cases, I have not debarred anyone from doing so. My own belief is that they would not do a service for the whole or, I suspect, for the individual case – which, because of a lack of evidence, could end up with a re-condemnation. Such an outcome is what I tried to avoid, and I think – and hope – that the generality of the statement of regret will be warmly welcomed by the public.

Several hon. Members *rose –*

Mr. Deputy Speaker (**Mr. Michael J. Martin**): Order. We are considering a deeply moving matter, but the House will appreciate that I must protect the main business of the House. I shall call other hon. Members, but remind them that they must put a question to the Minister. That question should be brief. I shall try to call as many hon. Members as I can before we return to the main business of the House.

Mr. Tony Benn (Chesterfield): May I join in thanking the Secretary of State – and particularly my hon. Friend the Member for Thurrock (Mr. Mackinlay) – for the very sensitive and imaginative way in which he has dealt with the matter? However, are we not speaking about a little bit more than the victims of war? Are we not speaking about the victims of the law, passed by Parliament, that conscripted young men and women who did not wish to fight and told them – under the then military code – "If you do not kill under orders, we will execute you"? They were victims of Parliament and of war, although the two were interconnected in that case. May I ask him also to recognise that the real victims today – for those who were shot have gone – are the families who have the anguish of knowing that their fathers, grandfathers, uncles and great-uncles died as convicted of cowardice?

In the light of Archbishop Tutu's institution of a Truth and Reconciliation Commission to bring out the truth and allow the past to rest in peace, could not the word "pardon" be used to recognise that – for the benefit of the families – those people really were not guilty of the military offence for which they were sentenced to death? I ask the Secretary of State to consider that proposal in the light of the families who suffer, still to this day, for what happened to those who went before.

Dr. Reid: I thank my right hon. Friend, especially for referring to me as the Secretary of State – but the reshuffle is not until next week.

My right hon. Friend raised some very serious points. I did use the word "pardon" – I used it several times, both in my statement and subsequently – and explained that it is more than a legal formality: it also means compassion and forgiveness. I hope that that has been noted by the families themselves.

Many of those who were executed were not conscripts but volunteers. I specifically drew attention to that fact. I specifically drew attention also to the House's role, by saying that it was appropriate that the Government are making the statement in the House that sanctioned the legislation – the Army Act 1914 – under which the people were executed. I made that point because, ultimately, responsibility rests in this place. It is therefore appropriate that we should have made our expression of regret here.

Rev. Martin Smyth (Belfast, South): I join, on behalf of my colleagues, in thanking the Minister for his clear statement and for underlining in his last reply the fact that many of those people were volunteers – among whom were the men of Ulster. I suggest that, in compassion, the House should reflect on the difference between calm debates in this place – where we sometimes use passion – and the battlefield. When we think of the victims of those days, perhaps we should remember that their officers also were victims, having to uphold military discipline in extreme circumstances. Does the Minister share my belief – it is also my plea – that those who have been so treated in the past will now be restored, even in books of remembrance and war memorials, so that, across the nation, no one may withhold recognition of the pardon that we are seeking to make?

Dr. Reid: Yes, indeed. The hon. Gentleman speaks for a part of the United Kingdom that suffered and sacrificed on a par with any in our history. Ulstermen stood in the vanguard of the efforts of the British armed forces in the first world war – not only at the Somme but at other horrific events in that war. It is not in my power to direct or to dictate, but I do hope that their names will be added to war memorials and books of remembrance, as that will be a symbol of the lifting of the stigma of execution.

The hon. Gentleman mentioned the officers – some of whom, too, were executed. The sentences of 89 per cent. of those who were sentenced to death were commuted by the higher chain of command – which should give pause for thought to those who claim that executions were merely a rubber-stamp process performed by a bloodthirsty officer corps. That is not borne out by reality. Although evidence from the files is missing, there are sufficient grounds for us to believe that great consideration was given to executions, and that – despite the need for discipline and to ensure that, for the benefit of the many, there were executions when such offences occurred – a great deal of compassion was shown throughout the chain of command.

Mrs. Llin Golding (Newcastle-under-Lyme): With one other hon. Member, I represent the House on the Commonwealth War Graves Commission. As I walk up and down those rows of graves – many of 16, 17, 18, 19-year-olds – I try to imagine the horror that must have gone through their minds at what they saw. It is not surprising that many of them deserted. Perhaps many more did not do so only because they died so quickly that they did not have a chance to appreciate the situation from which they would never escape.

I thank the Minister for his statement. On behalf of all those who now rest in Commonwealth war graves, I ask him whether he will now write to other Commonwealth countries and ask them to include the names of the comrades of those who died in that dreadful war on war memorials and war graves.

Dr. Reid: I thank my hon. Friend, and pay tribute to the work done by the Commonwealth War Graves Commission. Upkeep of those graves – particularly in France and Belgium, but elsewhere on the globe – is a tribute to the depth of feeling that we still have for all those who died in that war. She will know that no one who has walked through France and Belgium and seen the acres of white crosses around Arras, the Somme and the Ypres salient can come away without being profoundly affected by the experience.

As for the wider implications for the Commonwealth, I assure my hon. Friend that we have kept in touch with our Commonwealth colleagues as this issue has progressed. It is not within my power to direct other sovereign nations, but the remarks I have made today and the sentiments I have expressed were for all those who served in the British and Empire forces, and I have no doubt that they will be noted by our Commonwealth colleagues. I am sure that the whole House would welcome it if they decided that a similar course of action was appropriate in their case.

Mrs. Margaret Ewing (Moray): I, too, welcome today's statement by the Minister. I note the dignified manner in which he presented it, and the sombre mood in which the whole House has responded.

In thanking the hon. Member for Thurrock (Mr. Mackinlay) for his tireless work on this case, may I say, also as an historian, that I do not believe that we can leave history alone? As an historian specialising in the history of the first world war, when teaching that history to youngsters who are far more accustomed to the virtual reality of Hollywood, I have discovered that the reality of man's inhumanity to man was something that they found extremely emotional. Perhaps in the process they recognised that we have to consider all our actions in society, and what they mean to all of us.

On the question of names being added to books of remembrance and war memorials, is it anticipated that that will happen by Remembrance Sunday this year? As a Scottish Member of Parliament, I am sure that the Minister will be keen to ensure that action is taken in respect of the Scottish national war memorial at Edinburgh castle.

Dr. Reid: I thank the hon. Lady. I cannot add anything to her comments about the First World War. The matter of war memorials and books of remembrance is not within my power to dictate, but I hope that the sentiments expressed in the House today are shared by those who do have power in such matters. I was pleased to read recently, as no doubt did the hon. Lady, that those responsible for the Book of Remembrance in Edinburgh Castle have already decided to take action. I hope that their action is adopted as a more widespread practice.

I should add that, although we are concentrating on one aspect today, as I said in my statement and as I know the House feels, we remember and will never, ever forget the sacrifices made by those who died from the bullets or the bayonets of the enemy – those who found within themselves, in those awful conditions, the fortitude and courage to overcome fear, which afflicts all of us, and to go forward, sometimes into a hail of fire. We remember them today, as we shall on 11 November.

Mr. Kevin McNamara (Hull, North): In welcoming my hon. Friend's statement, and acknowledging the work of my hon. Friend the Member for Thurrock, I should like also to recall the work of our former right hon. Friend and Member for Mansfield, Don Concannon. When he was first elected, he tried, desperately banging his head against the wall of the Ministry of Defence, to resurrect even the idea of re-examining these cases.

The most important and significant thing that my hon. Friend the Minister said today came in those few sentences at the end of his statement, when he ensured that this would never happen again. May I say how much I welcome his statement that no longer will capital punishment be seen as a punishment within the British military code? By that decision, we shall never again make any of the sort of mistakes that may well have been made in the past.

Dr. Reid: I join my hon. Friend in paying tribute to the endurance over a long period of Don Concannon, who, if I remember correctly, was a former guardsman and who took a great personal as well as academic interest in these matters.

I thank my hon. Friend for his comments about the abolition of the death penalty. Lest there be any doubt, let me make it plain that that has not been imposed on the armed forces; they have been working on this matter and have given it their full consideration, and they are at one with Ministers on that point – indeed, the recommendation came from the armed forces themselves. I am pleased to have been able to make that announcement today. It is appropriate in the context of the subject that we are discussing and hon. Members' interest in it.

Rev. Ian Paisley (North Antrim): I thank the Minister for his words today. This has been a moving time in the House. I thank him also for the tribute he paid to Ulstermen, especially those who fought at the battle of the Somme, after which there was hardly a home in the locality in which I work in which there were not victims. I thank him also for the way he put his remarks today; I want to assure him of that.

There is one note I want to strike – that it will appear strange to many people in Northern Ireland that the House can find a way to let terrorists out of prison by law, through a political act, whereas we cannot have a political pardon for the cases being discussed today. Why can there not be complete coverage, so that all can say that those men will rest in peace? I was touched when the hon. Member for Newcastle-under-Lyme (Mrs. Golding) spoke of the awesomeness of visiting the cemeteries, and by the Minister's words, echoing those of a victim: "What will my mother say?" I think that we will do good to everyone if we find a political way completely to lift the stigma through a pardon.

Dr. Reid: I thank the hon. Gentleman for his words. He has, for many years now, been a staunch supporter of the idea of the rule of law, and I believe that, when he thinks the matter through, he will not want me to dispense with the rule of law in coming to a political judgment. There is a clear distinction between the expression of regret and the sentiments that we have expressed today, and anything that has ever been expressed in respect of those convicted of terrorist offences. In addition, those men have not been pardoned in any way. The comparison is not a fair one, nor do I believe that it is one that the House would want to pursue, because it is not in accord with the sentiments expressed today.

I have no difficulty in reiterating, and joining the hon. Gentleman in acknowledging, the vast sacrifices made by the men of Ulster – it was men – during the first world war. The loyalty they showed to the United Kingdom throughout that period should not and will not be forgotten. I am sure that it is at the back of our minds as we deal with contemporary developments, and that it occasionally comes to the forefront of our minds when we consider the role of Ulster and the north of Ireland within the United Kingdom.

Mr. Bill Michie (Sheffield, Heeley): I thank my hon. Friend for his statement. I share the view that none of us can understand the trauma that those soldiers experienced. I learned of that at second hand from my father when I was a child. He was in uniform throughout the war, and lost many of his comrades and two of his brothers. I am sure that, if he were alive today, he would be overjoyed by the statement. Will the Minister explain what communication will take place between his Department and the families concerned?

Dr. Reid: I thank my hon. Friend for his words. The number of families that have been in correspondence with me is relatively small – only 12 – and I am writing to them today enclosing a copy of the review and my statement to the House. I shall express the hope that, by extending our feelings of regret, by asking that the names be added to war memorials and books of remembrance, by recognising that those men were, like many others, the victims of a terrible war, and by announcing the abolition of the death penalty, we have left to rest in peace the relatives about whom they feel so deeply, and lifted the stigma of execution.

Mr. Edward Garnier (Harborough): With considerable diffidence, I join other hon. Members in congratulating the Minister on his statement and hon. Member for Thurrock (Mr. Mackinlay) on raising the subject so forcefully over the past year or so. I use the word "diffidence", because, among hon. Members here this morning, only the right hon. Member for Chesterfield (Mr. Benn) has served in the Second World War. He may be the only person who understands to some extent what the soldiers we are discussing went through in the First World War.

I thank the Minister for recognising the context in which the executions took place: 20,000 people were convicted of offences for which they could have been sentenced to death, but only a tiny proportion of them received the death penalty. I congratulate the Minister on recognising that the command structure was not the brutish, thoughtless, careless creature that so many people think it was.

I ask the Minister to bear in mind what others at the time may have thought, rather than what we now think at this distance. I think of my grandfathers, both of whom were decorated in the first world war and returned wounded, and one of whom was a founder of the Royal British Legion. I think also of my parents, one of whom has just, thanks to the Under-Secretary, received her war medals, and their contemporaries in the last war.

Mr. Deputy Speaker: Order. The hon. and learned Gentleman must be brief.

Mr. Garnier: I shall be. Does not granting a pardon imply guilt of the offence for which someone is pardoned? Pardoning may therefore not be the answer that many people want. Will the legislation to remove the death penalty for military offences, to which the Minister referred, be a Government Bill and a discrete Bill dealing only with that measure, or a private Member's Bill for which the Government will give time?

Dr. Reid: I do not want to test your patience, Mr. Deputy Speaker. The hon. and learned Gentleman asked a list of questions, and I shall answer a couple of them.

I made known my views on the chain of command. Like the hon. Member for mid-Norfolk (Mr. Simpson), I have spoken to several veterans. There are different views among those who served in the first world war, and I have tried to place them in context today. Without punishment of some nature for desertion, many more people might have died because of the collapse of military discipline. That certainly happened in the forces of some of our allies which did not use the death penalty.

It would be normal to use the Armed Forces Bill to abolish the death penalty. As the hon. and learned Gentleman knows, that comes before the House every five years. That is when that provision will be incorporated into military law. It has not been used in peace for many years. We have said today that Defence Ministers will be inviting the House to decide that. As it is an issue of life and death, there will presumably be a free vote, although I cannot prejudge that. All Defence Ministers will certainly vote to abolish the death penalty, and will invite our colleagues to do so.

If legislation is required to sign protocol 6, which relates to the death penalty in peace or other than in war or the imminent threat of war, that will be introduced as an amendment to legislation that will [be] introduced long before the Armed Forces Bill is introduced. That will allow us to ratify protocol 6.

APPENDIX 2

A listing of the men executed in the Great War, by type of offence, with details of the PRO reference number.

Name	Rank	Regiment
Stones Joseph William	L-Sgt	19/DLI
Frafra Aziberi	Private	Gold Coast Regt
Adamson James Stark	Private	7/Camerons
Anderson James A	Private	12/King's (L'pool) att 8 Loyal N Lan
Barker Robert Loveless	Rifleman	6/R London (1/6Bn City of Lond Ri
Bellamy W	Rifleman	1/KRRC
Bennett John	Private	1/Hants
Farr Harry T	Private	1/W Yorks
Hodgetts Oliver W	Private	1/Worcs
Lawton George H	Private	17/S'wood For
Mamprusi Allassan	L-Cpl	Gold Coast
Sinizki Dimitro	Private	52/CEF
Tite Reginald Thomas	Private	13/Sussex
Ward George	Private	1/R Berks
Botfield Albert	Private	9/S Staffs (B Coy) (Pioneer Bn)
Chase Herbert H	Private	2/Lancs Fus
Fatoma	Private	West African Regt
Hawthorne Frederick	L-Cpl	1/5 S Staffs
McCubbin Bertie	Private	17/S'wood For
Holland James	L-Cpl	10/Cheshire
Abigail John Henry	Private	8/Norfolk
Ainley George	Private	1/4 KOYLI

Execution date	Offence	PRO reference	Where commemorated
18/1/17	Casting away arms	WO 71/535	St Pol Com Cem Ext
28/9/16	Casting away arms	WO 71/538	Kumasi Mem Ghana
23/11/17	Cowardice	WO 71/620	St Nicholas Brit Cem
12/9/16	Cowardice	WO 71/497	Fienvillers Brit Cem
4/11/16	Cowardice	WO 71/507	Reninghelst New Mil Cem
16/7/15	Cowardice	WO 71/422	Brown's Road Mil Cem
28/8/16	Cowardice	WO 71/492	Poperinghe New Mil Cem
18/10/16	Cowardice	WO 71/509	Thiepval Memorial
4/6/15	Cowardice	WO 71/416	Royal Irish Rifles Graveyard
30/7/16	Cowardice	WO 71/486	Brown's Road Mil Cem
28/4/17	Cowardice	WO 71/575	Accra memorial, Ghana
9/10/17	Cowardice		Ecoivres Mil Cem
25/11/16	Cowardice	WO 71/527	Poperinghe New Mil Cem
26/9/14	Cowardice	WO 71/388	La Ferté sous Jarre Memorial
18/10/16	Cowardice	WO 71/508	Poperinghe New Mil Cem
12/6/15	Cowardice	WO 71/420	White House Cemetery
19/7/15	Cowardice	WO 71/429	Freetown memorial
11/8/16	Cowardice	WO 71/490	Warlincourt Halte Brit Cem
30/7/16	Cowardice	WO 71/487	Brown's Road Mil Cem
30/5/16	Cowardice	WO 71/470	Ecoivres Mil Cem
12/9/17	Desertion	WO 71/592	Esquelbecq Com Cem
30/7/18	Desertion	WO 71/658	Hagle Dump Cem

Name	Rank	Regiment
Alexander William	CQMS	10/CEF (Alberta Regt)
Allsop Arthur E	Rifleman	12/KRRC
Anderson William Edward	Private	5/Dorset
Ansted Alfred Thomas	Private	4/R Fus
Archibald James	Private	17/R Scots
Arnold Frederick S	L/Bmdr	1 Bde CFA
Ashton Harry	L-Sgt	11/Cameronians
Atkinson Alfred	L-Cpl	1/W Yorks
Auger Fortunat	Private	14/CEF
Baker William	Private	26/R Fus
Ball Joseph	Private	2/Middx (4th Coy)
Barnes John Edward	Private	7/R Sussex
Barratt Frederick Martin	Rifleman	7/KRRC
Bateman Frank	Private	1/4 Yorks & Lancs (Hallamshire Bn)
Bateman Joseph	Private	2/S Staffs
Beaumont Ernest Alfred	Private	2/Leics
Beeby Ernest	Pioneer	212 Coy RE
Bell John	Driver	57 Bty 43 How Bde RFA
Benham William	Private	1/3 R Fus
Beverstein Abraham (aka Harris)	Private	11/Middx
Black Peter	Private	1/4 B Watch (CWGC 1/7th)
Bladen F Charles H	Private	10/Yorks & Lancs
Blakemore Denis Jetson	Private	8/N Staffs
Bolton Edward	Private	1/Cheshire
Bowerman William	Private	1/Queen's
Brennan Joseph	Private	1/8 (Irish) King's (L'pool)
Briggs James	Private	2/Borders
Brigham Thomas	Private	1/10 Manchesters
Britton Charles	Private	1/5 Warwicks
Broadrick Frederick	Private	11/Warwicks
Brown Archibald	Private	10/B Watch
Burden Herbert Francis	Private	1/S N Fus
Burrell William Henry	Private	2/Sussex
Butcher Frederick Charles	Private	7/Buffs
Byers Joseph	Private	1/R Scots Fus
Byrne Stephen (Monaghan M)	Private	1/R Dub Fus (1 Coy)

Execution date	Offence	PRO reference	Where commemorated
18/10/17	Desertion		Barlin Com Cem Ext
15/6/17	Desertion	WO 71/561	Favreuil Brit Cem
31/3/17	Desertion	WO 71/554	Gezaincourt Com Cem Ext
15/11/16	Desertion	WO 71/517	Bertrancourt Mil Cem
4/6/16	Desertion	WO 71/473	Beuvry Com Cem Ext
25/7/16	Desertion		Boulogne Eastern Cem
8/7/17	Desertion	WO 71/573	Karasouli Mil Cem, Greece
2/3/15	Desertion	WO 71/402	Chap d'Armentieres Old Mil Cem
26/3/16	Desertion		Trois Arbres Cem
14/8/18	Desertion	WO 71/660	Lijssenthoek Mil Cem
12/1/15	Desertion	WO 71/392	Le Touret Memorial
4/7/17	Desertion	WO 71/568	Faubourg d'Amiens Cem
10/7/17	Desertion	WO 71/572	Louvencourt Mil Cem
10/9/18	Desertion	WO 71/666	Villers Station Cem
3/12/17	Desertion	WO 71/621	Rocquigny-Equancourt Road Brit Cem
24/6/15	Desertion	WO 71/418	St Vaast Post Mil Cem
9/12/16	Desertion	WO 71/528	Albert Com Cem Ext
25/4/15	Desertion	WO 71/412	Le Touret Memorial
12/7/17	Desertion	WO 71/570	Le Cauroy Com Cem
20/3/16	Desertion	WO 71/456	Labourse Com Cem
18/9/16	Desertion	WO 71/502	Trois Arbres Cem
23/3/16	Desertion	WO 71/458	Cite Bonjean Mil Cem
9/7/17	Desertion	WO 71/569	Locre Hospice Cem
14/4/16	Desertion	WO 71/459	Roclincourt Valley Cem
24/3/17	Desertion	WO 71/556	Loos Memorial
16/7/16	Desertion	WO 71/483	Barly French Mil Cem
6/3/15	Desertion	WO 71/404	Le Touret Memorial
4/6/18	Desertion	WO 71/649	Warlincourt Halte Brit Cem
12/9/17	Desertion	WO 71/586	Mendingham Brit Cem
1/8/17	Desertion	PRO 71/576	Dranoutre Mil Cem
1/6/17	Desertion	WO 71/565	Karasouli Mil Cem, Greece
21/7/15	Desertion	WO 71/424	Menin Gate
22/5/16	Desertion	WO 71/469	Mazingarbe Com Cem Ext
27/8/18	Desertion	WO 71/664	Vis-en-Artois Memorial
6/2/15	Desertion	WO 71/397	Locre Churchyard
28/10/17	Desertion	WO 71/613	Arras Memorial

Name	Rank	Regiment
Cairnie Peter	Private	1/R Scots Fus
Cameron John	Private	5 N Fus
Card Edward A	Rifleman	20/KRRC (Pioneer Bn)
Carter Harold George	Private	73/CEF (Quebec Regt)
Carter Henry	Private	11/Middx
Cassidy James	Private	1/R Inniskilling Fus
Cheeseman Frank William	Rifleman	18/KRRC (CWGC 14th Bn)
Clarke Wilfred	Private	2/DLI
Collins George Ernest	Private	1/Lincs
Comte Gustave	Private	22/CEF (Quebec Regt)
Crampton James	Private	9/Yorks & Lancs (orig. 6/Yorks)
Crimmins Herbert	Private	18/W Yorks (2nd Bradford Pals) 'A' Coy
Crozier James	Rifleman	9/R Irish Rifles
Cummings Thomas	Private	1/Irish Guards
Cutmore George	Private	2/B Watch
Dagesse Arthur Charles	Private	22/CEF (Quebec Regt)
Davies Richard M	Private	11/S'wood Foresters
Delargey Edward	Private	1/8 R Scots (Pioneer Bn)
Delisle Leopold	Private	22/CEF (Quebec Regt)
Dennis John James	Private	1/Northamptons
Depper Charles	Private	1/4 R Berks
Docherty John	Private	9/B Watch (D Coy)
Docherty Thomas	Private	2/KOSB
Dossett Walter	Private	1/4 Yorks & Lancs
Duncan John	Private	1/Cameronians
Dyett Edwin Leopold Arthur	Sub Lt	Nelson Bn RND
Earl William J	Private	1/7 Lancs Fus
Elford Lawrence D	Private	1/8 KOSB
Evans Andrew	Private	1/R Scots Fus
Eveleigh Alfred E	Private	1/Buffs (D Coy)
Everill George	Private	1/N Staffs
Fairburn E	Private	18/CEF (W Ontario Regt)
Fellowes Ernest	Private	3/Worcs
Ferguson Joseph	Private	1/R Scots Fus att RE
Flynn Hugh	Private	18/HLI (4th Glasgow Bn – Bantams)
Foulkes Thomas	Private	1/10 Manchesters
Fowles Stephen McD	Private	44/CEF (New Brunswick Regt)

Execution date	Offence	PRO reference	Where commemorated
28/12/16	Desertion	WO 71/532	Thiepval Memorial
4/12/16	Desertion	WO 71/524	Ribemont Com Cem Ext
22/9/16	Desertion	WO 71/503	Mazingarbe Com Cem Ext
20/4/17	Desertion		Villers Station Cem
26/4/16	Desertion	WO 71/461	Sailly-Labourse Com Cem
23/7/16	Desertion	WO 71/484	Engelbelmer Com Cem Ext
20/10/17	Desertion	WO 71/607	Coxyde Mil Cem
9/2/18	Desertion	WO 71/678	Bancourt Brit Cem
15/2/15	Desertion	WO 71/399	Locre Churchyard
3/7/17	Desertion		Aix-Noulette Com Cem Ext
4/2/17	Desertion	WO 71/543	Poperinghe New Mil Cem
5/9/16	Desertion	WO 71/495	Vieille Chapelle New Mil Cem
27/2/16	Desertion	WO 71/450	Sucrerie Mil Cem France
28/1/15	Desertion	WO 71/395	Le Touret Memorial
25/7/17	Desertion	WO 71/633	Basra Memorial
15/3/18	Desertion		Lapugnoy Mil Cem
15/11/17	Desertion	WO 71/617	Wizernes Com Cem
6/9/17	Desertion	WO 71/583	Vlamertinghe New Mil Cem
21/5/18	Desertion		Bellacourt Mil Cem
30/1/16	Desertion	WO 71/440	Lillers Com Cem
13/9/16	Desertion	WO 71/501	Beauval Com Cem Ext
15/2/16	Desertion	WO 71/444	Mazingarbe Com Cem
16/7/15	Desertion	WO 71/423	Perth (China Wall) Cem
25/6/18	Desertion	WO 71/650	Hagle Dump Cem
7/3/15	Desertion	WO 71/405	Le Touret Memorial
5/1/17	Desertion	ADM 156/24	Le Crotoy
27/5/18	Desertion	WO 71/647	Warlincourt Halte Brit Cem
11/10/18	Desertion	WO 71/671	Noeux-les-Mines Com Cem Ext
6/2/15	Desertion	WO 71/397	Locre Churchyard
24/2/16	Desertion	WO 71/448	White House Cemetery
14/9/17	Desertion	WO 71/593	Poperinghe New Mil Cem
2/3/18	Desertion		Villers Station Cem
26/7/15	Desertion	WO 71/426	Perth (China Wall) Cem
20/4/17	Desertion	WO 71/555	Wanquetin Com Cem Ext
15/11/16	Desertion	WO 71/519	Habarcq Com Cem Ext
21/11/17	Desertion	WO 71/623	Loos Memorial
19/6/18	Desertion		Villers Station Cem

Name	Rank	Regiment
Fox Joseph Stanley Victor	L-Cpl	1/Wilts
Fryer John W	Private	12/Queen's (D Coy)
Gawler Robert W	Private	1/Buffs (D Coy)
Gibson David	Private	12/R Scots (C Coy)
Giles Peter	Private	14/N Fus
Gleadow George E	Sergeant	1/W Yorks
Gore Frederick Coutts	Private	7/Buffs
Haddock James A	Private	12/Yorks & Lancs (Sheffield City)
Hamilton Arthur	Private	14/DLI
Hanna George	Private	1/R Irish Fus
Harding Frederick	Rifleman	1/KRRC
Harris Ernest Walter Jack	Private	10/Lancs Fus C Coy
Harris Thomas	Private	1/RW Kent
Hart Benjamin Albert	Private	1/4 Suffolk
Hartells Bert	Private	3/ Worcs
Hawkins Thomas	Private	7/RW Surrey
Hendricks Harry	Private	2/Leinster ('C' Coy)
Higgins James	Private	1/9 Argylls (att 1/8th)
Higgins John Maurice	Private	1/CEF (W Ontario Regt)
Highgate Thomas James	Private	1/RW Kent
Hogan Thomas /Murphy Thomas	Private	2/R Inniskilling Fus
Holmes Albert	Private	8/King's Own
Hope Robert (aka Heppel /Hepple)	Private	1/R Inniskilling Fus D Coy
Hughes Frank	Private	2/Cant (NZ)
Hughes George Edward	L-Cpl	7/King's Own
Hughes Henry J	Private	1/5 Yorks & Lancs
Hunt William G	Private	18/ Manchesters
Hunter George	Private	2/DLI
Hunter William	Private	1/Loyals
Hyde John J	Rifleman	10/KRRC
Ingham Albert	Private	18 Manchesters att 90 Coy MGC
Irish Arthur James	Rifleman	2/Rifle Brigade
Ives Frederick	Corporal	3/Worcs
Jennings John	Private	2/S Lancs
Johnson Frederick	Private	2/Borders
Jones Richard M	Private	6/S Lancs
Jones William	Private	9/R Welch Fus

Execution date	Offence	PRO reference	Where commemorated
20/4/15	Desertion	WO 71/408	Dickebusch New Mil Cem
14/6/17	Desertion	WO 71/562	Poperinghe New Mil Cem
24/2/16	Desertion	WO 71/449	White House Cemetery
24/9/18	Desertion	WO 71/668	Mendinghem Brit Cem
24/8/16	Desertion	WO 71/494	Louez Mil Cem
6/4/17	Desertion	WO 71/553	Le Cauroy Com Cem
16/10/17	Desertion	WO 71/609	Poperinghe New Mil Cem
16/9/16	Desertion	WO 71/499	Vieille Chapelle New Mil Cem
27/3/17	Desertion	WO 71/550	Noeux-les-Mines Com Cem
6/11/17	Desertion	WO 71/611	Neuville-Bourjonval Brit Cem
29/6/16	Desertion	WO 71/479	Quatre Vent Mil Cem
3/2/17	Desertion	WO 71/542	Carnoy Mil Cem
21/6/15	Desertion	WO 71/419	Perth (China Wall) Cem
6/2/17	Desertion	WO 71/537	Suzanne Mil Cem no 3
26/7/15	Desertion	WO 71/426	Aeroplane Cem
22/11/17	Desertion	WO 71/622	Bleuet Farm Cem
23/8/18	Desertion	WO 71/661	La Kreule Mil Cem
26/8/16	Desertion	WO 71/493	Cite Bonjean Mil Cem
7/12/16	Desertion		Quatre Vent Mil Cem
8/9/14	Desertion	WO 71/387	La Ferte sous Jarre Memorial
14/5/17	Desertion	WO 71/557	Ham Brit Cem
22/4/18	Desertion	WO 71/646	Chocques Mil Cem
5/7/17	Desertion	WO 71/571	Ferme-Olivier Cem
25/8/16	Desertion		Hallencourt Com Cem
23/11/16	Desertion	WO 71/521	Warloy-Baillon Com Cem Ext
10/4/18	Desertion	WO 71/638	The Huts Cem
14/11/16	Desertion	WO 71/516	Bailleulmont Comm Cem
2/7/16	Desertion	WO 71/480	Esquelbecq Mil Cem
21/2/16	Desertion	WO 71/445	Maroc Brit Cem
5/9/17	Desertion	WO 71/587	Mendinghem Military Cem
1/12/16	Desertion	PRO 71/526	Bailleulmont Comm Cem
3/10/15	Desertion	WO 71/434	Sailly-sur-La-Lys Can Cem
26/7/15	Desertion	WO 71/428	Perth (China Wall) Cem
26/6/16	Desertion	WO 71/477	Norfolk Cem
1/8/18	Desertion	WO 71/657	Vincennes New Com Cem (Paris)
21/2/17	Desertion	WO 71/630	Basra Memorial
25/10/17	Desertion	WO 71/608	Locre Hospice Cem

Name	Rank	Regiment
Kerr Henry H	Private	7/CEF (Brit Columbia Regt)
King John	Private	1/Cant (NZ)
Kirk Ernest	Private	1/W Yorks
Knight Harry James	Private	1/RW Surrey
La Liberte Come	Private	3/CEF (Central Ontario Regt)
LaLancette Joseph	Private	22/CEF (Quebec Regt)
Lamb Alexander	Driver	21 Bty 2 Bde RFA
Lawrence Ernest	Private	2/Devon
Lewis C	Corporal	12/HLI
Lewis Griffiths	Private	3/S Lancs att 2nd Bn
Lewis John	Private	5/Dorset
Ling Wilson Norman	Private	2/CEF (Eastern Ontario Regt)
Loader Frederick	Private	1/22 R Fus (The Queen's)
Lodge HEJ	Private	19/CEF (Central Ontario Regt)
Longshaw Alfred	Private	18/ Manchesters
MacDonald Harry	Private	12/W Yorks ('C' Coy)
Mackness Ernest	Private	1/Cameronians
Malyon Frederick	Sapper	12 Coy RE att RFA
Martin Harry	Private	9/Essex (A Coy)
McBride Samuel	Rifleman	2/R Irish Rifles
McClair Harry	Private	2/Borders
McColl Charles F	Private	1/4 E Yorks (CWGC 4th Bn)
McCracken JE	Rifleman	15/R Irish Rifles
McGeehan Bernard	Private	1/8 King's (L'pool)
McQuade John	Private	18/HLI
Michael James S	Private	10/Cameronians
Milburn John B	Private	24/27 N Fus (Tyneside Irish)
Milligan Charles M	Private	10/Cameronians
Mitchell Arthur	Private	1/6 Lanc Fus
Mitchell Leonard	Private	8/Yorks & Lancs
Moles Thomas Lionel	Private	54/CEF (Central Ontario Regt)
Molyneaux James	Private	1/Loyals
Moon William Alfred	L-Cpl	11/Cheshire
Morris Herbert	Private	6/Brit West Indies
Murphey William	Rifleman	1/5 R Scots
Murphy Allan	Private	9/Cameronians
Murphy Patrick	Private	47 Bn MGC

Execution date	Offence	PRO reference	Where commemorated
21/11/16	Desertion		Quatre Vent Mil Cem
19/8/17	Desertion		Trois Arbres Cem
6/3/15	Desertion	WO 71/403	Chap d'Armentieres Old Mil Cem
6/10/18	Desertion	WO 71/670	Fins New Brit Cem
4/8/16	Desertion		Poperinghe New Mil Cem
3/7/17	Desertion		Aix-Noulette Com Cem Ext
2/10/15	Desertion	WO 71/435	Vlamertinghe New Mil Cem
22/11/17	Desertion	WO 71/634	Ypres Reservoir Cem
11/3/16	Desertion	WO 71/452	Mazingarbe Com Cem
26/6/16	Desertion	WO 71/478	Norfolk Cem
19/4/17	Desertion	WO 71/539	Forceville Com Cem
12/8/18	Desertion		Cerisy-Gailly Mil Cem
19/8/17	Desertion	WO 71/578	Reninghelst New Mil Cem
13/3/18	Desertion		Noeux-les-Mines Com Cem
1/12/16	Desertion	WO 71/525	Bailleulmont Comm Cem
4/11/16	Desertion	WO 71/514	Louvencourt Mil Cem
1/10/17	Desertion	WO 71/598	Blaringhem Churchyard
4/4/17	Desertion	WO 71/551	Noeux-les-Mines Com Cem
20/3/16	Desertion	WO 71/455	Labourse Com Cem
7/12/16	Desertion	WO 71/529	Hyde Park Corner Cem
1/8/18	Desertion	WO 71/657	Vincennes New Com Cem (Paris)
28/12/17	Desertion	WO 71/628	Ypres Reservoir Cem
19/3/16	Desertion	WO 71/453	Mailly-Maillet Com Cem
2/11/16	Desertion	WO 71/513	Poperinghe New Mil Cem
6/11/16	Desertion	WO 71/518	Habarcq Com Cem Ext
24/8/17	Desertion	WO 71/577	Poperinghe New Mil Cem
8/11/17	Desertion	WO 71/612	Bucquoy Road Cem
3/6/17	Desertion	WO 71/560	Canadian Cem No 2
20/8/17	Desertion	WO 71/580	Achiet le Grand Com Cem Ext
19/9/17	Desertion	WO 71/590	La Clytte Mil Cem
22/10/17	Desertion		Ypres Reservoir Cem
15/6/16	Desertion	WO 71/476	Maroc Brit Cem
21/11/16	Desertion	WO 71/520	Bailleul Com Cem Ext
20/9/17	Desertion	WO 71/594	Poperinghe New Mil Cem
7/2/17	Desertion	WO 71/541	Bertrancourt Mil Cem
17/8/16	Desertion	WO 71/491	Quatre Vent Mil Cem
12/9/18	Desertion	WO 71/667	Sand Pits Cem

Name	Rank	Regiment
Murray Robert	Driver	81 Bde RFA
Neave Walter	Private	10/W Yorks
Nelson William Barry	Private	14/DLI
Nicholson Charles Bain	Private	8/Yorks & Lancs
Nisbet Joseph (or Nesbit)	Private	1/Leics
O'Connell Benjamin	Private	1/Irish Guards
O'Neill Anthony (or O'Neil)	Private	1/SWB
O'Neill Frank	Private	1/S'wood For
Palmer Henry	Private	1/ N Fus
Parry Albert	Private	2/W Yorks
Pattison Robert Gillis	Private	7/East Surrey
Penn Major	Private	1/R Welch Fus
Perry Eugene	Private	22/CEF (Quebec Regt)
Phillips HTW	Private	1/Coldstream Guards
Phillips Louis R	Private	6/SLI
Pitts Albert Henry	Private	2/Warwicks
Poole Eric Skeffington	2 Lt	11/W Yorks
Poole Harry	Private	7/Yorks
Randle William Henry	Private	10/S'wood For
Reid Isaac	Private	2/Scots Guards
Reynolds EJ	Private	3/CEF (Central Ontario Regt)
Richmond Malcolm R	Private	1/6 Gordons
Rickman Albert	Private	1/R Dub Fus (Y Coy)
Rigby Thomas Henry Basil (Harry)	Private	10/SWB
Robinson Arthur Harold	Private	9/N Fus
Robinson John	Private	3 Worcs
Robinson William	Private	1/S'wood Foresters
Roe George Ernest	Private	2/KOYLI
Rogers John	Private	2/S Lancs
Rose Frederick	Drummer	2/Yorkshire
Sands Peter	L-Cpl	1/R Irish Rifles
Scholes William	Private	2/SWB
Scotton William	Private	4/Middx
Seymour John	Private	2/R Inniskilling Fus
Sheffield F	Private	2/Middx
Simmonds William Henry	Private	23/Middx
Skilton Charles Walter F	Private	22/R Fus

Execution date	Offence	PRO reference	Where commemorated
3/2/17	Desertion	WO 71/545	Carnoy Mil Cem
30/8/17	Desertion	WO 71/584	Ste Catherine Brit Cem
11/8/16	Desertion	WO 71/488	Acheux Brit Cem
27/10/17	Desertion	WO 71/619	Longuenesse (Souvenir) Cem
23/8/18	Desertion	WO 71/663	Nine Elms Brit Cem Belgium
8/8/18	Desertion	WO 71/659	Bailleulmont Comm Cem
30/4/16	Desertion	WO 71/462	Mazingarbe Com Cem Ext
16/5/18	Desertion	WO 71/639	Hermonville Mil Cem
27/10/16	Desertion	WO 71/512	Albert Com Cem Ext
30/8/17	Desertion	WO 71/585	Maple Leaf Cem
4/7/17	Desertion	WO 71/567	Faubourg d'Amiens Cem
22/4/15	Desertion	WO 71/414	Estaires Com Cem
11/4/17	Desertion		Ecoivres Mil Cem
30/5/16	Desertion	WO 71/471	Wormhoudt Com Cem
19/8/15	Desertion	WO 71/430	Perth (China Wall) Cem
8/2/15	Desertion	WO 71/398	Ploegsteert Memorial
10/12/16	Desertion	WO 71/1027	Poperinghe New Mil Cem
9/12/16	Desertion	WO 71/530	Cavillon Com Cem
25/11/16	Desertion	WO 71/523	Cavillon Com Cem
9/4/15	Desertion	WO 71/407	Longuenesse (Souvenir) Cem
23/8/16	Desertion		Longuenesse (Souvenir) Cem
26/5/18	Desertion	WO 71/643	Ecoivres Mil Cem
15/9/16	Desertion	WO 71/498	Vlamertinghe New Mil Cem
22/11/17	Desertion	WO 71/618	Cité Bonjean Mil Cem
10/5/16	Desertion	WO 71/475	Cité Bonjean Mil Cem
26/7/15	Desertion	WO 71/425	Aeroplane Cem
10/4/17	Desertion	WO 71/552	Peronne Com Cem Ext
10/6/15	Desertion	WO 71/417	Perth (China Wall) Cem
9/3/17	Desertion	WO 71/549	Bailleul Com Cem Ext
4/3/17	Desertion	WO 71/547	Berneville Com Cem
15/9/15	Desertion	PRO 71/432	Cabaret Rouge BC/Fleurbaix Ch
10/8/18	Desertion	WO 71/656	Borre Cem
3/2/15	Desertion	WO 71/396	Menin Gate Memorial
24/1/18	Desertion	WO 71/679	Duhallows ADS Cem
12/1/15	Desertion	WO 71/391	Le Touret Memorial
1/12/16	Desertion	WO 71/522	Poperinghe New Mil Cem
26/12/16	Desertion	WO 71/531	Thiepval Memorial

Name	Rank	Regiment
Sloan J	Private	1/4 King's Own
Smith John	Private	1/Loyals
Smith W	Rifleman	2/Rifle Brigade
Smith William	Private	3/5 Lancs Fus
Smythe Albert	Private	1/Irish Guards
Spencer James	Driver	65 Bty 8 Bde RFA
Spencer Victor Manson	Private	1/Otago (NZ)
Spry William Thomas	Private	2/R Fus
Stead Frederick	Private	2/Duke of Wellington's
Stedman Joseph	Private	117 Coy MGC
Stevenson David	Private	13/Middx
Stevenson Richard	Private	1/4 Loyals
Stewart Stanley	Private	2/R Scots Fus
Swain John	Private	5/R Berks
Swaine James W	Driver	54 Bty 39 Bde RFA
Sweeney John Joseph	Private	1/Otago NZ
Tanner Edward	Private	1/Wilts
Taylor John	Private	15/Lanc Fus
Taysum Norman Henry	Private	9/B Watch
Templeton J	Rifleman	15/R Irish Rifles
Thompson Alfred Dennis	Private	3/ Worcs
Thompson William Landreth	Private	6/Buffs
Tongue James (Joseph)	Private	1/King's (L'pool)
Turpie William J	Private	2/Queen's
Wall John Thomas	Sergeant	3/Worcs
Walton William	L-Sgt	2/KRRC
Ward Thomas	Private	8/10 Gordons
Watkins George	Private	13/Welsh
Watts Thomas W	Private	7/E Yorks
Welsh C	Private	8/CEF (Manitoba Regt)
Westwood Arthur H	Private	8/Queens
Wild Arthur	Private	18/W Yorks (2nd Bradford Pals)
Williams Harry	Rifleman	1/9 R Fus (QVR)
Wilson James H	Private	4/CEF (Central Ontario Regt)
Wishard J (or Wishart)	Private	7/R Inniskilling Fus
Woodhouse John	Rifleman	12/KRRC
Worsley Ernest	Private	2/Middx

Execution date	Offence	PRO reference	Where commemorated
16/7/16	Desertion	WO 71/482	Barly French Mil Cem
2/7/16	Desertion	WO 71/481	Bully-Grenay Com Cem Brit Ext
3/10/15	Desertion	WO 71/434	Sailly-sur-La-Lys Can Cem
14/11/17	Desertion	WO 71/624	Reninghelst New Mil Cem
28/1/15	Desertion	WO 71/394	Le Touret Memorial
29/9/15	Desertion	WO 71/433	Côte 80 French Nat Cem
24/2/18	Desertion		The Huts Cem
14/6/18	Desertion	WO 71/648	Morbecque Brit Cem
12/2/17	Desertion	WO 71/546	Suzanne Mil Cem no 3
5/9/17	Desertion	WO 71/589	Poperinghe New Mil Cem
18/7/18	Desertion	WO 71/652	Bully-Grenay Com Cem Brit Ext
25/10/16	Desertion	WO 71/511	Poperinghe New Mil Cem
29/8/17	Desertion	WO 71/579	Kemmel Chateau Mil Cem
11/8/18	Desertion	WO 71/662	Montigny Com Cem Ext
9/6/16	Desertion	WO 71/474	Bully-Grenay Com Cem French Ext
2/10/16	Desertion		Dartmoor Cem
27/10/14	Desertion	WO 71/389	Le Touret Memorial
27/1/17	Desertion	WO 71/533	Bertrancourt Mil Cem
16/10/17	Desertion	WO 71/602	St Nicholas Brit Cem
19/3/16	Desertion	WO 71/454	Mailly-Maillet Com Cem
26/7/15	Desertion	WO 71/425	Aeroplane Cem
22/4/16	Desertion	WO 71/460	Labourse Com Cem
31/1/17	Desertion	WO 71/536	Agenvillers Ch'yard (Somme)
1/7/15	Desertion	WO 71/421	White House Cemetery
6/9/17	Desertion	WO 71/582	Poperinghe New Mil Cem
23/3/15	Desertion	WO 71/406	Longuenesse (Souvenir) Cem
16/10/17	Desertion	WO 71/601	St Nicholas Brit Cem
15/5/17	Desertion	WO 71/559	Ferme-Olivier Cem
30/8/17	Desertion	WO 71/581	Ste Catherine Brit Cem
6/3/18	Desertion		Mazingarbe Com Cem Ext
23/11/17	Desertion	WO 71/625	Bleuet Farm Cem
5/9/16	Desertion	WO 71/496	Vieille Chapelle New Mil Cem
28/12/17	Desertion	WO 71/627	Roclincourt Mil Cem
9/7/16	Desertion		Poperinghe New Mil Cem
15/6/17	Desertion	WO 71/563	Cabaret Rouge/Merris Chyd
4/10/17	Desertion	WO 71/597	HAC Cem
22/10/17	Desertion	WO 71/605	Pont d'Achelles Mil Cem

Name	Rank	Regiment
Wright Frederick	Private	1/RW Surrey
Yeoman Walter	Rifleman	1/12 R Fus (Rangers)
Young Elsworth	Private	25/CEF D Coy (Nova Scotia Regt
Young Robert	Private	11/Worcs
Briggs Arthur	Private	9/S'wood For
Browne Archibald	Private	2/Essex
Bryant Ernest	Private	10/Cheshire
Carey Joseph	Private	7/R Irish Fus
Carr James G	Private	2/Welch
Cunnington Samuel H	Private	2/Warwicks
Dalande Hector	Private	8/Seaforths
Donovan Thomas	Rifleman	16/KRRC (Church Lads Bde)
Fraser Evan	Private	2/R Scots
Graham James	Private	2/R Munster Fus
Harris Louis	Private	10/W Yorks
Holt Ellis	Private	19/Manchesters
Hope Thomas	Private	2/Leinster
Horler Ernest	Private	12/W Yorks
Irvine William John	L-Cpl	1/King's Own
Jackson Ernest	Private	24/R Fus
Jefferies Alfred Leonard	Private	6/SLI ('C' Coy)
Jones John T	Private	1/N'hamptons
Jones William	Gunner	43 Bty RFA
Kershaw James	Private	1/King's Own
Kirman Charles Henry	Private	7/Lincs
Latham George W	Corporal	2/Lancs Fus
Mayers James	Private	1/13 London Regt (Kensington)
McFarlane John	Private	4/King's (L'pool)
Mills George	Private	2/DCLI
Parker Albert Edward	Rifleman	7/KRRC D Coy
Reid James	Corporal	6/Cameronians
Roberts John William	Private	2/Can Mount Rif (British Columbia
Roberts William W (Ted)	Private	4/R Fus
Salter Harry	Private	6/E Lancs
Sim(mer)s Robert W	Private	2/R Scots
Smith James	Private	17/King's (L'pool)

Execution date	Offence	PRO reference	Where commemorated
28/1/17	Desertion	WO 71/544	Suzanne Mil Cem no 3
3/7/17	Desertion	WO 71/566	Achicourt Road Cem
29/10/16	Desertion		Bully-Grenay Com Cem Brit Ext
18/9/18	Desertion	WO 71/669	Karasouli Mil Cem, Greece
19/7/18	Desertion	WO 71/653	Hersin Com Cem Ext
19/12/14	Desertion	WO 71/390	Ploegsteert Memorial
27/10/17	Desertion	WO 71/616	Bethune Town Cem
15/9/16	Desertion	WO 71/500	Corbie Com Cem Ext
7/2/16	Desertion	WO 71/443	Auchel Com Cem
19/5/17	Desertion	WO 71/558	R Fus Cem Neuville-Vitasse (London Cem)
9/3/18	Desertion	WO 71/637	St Nicholas Brit Cem
31/10/17	Desertion	WO 71/614	Westhof Farm Cem
2/8/15	Desertion	WO 71/427	Perth (China Wall) Cem
21/12/15	Desertion	WO 71/438	Mazingarbe Com Cem
7/11/18	Desertion	WO 71/672	Ghissignies Brit Cem
4/3/17	Desertion	WO 71/548	Berneville Com Cem
2/3/15	Desertion	WO 71/401	Ploegsteert Memorial
17/2/18	Desertion	WO 71/677	Bucquoy Road Cem
20/4/15	Desertion	WO 71/411	Le Grand Beaumont Brit Cem
7/11/18	Desertion	WO 71/673	Romeries Com Cem Ext
1/11/16	Desertion	WO 71/515	Arras Road Cem
24/2/16	Desertion	WO 71/447	Mazingarbe Com Cem
20/4/15	Desertion	WO 71/409	Chap d'Armentieres Com Cem
26/4/15	Desertion	WO 71/410	Le Grand Beaumont Brit Cem
23/9/17	Desertion	WO 71/604	Ste Catherine Brit Cem
22/1/15	Desertion	WO 71/393	Trois Arbres Cem
16/6/17	Desertion	WO 71/564	Achicourt Road Cem
22/5/18	Desertion	WO 71/644	Nine Elms Brit Cem Belgium
29/9/15	Desertion	WO 71/436	Boulogne Eastern Cem
15/5/16	Desertion	PRO 71/467	Warlus Com Cem
11/5/18	Desertion	WO 71/642	Duisans Brit Cem
30/7/16	Desertion		Boulogne Eastern Cem
29/5/16	Desertion	WO 71/472	Bailleul Com Cem Ext
11/12/15	Desertion	WO 71/439	Green Hill Cem Gallipoli
19/5/18	Desertion	WO 71/645	Chocques Mil Cem
5/9/17	Desertion	WO 71/588	Kemmel Chateau Mil Cem

Name	Rank	Regiment
Taylor John	Private	2/S Staffs
Thomas J	Private	2/Welch
Troughton A	Private	1/R Welch Fus
Turner Frederick	Private	6/ N Fus (CWGC 6th Bn)
Watts William	Private	1/Loyals B Coy
Webb Henry J	Private	2/KOYLI
Wycherley William	Private	2/Manchesters
Cuthbert James	Private	9/Cheshire
Downey Patrick Joseph	Private	6/Leinster
Robins John	Sgt	5/Wilts
Hasemore John William	Driver	180 Bde RFA A Bty
Slade Frederick William	Rifleman	2/6 R Fus (2nd/6th Bn London Reg
Barama Dezari	Private	Gold Coast Mtd Inf Coy
Boos F (aka Alberts)	Private	1 Cape Col Labour Regt
Butler Alexander	Trooper	R Can Dragoons
Chandler Joseph	Private	10/Lincs
Chao Hsing I	Coolie	Chinese Lab Corps 161st Coy
Cheng (Tseng) Shu(a)n Kung	Coolie	Chin Lab Corps 60th Coy
Chisholm Alexander	A/Cpl	20 Army Troop Coy RE
Dale Arthur	Private	13/R Scots
Davids Abraham	Private	1 Cape Col Labour Regt
De Fehr B	Driver	1/Res Pk (Can ASC)
Denny Albert	Private	8/Brit W Indies
Flynn Richard	Private	2/R Dub Fus
Harris Willie Peter	Private	1 Cape Col Labour Regt
Hei Chi Ming	Coolie	Chin Lab Corps
Hui I He	Labourer	Chin Lab Corps 112 Coy
K'ung Ch'ing Hsing	Labourer	Chin Lab Corps
Knight Charles William	Private	10/R Welch Fus
Matthews N	Private	3rd S African Inf
Mitchell James A	Private	1/Brit West Indies
Moore Thomas	Driver	24 Division Train ASC 4th Coy
Morgan Richard	Private	2/Welsh (C Coy)
Murray Francis	Private	9/Gordons att RE (Pioneer Bn)
Paterson John H	2 Lt	3/Essex att 1st
Price William	L-Cpl	2/Welch (C Coy)

Execution date	Offence	PRO reference	Where commemorated
6/11/17	Desertion	WO 71/610	Lapugnoy Mil Cem
20/5/16	Desertion	WO 71/468	Mazingarbe Com Cem Ext
22/4/15	Desertion	WO 71/413	Estaires Com Cem
23/10/17	Desertion	WO 71/606	Bedford House Enclosure No.4
5/5/16	Desertion	WO 71/463	Maroc Brit Cem
31/10/17	Desertion	WO 71/615	Lederzeele Chyd
12/9/17	Desertion	WO 71/591	Coxyde Mil Cem
6/5/16	Disobedience	WO 71/464	Longuenesse (Souvenir) Cem
27/12/15	Disobedience	WO 71/441	Mikra Brit Cem, Salonika
2/1/16	Disobedience	WO 71/442	Twelve Tree Copse Cem Gallipoli
12/5/16	Disobedience	WO 71/465	Mazingarbe Com Cem Ext
14/12/17	Disobedience	WO 71/626	Bleuet Farm Cem
10/11/18	Murder	WO 71/674	Kumasi Mem Ghana
15/10/19	Murder	WO 71/686	Y Farm Mil Cem
2/7/16	Murder		Ribemont Com Cem Ext
11/8/19	Murder	WO 71/683	Les Baraques Mil Cem
9/8/18	Murder	WO 71/655	Les Baraques Mil Cem
23/7/18	Murder	WO 71/651	St Etienne au Mont Com Cem
17/5/15	Murder	WO 71/415	Chap d'Armentieres Old Mil Cem
3/3/16	Murder	WO 71/451	Mazingarbe Com Cem
26/8/19	Murder	WO 71/685	Y Farm Mil Cem
25/8/16	Murder		Hazebrouck Com Cem
20/1/19	Murder	WO 71/675	Taranto Town Cem Ext Italy
6/11/20	Murder		Haidar Pasha Cem
26/8/19	Murder	WO 71/684	Y Farm Mil Cem
21/2/20	Murder	WO 71/688	St Sever Cem Ext
12/9/18	Murder	WO 71/665	Les Baraques Mil Cem
21/2/20	Murder	WO 71/688	St Sever Cem Ext
15/11/15	Murder	WO 71/437	Le Grand Hasard Mil Cem (Morbecque)
3/4/16	Murder	WO 71/457	Chatby War Mem Cem Egypt
22/12/17	Murder	WO 71/629	Ramleh Cem Palestine
26/2/16	Murder	WO 71/446	Menin Gate Memorial
15/2/15	Murder	No record	Bethune Town Cem
1/10/16	Murder	WO 71/504	Noeux-les-Mines Com Cem
24/9/18	Murder	WO 71/1028	Terlicthun Brit Mil Cem
15/2/15	Murder	No record	Bethune Town Cem

Name	Rank	Regiment
Reid Alexander	Private	16/HLI (2nd Glasgow Bn – Boys Bde)
Skone James	Private	2/Welch
Wang Chin Chih (Ch'un Ch'ih)	Labourer	107 Chin Lab Coy
Wang En J(Y)ung (En Jung Wung)	Labourer	29th Coy Chinese Lab Corps
Wickings A	L-Sgt	9/Rifle Bde
Yang Chin Shan (Ch'ing Shan Yang)	Labourer	29th Coy Chinese Lab Corps
Bell Robert	Sapper	123 Field Coy RE
Chang Ju Chih	Coolie	Chinese Lab Corps
Wan Fa Yu	Labourer	Chinese Lab Corps
Wills Frank O	Gunner	X50th TMB RFA
Oyns Arthur Phillip	Sapper	50 Search Light Coy RE
Ahmed Mahmoud Mohamed	Labourer	Egypt Labour Corps
Braithwaite Jack (John)	Private	2/Otago (NZ)
Lewis William E	Gunner	124 Bde RFA/Details RFA
Short Jesse Robert	A/Cpl	24/N Fus (Tyneside Irish)
Davis Thomas	Private	1/R Munster Fus
Goggins Peter	L-Cpl	19/DLI
Hopkins Thomas	Private	1/8 Lancs Fus
McDonald John	L-Cpl	19/DLI
Povey George H	Corporal	1/Cheshire
Wilton Jesse	Corporal	15/S'wood For
Earp Arthur Grove	Private	1/5 Warwicks 'D' Coy
Downing Thomas	Private	6/S Lancs
Burton Robert	Private	6/S Lancs
Fox J	Private	2/HLI
Hamilton Thomas Grant	Driver	72 Bty 38 Bde RFA
Clarke Hubert A	Private	2/Brit W Indies
Mullany James	Driver	72 Bty 38 Bde RFA
Sabongidda Samuel	Private	3/Nigerian

Execution date	Offence	PRO reference	Where commemorated
31/1/17	Murder	WO 71/540	Bertrancourt Mil Cem
10/5/18	Murder	WO 71/641	Hersin Com Cem Ext
8/5/19	Murder	WO 71/680	Poperinghe Old Mil Cem
26/6/18	Murder	WO 71/654	Les Baraques Mil Cem
7/3/18	Murder	WO 71/636	Ste Marie Cem
26/6/18	Murder	WO 71/654	Les Baraques Mil Cem
22/5/18	Murder	WO 71/640	Toutencourt Com Cem
14/2/20	Murder	WO 71/681	Les Baraques Mil Cem
15/2/19	Murder	WO 71/676	St Sever Cem Ext
27/5/19	Murder	WO 71/682	Ste Marie Cem
20/10/17	Murder	WO 71/603	Coxyde Mil Cem
10/10/17	Mutiny	WO 71/600	Not commemorated
29/10/16	Mutiny		St Sever Cem Ext
29/10/16	Mutiny	WO 71/510	St Sever Cem Ext
4/10/17	Mutiny	WO 71/599	Boulogne Eastern Cem
2/7/15	Quitting post	WO 71/431	Helles Memorial
18/1/17	Quitting post	WO 71/534	St Pol Com Cem Ext
13/2/18	Quitting post	WO 71/635	Gorre Brit Cem
18/1/17	Quitting post	WO 71/534	St Pol Com Cem Ext
11/2/15	Quitting post	WO 71/400	Menin Gate Memorial
17/8/16	Quitting post	WO 71/489	Bray Mil Cem
22/7/16	Quitting post	WO 71/485	Bouzincourt Com Cem Ext
19/2/17	Sleeping at post	WO 71/632	Basra Memorial
19/2/17	Sleeping at post	WO 71/631	Basra Memorial
12/5/16	Striking a SO	WO 71/466	Arras Memorial
3/10/16	Striking a SO	WO 71/505	Ribemont Com Cem Ext
11/8/17	Striking a SO	WO 71/595	Kantara War Memorial Cem, Egypt
3/10/16	Striking a SO	WO 71/506	Ribemont Com Cem Ext
27/7/17	Violence	WO 71/596	Calabar Memorial, Nigeria

APPENDIX 3

A statistical analysis

These figures, like all statistics taken out of context, can be misleading, but
analysis of numbers reveals some significant trends.

Net effect of desertion per month through the war
(negative no. indicates more returners than deserters)

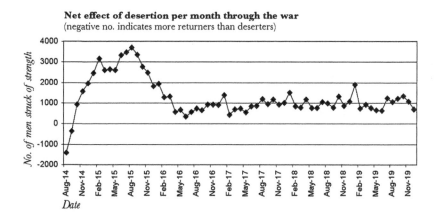

Showing the net effect of desertion throughout the war. In the early months of the
conflict, 'old soldiers' who had deserted before the war returned to their units, but
desertion quickly became a serious problem for the BEF, with over 3,000 deserters
in the month of February 1915. A peak was reached in August 1915, after which
the problem declined, reaching a 'steady state' of around 1,000 men per month
throughout the rest of the war.

Executions per 1 million soldiers in the Expeditionary Forces

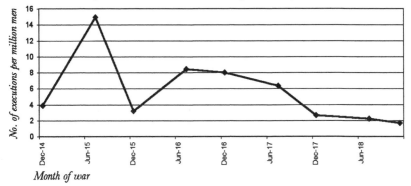

Month of war

Showing the number of men executed per million men serving in the Expeditionary Forces. As a percentage of men serving, the executions reach a peak in mid-1915 (when desertion was also a major problem). After that, the proportion of men executed in relation to the total numbers of men serving declined.

Death sentences during the war, by month
with mathematical trend line added

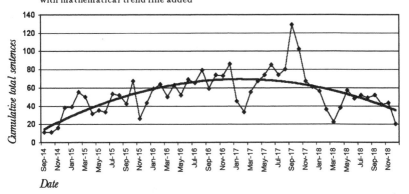

Date

The number of death sentences awarded each month during the war, with a mathematical trend line added, showing that the number of death sentences awarded during the war increased until the end of 1916, but fell thereafter.

GLOSSARY

A & QMG	Adjutant and Quartermaster General
A Staff	Army Administrative [personnel] staff branch
AA	Army Act
AAG	Assistant Adjutant General. A staff officer of the AG branch
ACI	Army Council Instructions
ADC	Aide de Camp; junior officer assistant to a general officer
Adjutant	Administrative Captain of a battalion or regiment
ADMS	Assistant Director of Medical Services
AF B122	A soldier's regimental conduct sheet, containing details of his offences and punishments
AG	Adjutant General
AG Branch	Adjutant General Staff [personnel, discipline, postings]
AIF	Australian Imperial Force
Anzac	Australia and New Zealand Army Corps
APM	Assistant Provost Marshal
AQMG	Assistant quartermaster general
ASC	Army Service Corps
AWOL	absent without leave
battle police	regimental police, controlling access to a battalion's trenches
Bde	Brigade
BEF	British Expeditionary Force
Bg, or Brig. Gen.	Brigadier General
Blighty	Slang term for British Isles
Bn	A battalion [about 1,000 men]
to be Cashiered	To lose ones commission and be dismissed with disgrace
'Cast'	Inspected and found unfit for army service
CB	confined to barracks
CCS	casualty clearing station

C.-in-C.	Commander-in-Chief
Coalbox	Heavy high explosive German shell
CM	court martial
Cmdr	Commander (Navy) (Comd is Army usage)
CMO	Court Martial Officer
CO	Commanding Officer, usually a lieutenant colonel
Coy	A company [a sub-unit with between 100 and 200 men]
CQMS	Company Quartermaster Sergeant
CRA	Commander, Royal Artillery
CRE	Commander, Royal Engineers
CSM	Company Sergeant Major
CSR	Combat stress reaction
CT	Communication trench, usually leading back from the front line
CWGC	Commonwealth [originally Imperial] War Graves Commission
DAA & QMG	Deputy Assistant Adjutant & Quartermaster General
DAAG	Deputy Assistant Adjutant General. Junior 'A' Branch staff officer
DCLI	Duke of Cornwall's Light Infantry
DCM	District Court Martial [UK only] or Distinguished Conduct Medal
Div.	Division
DJAG	Deputy Judge Advocate General
DLI	Durham Light Infantry
DSO	Distinguished Service Order
Dugout	A shelter dug into the side of a trench for men to shelter
FGCM	Field General Court Martial
FL	Front line
FP	Field punishment [either 'FP No. 1' or 'FP No. 2']
G Staff	General Staff [operations]
GHQ	General Headquarters. Overall HQ of a British Expeditionary Force
GOC	General Officer Commanding
GPI	General paralysis of the insane [tertiary syphilis]
GROs	General Routine Orders
GSW	Gunshot wound
HAC	Honourable Artillery Company
HE	High explosive

HL	Hard labour
HM	His Majesty [as in "Dismissed HM's Service …"]
IG	Inspector General
IHL	Imprisonment with hard labour
IWM	Imperial War Museum
JAG	Judge Advocate General
KSLI	King's Shropshire Light Infantry
KRRC	King's Royal Rifle Corps
LFFI	Land Forces Falkland Islands
LI	Light Infantry
Lt	Lieutenant
Lt Col	Lieutenant Colonel
M&D	'Medicine and Duty'; army doctor's prescription for mild sickness
Maj.	Major
MEF	Mediterranean Expeditionary Force
MFP	Military Foot Police
MM	Military Medal
MML	*Manual of Military Law*
MMP	Mounted Military Police
MO	Medical Officer
MP	Military Police
NCO	Non-commissioned officer [usually corporal or sergeant]
OC	Officer Commanding a sub-unit, usually a company commander [a major or captain]
Padre	A military chaplain or priest
PM	Provost Marshal. The senior military police officer
PRO	Public Record Office
PS	Penal servitude *or* permanent staff
PTSD	Post-traumatic stress disorder
Q Staff	Quartermaster Staff [supply]
QMG	Quartermaster General
QMS	Quartermaster Sergeant
RA	Royal Artillery
RAMC	Royal Army Medical Corps

RASC	Royal Army Service Corps
RCM	Regimental Court Martial
Regt	A Regiment: a generic title, as in the 'Notts and Derbys Regiment'.
RFA	Royal Field Artillery
RFC	Royal Flying Corps
RGA	Royal Garrison Artillery
RHA	Royal Horse Artillery
RIR	Royal Irish Rifles
RM	Royal Marines
RMLI	Royal Marine Light Infantry
RMO	Regimental Medical Officer
RND	Royal Naval Division [63rd Infantry Division]
RNVR	Royal Naval Volunteer Reserve
RP	Regimental Police or rules of procedure [for military legal purposes]
RSM	Regimental Sergeant Major
RTO	Road/Rail Transport Officer
RWF	Royal Welch Fusiliers
RWK	Royal West Kent (Regiment)
Sap	A small trench leading forward towards the enemy
Sgt	Sergeant (often spelled 'Serjeant' 1914–18)
SIW	Self-inflicted wound [usually to the hand]
SS	Shell shock or suspended sentence
SWB	South Wales Borderers
TCO	Travel control officer
TCS	Travel control security
TM	Trench mortar
VC	Victoria Cross. Highest British award for valour
WO	War Office or warrant officer
Whizzbang	Shrapnel shell
WW1	World War One
WW2	World War Two
2Lt	Second Lieutenant

NOTES TO THE TEXT

CHAPTER 1

1 L. P. Hartley, *The Go-Between* (London: Penguin, 1999)

2 Niall Ferguson, *The Pity of War* (London: Allen Lane, The Penguin Press, 1998)

3 Barbara Tuchman, *The Proud Tower* (London: Hamish Hamilton, 1966)

4 John Keegan, *The First World War* (London: Hutchinson, 1998)

5 For a powerful and well-argued refutation of many of the 1914–18 myths and historical distortions, see John Terraine's *The Smoke and the Fire* (London: Sidgwick and Jackson, 1980)

6 William Moore, *The Thin Yellow Line* (London: Leo Cooper, 1974)

7 Anthony Babington, *For the Sake of Example* (London: Leo Cooper, 1983)

8 PRO WO 93/49

9 Julian Putkowski and Julian Sykes, *Shot at Dawn* (London: Leo Cooper, 1989)

10 Gerald Oram, *Death Sentences in the British Army* (London: Francis Boutle, 1998)

11 A. B. Godefroy, *For Freedom and Honour* (Ontario: CEF Books, 1998)

12 Christopher Pugsley, *On the Fringe of Hell* (Auckland: Hodder & Stoughton, 1991)

13 The records of the trials which ended in execution are held at the PRO in class WO 71

14 PRO WO 71/490

15 Imperial War Museum Oral History Recordings, Western Front 1914–18, Dr M. S. Esler

16 'Victor's Deadly Secret', *Daily Express*, 16 August 1978 and 'The Grim Wartime Secret of Victor Sylvester', *Guardian*, August 1978

17 Jose Harris, *Private Lives Public Spirit* (London: Penguin, 1993)

18 Jose Harris, *Private Lives Public Spirit*

19 Carlo M. Cipolla (ed.), *The Fontana Economic History of Europe*, vol. 2 (London: Collins Fontana, 1977)

20 BBC Radio 4, *Illiteracy: the Great British Secret*, 27 March 2000

21 Peter Mathias, *The First Industrial Nation* (London: Methuen, 1969)

22 John Maynard Keynes, *The Economic Consequences of the Peace* (London: Macmillan, 1919)

23 Franck Allengry, *Psychologie et Education* (Paris: Librairie d'Education National, 1907)

24 Viscount Snowden, *An Autobiography* (London: Nicholson and Watson, 1934)

25 For an excellent summary of the social background to the British Army on the Western Front, see John Bourne, 'The British Working Man in Arms' in *Facing Armageddon*, edited by Hugh Cecil and Peter Liddle (London: Leo Cooper, 1996)

26 Henry Williamson, *A Chronicle of Ancient Sunlight* (fifteen volumes) (London: Macdonald & Co., 1951–69)

27 Paul Fussell, *The Great War and Modern Memory* (Oxford: Oxford University Press, 1977)

28 For British society in 1914, see Jose Harris, *Private Lives, Public Spirit*

29 C. Northcote Parkinson, *The Law and the Profits* (London: John Murray, 1960)

30 Sir Phillips Gibbs, *The Pageant of the Years* (London: Heinemann, 1946)

31 R. J. Unstead, *A Century of Change* (London: A & C Black, 1986)

32 Jose Harris, *Private Lives, Public Spirit*

33 Jose Harris, *Private Lives, Public Spirit*

34 Christian Spielman, *Deutsche Geschichte vom Ende der grossen Krieges bis zum des zwanzigsten Jahrhunderts* (Halle: Gesenius Verlag, 1908)

35 For a thoughtful discussion of the social dynamics which motivated the BEF, John Keegan's *The Face of Battle* (London: Jonathan Cape, 1976) has a wide-ranging and well-informed analysis of the real bonds that hold soldiers together

36 For a summary of the pre 1914 army, see Tim Carew, *The Vanished Army* (London: Kimber, 1964)

37 Cited by Gary Sheffield in his chapter 'Officer–Man Relations and Discipline', in *Facing Armageddon* (London: Leo Cooper, 1996)

38 War Office, *Statistics of the Military Effort of the British Empire 1914–20* (London: HMSO, 1922)

39 For a fuller understanding of the pre-war army and society in 1914, see Hugh Cecil and Peter Liddle, *Facing Armageddon*; John Keegan, *The Face of Battle*; Lynn MacDonald, *1914* (London: Penguin, 1989); and Kate Caffrey, *Goodbye Leicester Square* (London: Deutsch, 1980)

40 Professor Edwin Tannenbaum's *1900* (New York; Doubleday 1976) offers an unrivalled analysis of European social dynamics during the critical years before WW1

CHAPTER 2

1 Cited in: Professor Peter Rowe, *Defence – the Legal Implications* (London: Brassey's, 1987)

2 Robin Higham (ed.), *A Guide to the Sources of British Military History* (London: Routledge, 1972)

3 Michael Roberts, *Gustavus Adolphus* (London: Longman, 1992)

4 John Childs, *The British Army of William III, 1689–1702: Mutiny Act 1689, I William & Mary, c5* (Manchester: Manchester University Press, 1987)

5 *ibid., c13*

6 Ulric Blickensdorfer, *Blackstone's Elements of Law* (London: Stevens & Sons, 1889)

CHAPTER 3

1 War Office, *Manual of Military Law* (London: HMSO, 1914) page 18

2 War Office, *Manual of Military Law*, page 18

3 War Office, *Manual of Military Law*, page 18

4 War Office, *Manual of Military Law*, page 382

5 War Office, *Manual of Military Law*, page 379

6 War Office, *Manual of Military Law*, page 379

7 War Office, *Manual of Military Law*, page 380

8 War Office, *Manual of Military Law*, page 395

9 War Office, *Manual of Military Law*, page 382

10 War Office, *Manual of Military Law*, page 384

11 War Office, *Manual of Military Law*, page 15

12 War Office, *Manual of Military Law*, page 15

13 War Office, *Manual of Military Law*, page 385

14 War Office, *Manual of Military Law*, page 390

15 War Office, *Manual of Military Law*, page 391

CHAPTER 4

1 E. B. Sherlock, *The Feeble-Minded* (London: Macmillan, 1911) page 87

2 J. Rogues de Fursac and A. J. Rosanoff, *Manual of Psychiatry* (New York: John Wiley & Sons, 1916) 4th edition, pages 344–346

3 Robert Baden-Powell, *Scouting for Boys* (1908)

4 J. Rogues de Fursac and A. J. Rosanoff, *Manual of Psychiatry*, page 358

5 E. B. Sherlock, *The Feeble-Minded*, pages 272–281

6 Thomas Salmon, 'Care & Treatment of Mental Disease and War Neurosis ("Shell Shock") in the British Army', *Mental Hygiene*, 1917, vol. 1, page 509

7 Charles Moran Wilson, *The Anatomy of Courage* (London: Constable & Company, 1945) page 22

8 Clifford Beers, *A Mind That Found Itself* (publisher unknown, 1908)

9 William A. White, *Outlines of Psychiatry* (New York: The Journal of Nervous and Mental Diseases Publishing Company, 1909) page 7

10 William A. White, *Outlines of Psychiatry*, pages 14–15

11 William A. White, *Outlines of Psychiatry*, pages 210–211

12 Charles L. Dana, 'The Future of Neurology', *Journal of Nervous and Mental Disease*, 1913, vol. 40, pages 753–757

13 Leonard Woolf, *Beginning Again: An Autobiography of the Years 1911–1918* (London: Hogarth Press, 1964) page 160

14 G. Elliot Smith and T. H. Pear, *Shell Shock and its Lessons* (Manchester University Press, 1917) page 79

CHAPTER 5

1 Edmund Blunden, *Undertones of War* (London: Cobden-Sanderson, 1928)

2 Homer, *Iliad*

3 Osbert Sitwell, *Great Morning!* (London: Quartet Books, 1947)

4 The War Office, *Statistics of the Military Effort of the British Empire in the Great War 1914–1920* (London; HMSO, 1922)

5 Anthony Farrar-Hockley, 'The Shock of Battle 1914-1916', *RUSI Journal*, February 1998

6 G. Ferrero, *Peace and War* (London: Macmillan, 1933)

7 Theodore Lyman, *Meade's Headquarters* (Boston: Massachusetts Historical Society, 1922)

8 Harold M. Hyman, *A More Perfect Union: The Impact of the Civil War and Reconstruction on the Constitution* (New York: Alfred A. Knopf, 1973) page 149

9 Robert I. Alotta, *Civil War Justice* (Pennsylvania: White Mane Publishing Co. Ltd, 1989) page 16

10 G. Dyer, *War* (London: Guild Publishing, 1986)

11 Ed Parker, *Cambridge History of Warfare* (Cambridge: Cambridge University Press, 1995)

12 I. S. Bloch, translated by W. T. Stead, *Is War Now Impossible?* (London: Grant Richards, 1899)

13 A. Tardieu, *Avec Foch 1914* (Paris: Flammarion, 1939)

14 Malcolm Brown, *Imperial War Museum Book of the Western Front* (London: BCA, 1993)

15 Malcolm Brown, *Imperial War Museum Book of the Western Front*

16 See Brig. J. B. A. Bailey, Director Royal Artillery, *Deep Battle and the Century of Firepower* (SCSI Camberley, 2000) for a professional analysis of the impact of artillery in WW1

17 Malcolm Brown, *Imperial War Museum Book of the Western Front*

18 S. Bagnall [late of the 5th East Lancashire Regiment], *The Attack* (Hamish Hamilton 1947), cited in John Ellis, *The Sharp End of War* (London: BCA, 1980)

19 Malcolm Brown, *Imperial War Museum Book of the Western Front*

CHAPTER 6

1 Hans Binneveld, *From Shell Shock to Combat Stress* (Amsterdam: Amsterdam University Press, 1997) page 1

2 Anon, 'War Neurosis in the Battle of Marathon', *Mental Hygiene*, 1919, vol. 3, page 676

3 William Shakespeare, *Henry IV Part 1*

4   Hans Binneveld, *From Shell Shock to Combat Stress*, page 4

5   George Rosen, 'Nostalgia: a Forgotten Psychological Disorder', *Psychological Medicine*, 1975, vol. 5 No. 4, page 340

6   Anthony Babington, *Shell Shock* (London: Leo Cooper, 1997) page 8

7   Hector Gavin, *Feigned and Fictitious Diseases* (London: John Churchill, 1843)

8   Albert Deutsch, 'Military Psychiatry in the Civil War' in *One Hundred Years of American Psychiatry* (New York: Columbia University Press, 1944) page 377

9   William Hammond, quoted in Wendy Holden, *Shell Shock* (London: Channel 4 Books, 1998) page 9

10 Albert Deutsch, 'Military Psychiatry in the Civil War' in *One Hundred Years of American Psychiatry*, pages 367–384

11 Albert Deutsch, 'Military Psychiatry in the Civil War' in *One Hundred Years of American Psychiatry*, page 377

12 S. Weir Mitchell, *Injuries of Nerves and their Consequences* (Philadelphia: J. B. Lippincott, 1872)

13 *Medical and Surgical History of the War of Rebellion* (Washington, DC Government Printing Office, 1888) vol. 1, part 3

14 Charles A. Morris, 'Some War Sequelae', *Lancet*, 1901, vol. i, page 1559

15 Hans Binneveld, *From Shell Shock to Combat Stress*, page 139

16 Anon, 'Madness in Armies in the Field', *British Medical Journal*, 1904, vol. 2, page 30

17 Captain R. L. Richards, 'Mental and Nervous Diseases in the Russo-Japanese War', *Military Surgeon*, 1910, vol. 26, page 177

CHAPTER 7

1   *Lancet*, 1914, vol. ii, page 1388

2   Charles S. Myers, 'A Contribution to the Study of Shell Shock', *Lancet*, 1915, vol. i, pages 316–320

3   Charles S. Myers, *Shell Shock in France* (Cambridge: Cambridge University Press, 1940) page 13

4   Charles S. Myers, *Shell Shock in France*, page 16

5   Charles S. Myers, *Shell Shock in France*, page 83

6   Charles S. Myers, *Shell Shock in France*, page 84

7   G. Elliot Smith and T. H. Pear, *Shell Shock and its Lessons* (Manchester: Manchester University Press, 1917) Introduction, page x

8   G. Elliot Smith and T. H. Pear, *Shell Shock and its Lessons*, page 12

9   *The Times History of the War* (London: The Times, 1916) vol. 7

10 Quoted by Hans Binneveld, *From Shell Shock to Combat Stress* (Amsterdam: Amsterdam University Press, 1997) pages 107–109

11 Pat Barker, *Regeneration Trilogy: Regeneration* (London: Penguin Books, 1992); *The Eye in the Door* (Penguin Books, 1994); *The Ghost Road* (Penguin Books, 1996)

12 Lewis Yealland, *Hysterical Diseases of Warfare* (London: Macmillan & Co. Ltd, 1918) page vi

13 Joanna Bourke, *Dismembering the Male* (London: Reaktion Books, 1996) page 85

14 Sir John Collie, *Malingering and Feigned Sickness* (London: publisher unknown, 1917) 2nd edition

15 J. C. Dunn, *The War the Infantry Knew* (London: Abacus edition, 1994) page 586

16 Wendy Holden, *Shell Shock* (London: Channel 4 Books, 1998) pages 53–59

17 Pat Barker, *Regeneration Trilogy*

18 Wilfred Owen, 'Mental Cases', in *The War Poems* (London: Chatto & Windus, 1994)

19 Richard Slobodin, *W. H. R. Rivers* (New York: Columbia University Press, 1978) page 67

20 William H. R. Rivers, 'Psycho-therapeutics' in *Encyclopaedia of Religion and Ethics*, edited by James Hastings (Edinburgh: T. & T. Clark, 1918) vol. 10, page 437

21 Siegfried Sassoon, *Sherston's Progress* (London: Faber & Faber Paperbacks, 1983) page 48

22 D. Felicitas Corrigan, *Siegfried Sassoon: Poet's Pilgrimage* (London: Victor Gollancz, 1973)

23 Ben Shephard, 'Shell-Shock on the Somme', *RUSI Journal*, June 1996

24 Philip Gibbs, *The Realities of War* (London: Heinemann, 1920)

25 *Court of Enquiry into the failure of a party of the 11th Border Regiment to carry out an attack on 10th July 1916*. Wellcome History of Medicine, RAMC 446/18

26 *Court of Enquiry into the failure of a party of the 11th Border Regiment to carry out an attack on 10th July 1916*.

27 Charles S. Myers, *Shell Shock in France*, page 18

28 Charles S. Myers, *Shell Shock in France*, page 84

29 Charles S. Myers, *Shell Shock in France*, page 64

30 Charles S. Myers, *Shell Shock in France*, page 95

31 Charles S. Myers, *Shell Shock in France*, pages 95–96

32 PRO WO 293/8 ACI 54 of 1918

33 PRO WO 293/8 ACI 307 of 1918

34 G. Elliot Smith and T. H. Pear, *Shell Shock and its Lessons*, page 132

CHAPTER 8

1 PRO (NI) D. 2794/1/1/13

2 See Charles Carrington, *Soldier from the Wars Returning* (London: Hutchinson, 1965)

3 The War Office, *Manual of Military Law* (London: HMSO, 1914), Army Act, Section 46, subsection (7), page 423

4 The War Office, *Manual of Military Law*, Army Act, Section 47, pages 426–427

5   The War Office, *Manual of Military Law*, Army Act, Section 49, page 430

6   The War Office, *Manual of Military Law*, Army Act, Section 50, page 430

7   The War Office, *Manual of Military Law*, Army Act, Section 128, pages 496–497

8   The War Office, *Manual of Military Law*, Army Act, Section 56, subsection 3, pages 437–438

9   The War Office, *Manual of Military Law*, Army Act, Section 49, pages 429–430

10 The War Office, *Manual of Military Law*, Army Act, Section 54, page 435

11 William Moore, *The Thin Yellow Line* (London: Leo Cooper, 1974)

12 Anthony Babington, *For the Sake of Example* (London: Leo Cooper, 1983)

13 Julian Putkowski and Julian Sykes, *Shot at Dawn* (London: Leo Cooper, 1989)

14 See for example numerous soldiers' letters in the Liddle Collection, University of Leeds

15 PRO WO 374/1612

16 Charles Carrington, *Soldier from the Wars Returning*, page 172

17 Charles Carrington, *Soldier from the Wars Returning*, page 172

18 Guy Chapman, *A Passionate Prodigality* (Leatherhead: Ashford Buchanan and Enright edition, 1990) pages 73–74

19 See for example the intensely detailed and comprehensive exam requirement set out by Lt Col. Sisson C. Pratt, *The Military Law Examiner* (Aldershot: Gale and Polden, 1911), which in twenty-six chapters ranges from the history of military law to the customs of war, with over a thousand questions and model answers.

20 Charles Carrington, *Soldier from the Wars Returning*, page 173

21 Malcolm Brown, *Imperial War Museum Book of the Western Front* (London: BCA, 1993) pages 97–98

22 Malcolm Brown, *Imperial War Museum Book of the Western Front*

23 War Office, *Statistics of the Military Effort of the British Empire, 1914–20* (London: HMSO, 1922)

24 By far the best short but highly detailed and authoritative summary of how military law worked in 1914–18 is in Professor G. R. Rubin's presentation to the Royal United Services Institute in 1997. See G. R. Rubin, 'Military Law in WW1', *RUSI Journal*, vol. 143, no. 1, Feb 1998

CHAPTER 9

1   Henry Williamson, *How Dear is Life* (London: Macdonald, 1954) gives a semi-autobiographical description

2   Richard Holmes, *Riding the Retreat* (London: Random House, 1965) gives a good description of life in the 1914 army

3   Brig. Gen. J. Edmonds, *Official History of the Great War, Operations in France & Flanders 1914* (London: Macmillan, 1926) vol. 1, page 65

4 J. C. Dunn, *The War the Infantry Knew* (London: Abacus edition 1994) page 29

5 Capt. C. A. L. Brownlow in: Guy Chapman, *Vain Glory* (London: Cassell, 1965)

6 PRO WO 54/33 War Diary APM 5th Division

7 PRO WO 95/25 War Diary Adjutant & QMG 4th Division

8 PRO WO 95/25

9 PRO WO 95/25

10 PRO WO 95/25, BEF Army Routine Orders 59 of 4 September 1914

11 Brig. Gen. J. Edmonds, *Official History of the Great War, Operations in France & Flanders 1914*, page 260

12 PRO 71/387

13 PRO 71/387

14 PRO 71/387

15 PRO 71/387

16 Hansard, July 1919

CHAPTER 10

1 PRO WO 95/25

2 PRO WO 95/25

3 PRO WO 71/388

4 PRO WO 71/388

5 PRO WO 71/393

6 PRO WO 71/393, Commander 12 Inf Bde, 13 Jan 1915

CHAPTER 11

1 War Office, *Manual of Military Law* (London: HMSO, 1914) page 387

2 *Soldiers Died in the Great War,* CD-ROM (London: Naval & Military Press, 1998)

3 PRO WO 71/441

4 PRO WO 71/441

5 PRO WO 95/4303 Battalion War Diary 5th Wiltshires

6 PRO WO 71/442

7 PRO WO 154/116 War Diary DJAG Dardanelles

8 PRO WO 71/464

9 PRO WO 95/2090 Battalion War Diary 9th Cheshires

10 PRO WO 71/465

11 PRO WO 71/626

CHAPTER 12

1   The War Office, *Statistics of the Military Effort of the British Empire in the Great War 1914–1920* (London: HMSO, 1922)

2   PRO WO 95/116, War Diary DJAG Dardanelles

3   First Army Routine Order No. 57, 28 September 1915, in War Diary A&QMG WO 95/181

4   PRO WO 71/631 and PRO WO 71/632

5   Ex-Sergeant Crutchlow, *Tale of an Old Soldier* (London: Robert Hale & Co, 1937) pages 161–162

6   WO 95/5156 Battalion War Diary of 6th South Lancashire Fusiliers

7   Gerald Oram, *Death Sentences Passed by Military Courts of the British Army 1914–1924* (London: Francis Boutle, 1998) pages 19–20

8   PRO WO 71/400

9   The War Office, *Manual of Military Law* (London: HMSO, 1914) page 50

10 PRO WO 154/33, Extracts from War Diary of APM 5th Division and PRO WO 154/31, Extracts from War Diary of A&QMG 5th Division

11 Brig. E. A. James, *British Regiments 1914–1918* (London: Naval & Military Press Ltd, 1978) page 109

12 PRO WO 71/431

13 Julian Putkowski and Julian Sykes, *Shot at Dawn* (London: Leo Cooper, 1992) page 57

14 PRO WO 213/4, Register of Field General Courts Martial Abroad

15 Gerald Oram, *Death Sentences Passed by Military Courts of the British Army 1914–1924*, page 80

16 PRO WO 71/485

17 Gerald Oram, *Death Sentences Passed by Military Courts of the British Army 1914–1924*, page 35

18 PRO WO 71/645

CHAPTER 13

1   WO 71/473

2   WO 71/489

3   Lt Col. H. M. Davson, *History of the 35th Division in the Great War* (London: Sifton Praed & Co. Ltd, 1926) page 35

4   Gerald Oram, *Death Sentences in the British Army 1914–1924* (London: Francis Boutle, 1998) page 100

5   War Office, *Manual of Military Law* (London: HMSO, 1914) page 50

6   PRO WO 95/2485 War Diary 105 Brigade

7   PRO WO 95/2485 War Diary 105 Brigade

8   Lt Col. H. M. Davson, *History of the 35th Division in the Great War*, page 48

9   Ray Westlake, *British Battalions on the Somme* (London: Leo Cooper, 1994) page 260

10 PRO WO 71/519

11 PRO WO 154/114, War Diary of the Provost Marshal, Lines of Communication

12 WO 71/518

13 PRO WO 154/114

14 PRO WO 95/2490, War Diary of 19th DLI

15 PRO WO 95/2473, War Diary of CRE 35th Division

16 PRO WO 95/2490

17 PRO WO 95/2489, War Diary of 106 Brigade

18 PRO WO 95/2468, War Diary 35th Division

19 Lt Col. H. M. Davson, *History of the 35th Division in the Great War*, page 78

20 PRO WO 95/2489

21 PRO WO 95/2489

22 Lt. Col H. M. Davson, *History of the 35th Division in the Great War*, page 80

23 WO 71/535

24 PRO WO 95/2468

25 War Office, *Manual of Military Law* (London: HMSO, 1914) page 67

26 War Office, *Manual of Military Law* (London: HMSO, 1914) page 379

27 War Office, *Manual of Military Law* (London: HMSO, 1914) page 660

28 WO 363/S2462 First World War Service Documents (Burnt Documents)

29 PRO WO 95/2468

30 WO 71/534

31 PRO WO 95/2468

32 Lt Col. H. M. Davson, *History of the 35th Division in the Great War*, pages 81–82 and page 53

33 PRO WO 363/D1148 First World War Service Documents (Burnt Documents)

34 Professor Gerry Rubin, University of Kent at Canterbury personal communication, 2000

CHAPTER 14

1   Rowland Fielding, *War Letters to a Wife* (London: The Medici Society, 1930) page 374

2   PRO WO 71/416

3   Brig. Gen. E. A. James, *British Regiments 1914–1918* (London: Naval & Military Press, 1978) page 73

4   *Soldiers Died in the Great War*, CD-ROM. Naval & Military Press, 1998

5   Brig. Gen. James Edmonds, *Military Operations in France and Belgium 1915* vol. 2 (London: Macmillan & Co., 1928) page 37

6   PRO WO 71/420

7   Rose Coombes, *Before Endeavours Fade* (London: After the Battle, 1990) page 10, and Julian Putkowski and Julian Sykes, *Shot at Dawn* (London: Leo Cooper, 1992) page 44

8   PRO WO 154/28 War Diary A&QMG 4th Division

9   PRO WO 71/422

10 PRO WO 71/470

CHAPTER 15

1   PRO WO 95/2587, War Diary 17th Sherwood Foresters

2   PRO WO 71/486

3   PRO WO 71/487

4   PRO WO 71/490

5   John Masefield, *The Old Front Line* (London: William Heinemann, 1917) page 32

6   PRO WO 95/2686, War Diary 1/5th Battalion, South Staffordshires

7   PRO WO 71/490

8   PRO WO 95/2663 War Diary General Staff 46th Division

9   PRO WO 71/490

10 WO 329/1 Index to the Great War Medal Rolls

11 PRO WO 71/492

12 PRO WO 71/497

13 PRO WO 71/508

14 WO 95/2178 War Diary 9th Battalion, South Staffordshires

15 PRO WO 71/509

16 *Gunfire* magazine, No. 27, page 3

17 Brig. Gen. E. A. James, *British Regiments 1914–1918* (London: Naval & Military Press, 1978) page 57

18 PRO WO/951714 War Diary 2nd Battalion, West Yorkshire Regiment

19 *Gunfire* magazine, No. 27, page 4

20 Ray Westlake, *British Battalions on the Somme 1916* (London: Leo Cooper, 1994) page 77

21 PRO WO 71/507

22 PRO WO 71/527

CHAPTER 16

1   PRO WO 71/620

2   Memoirs of G. S. Chaplin, IWM ref. 74/100/1; PP/MCR/63

3   War Office, *Manual of Military Law* (London: HMSO, 1914) page 50

4   Frank Davies and Graham Maddocks, *Bloody Red Tabs* (London: Leo Cooper, 1995) pages 22–23

CHAPTER 17

1   WO 93/49

2   'Discipline & the Death Penalty in the British Army in the War against Germany in the Second World War', *Journal of Contemporary History*, October 1998

3   War Office, *Manual of Military Law* (London: HMSO 1914) page 18

4   War Office, *Statistics of the Military Effort of the British Empire 1914–1920* (London: HMSO, 1922)

5   PRO 293/2 WOI 197 of June 1915

6   PRO 293/2 WOI 204 of August 1915

7   PRO WO 154/8 War Diary of the APM 9 Corps, PRO WO 154/114, War Diary Provost Marshal Lines of Communication

8   WO 71/547

9   WO 71/428

10 F. P. Crozier, *The Men I Killed* (London: Michael Joseph, 1939) page 56

11 WO 71/419

12 WO 71/634

CHAPTER 18

1   PRO WO 95/1383 War Diary of the A&QMG, 3rd Division

2   Julian Putkowski and Julian Sykes, *Shot at Dawn* (London: Leo Cooper, 1989) page 50

3   Sir Gordon Macready, *In the Wake of the Great* (London: William Clowes & Sons Ltd, 1965) pages 21–22

4   John Peaty, 'Haig and Discipline' in *Haig: a Re-appraisal 70 years on*, ed. Brian Bond and Nigel Cave (London: Leo Cooper, 1999) page 215

5   WO 71/428

6   CWGC Debt of Honour Register at http://www.cwgc.org.uk and General Register Office records

7   PRO WO 95/1414 War Diary of 4th South Lancs

8   Correspondence from Commonwealth War Graves Commission

9   WO 71/426

10 WO 71/425

11 WO 329/2451 Medal Rolls, 3rd Worcester Regiment

12 PRO WO 95/1415 War Diary 1st Wiltshire Regiment

13 Correspondence from Commonwealth War Graves Commission

14 Piet Chielens and Julian Putkowski, *Unquiet Graves: Guidebook to the Execution Sites of the First World War in Flanders* (London: Francis Boutle, 2000) pages 16–17

CHAPTER 19

1 PRO WO 71/432

2 PRO WO 71/459

3 PRO WO 71/459

4 PRO WO 71/459

5 Malcolm Brown, *Imperial War Museum Book of the Western Front* (London: Sidgwick & Jackson Ltd, 1993) pages 97–98

6 PRO WO 71/463

7 PRO WO 71/653

8 CWGC register for Hersin Communal Cemetery

9 PRO WO 71/554

10 PRO WO 71/554

11 PRO WO 71/539

CHAPTER 20

1 PRO WO 71/404

2 PRO CAB 45/120

3 PRO WO 71/436

4 PRO WO 71/556

5 Col. C. H. Melville, 'Eugenics and Military Service', *Eugenics Review,* 1910–1911

6 Julian Putkowski and Julian Sykes, *Shot at Dawn* (London: Leo Cooper, 1989) page 236

7 PRO WO 71/677

8 Hansard, 17 April 1918

9 WO 71/661

CHAPTER 21

1 Brig. Gen. J. Edmonds, *Official History of the Great War 1916*, vol. 1 (London: Macmillan & Co. Ltd, 1932) page 443

2 PRO WO 71/495 and WO 71/496

3 PRO WO 71/495 and WO 71/496

4 Malcolm Brown, *Tommy Goes to War* (London: J. M. Dent & Sons Ltd, 1978) page 163

5   War Office, *Manual of Military Law* (London: HMSO, 1914) pages 18–19

6   PRO WO 71/525 and PRO WO 71/526

7   William Moore, *The Thin Yellow Line* (London: Leo Cooper, 1974) page 106

8   *Manchester Evening News*, 7 December 1916 and *Manchester Evening News* 16 December 1916

9   PRO WO 93/49

10   PRO WO 93/49

11   PRO WO 32/20624, Procedure for military executions

CHAPTER 22

1   *John Bull*, 23 February 1918

2   Frank Davies and Graham Maddocks, *Bloody Red Tabs* (London: Leo Cooper, 1995) pages 22–23

3   Douglas Jerrold, *The Royal Naval Division* (London: Hutchinson, 1923)

4   PRO ADM 156/24

5   All quotes from PRO ADM 156/24

6   Leonard Sellers, *For God's Sake Shoot Straight!* (London: Leo Cooper, 1995) page 77

7   *John Bull*, 23 February 1918

8   *John Bull*, 23 February 1918

9   *The Times,* 20 August 1983

10   Jeremy H. Bentham, Liddle Collection, GS 0123

11   A. P. Herbert, *The Secret Battle* (London: Methuen & Co. Ltd, 1919)

12   Anthony Babington, *For the Sake of Example* (London: Leo Cooper, 1983) page 102

13   *John Bull*, 23 February 1918

14   Thomas MacMillan, IWM Department of Documents

15   Thomas MacMillan, IWM Department of Documents

16   'Report of the Committee …constituted by the army council to enquire into … the Law and Rules of Procedure Regulating Courts Martial.' Parliamentary Paper, HMSO, 1919. PRO WO32/5478 (the Darling Report)

17   Douglas Jerrold, *The Royal Naval Division*

CHAPTER 23

1   Sir Ian Hamilton, *Gallipoli Diary*, vol. 2 (London: Edward Arnold, 1920) pages 17–18

2   *Soldiers Died in the Great War*, CD-ROM Naval & Military Press, 1998

3   PRO WO 95/4302 Battalion War Diary, 6th East Lancs

4   PRO WO 71/439

5 PRO WO 71/565

6 PRO WO 71/573

7 PRO WO 71/669

8 PRO WO 71/630

9 PRO WO 71/633

CHAPTER 24

1 *Mr Punch's History of the Great War* (London: Cassell & Co. Ltd, 1919) page 51

2 PRO WO 293/3, WOI/N046 September 1915

3 PRO WO 95/186, GRO No. 123 15 September 1916, in the War Diary of A&QMG First Army

4 PRO WO 95/186, GRO No. 129 20 October 1916, in the War Diary of A&QMG First Army

5 PRO WO 293/3, WOI/N046

6 George Coppard, *With a Machine Gun to Cambrai* (London: HMSO, 1969) pages 64–65

7 Peter N. Farrar, *Hull to the Somme* (Lambert (Hull) History Originals, 1982)

8 G. Adams, letters in the Liddle Archive, GS0006

9 'Victor's Deadly Secret', *Daily Express*, 16 August 1978 and 'The Grim Wartime Secret of Victor Sylvester', *Guardian*, 16 August 1978

10 PRO WO 363/S551 First World War Service Records (Burnt Documents)

11 PRO WO 363/2315

12 PRO WO 363/S551 First World War Service Records (Burnt Documents)

13 PRO WO 93/49 Summary of First World War Capital Courts Martial cases

14 Julian Putkowski and Julian Sykes, *Shot at Dawn* (London: Leo Cooper Books Ltd, 1992) page 31

15 See www.shotatdawn.org.uk 3 January 2000 and 'Saving Private Byers', *Guardian*, Thursday 11 November 1999

16 Letter from Commonwealth War Graves Commission

17 PRO WO 329/2677 Medal Roll 1914–15 Star, Royal Scots Fusiliers

18 PRO WO 71/397

19 Julian Putkowski and Julian Sykes, *Shot at Dawn*, pages 48–49

20 PRO WO 71/424

21 Julian Putkowski and Julian Sykes, *Shot at Dawn*, page 48–49

22 PRO WO 93/49

23 PRO WO 329/2623 Medal Roll 1914–15 Star, Northumberland Fusiliers

24 PRO WO 363/1999 First World War Service Records (Burnt Documents)

25 The *Catford Journal*, Friday 6 August 1915

26 *Soldiers Died in the Great War*, CD-ROM. Naval & Military Press, 1998

27 Commonwealth War Graves Debt of Honour Register, http://www.cwgc.org

28 Documents deposited by the Vicars of St Laurence's Church, Catford, in the
Lewisham Local Studies and Archives Centre

29 Commonwealth War Graves Commission Debt of Honour Register gives this
information under J. Highgate, brother of Thomas and Robert

30 PRO WO 93/49

31 Commonwealth War Graves Commission Register for Poperinge New Military
Cemetery

32 WO 95/495 War Diary 6th Battalion British West Indies Regiment

33 PRO WO 71/594

34 PRO WO 93/49

35 PRO WO 71/445

36 George Coppard, *With a Machine Gun to Cambrai*, pages 64–65

37 F. P. Crozier, *The Men I Killed* (London: Michael Joseph, 1937) pages 42–43

38 PRO WO 93/49

39 F. P. Crozier, *The Men I Killed*, page 44

40 F. P. Crozier, *The Men I Killed*, page 45

41 F. P. Crozier, *The Men I Killed*, page 46

42 PRO WO 71/450

43 Anthony Babington, *For the Sake of Example* (London: Leo Cooper, 1983) page 60

44 F. P. Crozier, *The Men I Killed*, page 50

45 F. P. Crozier, *The Men I Killed*, page 50

46 F. P. Crozier, *The Men I Killed*, page 51

47 F. P. Crozier, *The Men I Killed*, page 40

48 F. P. Crozier, *The Men I Killed*, page 52

CHAPTER 25

1 Charles Moran Wilson, *Anatomy of Courage* (London: Constable & Company, 1945)
pages 50–51

2 Joanna Bourke, *Dismembering the Male* (London: Reaktion Books Ltd, 1996) pages 78–87

3 John William Rowarth, 'The Misfit Soldier', IWM 90/40/1

4 Charles Moran Wilson, *Anatomy of Courage*, page 5

5 PRO WO 95/2443 War Diary of ADMS 34th Division

6 Charles Moran Wilson, *Anatomy of Courage*, page 186

7　PRO WO 95/2485 War Diary 105 Brigade

8　Edward Marjoribanks, *The Life of Sir Edward Marshall Hall* (London: Victor Gollancz Ltd, 1929) page 381

9　Edward Marjoribanks, *The Life of Sir Edward Marshall Hall*, page 387

10　Edward Marjoribanks, *The Life of Sir Edward Marshall Hall*, page 389

11　Charles Moran Wilson, *Anatomy of Courage*, Preface, page x

12　Ray Westlake, *British Battalions in France and Belgium 1914* (London: Leo Cooper 1997) page 257

13　PRO WO 71/389

14　G. Elliot Smith and T. H. Pear, *Shell Shock and its Lessons* (Manchester: Manchester University Press, 1917) Introduction, page 12

15　PRO WO 329/1 Index to the Great War Medal Rolls

16　PRO WO 95/1856 War Diary of 11th Middlesex

17　Sylvia Pankhurst, *The Home Front* (London: Hutchinson, 1932) page 309

18　PRO WO 95/1856 War Diary of 11th Middlesex

19　PRO WO 71/456

20　Sylvia Pankhurst, *The Home Front*, page 311

21　Sylvia Pankhurst, *The Home Front*, page 309

22　Sylvia Pankhurst, *The Home Front*, page 310

23　PRO WO 71/520

24　PRO WO 293/5 ACI 1537 of 1916

25　Julian Putkowski and Julian Sykes, *Shot at Dawn* (London: Leo Cooper, 1989) page 204

26　PRO WO 71/609

CHAPTER 26

1　The War Office, *Statistics of the British Military Effort of the British Empire in the Great War 1914–1920* (London: HMSO, 1922), page 669

2　Gerald Oram, *Death Sentences Passed by Military Courts of the British Army 1914–1924* (London: Francis Boutle, 1998) page 15

3　The figure for the total trials for desertion is taken from *Statistics of the British Military Effort of the British Empire in the Great War 1914–1920*, s is the number of executions for this crime. The number of death sentences awarded for desertion is taken from Gerald Oram, *Death Sentences Passed by Military Courts of the British Army 1914–1924*, page 15

4　PRO WO 339/35077 Officers' Service Records

5　PRO WO 339/35077 Officers' Service Records

6　PRO WO 71/1027

7　PRO WO 71/1027

8   PRO WO 71/1027

9   PRO WO 256/14 Diary of Field Marshal Haig for Wednesday 6 December 1916

10 PRO WO 339/35077 Officers' Service Records

11 PRO WO 339/35077 Officers' Service Records

12 PRO WO 339/35077 Officers' Service Records

13 PRO WO 339/35077 Officers' Service Records

14 PRO WO 339/35077 Officers' Service Records

15 PRO WO 339/35077 Officers' Service Records

16 CWGC Register for Poperinge New Military Cemetery

17 *Shot at Dawn*, Channel 4 Television 1998

18 O'Moore Creagh and E. M. Humphris, *The Distinguished Service Order 1886–1923* (London: J. B. Hayward & Sons 1978) page 324

CHAPTER 27

1   Wyndham Childs, *Episodes & Reflections* (London: Cassell, 1930) page 137

2   Wyndham Childs, *Episodes & Reflections*, page 137

3   PRO WO 71/427

4   Julian Putkowski and Julian Sykes, *Shot at Dawn* (London: Leo Cooper, 1989) page 51

5   PRO WO 71/440

6   Julian Putkowski and Julian Sykes, *Shot at Dawn*, page 62

7   Michael Gavaghan, *Loos 1915* (London: M&L Publications, 1997)

8   PRO WO 71/444

9   Brig. Gen. James E. Edmonds, *Official History of the Great War, France and Belgium 1915*, vol. 2 (London: Macmillan and Co. Ltd, 1928) pages 293–294

10 Brig. Gen. James E. Edmonds, *Official History of the Great War, France and Belgium 1915*, vol. 2, page 294

11 Brig. Gen. James E. Edmonds, *Official History of the Great War, France and Belgium 1915*, vol. 2, page 342

12 Brig. Gen. James E. Edmonds, *Official History of the Great War, France and Belgium 1915*, vol. 2, page 343

13 Brig. Gen. James E. Edmonds, *Official History of the Great War, France and Belgium 1915*, vol. 2, page 342

14 PRO WO 71/488

15 PRO WO 363/N95 First World War Service Documents (Burnt Documents)

16 Unquiet Graves Conference, Ypres, May 2000 and Shot at Dawn web site at http://www.shotatdawn.org.uk/nelson.htm, date 02/09/00

17 Shot at Dawn web site at http://www.shotatdawn.org.uk/nelson.htm, date 02/09/00

18 PRO WO 71/561

19 Anthony Babington, *For the Sake of Example* (London: Leo Cooper, 1983) page 123

20 *Soldiers Died in the Great War*, CD-ROM. Naval & Military Press, 1998

21 PRO WO 95/2120 War Diary 12th Battalion KRRC

22 PRO WO 71/610

23 PRO WO 71/652

24 PRO WO 71/652

CHAPTER 28

1 PRO WO 71/466

2 PRO WO 71/505

3 PRO WO 71/506

CHAPTER 29

1 The War Office, *Statistics of the British Military Effort of the British Empire in the Great War 1914–1920* (London: HMSO, 1989)

2 Julian Putkowski and Julian Sykes, *Shot at Dawn* (London: Leo Cooper, 1989) pages 33–34, and PRO WO 95/1235 War Diary of Adjutant General, 1st Division

3 PRO WO 90/6 Register of General Courts Martial Abroad and PRO WO 213/3 Register of Field General Courts Martial Abroad

4 Frank P. Crozier, *The Men I Killed* (London: Michael Joseph Ltd, 1937) pages 53–55

5 Frank P. Crozier, *A Brass Hat in No Man's Land* (London: Jonathan Cape, 1930) pages 208–209

6 G. K. Chesterton, 'The Sign of the Broken Sword' in *The Innocence of Father Brown* (London: Curtis Publishing Company, 1911)

7 PRO WO 71/437

8 PRO WO 71/451

9 War Office, *Manual of Military Law* (London: HMSO, 1914) page 98

10 PRO WO 71/446

11 Julian Putkowski and Julian Sykes, *Shot at Dawn* (London: Leo Cooper, 1989) page 67

12 PRO WO 95/2203 War Diary of 24th Division, Divisional Train

13 PRO WO 71/603

14 PRO WO 71/640

CHAPTER 30

1 PRO WO 339/111890 Officers' documents

2 PRO WO 95/1361 War Diary 17th Battalion Middlesex Regiment

3 PRO WO 339/111890

4 PRO WO 71/1028

5 PRO WO 97/4561 Soldiers' Service Records

6 PRO WO 339/111890

CHAPTER 31

1 War Office, *Statistics of the Military Effort of the British Empire 1914–1920* (London: HMSO, 1922) page 669

2 Archives du Service Historique de l'Armée, Paris

3 G. Pedroncini, *Les Mutineries de 1917* (Paris: Presses Universitaires de France, 1996)

4 War Emergency: WNC papers 1914, Labour Party Archives 7/1/7/11-68

5 *Weymouth Telegram* newspaper, January 1915

6 *Gunfire* magazine No. 40

7 PRO WO 32/9560

8 Ian F. W. Beckett, 'The Singapore Mutiny of February 1915', *Journal of the Society of Army Historical Research*, 1984, vol. 62, pages 132–153

9 PRO WO 32/9560

10 William Allison and John Fairley, *The Monocled Mutineer* (London: Quartet, 1978)

11 PRO WO 95/4044 War Diary Sanitary Officer Rouen Base 1916

12 For a good description of the Blargies mutiny, see Julian Putkowski, *British Army Mutineers* (London: Francis Boutle, 1998)

13 PRO WO 71/510 (All quotations from Lewis C M are from this reference)

14 K. Hyman, *The Hill* (MGM and Seven Arts, 1965)

15 For a full description of the case and the NZ executions in WW1, see Christopher Pugsley, *On the Fringe of Hell* (Auckland: Hodder & Stoughton, 1991)

16 Transcript of GCM 11 Oct 1916, 2nd Otago, JAG (NZ)

17 IGC to DJAG 17 October 1916

18 For an insight into Haig's thinking see the Haig diaries, National Library of Scotland.

19 For a good description of British attitudes towards the Australians, see the Haig diaries (various) and Brig. Gen. Ludlow's memories of the Ypres Sector, Oct 1916 (Liddle Collection Leeds, GS 0984). Gen. Sir Archibald Murray's letter to the CIGS – Robertson – in March 1916 gives a wonderfully honest and unblinking description of Australian vices and their equally remarkable virtues as soldiers (King's College London, Centre for Military Archives).

20 For an excellent review of Australian attitudes towards discipline in WW1, see Col. Peter Pedersen's paper to the Unquiet Graves Conference, Ypres, May 2000

21 PRO WO 95/4027 War Diary Commandant Etaples Base

22 *Manchester Guardian* article, February 1930

23 PRO WO 71/599

24 PRO AIR 1/720/36/1

25 Julian Putkowski, *British Army Mutineers 1914–1922* (London: Francis Boutle, 1998)

26 PRO WO 71/600

27 J. C. Dunn, *The War the Infantry Knew* (London: King Books, 1938)

28 War Office, *Statistics of the Military Effort of the British Empire 1914–1920*, page 667

29 For the best brief account of the impact of mutiny on an army in WW1 see Correlli Barnett's ground breaking socio-economic and military analysis of 1914–18 *The Swordbearers* (London: Penguin 1966) which describes (pp222–261) the full nature of the French Crisis in 1917

CHAPTER 32

1 WO 71/673

2 WO 71/672

CHAPTER 33

1 Hansard, 9 June 1915

2 Hansard, 17 June 1915

3 Hansard, 1 July 1915

4 Hansard, 7 July 1915

5 Hansard, 20 January 1916

6 Hansard, 8 March 1916

7 Hansard, 10 May 1916

8 Hansard, 31 October 1917

9 Hansard, 26 November 1917

10 Hansard, 18 December 1917

11 Hansard, 19 February 1918

12 Hansard, 20 February 1918

13 *John Bull*, 23 February 1918

14 William Moore, *The Thin Yellow Line* (London: Leo Cooper 1974) page 141

15 *John Bull*, 2 March 1918

16 Hansard, 14 March 1918

17 William Moore, *The Thin Yellow Line*, page 141

18 War Office, *Statistics of the British Military Effort of the British Empire in the Great War 1914–1920* (London: HMSO, 1922)

19   Sylvia Pankhurst, *The Home Front* (London: Hutchinson, 1932) page 309

20   Sylvia Pankhurst, *The Home Front*, page 313

CHAPTER 34

1   *Report of the Committee constituted by the Army Council to enquire into the law and rules of procedure regulating Military Courts-Martial* (London: HMSO, 1919)

2   Hansard, 13 April 1920

CHAPTER 35

1   T. J. Mitchell and G. M. Smith, *Official History of the War Medical Services: Casualties and Medical Statistics of the Great War* (London: Macmillan & Co. Ltd, 1931) page 285

2   C. Stanford Read, *Military Psychiatry in Peace and War* (London: H. K. Lewis & Co. Ltd, 1920)

3   E. E. Southard, *Shell Shock and Neuropsychiatry* (Boston: W. M. Leonard, 1919)

4   G. Elliot Smith and T. H. Pear, *Shell Shock and its Lessons* (Manchester: Manchester University Press, 1917) page 132

5   *Report of the War Office Committee of Enquiry into Shell-Shock* (London: HMSO, 1922) page 3

6   *Report of the War Office Committee of Enquiry into Shell-Shock*, page 5

7   T. J. Mitchell and G. M. Smith, *Official History of the War Medical Services: Casualties and Medical Statistics of the Great War*

8   *Report of the War Office Committee of Enquiry into Shell-Shock*, pages 16–18

9   *Report of the War Office Committee of Enquiry into Shell-Shock*, pages 48–51

10   *Report of the War Office Committee of Enquiry into Shell-Shock*, page 46

11   *Report of the War Office Committee of Enquiry into Shell-Shock*, pages 44–45

12   *Report of the War Office Committee of Enquiry into Shell-Shock*, page 44

13   *Report of the War Office Committee of Enquiry into Shell-Shock*, pages 85–86

14   *Report of the War Office Committee of Enquiry into Shell-Shock*, page 31

15   *Report of the War Office Committee of Enquiry into Shell-Shock*, page 33

16   *Report of the War Office Committee of Enquiry into Shell-Shock*, page 88

17   *Report of the War Office Committee of Enquiry into Shell-Shock*, pages 13–16

18   *Report of the War Office Committee of Enquiry into Shell-Shock*, page 25

19   *Report of the War Office Committee of Enquiry into Shell-Shock*, pages 26–28

20   *Report of the War Office Committee of Enquiry into Shell-Shock*, page 55

21   *Report of the War Office Committee of Enquiry into Shell-Shock*, pages 37–41

22   *Report of the War Office Committee of Enquiry into Shell-Shock*, page 43

23   *Report of the War Office Committee of Enquiry into Shell-Shock*, page 44

24 *Report of the War Office Committee of Enquiry into Shell-Shock*, page 138

25 *Report of the War Office Committee of Enquiry into Shell-Shock*, page 139

26 *Report of the War Office Committee of Enquiry into Shell-Shock*, page 139

27 *Report of the War Office Committee of Enquiry into Shell-Shock*, page 139

28 *Report of the War Office Committee of Enquiry into Shell-Shock*, page 140

29 *Report of the War Office Committee of Enquiry into Shell-Shock*, page 190

30 *Report of the War Office Committee of Enquiry into Shell-Shock*, page 190

31 Wendy Holden, *Shell Shock* (London: Channel 4 Books, 1998) page 77

32 Hans Binneveld, *From Shell Shock to Combat Stress* (Amsterdam: Amsterdam University Press, 1997) page 1

CHAPTER 36

1 E. Thurtle, *Military Discipline and Democracy* (London: Daniel Books, 1920)

2 G. Lansbury, in the Foreword to E. Thurtle, *Military Discipline and Democracy*

3 *Minority Report of the Darling Committee (Report of the Committee constituted by the Army Council to inquire into the law and rules of procedure regulating Military Courts-Martial)* (London: HMSO, 1919)

4 Hansard, 1929, various debates.

5 PRO WO 163/609 Report of the Army and Air Forces Courts Martial Committee, 1938

6 Carlo d'Este, *Bitter Victory* (London: Collins, 1988)

7 PRO WO 163/49

8 Ref: Liddell Hart Centre, King's College, O'Connor MSS 1/5, c 1971 quoted in the *Journal of Contemporary History* (LHMCA) October 1998, 'Discipline and the Death Penalty in WW2', where Professor David French provides an outstanding summary of this whole subject in the British Army in WW2

9 PRO WO 32/15773

10 PRO WO 2235 (Board of Enquiry 1942)

11 PRO WO 214/62

12 PRO WO 277/7 'Discipline' London 1950

13 For an excellent analysis of the problems of desertion in the British Army in WW2, see John Ellis, *The Sharp End of War* (London: BCA, 1980)

14 PRO WO 222/103

15 LHCMA, King's College, Adam MSS V/6, cited by David French

16 LHMCA, King's College, O'Connor MSS 21

17 PRO WO 32/15774

18 PRO WO 277/7

19 For a good account of the problems of the British Army in WW2, see David Fraser, *And We Shall Shock Them* (London: Hodder & Stoughton, 1983)

20 Gen. H. Essame, quoted in David French's article in *Journal of Contemporary History*, October 1998

21 John Terraine, *The Right of the Line* (London: Hodder & Stoughton, 1989) page 641

22 'Administrative History of Operations of 21 Army Group, 6 June 44 – 8 May 1945', plus Annex L(e) November 1945

23 PRO AIR 20/2859

24 PRO AIR 2/8038

25 Max Hastings, *Bomber Command* (London: Michael Joseph, 1979)

26 For a fictional description that is widely admired by ex-RAF aircrew, see Len Deighton, *Bomber* (London: Jonathan Cape, 1970), which outlines the LMF system.

27 John Terraine, *The Right of the Line*

28 For an outstanding discussion of the realities of warfare and the battlefield, see John Keegan's seminal work *The Face of Battle* (London: Jonathan Cape, 1976)

29 Hans Binneveld, *From Shell Shock to Combat Stress* (Amsterdam: Amsterdam University Press, 1997)

CHAPTER 37

1 Correspondence in PRO WO 93/49

2 Hansard, May 1972

3 William Moore, *The Thin Yellow Line* (London: Leo Cooper, 1974).

4 Julian Putkowski and Julian Sykes, *Shot at Dawn* (London: Leo Cooper, 1989).

5 Julian Putkowski and Julian Sykes, *Shot at Dawn* (London: Leo Cooper: 1989): book dust jacket

6 Julian Putkowski and Julian Sykes, *Shot at Dawn*, authors' statement

7 Hansard, House of Commons Draft Bill 161, 51/3, 11 July 1995,

8 All references are to Hansard, Ministerial Statement and debate, July 1998

9 http://www.shotatdawn.org.uk

CHAPTER 38

1 Hugh McManners, *The Scars of War* (London: HarperCollins, 1993)

2 James Stuart-Smith, see PRO LCO 53/99/1 LM 1 August 1984, cited by Professor G. R. Rubin, University of Kent

3 Frederick Manning, *Her Privates We* (London: Serpent's Tail, 1999 (unexpurgated version))

4 Private J. W. Horner, Private Memoir, Liddle Collection GS 0800, University of Leeds

INDEX